W9-BZK-432

Ethnomimesis

Ethno

Folklife and the Representation of Culture

Robert Cantwell

mimesis

The University of North Carolina Press Chapel Hill & London

The author gratefully acknow-
ledges the generous support offered
toward the completion of this work
by the John Simon Guggenheim
Foundation and the Office of Folklife
Programs, Smithsonian Institution.
Portions of this text, in earlier
versions, have appeared in *The New
England Review*, *The Journal of
American Folklore*, and in Jane
Becker and Barbara Franco, eds.,
*Folk Roots, New Roots: Folklore in
American Life* (Lexington, Mass.:
Museum of Our National Heritage,
1988).

Robert Cantwell is visiting associate
professor of American studies at the
University of North Carolina at
Chapel Hill and author of *Bluegrass
Breakdown: The Making of the Old
Southern Sound*.

97 96 95 94 93   5 4 3 2 1

Library of Congress
Cataloging-in-Publication Data
Cantwell, Robert, 1945–
    Ethnomimesis : folklife and the
representation of culture / Robert
Cantwell
        p. cm.
    Includes bibliographical references
and index.
    ISBN 0-8078-2112-8 (cloth : alk.
paper).—ISBN 0-8078-4424-1 (pbk. :
alk. paper)
    1. Festival of American Folklife—
History. 2. Festivals—United States.
3. Festivals—Washington (D.C.).
4. Folklore—United States.
5. Folklore—Washington (D.C.).
6. United States—Social life and
customs. 7. Washington (D.C.)—
Social life and customs.
I. Title.
GT4802.C36 1993
394.2'6'0973—dc20 93-9681
                              CIP

FOR LYDIA

Contents

And then, in affairs like this one, we realize our

strength; we realize how beautiful we are . . . even

tired old Washington is beautiful when the American

people gather to sing and fall in love with each

other again.

—ALAN LOMAX,

at the Festival of American Folklife,

July 7, 1968

Preface

Late in the spring of 1985, the Office of Folklife Programs at the Smithsonian Institution approached me about writing a history of the Festival of American Folklife, soon to mark its twentieth year.

It is difficult to believe now, nearly eight years later, that having reached the age of forty, I could have failed to recognize the many snares that lay in the path of anyone presuming to write an institutional history of any kind. The first of these was something, happily, that I did realize immediately: I could not possibly write a history of the Festival of American Folklife. The available documentation—housed not only in ten or twelve filing cabinets groaning with the weight of memos, letters, contracts, and reports, but in thousands of square feet of storage space literally spilling over with uncataloged audio and videotape, film, and still photographs from twenty years of the Festival—brought me to despair; not in a lifetime could I have brought to this mass of information the organization necessary to make out of it an intelligible historical narrative. I believed, furthermore, and still believe, that even a carefully researched history of the Festival, with its many yearly repetitions, would have an inevitable kind of redundancy and would be of interest, probably, only to the people who had been immediately involved in it.

While I was still ruminating on the possibility of a history of the Festival, however, the problem was in a sense solved for me, from a cause about which I still speculate, when a team of workmen came into the office one afternoon with handcarts and began to haul away the filing cabinets, the boxes of film, and all the rest: somewhere in the upper reaches of the Smithsonian it had been determined that the Office of Folklife Programs needed more office space and a new wall-to-wall carpet. Off it all went to Silver Hill, Maryland, to the back of a huge truck trailer where in fact I *did* ultimately conduct, with blue fingers in 28-degree weather, some "research." But my frozen fingers proved prophetic. Fate had decreed that I should not write a history of the Festival of American Folklife. At least not from the documents.

Well, then, I could interview the various people who had helped to create the Festival and who had been connected with it in its formative years; many of these men and women were still employees of the Office of Folklife Programs and were easily available to me—and I did, at the beginning, conduct a number of such interviews. But this was a delicate, disquieting, and disorienting process, as it soon became obvious to me that my informants regarded me, quite predictably I suppose, as their own personal contract worker, and in no instance did they fail to communicate their expectations that I would incorporate into my book not only the substance of their interviews but also something of their conceptions of what the book itself should be—and there were as many such conceptions as there were people to conceive them.

One important personage was anxious that the book should reveal, in a righteous, combative way, the institutional politics that had shaped the Festival. Another saw the potential book as an instrument for promoting the survival of the embattled Office of Folklife Programs within the Smithsonian. Still another, who did not really approve of folk festivals, saw me as a kind of telltale who would expose at last the institutional and personal folly that had compromised both public and academic standards of folklore scholarship and advocacy; yet another person definitely implied that the book should highlight his own role in the Festival and was most eager to tell me his story.

Of course, there were better suggestions—far better. One staff folklorist saw the book as an extension of the office's larger cultural mission to promote the survival of marginalized, disadvantaged, minority, and other cultures that had been deeply compromised by their material, political, historical, and social situation in the world. To this aim I was deeply sympathetic, but I did not see how an honest book could adopt a particular political program—especially this one, already ideologically and rhetorically well developed—without first arriving at its own conclusions about what had shaped the historical evolution of the Festival. Another person, unofficially connected to the project, saw the book as a chapter in the history of public folklore and particularly of folk festivals, a perspective I did indeed adopt in an essay that, in the end, I published separately. On the whole, however, so many different viewpoints were expressed, by people in a position to demand from me a particular kind of work, that I was left in a kind of paralysis; I could conceive of no book capable of satisfying all the demands implicit in these interviews. I could not write at all without first arriving at my own point of view, and so, when the opportunity presented itself, I ran away, after almost a year in Washington, to Iowa where, between sneezes (you could actually *see* the pollen in the air), I could write and think in peace.

As it turned out, the flight of the filing cabinets was fortuitous. When it came to submitting an outline for the proposed book, I tried to make a virtue of necessity by placing the Festival of American Folklife in the context of the "folk revival" of the 1960s, that is, the popular folksong movement that produced such cultural icons as Bob Dylan and Joan Baez and that, in fact, had provided the immediate historical occasion for the emergence of the Festival of American Folklife. The Archive of Folk Culture at the Library of Congress, after all, was a short Metro ride away from the Folklife Office at L'Enfant Plaza, and its files had not been carted off to some remote storage facility. With a stipend sufficient to rent a small apartment in Washington, I could research the folk revival, especially its intellectual and cultural background, and perhaps produce a book that would make sense of the Festival of American Folklife within that limited but important setting.

In the end, I did produce some writing on the folk revival, now scattered around in various essay collections and academic journals (titles appear in the "References" section), but this work, with the exception of a small portion of Chapter 7, does not appear in this book. The reason for that is not simple, but it is explicable. In the summer of 1985, to inaugurate my project, I involved myself in the Festival of American Folklife as a kind of participant-observer; I lived in the dormitory at Georgetown University with an African American blues band from Ferriday, Louisiana, Hezakiah Early and the Houserockers, sharing a room with the old minstrel-show trombonist Pee Wee Whittaker. I visited the Festival site every day, watching the demonstrations, engaging participants, staff, and visitors in hundreds of conversations, making notes, taking photographs, and ultimately becoming, like many people who work on or in the Festival of American Folklife, intensely involved with the event intellectually, emotionally, and morally. The depth of that involvement, the ways in which it touched me, and what I came over the years to understand about those experiences—particularly in relation to the personal testimony of others who convinced me that their experience paralleled mine in many ways—became, indirectly, the subject of my book.

I say "indirectly" because the book is not simply a narrative about two weeks in the summer of 1985, though in two chapters and in my conclusion I offer a picture of that experience shaped to the themes of the discussion. In many respects the book is, in fact, what I originally proposed. It places the Festival of American Folklife in a context: not the local and punctual context of institutional politics, or the microhistorical context of the popular folk revival, but a larger cultural context, the largest and broadest I could plausibly construct, one within which I was accustomed to working as an undergraduate teacher: that of the emergence of modernity, in which, it seemed to me then and still does seem to me, the meaning and importance of the Festival of American Folklife, and the idea of folklore itself, really lay.

Though I suspect he would be very surprised to hear it, this way of approaching my topic was suggested to me in my very first days at the Smithsonian during a brief conversation with the founder and for many years the presiding genius of the Festival of American Folklife, Ralph Rinzler. Rinzler at that time was the institution's assistant secretary for public service; certainly he was deeply interested in any public account that might be written of the Festival, which was the centerpiece, after all, of his exemplary career. He also was unofficially the man to whom, for whom, and perhaps *about* whom I would be writing.

Naturally I listened carefully to what Rinzler had to say. He told a story, one he has repeated to his colleagues and associates many times over the years: about the eighteenth-century Bishop Percy's rescue, just as his housekeeper was about to consign it to the flames, of a ballad manuscript; about Harvard's ballad-scholar George Lyman Kittredge, who edited Professor Child's ballads and encouraged his student John Lomax in song collecting; about Cecil Sharp, the English musicologist and reformist who in the early twentieth century, under the sponsorship of distinguished Boston philanthropists, set out to discover—and discovered—surviving British ballads in the Southern Appalachians; about the Popular Front folksong movement of mid-century, in which he, Rinzler, had been swept up and whose movers and shakers, the Lomaxes and the Seegers, are still his acknowledged models and personal heroes; about his own highly important and influential folklore work in North Carolina, Georgia, Louisiana, and Nova Scotia; and about the Smithsonian, the National Museum, for which he had conceived a folk festival compatible with both its cultural project and his own.

This was not *my* story, not quite; it did, however, suggest the larger historical patterns that the opening chapters of the book attempt to set out, and it drew my attention both to the Smithsonian museums and to the Festival's formative years of 1973 and 1974, upon which Rinzler himself had placed his emphasis. Of necessity, though, I have read his story in my own way, and to me it is a story of a specific continuing tradition, part literary, part political, unfolding at a very high, if not the very highest, social levels. Above all, it is a story of the invention in successive periods— the principled, the energetic, the learned, often the inspired and inspiring, but the invention nevertheless—of folklife. The story belongs to that perennial fascination of the developed imagination in a complex civilization with the original principles and the fundamental forms of culture and society, whose ideality we invariably construct, psychologically, socially, politically, scientifically, and philosophically, in opposition to, but often in ways that implicitly affirm, the lives we actually lead and what the world actually is. In the modern world, the idea of folklife belongs to the romantic tradition and, like that tradition, is a response to, an instrument of, and a phenomenon of modernity. And yet, in a larger sense, the idea of folklife surely belongs to the long and complex pastoral dream founded in Western civilization's primary myths.

This book, incidentally, does not repudiate the invention of folklife because it is an invention; on the contrary, it participates in it. Nor does it deny the existence of a vernacular culture that is the unmediated substance of what, in another order of signification, becomes "folklife"; on the contrary, it demands it.

In Rinzler, then, an elegant, outspoken, self-made patrician of impeccable taste, strong opinions, implacable anger, superb musicianship, and considerable intellectual and entrepreneurial energy, one might see Shakespeare's Edgar, the nobleman in the guise of pariah, and the sad Earl of Leicester, master of an estate made forlorn for the lack of tenants to populate it, his allegiance passionately divided between the powerful and the powerless, the high and the low, the rich and the poor—the division to which Rinzler from summer to summer brought a temporary but wonderful resolution on the National Mall.

I had, as I say, many conversations at the Office of Folklife Programs while I was there; but I'll mention just one other that has had a lasting impact on the themes of this book, and that was with the then director of the office, the folklorist Peter Seitel. Like the aforementioned conversation with Ralph Rinzler, my talk with Seitel took place within days of my coming to Washington, when I was eager to fathom the nature of the project being offered to me. Among several other observations, Seitel averred that the primary purpose of the Festival was to break down the social stereotypes that stand between one group and another and help to sustain the power of one over another. I found this to be a provocative and, upon further reflection, an immensely complex notion. I have tried to unravel at least some of those complexities here and to suggest how the Festival does, indeed, "break down" stereotypes—and further, to see it from the variety of perspectives Seitel offered, not only as theme park and living museum but as "cultural laboratory" and national "family reunion," as many in the office were fond of calling it.

These two memorable conversations took place during what was then my official relation as an independent contractor to the Office of Folklife Programs, and the substance as well as the organization of my book reflects an honest effort to incorporate them. Indeed, Rinzler later emphasized, in a longer interview, that he was more interested in a book of ideas than in a book of history; Seitel, too, encouraged me in this aim and urged me to take as much time with the project as I needed, indeed to think of my contract as a kind of grant.

I appreciated this liberality, and I took advantage of it. As it happened, however, four years later, when pieces of my still-evolving manuscript became available to Rinzler and others in the office, our relationship came to an unanticipated and somewhat mysterious end. I was unofficially and indirectly informed, through a colleague, that my book, for reasons never explained, was no longer wanted. This left my contract, and my hundreds of pages of drafts, in limbo—and so, with the fair-minded intervention of the new director, Richard Kurin, I arranged to discharge my obligation with another manuscript now in the archives of the Office of Folklife

Programs, an anthology of Festival-related pieces from program books and internal documents that included, among other things, the edited transcript of my extensive interview with Rinzler. I recommend it to anyone who wishes to catch the spirit of the Festival in the voices of many of the people most closely associated with it.

This outcome was initially painful, even frightening, but in time I've come to realize that, in fact, I probably was not writing the book for which I had been contracted, and that it was better perhaps for all concerned that the book, whatever it was to be, should be my own.

There are at least two other conversations in the background of this book that deserve mention. Roger Abrahams, from whom I have learned so much, whose friendship has meant so much to me, and whose confidence in me will, I hope, prove not to have been misplaced, gave me some highly insightful and fertile ideas of his own about the structure of stereotype and the anthropological locus of festivity, ideas that I have tried to develop in my own analyses. A man of huge intelligence, imagination, and intellectual mobility, Roger knows, better than anyone I know, what folklore is and what knowledge about folklore looks and sounds like. His understanding and his practice consistently traduce the received academic categories and take a coequal place with the best learned discourse in literature, history, and the social sciences. Because vernacular culture itself is a complex field of relationships among different orders of society, this is really the only authentic way to transform it into the cultural resource we call folklore.

From my old friend Myrddin Jones of Exeter University in England, with whom, alas, my conversations of late have been few and far between, I took some ideas about rank, class, and class relations that came as revelations to me, but that I now recognize to have been part of an important tradition of British cultural theory represented by such eminent critics as the late Raymond Williams, like Myrddin a Welshman, who despite the admitted historical differences between the British and American experience nevertheless has much to teach us about social hierarchy, class relations, and the social and cultural precipitates of capitalist democracy generally. Indeed, as I think back, I realize I have learned far more from Myrddin than I can express. He is a thoroughly excellent man, a model of scholarship, learning, energy, understanding, patience, generosity, and humor, whose example, though I cannot hope ever to approach it, has been consistently with me.

Indeed, this book has evolved far more from conversation and solitary reflection than from reading, study, or teaching, and this, I suspect, will turn out to be the principal objection to it. It contains, for example, very little in the way of scholarly apparatus. Indeed, in the process of writing the book I was much of the time myself, professionally speaking, an isolated, disaffiliated man, without any regular institutional connection, a fact that has been, like the other circumstances surrounding the making of this book, both a crippling practical liability and an unanticipated intellectual advantage. The debts I sustained in this project are numerous, but they are not of the sort that can be recorded in a bibliography. The book's little cache of idiosyncratic terms, its loose, almost wayward organization, its unorthodox mixture of discursive modes, its style, which is by turns intensely personal, ruthlessly technical, and extravagantly rhetorical, its mostly homegrown and hybrid theoretical position, all thrust this work decisively outside the realm of ordinary academic practice—but not, I hope, altogether out of the faith.

And yet, as I say, these liabilities bring strengths in their turn. When I left the academy—I hoped temporarily—more than ten years ago, I discovered almost at once that the pedagogical expedients of undergraduate teachers, infatuated as we all become with the little shows we put on for the edification of nineteen- and twenty-year-olds, aren't particularly impressive to people outside the academy, and for good reason. Outside the classroom, understanding is much harder to come by; it won't do simply to speak the language, cite the authorities, run with the pack, and toe the line. Setting my foot outside the academy forced me to consider the question of what I knew I knew—and it turned out to be very little. I am now much less confident, much less glib and voluble, more hesitating and often embarrassingly inarticulate than when I was a "brilliant" young professor, eager to impress the kids with how clever I was. But what I *have* learned has been forged in and tested against some real-life experience and leavened long and deep in memory, as, indeed, all good teaching and scholarship must be. I hope that some of it has found its way into this book.

Without the friendship, the generosity, and the support of people like Roger Abrahams and Myrddin Jones, and without the opportunity created for me, at Roger's instigation, by Ralph Rinzler, I would never have written this book. I am deeply grateful to these people. I was buoyed up, moreover, by the encouragement, the goodwill, and the love of men and women to whom, now, I can only express my love in return. Alicia

Gonzales, in those days program director at the Office of Folklife Programs, listened sympathetically and spoke encouragingly to me, buffering what would otherwise have been aggravating and injurious relationships with some of the thornier personalities in the field of public folklore, protecting me against intimidation and helping me to feel that I, too, had something to offer. I hope that I bolstered her self-esteem in return, for she is, to me, a highly estimable person. Like the others, she had many ideas for and about, and certainly an interest in, the book; but, for whatever reasons, she withheld them.

To Keith and Vivian Howard, who gave me their friendship and hospitality, who accepted me into the bosom of their family and shared their understanding of certain perennial human concerns, I shall always be grateful.

Beset in its final stages by organizational problems embedded in its very conception, this book has, I think, become considerably more reader-friendly thanks not only to its conscientious professional readers but also to the wisdom and good counsel of David Perry at the University of North Carolina Press. And to my editor, Pamela Upton, who turned my many obscurities to clarities, curbed my many mannerisms, alerted me to my many prejudices, and who offered the gift of many a felicitous word, both I and my readers are deeply indebted.

To Archie Green, finally, shipwright, union man, discographer, folklorist, teacher, my mentor and friend for more than twenty years, I owe nothing less than the direction my intellectual life has taken since we met and the professional identity he has helped me to wrest out of nagging ambivalence and confusion. That all-pervasive principle at work in the marketplace of ideas, proprietorship, Archie never embraced. Nor did he ever learn to drive an automobile—much to the benefit of those of us who from time to time have transported him, in feverish discussion, to this or that airport or bus station. Blessed with a great abundance of ideas, he regularly gives them away to young people in need of direction, and in the circles within which he moves it has become a standing joke that, if there's someone out there you need to know, Archie will make the introduction. He knows his way around in many circles, and he gets about the world, not alone, and never silently, but in eager curiosity, with friends or relations or in crowded public conveyances, continually discovering, wherever he may be, the genuine life—invariably the rich and interesting life—that others may have overlooked. In this way, he comes to know people as people, in all of their variety, as they would be known, and he shows us how, in our intellectual as well as our practical life, the human productive power lies in our love for and our allegiance to one another.

If I cannot point to any particular expression or theme or idea in this book that belongs to Archie Green, it is because, in a sense, *all* of its ideas and expressions belong to him; he has provided the ethical framework within which the book came to be and has guided me in answering, or at least in posing, the question that any writer must address in order to write at all, which is: *Who* is writing? And, still more, where do I stand? In the academy, it is almost a methodological imperative to avoid these questions. But in the end we must face them.

At last, and until then, there is Lydia. We met one exceptionally fine afternoon at the Festival of American Folklife. To her this book is lovingly dedicated.

Ethnomimesis

On Ethnomimesis

Introduction

Every year on the vast lawns of the National Mall the Smithsonian Institution produces a major cultural exhibition called the Festival of American Folklife. Like other such exhibitions, the Festival of American Folklife presents ideas, images, and enactments of human life as it appears across boundaries of social and cultural distinction, including those of rank and class, race and ethnicity, and gender and the life cycle, particularly where such boundaries mark the different tempos and trajectories of historical change, the textures and patterns of human migration and settlement, the coherence and persistence of communities and traditions. Like the idea of "folklife" itself, the Festival of American Folklife stands at the cultural frontier between self and other, particularly where self directs its gaze socially outward or downward.

The history of state-sponsored pageantry and festivity, for our purposes at least, probably begins with the court masques, royal entries, popular plays, and licensed vernacular romances of Tudor and Jacobean England, where more than a century of dramatically expanded cultural awareness, local and global, had come to require an officially sanctioned festive arena in which representations of the lowly, the marginal, the alien, and the exotic would help to incorporate their images symbolically with a newly consolidated political order.[1]

But it is not my purpose to tell again the story of modernity, already admirably told by Paul Mantoux, E. P. Thompson, Raymond Williams, Walter Ong, and Michel Foucault, among many others. I have chosen instead to concentrate on those configurations in the cultural text that, because they are imaginative, admit of many imaginative transformations—configurations in which the Festival of American Folklife, as an artifact of our civilization, is historically and culturally situated.

We begin, then, with Tom O'Bedlam, the beggar madman in Shakespeare's *King Lear*. The Tudors, as Stephen Mullaney points out, operated Bedlam Hospital as a concession, a "playhouse of Folly" in which the control and confinement of madness was bound up with the performance of it.[2] The old king's encounter with the naked Tom O'Bedlam on a storm-beaten heath, the ground of all the festive landscapes to follow, is a radical and originating instance, in an officially licensed and sanctioned theatrical performance, of the downward or descending gaze, of the encounter of self and other embedded in it, and of those cultural structures that inform and underwrite not only the Festival of American Folklife but the entire notion of culture, with its many classes, strata, grades, and formations.

Tom, the outcast and apparition, is a folk figure constructed from literary sources, exposed to the gaze of traditional embodied authority in a social order deteriorating under the influence of the emergent self-interested modern subject. In the play and in the dialogue surrounding him, Tom is the center of a profound ethical, moral, psychological, and metaphysical reflection and a central agent in the unfolding and resolution of the plot. And yet, in a far more important and interesting sense, Tom is not "really" there; he is an ethnographic construction, a disguise or mask adopted by a young noble who has been thrust into a nightmare of isolation, conspiracy, and unreality. In this complex fiction, whose moral anatomy of the early modern period looks forward to the dissolution of modernity in our own time, lies the central paradigm of this study.

The next chapter brings us roughly into the middle of the eighteenth century, a leap of well over a hundred years. Many of the characteristic developments of modernity have become visible on the landscape and have come to operate as principles in the organization of society, the economy, the polity, and the psyche. Through a complicated but well-documented historical and social evolution, the early modern individual and the increasingly rationalized universe that has been in the process of development since the late Middle Ages have produced a modern conception of property, a rationalized space, an enclosed landscape and scientific agriculture, an ascendant commercial class, and another solitary human epitome: not a madman, not Tom O'Bedlam, but a hermit-poet, or rather the imitated figure or enacted role of one, set out for the contemplation of a gentleman as a conspicuous feature in a landscape garden and engineering marvel accoutered with pleasant prospects, winding lanes, a peasant cottage, perhaps, or the front of one, supported by timbers, a Greek temple made of plaster of paris, and perhaps an imitated medieval ruin, done up at reduced scale in cobblestones.

Here, in the hermit and his gentleman, is that reiterated but subtly modified configuration: the solitary folk figure, a fiction, though connected now to some of the fixtures and properties of his putative existence and his situation in an imaginary time, the object now not of the astonishment of a king in his extremity but of a gentleman's cultivated, comfortable, and essentially self-centered reflections, sentiments wrought out of a highly sophisticated literary and pictorial culture. These sentiments are not, of course, unpleasant; indeed, they indicate the stirring of a romantic feeling that would ultimately give rise to the idea of "folklore." But above all, they belong to a structure projected out of the newly individuated modern subject, whose gaze presides over the entire scene and lends to it, by deliberate and concrete activity, the rational, empirical, and specular perspective that was the principal achievement of the early modern mind.

The expansive Enlightenment project that produced the enclosed and engrossed property, the landscape garden, its wealthy proprietor, and the idea of a constitutional democracy designed to secure his political ascendancy also produced, in America, after the social struggles of the Revolutionary period had largely subsided, the plan of Washington, D.C., as well as the political forms and iconography of power it embodies. With its Great House on a hill, its reflecting pools, its long vista terminating in our own towering national obelisk, the Mall in fact *is* our own landscape garden, a public one; culturally speaking it belongs, along with the museums erected around it and the folklife festival enacted upon it, to formations already visible in the social and economic life of late eighteenth-century Anglo-America. The Smithsonian Institution itself, appropriately, owes its existence to the bequest of an illegitimate eighteenth-century

British nobleman who sought to provide for the continuance of his scientific interests under the auspices of the newly independent United States of America.

It is within this framework, then, that five of the book's nine chapters pause to consider the complex phenomenon of the Festival of American Folklife, at which folk artists, dancers, musicians, and craftspeople work and perform under the public gaze on the "national front lawn." "Of King's Treasuries" surveys the National Museum, the Festival's immediate institutional context, materially and conceptually integral to it. Exiting the museums in the next chapter, we find ourselves on the Mall, visitors to the 1974 Festival of American Folklife, where a comprehensive plan of organization, undertaken in preparation for the vast twelve-week Bicentennial Festival of 1976, was in its formative stages; as the principles of this plan, with certain variations, governed the Festival's execution in succeeding years, I discuss them again later in the book in the context of the Festival's broader ideological background.

"Duncan's Hat" begins a Festival notebook, a narrative of the Festival experience shaped to the concerns of the study and setting out what is really the central event of the Festival: the encounter of visitor and participant. Succeeding chapters explore this encounter, beginning where most social encounter begins, with stereotype, and laying down in the analysis of stereotype a foundation for further exploration of the process by which the Festival provides for and shapes the visitor's recognition of the participant. Having arrived to this point, however, at which the Festival in a sense models one of the characteristic social events of our own historical moment, we are in the wider territory of festivity, identity, and memory, with which the remainder of the book concerns itself, concluding with some global reflections on tourism and postmodernity.

In these discussions of encounter, stereotype, and recognition, I have had recourse to Roland Barthes' famous theory of the sign as the union of the signifier and the signified. I frankly do not think that the theory of the sign, at least as offered here, has much to do either with language or more generally with culture as it actually is developmentally, psychologically, socially, or phenomenologically; nevertheless, it is a wonderfully ductile, versatile, and objective formula for explaining—to readers already sensitive to the complex metaphorical intangibles in the identifications human beings make between one thing and another and to the dynamic, elusive character of signification in its personal, social, linguistic, and historical milieus—the conditions under which we make and understand representations. All of this book is about representation, the movement of cultural material from one order of signification to another, a process that Barthes calls "myth," but that seems to me fundamental to the process of representation itself, whether undertaken on behalf of power or on behalf of resistance to power.

Central to that process is what I call *ethnomimesis*. The term is not meant to mystify. *Ethno* is self-evident, I think; it has to do with groups and the forces that constitute them. *Mimesis* is complicated but not occult. I use it in the three senses commonplace in the teaching of literature. In one sense, it means simply "imitation," which according to Aristotle was the primary form of learning—"this is that"; in this case, I refer to the learning that arises between, among, of, and by people in the realm of social relations, which includes most of what we call "culture," but especially that unconscious mimicry through which we take the deposits of a particular influence, tradition, or culture to ourselves and by which others recognize them in us.

Imitation, of course, transcends social relations and goes directly to the imaginative interplay between people and the material circumstances in which they live; as Hume pointed out with his example of the man who both imitates and attempts to influence the path of a rolling ball with movements of his body, the object world we shape then returns to shape us. Imitation, then, is that power by which, in different times and places, we take on and, consciously or unconsciously, perpetuate not only the habits, behavior, speech, ideas, and feelings of people close to us, but also the character of what is perceptibly around us: smokestacks and locomotives in one period; automobiles and airplanes in another; fantasies and spectres in another.

Closely related to this sense of "imitation" is another sense that Eric Havelock, in his *Preface to Plato*, emphasizes in relation to the Homeric poems: "impersonation," in which the poet imitates, as a part of the poetic performance, other persons such as the heroes of the Trojan War, whose voices and attitudes he takes on or "impersonates" as he sings, an impersonation in which his audience subliminally and physically participates. Impersonation is also the embodiment, in a person, of a total sense of life, which is the cultural infrastructure of personality. This sort of impersonation is at once mostly unconscious and spontaneous and thoroughly ubiquitous in human social relations. I regard it as the vital medium of social communication and hence ultimately of culture. Thus I have loosely identified *ethnomimesis* with folk culture, which I take to be the imaginative life, the social and material practices that grow up in the noetic vacuums of complex, diverse civilizations but that, at the same time, have a kind of originality or independence, at once a consequence of their special situation, a kind of primary instance of the cultural process generally, and a particular form of interaction between "official," disciplinary, or "hegemonic" cultures and the marginal, enclaved, or ephemeral cultures that arise within them and yet are, in another sense, an extension of them.

Finally, following the lessons of such now largely forgotten literary critics as Elder Olson and R. S. Crane, I take *mimesis* to be the figuring-forth or summoning up that produces our elite and popular culture of literature, fine art, film, music, and so on, the area of artistic illusion. These are ethnomimeses too, particularly because, like other features of the object-world, they return to us to inform our own conscious and unconscious life at the same time that they give formal expression to the ethnomimetic powers of the men and women who make them. This kind of mimesis is a specialized, formal, institutional, disciplinary, socially patterned development that grows out of a far more extensive and fundamental human process.

All mimesis, then, is *ethno*mimesis; I attach the prefix merely to call attention to that fact. Moreover, the distinct kinds of mimesis are often indistinguishable in practice, particularly in those instances of special interest to this book, where spatial and temporal, institutional and political, or other social structures—a structure as solid and permanent as a museum or as subtle and ephemeral as a few verbal or kinesic cues—become frameworks of conscientious mimesis or fiction-making. Among these structures, of course, are those formed from the boundaries between groups and classes, where representation is a function of the tension, conflict, or change occurring at those boundaries. *Ethnomimesis* is, in effect, my word for culture and for my conviction that, although it is embedded in social practices, manifested in art, and reproduced by power, culture is essentially imaginative. This book will emphasize that, in a complex society like ours, social distances, with their accompanying insulation of one group or community from another, cause people otherwise unknown to one another to conceive the other on the basis of perceptible signs that lend to that conception the character of a mimesis or fictional attribution, with all that such attribution implies; in the social hinterlands between self and other, verbal, pictorial, dramatic, and other representations of groups and communities arise to mediate that conception, including self-representations of one group to another, often in response to the other's stereotyped expectations.

Nevertheless, it is imitation, affinity, resemblance, sympathy, and love, rather than insulation and distance, that mark the relations described in this book. Ethnomimesis is the human energy that joins Edgar and Tom, Tom and King Lear, gentleman and hermit, tourist and tourized. On the National Mall, ethnomimesis is critically at issue in the meeting of visitor and participant at the Festival of American Folklife; but what most exhibitions of traditional culture more profoundly intimate is that ethnomimesis is an elemental force coming out of time to shape the morphology of consciousness. The processes of ethnomimesis originate in the basic human capacity and need for close community—a capacity implicated, from infancy, in our neurological and physical development, becoming, as we grow into social beings, the only environment in which language and personality can develop. There is no more complete communication between human beings than human corporality itself, the human sensory and intellectual apparatus having evolved primarily to join us to one another. It is in this capacity, certainly, that our survival as a species originally lay.

As ethnomimesis belongs to our corporal and spiritual endowment, I tend to identify it not only with folk culture, which arises ethnomimetically in what I have called the noetic "vacuums" or culturally vacant spaces of complex societies, but also with festivity, which occurs in times and spaces similarly set apart and gives special priority to the ethnomimetic process—hence, "folk festival." In festivity we are all in a sense "folk," and folk cultures are inherently and fundamentally festive.

On this last point, I fully expect to be misunderstood, at least until I have set out my argument in full. Sophisticated people are at great pains to avoid what, a generation ago, was freely avowed to be the salient characteristic of the folk performance: its immediacy, spontaneity, and ingenuousness, its "unself-consciousness." Today we are less comfortable with the implicit assertion of social superiority that such an avowal entails, though the very concept of "folk" also implies it. On the other hand, it is well within our more egalitarian outlook to acknowledge—even while recognizing the sense in which "folklore" is a construction of vernacular practice by impresarios and academicians—the often astonishing technical, emotional, and intellectual power of the folk performance. Ethnomimesis has given the true folk performer, in speech, song, or any other field in which she or he acts or makes, the spontaneity and ingenuousness that comes of immediate, unself-conscious communication with the forces—and they are cultural forces—that express themselves in human productions.

Such communication is not, of course, confined to folk performers, nor does every folk artist necessarily enjoy it; but because of the ethnomimetic nature of the folk community, where cultural learning takes place primarily by conscious and unconscious imitation rather than by rote, often within particular families or other prolonged, often lifelong alliances, the power is, I believe, exceptionally well developed there. If it is not so well developed in you and me, it is because we are more isolated; as richly and elaborately mediated as our lives are, they are mediated nevertheless. Between us and our much-cultivated, much-analyzed, much-formulated cultural performances, between us and whatever we do that is not utterly thoughtless, stands an idea, an abstraction, some form of deliberate and self-conscious technical projection: the pattern, score, scheme, or text of the performance, in conformity to which we strive to perform because it is inscribed with social power.

Therein lies the swift and imperceptible compounding hesitation, the awkwardness and ultimately the paralysis that we can overcome, and do sometimes overcome, only with training, diligence, repetition, and habituation, but rarely in a way that "comes natural" to us. And yet what Walt Whitman, who lived at the time when ethnomimesis was shaping the national character and its myriad differentiations, called "the indescribable freshness and candour of the new American" has not been altogether eradicated, and never will be so long as commercial control of the means of the representation of life does not entirely rob us of our ability to live life actually and to imagine it freely. There is yet, indeed, much freshness and candor in us, much genuine culture springing, as in the past, out of the local and global third worlds whose folklife has already begun to transform us. That is what we go down to the Mall, when the Festival is on, to find, and finding, to celebrate.

Folklore and Power in *King Lear*

Poor Tom

Who gives anything to poor Tom? He "eats the swimming frog, the toad, the tadpole, the wall-newt, and the water, swallows the old rat and the ditch dog, and drinks the green mantle of the standing pool"; he is harried by devils and bitten by lice, "whipt from tithing to tithing"; and when he is not "stock-punish'd and imprison'd" or wandering at large on the heath, he nags and whines his way through wakes, country fairs, and market towns, both a casualty of Elizabethan culture and a construction of its laws, which sought to control, for specular consumption, his enactment of destitution, diabolical possession, and madness.

The naked Bedlam beggar in Shakespeare's *King Lear* is a figure of folklore and a bearer of it. His deranged mind is a bird's nest of the threads, strings, scraps, and twigs of the song and speech that play around him: an old ballad about the young Elizabeth and another about the martyred weaver John Careless; a sailor's cry, a lullaby, an obscene song, and an incantation about breeds of dogs; catechistic injunctions, snatches from penitents' manuals, and fragments from the ceremonies of exorcism. In his wandering, Tom must have heard the old wives of Lancashire or Buck-inghamshire tell their witches' tales, for he can call out the names of Hoppedance, Fratercetto, and Flibbertigibbet, of Modo and Mahu, the demons that taunt and worry him, and discover their mischief: how they will lay knives under our pillows or set ratsbane by our porridge to induce us to suicide; how they bring the cataract and the harelip, or mildew the white wheat. His family name effaced by madness and destitution, Poor Tom is but a ghost, the ruin of a personality who was, perhaps, that serving man, proud in heart and mind, who curled his hair, wore gloves in his cap, and served the lust of his mistress's heart.

And yet Tom, of course, is none of these things. He is an invention, the desperate expedient of a young gentleman, Edgar, eldest son and legiti-mate heir of the Earl of Gloucester, who to escape his brother Edmund's jealous designs against him has assumed the identity—if identity it can be called—of Tom O'Bedlam, beggar and madman:

> My face I'll grime with filth,
> Blanket my loins; elf all my hairs in knots,
> And with presented nakedness outface
> The winds and persecutions of the sky.
> The country gives me proof and president
> Of Bedlam beggars, who, with roaring voices,
> Strike in their numb'd and mortified arms
> Pins, wooden pricks, nails, sprigs of rosemary.
>   (II, iii, 9–16)

Edgar, it seems, as perhaps is proper to a gentleman, is an ethnographer of the first water, an able student of the cultural landscape; but he is also something of a playwright—in this speech conjuring the king as we shall shortly see him, "outfacing the winds and persecutions of the sky"—as well as an actor, in whom royalty and beggary are here first conflated. So well does he understand the beggar's life, language, and the character of his suffering that one would think he had been a beggar himself; and, when new circumstances call for it, he can cast off his beggar's rags and drop into the dialect of a Somerset peasant or into the tender discourse of a nurse. His disguises protect him; they enable him to act upon his father and upon the King; and they keep consistently before us, in steady juxtaposition to duke and king, the person, the discourse, and the images of indigent and peasant life whose office in the play is to rise up, as does Cornwall's servant, into the plots of nobles and to shape the action according to impulses of ordinary human compassion and love.

If, through Edgar, the implements of household, kitchen, and farmyard, the forms of wild and domestic animals, the sounds of speech, and the scenes of marketplace and countryside flow onto the stage and dissolve its boundaries, opening the play onto the wider natural universe into which the old king, having become a naked beggar himself, wanders at the height of his passion, it is because *King Lear*, in its language and its story, is deeply rooted in folklife.[1] The banter of the Fool, for instance, echoes with its sounds—children's rhymes and games, popular verse and song, ballads, riddles, puns, jokes, and spells; in Lear's fantasies we behold its images—of a bowman taking his pay, of a farmer's dog barking at a beggar, of a beadle lashing a whore; we hear allusions to a crow-keeper, an apothecary, and a bridegroom. Indeed, the action of *Lear* seems to take place principally against the background of the collective experience, as if collective experience, playing on the margins of the king's awareness, suddenly had cast over it the spell of its own extinction. Old Gloucester's mutterings about eclipses of the sun and moon, and what they portend, seem to belong, with the rest of these glimpses, sightings, and sounds, to a culture that, though everywhere manifest, had suddenly taken sick with the "plague"—as Edmund, the individualist, puts it—of custom, in which such relics of feudal loyalty and obedience as Cordelia and Kent carry their doom in their mouths.

Lear's story itself, in fact, is folklore of very ancient vintage: a synthesis of one legend, about an early British king who brought rebellion upon himself by dividing his kingdom, with another about a favored daughter who likens her love for her father to her love for salt. That is, of course, Cordelia—the traditional patient daughter, a Cinderella, who suffers under the tyranny of the traditional elder sisters in an atmosphere darkened by the absence of a primal figure, her mother, the protecting parent whose absence in *Lear* remains exhaustingly unrelieved. *Lear*'s opening scene, moreover, with the king's central authority surrounded by contesting influences, reiterates the structures of the English folk drama, the mystery and morality cycles in which the biblical King Herod wavers between his good and evil counselors, or the human soul—as the allegorized Everyman—between virtue and vice.[2] These sacred dramas were played from pageant wagons in the marketplace on saints' days and other holidays in Shakespeare's youth and, with other traditional performances, belonged to the popular culture to which *Lear* seems to be a kind of valediction.

And yet Edgar, at last, is neither Edgar nor Tom, nor Lear Lear; both are actors in their roles, themselves "licensed," like Tom, to ply their trade in the unincorporated zones of an ever more repressive society. Nor is *King Lear*, though redolent with folklife and its imaginative forces, a folk play. Although Shakespeare's language is steeped in oral traditions both learned and popular, his genius is literary, and his sources, however indebted themselves to folk traditions, are mostly literary as well. Chief among them is an old chronicle play called *The True Chronicle History of King Leir*. The folktale had appeared as early as the twelfth century in Geoffrey of Monmouth's *History*, and the legend was several times retold near the end of the sixteenth century—among others, by Spenser in *The Faerie Queen* and by Holinshed, the popular historian to whom Shakespeare frequently referred. The parallel plot involving Gloucester and his sons, which had never before been integrated with Lear's story, Shakespeare took from Sir Philip Sidney's aristocratic literary romance of the late sixteenth century, *Arcadia*. Perhaps more than any of Shakespeare's other plays, *Lear* was the fruit of reading, a kind of isolate reflection, least suited of all his plays to presentation on the stage because it so far transcends the limits of the stage.

Certainly Edgar's Tom O'Bedlam would seem to be most closely connected to the authentic folklife of Shakespeare's time; given the rich naturalism of the character, it is tempting to think that Shakespeare was recalling in Tom a beggar he remembered from childhood, roaming the fields and forests of Warwickshire. But "Tom A Bedlam" was an Elizabethan popular song whose text survives in a seventeenth-century manuscript in the British Museum. And Poor Tom's wild lines, as has long been known, owe most of their substance to literature, particularly to a popular satirical pamphlet called *A Declaration of Egregious Popish Impostures*, published in 1603 by the Reverend Samuel Harsnett, domestic chaplain to Richard Bancroft, Bishop of London.

Bancroft was an outspoken champion of the doctrine that miracles, oracles, and prophecies, which in biblical times God had permitted to strengthen the faith of his people, had ceased; this was a cardinal point of Anglican theology during a period in which, as Stephen Greenblatt writes, the Church of England strove "to eliminate competing religious authorities by wiping out pockets of rivalrous charisma"—a competition underwritten by the various social and economic interests, old aristocratic families, mercantile adventurers, Puritan enthusiasts, and the like whose ideological combat was breaking up a variegated but still continuous cultural field.[3]

Of the miracles claimed by English Catholics during their religious revival in the last quarter of the sixteenth century, the most spectacular was the rite of exorcism, a form of psychological theater that displayed to spellbound audiences of Catholics and Puritan nonconformists the power of the true faith—"true," perhaps, because it resided not in the official ecclesiastical hierarchy but in specially endowed individuals: Jesuits, roving miracle workers, and charismatic Puritan healers such as John Darrel. It was an exhibition, moreover, mounted not in the cathedrals, at the heart of religious power, but in the great households in the countryside into which repression had driven it.[4]

At this historical juncture at least, the rite of exorcism, like many of the other enactments of Elizabethan culture, was neither medieval nor modern, being essentially ecclesiastical in its ceremonial trappings and institutional affiliations but popular in its dramatic manipulation of subjective states and its fairylike enchantment of the body, which during the course of the ritual might utter hideous but homely animal sounds of pigs, chickens, and cats or excrete mice or toads or nameless loathsome substances. Coupled with magical exhibitions of spiritual teachers who operated outside the boundaries of officially constituted religious practice, such recusancy, in the Tudor administrative aristocracy, was of course seditious; but it must also have seemed—insofar as it intimated a radical disruption of a social order whose political axis had for centuries turned on spiritual bearings—diabolical in more than a magical or folkloric sense, capable of releasing superhuman destructive forces.

The most famous of these exorcisms occurred in the household of Edward Peckham, member of a prominent and powerful Catholic family long connected to the Tudors.[5] Here a Jesuit priest named Weston and his associates, as they later claimed in a document called *The Book of Miracles*, cured five servants of diabolic possession: Marwood, a manservant; Trayford, Peckham's personal attendant; and three chambermaids—Anne Smith, Friswood Williams, and her sister Sara.

The precise connection among the five is not and probably never shall be known, but Marwood served a dashing and wealthy young Catholic named Anthony Babington, who was a prominent member of the large audience to the exorcisings and who was later executed as the ringleader in a conspiracy to assassinate Queen Elizabeth. Some seventeen years afterward, in any case, four of the five demoniacs came forward, "and upon gentle conference," Harsnett reported, "have frankly, and freely avowed, and have sealed it with their voluntary oathes, taken upon the holy Evangelists, that all in effect, that passed between them, & the Priests, in this wondrous possession, and dispossession, was naught else save close packing, cunning jugling, feate falsehood, and cloked dissimulation."[6]

Culture and ideology, whose union in the late Middle Ages constituted a thoroughgoing philosophical account of reality, were breaking apart; spiritual power, which had been a species of the respect, veneration, and awe that normally sustain traditional social and political hierarchies, was drifting away from the center, reposing itself in sects and in individuals defined not by dependency or domination but by resistance to it. At issue were the very sources of authority, which, in the church, the state, the university, and the marketplace, had been dislodged from their places in an idealized cosmic order wherein God's power was distributed by "degrees" through a hierarchy of legitimate agents, sacred and secular, which conjoined nature and society into a harmonious system of visible and invisible laws. The violent political rivalry between the Anglican and Catholic churches in the late sixteenth century, and the severe repression of one by the other, makes clear sense in this institutional context: to have any legitimacy at all, the monarch must control the institution in which divine authority is vested—this in an age when the fountainheads of divinity were inscrutably and irresistibly drifting out of institutions altogether and into the private recesses of the human breast.

Harsnett made a sensation by printing, along with his mocking narrative of the discredited events, the confessions before Privy Council of the servant girls—a "Transaction so rife in Every Body's mouth," wrote one of Shakespeare's early editors, Lewis Theobald, in 1733, "upon the Accession of King James the 1st to the Crown; that our Poet thought proper to make his Court, by helping forward the Ridicule of it."

"I need only observe now," Theobald continued, "that Edgar thro' all his Frenzy supposes himself posses'd by Fiends: and the greatest Part of his dissembled Lunacy, the Names of his Devils, and the descriptive Circumstances he alludes to in his own Case, are all drawn from this Pamphlet, and the Confessions of the poor deluded Wretches."[7]

It appears from the testimony, however, that although the conspirators may have been somehow deluded or mad, the demoniacs, especially Sara Williams, were not. Weston had written that the girls grunted like swine and croaked like toads; that a demon had exited Trayford's mouth in the form of a mouse; that a Black Man had tempted poor Sara to slit her throat with a knife and to throw herself down a flight of stairs; that the priests had magically restored her hearing and sight after a demon had deprived her of them.

All this Sara stoutly denied. The priests, she said, had held burning brimstone and feathers under her nose to make her sick and had forced strong stout upon her to muddle her head. They had run their hands lasciviously along the entire length of her body, seeking to exorcise the devil whom, they said, would in the manner of his departure render her—who in succeeding years gave birth to five children—incapable of conceiving. Indeed, Sara observed that possession seemed to warrant a certain license lewd, but not altogether diabolical, in character: one of the demoniacs, the pious Richard Mainy, she recalled, had openly tried to seduce her sister Fid; when he behaved in like manner toward Mistress Platter, "a very proper woman," Sara became convinced that Richard was "very wickedly bent." All of her protests, her complaints, and her cries of pain, Sara reported, the priests attributed to the devil, whom they attempted to expel "most unnaturally" by placing a holy relic, pieces of a martyr's bones, in her mouth.

Perhaps Weston, Peckham's chaplain Richard Dibdale, and the rest were suffering from a kind of religious psychosis, bound up as such disorders sometimes are with sexual obsessions; Sara testified that before going into service there, she had heard that the Peckham household was troubled with spirits. More likely, though, the Peckham household was troubled with folklore; indeed, they were quite the enthusiasts. Sara had found the names of the devils, those names that Shakespeare ultimately wrote into his play, under the hangings on the wall of Sir George Peckham's house. One name, Pudding-of-Thames—which after four hundred years can still be heard in schoolyards and playgrounds in the rhyme "What's your name? / Old Puddin'tane"—she recognized from her childhood as the fellow who puts holes in stockings, and another, Maho, from a tale her uncle had read to her from a book. Of still another, wrote the council secretary, "She wel remembreth, that her Mistress, as they were at worke, had told them a merry tale of Hobberdidaunce, that used his cunning to make a Lady Laugh."[8] Mischievous demons these—and no doubt still responsible for such evils as the loss of socks in the wash and the strange proliferation of coathangers in the closet—but not such spirits as can bring down a queen.

From Celtic legend and Saxon fable, from antique demonology, moral and religious drama, popular ballad, children's rhyme, Mistress Peckham's merry tale, and Sara Williams's recollection of it, through Shakespeare's own times and experience—especially, of course, his literary experience—to its birth in performance on the night after Christmas in 1606, the ontology of *Lear* begins deep in the womb of traditional culture. Its folklore is reborn in each incarnation through a series of syntheses that mark its intersection with literary and political forces, which seem diverted or disturbed in haunting and mysterious ways by its influence. The oral traditions themselves, however ancient or contemporary, remain out of reach; we must forever hear *about* Mistress Peckham's tale, but never the tale itself. Who named a devil "Hobberdidaunce," and when? Who first told the story of a foolish king who parcelled out his lands, or the one about a favored girl who compared her love for her father to the love of salt? The texts of *Everyman* and *King Herod* are before us; but these are only the barest bones of what we can never know except by inference, the richly embodied forms of medieval carnival, festival, and holiday. Even Old Puddin'tane, whose name I have heard my own daughters sing in a jump-rope rhyme, has, I trust, entirely lost his diabolical character.

Odd, that the very medium though which folklore reveals itself should, like the mists in which the rainbow forms, frustrate the search it inspires. It is one of the paradoxes of folklore that though we can discover it, and test its authenticity, and even incorporate it into our own cultural life, our literature, music, and art—though we can transmit and even revive it by these agencies, like carriers of a gene, we cannot deliberately create it, any more than we can create the chromosomes whose existence and nature we detect by their manifestations. Like Mistress Peckham's merry tale, it consistently eludes capture, disappearing like a thief among thieves when we pursue it into its own quarter.

It is not folklife itself, but its epiphanies—in elite cultural forms that are not its own and of which literature is, of course, but one—that render it perceptible to us. *King Lear*, in its sources and structures, and even, in a sense, in its meaning, seems to have been generated out of a series of such epiphanies, in which the ground of visible and official culture opens to the revelation of forms from the invisible and unofficial culture, whose only authority is its own—forms that are thereby permanently incorporated with the extant cultural ecology. *Lear*'s folklore, in other words, is something constructed out of the mimesis of the stage, just as, in a sense, Weston constructed his devils out of brimstone and stout; and it is constructed, as folklore always is, along the ever-emergent, ever advancing frontier, often but not always historical, between one species or level of culture and another. Both in the Peckham household and in *King Lear* that boundary is rank; but in the play another boundary—at once natural and cultural—between parent and child has been tragically inscribed upon it.

In the Catholic exorcisings, folklore is an instrument of power and privilege, allied with religious belief and, interestingly, with the spirit of resistance and rebellion. Diabolism, with origins in both theology and folklore, was in the Peckham household perhaps the diversion of young nobles and a kind of decadence whose foundation was, in any case, the exploitation of people beneath them; in the hands of Jesuit priests it became the handmaiden of political intrigue and an instrument of rebellion in a time of political and religious tension and strife.

The fundamental epistemological struggle at the end of the sixteenth century was, finally, between the customary voices of authority in the university, the nobility, the monarchy, and the church, and the autonomy and power of the individual mind to fashion the universe around itself. The cultivation of the subjective at the highest levels of culture; the intensity of the Puritan faith, which fixed the cosmic drama within the individual soul; the emergence of active self-seeking individualism in the commercial classes, many of whom rose by means of it into the aristocracy and the court; the increasing importance in government, manufacture, and trade of practical men, "empiricks" such as surveyors, mining engineers, and navigators: these were powerful forces. Enforce its will though it might, the Tudor monarchy—indeed, no historic institution—could resist the cultural consolidation of what Descartes would call "the simple and natural reasonings of a man of good sense, laboring under no prejudice concerning the things which he experiences."[9]

Harsnett's book registers the reaction, in an increasingly fragmented Jacobean official culture, to fundamental shifts in consciousness that had begun to disentangle the operations of reason from the traditions of learned dialogue and received wisdom with which they had been bound up; these shifts involved the deployment of newly abstract symbolic procedures, derived from old rhetoric and logic but ever more independent of language, broadly known as "method"—not yet a purely experimental and mathematical method, but after Bacon tending inexorably toward it— in pedagogy, technology, even in philosophy and theology.[10] Even the knowledge recorded in books Descartes would ultimately dismiss as a kind of intellectual refuse, the "accumulation of the opinions of many different persons." Where authority is contested, so is reality itself; hence method, which seemed independent of institutions, rushed into the epistemological vacuum to guide the operations of a rational faculty that was wandering out of schools and books to confront experience nakedly and alone.

Not surprisingly, then, reason in *Lear*—whether practical, moral, or metaphysical—is incapable of producing certain knowledge, blighted as it is by humankind's "goatish disposition." In *Lear*, "reason" and superstition undermine one another, the one directing its light only toward selfish ends and the other wandering in a darkness where truth can be stumbled over but never seen. If the exorcisings were indeed "rife in Every Body's mouth" and the ridicule of them thought politically urgent, it is because, at a moment of profound uncertainty, neither institutional authority nor the early stirrings of rational skepticism had yet—and still have not yet—dispelled the enduring human fascination with the ways of knowing immediately gratifying to the imagination: natural wonders such as "eclipses of the sun and moon"; uncanny omens or enactments like the displaced forms of sexual violation that seem to have been part of the Peckham exorcisms. Official culture required, then as now, a reinforcing affiliation with economic and political power, the more repressive as that power lost its legitimacy. No doubt the exorcisms drew large audiences because they offered relief from the intellectual domination of an established church that, like any form of official culture, demanded in some degree the alienation of desire from belief, rendering the one chaotic and the other mechanical; the spectacle of exorcism rent the tissue of ordinary perception with violent and terrible "miracles" that, if they did not, like the miracles of old, betray the working of God in history, could at least temporarily shake the authority of those institutions that stood for, and enforced, their own sovereignty in the realm of culture. Like the miracles of our own popular culture—miracle cures or sightings by "experienced pilots" of unidentified flying objects—the exorcisms enunciated the defeat of authority in the voice of authority.

The power of folklore in *Lear*, at once constituting and deconstituting, reflects the perennial place of folklore on the margins and at the base of the social pyramid, where stereotypes spring up to mollify the host culture, caricatures to mock it, and grotesques to mortify it. How lifelike, therefore, and how trenchant an image, is Tom O'Bedlam. How, like all of Shakespeare's lowlife characters, transparent, as if through the play we could look directly into the actuality of Elizabethan life—a kind of rent in the play's tissue of allusion, convention, and style. Tom is nothing if not authentic: and yet Tom is a work of art—Edgar's work of art, a fabrication designed to absorb the king's affliction, a "spirit," as the Fool names him, which Edgar makes palpable, fulfilling the wish of imagination to meet its conceptions in the street.

Simple loyalty—of Kent to his king, Edgar to his father, Cordelia to hers—is the lifeblood in this play of a feudal order, the "curiosity of nations" and the "plague of custom" of which Edmund, the villain, stands in contempt, an order that appears to be passing away with the passing generation represented by Lear, Kent, Gloucester, and the Fool. It is an order not of individuals in competition, but of communal obligation, interdependency, and, of course, hierarchy, in which the king is his own subject, with the obligations of a subject, and the subject is bound to the king by formal ties that express themselves in duty and ceremony, including such ceremonial address as Kent's "Royal Lear, whom I have ever honored as my king."

In the old hierarchy, authority proceeds from above, through God and the king; for Kent, being and station are one. But in Edmund, power proceeds outward from the exertions of the interested self, where it meets the disciplinary forces that both constitute and limit it. This is Hobbes's war of all against all: a war in which Edmund's special prowess consists of his ability, through dissimulation, to marshal such psychological instruments of the old social order as loyalty and faith on behalf of the new order of autonomous selves—an order in effect so fresh and primitive that self, newly liberated from traditional constraints, can practice little besides ambition, power, appetite, and animal passion. In a traditional society, such autonomy is deeply threatening, as dramatized, for example, in the recklessness with which Lear brandishes his map about the stage like a loaded gun; it is the first sign of his madness, a kind of intoxication wrought upon him by novel technologies of power.

What those technologies are, essentially, is perhaps suggested by the sisters' speeches. In Goneril's "eyesight, space, and liberty"—an original expression if ever there was one—the modern world, with its ideas of democracy, of individuality, of property and the drive to acquire it, seem to spread before us, quite as if Goneril had read Newton and Locke; the phrase seems to thrust her, by a kind of witchcraft, into the eighteenth century and the company of enlightened gentleman republicans. Regan, "made of the selfsame metal" as her sister, rings at once with gold and iron and, with what Cordelia calls her "glib and oily speech," might be a character out of Dickens, assimilated to the material in which she works, as if Shakespeare had made her of machine parts by which sisters, like pins, are exactly reproducible.

The origin of this psychotechnical magic is perhaps revealed in Regan's "precious square of sense," which evokes, like a perspectivist's screen, the rigid analytical framework of scientific inquiry, of senses abstracted from their seats in culture and fitted to the world with machine-turned precision; like Macbeth's dream, it seems to foretell a whole legion of windows, lenses, picture frames, Claude glasses, cameras, and video and computer monitors, not to mention the pages of scores, texts, equations, and formulas, the rules, scales, scopes, and other devices of measurement that, in the ages of science, have interpreted reality for us. Between them Goneril and Regan have already entered Newton's universe of uniform continuous space, integrated surfaces, and predictable mechanical motions, in which being flows from the social and technical fabrications—what Foucault calls the "disciplinary"—that extend its laws into culture, the self, and the body.[11]

From the outset, the atmosphere of *King Lear* is somehow already inimical to the ceremonial character of language and gesture, the traditionality of thought, in the old king's obsolescent world. Shakespeare spreads courtly speech like grease over the ribald and dishonest banter in which Gloucester recalls to Kent the "good sport" at the "breeding" of his illegitimate son Edmund; Edmund's mincingly polite "Sir, I shall study deserving" immediately sounds an effete and unwholesome note. In the opening lines of the play, the world has already been revealed in its animal fecundity, a foundation upon which the ceremony of the old court seems merely theatrical, far removed from the more strictly natural realm in which human motives are actually formed. Even before Lear divides his kingdom, a few lines later, the play has been riven by a division between nature and art, the one illicit and bestial, the other shallow and corrupt, which it is normally the business of human life to reconcile; the king himself is the emblem and embodiment of such a reconciliation.

In dividing his kingdom, Lear divides his "two bodies": the one divine, indestructible, the apex of the structure of human interdependency that describes all social roles; the other mortal, a father, and in decline, destroying the unity of person and role in which all, in the transpersonal world of communal obligation and traditional office, have their existence.[12] In what McLuhan calls a gesture of "left-wing Machiavellianism," Lear delegates his royal authority to his sons-in-law in order that his whole *mortal* identity may be withdrawn into its immortal role, "the name, and all the additions of a king," which without its legitimizing authority is, as Lear is shortly to discover, merely superfluous, a "robe and furr'd gown," a mere "addition" that Regan's coolly empirical "reason," all expedience and self-interest, can no longer understand.[13]

In his old age, Lear wishes to be gathered into Kingship itself. His histrionic posturing—"come not between the dragon and his wrath"—and his "hideous rashness" in the opening scene betoken the terror of oblivion that Lear's own actions have aroused in him, a terror that he seeks, urgently and in vain, to mollify by the wanton exercise of power on the one hand and, on the other, by soliciting reassurances of his daughters' love. That love, in Lear's universe as well as ours, is the fountainhead of being, particularly in the primordial maternal form that Lear, who like an infant proposes to "crawl towards death," was to seek in Cordelia, setting his rest upon her "kind nursery." With his illicit and sinister pun on the word *love*, Lear poisons the body politic by exploiting his divinely constituted power and the ceremonial language of the court, wherein *love* signifies the allegiance of subject to king, to master the natural filial love that cannot be invoked by fiat.

The strangely accelerated and inexorable pace of the opening scene, emanating from Lear—indicated by his impatience with Kent's speech ("the bow is bent and drawn, make from the shaft") and of course by his unreflective, peremptory, and hasty response to Cordelia's "plainness"—suggests a kind of preparedness, as if, indeed, the opening scene were "theatrical" not only in quality but in essence, as if Lear were carrying out a kind of plan or script, or, rather, being carried out by it. Anticipating rejection by Cordelia, he responds to her paralysis in a reckless way that far more indicates his anticipation than it does any actual failure of hers. Anticipating death, he symbolically dies as king, almost as if he were being pulled apart on the rack, at once executing and executed—"this coronet part betwixt you"—in both instances actuated by an unacknowledged consciousness of the illegitimacy, the tyranny, of his methods. If we feel that the old king is somehow out of touch with reality, it is because another reality, a hidden one, seems to be impinging upon him: his own fear of extinction, which he confronts with actions cunningly, if unconsciously, calculated to bring it about.

In Tom O'Bedlam, Shakespeare provides the image not only of "unaccommodated man" but of the wretchedness of a father turned out of doors by his own children, a man in whom infantile terror and rage have been aroused from their latency in the psychological reservoirs of natural love that binds parent to child and child to parent, in which the demand for demonstrations of love, the fear of its withdrawal, the terror of oblivion, and the urge to self-destruction are all one. "Old fools are babes again." In Lear's fantasy on the heath, even the household dogs, Tray, Blanch, and Sweetheart, bark at him—for in this condition of psychological nakedness, where we are all infants, the withdrawal of love is a lesson in the vileness of one's own flesh, a lesson that all of nature seems, and the self seeks, to affirm. "Is it the fashion," Lear wonders, "that

> discarded fathers
> Should have thus little mercy on their flesh?
> Judicious punishment! 'twas this flesh begot
> Those pelican daughters!
> (III, iv, 71–75)

"Our flesh and blood, my lord," says Gloucester, "is grown so vile that it doth hate what gets it."

The king's thrusting out is both the inevitable consequence and the outward image of the fragmentation of his authority; it reduces him to an "unaccommodated man" who "hath ever but slenderly known himself" *as* a man, and whose ordeal, therefore, will be a lesson in his own nakedness. This is, of course, the theme of his discourse on the heath—that of the chastened king who has "Ta'en too little care" of "poor naked wretches" with "houseless heads and unfed sides," and who learns that

> The art of our necessities is strange,
> And can make vile things precious.
> (III, ii, 70–71)

The image of Lear's "unaccomodated man," the "thing itself," Tom O'Bedlam concentrates, in Edgar, the play's dramatic, moral, and intellectual forces. Fleetingly, but full of intimation, his figure passes before us, almost at the play's beginning, in the speech with which Edmund introduces Edgar's first appearance on stage:

Pat! he comes like the catastrophe of the old comedy. My cue is villainous melancholy, with a sigh like Tom O'Bedlam. (I, ii, 135–36)

Edmund, like Lear, seeks immunity from conscience by framing his experience as theater, though, unlike Lear, he does so explicitly, with an unbecoming and not altogether convincing irony. In this frame he is

---

weirdly prescient, summoning up with his reference to Tom O'Bedlam the figure whose guise Edgar, under proclamation of death, will have adopted when next we see him. Edgar, it seems, is not the only character who can affect "villainous melancholy"; Tom is a role waiting to be played. It is often difficult to remember that, in *Lear*, there is no real Bedlam beggar, a fact that persistently brings home to us the untrustworthiness of appearances, including the appearances of the stage itself, which are, as always in Shakespeare, a metaphor for the process of appearance in the construction of social life, but which in *Lear* have taken on a very sinister character.

If Edmund briefly summons up the beggar in speech as an instrument of deception, so does Lear, awakened to compassion by his own unhoused state, summon him up outside the hovel, inquiring how "poor naked wretches" can defend themselves from "seasons such as these," and resolve upon a course of moral therapy:

> Take physic, pomp;
> Expose thyself to feel what wretches feel,
> That thou mayst shake the superflux to them,
> And show the heavens more just.
>
> (III, iv, 33–36)

As if in response to the king's summons, and arising as if out of Lear's own mind, Tom at once appears, discovered by the Fool under the straw of the hovel where he has taken shelter. At once the entire natural landscape—beginning with Tom's sailor's cry, "Fathom and half!" and extending far beyond the boundaries of court and stage, traversed by fiends and cold winds, imprinted with human lust and terror, spilling out of Tom's speech in swift and copious havoc—spreads over the play's noetic surface to mire the king, and all the characters, in a sticky, intractable reality that cannot be subdued by kings, baffled by conspirators, or cosmeticized by fops:

Who gives anything to poor Tom? whom the foul fiend hath led through fire and through flame, through ford and whirlpool, o'er bog and quagmire; that hath laid knives under his pillow, and halters in his pew, set ratsbane by his porridge; made him proud of heart, to ride on a bay trotting-horse over four-inch'd bridges, to course his own shadow for a traitor. (III, iv, 51–58)

Tom's speech is an auditory theater of polyvocality, layered over Edgar's inventions and invested with his authority, registering from the past the voices of Sara Williams, Father Weston, and Samuel Harsnett and bearing them, on the twinned voices of the young aristocrat and a Bedlam beggar, away from the play itself toward a frontier of unbounded actuality, natural and supernatural, vegetable, animal, and human. Tom's thick prose passages lend to the play a texture and density that relieve the nagging sense of weightless artifice Lear and Edmund have introduced and root the play deeply in a consciousness of its own culture. Edgar's disguise becomes a fable whose moral burden can be read back into the play as a depiction of the sordid relations that lie at the interior of the conspiracy; the "serviceable villain," as Edgar describes the murdered Oswald, "as duteous to the vices of thy mistress / As badness would desire," finds his unrealized destiny, and hence his moral consummation, in Tom the servingman:

> Wine lov'd I deeply, dice dearly; and in woman out-paramour'd the Turk. False of heart, light of ear, bloody of hand; hog in sloth, fox in stealth, wolf in greediness, dog in madness, lion in prey. Let not the creaking of shoes nor the rustling of silks betray thy poor heart to woman. Keep thy foot out of brothels, thy hand out of plackets, thy pen from lenders' books, and defy the foul fiend. Still through the hawthorn blows the cold wind. (III, iv, 90–99)

This is indeed "the thing itself," and Lear recognizes himself in Tom at once: "Has his daughters brought him to this pass?"

Tom is the issue of a process, a mitosis, whereby the king, by dividing his kingdom, has in effect expelled from himself his mortal body, which in Tom, who absorbs it, becomes available for his contemplation, inspiring the self-awareness that is the object of his spiritual education: he wipes the hand that "smells of mortality" and learns that he is "not ague-proof." It is precisely the catharsis of that unconscious fear of death from which the tragedy exfoliates and which Lear, through Tom, brings to consciousness and overcomes with mocking reenactments of his own authority.

But remember, there is no Tom. He is an illusion within an illusion; and in fact, we can have him no other way. Unaccommodated man, whether Bedlam beggar or noble savage, is a myth. More than a simple cultural negative, he is the oxymoron that renders visible as an image the reflexivity of two ideas, humanity and its accommodations, which until the moment of *Lear* could only be contemplated in terms of one another. "In the darkest region of the political field," writes Foucault, "the condemned figure represents the symmetrical, inverted body of the King." The beggar and king whom Shakespeare has juxtaposed on stage greet one another across the cultural hiatus in which a new distribution of power articulates itself in a newly constituted inviolability: the "spirit," in which we locate, and in which Lear for the first time recognizes, an essential humanity, no longer a function of its accommodations but of their stripping off, the object of all our humane impulses and the field of our humane knowledge. The King's two bodies, mortal and immortal, have, as Foucault puts it, been reduplicated in the subjected, punished, and absolutely powerless man, whose newly essentialized humanity "is produced permanently around, on, within, the body by the functioning of a power that is exercised on those punished—and, in a more general way, on those one supervises, trains and corrects, over madmen, children at home and at school, the colonized, over those who are stuck at a machine and supervised for the rest of their lives."[14]

We must, then, place Tom, the licensed lunatic, among the ranks of the supervised, the disciplined, the exploited, and the punished; but at the same time we must, if there is to be a folklore at all, search his soul, "the effect and instrument of a political anatomy," for the power with which he cultivates—even within the territory of domination, as Edgar acts within the domination of Edmund's plot—a cultural field in which to exercise his freedom. Edgar's lines intimate what breeds about the beggar's heart; even he may be said to have a psychosocial medium in which to shape himself, once we equip ourselves with the forms of knowledge his existence demands—unless, of course, we are content to view him simply as the blank upon which Shakespeare has scribbled a handful of allusions.

Tom, let us say, is the wreck of a sensualist whose disintegrating personality—the devastation, perhaps, of syphilis—discharges the hidden knowledge that the mind has recorded below the level of conscious awareness and that trespasses the boundaries of private and individual experience, just as in dreams we might encounter past lives or read learned treatises, which in fact we have gleaned by stealth, unawares, from things around us. In him the tide of the natural world, with its rats, lice, and howling dogs, has encroached upon the human interior, where the resounding voices of priests, witches, wives, beggars, servants, children, poets, balladeers, gentlemen, nurses, and inquisitors summon up the moral and emotional forces that rule at the deepest levels—what we usually call the unconscious levels—of human life. That is the level at which king and clown are one, a unity that medieval folk culture recognized and celebrated; it is the level upon which the heath scenes in *Lear* are enacted; and it accounts for the fact that Tom seems almost to have been projected out of Lear or that the Fool is somehow Cordelia (it has been suggested that the same actor played both roles), and that all the characters are, in effect, dimensions of one another. Together they are festivity without society, festivity transposed to a wilderness where clown is not clown and king is not king, where there is no power or authority, or any amusement to be had from trespass upon standards of taste or fashion, no social contract to be ratified in laughter. Tom is nakedness of body and mind, the "poor, bare, fork'd animal" whom succeeding centuries will accommodate with the entire tradition of our humane and social scientific learning; in him culture returns to nature—that is, to human nature, where it finds only the necessity for itself.

In a setting where society, families, and personalities are divided, where humanity itself is divided between men and women who are made of nothing but their clothes and the naked wretches in the hovel who are nothing without them, Edgar seems to have understood fully the nature of the disease. For him, as for all the characters except Cordelia and Kent, all the world's a stage; identity, which formerly marked one's place in a structure of human interdependency, has been exposed as a social fiction, "mere exhibition." Lear, in retreating into that fiction, hopes that death will overlook him. Edmund and the wicked sisters become master manipulators of it, defrauding for private gain; they are all cynicism and despair. Only Edgar, who is never so much himself as when he is not himself, accepts with equanimity the responsibilities that devolve upon him as a nobleman and uses "mere exhibition" to carry them out, inheritor both of a new form of individuality and of the informing traditions of moral authority he has acquired by birth. Hence it has fallen upon him to open the eyes of others: those of the king, of course, by showing him, in the person of Tom O'Bedlam, what a king is without his authority; but also those of his father, by showing him what he is, or rather, *that* he is, without his king. In so doing, he reveals that point outside of official culture upon which he has learned to stand in order to master its forms and expel its demons—a point that lies within a newly organized self, in a new relation to nature and society.

Without kingly authority above him or filial piety below him, Gloucester has lost his equilibrium—he is floating freely and terrifyingly in a universe that seems to have become completely arbitrary: "As flies to wanton boys are we to the gods." Edgar restores him by an artifice that reorganizes consciousness, pictorially, around a fixed point of internal subjectivity, assimilating it to that quiescent point of pure vanishing in relation to which the visible world, also subdued to stillness, takes on orderly and rational form. I am referring, of course, to one of the most peculiar scenes in English literature, that of Gloucester's mock suicide.

"Our foster-nurse of nature," a doctor has told Cordelia, "is repose," whose power will "close the eye of anguish." Edgar leads Gloucester to what he tells the blinded man is the bourne of a cliff at Dover; he then describes the view in what McLuhan identifies as the first rationally projected image of three-dimensional space in literature, extending through several planes, from the birds in the "midway air" that "show scarce so gross as beetles," to a man gathering plants on the cliff face who "seems no bigger than his head," to the fishermen on the shore who "appear like mice," and finally to a ship on the water reduced to the size of its own cockboat, which is in turn reduced to the size of a buoy and is almost invisible.[15] Though Edgar does not speak strictly in quantities, he has nevertheless summoned up a set of relations, which is the essence of quantitative measurement, in which there is no *moral* ground, only arbitrary scales formed from immediate approximations. In this specular world, all is silence:

> The murmuring surge,
> That on th' unnumbered idle pebble chafes,
> Cannot be heard so high.
>
> (IV, vi, 20–22)

Believing he is hurling himself from the high cliff that has been described to him, Gloucester falls; a moment later Edgar, his voice altered to the tone of a knight's, approaches him to find out whether he is "alive or dead," to assure him, with quantitative precision, that he has fallen from an altitude more than "ten masts" high—"from the dread summit of this chalky bourn"—without injury, and to conclude with him that his "life's a miracle," thus "trifling with his despair," and his credulity, "to cure it."

If the heath scenes are festivity without society, Dover cliff is comedy without humor, comedy in which we cannot detach ourselves, until the last moment, from the characters, and hence a kind of ordeal. On stage, Gloucester's fall is pure slapstick—pure stage deception, as if he were blindfolded—a form of comic irony at which we laugh, albeit uncomfortably, at the same time that we recognize in the mock suicide both a miniature of Lear's own story and an ambivalent reiteration of the Peckham exorcisings. Gloucester's despair and its catharsis parodies the king's; but it also relieves the play's tragic intensity, so that the madness of the weed-crowned king, who lurches onto the stage in the next instant, has an antic, a wild, an unearthly gay as well as a ghastly brilliance.

Edgar has painted a picture projected out of the eerie, vanishing repose of the fixed visual point-of-view and thus has given his father the vision that Gloucester's natural eyes, trained by the old culture, could not formulate—"I stumbl'd when I saw." The same intellectual technology that produced Lear's map has also produced Edgar's picture, and within a century it will have generated an altogether new nature and a new art. Shakespeare has taken pains to show us that Edgar's image is, indeed, *only* an image—what McLuhan reminds us is a "conventionally acquired mode of seeing"—a fiction that Edgar systematically constructs, by means of poetic simile, in Gloucester's imagination, drawing upon more than a century of intellectual discipline devoted to isolating the visual sense.[16] But it is effective. Gloucester visualizes; therefore he is.

And the *play* has changed. Edgar's speech, for a transitory moment, quells its turbulence and disorientation; the action stands still for the nonce, and the world is reconstructed before our eyes, reasonably and intelligibly, a world of "eyesight, space, and liberty." From that point on, the play's direction seems to change: the conspiracy begins to fall apart; Lear's madness has the power of new knowledge in it, a kind of clairvoyance, and is soon to pass out of him; and, though the king and his beloved daughter must die, a new order is poised to succeed the old.

King Lear, then, is among other things a play about the division of might and glory: might to become diffuse, faceless, impersonal, or masked, and glory something shallow, spurious, even cheap. It is this impersonal might that spreads through the disciplinary society and operates upon the subjective and subjected self; in so doing, however, it posits simultaneously a kind of cultural antimatter, an adisciplinary field still connected to, or reconstructing originally, forms of traditional power and transcendent authority within the disciplinary body. That is the radiant element whose existence Edgar has detected, and from which he fashioned his Bedlam beggar; it is the stuff of folklore.

Perhaps in the "close packing, cunning jugling, feate falsehood, and cloked dissimulation" of the Peckham household, where from power and privilege sprang exploitation, brutality, and rebellion, Shakespeare has found the very type of the diabolical. The exorcisings belong to a world in which the beadle lusts after the whore, the usurer hangs the cozener, the "image of authority" is a beggar in flight from a barking dog, and "robes and furr'd gowns hide all"—the world Gloucester has learned to see "with no eyes." Lear's brave and uncompromising vision recognizes those social institutions, just and right in themselves, which have become the bowers of otherwise unaccommodated men, lost souls who, identifying themselves and being identified with the institution in whose name they act, wield its power to destroy whoever threatens them, to enjoy what and whom they desire, to further conceal their own weaknesses with institutional displays and their guilt with shows of righteousness. Sara Williams was the victim of this evil of personal violation, and she recognized it; so were Gloucester, Edgar, and Cordelia, violated in the sanctity of fraternal and filial relations. Lear, too, ultimately descried it: it is a picture of power in the moment of its collapse, as office and officeholder cleave apart, the one reduced to flesh, the other to mere appearance—precisely where we found the king in act 1, scene 1, and where, it might be said, the Tudor dispensation stood at the moment of *King Lear*.

Diabolical possession symbolizes and exhibits this condition; the rite of exorcism dramatizes it; and the exorcist exploits it, promising implicitly to transform bizarre and frightful suffering into something harmless and familiar and to dispel its supernatural causes, in effect holding his audience hostage to its own dread. Though he achieves his performance through theater, granting to his audience that sense of immunity given by theater, he frames it as an institutional potency to which, within that immunity, the audience builds its assent and bestows its allegiance. But in this institutional frame the exorcist's own demons find a legitimizing avenue of expression, secretly shaping his performance and making their covert appeal; thus do the most ungovernable and destructive of human drives inexplicably acquire the immensity and inexorability of socially constituted power, the power of little gods.

It is precisely this effacement of the theatrical frame in the enactments of official culture—the thoroughgoing identification of the self, both as the object and as the agent of its power, with the institution that constitutes it—that renders the self vulnerable, as Lear is vulnerable, to unacknowledged aggressions, cravings, and fears now diabolically magnified in the institution made to serve them. For the playwright, this manifestation of the theatrical, apparently bound up with the rituals of authority and the organization of power but bent on deception pure and simple, must have been particularly troubling. In *Lear* we cannot so confidently disconfirm, as Harsnett does, the apparently real with the imputation of theatricality, for theatricality goes to the essence of culture and its power to project a universe onto the two-sided scrim between consciousness and self-consciousness. The theatrical frame is an extrapolation from the social frame; and there is no social frame, however transient, that cannot be pressed into service as theater. As in act 1, scene 2, in which Lear's court becomes a theater for the enactment of kingship, so in the ritual of exorcism does the sacred authority, which frames the exhibition, secure as actual what in theater would be merely hypothetical and direct its force toward actual psychological and political ends.

Cultural life is a continual transfiguration of institutional authority by such enactments, from the merest turn of fashion to the beliefs upon which social and personal lives are grounded. What can be said anthropologically about exorcism—wherein, as Greenblatt puts it, "the treatment is in effect an initiation into the performance of the symptoms, which are then cured precisely because they conform to the stereotype of the healing process"— can also be said about the initiation into and the performance of culture, which confirms itself by conforming consistently to our already inculcated expectations of its forms.[17] The imaginary, in art and in life, is our instrument for controlling this ever-unfolding transformation of consciousness into the conscious, for whatever the ontological status of culture as such, it must be embodied, enacted, performed, represented, and reproduced in order to have any social reality.

The scene at Dover cliff irradiates the structure of theatrical representation, exposing the disjunct relations between the physical stage, the scene enacted upon it, the putative reality summoned up in language, and the subjectivity of both characters and audiences that either reconciles or fails to reconcile these influences. Shakespeare has offered a glimpse into the cognitive machinery of theater itself and awakened a consciousness of artifice that allows him to explore dramatically a particular extremity of pain while permitting his audiences to contemplate that pain with an almost philosophical detachment and at the same time insulating them from the terrible punishments wrought upon the characters by a pervasive, unnamed, and unembodied force in the play—the force of authorship itself.

In this sense, then, *Lear* marks a moment of transition between a theater grounded in ritual and an original dramatic literature, the one corporate, the other authorial—a cultural moment in which a new social category, the category of the individual, appears to urge a reorganization of psychic experience, a new husbanding of imaginative resources on its behalf. As Foucault insists, the new individuality is not an illusion, not simply an "ideological effect." Just as a redistribution of power made the category of the self, it was an original human productive power, an imaginative power, that made the psychic substance it delimits and defines. The psychosocial processes that we locate historically in the early seventeenth century and that so fascinate us about the period, folklore continually reproduces; the relation between folklore and official culture is precisely that between the self, as a psychological substance, and the economy of power that constitutes it. The fact that official culture reinscribes and reenacts the folkloric in its own medium, as Edgar enacts Tom, that Shakespeare constructs Tom's lines from literary sources, that social identity, indeed, must continually reshape itself to the promptings of the soul, only indicates the dialectic of disciplinary and imaginary without which self and culture simply die, the one to become schizophrenic, the other totalitarian.

Out of this nightmare, Poor Tom shall lead thee: to the precincts of the common life, where ordinary human intercourse rounds the sharp edges of institutional power, or into the recesses where self and soul carry their dialogue to the very bourne of despair—and meet an old king coming crowned with weeds and flowers.

Enclosures, Gardens, and the Festival Market

Bring out weight and measure in a year of dearth.

—*William Blake,* Proverbs of Hell

The Ogre in the Tale

With Lear's map, with the speeches of the sisters and of Edgar at Dover cliff, in the very conception of the play, *King Lear* projects the intense light of a new system of thought into areas of the imagination long shaped by traditional practices, ideas, and values. During a period when "weight and measure" were establishing themselves as the instruments of economic relations on the one hand and of scientific investigation on the other, it was becoming possible to discern and to contemplate the forms of life and belief, of human community and expression, that the new system would in the course of the next century drive like a conquering army toward the margins of civilization and into the protecting enclaves of remote and inaccessible parts. Lear's fascination with the Bedlam beggar anticipates a tradition in which thoughtful people would find their attention drawn to the shadows and dim places of human consciousness as well as to the marginalized and residual ways of life into which the Enlightenment had not penetrated, attempting to know them either by subtle and intuitive means not favored by men of affairs, or by directing the light of reason toward those places which its very intensity had thrown into deeper darkness.

Let us remember that it is to cure despair that Edgar paints in words a landscape for his father's inward eye. The same science which transformed the time and space, not only of philosophy, but of social and economic relations, which displaced traditional society in the English countryside with a new system that profoundly disrupted and divided that society, also provided the structure of a new elite aesthetics in which the isolated heart would seek its own restoration. These aesthetics were the milieu in which the idea of culture as a discrete sphere of human activity would arise and— as industrialism fractionalized formerly interdependent ranks into separate, distinct, and fundamentally antagonistic classes—the framework within which the encounter of self and other henceforth would occur.

"The greatness of an estate," wrote Francis Bacon, "in bulk and territory doth fall under measure; and the greatness of finances and revenue doth fall under computation."[1] In the culmination of a process that had begun as early as the fifteenth century, the rural parishes of England, under the impetus of the expanding woolen industry, were by the end of the eighteenth century about equally divided between the open field system, a kind of tribal agriculture whose origins are lost in antiquity, and a modern system of enclosed fields that drew great tracts of land together as the private property of a single owner who was essentially free to manage it as he pleased: for plowing or for grazing, for rent, lease, sublease, or sale.

This monumental change, which decisively ended the Middle Ages in the countryside and prepared the way for the growth of industrial towns, was effected in Parliament through the passage, over roughly a century and a half, of what are called enclosure acts—many thousands of them by the early nineteenth century—whose purpose was "dividing, allotting and enclosing the open and common fields, meadows, pastures and common and waste lands" in the rural parishes. As plowland gave way to pastoral land, cottages, farms, and entire villages disappeared; many farmers of moderate means found it expedient to convert their fields to pasture and to raise sheep for commercial advantage. "Yes," wrote John Hales in 1549, "those shepe is the cause of all these meschieves, for they have driven husbandrie oute of the countrie, by the which was encreased before all kynde of victuall, and now altogether shepe, shepe."[2]

Commercial interests tended to divide the peasant classes themselves; wealthier yeomen who had turned their modest lands to pasture or to market crops, and who employed wage labor, adopted the outlook of gentlemen and merchants, growing increasingly alienated from the village knot of subsistence farmers, craftsmen, and cottagers whose survival depended upon the traditional system of open fields and common lands and who therefore stood in the way of their success. Failing farmers were forced to sell their lands, becoming tenants or laborers or seeking their fortune in the new industrial towns or across the Atlantic.[3] "It is no uncommon thing," wrote a pamphleteer, "for four or five wealthy graziers to engross a large inclosed lordship, which was before in the hands of twenty or thirty farmers, and as many smaller tenants or proprietors. All these are thereby thrown out of their livings, and many other families, who were chiefly employed and supported by them, such as blacksmiths, carpenters, wheelwrights and other artificers and tradesmen, besides their own laborers and servants."[4] This was the community whose remnants would come to be regarded by antiquarians of the nineteenth century as the "folk," keepers of traditional ballads, tales, customs, ceremonies, and other relics of an increasingly remote and increasingly imaginary past.

The enclosures seem to represent one of those great historical moments in which society divides like a living organism, a new group or class emerging out of it to dominate or even obliterate the old, an old way of life giving way and a new system, with its new thought, its new technology, its new values, supplanting the old so swiftly that, by the time the revolution has run its course, its effects and its causes cannot be disentangled from one another. English society in the eighteenth century underwent a morphological transformation, in which interdependent economic communities of an essentially local and regional character, rooted in feudalism, gave way to an interdependency of an altogether novel kind, in which new classes of people—never to be confused with the ancient social hierarchy—economically specialized, physically and socially insulated from one another, and concomitantly segregated and estranged, divided among them the tasks that any human society must undertake to supply its wants. The small manufactures linked to yeomanry and peasantry gave way, as the rural population drifted into market towns and commercial centers, to the factory system; the concentration of a newly proletarianized population in the cities created an expanding market for the agricultural products of a countryside now dominated by great farmers, graziers, and their prospering tenants, who formed a new commercial class with values and motives utterly alien to those of the ancestral nobility it replaced.

Society itself, in short, had been fundamentally reorganized, as knowledge had been reorganized, according to the same principles and, we may suppose, from the same promptings in consciousness itself. As its very name suggests, enclosure enforced a new conception of property based on the cultural project of the previous century, the detraditionalization of knowledge. Arable land, the bounty of God, the fruit of conquest, and the curse of Adam, had become mere surface—a surface, moreover, that could be analyzed, evaluated, dissolved, and reconstituted, not as text, as the monk had read it, but as the technological space upon which the cultural text would henceforth be inscribed. Possession—heretofore bound up with the traditional recognition and assent of the community, endorsed and ratified by it, grown out of generations of customary interdependence and privilege (privilege, it must be noted, present in some degree at every rank)—was now the simple consequence of a commercial transaction between individuals, duly recorded in writing; this was a concept utterly inimical to a tradition in which possession, privilege, and rank had their meaning in terms of one another and in relation to the cosmic principle expressed in social hierarchies.

Simply to *conceive* of enclosure, and still more to carry it out, demanded such rationalization: the professional surveyor, with his new mathematics that could calculate the value of land and the cost of improvements, emerged in the Elizabethan period as an instrument of the commercialization of land use. And, as culture seems to demand that the world reconstitute itself to satisfy its conceptions, so we might hazard that the aim of the enclosures, quite apart from obvious economic causes—the expansion of the wool trade, the commercialization of agriculture, the population explosion, and so on—was quite simply to achieve on the landscape what painters had achieved on their canvases: an organization of space, which, because it flowed from a fixed point of view, could be assimilated, like Descartes' "simple and natural reasonings of a man of good sense," to the newly privatized and individuated imagination that culture had already created out of literacy and money. A realignment of power demanded a new species of authority and the new kind of knowledge it could produce.

The long reification of language by print literacy and of economic value by capital, and ultimately the mechanization of the world picture by mathematics, with its consequent rationalization of time and space, had, as Foucault puts it, transformed "imagination into voluntary memory, spontaneous attention into reflection, instinct into rational knowledge."[5] This should be of particular interest to us, since in our own period the spirit of quantity, now swift and weightless as thought itself, is abolishing the world that quantity created, transforming memory into fantasy, reflection into passive sensory absorption, and knowledge into denatured and discontinuous information or "data."

Economically, then, the enclosures accomplished their purpose with higher agricultural and pastoral productivity; historically, with the gentrification and political empowerment of the commercial class through ownership of land. Culturally, however, enclosure achieved its highest aims wherever the fact of property could be most closely cultivated and experienced by the new bourgeois private person: where, as Joseph Addison put it in the *Spectator*, a man could make "a pretty Landskip of his possessions"—the gardens, pastures, and parks that, in the eighteenth century, were the aesthetic expression, the cultural finial, upon the enclosure and improvement of lands and that made them productive, not of wool or corn, but of aesthetic pleasure.[6]

The representation of reality in language, symbol, effigy, icon, simulacra, and other mimetica emancipates the human dream only to lose it, through resemblance, in the thickets of the world, from which art, like memory, can only briefly and imperfectly recapture it. Algebraic letters, numbers, notes, schemata, and other abstract measures dispel the dream, but with these signs confine the soul, Foucault writes, "in the interstices of ideas, in that narrow space in which they interact with themselves in a perpetual state of decomposition and recomposition."[7] Landscape gardens were living pictures; but the art of pictorial representation—and particularly the art of perspective, of representing three-dimensional space in two dimensions, which involved the mechanical division of the framed three-dimensional image into an abstract two-dimensional grid of coequal squares—was adopted by the surveyor and mapmaker as an instrument for organizing the space in which such representation could occur.

"The ground before you is like the canvas of a picture," one popular handbook advised, "upon which you may draw almost what you please."[8] Enclosure brought landholdings into comprehension by the eye, as an organization of surfaces; the landscape garden, as picture, consummated this development by enunciating the representational character of surfaces thus conceived. In the landscape garden, life and the representation of life seemed to become one.

Walks, lanes, avenues, and views and prospects: the landscape garden of the eighteenth century was chiefly a field for the eye—not only for the stationary gaze fixed at a drawing-room window, but for the stroller through the park who moved in anticipation of changing views and prospects, of surprising turns and fetching glimpses of a fountain, pavil-ion, tower, or bridge, a statue or an obelisk, a grotto or a Gothic ruin, or the more distant prospect of pastures, hills, and dales. Here, perhaps, as Humphrey Repton, champion of the picture window, puts it, the smoke from a woodsman's cottage spreads "a thin veil along the glen, and pro-duces that kind of vapoury repose over the opposite wood which painters often attempt to describe, and which in appearance so separates the two sides of the valley that the imagination will conceive it to be much wider and more extensive than it really is."[9]

With the introduction early in the eighteenth century of the sunken fence or "ha-ha," over which "from the windows of the house the eye could roam at will over the garden and park without the interruption of any barrier," the landscape garden could become a playground for the pictorial imagination, where the romantic yearning for scenes gracefully outflowing, or for the wild and picturesque, replaced the symmetrical formal and topiary gardens of earlier decades.[10]

In Wiltshire, for example, at Stourhead, the banker Henry Hoare strove to re-create Claude Lorrain's plangent transfigurations of the ancient Ital-ian landscape. He formed an artificial lake by damming the Stour, planted its banks with beech, conifers, and rhododendrons, and placed around it three classical temples—a Pantheon and temples of Flora and of the Sun—which a visitor might encounter in turn on a path that led through a damp grotto built around the six springs of the Stour.

The Hoare family was descended from a late-seventeenth-century pa-triarch, the son of a horse dealer who apprenticed to a goldsmith; out of his trade arose one of England's earliest private banking systems. Hoare's father had bought the estate early in the eighteenth century from the ancestral family, the barons of Stourton, who had held the manor since before the Conquest.[11] Although it was typical, after such purchases, for the new owner to demolish the medieval villages that stood in the midst of what might become an idyllic park—the Earl of Dorchester, for example, after buying up the entire parish of Abbey Milton, razed the village to make a fishpond—Hoare chose to preserve the village, with its parish church, in the midst of his park on the near side of the lake, so that it became, in effect, a feature of it; later he placed a fanciful Chinese alcove and Turkish tent of painted canvas near the main house and, as the fashion for the Gothic gained force at midcentury, erected a Celtic cross, an actual antiquity from Bristol, near the village, a Saxon tower on a distant hillside, and in the woods below it a rustic convent.[12] Hoare's grandnephew,

Richard Colt Hoare, the heir to Stourhead, apparently not content with the mere contemplation of pretended antiquities, took an interest in the neolithic and medieval antiquities of his district and published a book called *The Ancient History of Wiltshire*; during his tenure, trees on the riverbank were cleared to reveal a rustic cottage, probably the former home of a gardener or woodsman, to which were added a porch and a bank of Gothic windows.[13]

Many of these features, of course, were lath-and-plaster models, sometimes in miniature, depending upon the distance from which they were to be seen, while the designing and building process itself typically made use of canvas mock-ups. By the early nineteenth century, in any case, the English landscape garden had become a field for all manner of fantasies: Swiss barns, French cottages, and Italian dovecotes succeeded Chinese pagodas and Persian mosques, which had in turn succeeded Greek temples and Old English cottages; all these were succeeded by still more ambitious projects in the shaping of nature—"glass houses designed on a scale so vast that a passable replica of a tropical forest could be contained within their transparent walls."[14]

The cultural work undertaken by the landscape gardener, which was to reanimate and hence to sacralize the visible nature from which God had withdrawn by scoring it with the *notae* of a sentimental calculus, would ultimately be consummated by the romantic poets. "Straying from high ground into a gloomy dell," writes Robert Morris of a walking tour of William Shenstone's estate in Worcestershire, our smell is "regaled with the woodbine climbing up the trees . . . and our ears are delighted with the song of the throstle, re-echoed through the vale, and the whistling of the black-bird."[15] Sensory experience is mediated here by narrative, replete with the quasi-scientific nomenclature—which was becoming a poetic jargon—that places the landscape out of direct access to the senses, rendering it an object of desire, and fashions specific couplings between its features, or the names of them, and the appropriate sentiments, which must be conscientiously summoned up from the emotional reserves of the narratee. It is a narrative that, by a mechanism derived from associationist psychology, could ultimately allegorize the landscape—not, as in the Middle Ages, with reference to an orthodoxy already deeply invested with moral and spiritual significance, but rather to the contemplated, remembered, fancied, or otherwise aestheticized content, particularly the erotic content, of the private life.[16] "Issuing from this sequestered spot," Morris's narrative continues, "we rise a knowl and approach the light, and are cheared with a pleasing home-scene . . . a farm house with a road round it, and a neighboring village in the background."

The next scene is more solitary and mysterious; we descend into a vale covered with bushes, and here and there a tree, where an antique urn contains the ashes, perhaps, of two faithful lovers. . . . This wilderness thickens as we go, and becomes an impenetrable wood, the sacred asylum of happy pairs. . . . At the bottom of this solitary vale a little lake is formed which reflects the moon long before she sets, the shores are planted with poplar, and within their peaceful shade is erected a little monument dedicated to the remembrance of some valued friend.[17]

This *moving* picture mediates emotion with an ingenious structure of cultural scavengery. An artificial landscape has been realized in narrative that interprets the picturesque, and its particular pressures upon the heart, in terms of various moments of contemplated bereavement, which the scene does not dramatize but further mystifies with signs, signatures, memorials, and even a kind of miniaturization: the warmth and conviviality of hearth and village life; the purity of a lovers' faith sealed in death; a fantasy of uninhibited erotic play; the satisfactions of friendship. But these several varieties of love are several times removed: by the narrative itself; by death; by social arrangements and moral law; by their symbolization upon a landscape that is itself a fiction, a kind of museum of sentiment, which to have life must be reinscribed with the feeling of life—inscribed, that is, quite literally. "Those who are fond of inscriptions on buildings, backs of seats, etc.," Morris counsels, "though they can never please but once; and though the utmost they can pretend to, except where they carry emblematical allusions or commemorate a departed friend, is to point out the beauties and describe the effects of the spots where they are placed; these persons will find a variety of lines, adapted to almost every occasion, in Horace, Pope, Shenstone, and other English poets."[18]

The mainspring of this emotional mechanism, with its frustrated, withdrawn, and forbidden human attachments, is clearly the sensation of sundering or of separateness itself, a symptom of the psychosocial quarantine of the self and a clue to the nature of the abdicated relations in which the isolate self might ultimately find its fulfillment. In that sensation lay, conceivably, but in a primitive condition, reassurances of existence and, perhaps, a horizon of transcendence; to nurture and explore that sensation, however, was an achievement of "negative capability" that sublimated a pathology of self-inflicted pain by situating the attention in the field of fictive distances, silences, and absences that the romantic landscape is.

A projection of the solitary self, indeed, was to become one of the principal features of the landscape garden, designed not only to inspire contemplation of our isolate condition, but to provide the image of and even to enact it. The "thresher poet" Stephen Duck was employed as Queen Caroline's hermit at her residence at Richmond; Charles Hamilton, who owned an estate in Surrey, built a hermitage and drew up a contract for the post of hermit, who would pass a seven-year term "with a Bible, optical glasses, a mat for his feet, a hassock for his pillow, an hourglass for his timepiece, water for his beverage, and food from the house. He must wear a camel robe, and never, under any circumstances, must he cut his hair, beard, or nails, stray beyond the limits of Mr. Hamilton's grounds, or exchange one word with the servants."[19]

This poor fellow fled, apparently, after three weeks. Another, who sat in a cave "with an hourglass in his hand, and a beard belonging to a goat," survived, incredibly, for fourteen years; perhaps, like Concord's transcendental hermit, Thoreau, he was moonlighting at the local pencil factory. Most vacancies for the job of official hermit, writes John Dixon Hunt, were filled by dummies stuffed with straw, which gave "the right emblematic effect" at twenty yards, and, in any case, made minimal demands on the resources of their employers.[20]

The hermit in his hermitage may perhaps be regarded, actually or symbolically, as the last of a displaced folk who could not or would not be moved by enclosure. He is, in any case, a transitional figure between Shakespeare's Tom O'Bedlam, whose nakedness and incoherence seem to embody the infancy of a psychological self born out of traditional interdependencies and hierarchies, and such self-conscious and self-dramatizing romantic figures as the solitary poet of Gray's *Elegy* and the wandering young mendicants of Herder's Germany, or poetically constructed ones such as Wordsworth's leech-gatherer or Arnold's scholar gypsy. To him, too, we must trace, I think, the lineage of our own politically constructed folksinger heroes like Woody Guthrie, the dustbowl balladeer, or the self-created Bob Dylan.

It is as though the frame of reference represented by the landscape garden, once the modes of perception peculiar to it had been firmly established in culture, had been dismantled and "nature" established as a cardinal cultural category dissociated from its historical links to capital, property, and measure, though still deeply and invisibly informed by them.

The whole countryside of old Europe, with its lakes and mountains, and the half-perceived, half-created wilds of the Americas became a "landskip" to be celebrated, painted, written about, re-created, and toured for its sublimities; poets and philosophers—soon to be followed by folklorists, psychoanalysts, and anthropologists—would set out to explore the vast new regions of the human psyche, manifested in its "natural" products of language, folklore, and myth, as well as in the "natural" promptings of sensation, feeling, and memory. A "sentimental" or psychological self, the modern bourgeois subject, now projected an idea of culture broadly understood as a phenomenon of psychological time, symbolic exchange, and ritual production.

The mitosis revealed in the enclosures, then, is a displacement of what had occurred and was occurring in philosophy, where mathematical means of representing reality triumphed over mimetic modes of representation because they had the power, which mimesis did not, of actually influencing the physical world through internal manipulations. This idea delivered the ground of culture, if not culture itself, into the hands of scientific, technical, and especially commercial men whose quantitative methods, by which all their reckoning was carried out, greatly facilitated the alliance of science, technology, and commerce at the heart of modernity.

Money, it seems, had in the eighteenth century begun to rival nature for sovereignty over Creation; in two-and-a-half centuries the forces of culture, with its imaginative "works," its unmediated awareness, its unconscious knowledge, were beginning to seem somehow antithetical to the mechanical time, rationalized production, and capitalized exchange that characterized the new social order, albeit constructed in relation to it— above it, upon it, within it, or against it. As Raymond Williams explains in *Culture and Society*, culture itself, as an "abstraction and an absolute," emerged with special visibility in the "practical separation of certain moral and intellectual activities from the driven impetus of a new kind of society"; society itself, a matrix of abstract and technical forces and relations, had become a medium of which culture was not an effect but a content.[21] The enclosures, and the landscape gardens that grew up within them, are enactments of this new cultural situation: in which the ground of culture is not "nature" but the scientific, technological, and commercial civilization that human ingenuity has summoned out of nature; in which human artifice, in anthropology normally identified with the culture-making power, is now—with its rational structures of space and time, its technological networks of transport, communication, and exchange, its bureaucratic organization and planning, and its industrial production—the condition, not the realization, of culture, including that culture which grows up in the very bosom of science, technology, industry, and commerce.

"Since money does not disclose what has been transformed into it," writes Karl Marx, "everything, whether a commodity or not, is convertible into gold." Now money isn't everything; but it follows that gold may be in turn transformed, theoretically, into whatever may be transformed into gold. And as surely as money does not disclose what has been transformed into it, so does money wonderfully vanish when it is transformed into land, labor, or goods, time or information. Hence it was not only within the capacity of mercantile wealth to convert itself into land but also, through that conversion, to transform yeomen, mechanics, and merchants into gentlemen, the ownership and proprietorship of land being, in the eighteenth century, the cultural index and precondition of power. Gentlemen, therefore, who had come by their lands through money were quick to rifle the genealogies for distant relatives and noble names by which to authenticate their new social standing; in Scotland, newly titled graziers, merchants, and lawyers, inspired by the novels of Sir Walter Scott, began after a generation to wear the kilts of the same highland clans their fathers' enclosures and the British army had driven off the land. In fact, as Hugh Trevor-Roper shows, highland culture was itself a "retrospective invention" and the kilt a relatively late expedient of an English ironmaster that became the fancy of romantics and a symbol of the Highland Regiments—in short, an artifact of England's economic, political, and military hegemony.[22]

Thus does each inundation of capital absorb the cultural signifier, including not only the signifiers of its own historical stages but also those of the cultural enclaves that develop or survive within it; both of these acquire significance in the marketplace by virtue of their displacement by capital. In a world of conglomerates, junk bonds, and global markets, even the old corporate capitalism of steel, oil, and railroads acquires a cultural hue and can be recycled in the form of the symbols, styles, and signs connected with it.

The landscape garden and the highland kilt, forms of cultural recovery and invention, respectively, both illustrate that, as culture is that which lies outside the domain of capital, capital can create culture by negotiating its own concealment—precisely the magic that transforms an abstract ledger of appropriated quantities into a realized imaginative "culture." Because consumerism is built on dissociated production, cultural communities arising from the actual processes of production become, in effect, natural resources, the social center becoming in turn a colonial market into which the converted icons, artifacts, and images of culture, historically and aesthetically stable, can be offered up to baffle momentarily the dread of cultural instability and change endemic to the system. This process has been institutionalized in the fashion system, which has erected a marketplace at the gates of time that it variously calls "now," "today," the "season," "this year," or even "this generation," in a social field contoured by class and set out with its markers, called "taste."

Money alone can release the cultural object from the enchantment of its commodification. Hence capitalism, as has frequently been observed, parasitizes even those cultures that capitalism itself generates, because it at once creates and indicates a cultural value; emergent networks of commerce invisibly underwrite what is essentially a traffic in representations. As the power of capital consists fundamentally in the genesis of signs, the mass market very early learned to trade in imitations—plaster for marble, glass for jewels, gilt for gold, and so on—which *as* signs could be cheaply reproduced. The market consequently created a distinction between the spurious and the authentic cultural object, so that authenticity, too, could in a sense be bought and sold, and massive expenditure come inevitably to be identified with it.[23] The semiosis of contemporary consumer capitalism is of course far more supple, a phantasmagoria of dereferentialized cultural fragments, a kind of autovandalism in which information processing and megacorporations replace surveyors and estates; but the process, structurally, is the same.

The extent of our relations now vastly transcends the specific conditions of culture in community, in tradition, and in individual experience; to understand this, it is only necessary for the electricity to go out for an hour, or for a blizzard to close the roads or a wind to bring down the telephone wires, or for the water supply to dry up, or, for that matter, for us simply to run out of the money upon which access to the system depends. As the ground upon which it stands gives way, in the elongated instant of our barbarization, culture reveals itself.

All of this, then—the rise of the commercial classes, the enclosure acts, the gentlemen who with economic instruments displaced a people, their history, and their traditions in order to erect in their gardens and parks idealized pictures of history and culture, sometimes of the very culture they had displaced—should help us to understand our own cultural situation, which confronts us at every turn with the images or pictures of culture, not only as spectacle, but in forms so concrete that we can scarce distinguish them as images or pictures at all. For though the landscape gardens were picturesque—that is, "like pictures"—they took shape in a medium that pressed upon the viewer the conviction of reality—unlike the painter's canvas and paint, through which illusion could be appreciated as such. Among the new landed gentlemen of the eighteenth century grew up a new cultural mythology, by turns classical, Gothic, romantic, Oriental— what Roland Barthes calls a second-order semiological system, in which the signs of a deposed cultural language had become the signifiers in a new language, which, having been emptied of history, opens the possibility of a cryptohistory invested with values that, so long as they remain concealed in the sign, can advance one cultural project in the name of another. The landscape gardens of the eighteenth and nineteenth centuries are monuments to commerce, colonialism, and the factory system; yet we still identify them, culturally, by the traditions with which they allied themselves, history having been very nearly converted into myth by the men who spent money in order to make it.

This is the sense in which the enclosures, and the landscape gardens that followed upon them, point socially and culturally toward the Quincy Markets, the Harbor Places, the historical districts, tourist attractions, theme parks, suburban tracts, shopping malls, and, indeed, to the folk revivals and folk festivals of our own day, which make nonsense of such functional distinctions as that between "educational" and "historical" or between "commercial," "residential," and "recreational." Such complex retail pseudoenvironments as Baltimore's Harbor Place or Boston's Quincy Market—called "festival markets" by developers—promise to gratify, with shops and restaurants, the inchoate hankering, almost an anxiety, after unmediated experience underwritten by the slovenly physical persistence of the historically enchanted external forms of nineteenth-century trade in marketplace and port; this hankering is, as I have suggested, for the reunification of cultural knowledge with cultural practice, the two having been divorced by the very system that at Quincy Market or Harbor Place now offers to reunite them, but on its own terms.

In the "festival market," so called in recognition of its isolation of the "retail drama" from the diurnal world, diverse fragments of authentic cultures already fixed unawares in the imagination by half-forgotten popular arts—the movies, perhaps, or the magazine ads of a generation ago, always capable of arousing an association but never of articulating it—call out like impounded dogs to the bewildered consumer. A Nevada roadhouse, a Filipino bistro, an Italian fruit vendor's cart, a Marin County outfitter or Flatbush deli, each one evoked by the merest gesture of ornament, design, or logo, each one fleetingly pressing its cultural moment upon us, cluster together under the steel-trussed canopy of a freight-pier-turned-shopping-mall; outside, couples in athletic wear and other fashionable costumes—indicators of a social class, an exotic world, a vanished epoch—stroll as on a promenade of the Gilded Age past the three upthrust masts of a man-of-war tied fast to the wharf. Across the bay, the gigantic barnlike structure of a munitions plant joins the sugar and soap factories where freighters from the Far East lie idle as cranes dip languidly into their holds; around them an ethnic neighborhood, close upon the ruin of the docks, yields awkwardly to redevelopment—a bakery, formerly a trolley depot, sends the odor of warm cinnamon rolls into the air, and shops and taverns jockey for the quality of authenticity that seems to consist, not only in the excellence of the counterfeit, but in the possibility that we may make it, through a money transaction, our own.

Within and without, contemporary hyperstructures embody the cultural moment and delineate its sacred space as surely as the cathedrals of the twelfth century. The lofty, cavernous interiors of John Portman's Hyatt Hotels, built on a Dantesque scale that baffles conventional expectations of time and space and isolates discrete environments such as restaurants and shops each in its own lake of shadows, reproduce the culturally empty zones that capital opens in the social order in order to import, in the newly reified cultural forms that lie beyond its walls, its own commercial activity. And like the economic field it imitates, the Hyatt interior consistently unravels the social fabric so as to reconstruct it in the ways that its own technologies of communication and transport—the house phone, the elevator and escalators, the public address system—dictate. In order to do so, however, it must shut out the savage and poisonous environment outside, indeed the very atmosphere itself, which unbridled capitalism has created.

Detroit's Renaissance Center is literally a fortress against the city, surrounded by concrete buttresses that coldly acknowledge the social catastrophe it represents. Waterfront restorations, in similar fashion, take up residence in derelict structures, though often integrating or incorporating them into their own designs in restorative ways that, at best, reconcile the changing scale and amplitude of invisible economic systems with the needs of imagination for a whole and continuous world framed on the human scale and hence an extension of it. Both kinds of hyperstructures take on meaning with reference to the spoiled urban environment to which they are both a response; both indicate a new stratum of cultural life emerging within and over the old, in various relations closely analogous to those between commercial society and the other orders, such as folk culture, that live in and around it, and which it is in the power of commercial culture to frame, to isolate, and to appropriate.

Yet "commodification" only describes a process that, in the real human world of desire, remembrance, and death, where everything is charged with significance, is never complete or perfect, and in which money, even if it has become as ephemeral as the modulations of an electromagnetic wave, remains tied to human needs and powers. For, as the landscape garden was contained in the estate, the commercial hyperstructure is itself already contained in a commerce, and that commerce in a technology, in a structure of information as yet invisible to us—already an artifact of history spontaneously converted, by such consumer communities as teens and retirees and by flea markets and carnivals, to new uses through perennial modes of human association that long antedate the retail drama.

Let us return, then, to the landed gentleman of the eighteenth century, who, as the beneficiary of all these changes, gazes out upon the formal garden just below his windows, to the park that sweeps into the distance where few sheep graze, and, perhaps, to the point at which the scene breaks open into views beyond the boundary of his park—to the remains of a peasant cottage, or a distant village now uninhabited, or a facsimile of them. All has become the dominion of a man no longer tied, either by tradition or by necessity, to the ranks of folk now exiled to the industrial cities or to America or Australia, leaving behind them a rational landscape in which the human heart no longer casts its shadows. No Bedlam beggars roam at will across it, no ghosts or demons; the girls of the May, who once may have danced upon the green, now stand at the looms of Birmingham or Manchester. "It is a sad thing," remarked the Earl of Leicester, whose words Karl Marx saw fit to record, "for a man to be alone in the district of his residence: I look around, and can see no other house than mine. I am like the ogre in the tale, and have eaten up all my neighbors."[24]

The Earl is lonely; but, if he does not carry the actual charge of his ancient dependents, or their actual fealty, or any sense of his patrimonial obligation, he has at least an obscure and not unpleasant sensation, in the contemplation of the meadow before him and of the distant spire, of a kind of bereavement, almost a pain—and yet a pain that does not quite touch him, one from which he is protected by a bank vault of economic and social security. Indeed, that complex sentiment, compounded of natural beauty, formal aesthetic arrangements, romantic evocations of ancient and distant times and places, may be sweetened by the infusion of feelings warmer and more intimate: perhaps his daughter is at play on the lawn, dressed as a Roman princess or, like Marie Antoinette, as a dairymaid. Perhaps the Earl will establish among the locals of his district a revived May festival, which a curate of the next century will describe in a letter to an antiquarian journal, believing that the festival is a survival from ancient Saxon tribes.

The Earl's loneliness, by the end of the eighteenth century, has become a cardinal feature of the romantic tradition that joined the commercial and scientific mind by new ties—no longer those of obligation or of obvious and immediate communal interdependency, but rather of aesthetic and intellectual pleasure—to the phenomenal world. In the steeple raising its old head above the treetops, in the plume of smoke, in all of what Words- worth called "the fallings from us, vanishings," the "blank misgivings" that the rationalization of the world picture had produced, the romantic tradi- tion had located that point on the map of the human imagination where the lost treasure of human community had been buried.

This tradition and the social programs that grew up within it were the artistic and intellectual responses of culturally refined and economically privileged men and women whom commercial and industrial civilization had emancipated from immediate dependence upon nature or upon physi- cal labor and from immediate and perceptible interdependence with the several ranks and classes of society—men and women whose minds, more- over, had been shaped by the rationalist outlook of the eighteenth century, whose essence was the detachment achieved by the perceiving mind from its object. But in that object, romantic poets and painters as well as the socialists, antiquarians, and folklorists who directed the romantic gaze into history, society, and culture had found a silent rebuke in which the heart might explore, through the contemplation of its distance from its object, the very wound it had sustained in the creation of that distance. That "sense sublime of something far more deeply interfused," as Wordsworth called it, the "intimation of immortality" that comes to us in the elusive "vanishings" that seem to conceal the possibility of their own fulfillment, the romantics regarded as a natural, even a sacred prompting in their own breasts toward a union of reality and actuality, which cultural discontinuity had ruptured but which the heart's own obscure rememberings could fleetingly fulfill.

This same longing, once so exotic, so fragile, is now the common currency of our imaginative life, bewilderingly diffused in our art, our manufacture, our ideas, but particularly in or in opposition to the commercial medium in which most of our imaginative culture is made manifest, leading us obscurely through a landscape of shopping malls, real estate developments, restaurants, theme parks, tourist traps, and even to the Festival of American Folklife, which like a distant spire or ancient cross, or the smoke from a woodsman's cottage, beckon to us with the traces of completed ways of life. For Enclosure is the parent of culture: enclosure, if not by God or Nature, then by the gods, and the second nature, of our knowledge and our power, within which we must learn to design our garden and erect our ruin.

The National Museum

We are only human insofar as we are sensitive.

—John Ruskin, "Of King's Treasuries"

Of King's Treasuries

Interred in a crypt by the door of the picturesque red sandstone hall erected at Washington in his name lie the bones of James Smithson, illegitimate son of Elizabeth Keate and Hugh Smithson, the Duke of Northumberland, who at his death in 1829 bequeathed to the American government a half-million-dollar trust for an "Establishment for the increase and diffusion of knowledge among men." With its vigilant parapets rising above the linden trees along Jefferson Drive, the Smithsonian Castle might be the ancestral seat of some English gentleman— as indeed it is, in an expatriotic and posthumous sense; but the elegant park that extends from its doorstep, which at one point in its history was a luxuriant garden shaped by serpentine paths and hanging trees, belongs now to the intersecting sweep of the National Mall, whose indomitable longitude summons the entire city to attention along the intellectual line between the Capitol and the Washington Monument.

Outside the baronial walls of the Castle, where Andrew Jackson Downing's evergreen grove once stood, a blue-and-yellow carousel, mirrors winking at intervals around the cornice of its canvas top, turns in the widening spirals of old-fashioned waltzes: "The Daring Young Man on the Flying Trapeze" and "After the Ball." Some antic Smithsonian official must have placed it there, determined that even in the midst of the dreary national museums children should have fun; but where are the gypsies, the carnies, the Kewpie dolls, the Ferris wheel, the cotton candy? With its prancing antique ponies and its gay Gilded Age melodies, the carousel is itself a museum, a circuit of fancy that stills the flow of time and, to the parent who finds herself remembering the moment even while it is shaping itself in her admiring eyes, speeds it headlong with the rest of existence, as her child comes round again, into oblivion.

On the other side of the Mall, on a bench with its back to the National Museum of Natural History, perusing the *Washington Post* through the thick, round lenses of his hornrims, may be seen, every summer evening after six, an aged Bertrand Russell, or the perfect likeness of him, a likeness made still more perfect by the rumpled suit of clothes that seems to have accompanied him in his dim journey into the present out of some London street demonstration of the 1940s, retaining all the telltale marks—a threadbare elbow, a shine at the knee, a deteriorating hem—of time's passage.

Not ten paces beyond him, occupying another bench and surrounded like a caliph by the cushions of plastic bags stuffed with rags, bottles, cans, and other refuse salvaged from the sidewalk trash barrels, sits a woman of Afro-Caribbean aspect, with pendant earrings, a yellow turban, and a ruffled Jamaican skirt shot with yellow, red, and green. To no one in particular, she carries on, in a sharp and peremptory tone, a lengthy diatribe on a topic known entirely only to herself, from time to time addressing the pedestrians passing on the promenade before her, who studiously ignore her.

Occasionally, the old philosopher peers over his newspaper to watch a jogger pass: a young congressional aide, perhaps, with a walkman, who will pick up her pace to pass a lumbering federal bureaucrat, his step somewhat burdened with middle age and the cares of government; then both are passed by a fleet-footed trio of shirtless young United States Marines in red trunks who advance toward the Washington Monument with manly strides and heavy footfalls that cause the gravel path to quake.

On the lawn beside them, a softball game is in progress: Greenpeace, the environmental group, is taking on the State Department—the office ball clubs—and Chris, a Greenpeace volunteer from Michigan, has just hit an unanticipated double into right center field, sending two startled fielders racing toward the trees with reckless determination. One wonders whether the actual political life of Washington is in fact going on, not in the Congressional office buildings, or the executive branch agencies, or the federal courts, but on the softball diamonds here on the Mall: on the grass across Twelfth Street, the American Petroleum Institute has taken the offensive against its archenemy in the field of atmospheric pollution, the Environmental Defense Fund, whose outfielders must pause to return the dayglo frisbee that from time to time drops into the field of play, sailing through the bright atmosphere that seems to radiate over the Mall from the Capitol dome.

Between a government office and a Metro stop, or between a museum and the Monument, a lawyer in a black pinstripe suit, with his blue-shaven face, carries an expensive leather briefcase down the gravel path of the Mall; a black museum guard, still in uniform but with his cap tipped back, carries an unopened umbrella; a student in Nike Airs gazes at the ground as she walks, a bookbag slung over her shoulder. A young West Virginian, a mountaineer not yet eighteen, skinny as a flintlock, the broom of his hair bound under a red tractor cap, his muscleshirt hanging on his bones, his knees showing through holes in his blue jeans, has come here on his honeymoon with his corpulent bride, age seventeen and disarmingly pretty; they are all nestling and hand-holding when not recording the sights, and each other, with their Instamatic. An entire busload of eighth graders, gossiping about the familiar but unidentified public figure they think they saw on Pennsylvania Avenue, or about the romances budding in their midst, assembles by the Union Square reflecting pool to be photographed before the Capitol.

The varied timbres of human voices, the shapes of speech—thin and fragile, robust and rounded, elastic and melodious, from Macon and Jersey City, Galesburg and Dallas—drift and dissipate in the sunlight: families mostly, with their duets and trios and quartets of half-grown children in pennantlike clothing still stiff with the starch of shopping malls and discount stores, hinting obscurely of the tennis court, the golf course, the beach house, and the marina as well as of the bowling alley, the Little League diamond, and the scout camp. Their clothes, in fact, seem to be more wrapping than clothing, as if the consumers themselves had become the product to be consumed, taking on the quality of the traffic in which they are most deeply concerned.

Gradually, as the weather cools, all these people disappear. Summer ends; the trees around the reflecting pool drop their leaves; autumn packs its bags for the trip home; and a young man, black, homeless, his hair clotted, his skin scarfed and hands bruised, hugs himself to sleep on the grate that opens above the Twelfth Street tunnel, where the writhing air heated by innumerable auto engines ascends in a massive column toward the rheumy winter skies.

In 1967, when the popular resurgence of folksong and folk music now called the "folk revival" had begun its decline and a folk festival on the National Mall was proposed by the Smithsonian, members of Congress complained that such festival—along with the other novelties such as the carousel, theatrical productions, and evening concerts that Secretary S. Dillon Ripley had introduced—would make a "midway of the Mall." Since the 1930s, folksinging had been enlisted by various radical, populist, and progressive movements as an instrument of social change; indeed, in the years of the Popular Front it had been the explicit program of the Communist party to reach the working class through folksongs and music adapted for use at strikes and union rallies. McCarthyism drove the music of social protest temporarily underground; but the impulse to reform and the populist vision generally, with its Spartan personal attitudes, its political combativeness, and its idealizing love of American folk culture, survived to inform the commercial folk revival that emerged on college campuses after the Kingston Trio's 1958 recording of the mountain murder ballad "Tom Dooley" showed the power of traditional songs, sung in a commercial style, to rival rock-and-roll music in the marketplace.

For the political and social establishment, however, the folk revival still retained its old associations; to people who could remember the 1930s, *folksinger* was virtually synonymous with the Popular Front and with left-wing politics. In 1967, too, the term *folk festival* could still be associated with, for example, the massive countercultural powwows at Newport, where, a few years earlier, legions of college-age bohemians—rallied by the resistance songs of Pete Seeger, Bob Dylan, and Joan Baez—had massed to share their collective discontent with a society dominated by postwar social regimentation, racial segregation, and the nuclear terror. The Mall, moreover, had only recently achieved the abstract, almost spectacular formality that the capital's original architect, Pierre L'Enfant, had intended for it; it had become, itself, a kind of monument, with the old Victorian museums presiding over it, federal buildings standing at attention at its margins, and the great marble piles of the Capitol Building, the

Washington Monument, and the Lincoln Memorial brooding over it with inscrutable glory.

But Martin Luther King's March on Washington in 1963, undertaken in the gaze of the nation's television networks, woke the excited democracy of the 1960s to the public and, more exactly, the political character of the National Mall, virtually defining it as a stage for the dramatization of political will—whether an outcry for constitutionally guaranteed civil rights or, as in the Poor People's Campaign of 1968, for equality of economic opportunity. In the intervening years, with the video gaze still directed to the greensward at the center of Washington, scarcely a cause has not been represented by demonstrations on the Mall; Hare Krishnas and Vietnam War veterans, abortion rights activists and antiabortionists, environmentalists, law enforcement officers, military personnel, farmers, and hundreds of other groups have joined the softball and frisbee players, the bicyclists and joggers, the boomerang throwers and kite fliers, the dancers, singers, flute and guitar players, proselytizers, and picnickers on the lawn of our now emblematically national National Park, in a political field defined, perhaps, by the Inaugural ceremonies that, from Lincoln's day to the present, have made the Mall the scene of the awful moment in which power lingers for a moment, disembodied in its passage from one bearer to another.

It was this public spirit that Connecticut patrician S. Dillon Ripley sensed when he came to the Smithsonian in the year after King's march, and he promptly turned the statue of the institution's first secretary, Joseph Henry, to face the Mall and the people now vigorously encouraged to enjoy it. Catching, too, the Parisian quality of the city and the festive mood of the period, and recalling the balloon men, waffle vendors, and Punch and Judy shows in the Tuileries Gardens that he had visited as a youth, Ripley proposed that the spectacle of people at play on the National Mall might plausibly serve as a national example and perhaps encourage a body politic, agitated by civil rights and antiwar struggles, to live at peace with itself again. By the third year of Ripley's tenure, the old National Museum, the "nation's attic," had introduced evening hours for summer visitors, various outdoor concerts, puppet shows, barbershop quartet singing, musical comedy, jazz combos and opera, and the Festival of American Folklife onto the National Mall.[1]

Until the middle of the last century, when James Renwick's brick-red Norman castle with its eight crenellated towers was built on Jefferson

Drive to house the Smithsonian Institution, the National Mall was a commons upon which sheep and cattle grazed and vegetable gardens grew; marshes and tidal flats extended to the Potomac from the rise upon which the Washington Monument now stands to what is now the Tidal Basin at the base of the Jefferson Memorial. In 1850 a pleasure garden, with serpentine groves of American evergreens designed by Andrew Jackson Downing, was partially realized; but the Mall ultimately proved more useful—during the Civil War as a camp for union soldiers, and later as a railroad yard, with its engine sheds, switches, water tanks, and coal hills. Not until 1901 were the tracks torn up and the Potomac swamp reclaimed.

That the Mall should have remained, throughout the nineteenth century, a field reserved for public utility rather than the public pleasure was utterly appropriate for the young democracy, in which "all men are created equal" was less a philosophical proposition than a popular proverb; in which there was no man to "lord" over any other, nor any "airs" to put on; in which even the president of the United States could be addressed—and was addressed—by any ordinary person as familiarly as if he were a cooper or a farrier, and not a great general with grievous war wounds; in which our natural environment was popularly regarded, not as a pretty picture to please the eyes of gentlefolk, but, as it is now, as a resource to be turned to use and, at best, to profit by.

As the name of its architect, Pierre L'Enfant, may suggest, however, the Mall belonged to an original plan more republican than democratic, more patrician than plebeian, more philosophical than practical, a plan that, as presented in 1791, was replete with the rational idealism of postrevolutionary France—far more a late child of the Enlightenment than of the new popular democracy. Like the city that inspired it—Paris, not Charleston or Philadelphia—its message was Empire, not Nation; conquest, not community; it was a plan quite incompatible with the entrepreneurial capitalism that drove real estate development in the early Federal period. While other new American cities like Cincinnati and Buffalo grew wildly, Washington slumbered; in 1792, shortly after submitting his plan, L'Enfant resigned when blame for the slow sale of lots, upon which the financing of the Federal District depended, was laid upon him. Not until 1871 was his plan revived, when public works projects under the new territorial governor, "Boss" Shepherd, brought paved streets, water, gas, and sewer lines, landscaped parks, shade trees, and a $20 million debt to the capital.

Yet Fanny Trollope, who visited Washington in 1830, "saw nothing in the least degree ridiculous about it"; foreigners and natives alike had laughed at it, she acknowledged, "because the original plan of the city was on an enormous scale, and but a very small part of it has been as yet executed."[2] That design, nevertheless, "which was as beautiful as it was extensive, has been in no way departed from." In fact, she said, the city of Washington reminded her of nothing so much as one of Europe's fashionable watering places:

> From the base of the hill on which the capitol stands extends a street of most magnificent width, planted on each side with trees, and ornamented by many splendid shops. This street, which is called Pennsylvania Avenue, is above a mile in length and at the end of it is the handsome mansion of the President; conveniently near to his residence are the various public offices, all handsome, simple, and commodious; ample areas are left round each, where grass and shrubs refresh the eye. . . . To a person who has been travelling much throughout the country, and marked the immense quantity of new manufactories, new canals, new rail-roads, new towns, and new cities, which are springing, as it were, from the earth in every part of it, the appearance of the metropolis rising gradually into life and splendour, is a spectacle of high historic interest.

"The total absence of all sights, sounds, or smells of commerce adds greatly to the charm," she continued, catching the spirit in which L'Enfant's plan had been conceived. "Instead of drays you see handsome carriages; and instead of the busy bustling hustle of men, shuffling on to a sale of 'dry goods' or 'prime bread stuffs,' you see very well-dressed personages lounging leisurely up and down Pennsylvania Avenue."[3]

Like all artifacts of the Enlightenment, L'Enfant's plan flows like a dream, albeit a rational one, from the eyes of that newly perfected engine of history, Rational Man, but not, it seems, from those of the self-reliant, independent, energetic, and pugnaciously egalitarian rational men of unexploited natural America—the entrepreneur, tradesman, or pioneer— and certainly not from those of the land speculator, except as he transformed, in doubletalk and for ready money, midwestern swamps and woodlands into watercourses and pastures. As L'Enfant's own words suggest, the plan of Washington might have flowed from the heart of a Duke—one of almost unimaginable dominion, for whom America was, as it was for Fanny Trollope, a vast pastoral landscape garden fitted in its substance and particulars to the individual sensibility, in its form and structure to liberal philosophy, and in its spatial orientation to the Newtonian cosmos. "The view from the capitol," Mrs. Trollope observed, "commands the city and many miles around, and is itself an object of imposing beauty to the whole country adjoining."[4]

L'Enfant's plan was framed in a continuous visual field "commanding" the surrounding space, a kind of aesthetic fortress, with the instruments and conventions of pictorial art; it was perforce connected to the rational principles, political and cosmological, of which the visual field was a sensory projection. L'Enfant expressed the concept of the constitutional separation of powers, for example, and the distribution of power between the federal and state governments, by linking the Capitol and the president's house, both built upon prominent rises, with the ceremonial Pennsylvania Avenue; squares and circles situated throughout the grid system of streets, regularly intersected by broad diagonal avenues representing the states, were intended as the centers around which local communities—linked to the larger city as the states were linked to the federal government and to one another—might form. The entire structure, moreover, was, like a ship at sea, oriented to the cosmos along a meridian drawn by Capitol architect Andrew Ellicott from celestial observation—appropriate, certainly, for a new Ship of State. Moving about the city on diagonal streets remote from the Capitol, it is still possible to recall the symbolic connection between local and national, neighborhood and city, margin and center, as the Capitol dome, drifting like a great bright thunderhead on the horizon, intelligent like the dome of the human head, lingers at the terminus of some long, broad avenue to watch us, or from the surrounding hills sails over the skyline as if seeking a place to descend, or raises its face like a planet for the city to fall into place around it. For though we merely see it, it is to us itself an eye, its gaze ever directed outward and all around.

The eye dominates, the ear attends. Domination by the eye, realized aesthetically in the landscape garden, has its basis in the expression and maintenance of power. The fortress, always established on the highest point of land and affording a visual command of all possible approaches, is perhaps the archetype of visual experience—of a realm conquered first by war and then by art, of subject peoples or of subject nature—and becomes itself both the seat of power and its symbol. Terminated at one end by the Capitol Building and at the other by the Washington Monument, the Mall declares, like the private park of a Whig aristocrat, a People's victory over an entrenched nobility by a form of occupation that has in time, inevitably, taken on the character of the power it displaced. In this respect the city, an architectural spectacle arising out of philosophical speculation in the midst of speculation in land, carried out by means of specular instruments with the aim of specular reciprocity at every point, is a monument to the Enlightenment myth that expressed an unprecedented consolidation of powers—political, economic, technological—in an ascendant class as a revolutionary extension of power that abolished class. Washington's glorious avenues, like the boulevards of Paris, descend culturally from the Roman highways that carried Caesar's imperial legions, returning from the frontiers of the Empire, into the city; its majesty is an aesthetic effect formed through the gradual sublimation of the moment of surcease that finds the victor, after many battles, secure upon his promontory, with a "commanding" view of the country around—in the fortress with its armory, treasury, and keep, which many centuries will transform into castle, house, and hall, and finally, in the democratic ages, into chambers where judges, legislators, and an elected monarch sit. From this dome, the greensward of the Mall falls to the base of Washington's colossal obelisk like the roadbed of some terrific railway, where the Engines of Progress, on tracks long ago torn up, ran on the Wheels of Democracy.

In time, nature and history have worked their shaping influences upon the city of Washington. A river, the Anacostia, stands between a populous black neighborhood and the rest; another, Rock Creek, called by Mrs. Trollope a "dark, cold little river, closely shut in by rocks and evergreens," forms a narrow wilderness along whose margins the city's most desirable residential neighborhoods have grown up and, at the same time, provides efficient entry and exit to the city along a parkway built on the ravine floor. The city's original four quadrants that meet at the Capitol—northeast and southeast, northwest and southwest—now describe divisions of race and class, divisions reflected on the social landscape by the pervasive presence of a black population largely employed in service occupations, whose daily intercourse with the white, largely suburban, bureaucratic, commercial, and professional classes produces, not interracial harmony or familiarity, but at best mutual indifference, as two schools of fish may swim through one another without any apparent mutual awareness—what a local journalist, comparing it to the relations of toddlers in a nursery school, calls "parallel play."

L'Enfant's plan spreads a pattern of surfaces across the visual plane, fixing us as observers, always outside and above it, in a world that is in effect a map of itself. But the three Smithsonian museums—Natural History, American History, and Air and Space—draw over and around us spacious but finite interiors that, in containing us, urge out of us and provide a theater for the signification and dramatization of the knowledge that we ourselves contain. They form a triad whose psychic texture suggests the much older geography of the naive imagination, a hierarchical realm in which we dig for truth, which is at once agricultural and archaeological, and ascend, on technological wings, toward the heavens, which are at once ethereal and divine.

The Museum of Natural History, for example, at once anthropological, zoological, botanical, and geological, describes what to its creators was, mythologically speaking, the descent of consciousness into ever darker and more narrow confines: to the primitive, the animal, to the uninterred bones of men and animals, and finally, with minerals and gems, into death and the insensate earth. But in this place an ages-old extractive quest in Western culture, which searches for riches underground, locates the essence of its own being, literally and figuratively digging for it in the ground. The gaze that fixes upon the lucid interior of the Hope Diamond, whose very name suggests its meaning, in its sanctum at the Museum of Natural History is contemplating something that is at once a concentration of the chemical basis of life, of fossil energy, of sumptuary wealth, and of contemplation itself; at its heart is egress out of this world into one of ineffable purity and infinite extension, one which, according to medieval folklore, could bestow spiritual and bodily health, protect chastity, influence behavior, and protect from harm—the eye at the heart of Death becoming also the Polaris of desire. For this prize men descended into mines and set out to the four corners of the earth, eternally bonding, actually and metaphorically, the search for riches—whether gold, spices, or eternal life—with the penetration of the New World and its illimitable bounty. The historical quest for cheap labor and new markets thus was coevally bound to the exploitation of exotic and primitive cultures, which in turn variously supplied, as a counterforce to prevailing social ideologies, the images of heathen, savage, unfallen, and natural man. But as Northrop Frye observes, the essential object of this adventure is the renewal of life, which is the essential character of the earth. "The authentic form of the treasure hoard," he writes, "is the release of the life-giving powers that come with the spring and the rain."[5]

That a kind of childlike awe that radiates from the Hope Diamond can still be the principal basis for pleasure in the museum is apparent in the Air and Space Museum, the Smithsonian's most popular, where the violent displacement of outsized missiles, airplanes, rockets, and the like is brought home by the gentility of the interior, whose lofty windows and carpeted floors belong more properly to an opera house like the Kennedy Center. Machines that have broken the bubble of the atmosphere and trebled the speed of sound are tethered like clouds awkwardly gathered into a barn; a rock that lay on the surface of the moon now sits with arms folded under glass at the door as if it were a fragment from some original building now demolished; barnstormers and mail planes, immense rocket boosters and manned satellites, crowd under the museum roof as though wrangled in from some steely destructive rain to mingle with the visitors like so many celestial objects. In fact, the Air and Space Museum resembles nothing so much as a vast aeronautical showroom, where symbols of the unity of corporate and military power, inscribed with a mythology of technical and entrepreneurial adventure and personal daring, somehow offer themselves to the nameless illimitable dream of an imagination puerilized by wonder.

If the Museum of Natural History displays what time has buried, Air and Space makes a sinister allusion to the end of time by apocalypse from the air. While also a history recorded in technological artifacts and hence in some respects evocative of the past, Air and Space celebrates an enterprise—the conquest of the skies—traditionally associated with spiritual quests, with the meeting of gods and men, and with the adventures of the intellect that carry us beyond the bounds of earth, nature, and the flesh. The implied tense of air and space travel, which seeks the unknown, is consequently always the future, into which technological progress, always associated with ascent and in turn with the cosmological, carries us.

Curiously, though, as space-age technology slips into the past, archaeology and technology, death and desire, meet, and time folds in on itself. The age-old dream of walking on the moon has been realized—yet so strong is our sense of its futurity that it seems not to have been done at all; its future tense works upon us as a vision of paradise, located at the origins of time, aroused the earliest explorers of the New World, informing our visions of time's farthest frontier. The outer reaches of the solar system become provincial, and the galaxy—indeed, the edge of the observable universe—a region of pure speculation; and the future, insofar as it is linked to technological advance, seems to shrink and die or to reestablish itself, perhaps, in another realm—in the interior space of the microchip, where extensions of the mind proceed invisibly and without mass or volume. The Viking lander, on its barren little patch of Martian sand, has a quaint and familiar terrestriality, like an old farm machine sinking into the dust somewhere out in western Oklahoma, where a tenant family couldn't make it and moved on.

Between the extraterrestrial and subterranean realms, and in relation to which both are elaborated and to which each returns, lies the plane of ordinary experience, where wealth can be neither robbed, seized, discovered, nor dug from the earth, but only cultivated, gathered together, and planted again, and where the future, with its promise of freedom, is attained only by following the track of history and tradition; this is the realm of culture. It is a relief from the summer sun, the tumult of traffic, and the colossal scale of the National Mall to enter the cool, dark, central hall of the National Museum of American History and thence into its still more quiet, sequestered, and shadowed galleries; it is a relief, too, on another level, to escape the pervasive atmosphere of bondage, interment, and death in the Museum of Natural History, or the turgid glories of Air and Space, and to find, in American History, the material record of actual human relations.

Museum galleries; but theaters, too, dark as grottoes, where the fixed, inanimate museum artifact rises up as if enchanted and dances with other artifacts in an illusionary space within which unseen agents confusingly disconfirm, with an ingenious disorder, the historical actuality of authentic objects, turning our interrogation of reality inward to the process of perception itself. At "A Nation of Nations," an exhibit on immigration and assimilation in America, a silent inscription—Walt Whitman's "I am one of the Nation of many nations," from his *Song of Myself*—hovers at eye level, a voice made visible on a transparent plexiglass panel in the dark of the corridor. Here, outside Room 20 of the Dunham Elementary School in Cleveland, Ohio, it is 1915. But gazing through the pane of glass into the schoolroom, which I stand slightly above because I am at the edge of a short flight of steps—the viewpoint, in fact, of some proprietary spirit—I seem to enter my own childhood, and the world, with its fixed places and times, seems to melt over me in a warm wave.

I cannot remove my gaze from the scene. No question of authenticity arises, for there is no counterfeit: it is the schoolroom itself, almost identical to the rooms in which I spent all the years of my elementary education, with their elegant little desks and their inkwells, the flag with its forelock of gold hair, the round eye of the Bendix clock, the dyspeptic face of George Washington in Stuart's unfinished portrait. As I look about me at the young museum visitors for whom the schoolroom is something strange and oppressive, the episodes of my own life briefly form within me an intricate narrative ever more entangled, as it retreats toward its obscure origin, with a cultural history; the pane of glass between me and the schoolroom assimilates itself to the isthmus in my own being between the present moment and that dim region where dwell the unremembered memories that cannot find, except here in the museum, their own reflections on the surface of the altered world.

Filled with its coin and stamp collections, its cameras and printing presses, its machine tools, clocks, and early calculators, its farm implements and motorcars, "the nation's attic," as the Smithsonian used to be called, might seem appropriately named. Not all of the Smithsonian's collections, however, invite such a homely comparison. Like the Tower of London, which is both an armory and a treasury, the Smithsonian has collections that speak directly to the sources of political power and military domination. We have, of course, no crown jewels to deposit in the National Museum; but we do have the Hope Diamond in its stout, cavelike vault in the Hall of Minerals, and we have the moon rock, quarried by astronauts, to greet us, almost as if it were a doorstop, at the entrance to the Air and Space Museum. Above our heads, the shell of an instrument of war, the Bell X-1, hangs from the ceiling like some sinister piñata, an early experiment in aerodynamics shaped like a .50-caliber bullet; across the Mall, on the third floor of the American History museum, an arsenal of military rifles and other antique weapons stands at attention in the silent halls, guarded by headless soldiers, their chests bursting with military pride, in the uniforms of old wars. In these displays, the Smithsonian is, like the Tower, simply a fortress whose anthropological meaning is that a civilization initiated by the conquest of subject peoples, against whom the conquerors must henceforth fortify themselves, will be perpetually divided—a pattern that in less straightforward forms tends to repeat itself through all the stages of civilization and society, including the society of the contemporary District of Columbia.

All this is simply to say that the Smithsonian, like the treasuries, armories, fortresses, castles, hoards, and keeps of ancient societies, reflects a natural, perennial, and universal impulse to gather together and protect the wealth that is the foundation of any human order and to find in it a record of our past, through which, by writing and rewriting, we can in each epoch tell again the ever-unfinished story of who we are. It is further testimony to the universality of the impulse that we use our households— not only the attics, closets, and barns, but also the upstairs corridors—as well as our neighborhood restaurants and taverns as the repositories of our personal and local cultural artifacts. It is true that the taint of morbidity can hang over museum exhibits, whether of stuffed chickenhawks or plaster Eskimos, which embody the ideas that no longer speak to our understanding of nature, history, culture, or technology; it is always the task of museum curators to sustain, while carrying the colossal burden of exhausted ways of thinking on their backs, the life of their collections by reconstructing, according to the ideologies of the age, the manner in which they are exhibited. "The museum of the past must be set aside, reconstructed," wrote Smithsonian assistant secretary G. Brown Goode in 1896, "transformed from a cemetery of bric-a-brac into a nursery of living thoughts."[6]

In the nineteenth century and earlier, the collection of exotic objects or of animals implied an economic power and physical mobility peculiar to aristocrats and kings; but the agencies of such powers were, after the conquering armies and the crusaders, members of the mercantile and colonial classes, who brought back objects from faraway places that testified to economic, not military conquest. To display a collection is hence inevitably to reach, as printed texts may reach, across social lines, or, more precisely, to exhibit—literally to pull back the curtain on, as Charles Willson Peale is doing in a well-known self-portrait—private wealth, or the conversion of it, to an audience assembled on the other side of the economic and political barrier that has conspicuously favored the collector and tends to reenact and reinforce it. Peale's Philadelphia Museum, the first in America, seems to have contained the seeds of the Smithsonian's own triad of life above, upon, and beneath the earth: it included western birds, portraits of Revolutionary War heroes, and a gigantic mastodon skeleton that Peale himself had helped excavate.[7] Thus converted, wealth is of an entirely different order than land or money; it embodies an effort literally to possess, through various commercial transactions, capture, or rapine, the historical, cultural, and natural worlds and, ultimately, to re-create, control, and reproduce those worlds through such devices as the landscape garden, the greenhouse, the zoological park, and at last the industrial, commercial, and cultural festival or fair.

The evolution of museum displays suggests, of course, the changing social situation of the museum as an institution. In the Smithsonian's oldest museum, Natural History, one finds exhibits that are really nothing more than original naturalists' collections exposed to view, as they might be in a library; the labels affixed to particular specimens reflect only the exigencies of taxonomy, not of display. The monkey grimacing in a glass womb of formaldehyde, hugging himself against the cold of frozen time, is there as an emissary of his class, whatever the naturalists have determined that to be—not, like one of Barnum's sideshows, the lurid and ghastly offense to life that he is.

But one can trace in the halls of the Natural History museum the increasing effort to supply the context of the artifact or specimen as a way of mitigating the morbidity of the fact of its capture. Most familiar, of course, are the animal scenes arranged in artificial natural settings, to which most middle-class children have been repeatedly exposed. But the principle of contextualizing the museum specimen remains, in various elaborated forms, central to the museum enterprise; among the innovations of Dillon Ripley's watch were such sensory extensions as the many-faceted sounds of a departing steam train to accompany the 280-ton Pacific-type locomotive from the Southern Railway and the premonitory aroma of fresh chocolate to accompany a reconstructed nineteenth-century sweet shop.[8]

Contextualizing has its ultimate expression in the concept of the "living museum," in which living human beings are made to practice their art, say, in a setting created for artifacts, as was attempted in the Museum of Natural History's "Aditi: A Celebration of Life" in 1985; this exhibit placed Indian folk musicians, puppeteers, painters, jugglers, acrobats, dancers, a magician, a potter, a toymaker, and other practitioners in a gallery decorated to suggest a village of traditional rural dwellings and organized according to the stages of the traditional Hindu life cycle. But the spurious, disingenuous quality of artificial settings is, I think, lost on no one and cannot be banished with ever-more-perfect verisimilitude, because the very existence of these settings denies to the visitor the imaginative participation upon which the pleasure he takes in the museum depends; although the introduction of living beings into the structure of a diorama may reverse, in a rather crassly literal way, the awkward morbidity of a plaster manikin, it only amplifies the effect of objectification and domination that is the principal offense of such techniques. At bottom, the impulse to contextualize suggests that the force of the display no longer resides in a kind of admiration for the deeds and the powers that brought the specimen or the artifact into the museum—an admiration that implies a willingness to tolerate an overt assertion of class distinction; it aims, instead, for transport, suppressing its social affiliations while announcing in effect that to do away with itself has become the museum's principal project.

In the same way that the shopping mall insulates the "retail drama" from the many complex kinds of social and economic negotiations taking place outside its walls—the textual metaphor is appropriate here, too—so does the museum establish spatial and temporal boundaries within which the visitor is temporarily confined and outside of which lie the resources over which, consequently, the museum alone can exercise its power. The sequestration of its objects and the occlusion of the means and circumstances of their acquisition excite the desire for them or the wonder at them which, in a shopping mall, a money transaction can temporarily assuage but which, in a museum, become forces turned toward the replication of the power relations the museum embodies. The Hope Diamond and the ruby slippers, each one associated with a female Hollywood icon, Elizabeth Taylor and Judy Garland, the one glamorous, the other tragic, and the Gemini space capsule and Archie Bunker's chair, seats of a technocratic and a proletarian ideology, respectively, all mark, contain, and re-create their own cultural valuations.

To the eye of Empire, the Elgin marbles, installed in the British Museum, are trophies that somehow attach the glory of Greece to the glory of England, already ideologically melded; once the spell of Empire is broken, the marbles become first plunder, then debris. Similarly, the army barracks complete with latrine, the Dunham Elementary schoolroom, and the Italian American house in American History's "Nation of Nations," which would otherwise be quite absurd, both require and answer a conception of history assimilated to personal experience and to the life cycle, in a period in which the ubiquity of change lends a special density of reality to everything that escapes it. It is likely, however, that were it possible to display the Elgin marbles as Harrod's might display them—spotlit, on pedestals, importing the codes of the fashion system into the museum world—we might see them, as it were, in a different light. Art and history museums regularly employ commercial display strategies to lend the quality of the exquisite to their collections; that, in fact, is what the Smithsonian did with the "Nation of Nations," hiring the prestigious New York firm of Chermeyoff and Giesmar to design the exhibit.

The modes of organization in a history museum, whether of freeze-dried birds or of internal combustion engines, represent the choices, with their implicit evaluations, of the collectors and directors, which in turn partake of their own social and cultural affiliations. An automobile engine, for example, might be displayed with other machines, covertly becoming part of a paean to engineering and manufacture; it might be displayed anthropologically, alongside more primitive technologies that perform the same work, or historically, against those whose synthesis produced the idea of the engine; or it might be detached from related technology altogether and placed in the context of another dimension of culture. What, for example, would be the significance of a V-8 automobile engine were it placed in "A Nation of Nations" or in "From Field to Factory," an exhibit on the migration of rural blacks to the urban North after World War I? Either setting has the potential of transforming the artifact of technology into an agent of social change, an instrument of corporate hegemony, and a fetish of popular culture; one might even look ahead to the day when it will be reread as a symbol of environmental and social catastrophe.

Assuming it is true that the form of a museum exhibit illustrates the tacit and perhaps unconscious categories that at once circumscribe and enable any culture's thinking, let us look more closely at the state-of-the art contemporary exhibit at the National Museum of American History, "From Field to Factory: Afro-American Migration, 1915–1940."[9] Here artifacts from two conjoined contexts, the turn-of-the-century rural South and the post–World War I urban North, are assembled together with texts, artifacts, documents, recorded music, film, and material reconstructions to narrate the postwar African American migration not as a fixed text, or even mainly as a historical process, but as an unfolding modification of consciousness whose voluntary element makes the visitor a collaborator in its genesis, with the strange result that the visitor and the institution converge to discover together the moral center around which the exhibit turns.

Here a Washington taxi driver may reexperience, with an intensity that momentarily shakes his conviction of time and place, the motor trip that brought him, at age nine, to the capital city from his home in South Carolina. By a system of light and shadow, encasement and suspension, floating text and timely juxtaposition, "From Field to Factory" carries the artifacts of that movement and its period—diaries, public notices, newspaper clippings, household and personal items, farm implements, the interior of a sharecropper's cabin, radio music, a Baptist sermon—out of the inert collection and into the imaginative life of the visitor; it is almost as if the exhibit and his or her movement through it were assembling themselves, moment by moment, out of the visitor's own work of *remembering* the migration.

We encounter the exhibit literally before we enter it, in the form of an aerodynamic black sedan, a 1935 Chevrolet Master Deluxe, its roof carrier loaded with worldly goods packed in canvas and bound with rope, parked in the museum's first-floor west corridor. By saving sufficient money—about $600—or by repairing such a vehicle, a plaque informs us, a southern black family might secure it for the journey to the North. Turning into the exhibit—where, behind a screen, three manikins scrape the dirt with hoes against the backdrop of enlarged photographs of a cotton farm—we hear, as the light suddenly drops, the twittering of birds. At once we are out-of-doors; the air seems almost to freshen around us, and this, we realize, is meant to take us back to a South that, since the first minstrel shows of the 1840s, an ambivalent popular imagination has divided into an idyll of innocence and ease, on the one hand, and a backwater of cruelty, ignorance, and affectation, on the other.

On the wall nearby is a kind of shrine standing out of the darkness. It is a delicate little brace of shelves surrounded by family photographs, of women in kerchiefs and long skirts, of young men in World War I military uniforms—icons, it seems, of a lady's dressing table. An ornate vanity set, a lace hankie, pictures of a Detroit hotel and botanical garden in postcard lithographs, a wicker sewing basket, a package of needles, a coin purse, a tiny pottery watering can, a miniature water pitcher from the Chicago World's Fair, a bud vase and a pair of ceramic shoes, an appliqué napkin and chintz scarf, an embossed cigarette case set on its cover with a slim, elegant pocketwatch, a jewelry box and cameo, all of these things seventy-five or a hundred years old, bring us into intimate contact with a feminine presence and a personal life and, at the same time, with the subtlest suggestions, hint both at a spirit of the times and at the massive global forces poised to disrupt it.

Ahead of us, a farmer in a straw hat and overalls, standing from floor to ceiling in an enlarged black-and-white photograph—"From Field to Factory" is a rhapsody of photographs—drives a pair of mules. The wall beside him is paneled, most un-museumlike, with galvanized corrugated steel, the material from which shed roofs, watering troughs, chicken feeders, storage bins, and other furniture of the agricultural landscape is made, though we encounter only the material itself, not any of its real-life configurations. Turning the corner, we find the wall to our left nailed up with fresh pine boards reaching to the ceiling, their newness, with the still shining heads of nails rooted at each corner, somehow qualifying them for membership among the materials used to create the exhibit, however violently out of context. A voice—that of Moses Burse of Georgia—

speaks, as poets used to speak from the urns in gentlemen's gardens, from an inscription on the wall:

> We went barefooted. My feet been frostbitten a lot of times. My dad couldn't afford to buy no shoes. He'd get in debt and he'd figure every year he going to sell out. . . . They'd tell you, "You bought so-and-so," they get through figuring it up you lacking $100 of coming clear. What the hell could you do? You living on his place, you couldn't walk off.

Nearby, equally fresh and new, stands a kind of cabinet made incongruously of chicken wire on a board frame. There are no chickens in it, though, or plaster models of chickens, but actual artifacts from the cotton fields, including a pitchfork, a scythe, a hoe, an axe, a galvanized washtub, a wheelbarrow, and two plows, very worn and old, once drawn by mules. Overhead a framework of covered beams, through which a row of spotlights shines out of the blackness above, suggests an outdoor terrace, where fuschia or philodendron might spill over from hanging pots.

The armoring of the museum gallery with rustic materials, themselves smelling not of the farrowing house but of the lumberyard, both further invaded by artifacts either captured in the field or retrieved from some obscure corner in the museum's vast storehouses, lends "From Field to Factory" the immediacy of intelligence such as one finds in literature—the sense that, through the agency of the written word, one's own intelligence has been inhabited by another's, which is in effect doing our thinking for us, reserving to us only our consciousness *that* we are thinking: "A phenomenon," writes Georges Poulet, "by which mental objects rise up from the depths of consciousness into the light of recognition."[10] Indeed, the exhibit space, a realm of shadows haunted by islands of luminosity proceeding from invisible sources, seems almost to dramatize the somatic space in which the sensation of thought occurs.

Thus the lights that in various niches and corners push back the shadows, the explanatory texts on small palettes that rise up into the light as if out of depths of water, the photographs of black faces and the other documents that hang from invisible threads at eye level, the structures that stand at the turns of the passageway—the altar of a southern church, the twin doorways of a segregated railroad station in Virginia, the three-walled room of a sharecropper's cabin—all seem to materialize into the exhibit out of a process of introspection initiated by a moral anxiety, or, as the case may be, out of moral outrage and filial love. The more familiar components of the exhibit, such as account books, diaries, personal letters, handbills, railroad tickets, newspaper clippings, and the like, all in glass cases, or assemblages of family artifacts clustered around a central photograph or heirloom, seem strangely to abduct memory and scatter it amongst unfamiliar objects, at once familiarizing and alienating them. The scenes presented to us—of a woman wiping the sweat from her brow as she bends over a washtub behind the reconstructed cabin, or of a little girl in the railroad car or sitting on the front stoop of a rooming house poring over a letter—scenes either veiled by darkness or softened by screens, around which we hear voices preaching, singing, storytelling, seem to prey upon the imagination, winning our assent not with verisimilitude but with explicit fictionality in which otherwise contiguous functional elements are articulated as representations by systematic discontinuity.

It is discontinuity, in every instance, that defines for us the morphology of the exhibit. The pine boards and galvanized steel on the museum walls are discontinuous with the plaster, marble, and stone typically found there, but discontinuous, too, with the weatherbeaten and rusty pine and steel found on the structures they are intended to represent; the chicken coop is right—but normally the plow goes someplace else. Texts do not appear on walls unless sprayed or scribbled there by vandals; they are not stenciled by scholars and artists, nor do they appear before us in midair except as hallucinations. Major structural pieces of rooming houses, railroad stations, and Pullman cars, not to mention entire dwellings, moreover, are usually not found indoors, nor, certainly, are flocks of meadow birds—at least not in museums.

Ideally, the museum object should rally the initiatives of contemplation and organize the patterns of association in which any object has its meaning. To achieve this effect in the nineteenth century meant placing the object in linear sequence with related objects, for the underlying mythos of the real was that it was a process of evolution in which specific stages, embodied in specific objects or species, represented particular moments of development. In our day, it means uncoupling the object from all such patterns, fields, and sequences; for, to us, such constructs represent a kind of hallucination wrought by various cultural hegemonies that have reached—through language, the family, education and communications, and other institutions—into our very modes of perception. A fresh apprehension demands, it seems, that we expose not only the object, but the ways in which we have been trained, or influenced, to look at it: to exhibit, in effect, our own habitual ways of conceiving the thing, as well as the thing itself. To do so it is, of course, not sufficient merely to isolate the object; instead it must be carried up in a kind of cyclone of loosely confederated objects whose ordinary relations, in which normally they have their intelligibility and their meaning, remain suspended, in doubt, as mere intimations.

At that site, the site of the object, many strange and obscure forces converge, arresting the restless, hasty, and often cursory survey of reality in which our attention is normally engaged and drawing it toward a deepening reflection—not on the object itself, though we may be absorbed in it, but upon the way we have learned to construct its significance, which in this setting we must attempt, but will invariably fail, to do. In that moment of unbidden awakening, which we are bound to resist or even resent—it is as if the museum had forcibly detained us—the stubborn materiality of the artifact weakens and dissolves; a narrative, an explanatory text, the sound of music, or simply the silent copresence of objects now almost menacing in their transformation flows into it, virtually carrying the object away and supplanting it with a human story in which we must identify, for better or worse, our own complicity. It is always a sign of a good museum, a museum that works, that when we step outside again our own world momentarily shudders with its own unreality—unreal because our customary universe, in which our own actual circumstances are only an arbitrary point that will gradually drift back to the center of consciousness, has been dislodged, "decentered" as they say, capable again of discovery and change.

"From Field to Factory" tells, roughly, this story: The combined forces of a credit-driven tenant farming system, Jim Crow laws, official segregation and unofficial violence, and finally the invasion of the boll weevil made the post-Reconstruction South grossly inhospitable to rural blacks. New forces, in the meantime, heightened the appeal of the North: the First World War opened to young black soldiers a cosmopolitan outlook and a keener awareness of the South's racial parochialism, while labor recruiters from northern industries, the northern black press, and personal testimony—both in letters from the North and in a lively oral tradition—all promised high salaries, guaranteed jobs, and cheap housing in the industrial cities. Between 1915 and 1940, hundreds of thousands of blacks, individuals and families, in the face of the resistance of southern white landowners and their legal minions, migrated to Detroit, Chicago, Philadelphia, New York, and other northern industrial cities, seeking a better way of life.

Already wounded by "the severing of life-long ties," southern migrants to the North met the hard realities of a clock- and machine-driven factory life, menial labor, urban squalor and chaos, and the unanticipated resistance of middle-class blacks who feared deepening discrimination and who looked with contempt upon unsophisticated rural manners; they found, too, the hatred and prejudice of working-class whites, themselves often first- or second-generation immigrants, who competed with immigrant blacks for jobs and housing. Through initiatives from within the black community, such as those of the National Urban League, the NAACP, and the Travelers' Aid Society, and encouraged by various fraternal organizations, sororities, Masonic societies, athletic clubs, arts associations, and independent black businesses—restaurants, drug stores, savings and loan establishments, and beauty shops—as well as the durable traditions of church and school and nascent social venues such as the dance club and the movie house, there emerged in the North an African American urban culture that, the exhibit texts explain, permanently altered the perception of race in America, helped to shape the political consciousness that later informed the civil rights movement and other resistance efforts, and set the tone of northern urban life in the second half of the twentieth century.

This, from beginning to end, is a story of oppression, discrimination, displacement, and disorientation, and, in the face of these forces, the heroism of the community through social organizations and culturally influential people such as the Chicago disc jockey Sonny Porter and the beautician and humanitarian Marjorie Stewart Joyner. At a deeper level, however, the narrative historicizes one of black culture's most sacred stories, the flight to freedom—in this instance also a geographic ascent—whose underpinning is, of course, the biblical Exodus. And yet it is not quite accurate to say that "From Field to Factory" tells a story, especially not in the straightforwardly linear fashion we might expect of a historical text. Better to say that it provides several kinds of resources for a story, which it is incumbent upon us, through our imaginative participation, to construct and, in constructing it, to find the meaning that, were it simply thrust upon us by the authority of the museum, would meet whatever resistance to that authority, or to the story it tells, that we may have brought with us. Although text panels in the exhibit narrate the story of the Great Migration, the materials on display, and the manner in which they are displayed, complicate the story in ways that carry it beyond its historical and social boundaries, both into the moral life of the visitor, black or white, and into the larger society in which a racial distinction bifurcates a common culture whose two parallel histories continually absorb, distort, and transfigure one another.

Certain aspects of the exhibit, for example, such as the feminine personal objects set in the isolated glow of the small display case just inside the entrance, instantly dispel any quasi-scientific historical perspective that might insulate us against the impact of historical "forces" upon personal life and furthermore efface, at the personal level, the racial line. The axe, the plow, the rake, and other emblems of the old rural life—even the cotton gin with its curious mechanism of rakes and combs and its quaint decorative devices—fixed as ornaments in what amounts to a terrace garden, a visitor, particularly a white, middle-class visitor, might readily assimilate to kindred displays in the hundreds of suburban dens, roadside restaurants, and folk museums by means of which American popular culture, in commercial advertising especially, has for at least a century traded in nostalgia for agrarian past. Out of this nostalgia has developed a taste culture whose influence is vividly at work in the reconstructed settings—the southern Maryland tenant house and Philadelphia rental room—certain details of which situate these structures somewhere between scholarly historical reconstructions, which in any case can only be idealizations, and the explicitly commercial interior of a country antique shop.

In the reconstructed tenant house, for example, we find a braided rug, a patchwork quilt folded over a pressback chair, a black Raggedy-Ann on her own little coverlet, kerosene lamps, mason jars, a wooden rolling pin, a cane-bottom chair, a woodburning stove with nickel-plated fenders and a cast-iron kettle, and a windup phonograph; many of these items reappear in the Philadelphia rental room as mementos of the old life, but supplemented by a Victrola and a treadle-operated sewing machine. Both scenes are accompanied by rare blues recordings that touch the themes of the exhibit: Robert Johnson's "Got Leavin' on My Mind"; Blind Lemon Jefferson's "Matchbox Blues" ("I sit here wonderin', will a matchbox hold my clothes?"); and, in the urban context, alongside two barrelhouse piano blues, Bessie Smith's "Careless Love." Here there is painstaking accuracy, but no authenticity; there is no sense of invasion, because there is no privacy, while inscribed upon the icons of poverty is an ingenious and discriminating discourse in marketing, recontextualized as museology.

One of the familiar motifs of American longing, then, with specific historical origins, long connected to a particular set of traditional conservative values, invested in specific emblems long appropriated by commerce, and through commerce constructed as a standard of taste and displayed as a badge of cultural identity, the exhibit explicitly identifies as cultural icons of black folklife in the old rural South—abruptly arresting the movement of these forces by throwing in their way the visitor's own investment in the idea of race, either to expose it as racism or to restore it with tokens of cultural prestige. And, as if to guarantee that identification, the twittering of birds accompanies our first moments in the gallery, touching every object—where commercial forces, class affiliations, and institutional authority all merge—with the fresh, morning-scent of the bucolic.

Once this synthesis has been achieved, however, and the racial line at once articulated and effaced, we step "outside" the garden-terrace erected at the entrance into a shadowy hall in which several small lagoons of light compete for attention. Enacting a privilege conferred upon us simply in our status as visitors—further enforced by the materials, the technics, and the style of the exhibit—we enter a theater of underprivilege, and it is clear that, were the lights to go up, the spell would be broken. We might lurch to the right toward a small video screen, where a loop of rare film footage of southern black rural life is running alongside miniatures of a dogtrot and a shotgun house pictured in the film; or we might approach the unenclosed interior ahead of us, where five floor cases, their sides papered with enlarged images of newsprint, announce the documentary nature of the exhibits therein.

The documentary aspect of "From Field to Factory" has, in fact, already been introduced under glass—in conjunction with the cotton scale and gin—in the form of a planter's account book from 1914, its figures recorded neatly in pencil, a mortgage deed on a cotton crop, and sack ties with cardboard tags, all printed with the name of the McLauchlin Company of Raeford, South Carolina. Though in themselves commonplace, these materials provide, once we have a context for them, clues to the human story to whose moral dimensions artifacts have so far offered only an opaque substantiality and texts only a pattern of abstractions. A poll tax certificate, which along with the infamous "literacy tests" prevented the southern black from exercising his right to vote; a poster—"Safety First: Go North"—distributed by industrial agents; clippings from the *Chicago Defender*; an NAACP handbill urging support of the Dyer Anti-Lynching bill: these come to the visitor, engaged in constructing the relationships between the texts and artifacts before him, as the documentary links from which he, cast now into the historian's role, must forge an interpretive chain.

Gazing down though glass, the visitor finds exposed to view an illicit application for membership in "the Invisible Empire of the Ku Klux

Klan," with its unsavory appeal to white supremacy and "pure American-ism," which merely to behold seems almost furtive, as if one cannot shield oneself against the shame it radiates. Nor is any relief to be had above one's head, where, looking up, the eyes encounter, hanging behind glass in an upright case, the sinister Klan robe, now itself the victim of an institutional lynching, in which horror and brutality seem to linger like the odor of mildew.

Now in the depths of the museum gallery, where the chemistry of psalm song from an unseen congregation mingles with the sounds of housekeep-ing tasks and of a country blues, the boundaries between artifact, docu-ment, and text seem to disintegrate as it becomes possible to read into every aspect of the exhibit the unfolding narrative. Nothing is what it was before. The time-clock in its burnished oaken cabinet; the brass steam whistle; the primitive foundry ladle and brutish grinding and buffing machine; the apron, carpet sweeper, mop, and broom of the domestic servant; the ghoulish butcher knives: these otherwise quaint and innocu-ous antique objects have become symbols of what seems to have been a systematic punishment inflicted upon an entire class of people. And in being so transfigured, they shed a cold, inhuman fluorescence upon the entire system from which they descend and in which every visitor to the museum, as well as the museum itself, in some way shares.

Tins of hair cream and perfume, fraternal badges and ribbons, a group photograph of the New Amsterdam Music Association Orchestra of 1920, copies of Langston Hughes's *The Weary Blues* and James Weldon John-son's *God's Trombones*, phonograph records of vaudevillian Bert Williams and jazzman Chick Webb—these are no longer the detritus of a flea-market, but talismans of self-conscious cultural invention that, as the shadow of oppression falls over them, seem to stir in their places with a buried life the visitor now feels compelled to set free. The past itself, gazing into the museum gallery from its imprisonment in the huge photographs hung around it, silently petitions for redress of its unforgotten grievance. Meanwhile, the spotlights poised overhead and the great structural pieces of a church altar and the Virginia railroad station whose segregated en-trance doors provide egress into the urban North lend to the gallery the quality of an off-hours theatrical set, held in somber, almost nocturnal latency, as if the actors, like ghosts, had been shut out and could not gain access to their own story, or as if we ourselves were the actors, unable to play the part because of our vague and impoverished understanding— itself the issue of our own complacency or, as the case may be, of our pain.

In a dark corner just beyond the station doors, a narrow bench stands between disembodied voices of men and women narrating, from a tape player, their recollections of the migration—of the little stratagems, the "white lies," the careful planning required to remove oneself, one's family, and one's chattels to the North while under the gaze of white landlords and constables: "Those white people was watchin' you all the time." Train sounds usher us into a corridor constructed out of an old passenger car, where a child wrapped in a blanket, accompanied by a picnic basket, a bandbox, and a few suitcases, sleeps with her Raggedy-Ann, a note pinned to her blouse. We are led into a little hall: to one side is a film in progress; to the other, garishly lit by neon script proclaiming "The Finest Food Anywhere," stands a little case containing the scrapbook and photo album of Chicago disk jockey Sonny Porter—a record of middle-class black life in the 1910s, now irretrievably past and gone, lies opened on its pages. The little girl from the train has seated herself, now, on the stoop of the Philadelphia rooming house, where she is reading a letter from home, her doll's perambulator on the sidewalk in front of her.

Is this, then, the conclusion? The narrative momentum of "From Field to Factory" carries us beyond the gallery's succession of photograph panels, inscriptions, and summary text at the exit door into a realm of rumination and epiphany generated by the collaborative activity in which we have been engaged from the beginning. An anonymous voice speaks plaintively out of a brightly illuminated inscription—"I thought Chicago was some great place but found out it wasn't. Uncle told me he was living on Portland Avenue, that it was some great Avenue; found nothing but a mud hole. I sure wish I was back home"—and a gallery of photographic portraits terminates in a picture of a group of young men and women, their faces alive with hope and pride, at King's March on Washington in 1963. "The Great Migration lost momentum in the nineteen-thirties," reads the text on the wall; the depression, we learn, swept away many of the advantages the migrants might have won, and with the onset of World War II a second migration began, bringing three million African Americans from the South—twice as many as in the earlier period—to northern and western cities. The "problems of substandard housing, unfair employment practices, and social inequity persisted," the text panel declares, "creating an underlying sense of frustration and anger."

This, the very instant at which we understand that the exhibit's underlying mythos must remain unconsummated, is its most bewildering moment, for beside us, just beyond a translucent screen, we can see again the point at which we began and hear, again, the songbirds of Georgia and Alabama, whose singing now has a strange forlornness and a disquieting new ambiguity. The peculiar double consciousness—a kind of racial stereoscope—that to this point has doubled the perception of every feature of the exhibit now resolves itself into a single image, which implies some shared experience, and a dismaying intimation. An agitated, irrational longing to regain the primal garden—with its decent, uncomplicated life in the rural shade—returns, chastened by the understanding the story has brought us and soberly disavowed, but at the same time involuntarily renewed by the unconsummated promise of that story. With a grim irony, vaguely we discern that this idle, impertinent, even perhaps corrupt, but implacable desire is the instrument of an interest not our own; that it springs from the same conditions that made life in the South intolerable, that drew black migrants to the North seeking deliverance, and that ultimately disappointed their hopes; that racial oppression belongs to a broader human oppression built into the very structure of our society. The design of "From Field to Factory" is a circle, or more precisely a turning, and in our suspension between two worlds we can feel the blood of our two cultures cycling together into one system.

What has occurred here? It is, simply, that the exhibit's explicit racial division has concealed in it an implicit class distinction that rises more vividly into evidence as we near the end of the circuit, calling the premise of the exhibit silently into question. "From Field to Factory" is a story about the migration of southern rural blacks, framed by the social and domestic values of a black urban middle class. It highlights the individual and social initiatives of the black urban middle class while contemplating the old rural life and the experience of the rural migrant in the northern industrial setting through the mists of memory and of history, at once ideologizing and sentimentalizing them. This, then, is the source of some of the exhibit's strange dyslexia: the cultural practices it attempts to valorize, so long as the racial distinction remains in place, may appear to be a mere travesty of white middle-class models—and thus oppressive in themselves as well as symptoms of oppression; at the same time, however, the old rural system it repudiates, with the visitor's thorough ideological assent, is also represented as the context for—even, perhaps, as a condition of—sustaining cultural values.

"From Field to Factory" succeeds not in spite of these paradoxes but because of them. From the perspective of the black middle class, the racial distinction riven into the exhibit becomes both more vicious and more meaningless as that perspective emerges: meaningless because, outwardly at least, middle-class social forms, though differently nuanced, transcend race; vicious, because racism continues to shape the social, economic, and political condition of black people, whatever their social standing. Racism, it is clear, is an evil whose infinite power of discord begins, like all evils, with a lie: that all this has anything to do, fundamentally, with race.

As the exhibit itself, at the moment of its own narrative failure, seems to realize, we've been—all of us together, black and white—snookered. Whether romantic or parochial, grounded in distance or in proximity, racism has proved expedient to a society in which power distributes itself according to particular cultural advantages, which consequently become touchstones of a class system that discriminates on the basis of culture and that, owing to the tenacity of cultural tradition in social life, tends to perpetuate itself, in varying degrees centralizing some traditions and marginalizing others and urging, in the competition for advantage, assimilation to the advantaged forms. Racism is only the grossest and most invidious manifestation of a complex and subtle system of cultural discrimination, and it is a certain sign of the health and vitality of that system; for wherever and however it shows itself, racism is in no one's interest but that of the class which it palpably serves.

Strictly speaking, then, "From Field to Factory" has no end. It has only an exit: exit from the museum into the given world, where as of this writing lies, on one side of the racial line, the Nation's Capital of violence, murder, addiction, homelessness, poverty, sickness, anger, cynicism, depression, and despair, and on the other greed, fear, hypocrisy, fraud, and ill-will. The highest infant mortality rate, the highest murder rate, the highest school dropout rate, all within sight of the Capitol Dome: from this miasma, it seems, there can be no emigration, unless it is back into our own history to find the continuity that migration itself, virtual or literal, like the compulsive reenactment of an original grief, has again and again disrupted. For it is continuity alone that lays up in the soul the spiritual wealth whose expenditure redeems experience and brings it home.

What is the form of "From Field to Factory," or that of its antecedent exhibits, "A Nation of Nations" and others of the same kind? Let's call it *cyclonic* form—the form of a world that has been taken up, and set down again, by a whirlwind. The cyclone detaches objects from their grounding in traditional relation and recombines them in curious and bizarre ways: a palm leaf thrust through a tree trunk; a parakeet cage, with the living bird still in it, standing in what was once the parlor of a vanished house;

automobile tires hanging from tree limbs. This recombination and juxta-position of objects otherwise rationally related, but according to paradig-matic conceptual schemes, gives to the entire field of objects—a small town street, a farmstead—the quality of a combinatory system of signs, that is, a discourse, and hence exposes the significatory power of each independent object at the same time that it brings them into plainly metaphorical or paradoxical relationships. Although these metaphors and paradoxes may drive home a fresh conception of *literal* relations, which is part of the purpose of any symbolic inversion (and it should be remem-bered that the presence of *any* artifact in a museum is such an inversion), they do so in a way that calls attention to their own discursive character, rather than attempting—through, say, a diorama—to foster the illusion that we are somewhere other than in a museum.

These new exhibits are a stylized and dynamic mimesis of cyclonic wreckage, from which the disordered field must be reconstructed by moral participation. Unlike the eruption of Vesuvius, say, which arrested a mo-ment, the cyclone destroys the stereotyped rational field so that it may be reconstructed along political and moral lines. The exhibit is "cyclonic" in the sense that, like a centrifuge, it separates elements and recycles them with the visitor's moral being, for whom the material is detached from history and suspended in a somatic field, or a representation of one, from which concepts may continually be formed but which is not itself, except in a rough and casual way, conceptual. It is as if the curator wished us to encounter the materials as he encountered them, in an inchoate, unre-constructed stage, prompting us with gentle suggestions toward an idea, or toward many ideas, of a possible exhibit charged with moral impera-tives, which does not come into being except imaginatively.

These exhibits do not represent the boast of conquest or plunder, or a claim of total objective knowledge, but participation in the narrative of a historical community that, when the exhibit is entirely successful, again and again seems to become—or as in the case of the Washington taxi driver, actually *is*—our own. The cultural process itself cannot, of course, be exposed to view; but these contexts of immigration and emigration throw into bold relief the activity of culture in bestirring itself, giving concrete expression to itself, and sustaining itself in its transition from one historical situation to another. The exhibit accomplishes this purpose, fi-nally, by familiar means: the shadows of the gypsy's parlor, where fortunes can be read; the unexpected turns of the funhouse, where we anticipate the unanticipated; the graffiti of voices speaking across great social distances.

Like Xenia, Ohio, after the tornado, it is a scene of devastation, but of devastation formalized, often most dramatically, where the wonder that normally accompanies such scenes—the wonder at the cyclone's strange, inscrutable intelligence, even its sense of irony and of humor—may also attach to human actions and events.

The landscape garden, and the museum after it, attempted to restore the lost world imaginatively, as a picture, and thus in a sense to prolong its life; but "From Field to Factory" or the "Nation of Nations" turns destruction, disintegration, and dissolution into structural principles, projecting our own psychic disintegration into an aesthetic field and assigning it a special cultural value. What would have been, perhaps less than a generation ago, mere chaos or nightmare is to us beautiful; and yet, from the spire or ruin to the ruby slippers and the Dunham schoolroom, there is a direct line of descent.

Any social institution can be pressed into service as a theatrical frame, and culture, furthermore, largely consists in the transformations of institutional authority by such enactments; the Peckham exorcisms secured the authenticity of theatrical enactments by calling upon the sacred authority of the church to frame them. "From Field to Factory" represents such a transformation within an institution whose authority has traditionally been voiced—through such exhibits as the Fort McHenry flag and the First Ladies' gowns—in the tones of nationalism, patriotism, and technological progress. "From Field to Factory" exactly reverses this ethical tendency, framing a story told through the instruments and possessions of nameless people and the documents of a solitary inquiry that seems to become the visitor's own, of unrelenting oppression by and struggle against the very power that erected the museum to begin with. The cyclonic winds that lift up the Smithsonian collections and deposit them in the melancholy, almost funereal halls of "A Nation of Nations" or "From Field to Factory," where the galleries themselves seem to sigh with a consciousness of loss and disintegration, arise out of the agitation of the culturally dispossessed to construct the cultural narrative in their own ways. Insofar as the institution persists *as* an institution, it remains an instrument of cultural management, in which—in "From Field to Factory" and its kind—the *visitor* has become the exhibit. In another sense, however, "From Field to Factory" signals the end of the National Museum of American History, which, with its sister institution, the Museum of Natural History, slips itself into history, gradually to be displaced by a new kind of museology in which the visitor has become the curator and in which history itself can be understood only as the myth of the class that has fashioned it, an artifact of culture like any other.

Tower, castle keep, crown jewels, moon rock, Hope Diamond, ruby slippers—the treasury of weapons, or of gold, or of writings, arts, and artifacts: after Nature itself, these are, along with granaries, nurseries, gardens, and all the other means by which we accumulate, store, protect, and retrieve what we have produced or won, the sources and the strongholds of our wealth. They embody and symbolize the accumulation and husbanding of resources around which culture organizes itself. The community plentifully supplied by nature, secure in a harmony of cooperation, protection, and love, has no need of hoards; there is culture in Paradise, surely—but no museum. For the collection or hoard—at once treasury, armory, sanctum, and shrine—has as its own context an absence or vacuum; the hoard is an index of scarcity, vulnerability, exile, and isolation. The Anglo-Saxons, for instance, who had lost the metallurgical crafts necessary to make new weapons, hoarded the ancient swords and shields forged by technologically superior but extinct people and told stories of dragons who guarded the hoards until rust had fused the weapons together. The Jews, displaced and uprooted, hoarded the Law in the form of written manuscripts, which, fixed in writing but endlessly reinterpreted, might, in the uncontrollable and dangerous world of the spoken word, preserve them. The hoarding of money by individuals suggests expulsion from the social nexus; in a radically atomized and competitive society in which *everyone* is in a sense expelled, the savings, the insurance, and the pension all become, in effect, both a necessity and a social norm. "Equal opportunity," as political and social concept, suggests a society ranged around a central hoard of wealth, social, economic, cultural, to which, in the contest of life, each person either will or will not gain access. The cultural vacuum, then, is the underlying condition of the central hoard or plenum, which theoretically society must control and defend.

We live in such a vacuum, one that has since the seventeenth century—through the construction of the isolate subject and of a cultural system that has institutionalized its autonomy and deployed it ever more comprehensively as an economic, social, political, and psychological function—become ever more arid and sparse; with modernity, Shelley's "unacknowledged legislator," the psychological subject, became at once the fountainhead and the reservoir of culture, husbanding it through such isolate activities as writing and reading, at last compelling the King, the age-old emblem of the self, to place his crown upon the ego and to distribute his treasures to be secreted away in the private heart.

The consummation of the romantic revolution, in which the cultures of the book still live, was the theory of the unconscious: like language, a thing that could never be beheld in and of itself, but only through its performances, traces, and disruptions, which posited both universal psychic structures and specific cultural contents that in various protean forms at once transcended and informed the personal. But access to culture is contingent upon access to its sustaining institutions and technologies, an access economically and politically determined; thus, with the ever more extensive and efficient alienation of human relations in all spheres—principally through transportation, communications, and information technologies—and the ever more thoroughgoing disintegration of experience under the impact of these technologies, there rises gradually in our awareness the sense of an emptiness that more mobility, more information, and more efficient communication cannot replenish.

The curator's effort to animate a torpid collection, to deliver the artifact from its incarceration in matter to become an element in thought and feeling, suggests perhaps what real "wealth"—the treasure that museums primordially are built to protect and to exhibit—is. Wealth is not the mace, truncheon, or pike affixed to the wall of some tower catacomb, though these impress upon us the power of the state, nor is it the blinking gem gazing out from some subterranean chamber, absorbing by a kind of inverse radiation a kingdom's concentrated political energy. Nor is wealth even the beauty in art, architecture, music, and literature, what used to be regarded as the substance of culture, for which military strength can secure a place and riches an abundance. Wealth, instead, is the human productive power in which all these things—technological, semiotic, aesthetic—originate.

Culture is elusive. It passes secretly, often silently, telepathically, between a parent and a child who does not even realize she has been looking on or listening until years later, when she somehow discovers what she has learned and can now do herself; it ripens, untended, often unconsciously, in dreams, suddenly and unexpectedly to reveal itself in an expression or a turn of phrase, in a way of relating to one's children or one's spouse, or, at another level, in our musical and pictorial preferences, in the narratives we construct about ourselves and others or to which we turn for understanding. It may arise by accident, from a half-remembered memory, from fingers or hands idling with instruments and tools. Or it may simply persist, with a peculiar life of its own, in a circuitous transit over several centuries, from courtly to commercial to domestic culture and back again.

As Bess Lomax Hawes observes, folk art is often learned, but seldom taught.[11] Folklorists, with their emphasis upon small-group, face-to-face interaction, as they typically characterize it, seem to be suggesting the existence of some elementary and irreducible social form; at the same time, their social scientific practice of looking empirically at social interaction on this level and on this scale, as we might observe a conversation at a bus stop, prevents them from penetrating to what is actually occurring in the various forms of human intercourse—occurring, that is, not in behavior alone, but in the minds and hearts of the participants, something that can be known fully only *by* a participant.

The real stronghold of culture is neither tradition nor community, but a transpersonal ethnonoetic plenum of which each partakes, a vital medium of sensations of presence, feeling, intention, sexuality, intelligence, and a hundred other human forces extending outward from the self to the verge of our conscious relations. To discern the existence of the medium in which culture lives, we must abandon the social scientific perspective, with its specular, abstract, and empirical methods, and regard the human community from within, where a welter of proximities, contacts, connections, congresses, alliances, and intimacies—through exquisitely sensitive instruments of communication whose codes, though they still work in and upon us, we have mostly forgotten—extend the mind, not by magic, but palpably and sensibly beyond the limits of the individual nervous system and impart to consciousness a corporate character. Human ecology is underwritten by the sensory, and sensible, communion of human beings with one another—a "tradition" more durable than the mechanisms of cultural transmission or the structures of economic and social interaction can account for, and a "community" whose psychological intensity places it squarely in the realm of the erotic.

By means of exquisitely subtle, complex, and largely unmeasurable and undetectable communications that anyone who has ever loved and felt the withdrawal of love understands well, the human sensorium brings us into, sustains us in, and governs our interactions with one another, secretly vivifying our perceptions by liberating them into the corporate life. We are, of course, more than an optical, acoustic, and tactile apparatus, and our reality is more than an organization of information achieved by the isolation, extension, and discipline of these senses. We are more, too, than islands of consciousness; we are living organs of signification, bearing—

not only on our tongues, but in our eyes and on our faces, in the sounds of our voices, in the color, texture, and smell of our skin, in our posture and bearing—social, emotional, sexual, and psychological information whose subtlety, complexity, and richness art can approximate but rarely, if ever, achieve. Even the moral nature seems to flow into our touch, to warm or to chill an intimate relation; we are all doctors and fortune tellers, and, though we have largely lost the talent, we can still smell a fault or, as the case may be, a promise. That human beings have so evolved is perhaps not more fully revealed than in the fact of our prolonged dependence upon nurture, which begins with sensory stimulation and in effect never ceases, but only becomes more displaced and differentiated, and without which our natures, even the nervous system itself, cannot develop. The human animal is definitively the cultural animal, with senses that have evolved so that all knowledge, even knowledge of nature, cannot but assume a cultural form.

This process—through which we imitate, impersonate, incorporate, and figure forth our culture, which language typifies but which is far from exclusively linguistic, the process in which our cultural knowledge has its life, which sustains it, and which opens access to it—let us call *ethnomimesis*. It is, among other manifold effects, the process by which our children, most imperceptibly, become like us and, at a distressing later stage, like their peers; through it, we learn to act like and even to resemble those with whom we most consistently associate—our spouses, perhaps, or our coworkers. Ethnomimesis teaches hospitalized or institutionalized people how to be ill, criminal, or mad. It can be the origin of violent irrational antipathy or attraction between people whose spontaneous and unconscious imitation of the other arouses deep self-loathing or self-love. It is the process by which we adopt the melody and rhythm of a speech accent and orchestrate our own speech with it in order to enter a community of discourse; it is the process by which we unconsciously incorporate into our behavior and our expression the forms of others' behavior and expression, as well as those of significant natural and technological forms; it is how, at the height of the industrial age, men came to look like boilers and women like parlor furniture, how in the automobile age all of us became aerodynamic, and in the information age cybernetic. It is what gives actors, models, and other prestigious figures their tremendous power and sends their images into the manner and bearing of thousands of people—and it is also the process by which they originally acquired that power.

The manifest works we traditionally associate with culture are not identical to the ethnonoetic plenum, the culture, that ethnomimesis generates and sustains, any more than a mathematical equation is identical to the relation it expresses, even though that relation may not be accessible, or communicable, except through the equation; hence, through ethnomimesis the content of culture—its unconscious codes and impalpable images as well as its manifest works—replicates and modifies itself within the community and migrates across the boundary of one community or another to become, though transfigured by its new environment, an element in the life of adjacent cultures.

All human communities maintain themselves with the formally instituted learning that constitutes the sociocultural system; but the ethnonoetic plenum maintains itself, well below the level of formal learning, by the unconscious mimesis by which every member of the community, from infancy on, reperforms and incorporates it, from unconscious communications lodged in physical behavior and language itself to all the techniques of material facture, social interaction, and the expressive arts. With the possible exception of pristinely self-contained primitive cultures—themselves in all likelihood a figment of the anthropological imagination—actual human societies are diverse, built of many such plena; many and varied economic, social, political, and other factors—such as ethnicity, family, the life cycle, formal institutions, economic functions, social and racial discrimination, voluntary associations, and the like—bring groups of people into consistent association and interdependency with one another and sometimes set them against each other in a struggle for continuity, control, and dominance. The individual imagination moves among and through them, shaped more or less permanently in childhood but changing nevertheless in response to changing affiliations, while relations among individuals often reflect those affiliations to a far greater extent than they do the discrete personality upon which we typically lay most of the burden of individual difference. Technologically extended, as by literacy, the ethnonoetic plenum loses its immediacy, takes on the character of the extension, and forms the basis of social systems such as education, designed to shape consciousness to the medium in which the mimetic culture has been technologized. Fundamentally, however, *all* authentic human communities generate a noetic body undifferentiated by the complex rational forms, social, political, and technological, that extend, elaborate, and ultimately reify it.

Unlike the institutionalized arts and artifacts of palpable culture, the ethnonoetic plenum is embedded in the rounds of diurnal life and all the operations, duties, rituals, ceremonies, and occasions, sacred and profane, attached to it, including specific uses of language, kinesic and proxemic repertoires, particular performances, and technical skills. To gather all these resources and to spill them out in full display is one of the functions of festival, when at a specific juncture in the calendar—as one season, perhaps, turns over into another, with the customary laws, prohibitions, duties, and responsibilities temporarily suspended—the cultural treasury is opened to view.

Let us leave the National Museum of American History, then, and stroll across Madison Drive onto the Mall, where the Festival of American Folklife is under way, and where, as S. Dillon Ripley put it, the instruments have been taken out of their cases and made to sing.

The Sites of Culture

Café Tunis

"To Carthage then I came, where a cauldron of unholy loves sang all about mine ears." Surely at least one Festival visitor in 1974, as she sat at the Café Tunis among the trees at the foot of the Lincoln Memorial, within earshot of the playground cries of children on the one side, the mystical chants of Tunisian Sulamiyyah singers with their tambourines on the other, recalled Augustine's line or, at the very least, T. S. Eliot's allusion to it in *The Wasteland*, with its arcane footnote. More likely, though, the visitor shared the sentiments of the "enthusiastic teen-aged Festival-goer" interviewed by Bess Lomax Hawes, whose favorite exhibit was "the Tahitian belly-dancers." Other visitors, Hawes remarked, might have remembered that the dancers were Tunisian, not Tahitian—but, she added, "I wonder how many attending the Festival had any idea where Tunisia actually is?"[1]

In such a situation, one casts about for something familiar; and in the Café Tunis, no shopworn type, no image from songbook or novel, tavern humor or Broadway musical, appears to guide the experience safely home to harbor in our intellectual routines. A vague aura of adventure—in which dwell apparitions of, perhaps, the North African campaign of the 1940s, with its desert soldiers and cigarettes, or of Rick's café with its lethargic fans—surrounds it; the woven carpet, the fringed pillows, the robes and caps of the singers, their names—Habib, Ahmed, Abdellaziz—all have the hue of fable, as comfortably unreal as Aladdin's lamp and, in late afternoon, nearly as soporific, perhaps, as the monotone in which Father read the fairy tale.

And yet, exotic as they are, the tastes and smells of Café Tunis—thick, sweet coffee tasting of rose water, mint-flavored tea, the scent of jasmine hanging thick in the air—are as real as the yet-undiscovered parking ticket under your windshield wiper, while in the music—a quaking Ma'luf song of love swimming in the air like some bright aquatic snake, the court music of "caliphs and beys," as the Festival's daily newsletter explains—there is something hauntingly familiar, ancient, like the choral songs of the medieval Christian church or even the phonograph record of Gregorian chants that someone gave you for Christmas twenty years ago: "Strains of medieval liturgical music," the newsletter brusquely explains, "absorbed by the Andalusian Moors."

Strange and familiar, familiar and strange, somehow medieval, somehow Spanish, somehow Arabic and somehow Turkish, and yet none of these things, utterly fantastic and yet as real as the dish of couscous in front of you (which you recognize because you had it at a dinner party six months ago and liked it), Café Tunis arouses from these diverse sensations and associations an experience rich in recognition but poor in the conventional formulations, linguistic and otherwise, by which we might lock the experience away in the vault of consciousness to rest with other formulated experiences. Instead, our senses and our facility for association must remain open until, by imaginative acts of our own, we are able to make sense of the otherwise scrambled message, forging its meaning originally from a variety of responses at several levels of awareness.

The bowl of couscous, for example, which one can find among the exotica of the gourmet kitchen, places Café Tunis and the Tunisians, though certainly half-consciously and by association, in the world of cosmopolitan culture and taste, as if it had been featured in a newly published collection of Middle Eastern recipes or on the table of a fashionable Tunisian restaurant. Indeed, all the unintelligible signs, sensations, and indications of Café Tunis can be said to form a whole out of the fragments of our own cultural experience as class, history, and opportunity have shaped it; this may suggest why the Festival of American Folklife, in some of its aspects at least, tends to attract an audience of people whose childhood educations, home libraries, museum visits, and college degrees, among other advantages, have already aligned them with the aims of the Festival and acquainted them, however superficially, with its content. The coffee and tea, the taste of mint, and the aroma of jasmine, homely as these are, may remind us, in the setting of Café Tunis, that once they were exotic too, prizes won from distant parts of the globe, especially as the coffee is strangely thick and sweet and the jasmine, no longer a schoolroom or parlor scent, drifts in the air like incense—homely, perhaps, but at the same time imbued with a bracing sense of the illicit. These sensations can take us into their confidence and, by a kind of conspiracy, throw a thick obscurity over the surrounding world. At the Café Tunis one might willingly entertain a dream of adventure—of the dark face appearing from behind a veil or a white suit out of mist and smoke—and, surrendering entirely to the spell of fable, take one's tea and coffee upon a carpet that flies through the air.

For many Festival visitors, certainly, the cultural encounter prepared on the Mall does little more than illumine, like so much electrical circuitry, those systems of association that cultural experience has already laid down; the Festival is, for them, a kind of probe, arousing parts of their own cultural anatomy to spontaneous activity. The encounter might be purely imaginative, and the visitor might enjoy the insularity granted by pure fictions, were it not for the Tunisians themselves, who have come to the Festival from their adoptive city, Montreal, and who have brought with them their woven rugs, musical instruments, costumes, embroidery, and particularly their music and dance. Fantasy and play lead us squarely into an encounter with culture not poetically or scientifically pictured for us, but embodied in real presences: Abdel-Aziz Ben Mahmoud, the Sulamiyyah singer; Habib Chouaya, the Tunisian chef from Montreal; or the dancer, Ferida Zdiri. These are people who, as an observer later documented, suffered shock and embarrassment at working alongside young women Festival volunteers who wore halter tops and shorts, and who in turn showed no understanding of the ways in which their comparative informality and personal freedom affected the Tunisian guests. "They are sad because they are hungry and physically exhausted," one of the Tunisian participants reported of the members of her contingent. Though they were able to tolerate the hot Washington climate, "they all the time worry who will wash shirt."[2]

These are faces that in some other setting—on a subway, for example—

would be merely foreign and would hasten together the thousand petty judgments and sordid fears with which we have built the walls that separate us. But here we are disarmed, and the wall, stone by stone, is silently carried off; we are compelled to acknowledge in the marvelous and skilled work before us, even without a context in which to understand it, the signs of a grand and full humanity, as full as our own; and though we may have to reach into the remotest corners of our being to find the neurological chord that will resonate to the strange, strained vocality of the Ma'luf singers, we understand by a kind of revelation that, for them, it has some encoded cultural meaning; we realize, finally, that the Tunisians in some profound sense are, however unimaginably, like us—or, more accurately, that we are, though woefully incompletely and imperfectly, like them. That is where cultural education begins, with the chastening of our own provincialism: where the stranger not only cannot be dismissed, but must be admired and even loved, for we have entered his domain, and he is looking back at us with his excellence laid at our feet and our own foreignness reflected in his eyes.

For this disquieting sense of exclusion the Festival newsletter, with a brief explanatory text, provides some relief. Tunisian custom, it says, prevents men from visiting one another in their homes—though it does not say why. The coffeehouse becomes, then, a forum for news, gossip, and business among the men of the community, a custom that has continued in Montreal, no doubt in the local McDonald's and other short-order restaurants. The coffeehouse has something of a private character, like the household, and yet also a public character, like the marketplace; each man appears independent of his household relations, but at the same time as the representative and guardian of them. Unlike a restaurant, which gathers up families, however strictly or loosely constructed, around its tables and to some extent exposes a domestic scene to public view, the coffeehouse, with its fluid, informal, and voluntary associations, exposes the social patterns of the community—particularly, in this case, the male community—apart from the environment in which those patterns took shape; it provides a setting in which social interactions may be experienced in and of themselves and cultivated as such, and in which new associations and alliances, and new antagonisms, may form.

Because the café is a meeting place for familiars, not strangers, each man brings to the table the narrative his life has been to the community, a narrative that he can only partly know and that he may, in fact, have constructed along different lines than his fellows. Hence his meeting with them is partly for him to divine, by various subtle indications, what he is to them, and partly to promulgate the self-estimate that he is at pains to communicate to his fellows. His narrative is one that does not admit of wholesale revision—he cannot present himself as a fisherman if he is a cobbler, or as a bachelor if he is a husband, or as a father of three sons if he is the father of two daughters—but at the same time it omits most of the particulars of his intimate life and thought, which consequently it becomes the prerogative of the community to supply in its own way—to judge him on that basis, perhaps, or even to dull or to brighten his own self-estimate, perhaps even shape his destiny, with that judgment. Thus, though he is confined by his narrative—he can only be what his fellows understand, and implicitly demand, him to be—their representation of him provides him with a role that, through his playing of it, and yet not over- or underplaying, for the boundaries of his coffeehouse identity are strictly circumscribed, wins him a place among them. In the coffeehouse, we must be what we are said to be.

Understood as the framework and underpinning of personality, culture becomes real when personality rises to meet those occasions of assembly, congress, congregation, and encounter through which society carries out its purposes, chief among which, of course, is the perpetuation of its culture through, in turn, the nurture, exercise, cultivation, and expression of personality, whose various dimensions reflect those occasions and their variety. The vitally organic function of such occasions may be suggested by the fact that they can be understood metaphorically in terms of one another or substituted metonymically for the culture as a whole, as when we say "commercial" culture or "religious" culture, lending their character to the people and cultures that most habitually traffic in them. Crosscultural comparisons are perilous, but perhaps we can agree that, in Western societies at least, the coffeehouse and its near equivalents—pubs, cafés, cabarets—are among the many such occasions, arenas, theaters, hubs, communications exchanges, or ethnomimetic sites of culture. In the same way that the idea of language, as a body of forms and resources, a system, is an inference from the indefinite, ephemeral, and contingent play of speech in moments, events, and relations, hypostatized by the memorialization of these events in writing and books, so is "culture" an inference and abstraction from the multitude of artifacts and performances hypostatized by the proliferation of their images in ceremonies and pageants, museums, books, recordings, transmissions, and other forms that take the impression of the cultural surface and introduce it into its own and into alien settings. But as there is no "language" without the multitude of linguistic events from which we infer its existence, so there is no culture without the intelligence to figure it into the noetic moment—with genius or not, as the case may be—upon those occasions when, through social intercourse, the bearers of culture communicate, mimetically or deliberately, its substance to others. These are the sites of culture.

It is not from mere idleness that we sometimes even identify cultures with such places—for example, England with its pubs, France its cafés, or Germany its beer halls—and measure the congeniality and richness of those cultures with reference to them, while lamenting their lack in our own. It is to the pub or the café that we go when, as a visitor to England or France, we wish to catch the spirit of the culture, to experience it intimately—almost literally to eat and drink it at the same time that we look at and listen to it, on an occasion at once centered upon and framed by a casual communion of coffee and cake. This is enactment in a purely theatrical sense; but the incorporation of the symbol as substance invests its symbolicity in tangible, even organic, transformations. Enactment becomes ritual; insentient becomes sentient substance; incorporation becomes communion.

A visitor to the 1974 Festival of American Folklife would have found, in addition to Café Tunis, a *kafeneion*, or Greek café, and a Finnish coffeeshop, or *kaffestova*, as well, a grouping that served to transform the Festival-goer from an urbanite who knows his way around ethnic neighborhoods into a supernaturally mobile European cosmopolite who can leap from Scandinavia to the Mediterranean in a few moments—a tourist whose sense of transport, of weightlessness, situates her above and beyond culture and at the same time strips her of it; like the gentleman at his garden window, who has eaten up all his neighbors, culture becomes for him an object of longing at the same instant that he becomes conscious of it as a thing in itself. But unlike the tourist trade, the Festival does not answer that longing with stereotyped adventures. There are cultures that, by spatial or temporal insulation from the great tradition from which they descend historically, or by the creolization of several contributing traditions, have fashioned practices and expressions that will not yield to the guidebook's complacent formulas. It is often, at the Festival, just the deterioration of those formulas that cause those practices and expressions to stand out more boldly in their own loveliness or power, with disconcerting force and unanticipated beauty, fleetingly lifting the veil on the deliberateness and fragility of what might otherwise seem changeless, permanent, and God-given.

Such is the culture of Tunisia and, even more, of Tunisian-Canadians in Montreal; such, too, is the antique culture of the Karpathian Greeks or of the Pontic Greeks who, after World War I, returned to the Motherland and thence to a handful of American cities, after a sojourn of two thousand years in Asia Minor. Café Tunis indicates that, in the presentation of folklore and folklife, the sites of culture, where society manifests itself in cycles of social gathering and dispersing, meeting and parting, may be ideal ethnomimetic conveyances, because they do, after all, create situations in which society presents or transmits its culture to itself. Seated before our couscous and coffee in the erotic pantomime of the coffeehouse, we gain, even as strangers, silent temporary admission into the intimacy of a community and can observe the myriad human types of a strange society pass before us in review even as we are ourselves observed, or imagine that we are—for the coffeehouse is often contiguous with, or an extension of, the marketplace or street.

At Café Tunis we can hear, winding through a small grove of trees beyond the Old Ways in the New World demonstration area, distant strains of exotic music: drums babbling like agitated voices; calls, cries, and shouts that will not retire to any of the scenes of life. Exotic, because it is among exotics, but even more because everything on the Mall is at once outside and out-of-doors—evicted, exiled, and interned—located squarely in its own dislocation. Exotic but, as we perhaps realize for the first time, full of a familiar promise. The Old Ways area, in which the ethnic coffeehouses are situated, opens out onto a wide thoroughfare, intersected by a canopied performance stage, that leads to the Caribbean Marketplace, which is flanked on one side by a traditional African house and on the other by a wooden church from the black South.

This marketplace is not a faithful reconstruction of a marketplace in Charleston or in Accra, Port of Spain, or in rural Mississippi; rather, it stands at the intersection of these others, as if they had been gathered and placed at the termini of trade routes laid along the history of the slave trade. The close contiguity of house, market, and church in the Afro-Caribbean-American street thus becomes an equation—the factors of time and space figured out of it—of the underlying unity of African world culture; it is an equation, moreover, whose solution consistently leads us, like the mathematics of cosmology, into processes that we cannot observe or comprehend but that seem to carry the forces of culture beyond its material expression, even beyond learning and memory, into a forbidden zone explained in the last century by metaphorically linking culture, through evolution, to race.

We enter the marketplace, as we entered Café Tunis, as tourists; but by dismantling the historical structure that couples particular dialects of African culture with particular places, and by tendering a conclave of those dialects around the sites they have in common, the African Diaspora conducts us beyond tourism into a kind of ethnography embodied in the exhibit itself, in which we begin to see the familial strains in culture and hence to see it as a whole, at once writing and reading it. In the confusion of dialects we can gradually detect an original and essential influence that draws all forms, familiar and unfamiliar, out of their various illicit relations with us—the relations by which we know them—and into their family relations with one another, wherein they are newly revealed by the resemblances among them. This can be dismaying, for a familiar form—the blues style, the Philly dance step—cleaves to its long-lost relations, and the vocality or posture once so native, so familiar, becomes suddenly something alien as it finds its cousin in a Ghanian religious ceremony; but with this estrangement, too, comes a new kind of knowledge as the familiar form takes on an unforeseen dimensionality, traces of African antiquity still clinging to it even in the Mississippi Delta or the Philadelphia ghetto, like the shallow surface of a painting that, with a final stroke of color, falls dizzyingly into the third dimension.

Though we may recognize a particular way of making a basket as ingenious, or a method of combining and cooking vegetables as resourceful, rarely if ever can we see these homely inventions as parts of a tradition that reaches over generations and continents. Charles Freeny, a soul food cook from Chicago, makes a dish of collard greens and okra that is widespread in the Deep South; but so does Juliet Amoah, from Ghana. One of the coil baskets woven on the Sea Islands of South Carolina, for example, wound of sweet grass and sewn with palmetto fronds, reinforced with rushes when they are to be used for winnowing rice, might stand unprepossessingly beside an easy chair filled with magazines, having arrived last Christmas from a gift shop in Charleston; but it is identical to baskets woven for centuries on the West Coast of Africa by the Mandingos, the Yoruba, the Ashanti, and the Ibo, except for the rust-brown decorative threads that run through it, made from longleaf pine needles native to South Carolina.

These instructive juxtapositions expose the continuity of cultural practices invested in artifacts: not only in vegetable preparations and winnowing baskets, but in woodcarving, mask making, fishnet weaving, and hair braiding. But artifacts alone do not always speak to such relationships; resemblances can be misleading, and apparent differences may conceal deeper structural unities. This is particularly true in the most familiar forms of the culture of African descent—music, song, and dance—in which superficial structural differences overlay deeper unifying uses of rhythm and melody, of vocality and the human body itself. To detect the bloodlines running through the gospel songs of the Reverend Leon Pinson or of Washington, D.C., street singer Flora Moulton and into the vending cry of Baltimore's arabber Sonny Diggs or the shouts of Lefty Diaz and Shock Treatment, a blues band, may not be difficult: all the familiar traits—responsorial singing, melismatic ornamentation, descending melodic phrases, strong counterrhythms, the flatted or "blue" notes—are there. And with a little prompting, we can identify the rasping or quavering blues vocality with kindred sounds in Ghanian song, in which voice masking is a sign of spirit possession.

But it may require a deeper listening to understand that the rhythmic interplay among the trumpet, clarinet, and trombone of the Leonard Goines Quintet, a jazz band, arises from the same principle that unites the many rhythms of the Nigerian drum ensemble or those of the Trinidad Steel Band. The peculiar posture of G. D. Young of the Rising Star Fife and Drum Corps, as he bends over his bass drum, is not a sign of his age but the retention of a certain alignment of the body—shoulders thrust forward, hips behind, arms up with palms out, head turning from side to side—common in sacred and secular West African dance, a posture that was echoed in the plantation religious dance or ring-shout and that made its appearance in the popular culture of this country in the 1820s, when T. D. Rice introduced it onto the stage as "Jump Jim Crow"; it has reappeared in ballrooms, juke joints, and gymnasiums as the jerk, the lindy, the jitterbug, and the frug, among others. The social affinities of this posture, moreover, may blind us to the fact that its moral origins are not, as the stereotype dictates, in animal passion but in sexual modesty: while moving always in intricate and subtle relation to one another, the Ghanian man and woman, in traditional dances, never touch.

From the deep, inextricable mingling of African and European threads sometimes arise the haunting, inscrutable forms that occupy the gulf between two cultures that are themselves perpetually mingled and perpetually estranged in the New World. Consider again the rural Mississippi Rising Star Fife and Drum Corps, whose leader, G. D. Young, first appeared at the Festival in 1967 with his brothers Ed and Lonnie. Three small black men, stoop-shouldered, slight, their faces half-hidden under the narrow brims of fedora hats, the cuffs of their billowing trousers riding over their black shoes, move slowly together across the marketplace, turning languidly in opposition to one another but tied together by invisible lines like three dinghies bobbing in the water, knees, bodies, and heads bent, their gazes focused on the ground or turned meditatively inward. One might see these same men standing in the gray snow on a cold December day on a street corner on Chicago's West Side; they are an apparition, stragglers from some unheralded battlefield of the Civil War, whose music—the low, counsel-giving bass drum, the nagging snare, the chirping fife—seems to float over the yellow grasses of an African savanna.

The African Diaspora area, anchored by the Caribbean Marketplace, somehow brings to completion the sense of estrangement white and black Americans have known and felt all along on the streets of our cities, where our two peoples live within one another's gaze but out of mutual understanding and sympathy, unconsciously exchanging our visible forms while assigning to them our own meanings; it exposes the roots of that estrangement in the indelibly African character of African American culture and thereby, perhaps, at last thaws the freeze—for, however fearsome, the named thing cannot master us like the nameless. That is the thesis of the African Diaspora: that estrangement—which is, after all, the historical issue of ethnomimetic communication, conscious and unconscious—shot with ridicule and woven with unacknowledged continuities and identities, across a racial gulf flowing with fear and hate. That is why, too, the marketplace is the ideal site in which to present the African family reunion for the eyes of Americans, for the marketplace, and the street within which it stands, is the field of our relation and the scene of our two cultures' reflections upon themselves and upon each other.

As Bernice Reagon points out, in the black community the street forms the "link between home and the rest of the world"; "being 'in the streets'" means "living in the open, where anything can happen."[3] The street is a festive setting. As Roberto Da Matta observes, the street is a place of "movement, novelty, and action," whose basic rule, which we observe both as exhibitors of ourselves and as traders in the marketplace, "is to deceive and to take advantage of others."[4] As a site of deception, then, the street is a theatrical field whose density, although it may be modulated by conventional frames such as storefronts or graffiti, is more typically a density in the field of attention, as it is thickened by deliberate inversion, incongruity, color, dislocation, displacement, and the like or thinned by the commonplace and inconspicuous.

If culture at Café Tunis is convivial, a matter of conversation, consultation, and fellowship, in the Diaspora marketplace it is a matter of spectacle, where we are, not what we are said to be, but what we appear to be in relation to what appears around us, or what we say we are, and no more. Speech, here, if it has not actually been reborn as song, is cozening and declamatory or, where it engages with the stranger, propitiating; music, dance, song, and speech all cooperate to negotiate the transient moratorium that provides for trade, but within which cultural forms free themselves and fly about on the air like words. Among these forms is, of course, identity itself, which, if it is at once constrained, enshrined, and nurtured by the narrative community at Café Tunis, is in the marketplace plastic and protean, a flower of fantasy and wish or, more typically given the heterogeneity of the marketplace, a scene for satire and burlesque and, beyond that, for the proliferation of signs for signification's sake, wherein the very fact of identity becomes, in the cultural superabundance of the marketplace, ludicrous. In the marketplace we acknowledge what in the café we do not: the division between what we are and what we wish or pretend to be; and in dramatizing that division, we tend inevitably toward a parody of the social situation itself.

Hence it is in the street, too, as Reagon observes, that the community makes its "major statement of cultural identity," and where culture as spectacle has its fullest development.[5] In the culture of the African Diaspora, that statement is called Carnival: the Shrovetide or pre-Lenten festival that falls between the Feast of the Epiphany and Ash Wednesday in the Catholic calendar. Carnival was enacted at the Festival of American Folklife in 1974, 1979, 1980 (when it was the largest Caribbean Carnival parade in the United States), and—as Mardi Gras or "Fat Tuesday," the last day of Carnival—in 1985.

From its beginnings early in the nineteenth century, Carnival has been a dreamwork of cultural mingling, particularly of white and black cultures, in the New World. Like the display colors of courting birds, fantastic masks and costumes proliferate out of the myriad distorted reflections of human visages, and representations of them, that arise out of the alignments of African and European cultures with the class stratifications of Caribbean society. Like an electromagnetic bell whose oscillating switch closes its circuit by breaking it, the meeting of cultures across the inefface-able social gap created by race sets up a frenzied ringing of human images that reverberates through all the peoples represented there.

Carnival, a word whose literal and figurative senses combine the Lenten proscription against meat with the pre-Lenten consummation of the flesh—"farewell" (*vale*), in two senses, to the "flesh" (*carne*), also in two senses—came to Trinidad late in the eighteenth century with French planters, who celebrated the festival with masked balls and street proces-sions, the amusements of European mandarins in the Age of Reason: a time when the artful and the artificial were rarely distinguished, when art itself was understood as the best expression of human Nature, and when masks, wigs, powders, perfumes, and other paraphernalia of artificiality were a regular part of ordinary social life.[6]

But in the racially bifurcated slave society of the Caribbean, Carnival could not retain its European character. Over the course of the nineteenth century, an annual black festival called Cannes Brule—an emancipation celebration named for the burning torches that symbolized sugar cane set afire by rebellious slaves—came to be combined, in spite of prohibitive laws, with Carnival, bringing the satirical spirit of Cannes Brule into the licentious pre-Lenten season. The Cannes Brule of 1834 featured the parade of a costumed "artillery band" that parodied the ruling militia, sending before it, in the glow of burning torches and under the sting of whips, field slaves in blackface and chains.[7] The syncretic Carnival that emerged late in the century—with its ritual combat, the satirical singing that we call kalinda and calypso, African drum rhythms transfiguring formal procession into communal dance, and, of course, festive masking—threw over the methodical licentiousness of French pre-Lenten celebra-tion the lurid glow, wrought in anger, of Cannes Brule, presaging the ambivalent joy, the monstrous comedy, the straining revelry, and even the desperate abandon that have thrust Carnival onto the verge of nightmare.

Both because it has its origins in the medieval Catholic sacred calendar and because it is the symbolic exfoliation of a steeply hierarchical racist society, Carnival is more than just an interval of riot that opens and closes over a few days' time in the early spring. It is an unmanifest countersociety, running under and across the manifest social order to assert itself at a moment in which the prevailing order temporarily withdraws. In Rio, for example, as Da Matta reports, the Samba Schools that, with other associa-tions, form the Carnival parade are hierarchically organized in larger groups of twelve or fourteen schools, with participants, numbering between seven hundred and twenty-five hundred, who from year to year drift up and down in the hierarchy from one group to another, gaining status and losing it. Internally, the schools are further divided according to complex segments of social class, reintegrated for the parade into ranks of synchronized dancers, Samba dancers, theme characters, flag-bearers, allegorical floats, and, finally, elaborately or provocatively dressed—or undressed—isolated marchers, usually women and homosexuals.[8] The *blocos*, too, or "carnival blocs," though more informally organized out of neighborhoods, nevertheless fall into three classes based on social level, with the lowest group, the *bloco sujo* or "dirty" ones, being given to shocking and intimidating spectators with outrageous behavior; within each class, individuals fall into groups of chairmen, singers, musicians, and finally, among the general revelers, the "richer" and "poorer."[9]

Mas players, as the Trinidadian revelers are called, belong to permanent bands or clubs, each of which has its own internal hierarchy, ascending through separate sections that carry out, under an elaborately costumed leader, some motif belonging to the band's larger theme—a national myth, a sport or fantasy, a historical period, or the black "Zulus" and "Indians" of Mardi Gras, for example—to a King and Queen, who are the most elaborately costumed of all: so elaborate, in fact, that some have evolved into wheeled floats that carry the presiding figures at a regal elevation above the parading bands, becoming, in effect, a secular version of a religious procession.[10]

Though they have no political power, social prestige, or institutional permanence, the Carnival groups nevertheless are sometimes more long-lived than the schools, clubs, creeds, parties, and the like that form the official social structure. They are, in fact, folk groups in the important sense that they arise, as Da Matta puts it, from "the interest born from within that obeys the genuine impulse of the person or group itself."

In this sense the Carnival groups are among the most authentic and spontaneous forms of association. They do not follow any external model. They did not originate in any political or sociological handbook. They were not implemented through a specific and conscious plan of development. Furthermore, they did not come from those imitated countries, France and England. Thus they are not a means of responding to a world that certain groups believe exists as an absolute and unique reality. On the contrary, they are a way of opening a dialogue with the structure of social relations operating in Brazilian reality.[11]

That these groups are spontaneous, however, does not make them incoherent. They have, like the Samba Schools, a center composed of family, neighborhood, racial, and class alliances, the founders and parents of the association who form its administrative structure, and a margin of members and sympathizers who enter and leave the group from other neighborhoods, races, and classes with considerable flexibility and freedom—which they have precisely because the Carnival group is *not* a formally constituted element of the dominant culture. Bound internally by affinities of kind, unofficial or marginal but freely accepting and discharging its membership from and into the larger society in which it resides both interdependently and independently, the Carnival association is the social agent by which an ethnomimetic community declares, and through declaration reaffirms and secures, its institutional and unofficial, though permanent, place in the social order.

Consider, then, what happens in Carnival. The normally powerless, even the destitute people of the city or town emerge into prominence, openly competing with one another in a show of talents and abilities universally and perennially admired and envied but wretchedly incommensurate with the rewards of wealth and power that fate and the world have actually granted to them: skills in music, dance, and song; in originality and invention; in fantasy and industry; in physical strength, endurance, and beauty; in erotic power—Carnival represents the triumph of God-given gifts. Fixed racial, economic, and social categories dissolve in the manifestation of normally unmanifest associations; the cityscape itself, normally a beehive of economic activity, becomes, as if conquered by an invading army, a playground of idleness and pleasure, where the imaginative and erotic life, normally confined to the intimacy of households or within the boundaries of formally constituted art or never revealed at all, reveals itself not only in masks, costumes, floats, and sexual cross-dressing, but also in public urinating, defecating, eating, sleeping, and lovemaking.

An "immense social screen, where multiple visions of social reality are projected simultaneously," Carnival is a festival of types, in which wild Indians, frenzied savages, Chinese mandarins, astronauts, eighteenth-century French courtiers, Prussian grenadiers, Roman emperors, Spanish vaqueros, bedouins, plantation slaves, devils, clowns, and outsized costumed figures so fantastic that their wearers disappear into them—as if the swimming, undifferentiated surfaces of human sensory perception could spring hallucinogenically out of the brain and hover around us like a magnetic field—disport themselves in the joy that comes of their momentary victory over the order that has oppressed them. It is, in effect, a paradisiacal moment in which no social order exists at all, nor do any of the concomitant divisions between self and the world or self and other.[12]

Carnival, it appears, is the traditional and temporary conquest of official society by the ethnomimetic culture that lives within its social and noetic vacuums, and with which it has a broadly ironic relation—a relation expressed, of course, in the Carnival masquerade itself, in which the cultural plenum opens itself to view:

> On the other side of the street, a few meters farther along . . . two young women were walking. They were dressed as seducers, wearing clothing that did not cover, but instead revealed. There, in the middle of the multitude they were not assaulted. On the contrary, they assaulted the men, the Brazilian *machos* who during Carnival let their masks fall and showed themselves to be incredibly and surprisingly timid in sexual encounters. Farther along were four or five youths dressed as Arabs. Each had a long robe and carried a briefcase. Their faces were serious and they carried on their backs a sign that read Owners of the World. At another corner, an elderly gentleman solemnly puffed a pipe and looked on the passing spectacle with a grave face. He was an executive, with his characteristic briefcase. But he had no pants.[13]

Since the passage of the Immigration and Naturalization Act of 1965, Caribbean culture—a creole culture that attempts "to reconcile old world traditions, new world influences, and the exigencies of modernization," a cosmopolitan culture accustomed to the "adopting, confronting, negotiating, sharing and shaping" of ways of life that goes with creolization—has increasingly established itself in American and Canadian cities; with it has come, in New York, Washington, and other cities, an effort to restore the Carnival—not only in radio programs, private clubs, and school projects, but in full-fledged Carnival parades, which, because they draw participants from all over the Caribbean region, are "more Caribbean" than their originals in Trinidad and Tobago.[14]

In the Caribbean Marketplace we are very close to the secret operations of ethnomimesis. Most of the processes by which these traditions of music, crafts, art, and ritual pass from one generation to the next, and across the gulf between continents and epochs, by forces mostly invisible even to the tradition-bearers themselves, occur in the close, usually intimate communication within families, and even in the secondary relationships within families, such as those between grandparents or aunts and uncles and children. When ideas about music or hair braiding or basket weaving—all of them culturally interconnected and hence mutually reinforcing—are not actually passing from one person to another (and even that transition can be invisible, as between mother and baby), they are hidden in the memories of the bearers.

Thus the entire racial, ethnic, or linguistic community seems to be swept up in an imperceptible force that persists in expressing itself in a variety of circumstances in which direct communication seems impossible. Different epochs have accounted for this force in different ways. Where direct transmission seems impossible, some durable form, an archetype, is posited, perhaps an organ of the human mind that seeks consistently to project itself; or, should the racially other society appear savage or primitive to the Western eye, such forms are regarded as the prototypes or the universal original forms of human mechanical and imaginative power, which in its higher stages evolves into its complex Western forms. Both of these ideas, the one psychological, the other biological, emerged in the nineteenth century. Our current perspective, a sociological one, treats the human community as the site of complex human communications, by means of which economic, social, and political power distributes and sustains itself. Yet a mystery somehow remains; even though various moments, devices, and occasions of cultural transmission can be posited, few have actually been seen. The old theories retain something of their force, even if only as expressions of the sense that human communities have a larger life independent of and invisible to but continually bearing upon the lives of individuals.

The power of the Festival of American Folklife to translate and transform a visitor through the folkloric enactment of forms more or less remote from her experience may be conceived, perhaps, as a series of reverberations that extend outward from the familiar world to worlds most exotic and inscrutable, and inward to the hidden workings of familiar things—outward to a Tunisian devotional chant, say, and inward to family anecdotes, children's jump-rope rhymes, and the operation of a letterpress or the splicing of telephone cables. Of the unfamiliar things to which a visitor is exposed, closest to home are the ethnic and regional foods such as those offered in 1974 by Tunisians, Greeks, Swedes and Finns, West Indians, and Mississippians: *mashwiyya*, a Tunisian grilled vegetable salad; Greek honey pastries; Finnish braided cardamom bread; West Indian callalou stew; barbecued chicken. Sampling these foods literally cultivates our taste and hence makes us more urbane; attending a workshop on their preparation and perhaps taking home a recipe book expands our skills and enriches the vocabulary of our own kitchens. These are exercises in domestic culture, and they civilize us; they belong to our cultural education in the same way that the ballet school, the art museum, and the adult education course belong to it, and they embody what is at bottom a class motive that links a rise in social standing to sophistication in travel, cuisine, language, and art—all markers of cultural privilege. At the Festival of American Folklife, that motive is displaced, differentiated, sublimated, and diffused, but it remains a class motive nevertheless, grounded in the power to exchange economic resources for cultural capital.

The tourist aspires to enrich his experience through travel, engaging with a foreign culture by means no different from those he employs in his own city—tasting food and drink, imbibing the restaurant atmosphere, acquiring local crafts and art, having transient encounters, usually through trade, with native people; it is in this spirit that the Festival of American Folklife brings, as we have seen, the Tunisian café, the Karpathian coffee shop, or the West African nightclub to the National Mall, extending dramatically the range of the Washington tourist, if the visitor is a tourist—or transforming her into one if she is not. But our itinerary carries us at an oblique angle to the beaten paths of international and domestic tourism by opening to us, and conferring upon us the implied privilege of such exposure, those precincts of the national and international life, the close, intimate life of particular folk communities, that are normally invisible, inaccessible, or, more typically, hidden behind the very mask the community has fashioned to protect itself against the tourist's self-reflecting gaze.

It is in that quality of privileged access, of penetration into the privacy of communal life, that the transfiguring power of the Festival of American Folklife is greatest, and all the Festival's artifacts and icons—the T-shirts, jewelry, pottery, woven baskets, and other handicrafts that can be purchased on the Mall, or the Festival's internal indicia such as identification badges, Mardi Gras beads, tattoos, and the like—testify to it. The Karpathian *glendi*, the Caribbean Carnival, the Appalachian fiddle contest, the Mississippi cattle auction, the Chicago blues club or Louisiana dance hall, the black Baptist service, the rehearsals of a Washington professional theater production, the cakewalk and hootenanny—all of these events were presented on the Mall in 1974 and in succeeding years; the power to attend these enactments in their authentic or very nearly authentic forms, into which we are more or less successfully integrated as participants and as spectators, is exhilarating, all the more so because we share our privilege with others, with whom we enter into a transient but happy sense of belonging.

This is interesting. With its mostly affluent and educated visitors gazing into the lives of mostly working-class, immigrant, and rural peoples, the Festival adopts the class structure as an organizing principle; but to enjoy our privilege in such a conspicuous way is alien to our democratic tradition. We do it, therefore, together—in a sense democratically, enjoying not only our extraordinary social puissance but the blessing bestowed upon it by its collective exercise and the willing participation of the craftspeople, artists, and musicians themselves. That their participation is contractual, and that it involves a regular weekly wage, is not immediately apparent: the Festival, after all, is free.

In some sense, the Festival narratives, with all their infinite variety, each spun out of the succession of encounters between visitor and presentations, are about belonging—our own and others'. They may awaken us to the meaning of belonging and perhaps arouse a longing for the home in which we are rooted or grief for the home we have lost. There are some Festival visitors, it is sadly apparent, who have come in search of that sense of belonging, which, it seems, has not been given to them in their day-to-day existence; and there are few regular visitors, I suspect, for whom the Festival does not supply something of the sense of community that most of us permit ourselves to yearn for—not only the folk community into which we are virtually, if not actually, admitted, but also the communities of visitors formed around Festival events and the community of participants and staff.

Though fragile and sometimes perfidious, it is certainly that sense of belonging that argues most forcibly for the festivity of the Festival. The Festival is a field of social dislocations that thrusts self and stranger, participants and visitors, as well as the enigma between them, into naked visibility; at the same time, it compels each to orient himself or herself in relation to the other, dispelling that enigma with sometimes fantastic constructions of thought, which devices of display and associated texts and trained presentation cannot always control. Thus, for that exhilarating power of access and sense of privilege, we pay ultimately, as the mighty always pay, with isolation, for to be an outsider is precisely the condition of our privilege; it is the precondition of *all* Festival relations, which otherwise would deteriorate, as on occasion they have, into icy antagonism among isolated groups.

But this dialectic of dislocation and situation, the tug of nostalgia and the call of adventure, may have a resolving synthesis. Our godlike mobility, our unheard-of power of access, the succession of radical, even violent cultural transformations, ought to bring us the detachment—and the conviction of human culture as such, with its dim but detectable shapes of a universal humanity—that is an index not merely of social, economic, or political power but also, perhaps, of the moral wisdom such power ideally ought to confer. The Festival of American Folklife may be, broadly speaking, an arena for a kind of concentrated and localized international tourism; but it transcends tourism, too, by breaking through the tourist's psychic insulation with aesthetic forces for which that insulation provides. This suggests that tourist and native share, below the level of their divergent cultural lexicons, a deeper syntax that permits, at moments of great aesthetic intensity, or with patient tutoring and dedicated study, the understanding of one by the other.

Yet there are cultures, perhaps, with whom we do not share an underlying history and syntax; with whom, to communicate, some such basis must be fashioned or found; cultures shaped by wholly different influences, whose divergent traditions cannot be traced to a common, if hypothetical, root. Such a foray into the unknown is not a tour; it is an expedition.

Crossing the Lincoln Memorial reflecting pool on a raft cannot actually be compared to Major John Wesley Powell's expedition down the Colorado River through the Grand Canyon in 1871; but it can be likened symbolically. That was the route, at the 1974 Festival of American Folklife, between the African Diaspora and the Native American areas; the knee-deep waters of the pool symbolized the gulf between Anglo-American and Native American cultures, which, if it has been periodically crossed, has never been bridged. "In future," Bess Lomax Hawes cautioned the Festival producers, "if any group has to be geographically separated from the rest of the Festival, don't make it the Native Americans. Older Indians complained to me that they couldn't get around to see the rest of the Festival; younger ones invited me in biting terms to 'come visit our reservation.'"[15]

In the year after the museum's founding in 1847, the Smithsonian's Board of Regents declared its interest in "ethnological researches, particularly with reference to the different races of men in North America, also explorations and accurate surveys of the mounds and other remains of the ancient people of our country"—a statement that initiated the Smithsonian's ethnological programs, of which the Native American area of the

Festival is a descendant, but at the same time unconsciously fixed an epistemological ocean between ourselves and this continent and pronounced, also unconsciously, an elegy upon its aboriginal peoples.[16]

What we can't name, we can't know. "Indian" was wrong—the usage of a well-known fellow who didn't know where he was. "Native American" is an honorable, if awkward, political euphemism, but it is wrong, too. Both names, like the regents' charge, thrust the aboriginal people of this continent, like Daphne in her laurel, into the insentient Nature from which our own religious and scientific tradition has estranged us and which, though powerful hypotheses may be brought to account for it, can never be known in and of itself; following inevitably from such a hypothesis, our imposed names assign to these peoples the same unconsciousness of their place in the universe and in history as that shown by their own burial mounds, dooming them, of course, as the surviving relics of an earlier stage in the evolution of civilization, to extinction.

That is precisely the view embodied in the North American Indian Hall at the Museum of Natural History, where until recently the skeletal remains of Indians were used to illustrate early human evolution, graphically bloody and savage medical practices, and population changes; among the exhibits were rows of human skulls, arranged as tokens representing human births in millions, and dioramas, after the manner of animal dioramas, dramatizing primitive life. "It means something to the rest of the world," says Suzan Shown Harjo, executive director of the National Congress of American Indians, "to have us next to the elephants and the dinosaurs, things past and things not quite human."[17] The cultures of the descendants of Asian peoples—Ojibwa, Chippewa, Shoshone, Kickapoo, Navajo, to give them their proper names—whom Europeans encountered when they arrived in America, moreover, were so intimate with the natural world, materially and spiritually, that the Europeans could scarcely detect their culturality or discern the social, aesthetic, political, and linguistic structures that testified to the complexity, the extension, and the ecological genius of the native civilizations.

Technologically conservative, animistic, oral and intuitive, following cultural traditions in which Europeans had no share, red Americans were at best a mystery; decimated by European diseases and consistently driven beyond the frontier of European settlement, they became the shadows into which the Europeans projected their own personified wishes, dreams, and nightmares. The red American has been more than a stranger, then; in reality we have not seen him at all, for when we look, we see only our own erotic dreams—costumed, like schoolchildren in a holiday pantomime, in the innocent flesh of sensual savage and animal nature. Untempered by the regular interaction that has characterized relations between white and black cultures, images of the Indian have proliferated in the void between us, images so little connected to the visible foreground of red American culture that they are more akin to pure romance than to stereotype, bifurcated by the deep ambivalence of romance and suffused with its erotic character—a symbol that, perhaps better than any other, embodies our old identification of the New World, which we have loved, exploited, and lost, with female Nature.

Hence, as Rayna Green points out, the New World, in cartoons, maps, and travel books, took as its emblem an Indian queen figure, "a large, full bosomed, naked barbarous woman with her hand on a spear and her foot on the head of an Alligator," an allegorical figure synthesized from classical allusion and literary citations strongly reminiscent of that other victor over the English, Joan of Arc.[18] Her putative daughter "Liberty," a slender Indian princess "draped in a classic gown, tiara on her head, torch in her hand and surrounded by Revolutionary heroes like George Washington," might as easily have been a daughter of the French aristocracy on the eve of the Revolution, dreaming on Rome: Republicanism was a patrician idea, as socialism was a bourgeois one.

In popular culture—medicine and Wild West shows, stage melodramas, dime novels and Western movies, picture books, calendars, travel literature, popular painting and history, commercial iconography, and the like—the emblematic Indian descended from her eminence in allegory, where the symbol always enjoys the immunity conferred by intellectual analysis, into the broil of pure passion, where she took on the shapes of fear and desire. Respectable Protestant values such as spotless love, steady faith, selfless duty, and unflagging loyalty appeared in the legendary and imaginary figures of Pocahontas, the Dying Cherokee, Little Beaver, and Tonto, while sinister figures like Sitting Bull or the savage warriors and wild riders of the Wild West Show personified the admiration and wonder, as well as the fear, of those extremes of human power and will that lay outside the boundaries of the respectable bourgeois life. Even the fear of death, institutionalized in the commercial classes as a restless seeking after elixirs and nostrums wherein lay the secrets of good health and long life, found crass expression in "Indian doctors" and their patent medicines, which were presumed to have been cooked up out of the Indian's ancient wisdom in the ways of Nature. If, as Green points out, "playing Indian . . .

seems to be a compelling activity for the American people," it may be because the Native Americans are, at least in fancy, precisely that natural aristocracy—warlike and brave, passionate and wise, faithful and true—which democracy was to deliver to us.[19]

How, then, to present the Native American on the Mall? How to penetrate the thicket of myth and fantasy surrounding him, to make a presentation that will not simply become a more genteel or more high-brow or more "educational" version of the Wild West Show? Two years earlier, Smithsonian fieldworker Tom Kavanaugh had written that "the job of adequately presenting the Indian cultures . . . is impossible. Not only are those cultures complex and interrelated, but the gap between the Indian cultures and the general white population is wide enough to dis-courage most attempts at presenting them."[20] What ethnomimetic site can be re-created on the Mall that will bring our cultural endowments into alignment—as was the case at Café Tunis or in the Caribbean Market-place—when in effect we are reaching not across continents and histories but across the ages to a civilization not two thousand or four thousand but forty thousand years old, and to people who preserve in their languages and cultures not the memory of a Mediterranean garden that betrayed them or the determination to subdue the wilderness that it might become a garden again, but the love of a planet that heaved itself up out of the ice to welcome them?

At our landing spot on the opposite side of the Reflecting Pool and through a line of trees, a tepee has been erected—almost a joke, as if the Native American area were a theme park, a sort of Adventureland or a roadside tourist trap where jade jewelry and silver work can be had on the cheap. Its irony is, of course, directed against ourselves, as our own prejudices spring up spontaneously before us in a silent rebuke; it is a sign not of what to expect, but of what to leave behind.

The tepee, in fact, is the traditional summer dwelling of the Basin and Plateau peoples of the far West—the Paiute, Shoshone, Kaibab, Ute, and Nez Pierce—whose baskets, beadwork, hide tanning, and buckskin work appear just beyond it, along with the crafts of the California tribes—the Toloowa, Pomo, Hoopa, Yurok, Karok, Luiseño, Maidu, and Cahuilla—including fish traps and nets, beadwork, baskets, a fishing boat being woven from reeds, and a dugout canoe being adzed out of redwood. Between the tepee and the crafts area, under a canopy, a kind of school or "learning center" has been established, where text panels, photographs, and television videotapes supplement the classes and workshops conducted there. These include short courses in Hoopa, Ute, and Nez Pierce languages and discussions of the issues that join Native American culture to contemporary American society: Indian stereotypes; sexual roles; non-verbal communication; Indians in sports and the military; Indian professionals, artists, and writers; life on the reservations and in the cities. Acorn bread is baking nearby, and California salmon is being roasted on open fires; in the evening, gorgeously feathered Apaches dance in a pow-wow, the pantribal celebration of an emerging national Native American identity.

All of this is interesting, all informative; but, either because we conceive all that we see in the almost compulsive language of stereotype, or because we can find in ourselves no echo of the devotion, piety, and power in the drum rhythms, nor hear the divine voices in the songs nor understand their spiritual message, the beauty, the true beauty that would melt our hearts, is lost on us. There is education and demonstration, but little empathy or transport. To pass beyond the tepee is sobering and certainly cools a tourist's ardor; but the encounter is not transforming—not like the pioneer meetings of Frank Cushing, Major Powell, and other Western adventurers who left everything familiar behind.

One must go still farther, advancing with a brave, young, and, as it happens, a manly heart. Down the path in the direction of Constitution Avenue and the State Department lies the Native American playing field; only here, a new site of culture where young men meet beyond speech in the realm of physical strength, stamina, and skill, in *games*, can a genuine encounter between white and red occur. Young Indian athletes—Creek stickball players, Cherokee archers, an Acoma sprinter, and Laguna long-distance runners—are there to challenge young and adventurous Festival visitors to competition in their various sports and, perhaps more often than not, to exceed them. There is nothing, in the strict textual sense, to be learned about Native American culture from these events. But for the handful of volunteers who pitted themselves against Indian athletes in foot races and stickball, culture was tied to a moral structure of pride and shame that reconstrues cultural encounters in terms of outright masculine adventure, challenge, and conquest.

In the sites of culture, a dialectic of personality and society promulgates versions of identity belonging to that site. In Café Tunis we are what the narratives exchanged about us in the community say we are; in the Caribbean Marketplace we are what we say we are, in speech and in spectacle, through the propitiatory and parodic masks of economic and social negotiation. On the playing field, however, culture becomes a structure whose content is an autonomous system of challenges which in confronting we exhibit, to ourselves and to others, the particular physiological and intellectual powers that ideally bring victory and honor in the social sphere, usually because they are economically potent and hence erotically charged. Swiftness and endurance in foot racing; quickness of perception, alertness, and cooperation in the ball games; patience, concentration, strength, and precision in archery; dexterity in the hand games: all these qualities point to the imperatives of hunters, fishers, and herders and to the crafts that translate natural resources into clothing, tools, and expressive artifacts. Except insofar as the game itself is a cultural product, both the form and the matter of culture have been artificially banished from the playing field; through the contest, we expose the efficient causes, the human agencies, of culture and hence measure, and certainly cultivate, our ability to succeed or fail in it.

The polarized and masculine world of the playing field, where glory belongs to the victor and disgrace to the loser, should remind us, moreover, of the ambivalent romantic world into which the white masculine imagination has thrust the red American. On the playing field, the bipolar romantic stereotype cannot survive, for in athletic contest the figurative basis of stereotype, which depends on various symbolic modes of representation, has been literalized; challenger and opponent alike, presenting themselves metonymically to one another, are embedded, not in one another's moral universe, figuratively, but in a system of concrete and literal aims that they mutually embrace and mutually pursue. The gulf between them has narrowed to a fulcrum, upon which defeat and victory are balanced. Victory for the outsider brings acceptance and, with it, honor; one thinks of Frank Cushing, the adventurer, posed for a photograph wearing the Zuni costume that signified his acceptance into the tribe—or at least his boast of it. Defeat may deepen the challenger's alienation or dispel it; but either way, having thrown in his lot with the Indian in the game, he cannot but depart with a new sense of the human powers, measured on his own pulse, that have figured into his opponent's otherness—in the harrowing moment, the moment of his most intense striving, when young Gordon Joe of the Acoma, feet working on the hard ground like hammers, all the muscles of his back crowding toward the exits, draws ahead and recedes to the finish line like the ring that a lover, betrayed, flings over the precipice into the chasm between them.

And yet the game supplants the romantic stereotype even as it displaces it. Whatever we may be in the café or the marketplace, on the playing field we are characters in a drama of cultural values and, potentially, the heroes of narratives that partake again of what has been invested in us as embodiments of an ideal. Though we leave our social identity behind us on the playing field, along with, perhaps, all rational speech except the ejaculations of partisanship and enthusiasm, we may become through honor the moral grains around which the social identities of others form, thereby actively participating in the making of culture.

The athletic contest between white American and Indian is perhaps the best scheme of all the encounters between self and stranger at the Festival of American Folklife. Within its exclusively masculine framework, it summons up the entire culture of subjection that defines *all* Festival relations, where, in a context of unshakeable dominance, the dominant offers himself up for a temporary and symbolic humiliation and defeat. In that transient moment, the nakedness of the runner stands simply for the cultural nakedness of the displaced person—which all of us, men and women, at the Festival are—and the game itself for all the games of admiration and love that are played to win our hearts or that we play to win the heart of another; all of us seek redemption in the festive community, which excludes everyone and embraces everyone and makes everyone anew.

Like all great festivals, the Festival of American Folklife turns the world outside in, inside out, and upside down, gathering up within the five realms of American folklife—African Diaspora, Old Ways in the New World, Working Americans, Native Americans, and Family Folklore—the cultural sites at which, in carrying out various social functions and roles, the many dimensions of human personality can be made manifest. Many far-flung scenes and occasions flow toward us on the Mall, transforming us from urbanite to tourist to adventurer—a progress whose terminus lies, for some at least, on the Native American playing field, where we leave all representations behind and instead negotiate our meeting with the stranger in formal contest, coming to know him not by images, figures, or texts, but silently and immediately, almost as we know ourselves, and just as obscurely. Self and stranger can meet in the café and the marketplace, or on the playing field, because these are sites in which society and culture open out of themselves, not only upon their own communities but also into the avenues that join the community to society, in which visitors and strangers meet, linger, and vanish.

But, as I have suggested, the Festival visitor's power of access extends inward well as outward, into sites of culture insulated or sequestered by such factors as the human life cycle, technological structures, and the natural environment. In 1974 and in the years to follow, Festival-goers not only visit, like tourists, the café and marketplace, or like adventurers compete with Indians in foot races and archery, or like vacationers gourmandize in rural Mississippi or Louisiana; like disembodied spirits, we also pass through social and psychological barriers into religious ceremonies, into the lives of children on street and playground, and into the worksites of industrial occupations. At last, at the Family Folklore tent, we become participants ourselves, interviewed by folklorists for the tales, legends, and rituals of our own families.

As we move from the exterior to the interior sites of culture—from, roughly, the social to the occupational, domestic, and sexual spheres—the reflexivity of the Festival begins to suggest itself, as if to explain that the Festival only required its various elements to be brought into certain theoretical and metaphorical alignments with one another, all those elements being, in effect, articulations of one another. We have already seen that the entire Festival, as a scene of social and cultural interaction, can be compared to the conversations in a café, or to the negotiations in the marketplace, or indeed to the spectacle of a street Carnival or the contests on an athletic field; all these are both elements of and metaphors for the Festival. Looking into the more sequestered areas of folklife such as childhood and the family, however, we can see that play, the universal theme of childhood, spills over into the Carnival and onto the athletic field and even, perhaps, into the café; that relations within a household significantly influence social identity in the café or the marketplace, which in turn shape relations within the family; indeed, that the politics of a close community—say, of the congregants in the African Methodist church, or a Brazilian Samba School—closely conform to and may even deliberately adapt the politics and the erotics of the family or of the playground.

Nor, as it happens, can the occupational group always be neatly discriminated from the ethnic community, or the ethnic community from the constraining and shaping influences of a particular neighborhood or region, where out of economic, political, historical, technological, commercial, and environmental forces arises an elusive but perceptible regional identity.

Even more powerfully do these interior spaces, when we look into them, seem to blueprint or model human cultural behavior, and like the café, street, and playing field they further elaborate the dimensions of human identity. In the region, for example—a cultural interior of the national polity—our identity, as a *regional* identity, remains largely imperceptible to us, except as a kind of seismometer of difference, rising to the level of perception only when an outsider stirs it to activity. We can know it only in relation to other natures similarly formed—or, perhaps, in relation to the stereotypes formed around it, which from within will always have a quality of distortion or exaggeration, but which paradoxically can become the legal tender of our negotiations with the outsider, the means by which we awaken in him or her recognition of us. Regional identity records and synthesizes, at what is perhaps the ecological limit of the ethnomimetic process, patterns of settlement, cultural retention, and creolization and the accommodation of these historical forces, through economic and attendant social formations, to the natural resources and features—such as the Appalachian mountains of Kentucky with their coal and lumber, the Chesapeake Bay with its fisheries, recreation, and tourism, the Texas oilfields, the old industrial cities of Ohio, or the fertile farms of Pennsylvania—that identify a region as such without reference to its political boundaries.

Regionality, then, draws up all the elements of culture represented elsewhere in the Festival into a net of interwoven historical, economic, political, ethnic, and natural forces and illustrates, in microcosm, the interdependency of culture with these forces. With its corporate and state sponsorship, including the contributions of several giant lumber companies such as Weyerhauser and Georgia Pacific and agencies such as the Mississippi Agricultural and Industrial Board, the Regional Americans area, in 1974 and in succeeding years, inevitably has had a promotional aspect. Mississippi, the featured state at the 1974 Festival, has trailing behind it, like other southern states, a legacy of sentimental images in literature, film, popular music, and art—elegant hanging mosses, vast cotton plantations, tender summer evenings, the rustic Negro, the canebrake, the river bottom—that cannot help but form at least one element even of the folklorist's concept of the state. "Folklore," insisted folklorist and native Mississippian William Ferris in 1974, "is the key to everybody in the state of Mississippi, black and white. It is the key to Faulkner, Eudora Welty, Richard Wright, B. B. King."[21]

But the Mississippi presentation expanded dramatically outward from the literary and folkloric spectres incarnate on the Mall to encompass many traditions that the state has inherited by emigration from other regions and that it shares with regions normally distinguished from it on the basis of those very traditions, becoming in effect a kind of microcosm of regionality itself. Of the singers who developed the signature folk music of the region, the Delta blues, Sam Chatmon, Son Thomas, and Chicago bluesman Houston Stackhouse all appeared at the Festival in 1974. A cotton patch, planted on the Mall in the spring by the Department of Agriculture, provided the raw material for exhibits in the classing, grading, ginning, carding, and spinning of cotton, during which the Festival visitor was invited, by his or her participation, to take the place of the slaves, sharecroppers, and workers who performed these tasks in the past. Narratives of culture in the cotton country, including cotton picking, playparty dancing, and a funeral, were wrought heiroglyphically in the elaborate tapestries of Ethel Mohammed of Belzoni, Mississippi.

Other forms reached, emblematically, to distant parts of the country: to Appalachia, the Southwest, the Midwest, the West, and even the Northwest; Mississippi, in short, proved itself a reservoir of traditional culture in America. The fiddlers' contest, well established at the Festival after three years, brought out of Mississippi Scots-Irish, Cajun, French, bluegrass, swing, jazz, and ragtime fiddlers. The origins of country music were explored in the performances of two original old-time string bands, the Leake County Revelers and Hoyt Ming and the Pep-Steppers, and in concert tributes to the Mississippi Sheiks and to the father of country music, Jimmie Rodgers of Meridian, Mississippi. Quills and bones players Derrick Bunch and Eddie Knight divided their time between the Mississippi and African Diaspora sites at the Festival.

Yet the Mississippi area seemed to transcend not only regional stereotypes but regionality itself. Would anyone have thought that there are cowboys and lumberjacks in Mississippi? With eight breeds of cattle stabled on the Mall, the Festival presented rodeo events such as horseback calf-cutting, a barrel race, and a cattle show, along with associated crafts such as saddlery and smithing. Opposite the cotton patch a stand of timber—bare poles, actually—occasioned the felling of trees by crosscut saw teams, a workshop on lumberjacks' tall tales and other timber lore, the crafting of an ox-yoke and whips, and a demonstration of ox-driving established Mississippi's place as a lumbering state.

The tourist seeking authenticity among strange people in exotic places finds himself blocked by his own status; the distance fixed between him and his object is at once the precondition of its charm and the barrier to his experience of it—hence his need to eat and drink, to photograph, and to buy, all ways of immediating the stubbornly mediated experience. But how are we to invest the immediate and familiar with the quality of authenticity—to lend charm to those realms of society and culture that lie so close to home, or indeed so literally *are* at home, that we rarely if ever experience them through representations, indeed cannot be said to experience them at all unless we are separated from them, in effect fetishizing them in memory?

In the Regional Americans area, whole regions have been modeled out of the scenes and icons arising from the natural and economic conditions that through schoolbooks, postcards, movies, and other popular imagery have come to characterize those regions: an oil derrick, a tobacco or cotton patch, a fishing boat, a horse-racing track, a Mardi Gras float—positioned in a setting of folk music and such crafts as woodcarving and whittling, pottery, basketry, broom and chair making, quilting, and needle and leatherwork, which, though they may flourish in a particular state and reflect its natural resources, are the very lexicon of traditional culture as folklorists have constructed it. Lengthy conversations between craftspeople and visitors are commonplace. The visitor is also invited to participate directly by operating a tool—in 1974, a spinning wheel—or helping to build a kite, or by sharing regional foods like Mississippi's fried catfish and barbecued chicken. All this occurs in an area of the Mall roughly the size of a soccer field—it *is*, in fact, a soccer field—framed by wide public footpaths and lined with shade trees. Much, of course, is excluded: there is no suggestion of poverty, though poverty is certainly implicit in many folk crafts, no welfare office, no high-tech or service industry, no local television or radio station, no mass culture of any kind—nothing, in short, which does not contribute to the myth of the region as the field of a coherent and extensive traditional culture.

This is a compound formula with a complex meaning. The memorable transformation of the Mall with the erection of an oil derrick, cattle barn, rodeo ring, or tobacco patch—or a boardwalk when New Jersey was the featured state in 1983—has a kind of gorgeous impertinence reminiscent of the entrepreneurship of P. T. Barnum, with even something of Barnum's vulgarity. In 1984, with Alaska as the featured state, a piece of an iceberg reached the Mall, with the help of trucks and heavy equipment. In the context of the regional and other areas, a log cabin, several varieties of vernacular houses, and a steel-girdered structure have been built on the Mall; pipeline, phone cables, and a railroad track have been laid there, a railroad train, semitrailer trucks and aircraft parked there, and rice and corn grown there in addition to the aforementioned cotton and tobacco.

Like Haverly's Colored Minstrels of the nineteenth century, a pageant that offered to present an entire plantation scene with "overseers, bloodhounds, and darkies at work" in a field near Boston, or indeed like the Greatest Show on Earth itself, the National Museum, on the Mall at least, seems to want to impress us with its ability to wield the world about like a toy.[22]

Well, yes. This is in the nature of the Smithsonian: to be the repository of the enchanted objects around which the narrative of our history has formed. In the National Museum, where a rock from the moon is used as a doorstop and an African elephant as an umbrella stand, where the X-15 hangs from the ceiling as children hang model airplanes in their bedrooms, where touring cars and combines are parked in the corridors, and where the parlors are hung with the fine art of Europe, Africa, and the Orient, one can only wonder behind what curtain or door lie the private rooms of the great Curator, whether he ever emerges to hobnob with the visitors, whether his smoke-yellowed mustache has turned white. The oil derrick thrusting up against the axletree of the Washington Monument, upon which the entire city seems to turn, or the figure of the cowboy with his lariat overhead, chasing a calf, the dust from his horse's hooves obscuring the somnolent Capitol Building in the distance behind him (I am alluding to images out of the Festival's own promotional material), or, indeed, the Cajun waltz or mountain breakdown holding all the monumental buildings in their spell: these elements anchor the regional exhibit in the traditions of representation surrounding it.

But the Festival exhibits, set out in the name of cultural context, precisely reverse the centrifugal direction in which the Smithsonian sends the museum visitor, calling her back from the successive wonders of technology, the frontiers of science, the monuments of art, and the detritus of history—all, by their own view, advancing unilaterally out of themselves—to the technology, science, and art that, in the view of the folklorist, issue from people providing for themselves, practically and culturally, out of immediately available natural and cultural resources. In this setting, the knobbed hands that carve a cork float for a fishing net with a penknife or, bathed in clay-red water, shape a pot, or the easy talk about matters of mutual concern, not to mention the cheering or inspiring music of gospel choirs, Cajun bands, Irish fiddlers, and the like, are not only strongly evocative but restorative; the grandeur, majesty, and scale of the Mall, framed to communicate the power of the Republic, opens a desert in the soul wherein we feel a cold forlornness that the grass and the trees do little to relieve. It's grand to be on the Mall, grand; but it's lonely.

Probably there is no place in the country in which the idea of regionality could be brought home more decisively than on the Mall, for there is no place from which regionality has been so thoroughly evacuated. The site of Washington was an arbitrary point between North and South, a swamp. No early settlement, not even by Indians, no colonists, no seaport, no agriculture, no natural resources, no industry, no European migrations: the city has virtually no history. It is simply the Capital. If regionality is a species of social organization based on the visible interdependency of human culture with the givens of nature and history, culture that suggests its own explanations in surrounding conditions, then the city of Washington, and especially its architectural apotheosis on the Mall, is its precise antithesis.

Except insofar as it defines its own place, the National Mall transcends place. The Mall is an idea—and a European idea at that. It is, as noted earlier, the architectural expression of Enlightenment philosophy, dominated by the eye, associated historically with Greece and Rome and with Republican and Napoleonic France, a vista conceived on the model of the Garden but framed on the scale and furnished with the monuments of the State. We are all, whether visitors to or residents of Washington, mere provincials on the Mall—pilgrims in an imperial city whose architectural glories cannot entirely ease the pang of our displacement, which we see on the long, blank faces of the museums or in the evening light reflected from distant domes and towers.

In this state of mind, we find the grass and the trees particularly consoling and familiar; so is the texture of the museum exhibits—whatever they may be—especially warm. But in this state of mind, too, as every pilgrim knows—the tourist who will watch any outdated film or television program only to see the backgrounds, who will tune in to every broadcast of his native entertainment, even those kinds he never cared about before, who will read her country's authors and visit exhibits of its art, who will, in short, love his own country as he never could at home—in this state of mind, I say, we are ready to have the idea of America created for us.

And that is precisely what happens in the Regional Americans site, where, as Festival promotion has put it, "America comes home to itself." Actually present to the senses, but with their actuality baffled or compromised by their symbolicity, the regional scenes and icons shake the rational foundations of place so that it clings, with a vague anxiety, to the scenes and icons themselves; familiar geographical coordinates swim out of their places and reposition themselves like spirits around the exhibits and exhibitors. This is, if you will, a kind of transubstantiation. Thus embodied, the sense of place arises out of the wells of music scattered throughout the site to flood the area with its evocations; what can be more replete with regionality, as a union of natural resources, historical memory, and cultural performance, than a traditional song accompanied by traditional instruments? The sounds of barrelhouse, juke-joint, dance hall, brothel, bar, cantina, church? This is the transfigured atmosphere, then, held in an auditory synthesis, in which we engage the Mississippian or the Louisianan or the Marylander in conversation about her basket, pot, or net, or in which we observe the sawyer or the logger at work while we chew on a crab sandwich and sip a glass of iced tea.

There is delight, of course, a kind of comic impertinence, in the unlikely presence of an oil derrick or a tobacco patch in the shadows of the Capitol and the Monument, and in the wit and ingenuity of such human adaptations as competitive cable-car bell ringing from San Francisco or the Barnegat Bay "sneakbox" boat from New Jersey. But the real charm of Regional Americans is that, through the Smithsonian Institution's invisible agents, all this has become—as we linger at the music stages, the discussion workshops, or craft demonstrations, outsiders no longer—our own, as surely as if we had buried its bones at midnight under the old iron bridge.

It is by reflection, then, on a surface curved by the cultural imagination that the interior sites of folk culture, of which the "region" is the most extensive, become authentic to us. The centripetal momentum of the Festival brings us home to fables of identity that release us, like the myths of ethnicity and race, from a selfhood constituted by education, or social standing, or achievement, or wealth, or the want of these: the fable that we are where we come from. If, at the Festival, the region is the historical and topographical setting of this story, so are the family and the phases of the life cycle that differentiate it its personal and psychological setting, the most sequestered of the sites of culture.

Identity, here, is shifting and obscure, either all in the future or all in the past; it is a story of lives remembered, told and retold, or only imagined. Within the family, it is a phantom born out of love and hate, rivalry and need. Society, embodied as values, expectations, and influences, incarnates itself in the particular personalities that work upon the child, distorted by the very medium in which it is embodied; the prepersonal child projects the forces working in her onto others and, through play and fantasy, into the world around her, surrounding herself with a nuclear society that is the expression of those forces and learning, by conscious and unconscious imitation, to find her role in it. This is no "dialectic" of society and personality, as if each were an independent agent or center, but the scene of their mutual growth and differentiation. We are in the marrow of culture, where it is being formed and where, in the obscure shapes of a child's experience, a spurious and ephemeral present—through the impalpable wishes and vague designs it deposits in memory—becomes the pattern of the future, a fate.

In 1974, at the new Family Folklore tent, Smithsonian folklorists conducted more than three hundred tape-recorded interviews with Festival visitors, soliciting such matter of folklore as names and expressions, including nicknames, pet names, names for automobiles, endearments, euphemisms, greetings, and, from the children, remedies for bad dreams and procedures for dibbing; foodways, including traditional holiday foods, ethnic dishes, and treats for children; and family anecdotes, including the "family saga"—stories of ancestors, adventures, emigrations, fortunes won and lost. In the following year, the program included family photographs collected by fieldworkers, around which family chronicles form and invite their own recounting in narrative. Hence, through the medium of the recorded interview and later in a Smithsonian publication, Festival visitors found themselves presented *to* themselves—tourists, in effect, in their own lives.

Within view of the Family Folklore tent stands what one might find in any city park: a children's playground, with a sandbox where forts and castles are going up, a small pool where boats are sailing, a haystack, pony rides, and a small stage. In its second year, the Children's Folklore area added a game ring and crafts tent; by 1976 the playground included a marble ring and a swap tent for the exchange of secret languages, riddles, counting rhymes, and ghost stories. Collected from local campers, scouts, and schoolchildren or contributed by folklorists, teachers, and parents, the traditional play of city streets and suburban dens here appeared at once ideological and idyllic. On the stage, children perform their jump-rope rhymes and their ring and clapping games, as well as dancing, singing and cheerleading; in the craft tent they make slingshots, dolls, paper airplanes, cootie catchers, and water bombs, in addition to drawing and whittling. Someone is working on a soapbox derby racer. In the game ring they are playing ball, or hide-and-seek, kick the can, Red Rover, tag, and Mother May I, as well as hopscotch and squirt-gun; some are actually building a treehouse. In the swap tent they are talking with grown-ups: telling elephant and knock-knock jokes, recounting the plots of books, movies, and TV shows, telling the story about the woman who found a spider's nest in her beehive hairdo, or one about the Bermuda Triangle. Some tell about their collections of baseball cards or rocks or stamps or coins; some talk about their bikes. There is little, perhaps, in children's play that does not appear in the children's area, unless it is their caste system and its rituals of shunning, their exchanging of dirty words, or playing doctor.

In 1984, the Festival of American Folklife introduced a program on folklife and aging called "The Grand Generation," bringing to the Mall craftswomen and craftsmen, representatives of various occupations, and performers, all elderly people whose traditions transected the Festival's ethnic, Native American, regional, and other categories. These included black, Native American, and Anglo-American quilters, basketmakers, needleworkers, woodcarvers, and cooks, among them needleworker and veteran Festival participant Ethel Mohammed; southern potters, Chesapeake Bay watermen, Pullman porters, and a group of stonecarvers from the Washington Cathedral. Among the musical performers were Laotian musicians, singers, and dancers from Washington's Indo-Chinese Community Center; the traditional musicians Tommy Jarrell, fiddler from Galax, Virginia, and black songster John Jackson; old-time banjoist Wade Mainer and his wife Julia; the Moving Star Hall Singers, spiritual singers from Johns Island, South Carolina; the Popovich Brothers, a Tamburitza orchestra from Chicago; the coal miner–ballad singer Nimrod Workman; Doris Kirshenblatt, storyteller from Ontario; and Hauoliaonalani Lewis, a Hawaiian hula dancer. The complete roster included the most exposed, most respected, best-studied, and best-recognized folk artists of the period, owing largely to their participation in the Festival and, for some, to their recognition by the National Endowment for the Arts as National Heritage Award winners.

"How does it happen," asks Bess Lomax Hawes, director of the Folk Arts Program at the NEA, "that in the Heritage Fellowships there has been such a concentration on older artists?" There does seem to be, she notes, "an especially close relationship between the folk arts and the elderly," generally explained by the fact that the transmission of culture occurs, through a process of informal observation and learning, between the grandparent and grandchild generations. Grandparents the world over, Hawes reports, citing Margaret Mead, "inspire and instruct the children while parents work to support and protect both the young and the old, until such time as they themselves become grandparents and their own children take up the middle year tasks and a new generation of young ones comes along."[23]

"American society," she continues, "does not ordinarily place much stock in informal learning."

> The notion that an artistic activity or style might be absorbed simply by a process of hanging about and observing sits uneasily with our feeling that the really important things ought to be conveyed in a formalized manner. Just a bit of reflection impresses upon one the universality of those early childhood experiences when one drifted off to sleep to the strains of grandfather's fiddle practicing waltzes, or the family's favorite gospel hour on the radio, or the matachine society next door getting ready for the fiesta tomorrow. . . . As the child watches the swift fingers of a basketmaker selecting and rejecting grass stems, or sees the seamstress making the vital decisions between contrasting or complimentary colors, or absorbs, just by living with it, the spare dignity of furniture built in the Shaker style, an equal number of elegant distinctions are being learned, even though not taught.[24]

Almost without exception, as folklorists have continually observed, the elderly folk artist was exposed to her tradition in childhood, then neglected or abandoned it in middle life, only to return in old age—after retirement, widowhood, or some other milestone—to the childhood interest, pastime, or play, the period of dormancy being also, it appears, the period during which the art or craft came secretly to maturity. It is a story that probably all of the participants in "The Grand Generation" could tell, and it is one with a happy ending: "I love it, oh boy!" exclaims Carmen Maria Roman, who emigrated to Cleveland from Puerto Rico in 1952, of her embroidery; "No more pills, no more nervous, I'm happy!"[25]

Many folklorists have treated children as a kind of transcontinental and transhistorical folk community; so in a parallel way does the family constitute a kind of elementary folk culture whose relationship to the surrounding order parallels the relation between folk and host cultures generally.[26] The family's private language—pet names, endearments, euphemisms, and the like—defines the boundary between itself and the broader linguistic community in which it shares. Much family lore and language personalizes with the family's own signature the larger impersonal forces that mark its intersection with history and culture: when we call the Chevy "Old Paint," for example—or, for that matter, when we *customize* it; or when we present as family photographs such pictures as those exhibited at the Festival, of an Eisenhower motorcade or of "the first Third Avenue Elevated train leaving the northernmost 241st Street station in the Bronx."[27]

Stories of family ne'er-do-wells, rogues, and adventurers testify simultaneously to the achieved social status of the family and to the restless or even lawless spirit that lends savor to that achievement; the family saga or epic, moreover, like the sagas of peoples, supplies the myth of origin that locates the family in the present and expands the moral field in which we summon our own beings into existence. The wholeness and integrity of this entire imaginative world, which is perpetually dissipated in the business of living, perpetually coalesces in the hearts of the aging and the elderly, who, as they pass beyond the householding years, find access to the distant past broadening and deepening in memory, just as access to the near past becomes spotty and capricious. If the elderly seem always to be the bearers of tradition, it is because in a sense they have created it, or, more precisely, they are the psychosocial sites of its creation, as the young are the sites of innovation.

If the family is the basis of culture, it is so simply because it creates the immediate emotional environment that will in time establish itself as the immediate mental environment of the forces, drives, and impulses of personality. And if, culturally speaking, the child's world is the scene of cultural transmission, it is because that world is uncompromisingly and comprehensively a world of learning by experience and example—not only of a folk craft or art, but of literally everything: of what men and women and their relationships are; what hate and love are supposed to be; what self is and how one is to behave; indeed, what the world itself is and whether it is friendly or unfriendly. This knowledge is usually so unconscious that we are wholly unaware of the ways in which it determines the fates we attempt to realize in an adult world that, if only because time has passed, invariably fails to meet our expectations of it.

The child's world is the original world against which all experience henceforth will be measured and toward which all imagination will tend— to which the child, and hence culture itself, is inextricably bound by the natural mimesis that arouses the child's perceptions and shapes her mind. No matter how far afield the experience and venturesomeness of youth may carry her, she ultimately returns, albeit perhaps in some wildly original displacement colored with her own unique experience, to her inheritance. Cut and comb our hair as we will, it will always part where our mothers parted it.

"Floating over our playgrounds," Bess Hawes writes, "are the shrill intense voices of a thousand decision-makers at work—testing, probing, rearranging, counter-posing, adjusting. No wonder the decibel rates of our schoolyards and playgrounds are so high."[28] Indeed. Where there are voices, there is culture: voices in the café, in the marketplace, on the playing field, in churches and taverns, around the supper table, and on the playground; voices on the omnibus (a real cacophony), in the legislative chamber, in the pub. And not only human voices: the world's great cultures have attended as well to the voices of animals and spirits, ancestors and gods; when these voices are silenced, culture dies.

Utterance and expression are, of course, essentially human, the results of what must be a neurological drive to make palpable to the senses and deliver into our hands phantasms of thought and feeling, and even to reproduce in the living world instruments that extend our own God-given instruments of perception, communication, and thought. When to human culture reality lay principally in the spiritual realm, so our human inventions were spiritual in character—inventions of image, symbol, icon, tale, legend, and myth. But when, early in the modern world, reality came to reside principally in the material realm, so did our manipulations of matter send forth into the world vastly amplified embodiments of our own mechanical functions, including the functions of perception and communication.

Our world, consequently, is a technological world, and it is perhaps from the cultural position afforded by it that we can best perceive the Festival of American Folklife. Our world is alive with voices, too—but many of them move in silence across vast reaches of time and space, embodied in writing and print, divorcing the utterance from all the contexts in which it has its meaning, particularly the context of immediate human dialogue, and compelling us to reinvent them on the basis of it. Some move invisibly in electrical currents, to issue forth in the tiny sites to which we attend in order to hear them, forming intimate dialogues between people widely separated; others emerge out of boxes, sometimes accompanied by images, drawing widely scattered audiences together into a blind association or actually supplanting, in the tavern or the household, those occasions that might otherwise have aroused the natural human voice.

The folklife of many occupations, including highly technical occupations such as airplane piloting and truck driving, has been presented on the Mall. In 1974 communications workers plied their trades in language and expression: printers, broadcasters, telephone technicians, ham radio operators, professional actors, and musicians opened the interiors of their occupations to the eye and ear of the visitor. Visitors participated in the making of paper and ink and compared traditional "lock-up" printing to contemporary computerized composition; each day a modern high-speed press, set for comparison next to a six-hundred-pound lithostone, issued a Festival newspaper that was distributed throughout the site. From a fully operational Festival post office, mail was delivered to and fro in the site, perhaps between new lovers bonded in the energy of festivity. National Public Radio set up a studio on the Mall and broadcast highlights from Festival performances and interviews with participants across the country, while in the second week of the Festival ham radio operators talked, by satellite, to their counterparts around the world.

An entire telephone company set itself up on the Mall as well, with operators, installers, linesmen and lineswomen, and rescue crews, so that a visitor in one area of the Mall might call someone in another area and trace the path of the call. Perhaps they wished to talk about the stage play under rehearsal, "Once Upon a Mattress," which brought onto the Mall, comedically, the one site of culture that could hardly be presented any other way.

In the cultural calculus of the Festival of American Folklife, one looks in vain for the single element in which the others can be subsumed. For a ruling metaphor, one must step outside the boundaries of folklife and turn toward it the reflecting surface of a culture evolved along different lines and according to different technical principles—and for this, the technology of communication serves very well, for it reveals, perhaps better than any other technology, the extent to which folk culture in all its sites is epitomized, not in the disembodied voices that speak across the alphabetic and electronic matrices of our society, but by the somatic encounter of human beings who, through their own senses, share a noetic space abundantly supplied with the human presence.

I choose a homely figure: the manhole. Like the other hidden and sequestered processes of culture, the manhole lies beneath our feet, under the street. For it to spring up into view, as it did in 1974, is fitting, for it is in the nature of festival to throw back the veil, to expose what was concealed, and to invert the verticality of things, whether the social hierarchy or the geology of the city street. That the manhole lies under the street is, I think, especially appropriate—for, as we have seen, the street is the scene of the social spectacle, and the manhole is the vortex through which passes, though we can't hear it, the babble of conversation, consultation, and counsel. *Were* we to hear it, as sometimes we do when wires cross, we might vaguely discern, in the innumerable voices of the invisible electronic network, what Thoreau calls "the infinite extent of our relations."

A manhole, then, has sprung up out of the ground. Here is the site of sites, in which the ethnomimetic process has been materialized, exteriorized, and technologized. A safety barricade is set up around it, a high warning mast redirects automobile traffic, and a ventilator is placed to provide fresh air. Two splicers—the master and his assistant, called a "grunt"—descend in their yellow helmets into the chamber, whose interior, reminiscent of the interior of a space capsule, might have been thrown into the stratosphere atop the Atlas rocket. A splice case is knocked off to reveal an extended cable spitting out in a hundred colors the naked ends of circuit pairs that must be twisted to their mates in an opposing cable. The men may reminisce about having seen a roach big enough to install a phone, or about rats the size of dogs darting down the wells. They end by sealing the splice in a soldered lead enclosure: this is called "wiping their sleeves."

There—done.

Here, and at every site on the Mall, is the essential work of culture: to splice us together, nerve to nerve, gathering up in the delicate luminous net of human sentience the spiritual life of the social body.

Duncan's Hat

Duncan cuts quite a figure in his white hat. It has a broad brim—broad almost as an auctioneer's under the sun on a Saturday morning at a Missouri farm sale—and a black band, very wide, such as one might see in the box-seats at the racetrack. It makes him urbane and, though he tips it back on his head at a slight angle, lends him a certain authority, a slight air of corruption; he might be the police captain of some remote district, or a government's petty bureaucrat, or the agent of a mining company or fruit grower, or even the planter himself—Belgian or German, dressed for the tropics in white. His suit, tailored to him, is white as well, with a white vest and a cream-colored silk lining.

The hat is appropriate here. The sun is beating down; everyone is dressed for the Washington summer in T-shirts, shorts, and sunglasses, thighs, forearms, and foreheads greased with suntan lotion, hair bleached and wind-blown. We sip cool soft drinks or lemonade from the concession stands and, in the afternoon, once the dance parties have begun, cold beer, seeking the shade of canopies and tents or of the glades along the periphery of the National Mall.

Most everyone wears a hat: tractor caps, baseball caps, cowboy hats, straw hats, and sunbonnets. But though Hollywood's Indiana Jones has made men's hats, for the few, fashionable again, one rarely sees a Panama hat. On Duncan's head—where it sits from morning until evening with perfect constancy and confidence, so that one rarely sees the top of his head with its thick mass of auburn hair shaped by the crown—the white hat, by an intrinsic power that seems to radiate from its whiteness, rules the occasion, lending a tropical density to the atmosphere and a quality of intrigue to the private dialogues in which Duncan, from time to time, may be seen to engage. It inspires an atmosphere of adventure, as if the hat itself had transported us to the equatorial regions and banished all the illegal trade, the turbulent politics, the technological revolution that stands between us and the superbly arrogant epoch when young men loitered at street corners in suits with ballooning pant legs and strutting lapels, their hats tipped back and brims turned down, heads bent over the comic strip on a folded tabloid, chewing on a matchstick, idly plotting the overthrow of a rival gang, a bank, or a government—one of them, perhaps, from time to time consulting the timepiece hanging at the end of a watchfob because the woman in red for whom he has been waiting is half an hour late.

Duncan's hat, indeed, seems almost to have summoned into existence the intrigue and conspiracy it symbolizes; this morning there is a story circulating about a man in a Hawaiian shirt and a black mustache who gained illicit entry to Duncan's room, took photographs, and disappeared. This same mustachioed fellow, affable as a flower vendor, has been around asking questions but has not identified himself. What is he, a spy? To his white hat and suit Duncan seems somehow entitled; something connects him honestly and intimately to it, so that he can concentrate himself in it without pretense or fraud and, without deception, charge our reality through his presence with its intimations, its associations, its significations.

Duncan's hat is an authentic hat. It is actually disconcerting in its authenticity, as if everything that is not Duncan's hat, or Duncan's suit, or Duncan himself were somehow stricken, feverish, faulty. Although there is a persuasiveness in his manner of wearing it, there is a persuasiveness, too, in the hat itself: in the materials of which it is made, though one cannot be entirely certain what those materials are; in its proportion and shape, though one cannot quite divine what is shapely and proportional in them; and in its actual fashioning, though by what process it was made we never learn and probably can't imagine. Duncan's hat is authentic, and we are ignorant; and yet somehow we know. The hat communicates itself to us as precisely as a musical pitch and stands out in the traffic of things as sharply as a musical note stands apart from ordinary noise.

It is clear that Duncan's hat was not bought from a sidewalk vendor somewhere on Constitution Avenue, though the vendors there sell similar hats, along with Kewpie dolls, T-shirts, pennants, and fanny packs; it was not recovered from an attic, secondhand store, or consignment shop; it was not plasticharged at a department store or shopping mall; indeed, if it was bought at all, it was in a transaction belonging to an economy very remote, archaic, a marketplace outside the walls of time.

Alone in a darkened screening room at the Office of Folklife Programs on the day before the opening of the Festival, lantern-jawed Cal Southworth, the technical man, is reviewing a pair of films designed to promote the Festival of American Folklife to potential benefactors. It will be shown to the participants as part of their orientation. I wander in and sit down in someone's abandoned desk chair.

The film on the screen was made a few years ago, in 1982. It opens with a succession of emblematic scenes: the Mall, a mountain fiddle band and a buckdancer, Koreans in native costume, railroad workers leaning on their picks, the audience, kids in a hay wagon, Mall overview, mariachi band, hat dancers.[1]

A deep male voice begins speaking, accompanied on the screen by a Korean masked dance: "The Festival," it tutors us, is "an opportunity to experience in a personal way the beauty and the joy of another culture." "Through the Festival," the voice continues, "participants from other countries are reunited with ethnic Americans who have preserved their old ways in the new world." Greens frying in a pan follow, and a Korean weaver; people dance along at an Indian ceremony—"an opportunity for Native Americans to reaffirm the value of their ancient culture." The railroad men say, together, "We're here to demonstrate what we do for a living."

Police officers, paramedics, railroad switchmen, oil drillers and oilfield workers, cowboys from Oklahoma, cattle branding, a horse race on the Mall, a western swing band. "And craftspeople, whose work is often unrecognized in their own communities, are honored by the attention they receive at the Festival." Chairmakers, potters, embroidery, children in attendance: "Even very young visitors get a taste of the featured state," says the voice, as a young boy awkwardly spins a lariat. "It's a chance for them to learn and experience something they might not normally encounter."

The film concludes with images of gospel singer Matthew McClarity, repeated shots of the Washington Monument, and a Cajun band, the Balfa Brothers. Says Dewey Balfa to an unseen interviewer: "It matters not what nationality you are—you should be proud of your nationality, your region. I want to respect your culture, and you to respect my culture." As the credits come up, Cajun fiddles and the chiming of a triangle swell into the dark spaces of the room.

This film, it seems, partaking deeply of the post-Vietnam mood, treats the Festival as a kind of cultural summer camp. It finds salutary effects in the Festival for everyone involved; participation in it is, like the great outdoors, somehow good for our health and happiness. Visitors experience the "beauty and joy" of another culture; Native Americans reaffirm their half-forgotten way of life, while other participants find recognition they otherwise would not receive and fulfillment in their reunion with their Old World counterparts. Though the film focuses on the Festival visitor, it tacitly assumes that the Festival, in a general way, revitalizes an almost universal cultural morbidity. Balfa's message, obviously informed by the anthropological and political discourse of the Festival creators as well as by his own experience with the Festival, seems to reflect a personal adjustment to the special challenges of the Festival setting, in which cultures are embodied as people.

A second film, "Festival in Washington," made in 1968, the Festival's second year, sweeps across the screen. Its images: the Mississippi fife and drum corps; three old gentlemen in hats; a clogger and a guitar and the hands that are playing it; a Kentucky balladeer and fiddler; a potter; and visiting children "who," says the narrator gravely, "had hardly seen music, or anything else, made by a pair of human hands."[2]

He goes on: "Crafts are hobbies for most Americans; for these people they are part of a way of life." A group of children watches a blacksmith hammering a glowing red horseshoe: "There are very few village smithies left to stand under spreading chestnut trees—and the children of suburbia might as well read poems about punch-card operators standing under conveyor belts."

Bluesman Mance Lipscomb appears for an instant; a mule treads glumly around a cider press while another blues guitarist, Skip James, plays in the background; James's face momentarily fills the screen, followed by pedestrians on the Mall. Muddy Waters sings "I'm a Man"; a shingle splitter rives cedar shakes while Bill Monroe and the Bluegrass Boys sing "Roll On, Buddy." Says the narrator: "The feeling of history is a hard thing to come by; in the pre-fab era, watching a man split a shingle gives that feeling . . . the feel of a world where no one hardly ever bought anything. . . . imagine a world when there was no litter problem . . . where nothing was ever wasted."

This earlier film, though, takes a disconsolate and despairing view of life in contemporary America—a life machine-dominated and impersonal, in which children are denied the immediate experience of human authenticity and adults "the feel of history," which presumably lends density and texture to existence, as if contemporary modes of production were not only alienating but unreal. Contemporary existence is spurious, it seems, a matter of mere idleness—crafts and hobbies—whereas the preindustrial past, embodied in the "village smithy," represents a whole and genuine way of life. Until the end of the film—a night scene in which Fourth of July fireworks are bursting over the Monument—we see little of the Festival setting and much more of the performers themselves than we saw in the more recent film.

This earlier film quite explicitly identifies folklife with an imagined precapitalist world, a paradise without money and without waste. Although it pays only a desultory attention to the effects of the Festival on the participants, the preoccupation of the later film, it focuses upon them more intently in visual images. The narrator's tone is strangely combative; he adopts an artificial idiom, a sort of stage dialect reminiscent of the actors in "folk dramas" like *Oklahoma!* who try to sound rural and midwestern but whose diction betrays their expensive northeastern educations. It is a rhetorical pose that hopes to win the trust of its audience by seeming to eschew such things as the careful speech inspired by books as well as abstract ideas, especially in the social and political realm—insulting its listeners while glorifying occupations to which they no longer have either the access or the skills, materials, desire, or necessity to pursue.

Folklife, the film seems to say, is real life, while the actual life of suburb and bureaucracy, the life from which most of the Festival visitors are assumed to have emerged and against which speaker and audience seem tacitly united—the very life promised to America's farmers, tradesmen, factory workers, and other "folk" since World War II—is false and perfidious. Our business, the business of the Festival, is to salvage such scraps of the precapitalist paradise as we can and to expose our children to it in the hopes that they may bring about a change, by implication a revolutionary change, in the social and economic order.

We watch a chairmaker weave a split-oak seat, while in the background Doc Watson and Jean Ritchie sing an old ballad, "The Storms Are on the Ocean." The Festival, says the narrator, "makes it possible for the performers to get together, swap stories, to work together." In sheepshearing we get "a refreshing dose of reality." The film follows the wool from the carding, to the spinning and weaving, to the waulking accompanied by call-and-response Gaelic songs as the Scots weavers, seated around a table, shrink the tweed. "Today," says the narrator, "it is done by machines, which cannot sing."

At a lunchtime staff meeting we eat ordered-in pizza and exchange reminiscences from the Festivals of the past. Remember the Black Angus cows that escaped the flimsy stockade built for them, and how a vaquero lassoed one of them in the Kennedy Center parking garage? Or the "pregnant" cow—a steer—who got an uninvited enema with a garden hose? Or the rain-soaked sheep who collapsed from the weight of the water in their wool and the sheepshearer who, to the horror of onlookers, literally threw the animals backwards over his head? What about the Mexican cowboys who were afraid to ride the horses we brought in, because they were too big? And remember the derelict with a briefcase and a degree in math who looked like the well-known linguist Dell Hymes and was actually mistaken for him by one of the staff? Or the marijuana smoke-in? Or the day the site was cleared because the police found cases of dynamite—actually dummies used in the previous day's occupational demonstration? No one here really remembers the incident, but stories have been told about 1968, when tear gas directed by the police at the rain-soaked, mud-besotted Resurrection City—the vast tent settlement of protesters against poverty planned, before his assassination that April, by Martin Luther King—drifted onto the Festival site and drove everyone away.

When we reconvene for the last meeting before the opening of the Festival, the office director, Peter Seitel, compares the ongoing discourse on "cultural conservation" to the "Silent Spring" issue of the 1950s. He looks forward to the day "when they build a road they'll have to do a cultural impact study as well as an environmental impact statement." All nod their heads in assent.

Marjorie Hunt, with a large sketch, presents her plan for leather worker Duff Severe's saddle shop: Duff has sent photos of his real shop, which have been blown up to form the backdrop; benches have been set up so that the other cowboys can come in to sit and talk. The shop also constitutes, she notes for the record, a display of tools. Duff has brought most of his tools with him.

Taking up this point, Peter reminds the staff that he wants Festival-goers to have an "intimate" encounter with craftsmen, not the "two-dimensional" encounter that one finds at places like Williamsburg, which are too theatrical. A long discussion follows that relates the arrangement of the shop to problems of authenticity, space sufficient for work, ease of presentation, and so on. Margie wants "life" going on in the shop.

The cornrowers will be placed in a small, "embracing" semicircle on platforms at the height of about a foot; we discuss the relative merits of six or twelve inches. Bernice Reagon, someone reports, wants the place to be a hangout, the way it is in a neighborhood. The girls, one of whom is Tanzanian, will begin with their own clients. Charlie Camp, Maryland's state folklorist and consultant to the Festival, notes that the platforms at least distinguish the real performers from the guys who come to the Festival with their guitars and sit under a tree to play. Peter recalls a three-hour session on black foodways in which all the observers felt as if they had actually entered the demonstrator's kitchen at home. He cites Tristram Coffin's three areas of metaphor: food, sex, and knowledge.

Of the Makah woodcarvers, we learn that anthropological work among them has inspired a woodcarving revival. Peter argues for encouraging the "experience" of the woodcarvers, finding ways to hold a visitor's attention for twenty minutes or more—this in response to Charlie's observation that carving, unlike the foodways demonstrations, normally doesn't have a beginning, middle, and end for most who see it. Peter: "We don't have a good technology for presenting crafts." Says Margie: "Craftsmanship *is* performance." A persistent problem, everyone agrees, is that craftspeople get so involved in their work that they become reluctant to talk. A presenter may talk too much or, conversely, assist in the work and so also become too involved to talk; sometimes a volunteer or simply a visitor, Charlie points out, may take on the role of presenter when these lacunae occur, especially when other visitors ask questions.

For the Puerto Rican mask makers, Margie wants a "forest of masks" hanging on trees behind the workers and the display of a full costume with the traditional pig bladder at the end of a stick for thrumping people over the head. Peter notes that the task is relatively simple but the context complex—there is a need for talk about Carnival. How to do this?

There are eight representatives of the Kmhmu, a Laotian mountain people—musicians, spinners, weavers, basketmakers, and so on; they are to be placed in a "compound" (a word to which Tom Vennum, senior ethnomusicologist, takes strong exception) that will include a garden and a blacksmith shop, partially under a tent. The participants will include young people concerned about the survival of their culture. Peter's concern: "It sounds like 'don't feed the animals.'" Charlie agrees that the language problem will make it a "living diorama." Peter: "I'd like to see people surrounded by Kmhmu." On the basis of this discussion, they move the platform.

Peter briefs Charlie on the Mayan problem, the systematic extermination, putting it in the context of cultural conservation, and cites the planned photo of a Guatemalan soldier holding up an embroidered shirt. Charlie asks: What is being celebrated? Survival? Resiliency? The issue is acknowledged to be a thorny one.

About the Melā, the Indian fair, discussion centers on the difficulty of presenting something that we don't actually understand. Karen Brown explains how, when she tried to demonstrate Cajun music to the Indians with a cassette tape, a little boy dancer came up and turned it off; the interpreter explained that he didn't want to hear it. He wanted to perform more for her. They apparently didn't understand that other performers were coming, and they are unaccustomed to people performing *for them*.

Diana Parker, the Festival director, defines the Melā as an event balanced uneasily between a presentation, in which there is too much mediation, and a "cultural zoo," in which there isn't enough, especially because the Indians don't speak English. Outside the window, great stone buildings—the Treasury Department, the great blank wall of Transportation, the Washington Monument in the distance, seem to drift past a stationary sky, while from time to time our conversation fades into the intermittent roar of jet airplanes. Charlie shifts restlessly in his chair, adjusting the brim of his Baltimore Orioles cap.

Discussion of the Louisiana exhibit is introduced by Susan Levitas, who calls the Mardi Gras an "exaggeration, reverse ethnicity," saying it is "about stereotypes." Charlie, under the head of "cultural appropriation," points out that the "Mayan snake" on the Mardi Gras float represents the transformation of one culture's religious symbols into the comic exaggerations of another. A long, heated discussion ensues. "If we had known the float was going to make fun of Indian culture, "we wouldn't have had it," say Susan and her associate, Larry Deemer. "The greatest danger of a festival," Peter cautions, is that it may do what the media does: demean and "commoditize" a people's symbol. The Festival is attempting to keep symbols and their meanings together. Mardi Gras, Peter goes on, is a "discourse in ethnicity. . . . Its symbols are manipulated in a racist way." The float, it happens, is also decorated with Mayan glyphs. Everyone looks at everyone else.

Susan argues that the basic idea was to show a family making floats in the traditional way, not to focus on a certain theme. It is pointed out by someone that the Mardi Gras "Indians" are also coming—six blacks, four of whom dress as Indians—this in spite of the fact that there are four Native American tribes in the Louisiana exhibit, as well as the several tribes in the learning center and one, the Luiseño, in Cultural Conservation. These issues, it is hoped, will be discussed in the narrative sessions; consider the Mardi Gras "Zulus," for example—middle-class blacks who costume themselves in an outrageous Negro caricature.

But the Zulus weren't invited.

Principally because he fears the possibility of embarrassment to the Festival, especially through the media—the admittedly remote possibility that some clever reporter might catch the relationship between the Guatemalan presence and the Mayan symbols on the float—Peter rejects the float. Some effort must be made, at this late date, to modify the construction of the float or even to substitute a new one. Larry and Susan fear it may be impossible; their understanding is that a flatbed truck has already been hired and that the float is on its way to Washington.

A dark, eyeless stone building stands on a hill at the center of Georgetown University; its forbidding clock tower is visible from every point along the Potomac and from Virginia. Around it are arranged the campus buildings: a dormitory of the same period and newer red brick residences that reach down the hill alongside it and behind it to the vast medical complex. Obtaining a permit for the privilege of parking in the fifteen- or twenty-acre lot at the bottom of the hill requires at least three visits to the campus housing office and several conversations with the Festival's hospitality staff at the dormitories. Finally, having collected at least three parking tickets, I post my permit in the windshield, only to receive a new citation the following day from a campus policeman who now apparently tickets me on sight, out of habit.

After checking my room assignment, I carry my suitcases up the several hundred stairs that lead from the parking lot to the dormitories and again up the several flights of iron steps to my suite on the third floor, which I will be sharing with Hezakiah and the Houserockers, a blues band from Ferriday, Louisiana—the birthplace, I later learn, of Jerry Lee Lewis.

My key is poised for the lock, but I find the door open; three men in white, painters, are in the apartment, and when I ask them whether or not I will be able to stay in the room tonight they respond, in chorus, angrily and unintelligibly, in a language which my best guess says is Portuguese. The women in hospitality, to whom I report the confrontation, are exasperated; here is yet another glitch, apparently, in the arrangements with the university. I wonder: Will the fumes from the drying paint kill me as I sleep?

Soon the corridor of the dormitory in which the hospitality desk stands, which one cannot enter without a name tag, is filled with people: black men and black women; one very tall and angular fellow in a cowboy hat and alligator boots; another in a silver-painted hardhat, the kind they wear in the oilfields, and a Hawaiian shirt casually left untucked; many Hindustani and Bengali and Punjabi people, small of stature, with beautiful, fragile features, the men in their white pajamas and the women in saris of red, purple, yellow, and turquoise, with sequined borders. One of them, a handsome woman in middle age with silver hair recently done in a contemporary style, the red token of blessing on her forehead, walks with a limp, on a clubfoot. A very tall man with a leathered face and drooping eyelids who appears to have lived outdoors all his life, dressed in blue jeans and a cowboy hat and carrying a fiddle case, arrives with a stout woman no taller than his elbow. Her hair is tightly curled about her head in a brand-new perm, and her round face is smiling.

I hear an Indian language—Bengali, perhaps—clattering on tiny innumerable wheels across its speakers' tongues, and Spanish, and a looping, elastic French: Cajuns!

In the yellow glow of a mosquito bulb under the iron stairway between dormitories, Barry Bergey, a Missouri folk arts administrator who has just come to Washington to work for the National Endowment for the Arts, stands with Alicia Gonzalez, the program director in the Smithsonian's Office of Folklife Programs, and Duncan Earle, the young Dartmouth anthropologist who will present the Guatemalans at the Festival; they are awaiting the arrival of Duncan's group. The evening is so palpably warm and moist that nature itself seems to have evaporated into the dark; from the rooms above and below, where a few steps lead down the bank upon which the building has been erected, electric lamps throw their soft light onto the concrete, and unintelligible voices migrate back and forth. Across the driveway, in the cellar of a large hall, there is girls' laughter and the thumping of sexual music.

A folk festival is idyllic, Barry observes; everyone is euphoric. All the usual fear and mistrust are somehow suspended, and people, no matter how different from one another, find themselves brought together in happy community—so happy, in fact, that even now, at the beginning, it is possible to anticipate the sadness and disappointment when the Festival breaks up. While we talk, a copper-colored van with Florida plates and a bumper sticker that says "Indian Power" pulls into the drive, and four of the Guatemalans climb out; they have brought the marimba with them. Factor and Josefina Gomez, a young couple with three small children, trundle toward their room, obviously road-weary, one child asleep on her mother's hip; the father is carrying under his arm a huge, unopened box of Pampers. Around Josefina the brick walls and concrete walk seem to weaken and grow pale, for, as she and her husband are traditional Mayan weavers, she is wearing a bodice and an ankle-length skirt that she has woven herself; their colors and designs have an almost electronic intensity, as if they had been generated in a computer lab. Two younger men follow, both in cowboy hats and yoked shirts with floral embroidery on the shoulders, carefully maneuvering the instrument out of the van.

The marimba seems to have been drawn from the innards of some unbelievable fossil, its grotesque carcass discarded for the sake of this fantastic collection of bones—a skeleton of woods, dark and light, that makes a celestial sound when struck. The young men's faces, with their high cheekbones and long noses, are strikingly Asian; one of them, when he looks out from under the brim of his cowboy hat, has an almost frightening antiquity—his is the face one might encounter carved and painted onto the lid of a sarcophagus hidden deep in the recesses of a colossal tomb. His gaze gives rise to the fantastic speculation—did not someone once propose it?—that the natives of South America are the descendants of Egyptian sailors who landed on the continent ages ago in ships of reed.

The men carry the marimba down the few steps and through the open door of a dormitory room and immediately begin to play, while several people gather around them. Miguel Caraballo and his son, the Carnival mask makers from Puerto Rico whose room it seems to be, stand in the back of the group, smiling and greeting their unexpected visitors, Miguel senior taking photographs with his Instamatic. The tones of the marimba drop like fibrous, unripe fruit from the green roof of a tropical forest, spare, lively, balanced melodies in wholesome, familiar modes, while the young men follow their pairs of hammers across the bars as if they fear the hammers will escape and flee; all around rises a sonorous buzzing or rattling, like the talk of thousands of tiny invisible beings: it is the vibration, Duncan explains, of membranes made from pigs' intestines, built into the marimba's resonators.

Subrata Bhowmick, whom I have just met out on the half-finished Festival site, is the young industrial designer connected to the Handicrafts and Handlooms Export Corporation of India, who has come with the folk artists of Shadipur—the shantytown outside of Delhi to which government acts against beggary have driven them—to oversee the construction of the Melā celebration on the Mall. When I first saw him, he was standing, arms imperiously crossed, wrapped in his white and gray linens, one foot regally set forward, over a shallow pit where Fred Price, one of the young black grounds crew men, labored with a spade under Subrata's personal direction.

I had seen this posture before when, as a student supporting myself with mechanical work, I lay under the dripping oil pan of an expensive touring car while its owner, an Indian doctor of, apparently, very high caste, stood over me with his arms folded, glowering at every turn of my wrench, though he had not the faintest idea what I was doing. It had been exquisitely uncomfortable; but my ancestors had not been, at least not within living memory, slaves.

Subrata seemed to be a figure of some importance, someone I might interview. I explained myself at length, and he granted me a few minutes of his time, which Fred quickly used to finish his task. I learned that Subrata had worked with several textile companies in India; that with bamboo slats and clay tiles, an effort will be made to imitate vernacular Indian architecture; that all sorts of merchants and craftspeople will be brought in to create a street fair such as might be seen almost anywhere in provincial India; that a religious altar will be set up across the way, where there will be a learning center of Indian life and culture.

All this I found interesting, but I could not help but be distracted by the extraordinary beauty of this slight, delicate man with the intelligent brow, the thinning, ephemeral hair, the pencilled nose and sharp eyes. I thought it only a fluke until, a few days after the Festival had begun, I realized that beauty, in men and women alike, was everywhere to be seen in the Melā, that it was a kind of covert theme of the fair—indeed, a kind of conspiracy that, to one apprised of it, revealed itself at every hand: in every smile of the young women in the fair booths; in the handsome faces of the magician and the juggler, with their strong arms; in the acrobat children, the actors, and the puppeteers; in enigmatic Shyam, the Baul singer with the long, shining black tresses that flowed down his back, who could as easily have been a woman; in the round belly of the Durga goddess made of straw and clay, her woman's body perfectly formed before the icon-makers covered it with a gown of muslin and silk and sequins and gold thread.

So sensitive did I become to this conspiracy of beauty that I felt self-conscious and guilty when, in what I was pleased to call my work, I undertook to photograph the various booths along the midway at the Melā, each of which was attended by some exotic and beautiful young Indian woman, or by an equally beautiful Indian-American volunteer in traditional dress. One sunny morning a few minutes before the Festival opened, as I peered through the lens of my camera at a display of musical instruments attended by a young woman, also within my field of vision, whom I could scarcely avoid watching, protected as I was by the privacy of my camera, I felt someone's hand fall heavily on my shoulder: it was Subrata—and he wished to engage me in conversation, about a matter, it seemed, of the utmost urgency. He talked with great animation about I know not what as he led me across the Melā site until the musical instrument booth was well out of range and then suddenly, as I was about to discover the meaning of this hurried exit, abandoned me.

Subrata and I became passing friends, as people will at the Festival, though we did not talk much; and I sensed, by those fleeting indications, mere intimations, that vanish the moment we attempt to fix them that Subrata had become, after a week or so, isolated in his imperiousness and, perhaps, ultimately so chastened that he knew not what or how to be, lacking the easygoing tolerance and informality that belongs to our roughshod democracy, which so often brings us elbow-to-elbow with others who are, whatever their situation in life, obliged like aristocrats to treat us as equals.

He became moody and withdrawn, with an expression of injury on his face that suggested an almost physical pain. And yet, as the Festival entered its second week, I saw him—at one or the other of the many social functions, the dance parties, the receptions, even on the Melā site itself—winning the attention of a certain young Festival volunteer who had been herself, being rather beautiful, the object of some attention from several young fellows, and from one or two young only in spirit, whom she politely but firmly rebuffed. Subrata's mood brightened, and he took on a relaxed affability that was almost American, though necessarily stagy in its zeal, and as I sat on a bench outside one of the dormitory buildings where we were all gathered to enjoy each other's company for the last time, he bade me, with this same young woman happily on his arm, an expansive, sunny hello—as if he'd been born in Indiana.

Long after Subrata had returned to India, I learned he had vowed never to work with Americans again, for, as he put it, "one becomes too close to them."

Karen Brown has summoned the staff to an informal meeting behind the administration trailer to discuss certain emergent problems in the setting up of the Melā. Four or five young women are there, and several young men, volunteers, grounds crew, carpenters. All have come with essentially the same question: How can we communicate with the Indian people? First, says Karen, take off your watches and in general abandon your notion of time. Time, for them, moves much more slowly; two or three weeks to us are as days or hours to them. They work more slowly and less efficiently—in India, five hundred people would be doing this work, not twenty-five. Abandon if you can your levels, squares, and plumb lines: the Indians are not overly concerned about right angles, level planes, and the like. Play it by ear. Watch how you use your left hand—it is the profane one, associated in their minds with elimination; use it to clean up, but if you're eating together, use your right, and keep it washed.

But what about Subrata? asks one worker: he watches us like an overseer. "I'd like to clobber him with my shovel," says another. Tools, it seems, especially electric ones, have been disappearing—sixteen, altogether, by latest count. "They're fascinated by our tools," says Karen. "They can't afford to buy them at home, and they accomplish the work in what to them is no time." As for Subrata: endure.

Across the way, a bamboo hut nears completion. It has a woven mat floor on a frame of two-by-eights made by grounds crew carpenters. The six upright bamboo pillars have been raised and the interlocking tiles of the roof laid by the Indian craftsmen. Young workers in T-shirts and tractor caps are covering up the electric cables, now supine in their trenches, with rakes.

The grounds crew calls it the "stockade": a high fence of raw wooden poles hewn to a point at the top, with three gates that permit entrance by trailers, vans, and "pargos"—golf carts—one leading from the street and another onto the Festival site and one, near the back of the supply trailer, that opens onto one of the paths that crosses the Mall at Twelfth Street. Festival construction and Festival business are both conducted from within this enclave, called "Administration" on Festival maps, which itself harbors subordinate internal spaces, each with its own character. A house trailer set on the Festival side of the stockade becomes, in effect, the Festival encampment of the Office of Folklife Programs; an entire telephone switchboard is installed here, as well as the desks of a service manager, an acting administrative officer, and a clerk-typist. This trailer houses the only working toilet on the Festival site and so becomes a center for visitors; it is also the only air-conditioned building on the Festival grounds.

Directly across from the administrative trailer is one that serves as the headquarters of the grounds crew. It is a kind of sanctuary for them, too, and admission to the trailer is tacitly restricted. Each day, meal tickets are distributed to the staff here, two-way radios are recharged for the next day's use, certain small tools are stored, and grounds crew chiefs discuss developments over coffee at the small table attached to the wall. Between the two trailers is a working area where various carpentry tasks are completed, such as the manufacture of benches or other fixtures required for particular displays. Part of this area is covered by a tarpaulin for shade, which is itself fixed to the side of the large supply trailer brought from the Smithsonian depot at Silver Hill; during the course of the Festival, a collection of Polaroid photographs of the grounds crew at work, most of them satirical, collect on the side of the trailer. These are complemented, this year, by a shrine made of beer cans, inside the crew trailer, that parodies the shrine at the center of the Indian Melā, one that has actually been consecrated by a Hindu priest. At the other side of the stockade is another supply trailer with pargos parked in a row just outside it and, this year, a huge bundle of bamboo required by the Kmhmu for their traditional crafts.

Many of the young men and women on the grounds crew have come from the art schools and theaters of the Washington area; one is the son of a successful novelist; another is a sculptor who winters in Maine; still another is on the tech crew of the Arena Theater; another, an actor, has just been featured in *People* magazine. But like Van Mertz, the grounds crew chief, a professional carpenter who in his youth was a folksinger in the revival movement, the grounds crew leaders are men and women with streaks of gray in their hair who retain the countercultural style of the sixties and seventies, and who, for the duration of the Festival, may even give fuller expression to those inclinations than they do at other times.

Richard Derbyshire, for example, the archivist for the Office of Folklife Programs, dresses conservatively though casually in the office, keeps his brownish-red beard scrupulously trimmed, and conducts his business with officious and proprietary efficiency. At the Festival site, however, where he is the technical coordinator of the entire physical operation, he appears in what seems to be a lumberjack's outfit, with a stylish alpine quality that boldly declares his changed role and, one supposes, fits him for it. After several years' experience in this position, Richard has come to regard the Festival as "a construction site where from time to time we permit a festival to happen." A woman with the arms and shoulders of a wrestler, wearing an ancient leather hat, darts in and out of the stockade on a pargo and performs work that would be daunting to most of the delicate and artistic men on the grounds crew, such as lifting barrels full of drinking water onto the bed of the pargo for delivery to various places on the Festival site.

The stockade, then, seems to be a kind of haven for that class of young people caught in the eddies of history symbolized for most of us by the decade of the sixties, from which they either have not yet emerged or to which they from time to time retreat; others, as in the case of Derbyshire and other folklife professionals, have found a career that keeps the essential spirit of that epoch alive for them. From within the stockade, the Festival space outside begins to define itself, first with lengths of snow fence enclosing what will be the three display areas, where the raw materials of stages, signs, and tents are delivered by forklift truck—a task so coveted by members of the grounds crew that they have come to call the Festival the Festival of American Forklift.

It is just about noon, and on the path outside the opened gate of the stockade the young bureaucrats and professionals of Washington, fashionably dressed and coiffed, meticulously groomed, many with leather briefcases, are strolling toward or away from their luncheon dates—discussing, perhaps, some new way of spending money for recreation, travel, clothes, exercise, transportation, or hobbies—with copies of the *Washington Post* or *USA Today* folded under their arms.

The Festival volunteers—matrons, retirees, vacationing college students, preponderantly women, many of them people who have been participating for seven to ten years—appear in great numbers at the

Cultural Conservation stage on the Saturday morning before the Festival begins. They seem to have come from another decade, with a different political stamp upon them; they are representatives of the other Washington, the political culture that, with the election of Ronald Reagan, retreated into Bethesda and Cleveland Park.

Remember, warns Tinika Ossman, the volunteer coordinator, that many of our participants come from very conservative cultures, and that we represent the Smithsonian. It can get very hot—dress comfortably, but not provocatively. Be helpful, but remember that the participants aren't helpless.

Following the "living museum" theme, Ralph Rinzler in his brief address to the volunteers notes that, in the electronic age, people think that unless their work appears on a phonograph record or on the "silver screen," it isn't important. The purpose of the Festival, he says, is to show them that it is. He calls the Festival a "collection of treasures" that reside in the "hearts and minds and hands, and in the dancing bodies," of the participants.

At the opening meeting for Festival participants on the Georgetown campus, we are all ushered upstairs in the towered stone building to a vast lecture hall, ribbed with walnut struts and decorated all around by heavy-limbed representations of mythological figures in awkward, self-conscious Victorian poses, ornate hanging lamps, and linked seats whose narrow girths reveal, oddly, that we as a race seem to have outgrown our own forbears, who were students in this place. The copper-green walls, darkened by age, seem to belong in the lobby of some grand old hotel long since abandoned to salesmen and conventioneers; the high ceiling seems almost avian—surely there are birds, or bats, who have made homes in the upper reaches.

The Indians have gathered together near the front of the auditorium, talking animatedly among themselves and laughing, some of them, with bright, unspoiled mirth. At the back on the same side, accompanied by the earnest and anxious folklorist Frank Proschan, who has been their preserver and protector during the difficult early months in Stockton, California, sits the band of Kmhmu: a tiny man and woman, he with long gray hairs stiffly hanging from his chin, she with tiny black teeth and rounded shoulders, both of them as small as children; a young man with a warm, ingratiating smile, whose bones appear to have been hastily gathered together for the flight from his native country; another who purses his lips and anxiously casts his eyes about the room. They seem almost a miniature people whose world, necessarily reduced in scale, is closed to us, somehow separated by the invisible barrier that divides one order of perception from another, so that we exchange smiles and greetings, we with our wave, they with their little bow, the Punjabis with their palms held momentarily in prayer, with gestures that seem to acknowledge the frightening proximity of worlds which, were we to accidentally be drawn into them, would, like cultural antimatter, annihilate us.

At the door, where people are mingling, many passing in and out with no apparent business except to appear to be about some business, a tall man in a white western shirt and wide-brimmed felt cowboy hat, faded Levis, and cowboy boots stands in conversation with a young woman in a hair band and eyeglasses who, by her name tag, must be here in some official capacity; it is the famous cowboy Glenn Ohrlin, whose massive, sunburned red face and snaggle-toothed grin hold the woman in a kind of wonder of which she herself appears to be distrustful. Near him, the cowboy versifier and storyteller Ken Trowbridge engages in his avocation for the benefit of Waddie Mitchell, a younger cowboy from Nevada who wears wax on the twisted ends of his long blonde mustache. Trowbridge's huge hands from time to time rise into the air as if blown up by gusts of wind.

The burly man with the construction hat has arrived, too; it is Silas Hogan, the rhythm-and-blues pioneer from Baton Rouge whose records, widely covered by white rockabillies, won a cult following among the blues aficionados of the sixties and are now collectors' items. I used to play his "Lonesome Ya-Ya" ("Sitting by my window, watching the sun go down") over and over again on my little record player. Silas joins the sizable group of black men and women, gospel and zydeco musicians and singers and the young Mardi Gras Indians, who have gathered in the center seats, a few rows from the stage.

Festival founder Ralph Rinzler, who with his graying hair and well-trimmed beard more and more resembles his mentor, the ethnomusicologist Charles Seeger, is chatting with Frank Proffitt, Jr., the jovial young banjo player and balladeer whose father's "Tom Dula," a murder ballad about the 1868 Wilkes County murder of Laura Foster by Tom Dula, collected by YMCA recreation specialist Frank Warner and from him by Alan Lomax, became an international hit for the Kingston Trio and the keynote of the folk revival. "I feel as if I've known you all my life," says Rinzler, but this is a quote: he is recalling the balladeer Texas Gladden, whom he had visited some years ago during her final illness. "I never met a stranger," the dying woman had said. This is all in reference, it seems, to what Rinzler calls the "amazing mix of humanity" in the hall tonight.

Each group, at Rinzler's invitation from the stage, stands to reveal itself: the Guatemalans, the Native Americans, the Indians, the Kmhmu, the foodways cooks, the Cajuns, and the rest. Ohrlin, Trowbridge, Mitchell, and Duff Severe, the saddlemaker from Oregon, hidden in the far back corner of the room, are amusing themselves with Diana Parker's speech, in which she introduces the dance party participants. Ohrlin edits her report on the afternoon dance parties: "The drinkers from their home communities," he interprets to the other cowboys, "will join with other drinkers to demonstrate the drinks, and we hope that everyone will join in the drinking."

Uproarious laughter. All heads turn toward the cowboys.

Before the speeches begin, I learn from a Festival veteran that participants bring many of their social problems with them to the Mall: alcoholism has been a problem with many groups; occasionally a participant, filled with the goodwill of the Festival or with the glamour of Washington, has refused to go home, and on one or two occasions has disappeared into the city. Some have become involved with prostitutes or with the police; once a young gangster from Philadelphia brought a pistol, which he would not surrender. Many people from distant parts of the country or of the world have fallen ill with intestinal viruses, colds, flu, and allergies; some have been injured; some become desperately homesick. One elderly man, after a day of working in the summer heat, died of heart failure.

The assembled participants and staff, altogether an audience sufficient to fill the entire auditorium, quiets as the tall, distinguished-looking Ralph Rinzler again approaches the podium. Seconded by an interpreter, Rinzler charges them: "You are going to become a community in yourselves, and relate to the community outside. . . . We hope that what will happen is that you will communicate across all sorts of barriers and reveal the real genius that is in each of you."

Peter Seitel amplifies Rinzler's point: "The Smithsonian is the National Museum of the United States. Its purpose is to present things of importance in science, art, and the humanities. . . . We feel that the traditions you people carry on are as important as a lunar lander or the work of sculptors and painters."

The meeting of the Cultural Conservation participants, roughly sixty people, includes Makah, Luiseño, and other Native Americans; two

Puerto Rican men, mask makers, a father and son; black beauty-shop operators, two American and one Nigerian; several Mayan Indians from Guatemala; a band of Kmhmu from California; Italian, Chinese, and Salvadoran cooks; two Appalachian musicians, a young banjoist-singer and an elderly balladeer; two bluesmen from the Washington area; a Cajun band; an Irish band; a gospel quintet; a Hispanic family band from New Mexico; and a group of cowboys. Many groups and cultures—but what is apparent to everyone present is the fantastic unlikelihood of this association of particular people who, after all, do not carry on their brows the whole message of cultural tradition and personal achievement that has made them Festival participants.

What is actually visible here? Seen now apart from their functions, skills, and performances, a group of elderly ladies such as we might find at a church supper, in their print dresses and handbags, are in attendance; there is a teenage girl, too, in her high-school sweatshirt, blue jeans, and Nikes; there is an older man in shirtsleeves, smoking, apparently not wholly comfortable; there are two men in knit shirts, one much younger than the other but very much resembling him, both very dark, with flowing sable hair; there are four black men, two stout and two lean, dressed as if for church in suits, with white handkerchiefs in their pockets. All, in fact, appear to be quite ordinary, unprepossessing men and women, people whom one might plausibly and even predictably encounter in the course of a given day at a shopping mall. Hence the meeting has a strangely cosmopolitan quality about it—strange because few of the people present appear to be urbane or cosmopolitan themselves; what we see is a tiny cosmopolis of marginal people, society turned inside out, with the margins drawn to the center, like the swearing-in ceremonies of naturalized Americans.

Among the people in this transient congregation there is little or no basis for mutual understanding; but the atmosphere is charged with exhilarated feelings, with joy and anticipation. Each person appears with fresh, April-like intensity, clarity, and individuality, inspiring a mood of goodwill and mutual charity. If there are any hidden fears or resentments here, or feelings of isolation and uprootedness, they are not in evidence.

The meeting opens with a short address by Dewey Balfa, the Cajun fiddler who has been associated with Rinzler's folk festivals for twenty years, and whose view of his own life and culture has been deeply influenced by his festival experiences. He remarks that his experience with folk festivals has helped him to become aware of the importance of his own culture, as well as the cultures of others, and of the importance of preserving it. One can't be entirely certain what Dewey means by "culture." It is certainly not precisely what anthropologists and folklorists mean when they use the term; for him, the term seems closely allied to "rights" or "opinions." In any case, he speaks with conviction.

Unexpectedly and wonderfully, the others, as they introduce themselves, follow suit with some statement on their feelings about being present; the joy in their faces is evident, even if mixed with anxiety. When the introductions are completed, Margie Hunt, who heads the Cultural Conservation program, speaks to the assembly. Cultural conservation, she notes, is analogous to natural conservation and has been the central project of the folklife program from the very beginning, though never as explicitly as this year. Conservation implies controlled change and evolution, recognizes that cultures change and adapt, and implicitly compares culture to ecosystems; its ideal is variety. She cites instances in which the destruction of an environment threatens to destroy culture: The Kmhmu, a tribe from Laos, employed during the Vietnam War by the CIA and now expelled from Laos to places like Stockton, California, have no native materials such as bamboo from which to make their traditional crafts; the Cajuns, traditionally hunters, trappers, and fishers, evolved their culture in swamps and small waterways that are now disappearing; native Alaskans, too, are losing the grasses used in traditional crafts, as well as animal resources, such as ivory, now protected by law.

The Maya of Guatemala, systematically harassed by the Guatemalan army and economically exploited by the government, represent another embattled and now uprooted people. There is a refugee settlement of Mayans in Indiantown, Florida, whose residents make traditional embroidery for tourists, adopting designs such as American eagles and flags for the American market.

Margie concludes by saying that she feels honored to be in the presence of so many brave, gifted, and accomplished people, and she hopes that the Festival will honor them in return—a remark that inspires a spontaneous burst of applause.

It's beastly hot, and the participants, some of them elderly men and women, have to stand in a long line in the sun and dust outside the administration trailer to get the advances they need to get settled in Washington. They should get them in personalized envelopes, I complain to Charlie Camp, waiting for them in their rooms. They are guests, I insist—*guests*, not employees.

"Wait until you see the reception at the Castle," he says. "They're invited for the amusement of the VIPs, and some of them don't even have time to wash up. After spending all day out on the Mall." One year, he remembers, a group of participants, tired of being treated like animals on the Festival site, refused to ride in the bus provided to transport them to the dormitories: a vehicle from the National Zoo that, until they covered the words with a magnetic sign, spelled out "ZOO BUS" in giant letters across its sides.

"Welcome to the Plantation," Charlie says.

I have breakfast with my dormitory roommates, Hezakiah and the Houserockers. After Pee Wee arrives—Pee Wee Whittaker, an old minstrel show trombonist, accompanist for Ma Rainy and member of Louis Jordan's road company, now eighty-odd years of age—the conversation turns to "devil's work," magic, and voodoo. They're talking, I think to myself, about tricksters: dudes with clever moves who can cheat, change, or control you. Pee Wee tells the story of a man who once stopped him on the street in New Orleans, literally paralyzed him with a look, and took the money out of his wallet without removing the wallet from his pocket. When he looked in his wallet later, he found only tissue paper—"the kind you wipe your ass with."

Hezakiah has a similar story about how he found only brown paper, the kind with which they wrap laundered shirts, in his wallet where money had been, after a conversation with a stranger on the street. Both men relate the tale of a trickster from Shreveport named "Pinola" who, with a few gestures of his arms, could stop you in your tracks or make the newspaper you had been reading disappear or take the coins out of your pocket without making any holes. Hezakiah observes, though, that all these guys carry little bags or grips, without which they won't attempt their tricks. Pinola could also chew up razor blades and light bulbs and swallow the pieces with a drink of water—but all of it in the end, they agree, is designed to rob you.

James Baker, the band's lead guitar player, supplements this discourse with a story about how he once lost all his money to a prostitute—hardly witchcraft—which he takes as another indication of the power some people have to control others. Hezakiah cites several examples from his family: his sister-in-law, for one, had a sort of epileptic fit one day and "hasn't been right since." A local witch doctor, whom they consulted, directed them to a Prince Albert tobacco can, with a lock of hair inside, buried under an old bridge. His mother-in-law, too, was having trouble with her feet and was missing a shoe; her daughter had seen her stepfather outside the house with the shoe and had noticed that it had some writing in it. James adds that he once saw his own name written thirty-seven times in one of his shoes—a device for preventing a spouse from wandering. A woman can control a man, too, so that he "can't do anything"—that is, anything sexually. If she nails a bag of salt over the door, she can control him so that "he just holds his head down all the time." "A woman do *me* that way," says Pee Wee, "and I be gone. That stuff don't work on me."

All three tell of doctors who can tell you what your problem is as soon as you walk through the door—in fact, they know you're coming; they can give you something that will help, like a note in your pocket that can win back a woman.

All these attributions seem to me to arise from self-delusion, guilt, or sheer wish transferred to human agents, usually through a suggestion inherent in figures of speech. The trickster who takes our money is only that mysterious force all of us have encountered when we open our wallets to find we have spent more money than we can account for, much faster than we anticipated. If he takes the form of a city dude, it is because it is in a city that such spending is most likely to occur: is it not the city itself that takes the money away from you? The tissue paper we find in its place, I reason, must be what we placed there ourselves, though we will not admit to having done so, in order to impress someone—ourselves, perhaps—with our prosperity and to take comfort in it. If it is no more than the stuff we wipe our asses with, well, that is because it is, in fact, worthless—a truth that we unconsciously know but half-consciously suppress—and it stands for something, unparalleled in our contempt, which more than once has been compared to human waste.

Shoes, of course, are agents of wandering; doors and bridges open a way for it. An inexplicable mood, certainly, is a curse, especially when we cannot fathom the cause, which, if we could, would no doubt dispel the mood. And who has not tried to gain possession of his beloved by writing a name over and over again?

Very few people attend the opening ceremony. In fact, it seems not to be happening at all; it is more like a rehearsal, something casual, careless, improvisatory. A few technicians in T-shirts and Levis are wrangling over-the-shoulder television cameras with their assistants, under the direction of a young woman in a navy blue suit, carrying a clipboard. The participants themselves—the Zion Travellers, a gospel group from Louisiana,

Mick Maloney's Irish Tradition, and the Bengali drummers—linger outside the canopy in the morning sun.

A tall young man, very familiar, stands in conversation with Ralph Rinzler on the grass behind the stage; it is Senator Gary Hart from Colorado, last year's unsuccessful presidential candidate. He has a sheer physical amplitude which, at the same time that it provokes a kind of instinctive reverence, the reverence of the serf for his lord, arouses vague doubts about his existence: whatever his politics, however attractive a television image he may project, in this setting Hart looks like a fake, a mere model, a manikin, even as his stature, physical and political, shrinks the ordinary presences around him almost to invisibility and transforms their ordinary labors into a kind of pantomime of servitude.

The stage has been decked with urns and pots, with great fountainous ferns and plants, so that it has something of the look of a Belle Epoch hotel lobby. A row of chairs waits to receive the weight of the attending dignitaries. A group is arriving now: Indian women in saris, with gray hair, a jewel in one nostril, the red *tiki* of marriage on their foreheads. Rushing to greet them, his hand clutching the two ends of a white shawl to his breast, with a bustling self-importance in his step and agitation in his face, is Rajeev Sethi, the Brahman with the supercilious manner and the great mop of curly black hair who has somehow, at the administrative level, helped with the Melā. He kisses each of the women in turn as if their arrival had saved him—but from what? From the barbarism of the Americans, perhaps. Yesterday afternoon, as the final preparations for the Melā came to a close, Rajeev could be seen at the Hindu shrine at the center of the site that had been sacralized by a priest from Washington, sweeping it clean but holding the broom in such a clumsy and unaccustomed way that he could scarcely control it: could it be that he had never held a broom before?

Several other notables follow Rajeev to the stage: aristocratic Dillon Ripley, slender and erect, with a gracious restraint in his movements; Bess Hawes, chair of the folk arts panel of the National Endowment for the Arts, champion of embattled cultures, one of the original Almanac Singers, and sister to folksong collector Alan Lomax—a matronly, self-conscious woman with an eloquent and commanding speech; and Rinzler himself, with his elegantly trimmed beard, white now, and the sharp, angular frame that seems almost to store his suit, like a closet, rather than to wear it. Never, it seems, could he become overwarm in the sun or shiver in the cold—he shares with Ripley the careful insouciance of a patrician. A third man, also tall and well tailored, with a bold, iron-gray mustache, a man less at ease in this public and ceremonial occasion, ascends the platform, a glamorous woman wearing a corsage at his side; he is Robert McCormick Adams, descendant of the Chicago McCormicks who patented the reaper, an anthropologist formerly at the University of Chicago and now the new Secretary of the Smithsonian.

Suddenly the drummers commence their rattling and ringing, snaking their way toward the stage in a cloud of rhythms that, once they are settled in front, dissolves to reveal at its center a young man with carefully combed Oxonian hair, thick eyeglasses, and an immobile face, whose two tiny drums, which he plays with small sticks, seem to be reciting an epic poem and at the same time commenting on it with Talmudic subtlety and amplitude. His Bengali companion, wearing a golden turban, bangs his drum boastfully, his chest expanded, as if it were the instrument of some warrior's ritual challenge, while the third player, more boy than man, bony and urchinlike, with tangled hair, loses himself in the sober discourse of his long drum, closing his eyes and training his ear to its complex instructions.

Other entertainment follows—the Zion Travellers from Baton Rouge, the Irish band—along with a series of speeches. "In India," begins Pupal Jayakar, a sari-wrapped emissary from the Indian government and author of *The Earthen Drum*, "we believe that all manifestation arises from sound." For an instant it seems as if the still-lingering codes of the drummers will somehow populate the Mall with their incarnations—legions of spear-bearing warriors, dusty cities, elephants. Adams follows her with a scrupulous address on cultural conservation, redolent of the young anthropologist-ideologues who staff the Office of Folklife Programs. The woman with the corsage, Representative Corrine Boggs of New Orleans, makes an obligatory reference to the "little bit of gumbo" that is the culture of Louisiana; more than the others, she seems to grasp the nature of the occasion, dressed as she is in bright colors, speaking in ebullient tones, in the formulaic idiom of national pronouncements, all designed to register her presence on the turbid surface of video broadcasting.

Rinzler, by contrast, seems scarcely present at all. With a few modest remarks, long familiar to his associates, he situates the Festival in its traditions—in the scholarly tradition of Bishop Percy, in the romantic one of Cecil Sharp, in the popular one of John Lomax, whose daughter Bess, as if by a summons, follows Rinzler with a visionary address that maintains that, after centuries of cultural leveling, "the preservation of cultural difference may be the unique problem of our time—our own great adventure."

The camera crews and reporters, however, busy with their equipment and their notebooks, seem oddly inattentive or even indifferent; these events are, after all, only the beginning of a daylong series of words and images that this evening will find a few moments of exposure in the hallucinatory puppet theater of the television screen. Indeed the entire performance, even the speeches, has the quality not only of a rehearsal but of an *audition*, as if each speaker and each musician hopes that by winning a moment, fleeting and bright as a meteor, in the videosphere that surrounds us, he or she might leave behind the narrow straits and obscure brief passage of ordinary mortal existence. For it is our web of electronic relations, mimicking and mechanizing the net of sentience that encloses human existence, that catches us up through lines of invisible communication in an immensity we cannot conceive; the event itself, in its own setting, is as unreal as a child's fantasy, and even a bit demented—in the way that the reporters on the Capitol lawn, talking into cameras, are demented.

What, then, is occurring under this green canopy on this summer morning? Dignitaries are speaking; cameras are rolling; an energetic young woman, a signer to the deaf, is performing to the right of the stage her graceful Indonesian dance of the hands, though there seems to be no one in attendance who requires her interpretation. Below her and alone on one of the benches, like someone who has seen the show ten times before but cannot omit seeing it again, is a man with a large, suntanned head, white at the temples, and a wide, straight mouth, the mouth of a Calvinist, the stern expression of moral vigilance, seated where he cannot readily be seen; it is J. William Fulbright, former senator from Arkansas, descended in the flesh from the videosphere to endorse the proceedings with his presence. Fulbright seems large—physically large as a marble bust—but somehow reduced to silence by the acute embarrassment of his fleshly embodiment, as if to appear among us, without the mediation of television, is in effect to appear naked.

The Festival is not, it seems, happening here at all, though this event is the first one on the public calendar. The Festival is happening behind us, at the Metro Stage, where the St. Landry Playboys, a zydeco band from Opelousas, Louisiana, has begun to play. Their music rolls toward us like a wave, scattering our wits and calling our attention away from the pantomime before us to the place where people have gathered together to hear the tall J. C. Gallow, washboard player, and tiny Calvin Carriere on the fiddle, inscrutable in their sunglasses, a drummer, accordionist, and guitar player, the musicians. . . .

The Festival has begun!

Folklife and Stereotype

6
The Ink Spots

At the Festival of American Folklife, before we have so
much as learned the name of the man in the cowboy hat or
of the woman with the sari wrapped around her, we have
come, or feel we have come, to know them. Sentiments of
tolerance, charity, and goodwill arise at once to fill the
vacuum created by the absence of any real social nexus
beyond the daily routines of the Festival itself, very likely
to displace any feelings of antipathy or fear that might
otherwise characterize the meeting of people so diverse.

Were the Festival to last longer than it does, perhaps,
and the opportunities actually to know one another
greater, the willingness to bestow the kind of conscientious charity in which most everyone indulges might di-
minish, to be replaced by less salutary feelings. For that
charity, which must originate anew at every moment by a
kind of improvisation, without the prompting of a reliable code of etiquette, demands vigilance and requires us
to call upon some sort of conception of the stranger that
will allow us to see him or her in relation to something
familiar; a stereotype, no matter how skewed or impoverished, no matter what its relation to the actual facts of a

culture, often does service in this way. In the early hours of the Festival—and afterward indelibly influencing every successive impression, figuring in the interpretation of every encounter—the generative signs of human presences in their bewildering variety become a kind of chaos that, like a vandalized house, one hastens urgently to set in order. Duncan's palm-frond fedora, Silas Hogan's oilfield hardhat, Trowbridge's spurs, a *tiki* on a woman's brow, the little deferential postures of the Punjabis or the Kmhmu, the handkerchiefs in the breast pockets of the gospel singers, a Mickey Mouse T-shirt or a woven poncho, an Orioles cap or cowboy hat, a pair of Nikes, blue jeans or a polyester jacket, marks of age, charms of sexuality, dialects of speech, foreign languages familiar in their very unintelligibility: these constitute the cabinet of wonders that one must interpret from whatever resources of connection one has at hand. And, as signs, they never really dissipate; they only grow deeper and more resonant, more dense in their intrinsicality.

The conceptions to which such signs give rise in the Festival's environment of radical dislocation, the imaginary pictures of the whole people and ways of life for which the other has been made to stand, are essential to the feeling of goodwill, which is, in turn, socially essential; hence, the festival setting actually inspires us to form conceptions of others that are more or less developed versions of stereotypes.

Curiously, then, when we encounter someone comparatively familiar—in my case the Roths, polka dancers, midwestern, German American, urban, proletarian—the congenial festival mood comes awkwardly and uneasily into conflict with the set of attitudes the stranger evokes by virtue of our experiences in the world outside the Festival, where judgments of taste and class have already fixed our relationship to the other. Those judgments, under the pressure of what amounts to the Festival ethos, may come to seem embarrassingly selfish, backward, even bigoted. Vaguely I begin to surmise that the corpulent, red-faced Ken Roth—whose accent and idiom, whose gait, whose preoccupations and interests are as familiar to me as my own family, which is similarly situated culturally, and in whom, indeed, I see a large part of myself—is also "culture," as trenchantly so as the Cajuns or Mayans or Luiseño or Punjabis: that his nature, like the others', reflects the unique human productive power we call culture, enabling him to respond, to the fullest extent of his humanity, to the time, the place, and the generation in which he finds himself; that insofar as he possesses that power he is indistinguishable from me, whatever may be the particular substance of its expression; that my tastes—the entire endowment belonging to my class, my level of education, my economic oppor-tunities, the cultural influences that have worked upon me—must be traduced and reinterpreted as something contingent upon these accidents and situations. What ordinarily I interpret vertically, placing this or that person below or above me, I now see laterally, him with me on the same plane, where differences in tastes and style, idiom and manner, reflect only differences in patterns of necessity and influence; were I German Ameri-can, proletarian, and midwestern, I too would be what Ken Roth, as a cultural being, is.

And yet a kind of dread accompanies these revelations, as if I were being called away from something in which I have rooted myself; it is the terror of falling, of floating freely in a medium in which every value has been fixed in equilibrium with every other so that none has any value in itself. It must be—though I cannot perceive it directly, but only by inference from the others around me, to whom I am also an "other"—that as I too am a cultural being I must embrace what is my own: my own habits and tastes, insofar as I know them, and my own values and beliefs. There are occa-sions, at the Festival, when even the buoyancy of fellow-feeling cannot dispel the suspicion that among many social and cultural achievements of great scope and subtlety there are also, sometimes, cultural weaknesses, failures, and diseases: that certain cultures, languishing perhaps in condi-tions inimical to culture, seem to curb human fulfillment rather than to promote it; or that they rely on destructive forces for their forms or are so beset that they lose their center and become distorting mirrors of the cultures around them.

This festive mood, in any case, once upon us, is difficult to put off—indeed one does not wish to put it off after the Festival has ended. We carry it with us away from the Mall into the airports, the subway stops, the turnpike restaurants where people in all their variety seem to make a folklife festival of America itself, wondering why others do not return the goodwill, the sense of approbation, that we bring into these new situa-tions. Here an old order, which at the Festival has been temporarily in abeyance, reasserts itself. Certain racial and national groups retreat into the familiar menial occupations; the classes, identified by ten thousand subtle signs, assume their various niches in the social ecology, as oblivious of one another as species of fish; the entire society, by a kind of herd instinct, seems to rush into the devouring vortex of commerce, where access to the cultural sign is granted only to those who have money to exchange for it.

Alas, it becomes apparent that even in culture there are inequities—that we are not all equally endowed with the power to create and re-create it; that power belongs, it seems, to the individual imagination, which, if not identical to culture any more than the electronic circuit is identical to the energy it retains and communicates, is its seat and its instrument.

Charlie Camp, the Maryland folklorist whom the Smithsonian retained in 1985 to observe the reactions of Festival visitors, notes that the need to identify the participants is urgent enough that it inspires almost immediate stereotyping, despite the efforts of texts and presenters to forestall stereotyping and the complex particularity of the performance designed to dispel it.[1] Very swiftly the Tunisian Sulamiyyah singers become, for one young visitor, "Tahitian belly-dancers"; for another they become, perhaps, figures out of 1940s cinema, immigrants from a storied world of treachery, luxury, and cunning. Certainly, for many visitors, Latin American or Middle Eastern participants merely assimilate themselves to restaurant busboys and taxi drivers; labor union representatives and European ethnic participants become simply the "Polish," whom stereotyping has confined to bowling alleys and working-class bars. Even in the immediacy and intensity of their actuality, black gospel groups, jazz and blues bands, or old-time string, bluegrass, and Cajun bands all readily attach themselves to black and hillbilly stereotypes. The entire Festival, indeed, is subject to public stereotyping; typically, the newspapers and broadcasts patronize the Festival's folk dancers and blacksmiths and dollmakers with sentimental or moralizing portraits, treating the Festival as a refreshing respite from Washington politics and amusing their audiences with the occasional incongruities that arise from it. They are more interested in the mule, escaped from a sorghum mill and crossing with the pedestrians at Twelfth and Madison, than they are in the predicaments of Kmhmu, Maya, or Cajuns.

I myself overhear one visitor in a polo shirt, a young father with a toddler hanging on his arm, say to another as they stroll by a performance of the Fairfield Four: "Hey, look—the Ink Spots." It is perhaps an indication of the visitor's social class that the identification was intended to be funny—a kind of offhand dismissal that swiftly relegates the gifted, inspired, and long-lived gospel quintet to an outdated epoch of popular entertainment and at the same time reaffirms the racial and social standards belonging to that epoch, in which a young white man could depend upon, and perhaps enjoy, the easy deference and servility of his black peers and elders. The visitor's glib identification, however, is a complex product of the image with which popular culture has furnished him, his own class anxieties and aspirations, and, certainly, the sense of social immunity granted by the Festival, from within which the stereotype can be so freely bestowed.

Like many other social situations, the Festival brings together for a transient moment people normally isolated from one another, known to each other chiefly through popular representations, into a close contiguity that permits the immediate assimilation of impressions to prejudices and the shaping of the resulting ideas according to those representations, the stereotypes. These are ratified, in the case of our young father, by the assent of his auditor, who is implicitly being invited to share the speaker's own attitudes.

The stereotype, of course, is simply a way of sorting information; once the gospel group or the basketmaker or the Cherokee and Acoma athletes have been identified as such, with little more in the way of concretion or amplification, they have been classified and hence in a sense completed. The urgency that drives this process is almost certainly one effect of the magnitude and amplitude of the Festival and the corresponding need to experience it in a kind of shorthand, which is what we do in museums, too—taking note simply of what is to be seen so that at some later point we may pause to meditate on our experiences, torn between the interest of what is before us and the sense of limitless discovery beyond us.

The operative element here is insulation; the frame implied by some minimal device such as an elevated platform objectifies the content of the exhibit, however alive and present its participants may be. For some visitors, this frame may dissolve so imperceptibly into the internal categories already firmly in place—such as, perhaps, a secure sense of social class and class distinction—that it may offer no offense nor produce any uneasiness; the Other is *always* thus framed by the impermeable boundaries of class, a structure to which, in our society, distinctions of race, by an insidious historical association, all too readily adapt themselves.

The impulse toward stereotype, however, may be more than urgent; it may be imperative—suggesting that there is something at stake more critical than one's own immediate social and psychic equilibrium. As Glenn Ohrlin observes, "People get mad when you ain't what they expect you to be." Even folklorists, Ohrlin adds, can become very possessive: "They'll damn near fight over you . . . as if folks couldn't take care of themselves."[2]

In the art museum or out on the National Mall, it is social privilege or the sense of it, projected by the accumulation of cultural capital, which a museum or a folk festival represents, that permits the naked exposure of the object as object, or the folk as folk, plucked out of the cultures and communities in which they are at home. That folk artists themselves might feel honored or legitimized in the transaction is not at issue; such effects are on record and form an important element of the Festival ideology.[3] In the Festival of American Folklife, the limits of museum display have been expanded, but in order to expand them it has been necessary to expand, too, perhaps, our willingness to objectify people socially "below" us and to coax out their complicity in the process.

To visitors for whom social distinctions are at issue, who may have invested something of themselves in the idea of social mobility or who are themselves uncertain of their own social status, the folk festival can at times be disquieting, as it seems to have been for some visitors to the Kmhmu area, or profoundly disturbing—as has been the case, for example, when religious ceremonies mounted for visitors cross the boundary between demonstration and reenactment and become harrowingly authentic, or when participant testimony such as that of the Guatemalans, points un-compromisingly to execrable social injustices and carries the keenly politi-cized attitudes and combative rhetorical tone such injustice demands. The physical frameworks that materialize the conventions of festival display, moreover, not only permit but compel us to objectify, almost as a social duty—but one which a person of any imagination can undertake only with extreme uneasiness.

In a word, the circumstances place the visitor in a position of power, either familiar and habitual or bizarre and unreal; however admired they may be, moreover, however well remunerated, the artists are in a position of apparent internment, even servility, and visitors often speak of them, and observe them, as if separated from them by a one-way mirror. One feels, as an observer, that the artist must silently dismiss the audience as members of a class so positioned socially that they can enjoy his or her own socially inferior status as an amusement, diversion, or entertainment. But the devices that frame the participant also isolate and exclude the visitor. For the visitor, too, is isolated from his or her individual history and community and can perhaps feel frustrated to have been placed in circum-stances that imperfectly represent, or seem to misrepresent, him or her *to the participant*. Rarely do we feel that a playwright, to draw an analogy, has deliberately "excluded" us from the action of the play, yet excluded we are, as a condition of the fiction. In a "living museum" exhibition such as the Festival of American Folklife, such a sense of exclusion, which is an important psychological ingredient in the event, suggests that the expectation and desire aroused by stereotypes become, in cultural performances framed by theatrical devices, an anxiety about the framework itself that dilates into all the boundaries, differentiations, and imbalances that describe the structure of power and advantage in our society.

As Alexis de Tocqueville consistently pointed out—indeed, it was the main theme of his work on America—democracy created social ambiguities, which much of cultural life in a democracy could be explained as an effort to overcome. Our "place," it seems, supplies the role within which we discover our identity as social beings; without that role we are psychologically at sea and must surround all social encounters with various maneuvers designed to create a framework for communication. The Festival of American Folklife is, in a sense, paradigmatic for American society as a whole. Disrupt or dissolve already contested and fragile social distinctions, and people will seek to re-create them in some form and to represent those forms in ways that will enforce them in representations, in beliefs, and in behavior. In a culturally diverse society, where social distinctions are linked in complex ways to cultural differences, social representations, beliefs, and behavior will also be representations of, beliefs about, and efforts to bring order to culture and the relationships among cultures.

Artificial devices of dramatic distancing like the proscenium arch or the folk festival stage are not limited to theaters and festivals; such insulating lines between social groups form a tangled web across the face of society and make of ordinary life an ongoing series of encounters with people who make unconscious or deliberate representations of their own cultural identity to others. But these same insulating factors can, in the Festival context, function as an aesthetic frame. Just as drama, literature, film, and television can promulgate stereotypes either out of their own fancies or by echoing the images of the street, so can art and the folk festival break through the veil of social hallucination and explore the common humanity that the hallucination strives, in ignorance, to mediate. If it happens that, on the street or in the marketplace, people self-consciously adopt the stereotypes developed though their interaction with the dominant culture, it may be that in the larger vocabulary of stereotypes it is the image entertained by the socially powerful that permits the socially powerless to exhibit otherness—for only through the stereotype can difference be identified as such, or even detected on the social landscape at all.

Thus, among the many forces that contribute to the resilience of a stereotype is the tacit social contract among culturally diverse people that guarantees that a system of stereotypes shall be a language of communication across sociocultural lines. Hence a folk culture may forcefully put forward its popular or official image, perhaps in a hyperbolized form that arrests the corrosive influence of a negative stereotype by turning it back upon its creator; or that image can be transformed into a kind of parody of itself, and beyond that into an icon or effigy, a center around which cultural self-awareness can form. But the image itself, as an element in a social vocabulary, cannot be expunged, any more than we can expunge our names and still function socially. If stereotypes are not in some sense identity itself, they are the coupling through which personality and society conjoin to produce identity.

The impatient visitor's hasty identification of the Fairfield Four as the Ink Spots perhaps indicates less an urge to fix something than a need to set something in motion. It is the unidentified unknown that sits in consciousness, an inert weight without connections to anything outside of itself. That is the urgency: to translate a percept into a concept, as we might in the early morning struggle to interpret the inchoate colors and shapes of an object on the bureau that we cannot identify or remember having placed there, for it is this act of construction that secures us to reality; to have lost our trust in it is deeply terrifying, a kind of insanity. In pausing to attend to the "Ink Spots," which he can do because the stereotype secures his social relationship to them, our stereotyping young man might find himself engaged, moved, instructed—even the Ink Spots, when he begins to make historical and musical sense of their relation to the gospel quartet, will become more interesting to him, an image on hinges that can swing open onto a world. That is the motion into which the act of identification sets our experience; it is a motion of learning, a yoking, and however well or badly amplified and developed, it is the fundamental act of engagement with the other and the other's culture.

Stereotypes are configurations of traits: racial traits; social roles and economic functions; kinesic, sartorial, and tonsorial styles; expressive forms—all taken as typical and marked by certain social and cultural valuations. All traits express relations, to self primarily, but also the relations of traits to one another and finally the relations among those relations, which carry all of our social reality into the realm of metaphor. Among these relations are, with other determinants, the relation of the trait to the sign that identifies it, so that the elaboration of further relations in the realm of the sign, particularly in language, extends the primary perception beyond the self into the social nexus and its communications.

We learned, for example, "big" and "small," perhaps, first in relation to our own bodies and enacted the concepts, to the tune of the words as our parents sang them to us, with gestures of our hands and arms; all further perceptions of these concepts will follow, perhaps infinitely, from this original relation. With "red," "green," and "yellow," again, we name the retina's natural accommodation to visible light and install it in culture; but magenta, burnt ochre, fire-engine red, saffron yellow, and bone white are configurations of culture itself, figurative couplings of the retinal touch to the shared experience in which the names, as names, have their meaning. Whether directly linguistic or metalinguistic, a conception of the isolated trait has been secured by coupling the perception of it, and the entire system of such couplings we call culture, to what is in effect another perception—that of its expression in the articulating and signifying activity of the community.

Hence there are no isolate "traits," strictly speaking, apart from culture, which should be regarded as the total pattern of figures in which traits—what semioticians call "markers"—have their existence. We do not "perceive" traits; rather, we recognize them, consciousness having been cultivated by various systems of signification for the germination in it of sensory experiences. This person may be "phlegmatic," that one "sanguine," and still another "choleric"—verbal relics of the Renaissance psychology of humors that still have their meaning in relation to that system even though, as a psychology, it has been many times replaced; we call upon it, nevertheless, because such descriptions as "repressed," "compulsive," or "neurotic," although they have the authority of a still-official psychology (official because we haven't yet exhausted its lode of figurativity), cannot express the traits that our culture, as embodied in language, has already taught us to recognize. All apples that are not green or yellow, categorically speaking, are red; and yet, should they come from a Devon orchard, with blushes of gold, pink, and rose upon them, we shall require a poet to describe and a painter to depict them. Thus is culture, which is our reality, created: each new figure adjusting the medium of culture to the accommodations imagination has made, or must make, to experience—a pattern of inference formed where conceptual categories and perception meet.

There are, then, no "cultural traits" distinct from other kinds of traits—

all traits are inherently cultural. They belong, with the other constituent elements that represent a particular culture's analysis of reality, to the particular vocabulary in which all cultural discourse is carried out. This is particularly true of social and personal traits, whose norms are simply those of the community that embodies and names them. Their organization into classes, categories, and kinds, their representation in discourse or in more or less abstract and autonomous symbolic systems, their projection into narrative—all these are the means by which a culture expresses, *as* itself, its knowledge *of* itself. The authority of that knowledge, moreover, consists in the illicit relation of the discourse in which it is framed with the social, political, and psychological forces which have shaped it and which in turn are shaped by it. Even conflicting ideologies share a discourse, however sophisticated or primitive, however articulate, in the absence of which they could not have come into conflict, or into any relation whatever.

How then can culture, as itself, express—in a folk festival or in any other way—its knowledge of what is not itself, and how can that knowledge, supposing it could be developed, have any authority save that derived from its own historical and cultural situation? What can we know, especially, about social reality, when the discourse by which we know it is itself social? Insofar as human communities of whatever kind, on whatever scale, express, preserve, and transmit their experience in culture, and insofar as culture *is* the medium of knowing, one community can only know another negatively—only in terms of its own traits, of which the outsider's will be perceived as distortions, violations, or failures and to which that perception will be indissolubly tied. The social reality of the outsider cannot be known in and of itself; it can be known only as a pattern formed from the disturbance wrought upon the surface of the insider's own established attitudes and assumptions; it is a reality in translation. Within the domain of culture, culture cannot develop any knowledge that is not knowledge of itself, nor appeal to any authority not its own.

If the possibility of knowledge of the outsider exists at all, it is only *through* culture's knowledge of itself, for culture, at its own frontier, may figure obscurely beyond the domain of culture to that common human nature that, though it cannot be grasped in itself, is intimated by cultural difference. The distortions that arise out of the effort of the inside cultural community to know the outsider may themselves become figures in the weave of the insider's cultural discourse—figures that, like all metaphor, drive thought toward those inventions of analysis which, if they cannot actually pacify the warring terms of the cultural comparison, can interpret them in ways that create a transient mediating third term owing its existence to the comparison. Although we normally contrast figuration, which discovers similitudes, to analysis, which discriminates differences, it appears that the apprehension of figure demands that each of the coupled terms be dissolved by analysis into elements invented for the purpose of making that coupling intelligible.

Stereotype is a science of distortions, but a vernacular science—one that reasons from a primary cause, which is the distortion itself, supposing that all difference can be explained *as* difference. It does not ask what are the traits of the outsider, for it already knows them, as effects of causes it has adduced from the laws of its own world; reasoning only unknown effects from known causes, denying any causes peculiar to the outsider's own history, circumstances, and occasions, particularly those hidden causes that lie in the crosscultural encounter itself, stereotype denies the outsider, in effect, an independent existence. For there is no investigation; stereotype forms its theories out of those judgments of similarity and difference by which we assign individuals to groups and classes—the act of assignment being, in stereotype, the way we conceive or "know" the individual. Stereotype consists entirely of such assignments, its essential error being the simple fact that it knows social reality *only* in groups or classes, apart from which it has only the existential encounter with the individual: "Some of my best friends are stereotypes."

Things differ in what they have in common. In stereotype we assign individuals to groups on the basis of perhaps a single marker such as skin color, a profession of religion, or a native language, all perceived in relation to their contraries in the self. Hence, by a simple tautology, we suppose all such traits to be held in common by the class they indicate. Traits held in common, in any case, form the class.

But in order for traits to be held in common, they must be fixed and unchanging—for if traits were subject to change over time, they could not form a reliable basis for group or class distinctions and could not serve to indicate membership in such groups or classes. Hence, to paraphrase the anthropologist E. E. Evans-Pritchard, individuals will behave as they will, but groups as they must, for the traits of groups are by definition fixed traits. A group or class formed from the identity of traits exhibited by individuals, moreover, necessarily bestows those traits, conceptually, upon every member assigned to the class, whatever the basis for that assignment; membership in a class constituted from common traits implies common possession of those traits, since in stereotype, the class, though it may be indicated by a single trait in common, actually exhibits specific *sets* of associated traits, so that the act of classification prompts perception of all the traits belonging to that class. Hence all the traits belonging to a particular class—but especially the trait that indicates membership in that class—can be projected metaphorically upon individuals who do not display a particular marker but who may be supposed to belong to that class on some other basis; of them, we say they are "essentially" this or that, or "fundamentally" thus-and-so—that Native Americans are essentially "intuitive," that blacks are inherently rhythmic, that Latinos are passionately irrational or childlike.

In the fixity of traits and of their associations, then, stereotype falls into error; but it errs more deeply in the process of comparison itself. Traits shared are, conceptually, traits identical, not different; an ever finer discrimination of traits will produce ever narrower classes until no group or class can be said to have been formed at all—unless classes of one member are still classes. Hence the always expedient and arbitrary character of groups formed on the basis of shared traits: the process of discrimination has been arbitrarily limited so that traits that might otherwise be further distinguished can instead be identified with one another. As we have suggested, these limits are cultural—a trait distinguished on the basis of difference is also defined and bounded by it. In other words, we cannot perceive a trait that we suppose to be shared by all members of a given class on the basis of its difference from that same trait as exhibited by other individuals belonging to that class, else that trait would not be shared; we have distinguished it instead on the basis of its difference from analogous traits *outside* its class, in another, opposing class with which it otherwise has something in common.

Hence the apparently arbitrary limit upon a given class is really the boundary it shares with another class; groups and classes, like the traits that define them, have their existence in relation to the system of markers to which all belong. Red, yellow, and green apples can be divided by color first because apples belong to a system that includes pears and peaches as well as oranges and melons—and hence can be distinguished *as* apples—and second because red, yellow, and green belong to the system of colors and can be distinguished as red, yellow, and green. Any further distinctions of shades among these colors will produce as many kinds of apples as there are apples. In groups, then, traits are of necessity fixed and unchanging, uniform throughout the group, and significant only insofar as they can be distinguished from traits belonging to other groups that otherwise share some traits in common: differences in color have color in common, as against, say, texture; differences among apples have appleness—as against orangeness, or potatoness, or aspects of structure, texture, taste, and the like, as well as of color—in common. Differences of race or religion also have race and religion in common—as factors, perhaps, in the economic or social competition underwritten by a shared cultural discourse that defines the arena, the rules, and the objects of that competition.

Were stereotype simply a matter of these natural and commonplace intellectual processes, however, we might easily subdue it. But social and individual identity is itself involved in complicated ways with what seems to be a universal human impulse to identify the self with a group or class and, beyond that, actually to construct the self and ultimately to act on the basis of that identification; and let me observe, by way of anticipation, that any conscious and deliberate identification of self with group, as opposed to simple unconscious participation in it—ethnic and sexual politics both amply illustrate the difference—implies the awareness of some contrastive group or class and hence is on some level a dialogue in stereotypes. Stereotype consequently reflects, in the process of its formation, relations among groups, and it can be read as the record of the attitudes of one group toward itself as well as toward another, and of the evolution of those attitudes; once formed, stereotype influences those relations and supplies an instrument for assigning individuals, among which is the self *itself*, to groups when they display the traits belonging to the stereotype of that group. As a social theory, stereotype may organize and offer to predict social reality, but it is also a model for creating and controlling social reality.

Human traits, of course, are not like the mass or volume, the color or texture, of apples and oranges—nor, for that matter, are the traits of apples and oranges. Human traits are never fixed, never unchanging, any more than life itself; they are variable, dynamic, elusive, transient, resourceful. As Clifford Geertz demonstrates with the example of a blinking—or winking?—eye, the very concept of a human trait is problematic.[4] A given trait may be assigned to a group or supposed to be characteristic of that group; but the marker of that trait, as one group interprets it, may to another group indicate another trait altogether, while within the group itself it may signify yet another trait—if indeed it can be regarded as a sign at all within the group. As Robert Merton and other sociologists have observed, the signs of virtue among friends wonderfully become, among foes, the signs of vice: a friend's industry, intelligence, and honesty become in a foe opportunism, cunning, and vulgarity.[5] The very signs of such traits, such as long hours on the job, or wide reading, or outspoken conversation, may in different contexts have entirely different meanings— as people who have attempted to import these signs, or the appearance of them, into new situations perhaps have found.

In short, the information that passes laterally across the boundaries between groups, and vertically between individuals and groups, is wretchedly imperfect. Consequently, to understand stereotype we must proceed beyond the classificatory processes that produce it to those judgments of similarity and difference upon which classification depends: judgments that, because they turn upon principles of resemblance, and because they create alliances among traits by equivalence, association, and extension, are fundamentally metaphorical. Though it strives for the literal statement, stereotype is always expressed in figurative statements, which make up the difference between the fullness of another human being or human group and the poverty and superficiality of our information about him or her by denying, partially or wholly, his or her humanity and, at the same time, completing it by inference from our own—in short, by transforming the other into a metaphor in our own social discourse, at once eroding and reinventing the warring terms of the comparison in order to make sense of it. Precisely as language produces figurative statements out of the dissonance between syntactic structures and semantic forces, so does stereotype, though grounded in cognitive structures, produce, in the realm of social forces, socially figurative statements.

All this arises simply from conceiving, however accurately or inaccurately, human beings in groups, an intellectual propensity unspeakably complicated by the fact that human beings are, indeed, social—but can be conceived as such only by assigning to them traits fixed in uniform relationships to one another (already a dehumanizing factor), the very perception of which is an illusion borne of a consciousness of difference and whose meaning is a function of it. Lying concealed in the nucleus of the social hallucination it has itself generated, nevertheless, is a structure of figures that carry the enabling codes of our own sociality.

We may perhaps detect the genesis of stereotype, in a context that points toward our own folk festivals, in a nineteenth-century writer's effort to reveal for one social class the order and intelligibility in the apparently chaotic social reality of the class below it. In his *London Labour and the*

London Poor, begun in 1849 as a serial in the *Morning Chronicle*, Henry Mayhew, the London novelist and journalist, attempts a sweeping economic classification of London street folk, particularly the costermongers or vendors who bring "the greengrocery, the fruit, the fish, the watercresses, the shrimps, the pies and puddings, the sweetmeats, the pineapples, the stationery, the linendapery, and the jewellry, such as it is, to the very door of the working classes."[6]

Mayhew is remarkable for the richness and depth of his exploration of the lives of London dustmen, chimney sweeps, costermongers, acrobats, puppeteers, and others; through painstaking interviews and with a fine ear for narrative he takes us into their marketing practices, their opinions of their clientele (particularly of ladies and gentlemen), their language, their family histories, their living conditions and diet, their entertainments, their religious beliefs, and even their sexual arrangements.

His great project is "to arrange the several varieties of work into 'orders,' and to group the manifold species of arts under a few comprehensive genera—so that the mind may grasp the whole at one effort . . . a task," he says, "of most perplexing character."[7] Undaunted, Mayhew enumerates seven kinds of street people: street sellers and street buyers, whom he distinguishes according to the commodities in which they trade; street finders, divided according to what they salvage; street performers, divided by the arts they practice; artisans and peddlers, divided into makers at home, makers in the streets, and menders; and finally the laborers, discriminated by their functions. This means of classifying a social group has the obvious appeal, as Marx would discover, of an apparent rigor and precision, approaching the ideal of natural science: associated with commodities on the one hand, or with functions on the other, human beings fall into categories whose basis is not abstract or notional but nearly as concrete as the objects and functions themselves.

Mayhew's exceedingly fine subdivisions of these groups by commodities and functions seem, from a literary point of view, very closely tied to human character; he seems to locate that point at which, in the economic sphere at least, particular tasks and long association with particular perishables, natural and manufactured articles, and the like at once reveal distinct qualities in the human personality and impart their own to human identity. This is the point at which the classificatory impulse and the apprehension of social groups as such meet, and hence it is the very point at which stereotype is most firmly anchored to our imaginative life.

Mayhew's economic Baghdad of penny pies, bird cages, acrobats, trained bears, broom makers, lamplighters, and shoeblacks, among myriad others, has a distinctly festive air. In it, men and women become what their trade identifies them to be; one can almost detect in the lengthy inventories, which are themselves masterpieces of the analysis of material culture, incipient literary characters about to "materialize" out of the medium in which they work, as Dickens's Orlick arises out of a blacksmith's forge, even as they evoke in their totality the material world in which the Victorian middle class, Mayhew's readership, lives. Indeed, the middle-class household could serve as a memory system for retaining metonymically, in each of its many ordinary household objects, the idea or the picture of the class, if indeed it *is* a class, that produced it.

Mayhew's street folk reveal, at the heart of stereotype, a figurative assimilation of the human character to parts or pieces of itself, even when those parts are not, strictly speaking, *of* the human character—human character having always been subject, like nature, to a fallacy of the poetic imagination that dissolves distinctions in order to absorb the animate into the inanimate or the whole into the part: the wood and the wave are, tropologically speaking, made of the same stuff as the graybeard and the maiden.

Not content, however, with mere economic abstraction based on economic function, Mayhew seeks to situate the classes he has formed from sets of economic traits in a social, political, moral, and even a biological reality, as the abstraction alone seems inadequate to account for what appears to him to be a natural division of street people into classes. Now observe:

> Among the street-folk there are many distinct characters of people—people differing as widely from each in tastes, habits, thoughts and creed as one nation from another. Of these the costermongers form by far the largest and certainly most broadly marked class. They appear to be a distinct race—perhaps, originally, of Irish extraction—seldom associating with any other of the street-folks, and being all known to each other. . . . The street-performers differ again from those; these appear to possess many of the characteristics of the lower class of actors, viz., a strong desire to excite admiration, a love of the tap-room, though more for the society and display than for the drink connected with it, a great fondness for finery and predilection for the performance of dangerous or dexterous feats. Then there are the street mechanics, or artisans—quiet, melancholy, struggling men, who, unable to find any regular

employment at their own trade, have made up a few things, and taken to hawk them in the streets, as the last shift of independence. Another distinct class of street-folk are the blind people . . . mostly musicians. . . . Their affliction, in most cases, seems to have chastened them and to have given a peculiar religious cast to their thoughts.

Such are the several varieties of street-folk, intellectually considered— looked at in a national point of view, they likewise include many distinct people. Among them are to be found the Irish fruit-sellers; the Jew clothesmen; the Italian organ-boys, French singing women, the German brass bands, the Dutch buy-a-broom girls, the Highland bagpipe players, and the Indian crossing-sweepers—all of whom I here shall treat of in due order.[8]

At this level the stereotype, which literally forms here before our eyes, is an ingenious intellectual subterfuge, through which we apprehend an unknown by linking its traits—each unknown in itself—together in a fixed, that is, a stereotyped, association with one another, so that we seem to know them in terms of one another; what is known, of course, is not the organ boy or the singing girl in themselves, but the coupling of nationality with economic function—*Italian* organ boy, *French* singing girl—as we might "know" the capitols of the fifty states.

All of the moral and psychological traits that Mayhew cites—love of the taproom and of finery, a "desire to excite admiration" through dexterous or dangerous feats, even the artisan's melancholy or the blind musician's chastened religiosity—emerge, once Mayhew has imported them into his own moral universe, as the very features that, tautologically, enabled him to distinguish the exhibitors of those traits as a class in the first place; the difference is that, in the process of distinguishing them *as* traits, he has brushed them with colors from his own moral palette. Perhaps the street artisan is melancholy because he has been closed out of the shop, or perhaps it is a melancholy thing to Mayhew that he has been—doubtless there were cheerful artisans and dour acrobats on the streets of London in 1849. The religious temperament that Mayhew attributes to the blind is proverbial in any case and almost certainly reflects a spontaneous identification of the signs of blindness with the signs of introspection, prayer, and sleep. Indeed, the artisan's melancholy may in fact be concentration or absorption, and the acrobat's love of the taproom simply a mighty thirst. Certainly a love of finery and a predilection for "dexterous or dangerous feats" are, above all, signs of a good business sense.

Each of these traits is the kernel of a characterization which dilates through an economic class in the moral medium of Mayhew's own sensibility; the apparent natural unity and integrity of that class arouses him to account for it by embedding each of its members in a national or what we would call a cultural community grounded in ethnicity or race. That is the formula from which, like a solved equation, the stereotype arises: it is Mayhew's journalistic project to pursue the stereotype into the taprooms, the lodging houses, and the theaters of London, expecting to discover— and, indeed, discovering—its realization in actual communities whose existence palpably establishes his conceptions in society and nature.

Curiously, Mayhew accepts these alignments of race or nation on the one hand with economic function on the other, associations that are consistently enough displayed on the social landscape to permit him to fix them in stereotypes, almost as if they were natural phenomena and not the effects of historical causes. What seems clear, historically, is that cultural and social dislocation, along with racial and ethnic discrimination, have pushed certain national groups such as the Irish and the Italians to the margins of the British economy. But for Mayhew, as for most people in the nineteenth century, the biological notion of race and the political concept of nationality were often confounded, both imaginatively in literature and theoretically in science, with ideas of class, society, and species governed by certain economic, historical, and evolutionary theories that readily swept in to fill the anthropological vacuum with new syntheses such as class warfare and racial supremacy.

The word *stereotype* itself was originally coined in 1798 by the French printer Didot to refer to metal casts of print from which fixed texts could be repeatedly struck off. In psychiatry the term came to refer to pathologically fixed or repetitive behavior, and it entered the vocabulary of social science in 1922 through Walter Lippmann's *Public Opinion*, in which Lippmann saw stereotype as an element of the "pseudoenvironment" that human beings interpose between themselves and the world in order to make sense of it.[9] Stereotype is the *stereo*, the fixed or solid, *type*, the stamp or seal, from which every individual impression takes its form in thought, so that the particularity of the impression, even when it occludes, distorts, or breaks the image of the seal, is nevertheless always conceived as a more or less imperfect record of its pressure or imprint. As such it is the mechanism by which we describe, assess, and situate others in relation to ourselves, figuring each individual as an expression of a particular class.

Stereotypes can form around actual social groups, as most ethnic stereo-types do, or around social or economic abstractions, such as Mayhew's, which may or may not constitute living social realities; in fact, some of Mayhew's economic classes, such as costermongers and sweeps, do form primitive urban communities, while others, such as street performers, may or may not. But the mimetic force of such images, working both within social communities and upon them, particularly in relation to outsiders in whom the image originates, may give to the stereotype a curious and insidious tenacity both inside and outside the group. We tend to enact others' expectations of us and, in enacting them, to internalize them so that we may transmit them mimetically within our intimate community, which in turn exhibits them again to the outsider. A group caricatured by the stereotypes of another may become more conscious of itself *as* a group, while isolated individuals may find themselves identifying with the group to which they have been assigned by a stereotype, even though that group may have no concrete social reality.

Cognitively considered, stereotype is a three-dimensional figure drawn upon a two-dimensional plane and consequently a kind of illusion; like the two-dimensional image of a transparent three-dimensional figure, its inte-rior and exterior are interchangeable—either it is an image distorted by a judgment acting upon it from within, or a judgment distorted by an image acting upon it from without. It is a compound structure that relates a human trait or traits to the subject and associates that trait with a social group, either because the person who has displayed it can be identified with a particular group or because the trait itself can be identified with other traits and a social group formed, by generalization, out of that identification. Its integrity is a function not of any necessary alignment with anything outside itself but, like a pictographic figure, of the comple-tion of certain interior relations that constitute *in themselves* a moment of recognition.

Yet we read stereotype referentially even while acknowledging its fic-tionality, just as we do any work of art or literature, because with the relations belonging to one realm of experience—lines in two-dimensional planes, for example, or words in syntactical arrangement—it calls up the relations belonging to another—surfaces in three-dimensional space, or consciousness articulated in meaning. Stereotype is consequently always true, even perfectly true, since it is essentially self-referential—as long as we are willing actively to experience, or are compelled to experience, one species of reality as if it were another.

Stereotype, then, frames a hypothetical or actual social group according to the subject's own characterological laws as a human type that embodies the subject's sense of relation to the other. If, however, stereotype is a figurative and not a literal statement, we may perhaps best understand it rhetorically, as a certain system of metaphors or implicit comparisons. Let us see if we cannot catch a fairly familiar and harmless stereotype on the wing: that of the absentminded professor.

Ahead of me in the cafeteria line at Georgetown University, where the Festival participants are lodged, is an owl-eyed, bespectacled man who seems to have forgotten his meal ticket and with helpless, embarrassed gestures is searching his various pockets for it. I recognize him: he is a well-known folklorist from a prestigious graduate department, one of the Festival's distinguished guests. I myself—in contrast to the man whose difficulty may, I fear, cause me to miss my supper, for the cafeteria doors close promptly at six—have been efficient, competent, and thorough; *I* have remembered my ticket—and to reassure myself of this fact, I take it nervously in and out of my breast pocket, just to be certain that some obscure magic has not returned it the envelope in my dormitory room.

Now, as the lost ticket stands in the way of my purposes, and as the situation affords me an opportunity to translate my frustration into a judgment flattering to myself, I attribute the loss to an agency in the man ahead of me which, measured against my own competence, becomes incompetence; a word, "absentminded," suggested perhaps by his ab-stracted demeanor, comes to me and summons up the verbal formula, "absentminded professor," in which the stereotype lies preserved. Perhaps my perception has been prompted by the fact that he is dressed in a hapless rayon sport shirt and carries a pipe in his side pocket, as these are the stereotyped traits of professors, a class that, being notoriously absent-minded, most probably includes the man ahead of me, as my interpreta-tion of his behavior tautologically confirms. That is: he is absentminded because he is a professor and he is a professor because he is absentminded. Or perhaps he is not dressed in a basement-sale sport shirt or carrying a pipe. But this does not prevent me from saying in jest to the young woman behind me in line, to whom I wish to appear clever, that the man delaying both of us must be a professor, because he is so absentminded. At the same time there swells in me a contempt for the entire class of men and women to which the man ahead of me belongs: people who, secure in their ivory towers, while away the time in intellectual self-indulgence while the rest of us hustle to get a living in whatever way we can.

Once comfortably seated at the table, however, with steaming mashed potatoes in front of me, I begin to reflect on the man ahead of me, and I draw the generous conclusion that professors, being creatures of thought, always lost in the pursuit of knowledge and understanding, only *appear* to be absentminded; it isn't that they are absentminded, really, but that the trivial matters occupying most of us are to them just that, trivial, consistently excluded from consciousness in favor of the great questions that young minds are most eager to confront and in which they require the most tender guidance. I've read this fellow's work, in fact, and admired it. It's easy to be charitable; a hot and exhausting day is over, and as I begin to devour the food on my plate I feel my contempt turning to a kind of affection, even love, for the professor and his profession—after all, I am a professor myself.

This pantomime of rationality is a four-cornered structure of perception and generalization, self and other, whose coupling is a dynamic and meaningful sign that is pulled in opposing directions—toward the perceived world and away from it, toward the self and toward the other—but remains whole because the stereotyping process fixes the relation among the four antipodes of which that sign is the intersection and center. At one corner of this structure—which, for the sake of analysis, I invite the reader to visualize as two opposing triangles meeting at a central point—is a mere percept or impression, something conceived across the isthmus between one person and another: in this case, a missing meal ticket, an effect of what in actuality can be any one of ten thousand different causes. At the opposing corner I myself stand to observe and to be affected; incorporated into my own moral universe, itself excited to judgment by my own investment in the occasion, the missing ticket becomes a sign—in this case of incompetence or "absentmindedness," a moral trait. A sign, which stands at the center of our figure on the point at which two triangles meet, has been formed from the union of a signifier, the mere percept or impression, and a signified, which is its moral position relative to the competence that keeps me in possession of my ticket.

This union of signifier and signified, however, presupposes a deeper identification of myself with the man ahead of me, of the man ahead of me with myself—a metaphor of identity through which my anxiety like a dybbuk possesses the missing ticket, lending it moral animation within the subjective realm suffused with that anxiety. Embedded in metaphor, the sign thus formed, with its moral significance, is highly unstable; it is a compound that would, without the energy of my anxiety and antipathy, deteriorate—and indeed does deteriorate once I am in my chair—into component parts, each seeking to literalize itself, to find its meaning in its proper sphere. But it is highly dynamic, too: because it is a moral sign, a sign of a trait, it seeks to ally itself on the one hand with a moral being, the man ahead of me, who stands at the third corner of our four-cornered structure, and on the other with identical traits that form the class of the absentminded professors, who stand at the fourth. Our sign, then, the moral trait, is actually the kernel of another figure, a synecdoche or metonymy, which makes it the identifying feature both of the man ahead of me and of the class to which he belongs.

This triangular figure, extending from a sign that stands metonymically for individuals and for the groups to which they belong, is the heart of stereotype, assigning traits to individuals, individuals to groups, and groups to traits—or, in response to stereotypes already in place, assigning individuals to groups, groups to traits, and traits to individuals. The man ahead of me, whose moral nature is wholly absorbed in his absentmindedness, may enter the professoriat through his rayon shirt and his pipe; but, given the prior existence of the stereotype as classifying device, he may enter it by inference from absentmindedness alone. More typically, though, it is the fixed association of the sign—a physical feature, a point of conduct, speech, or dress, always distinguished with reference to the observing subject—with some generalizing factor such as race, nationality, or occupation that extends the characterizing metonym to an entire group, as it does with Mayhew's Italian organ boys and French singing girls.

Notice, however, that once the stereotype has been established, it becomes itself a generalizing force, making all organ boys Italian, all singing girls French, all southeastern European people Polish, all Orientals Chinese, all Latinos Puerto Rican (or Mexican, if you live in Texas or California), just as it makes all young males of African descent into potential muggers, musicians, or basketball players, all women either seductive or submissive, all men aggressive, and all Jews grasping. These identifications express the priority of specific social relations in the thought that follows from them.

Because it is unstable, because it seeks to form a metonym joining persons to traits and traits to groups, I call the generating sign at the center of stereotype the *ethneme*, the elementary conceptual particle which with other particles of its kind composes the nucleus of the social stereotype. The ethneme is a signifier that migrates across the social boundary between two groups and becomes by virtue of that passage a characterizing sign. Consequently the stereotype marks the distance between two groups, which it is its formal aim to fix and maintain; there is no stereotype without distance. In stereotype, Italian and French do not denote nationalities, strictly speaking, but marks of difference between them and "English" or "American"; "blind" is the contrary of "sighted"; "black" and "white," "man" and "woman," are not biological classes—not in stereotype—but markers of persistent class and cultural differences underwritten by economic structures and social forms and powerful enough in themselves partially to transform one into the other. At the same time, an isolated trait such as obesity, an aquiline nose, or long limbs, which may or may not have some background in social history, can in a variety of contexts appear as, say, a class marker. And herein lies the paradox of stereotype. The ethneme that migrates across the social boundary is perceived as a mark of difference, this being the very basis of its emergence out of the social cosmos *as* a trait; but often it crosses the social boundary *because* it is perceived as such—thus lending to stereotype, when the affirmation of difference is at stake, a self-perpetuating and self-aggrandizing force.

"All men are aggressive," says the stereotype, even though the evidence, of course, may show that some men are aggressive and some are not, or that all men are sometimes aggressive and sometimes not, or that men can be distinguished by varying degrees of aggressiveness, or even that "aggressiveness" has no meaning apart from the sexual or another competitive context. But the metonymic subtext of this stereotype is something to this effect: when men are perceived *as* men, it is in the moment of aggression, because aggression is, in one part of our cultural tradition, a sign of manhood; hence each act of aggression tends to assert or confirm manhood. Consequently the only men we perceive *as* men, and not simply as belonging to the class of men, are aggressive men—"aggression" being in this instance a mark of sexual difference, as opposed to, say, submissiveness, never perceived except with reference to the observing subject, sensitized by stereotype to male aggression. Hence "all men are aggressive"; hence, too, the tactic of "proving" one's manhood through acts of aggression.

The same process obtains in racial stereotyping, in which marks of difference, biological and cultural, become the identifying traits of the other race and, as indicators of difference, are maximized or minimized, in theory and practice, depending upon the degrees of social and psychological tension surrounding that difference.

In this paradox lies the tortured ambivalence of the stereotype, in which aggressiveness or submissiveness, or musicality or athleticism, or any other stereotyped trait, because it lies on the opposite side of a social boundary, is at once bemoaned as a lack and despised as a difference, at once wanted and wanting. That is why stereotype tends to fall on one side or the other of a moral line, to the "negative" or the "positive" side; stereotype enforces the distance between groups, either because those groups are competing in some fashion, socially, politically, or economically, or because the outsider group is sufficiently distanced socially to inspire the projected dreams and wishes or the unacknowledged horrors of the observing subject. If the ethneme records a social relation, it also changes form when social distances expand or contract through historical change, even though that change may far outstrip the capacity of the stereotype, firmly rooted in tradition, to follow it.

The metaphor of identity, which fuses signifier and signified to produce the morally charged ethneme, may produce simple tautologies or inferential errors—what Roger Abrahams calls "shallow" stereotype, which is often only a fixed, unyielding, and simplistic picture of what is in reality dynamic, supple, and complex.[10] Mayhew's pious musician, melancholy tradesman, reckless acrobats, and the like are all shallow stereotypes, which typically extend from more powerful to less powerful groups and usually in some way express the verticality of the relation.

But metaphor by its very nature produces distortions, always signaled in language by the figurative character of the expression. Kindred metaphorical distortions in stereotype, which are magnified by social tension, and the effort to express and embody them carry stereotype into the realm of representations and fictions, where, no longer limited by empirical observation across a social hiatus, it becomes a projection of purely subjective forces; that social line becomes in effect an aesthetic frame and the distance it describes an aesthetic distance insulating the observing subject from the competing group—an insulation that the observer will strive the more jealously to maintain as the competition intensifies.

Because it fixes the character of entire groups, stereotype facilitates the manipulation of social ideas in language and hence tends to flourish in speech as oral formulas; but cartoons, jokes, theatrical stock characters, and similar manifestations, because they are fictions and hence plastic, can also embody and dramatize the synthesis of idea and judgment that produces stereotype and can further promulgate it in thought and influence it in action. Nothing speaks more directly to the nature of stereotype than its curious affinity for various comic and grotesque forms, particularly masks and cartoons. In these forms, extraneous particularizing details of figure or of movement have been eliminated, while traits significant to the observer are released by the art of the mask maker, the cartoonist, or the animator from the thousand petty qualifiers of actual observation to achieve a kind of perfection of exaggeration; the identity and the movement of the caricatured figure are fantasies realized—light and airy as thought—and, as embodiments of our stereotyped conceptions, almost supernaturally fulfilling and unforgettable.

The "deep" stereotype, as Abrahams calls it, shapes itself blindly in the inarticulate darkness of our most deeply held beliefs, bringing them to light in monstrous or godlike types and antitypes. The deep stereotype demonizes or animalizes or, alternatively, glorifies or deifies its objects, assigning to them, for instance, the odor of animals or animal sexuality and strength, or perhaps godlike wisdom, goodness, purity, or power—places them, in short, above or below the plane of the human. To the extent that the subject's attention turns inward, the ethneme loses most of its empirical content and becomes simply a summons to psychic material normally tacit or repressed. With the deep stereotype we enter a realm of intellectual licentiousness entirely compatible with festivity, in which we re-create the world entirely according to the dictates of fears and desires, hatreds and loves, which, having detached them from social reality, we are at last free to affirm.

As Rayna Green's discussion of Native American stereotypes cited in Chapter 4 illustrates, the deep stereotype can descend into evil or ascend into good. The deep stereotype is the imaginative footprint of historical change: the plantation black of the minstrel show, well known to us, was an extremely ductile figure, presented in the early antebellum period as a raving dandy or rubber-limbed rube, by abolitionists in the prewar years as a paragon of Christian patience and humility, after emancipation as an animal with claws and canine teeth, and finally—once the economic and social inferiority of the African American had been reconsolidated late in the nineteenth century—as a bashful, ingratiating clown with flashing teeth and rolling eyes.[11] In all these incarnations, the African racial traits, distinguished by their difference from their European counterparts, were exaggerated to amplify the sensation of strangeness that so baffled and intrigued minstrel show audiences, so that the resultant caricature had the character of a homunculus, proportioned almost as if it were a projection of our own bodies, racially and culturally reimagined. Though deep stereotype finds expression in popular imagery and idiom and remains conventionally associated with particular groups, it is really a dream-monster, which, if it survives the encounter with the human reality it is supposed to represent, can transform the social landscape into a dark field upon which humanity enacts its nightmares.

Though inherently unstable, the structure of stereotype—two figures complete in themselves, joined by means of a shared term to form a third figure also complete in itself—is held together by powerful psychic forces, organically rooted intellectual processes on the one hand and, on the other, the instinctive antipathy toward the outsider that compels us to strive for social and cultural mastery. Like a neurosis, the stereotype arises from calculations of thought so swift that neither its origins nor the assumptions upon which it rests can penetrate without great difficulty into consciousness to reveal the illicit purposes of the observing subject. It is the deeper office of stereotype, as it is of neurosis and dream, to protect us from our own fears, or to fulfill our abiding wishes, by projecting into the phenomenal world a cast of characters in whom and in relation to whom our own drives can meet their otherwise mysterious or inaccessible objects. In order to create this structure, we must accomplish, in effect, what the folk festival accomplishes: we must extract our image of the stranger from its own matrix of society, history, and economy, with its own peculiar play of psychological and moral forces, and place it in ours; we must in effect create a social myth: a figure that embodies and dramatizes the impact of social forces upon us, in the contemplation of which we apprehend our own social values.

Stereotypes are usually not as harmless as that of the absentminded professor—certainly not for the brilliant young woman discouraged in intellectual pursuits because she is beautiful, or for the innocent young man detained by police and searched because he is black. Let's look at the "Ink Spots" again. The Festival visitor's image of the swing-era singing group is in fact an insidious coupling of two traditional black male stereotypes. First is the compliant, agreeable, obsequious Uncle Tom, the minstrel-show figure incorporated into Harriet Beecher Stowe's novel, who, it seems, appreciates white folks for having looked after him and, in many minstrel songs, longs to return after emancipation to the old plantation, to the old folks at the hearth, even to be near his old Master's grave. By accepting his subservience philosophically and, with a bluebird on his shoulder, playing the submissive role demanded of him, Uncle Tom mollifies the racist conscience and affirms the white man's confidence in his moral superiority, which is racism's justification. Hence he turns racism into benevolence. The image of the wise but ineffectual elder, moreover, with his strange predilection for children and banjos, dulls the edge of whatever threat, sexual or otherwise, so critical in the structure of white racism, the black male may pose.

But absorbed into the Tom figure, too, in the "Ink Spots" stereotype, is a 1940s variant of the dancing, singing Negro who, when he is not asleep on his mop, is at the nightclub dancing the jitterbug or playing his jazz horn, a stereotype that is itself a variant of the diffident, irresponsible Sambo of minstrelsy, the "lazy darky." This stereotype occurs within the cheerless context of Calvinist mercantile values such as thrift, punctuality, diligence, temperance, and the like, utterly contemptuous of the miserable legacies of racism, poverty, and forced, exploitative, and often brutal labor, of withheld rewards, dead-end wage slavery, and shattered self-respect, and of violent geographical, social, and cultural displacement that have shaped the African American traditions of work and play. It is ignorant, too, of the African American cultural heritage itself, which emphasizes radically different human gifts and powers, among which are rich traditions of elaborately rhythmic, participatory social music, improvisation, competitive play, and satiric impersonation. Identifying the Fairfield Four as the "Ink Spots" accomplishes many purposes at once for the Festival visitor: in the Festival context, where black culture is represented in all its immediacy and particularity against the historical backdrop of the civil rights, black power, and other assertive African American political and cultural movements of the post–World War II period, the stereotype returns the visitor instantly to the womb of complacent race relations from the 1940s, when a black man knew his place.

With other opportunities for distinction in our society having been closed off by racial discrimination, American blacks have often found in music and dance two of the few avenues open for success and the related but oft-unfulfilled promise of access to such benefits as education; for this reason, musical performance is precisely the ethneme most likely to penetrate the social barrier between white and black, because the dominant culture permits it to penetrate—or, it might be argued, *demands* that it penetrate, just as, a generation ago, black actors and musicians were required implicitly to play the minstrel offstage as well as on. In that sense, the overrepresentation of African Americans in music does not necessarily represent the musical superiority of that group, but is yet another artifact of racial discrimination. For though widely admired, the great popular musician or athlete normally remains, with some admitted exceptions, near the periphery of real power and influence.

It is patently absurd to maintain that all black people have "rhythm." But stereotype, as we've seen, dictates that all members of a particular group exhibit a trait that is in reality exhibited only by a few, or which at the very least is held in varying degrees by many individuals. That is not to say, however, that the trait, even as observed, does not *somehow* speak to the special experiences in response to which a community or a culture has fashioned its way of life. Human groups, finally, *do* of course have traits in common, by virtue of those common experiences that have inspired a generally uniform response, which is in turn communicated mimetically throughout the group or is formally instituted and transmitted, becoming a traditional and customary practice of the community. Against the background of African American cultural heritage, the Festival visitor might have surmised, had he taken a moment to explore the idea, that the "Ink Spots" are not shuffling, affable shoeshine "boys" or men's room valets who happen to sing—though this is the racial system whose historical moment the Ink Spots embody—but rather tricksters, meeting their condition with resourceful evasions and their oppressor with keen negative irony, and that the real Ink Spots, like other black musicians who have won acceptance in white popular culture, particularly in the 1940s, represent a phenomenally courageous and original adaptation of a cultural tradition to the imperatives imposed by a racist society.

The achievement of the Fairfield Four, which the visitor attempts to deflect, belongs to an area of endeavor required by the dominant society, as by any society, but which that society has for its own reasons placed in the realm of amusement, play, or recreation, refusing to grant it the importance it grants to, say, science and technology. In their musical performance, however, the Fairfield Four display precisely those aspects of their cultural endowment that most sharply differentiate them from the white European American to whom they have been invited to make that display: a certain quality of cool liquidity, of smooth, unruffled precision, of witty competence and powerful conviction, which, in the context of popular entertainment, brings home to the Anglo-American observer, perhaps, a dull, nagging, perhaps even painful self-consciousness—a conviction, whether warranted or not, of one's own woodenness and uptightness, one's utter want of spontaneity and woeful lack of conviction. Indeed, where male performers are concerned, the vague terror aroused by the black musician may lie in the deeper erotic threat suggested by his performative powers, which is often an explicit element of the black male stereotype.

Although confined to arenas of amusement and play, the stereotyped black performer exhibits—through those aspects of the African American cultural endowment that white culture has permitted or demanded—precisely those powers that, in the spectrum of human possibility, white culture will not permit itself *except* in their degraded forms as play or amusement, powers whose lack is implicitly acknowledged in the stereotype. This, then, is the agitation and confusion in which the stereotype completes itself, spreading metonymically in the mobilized imagination, along arteries of jealousy and fear toward lurid sexual and animal fantasies and other apparitions, from which we can protect ourselves only by coupling that vision to ourselves metaphorically and laughing at the clown that results: one who isn't as intelligent or as educated or as articulate as "we" are, who isn't as affluent or ambitious, as cultivated, as tastefully dressed, as dignified. . . . We are like adolescents in the throes of disappointed love, constructing a spurious counterself out of defensive rationalizations in which we only further alienate our already languishing humanity.

In its primary connection to the observing subject, the stereotype—in any case not independent and autonomous but part of a total system of classes—normally tends toward a broad social mythology, often allied to some form of popular anthropology, which seeks to locate social reality in nature, either to reinforce the prevailing structures of prestige and power or to overthrow them. The consolidation of a national consensus, as in pre–Civil War or post–World War I America or in Nazi Germany, may inspire a rhetoric of stereotype that demands the subduction, the expulsion, the destruction, or the absorption of the outsider in relation to whom the new order conceives itself. But the same process that delineates the frontier of the social order also works within the social order to cultivate a network of discrimination and differentiation.

In the nineteenth century, for instance, popular evolutionism and phrenology joined to create a psuedoscientific ethnemic system that claimed to locate human beings on the evolutionary scale on the basis of the physical conformation of their faces and heads; not surprisingly, the evolutionary scale turned out to have striking parallels to the class structure, with criminals, the insane, prostitutes, and other social outcastes at the bottom and statesmen, poets, and industrialists at the top; the physical traits of these groups, in turn, curiously resembled the racial characteristics of the oppressed Famine-Irish on the one hand, and the ruling Anglo-American oligarchy on the other. If such discriminations could be made at all on the basis of physical characteristics, it was certainly because the historical construction of the social hierarchy in relation to the movements of ethnic, racial, and national groups—as well as the consequences for physical growth and development attendant on social and economic advantage or disadvantage—had shaped a society in which physical characteristics could be impressionistically allied to social standing; in Anglo-America it continues to be true, for example, that the physical traits stereotypically associated with the British upper class, in popular representations at least, are signifiers of aristocracy. Such ethnemic systems set their various stereotypes in a bounded, hierarchical universe of status or rank, which, although it may incorporate such factors as power, wealth, and influence, or education, culture, and taste, cannot actually be assimilated to any one or more of these scales; in fact, social status in hierarchies of stereotypes, though it has a corrupt and invidious predictive power, is strictly a matter of the hierarchical arrangement that is itself the scale of status.

Social Darwinism and phrenology are no longer with us except in vestigial expressions like "highbrow" and "lowbrow." The stereotypes that nevertheless still form the building blocks of the class system are expressions of the very forces, historical, ethnic, and economic, that we must thrust aside in order to construct the system. "I am going to deal with some of the visible and audible signs of social class," announces Paul Fussell in his brilliant satire on class stereotypes, *Class*. "That means I will not be considering matters of race . . . or, religion and politics."[12] Precisely. The class system is an inventory of stereotypes drawn out of their historical and political relations—read race, religion, and politics—and set among one another in a hierarchy of status that, as it is internalized to greater or lesser degrees, tends to reproduce those hidden relations. This same system of stereotypes, detached from its objects and deployed as masks, costumes, and other signifiers of signs, can become in festivity an instrument of social inversion, demystification, or satire, as in the example of Carnival's seducing women, briefcase-carrying Arabs, and untrousered capitalists. As a system of stereotypes, class is a sheer wall of arrested time—as if we could slice through the twisted strands of history and contemplate the pattern of its many deposits in the present moment as something meaningful in itself.

We can regulate, but never legislate, the dreamwork of stereotype. Stereotype belongs to the world of appearances, and like other illusions wrought out of appearances—the idea that the sun orbits the earth, for example—it places us, as the subject, at the center of the social cosmos, secure in the capacity of our own minds to know and hence to the master the world in which fate has placed us. Indeed, it is difficult to imagine *any* representation of the human character without recourse to stereotype, in which the process of recognition seems to begin. Bound together by tropological forces, the stereotype is a primitive form of thought, the social form of the very process that originally mediates, through the genesis of gods and spirits, the primordial relations between humanity and nature, and it can no more be abolished than can lust or greed. At the same time, stereotype is a peculiar and special product of modern technological society, which brings us into daily contact with people who belong to other communities, classes, cultures, and indeed to other civilizations—a society in which the ancient concepts of the "barbarian" or "savage," or more modern biological, social, economic, or political prejudices, will no longer serve to conceive the outsider, who is ever in our midst, no longer, in fact, an outsider at all. Any campaign to "abolish" stereotype is, of course, futile. Stereotype has arisen spontaneously in response to the ever more complex social negotiations that contemporary global civilization demands, and it can only become more sophisticated as that complexity increases, as we learn to transcend its primitive form through deliberate reconstructions and even original constructions of it.

Stereotype governs, as a kind of script, the relations among the members of different social groups and among the hierarchical levels within those groups, supplying, by dint of the pressure of expectation, forms of self-presentation and conduct—a fact that is as true for young lovers as it is for Jews, blacks, Latinos, and the white middle class; even in saying so, I unwittingly summon it up. Thus traditionalized, the stereotype is diffused in the imaginative life as a complex system of codes, roles, and masks, institutionalized in particular settings to define and limit particular identities: to dictate, for example, what the student, the bohemian, the lawyer, or the wage earner will wear; what expressions he or she will use; even which attitudes he or she will adopt. Stereotype is the latent idea that tradition, custom, taste, and the like, shaped by time and experience, imperfectly and approximately manifest; it locates us with others in social reality and provides a structure for acting with reference to it. To those who don't know us, we are, even in close social interaction, simply what they are to us—a stereotype; but let the smallest intimacy pass across that social boundary, one genuine thought on a matter of mutual concern, and the stereotype swiftly and shamefacedly retires, only to reappear when an unknown other again enters our domain.

Because it is a structural element in social thought, stereotype both records what we perceive and shapes the form in which we perceive it, so that by its very nature its truth keeps coming home to us, again and again displaying itself in the human scheme and thus consistently affirming itself at the same time that we unconsciously conform to its secret influence. So thoroughly do we identify social reality with our traditional constructions of it that the rare union of the actual with the stereotypical produces a vivid sense of authenticity: The "real man" or the "real woman," the real mountaineer or real cowboy or real Caribbean marketplace, is usually the perfectly stereotypical man or woman, mountaineer, Indian, or Caribbean marketplace, just as the spurious or phony equivalents of them are simply crude, careless, or meretricious attempts to reproduce the stereotype. Because stereotype is imaginative, part of the instrumentality of our own minds, and because we recognize it as such, its appearance on the human landscape has an oddly hallucinatory, and yet oddly vivid and palpable, impact on the senses. For though it is exterior to us, an object of sensation, it seems at the same time something interior, as dear and familiar as the memory of a childhood toy. We cannot help but desire it, for in a sense it seems to have been taken from us—and that is the sensation of recovery, of authenticity. And yet, because we normally distinguish the actual from the authentic, our conviction of the actual usually arises from emendations of or departures from the stereotype—an age-old dramatic and narrative technique—whereas deliberate antistereotypes, such as the assertive woman or the weeping man, may restore a sense of the actual to a field eviscerated by stereotyping.

We live in a cultural ecosystem of stereotype and kindred forms, in relation to which we have our identity and our individuality on the one hand and our community and society on the other. Stereotype anchors us in society; by exploiting its powers, we fashion and promulgate an individual identity in relation to it. Were they not so interiorized, the cruel or the idealizing stereotypes would not be so cruel, isolating, and dehumanizing. We adopt the stereotyped traits of our profession, trade, class, or family, both to secure membership in them and to declare that we *are* members; by synecdoche and metonym we identify ourselves, and expect to be identified by others, with some facet of our being or our experience that we persistently call into the limelight of consciousness and persistently present—something we have made or done, something we possess, the work we perform or pastime we pursue. It becomes, as we say, a part of us, which we offer as a sign of the whole, projecting onto the other our own stereotype of him or her and soliciting a reciprocal judgment on the basis of it, presenting the different faces of ourselves, each with its metonymic signature, to the different faces we ourselves have fashioned for the other to present. The augustness of an institution, the dignity of a trade, the respectability of a profession, the boldness of an act, the rarity of an object in our possession, even the power of a machine under our control, the texture of the weave, the pattern on the print, the angle of a hat brim somehow magically attach to us. Seen in this light, personality is the reconciliation of our many stereotyped modes of social presentation with our inward drives; it individuates the one and socializes the other. Stereotype is a way of reading the social text; but it is a way of writing it, too.

Because it is a primitive form of thought rooted in metaphor, stereotype must, in our rational culture, retreat with other tropes into the background of tacit assumptions and unexamined hypotheses—in short, the myths— upon which all our thought is based; but it does not, and cannot, go out of existence for all that. Thrust into darkness, it will control thought in an even more covert and sinister way and will eventually spring out again in a new shape, with all the energy and power of human intelligence, which will, in the end, insist upon the evidence of its senses even as it capitulates to the rule of fear and desire. Cruel, venial, and demeaning stereotypes we must repudiate—but that is because they are cruel, venial, and demeaning, not because they are stereotypes. The moral and political projects surrounding stereotype cannot succeed by destroying stereotype, but only by reconstructing it to meet its own moral and political aims. It is, again, intimidation, racial, social, sexual, that compels a man or woman to mediate racial, sexual, or social difference by cleaving slavishly to the demanded stereotype, and intimidation that compels us habitually to conceive of one another stereotypically. For so great is the influence of mind upon mind, so compelling the mimesis between action and actor, that we are perpetually in danger of becoming our stereotypes; yet without stereotype we have no way to negotiate the difficult passage between psyche and society.

Like other projections, stereotype is the object of the soul's effort to make itself known to itself. And, like other projections, it is no mere chimera. We do not bestow our unacknowledged and unconfronted fears and desires arbitrarily, but upon those objects that have secretly touched us and aroused us by signs whose swift diffusion through our souls forecloses the painstaking interpretation that, could we perform it, would lay the map of our social being open before us. Unlike the personal projection that figures, say, in sexual love, however, the projection in stereotype ventures across a broad social frontier, across often unfathomable social and cultural differences, so that the stereotype, with all the force of an unconscious projection, nevertheless transcends the personal and is installed in popular tradition, where it is consistently amplified, elaborated, and reinforced, proving far more durable than the social differences that originally gave rise to it.

Having admitted, however, that, through a certain qualified consistency and uniformity in human nature, traits common to particular communities arise in response to common experiences, we must also admit that, however profoundly divided culturally, human communities nevertheless share a wide realm of perennial and universal experiences in which the answer of human nature, though modified superficially from place to place, culture to culture, is always the same. Moreover, the same social barrier that garbles the messages that pass from one group to another also insulates one group from another, laying open its life to the gaze of the other as a kind of fable or, more typically, as a satire or travesty of itself. We make metaphor not merely by yoking unlike things together but by detecting in their unlikeness the hidden sympathy that invited the comparison to begin with; the same metaphorical power that, in stereotype, reconciles differences through distortion has discovered in each point of difference, whether we wish to acknowledge it or not, a sign of the common humanity that dissolves all social barriers and all the stereotypes that grow upon them, at the same moment that the stereotype seems to be again affirming itself.

Though, like other kinds of artistic expression, it can be formally insulated and framed when it appears in representations, stereotype is normally part of the traffic of commonplace conceptions and ordinary life. It is nevertheless the work of what Shelley called "the great instrument of moral good," the imagination, "which has for its objects those forms which are common to universal nature."[13] Its truth, like the truth of all works of imagination, is not descriptive or scientific but formal or poetic, that is, a process of making or construction meaningful in itself. We willingly participate in its artifices, willingly follow them into what we know is an illusion, in order to grasp the truth of its dynamic form, which captures, like the two-dimensional drawing of three-dimensional space, the moment of recognition itself and objectifies the participatory element in it. That moment consequently becomes available for our contemplation as the only way we can master our fear, or satisfy our desire, of the stranger. No wonder we are so attached to our stereotypes; no wonder we are so convinced of their truth. For they *are* true—true for us, if not for the other: truths that we cannot otherwise know; truths that, moreover, we can vitally confront not in some shadowy underworld of introspection, but palpably and dramatically in the medium of a human relation.

Stereotype is a sociological concept, but we may detect its processes working in personality, too, where perhaps we must abandon the term *stereotype* altogether. The moments of cognition and figuration that form the stereotype form also, in relation to it, the many incarnations of self whose right name is perhaps "identity." From the dawn of consciousness, we discover our own traits and identify ourselves in classes with reference to others—as children with reference to parents, as boys with reference to girls or as girls to boys, as one household or family with reference to another, and so on through the ten thousand comparisons from which we gradually build a social identity out of many layers of affiliation. Growing to maturity, we consistently annex the self to images of the self constituted as other, not only in specifically mirroring and modeling activities, which include all forms of expression and relation, but in the more deliberate modes of self-representation written into memory and desire from which we transcribe the moral record of our lives.

There is no self-knowledge without other, and no knowledge of other without metaphor. The signifiers that pass from self-image to self do not, perhaps, migrate across a *social* boundary; and yet in consciousness lies a frontier between self and the consciousness of self, a boundary between life and mind along which, out of primordial human relations, the union of life-forces with the forms of imagination begins. Such unions are not always fruitful. Always we are borne back toward images that the soul has already jettisoned; always we discover what we are in the unexpected recognition of the other; always the recognition of the other reconstitutes and predicts the recognition of the self.

One wonders if stereotype does not begin at the moment a fissure opens in the total identification of infant with mother, an identification whose traces linger in all subsequent human encounters; at that moment, difference is wed to desire, and the other's identity to the life-granting sign, the original ethneme that propagates through all subsequent human identifications. If this is the beginning of knowledge, then culture begins in a metaphor whose primordial unity persists through all its differentiations in figures that record, at the point of their coupling of one idea with another, a moment in the soul's recognition of itself.

Queen of the Spelling Bee

Spellbound children watch as Buddha Chacha, the old potter with the yellow teeth, the broken, hand-rolled cigarette that is bitten by them, and the long face streaked like leather with the rains of time, turns his heavy wheel, a kind of millstone with a notch on its edge into which he inserts the end of a long stick, like a walking stick, and stirs it until the stone is spinning. A lump of red clay, inert as a hedgehog, gradually grows erect, stands up like a flower, and, as the old man's fingers undulate around it like strands of seaweed, blooms and seems to burst and is suddenly transformed into a womanly containing vessel capable of breath and speech. With a length of wire, the old man sweeps it up, rescues it from its trance, and lays it aside with the others like something transmitted from the world of spirit to the world of flesh. I can't divide the pot from the potter's hands—it *is* the caress that brought it into life and can never be merely an object. The action of his hand and the shape of the pot are one and the same; each shares in the same beauty. Continually and perpetually, the pot re-creates the caress that made it, and in perceiving it we feel ourselves caressed, so that the pot possesses—it loves—us.

Their bodies smeared with mud, the age-old gesture of mortification, and wearing black masks ringed with fur, the bahrupiyas, with monkey chatter and gestures, their tails erect behind them and curling up behind their heads, squat in the branches of a small tree and glare at passersby. One leaps down and places his fingers in a child's hair, grooming her as monkeys do, while on the other side of the Melā fence, along the path that passes in front of the Smithsonian Castle, marches the New Orleans Jazz Band, led by two black minstrel men with parasols and followed by a hundred people.

Nearby, with slow, deliberate movements, two craftsmen are making a clay effigy of Durga, the mother-goddess who destroys evil, spreading the clay with clay-reddened fingers over a structure of reeds and straw. She is no mere scarecrow to be dressed in finery, but fully a woman, with great round breasts and hips, over which the hands of the sculptors pass with religious sobriety.

They sing together in rhymed couplets, like a giant rap group, in call-and-response style, with a clattering of tom-tom and bongo rhythms. The prodigious plumage of their costumes, spreading out around each man in fountains of red and white, glistening with gemlike points of light, becomes a dancing wall of feathers through which faces and arms seem to be trying to break through.

These costumes require weeks, or months, to create. The sewing seems to be a kind of ordeal—so tedious, so painstaking, so time-consuming that it can "give you a nervous breakdown," says Charles "Chief" Taylor, chief of the White Cloud Indians, a Mardi Gras Indian "tribe." With him is Keith "Spyboy" Barnes, Tony "Lil' Chief" Guy, George "Flagboy" Harden, and Lionel "Uncle Bird" Oubichon. Each costume is a concentration of pearls, sequins, beads, feathers, and stones of different shapes unique to each man, and each can weigh as much as fifty pounds, so that one has to keep moving to bear it. "With my type of sewing," Charles adds, "there's no sitting down." Allison Kaslow, presenter of the Mardi Gras Indians, locates the tradition in the Brazilian Carnival where, as in New Orleans, the several "tribes" compete with one another for a trophy. She compares them to the "Zulus," the Zulu Social Aid and Pleasure Club, whose

African-caricature costumes have been a familiar sight in the Mardi Gras parade since their founding in New Orleans 1917.

But what *are* the Mardi Gras Indians?

"Renegades," Charles says gravely, men who do not belong to a tribe, "make confusion. They may end up in the hospital. Or dead."

Glenn Hinson, folklorist, opens the ballad workshop like a circus barker, calling to the strollers outside the canopy to join us for the ballad singing. The amiable banjo-player and singer Frank Proffitt, Jr., a young man of about thirty, remembers when the Kingston Trio recorded his father's version of "Tom Dooley." "Folks got interested in the old mountain culture," he recalls. "We were under assault from the modern world"—rock-and-roll, country music, and gadgets. "Gadgets, everywhere."

"I was so proud of my Dad," says Frank, "I wanted to carry on with it."

But just as he begins to sing "Tom Dooley," a sudden thunderstorm overtakes the Mall, its successive sheets of rain flinging themselves across the vast, steaming lawns. To prevent electrical shock, the sound system is abruptly shut down. Rain drums on the canvas canopy and airplanes fill the sky with their engines' roar; trucks, buses, and honking taxis on Jefferson Avenue, not a hundred feet from the Festival site, all conspire to drown him out. And so, while the canvas curtains are lowered around the edges of the tent, we rise from our benches and huddle close to Frank near the small stage; his voice expands to fill the shelter of silence our intimacy creates, where appear to our minds, ghostly, the murdered girl, Laura Foster, the repentant Tom Dooley in his cell, and the lonesome valley where he visions himself hung from a white oak tree.

On they come, the Fairfield Four, though there are five of them, the gospel quintet from Nashville. Slim, gray-haired Rev. W. Lawrence Richardson, bending toward us with his arm extended and fist closed, throttles us with a preaching song—"Dig, dig, dig a little deeper, in the storehouse of God's love"—shaking his head as if in memory of some awful personal transgression, grimacing like one in pain, glaring at us like an outraged father, but inwardly ebullient with the happiness that is, in music, fully formed. The others, with voices and hands, have created a city of sound, traversed by many thoroughfares of rhythm and melody, set by rotund harmonic architecture and brilliant streaks of voices that are reedy, gravel-strewn like a road, and deep like a well. With his mouth set out before him like the horn of a trumpet, rocking gently from one foot to the other, bringing his hands together like two great wings, bass singer Isaac Freeman stoutly institutionalizes each phrase in the deep archive of his chest. Is this a legacy of West African culture: this special capacity for speech and sound, for communication and voice, perhaps from unremembered times when these were the instruments of civilization, of memory, of counsel and decree, alarm and call, ceremony and celebration?

"All manifestation arises from sound."

In the years that the Festival has been operating, sound technicians have mastered the precise equilibrium of spatial and audial extension that makes the otherwise static emptiness of the Festival space, "filled" with exhibits, into a living body of discriminate but not discrete organs, which meet one another at invisible frontiers that subdivide the Festival space like the cells of a beehive. The dark batteries of speakers, the elaborate consoles, the heavy cables crawling over the ground create a vibrating, variegated atmosphere of aural fields, pools, and fountainheads of sound that are the real, albeit the invisible, architecture of the Festival. When the sound is up, the Festival is up; when the sound is down, the Festival is down; the platforms upon which the sound technicians at their tables sit before their panels of needles and dials, with tape reels turning, are the cockpits of the Festival juggernaut.

This is most apparent at the instant each day when the Festival opens, when, upon several stages poised for the beginning of the day's performances, music suddenly swells and fills the air—but it does not launch itself upon the breeze and flow desultorily along transient channels around the atmosphere of the Mall. It expands like a balloon to its limit, at which point it meets the gentle pressure of sound emanating from other sources, and their precisely equalized mutual force brings them both to a stand, so that each swelling, each bubble of sound is curbed and held steady in the total synthesis of sound in each area. One can stand at a certain spot between stages and—by moving slightly to the left or the right, forward or back—cross the boundary between one and the other: to the left, hear the zydeco band; to the right, hear conversation about the blues, punctuated with a blues song—or hear them both, though they don't interfere with one another.

There is no silence. The sound system at each of the stages is adjusted to its size and its spatial orientation, so that the groups that gather at each one, ranging from mere handfuls of people to small crowds, are in effect held in an audial force field that does not extend far enough beyond the actual boundaries of the overhead canopy to stop passersby and create a fringe of standees; one must actually enter the arena, which is not unlike a small livestock auction barn, in order to participate fully in the music. These same virtual boundaries act upon the small audiences under the canopy, too, insulating them from the activity outside, which is at their backs, and drawing them together into the resultant intimacy that seems to invite and perhaps to stimulate encounter and communication. One responds not only to the music but to the responses of others to it; in one's own response there may be a kind of half-conscious amplification—the clapping of hands, say, or snapping of fingers—which is nothing more than a way of winning membership in the temporary society formed by the spell of music and voice. A similar phenomenon occurs in the foodways demonstrations, slightly smaller in scale, in which a cook prepares a meal in full view of a tiny audience with whom she engages, through a lavaliere mike, in an ongoing, intimate conversation. Audially, then, the Festival actually occurs indoors, in a kind of laboratory whose walls are formed of the meeting in air of expansive surfaces of sound.

Spatially, the ground plan of the Festival reflects its larger intellectual order and organization—its theme and major divisions, its specific parts; audially, its rooms of sound body forth its deeper imaginative life, beckoning the visitor over scarcely measurable barriers from one experience to the next, in effect incorporating her into its imaginative system, wherein each musical form signifies and suffuses the cultural atmosphere around it.

The new Mardi Gras float arrives with a gigantic effigy of the Virgin Mary on its prow, her arms raised in the gesture of blessing as tourists and Festival visitors pass under them. Near it, under the float maker's tent, lies a head of Abraham Lincoln, staring sadly over the grotesque face of a monkey's decapitated head lying beside it toward the faces of demons hanging from racks on the canvas wall opposite. All icons and symbols, it seems, fall within the float maker's purview; her art turns on the typicality of the image and her ability to occlude the particularity of its embodiment—for the more particular the image, the closer it moves toward symbol or icon itself. The relative crudity of the medium requires her to mime with the signs that make up the image—the beard, the stovepipe hat, the mole—and not with representations. What she makes, then, is an effigy: a sign of a sign.

In the Cultural Conservation section, two of the exhibits fulfill Marjorie

Hunt's expectations wonderfully. The cornrowing parlor has become what Festival producers dream of—a genuine living place where people, children especially, linger and look on, ask questions, and engage in conversation with the hairdressers, while girls and young women, black and white, submit their hair to braiding with tender and trusting docility. I sit on the edge of the platform for a full half hour, with a sense of relief. At Duff Severe's shop, Trowbridge, Mitchell, and Ohrlin, the cowboys, linger and talk just as Margie intended, although the success of the shop in that respect seems to have had a chilling effect on visitors, who may feel as if they are intruding. But the Puerto Rican mask maker's booth and the Makah woodcarvers' are simply too spare: what is occurring there is, simply, men working—one doesn't want to disturb them. At the Makah woodcarvers' tent, I watch at a distance as Greg Colfax brings the image of a raven, its body embossed with larval shapes that mimic its enclosing form, out of a pine board.

The Kmhmu stage, alas, has become what Charlie feared it would, a living diorama; communication between the participants and visitors is difficult, even painful, and in fact, except for the old toymaker, the participants tend to ignore visitors as, it seems, a matter of propriety, with a kind of modesty. To approach the Kmhmu as closely as the Festival setting permits is profoundly disquieting. They are, after all, an Asian mountain tribe catastrophically dislocated by a bizarre war, culturally and physically enigmatic. Only children, unburdened by Oriental stereotypes and undaunted by language barriers, make communication with them; even Bess Hawes, whose interest in the Kmhmu is largely responsible for their presence, is visibly uncomfortable at the special flower ceremony prepared for her and other dignitaries.

A hierarchy of vertical arrangements—physical structures that shape the space around the meetings of participants with visitors—control our personal encounters. The rule of thumb is a simple one: the higher off the ground you are, the more passive is your audience. Even if you are a basketmaker, sitting on a wooden platform six inches high, and hence actually well below the visitor who must bend down to talk to you, the platform has something of a chilling effect on conversation; it insulates her from you, so that she can inspect your work closely, far more closely than ordinary social distance would allow, without offense, while you can continue with it in silence without giving insult. Some craftspeople sit at tables or simply upon freestanding chairs at their work; in such situations, conversation with visitors is almost inevitable, and typically children, who in a general way do not observe the etiquette of verticality, will gather around. This arrangement holds even when, as in the case of the iron-workers or the cowboys, a wide interval separates the participants from the visitors; if visitor and participant stand on the same ground, they are invited and even compelled to communicate—even if it means shouting or calling. Musicians, on the other hand, who perform from a conventional stage, have a kind of celebrity status, and when they are not performing they can be seen in small groups somehow set apart from both participants and visitors. To open conversation with a musician, even offstage, seems somehow brazen or foolhardy.

Other sensations, too, shape the Festival space. The aromas of food surround the foodways exhibits and the concession stands; the bold colors of a quilt or a tapestry may attract attention to a crafts exhibit from a great distance, as will the ringing of a smith's hammer or the scraping of a boatmaker's drawknife. At regular intervals of three minutes or less, the entire Mall is filled with the roar of a jet taking off from National Airport on an inclined path that takes it over the Monument; its volume is so great that all Festival sounds are absorbed momentarily into it. The noises of trucks and buses on the streets, or a police siren, occasionally swim in from a vague perimeter with their disquieting message. Even as the persistent world outside reminds us of the Festival's own transience, the Festival atmosphere spills out onto the streets and catches the traffic, the pedestrians, and the museums, like an old movie travelogue, in a distant dream.

At the same time, the Festival permits egress, actually and imaginatively, from its own space into other spaces. Behind the discussants in the workshop stages, wide photographic panels carry us to a Louisiana bayou or into a vegetable garden; other photographs may take us into the Guatemalan jungle or into the mountains of Laos. Music of all kinds leads us into many imaginary regions and human situations. Crossing the Mall from one area into another, we become conscious that we are, after all, in Washington, where, on the Mall at least, there are no natives; the Mall makes visitors and patriots of us all, and in passing over it one experiences the self-consciousness of exposure to the view of the great princes, the Capitol and the Monument, whose silent protocol one must observe in every step.

With its striped canopies and broad tents, the Festival, which momentarily we see as outsiders, has the courage and courtesy of a medieval tournament. It is a great national spectacle, a fair of the only kind that could take place on the Mall—a people's fair, unconnected to commerce and in some ways inimical to it, not political and yet rife with political implication, a national treasury and yet as homely as a kitchen garden, bringing to the Mall the life so conspicuously absent from all the world's parks and gardens that are tributes to empires and kings. Thus the Festival may have a curious effect on a Washington tourist, who has perhaps had her fill of hotel rooms and historical tours: it may make her want to go home.

As small and fine-boned as birds, their castoff Western shirts and trousers, blouses and skirts rudely tied and wrapped about the delicate framework of their shoulders and hips, their incomprehensible faces lit from within by a pale flamelike light, five people—one a woman no larger than a child, whose face seems about to break into a shriek, another an old fellow with tiny wire-rimmed spectacles and long thin whiskers hanging from his cheeks and chin, another a slim young man with wavy black hair and a blue shirt—climb hesitantly onto the stage, looking about them, occasionally smiling and nodding. With them is another young man with a well-trimmed moustache and an anxious expression, with gleaming black hair and delicate hands and skin: he is Frank Proschan, a folklorist; the small people are Kmhmu—a mountain tribe from Laos expelled from their homeland by communist insurgents after the American withdrawal from Southeast Asia, seeking now a new life in Stockton, California, where Proschan has taken up residence in order to help make comprehensible to them the strange and ubiquitous automation, the dreamlike bounty, the shocking personal ostentation and license of their new country, as well as the invisible legion of microbiological agents that have visited and revisited them with innumerable vague illnesses since they arrived.

They look at one another once on stage. Suddenly the secret to survival in a strange land has become simply to be what you are: to show them your dances, which you scarcely remember, the sword dance that grandfather used to do when he was drunk; to sing the few songs you can remember from the old days; to dance and sing for them—for otherwise they may enslave or murder you. Their voices depart their throats like a flock of hummingbirds, sweeping upward, falling with wounded flutterings, momentarily settling into a dense tangle of snapping, clattering, and clicking consonants. We are as barbarians to them, thick, white, outsized, and uncomprehending—their destroyers, puzzled by these fragments of a culture made of glass. Pipes made from lengths of bamboo lashed together make the songs of herons and cranes in a scale fringed with faint green familiar hills. Two of the men, the younger and the older, greet one another, smiling, in the circuitous sword dance to cymbal and gong, feinting and tempting each other, stepping, turning, and gesturing in a gathering of invisible intersecting circles above, below, beside, and around them, on whose circumference swords flash like an orbiter in sunshine.

There can be no more Laos for them. The Kmhmu must find the Laotian highlands in the recesses of the American psyche and draw it out with the invocatory songs and dances, with the very image of their faces and their persons, the sounds of their voices, the taste of their food, or with some particular craft that will find its way onto the backs of fashionable ladies, as the Hmong embroidery of Cambodia has done. And, in time, American life will send out its tributaries to embrace them—soon the young man, Khampheang Khoonsrivong, will be found at the K-Mart, in his vinyl jacket, buying a cassette to play on his new boombox.

Later, the young man describes the place of the Jew's harp in his culture. It is used in courtship—it speaks gently so that the young lady will come closer. The harps used to be made by hammering out the old French coins still circulating in Laos. One does not, in Laos, propose directly; one proposes by indirection, either through a gift to the girl's father or to the girl in a special language of figures. A tattoo that a young man wears signifies that a girl has loved him; a man without tattoos believes he will become a worm when he dies. It falls to the parents to select a spouse, but children try to give some indication of their preference, or they may ask outright for a particular person. In America, says Khampheang, he feels ill at ease—how can he choose a wife on his own?

Everyone seems urgently to want to involve themselves somehow in the lives of the participants. Volunteers and presenters indulge in highly conspicuous shows of affection, hoping for its return, in circumstances in which such demonstrations seem to be appropriate—at the end of a performance, for example, when the singers or musicians are coming off the stage. These impulses go to the very heart of relations among cultures and to one of the central paradoxes of folklife: that the host culture, in relation to the enclaved folk group, is always an outsider; and that in thrusting a folk society to the margins, the host culture at the same time closes off its own access to that society.

This sense of exclusion, which is especially keen when the folk group comes under the gaze of the tourist in settings such as the Festival which make of that culture a kind of romance, with all the attractions of romance, accounts for some of the most powerful emotions that arise in response to displays and performances of folklife. We may love them, exactly in the way we love the image on the opposite shore—because she is a world, a world that beckons us in large part because she is so difficult of access, even though, in a deep, unconscious way, she is really a thing of our own making. We want to be like these performers, to win their approval and acceptance, to show them we approve of and love them, at the same time that we create them out of the excommunicated life of our own hearts. Seen from without, the life of the folk group may appear as an idyll of happiness from which our exclusion only throws our own loneliness, dejection, and failure into higher relief.

A woman with a conjuring face and tripping step has caught my fancy—one of the chief volunteers, daughter of a State Department bureaucrat, who, when she is not carrying things for the Kmhmu people or issuing assignments to the other volunteers or filling the water kegs, lingers about the door of the trailer where I keep my extra shirt and my bottle of ink and my sunglasses and my extra rolls of film, observing the festivities from that beseeching faraway place in which she lives.

She is young, with fine light hair under a headband; her face looks sorrowful and scholarly behind her plain glasses and conceals a mystery and a familiarity. Have I met her somewhere before? Yes, of course I have met her before, in my dreams, in the secret meetings of my guilts and my desires in the inaccessible places of my heart. Or does she remind me of someone? Of an old lover, perhaps, with the same name, to whom she bears an appalling resemblance, or perhaps that sweetheart of long ago, ten lives past, in the schoolroom—Susan Sailors of the golden tresses, undefeated queen of the spelling bee, budding into the April of her life?

Ineluctably in a matter of days, quite in spite of myself, I find the Festival topography shifting about, new pathways unfolding, new missions formed out of my cunning, paths that seem to lead toward her, or in her vicinity—work to be done, or conversations with people primarily or secondarily related to her, the closing circle that, deep in my intentions, spirals down to the fated moment of an accidental encounter. She does not see me, of course, and for comfort I inscribe her name in my notebook again and again. I am as an invisibility; and furthermore, the idea is absurd.

And yet such things have been.

The infatuation inspires me, and I carry its energy to the blues dance party, where Boogie Bill Webb has all of us rocking and reeling at a high sexual pitch. I imagine, mistakenly, that I am a tolerable dancer to the blues, and when the hour arrives at which, as a part of my duties, I must wrestle a beer keg out of a refrigerator truck, into a van, out of a van, up a flight of stairs, and into the dormitory common room, I undertake the task bravely, already slightly intoxicated from one or two cans supplied by friends at the dance party, with a heady recklessness that allows me to lift, to roll, and in general to manhandle a weight that, were I sober, would simply crush me.

When I finally enter the cafeteria, about eight, I am tuckered out. As I walk into the lobby the Rev. Burnell Offlee, lead singer for the Zion Travellers, is holding forth for the benefit of seven or ten black men and women, participants or their spouses, who have gathered on two benches to hear his discourse on the expulsion from Eden. I can't make out precisely what he is saying, but he is saying it passionately, after the manner of the African American preacher, and it has to do with those two pioneers of all our woe, Adam and Eve.

By the time I have emerged with my tray into the dining room, I find only a few stragglers left. Two Finnish couples, members of the Oulu Hotshots, a polka band from northern Wisconsin, whom I met earlier on the shuttle bus, beckon to me. As I eat, they describe their community to me and the rugged history of their grandparents—of a man who lived alone for two years in order to clear the land, who built a two-story house out of hand-hewn, twelve-inch virgin pine logs for his huge family of twelve or thirteen children. Even the Kangases—Kangas is their name—express amazement. How did those old pioneers do it? Even more, *why* did they?

Nearby, the long-haired Baul singers are beating out intricate rhythms on the table while one plays an eerie flute, sending its long sinuous tone into the air like a pheromone.

"Down day." Everyone rushes to the coin laundries. Many go on tours to the zoo and to the White House or the Washington Monument. Everyone is hoarse. The hospitality staff have taken to wearing saris—people seem to be blending into one another. The bahrupiyas, in costume, walk across the Key Bridge and take the Metro into the city, carrying their fare cards. In the late afternoon, James, the Houserockers' guitarist, returns to the room, where I'm sitting with a jar of iced tea and my notebook. With him is a statuesque black woman whom he has met down on Twelfth Street. She seems very interested in what I'm doing; I tell her. Her skirt is a brilliant kelly green.

Kartika Nandi Das, one of the Bauls, wanders through the dining room that evening, holding his new cassette recorder to his ear. Karen Brown has taken the Bauls and a handful of others to the K-Mart this afternoon. Kartika, enjoying his paycheck in the American way, has returned with a tape player, which he carries with him wherever he goes, listening to recordings of his own voice.

Talk, talk, talk—everybody's talking! It is only a matter of a few days before virtually all the participants have become hoarse or nearly hoarse, whatever his or her role in the Festival. Many participants have been talking all day to Festival visitors, explaining their craft or art; many have been performing according to a rigorous daily schedule.

But narration has a special role here, which is to fabricate, for presentation to others, the history of oneself; and this narration occurs in special circumstances wherein each one is a stranger to the other, presented only in visible form, usually in codes that have no meaning to the others except that they *are* another's and not one's own, so that the narration of oneself is also perforce the interpretation, discovery, and invention of oneself. In many instances, we must fashion in narrative not only ourselves but our auditors, too, and in turn must permit ourselves to be shaped by the narrations made to us. Every turn in a narrative offered to a stranger seeks the common term between us; and where wide cultural gulfs divide us, we are compelled, in narrative, to speak of ourselves as we suppose the other would speak of us.

From one musician I heard, for example, the entire saga of his life to the present moment—an odyssey of crosscountry motorcycle trips, communes, various bands, girlfriends, drug and alcohol experiences; from others, like the Finnish dance band, I heard not the story of their own lives but of the lives of their grandparents, pioneers who settled in the wilderness and endured its hardships. Both these narratives reflected, I believe, the narrators' sense of what I might approve, based on the stereotype by which each conceived me.

Only James Baker, the guitarist for Hezakiah's band, makes no allowances for my difference but speaks to me always in his own idiom and accent, so that I am very hard put to understand him, even though he has accepted me as one of his own. I can only nod enthusiastically when he takes me into his confidence concerning the matter of—though I did not catch all the details—a certain way of tuning the guitar with which he promises to make his fortune, a tuning, of which he is at present the sole possessor, bequeathed to him by a local elder now passed on.

At the same time, the ubiquity of narrative at the Festival seems to suggest, too, some propinquity for narrative among the participants themselves. This I have observed in other folk communities; as one participant put it, "We are very talkable people." Hezakiah, my roommate, a drummer from Louisiana, narrates his life constantly, almost as it happens; he almost never describes himself with any degree of abstraction, but rather tells the story of what occurred an hour ago, or yesterday, or five years ago, usually with much interpolated dialogue, actual or imagined, whose principal aim, like that of narrative itself, is self-characterization, and beyond that, self-dramatization and, still further, self-realization. He is even more voluble with the other members of his band, and they are more voluble than he, when they talk among themselves. Because I can't understand their Delta dialect, I am more conscious of the quality of play in their speech, how fully it is undertaken for its own sake. All three talk simultaneously at top volume, repeating the same phrase or notion again and again, boasting shamelessly, blaming fearlessly, raising and lowering the pitch of their voices with a melodiousness that makes nonsense of any distinction between speech and song.

Later Hezakiah apologizes to me—all this transpires at six in the morning, or earlier, when I'm still in bed—for their "arguin'": but I have heard nothing of what I would call argument. I have heard what sounds to me like an improvised chorus of words, a verbal rideout, by three virtuosos who live in and through—who *are*—language.

The magician accompanies his performance with a constant chant, at the top of his lungs, voiced in upward cadences and shouts. Out of his mouth he unpacks marbles, ball bearings, and long sharp pins made of bone; he transforms coins, held in the palms of giggling children or wary men, into rocks, which, after having stowed them in a young woman's sweater, he transforms back into coins. He moves a five-dollar bill from one black bag, like a thief's bag, to another across the ring of people around him, and with a series of subterfuges he tricks a black hipster, whom he has been holding captive by keeping his cigarette lighter, into symbolically laying a missing chicken's egg into a sack. He prays for rain, and an empty clay pot standing alone in the dust at the center of the ring fills with water.

The young acrobats, a girl and a boy, are crossing a tightrope strung across the Melā entrance like a clothesline. Near them, the juggler is swallowing a sword, his head thrown back in a kind of agony, as if the sword had impaled him. Then the group joins together to put on a puppet show. Standing on the edge of the sizable crowd that has gathered around the spot is the famous folklorist Alan Lomax, who with his father toured the South in the 1930s with a disc recorder built into the back of a sedan, gathering the field hollers, prison songs, blues shouts, ballads, and string-band tunes that would become the motherlode of the Archive of Folksong at the Library of Congress. Smiling with delight, Lomax is holding over the heads of the people in front of him a tiny portable tape recorder with its built-in microphone.

From within the Melā, where wooden pavilions with tile roofs are arranged in a fashion that simulates a rural Indian village, one cannot see the Mall; a canvas wall, well above eye-level, surrounds the entire site. The Melā exhibits are organized loosely around the five senses, each one centered in a particular area of the site; while each pavilion engages in the trade that would be typical of an Indian street fair, many of the performers, magicians, jugglers, acrobats, actors, and musicians open their performances with apparent spontaneity in the midst of things, drawing an audience to them.

The Melā is a realm set apart—it is as if vast numbers of Americans had suddenly been transported to an Indian village, where the dust billows up from the ground and deposits itself between your teeth, in your throat, and over the top of your head. Its internal time is leisurely and irregular, its space dynamic and plastic. It does not take its form from the sweeping lines, the elegant angles, the heroic vanishing points, the austere silence, of Enlightenment ideas. The acrobats and the juggler, like the magician, accompany their performances with constant chants and shouts as well as an audible patter among themselves; a small boy sings and plays castanets as his sisters pass back and forth across the highwire. But the Melā is becoming intolerable to me—why do I so urgently want to get out?

At a workshop, Kiowa Indian Gus Palme from Carnegie, Oklahoma, explains that, because whites believed it would lead to an uprising, the Sun Dance was broken up in the 1830s, when the federal army came in. This, he says, was a kind of deicide, because the sacred circle, with the Sun Dance at its center, was the life-force of the tribe; all the tribes and families gathered within the circle at a certain season of the year. Now a cultural revival is going on, he reassures us, that emphasizes the lore of the elders, in whom all cultural knowledge resides.

Joan Madden, the Irish flautist, is apprenticed to the nervous, red-faced, chain-smoking Jack Coen, with the shock of white hair, who is seated next to her. She recalls hearing the music as a baby in her family's house; when she apprenticed to Jack, all the tunes were "in the back of my mind," and came right out the first time she heard them.

"Americanization," says Mick Maloney, picking up the theme, "has in the third generation never really occurred—the old culture is stronger than ever." Irish music, he observes, is very important in maintaining Irish identity—a fact that has been true since Queen Elizabeth I or earlier; the music has always symbolized freedom from colonial rule. Even the commercial Irish-American songs from Tin Pan Alley or vaudeville, such as "I'll Take You Home Again, Kathleen," have become the focus of Irish identity, as most Irish Americans *believed* the songs had come from the homeland.

The Cajuns, by contrast, had no contact with their home country: in their case, says Dewey Balfa, isolation preserved a culture in which over two million people still speak French. Huey Long provided access to public education and initiated the assimilation of the Cajuns, who were prevented from speaking French in school. Many tried to lose their accent; the "chanky-chank" music fell into disrepute in favor of Western swing and honky-tonk singers like Hank Williams, who permanently changed Cajun music. Now, though, there is a Cajun revival—even teenagers want to be identified as Cajuns.

"The folk festivals have done so much for the ethnic people," says Dewey.

"I'm very impressed, inspired, and gratified" by the example of the Cajuns, says Roberto Martinez of Albuquerque, New Mexico. Chicanos, he continues, also tried to shed their ethnic identity, to deny what they were—"I myself tried to get rid of my accent." For a time, his people were actually prohibited from speaking Spanish in school and were punished if they did. In Wyoming all the other kids had sandwiches for lunch—but they had only burritos. Charles Boyer, the movie star, was a hero to them because he spoke with an accent. In Los Angeles, though, Martinez saw burritos being sold by a street vendor, and he began to feel better—after all, all the Californians sunbathing on the beach were trying to get the color which was his naturally!

Khampheang Khoonsrivong, now of Stockton, California, was pursued by the communists for ten years before he finally escaped to Thailand. In 1980 he came to the United States and began to discover, in the Kmhmu community in Stockton, the old culture; it was in Stockton, in fact, that he first heard the bamboo flute.

Duncan's hat is made from palm fronds from the Guatemalan seacoast, stripped and braided into tiny coils that are then sewn together and molded on a hand-driven machine. The hat comes from Santa Cruz in the Quiché region of Guatemala, from the one hatseller in the marketplace who specializes in the slightly larger sizes required by the occasional gringo buyer. The energy concentrated in Duncan's hat is that of the many hands of the many men and women who labored to make it. Gathered together in the marketplace at Santa Cruz by the seven or so hatsellers lies the work of the fifty or sixty hatmakers in the region, men who work at treadle sewing machines and who gather their palm-frond coils from the hundreds of women in the countryside who weave them.

"My culture," says one of these women—though she may have said, in her Quiché dialect of Spanish, "my art" or "my work," which Duncan, who acts as her interpreter, has translated to "my culture"—"my culture is all made by hand . . . and the colors will not wash out."

The colors she refers to—an intense royal blue, a soft lavender, bright tomato red, a yellow as broad as a traffic signal, orange, white, midnight black—all dart across her bodice and over the shoulders of her woven shirt in an infinitesimal calculus of shocking contrasts. She has built the garment out of lateral bands, each of which carries a particular pattern of diamonds, triangles, and sawtooth lines in a series of orderly redundancies. Lying across her breast is the broadest and most ingenious of these bands, boldly bordered in black, in which a commanding strip of interwoven red and blue thread zigzags across a yellow field set with scarablike emblems of orange and black embroidery.

"My work is to weave," Josefina continues, and she names some of the many articles she produces: skirts and aprons, ponchos, blankets and belts. "I always wash my threads before I weave them," Duncan repeats in English after her, "so that the color won't come out. Not everyone takes this precaution. I do it because I don't want anyone to disapprove of me. I am very happy to be able to show you the work I do."

Josefina's blouse—her name is Josefina Díaz Gomez, and she is a Quiché Indian—is a concentration of geometry and color so intense that all the visible world beyond it, natural and artificial, becomes pale and slovenly by comparison. It is an island of intelligibility, whose degree and density of organization seems to exhibit the structure of human intelligence itself, as if the actual design of our neural network had been projected into it, charged with a spectrum of unblinking discontinuities that seem to lull nature's gradual organic forms to sleep. Yet intelligence has many modes. Unlike the ecstatic mode of her shirt, Josefina's ankle-length skirt is a somber navy blue, written around in ghostly glyphs of white thread, which, like the impressions in a cuneiform tablet, seem to contain some obscure historical narrative or record of commercial transactions, though the characters themselves float in their dark medium as if a laser beam had etched them onto a steel plate.

Josefina is a modest, matronly young woman who has come from the rural highlands of Guatemala with her husband and three young children. Before answering the first of Duncan's questions, she offers a warm good day to everyone, salutes all of our faces—that's how she says it, our "faces"—and gives thanks to God that she is able to join us. In her bright woven costume, though, she seems a kind of royal figure, or even a sacred one—a goddess, whose costume has been bestowed like some impersonal thing upon her, like the robe of a queen that belongs at once to a community, to a tradition, and to its own antiquity. Her weaving dignifies her and, like a wreath of flowers or a bridal gown, celebrates her, expanding her personal presence not toward a social class, if indeed she can be said to belong to such a class, but into a people, their past, and their situation in the universe. The designs she wears are, in fact, both ancient and universal, dating, some of them, from the time of the Conquest. But they are her own as well. "I wear the patterns my mother taught me," she says, "which were the ones her mother taught her. I keep them all in my head, and combine them to make many different designs."

Smiling demurely in a consciousness of the attention being paid to her clothing and of the photographs being snapped of her, Josefina sits with hands quietly folded in her lap while Duncan explains that the patterns of traditional Mayan weaving have not only an obvious beauty but a particular cultural significance. Each variation signifies a particular village, a family, and the individual identity of the weaver—a fact that in recent years has proved to be an unanticipated source of dread, because the Guatemalan army, intent on quashing subversive activity in the countryside, has studied the traditional patterns in order to use them for political identification. A photograph enlarged on a panel nearby shows a group of young men in uniform poring over colorful blankets and cloaks with the inquisitiveness of ethnographers. One response of the women to this situation, Duncan observes, has been to abandon the costumes of their native villages in favor of those belonging to villages that the soldiers have so far left alone. It is the same with the young men, too, Duncan continues, briefly summarizing to Josefina in Spanish all that he has been saying, who nowadays wear cowboy hats and Levis, like their Mexican neighbors. "The young people want to abandon the old ways," Josefina adds; "they are even giving up the old language."

Since the time of the Conquest, Duncan explains, it has been the traditional role of Mayan men to mediate with the outside world: to pay its tithes, to engage in trade, to adopt its costume. So the cowboy hats are not surprising; in a sense they are quite "traditional." But until now the traditional costume—traditional, at least, since the 1940s, when the color-ful dictator Ubico and his retinue paraded through the streets in white zoot suits and panama hats—the formal costume a man might wear to a wedding, has been essentially a European dress suit: double-breasted jacket, white shirt and hat, and leather shoes, in the Italian style. This suit the man would weave himself, not on the backstrap loom the women use but on a standing loom, a sort of frame on table legs, that had been warped by his wife and children.

This is not to say that his formal attire was wholly European, or "Alle-mande" as he would probably say—a word that must have come, Duncan speculates, from "Allemagne," for the Germans who settled on plantations in the nineteenth century. He would cut out the toes of his shoes, which he wore, like sandals, without socks, and tie his trousers with a red belt his wife had woven for him. He might also wrap about his waist a brocaded apron in fifty or sixty colors, this apron being a lineal descendant of the kilts Mayan men wore in antiquity.

Now, though, Duncan concludes, the people are not anxious to call attention to themselves; there has been too much violence directed against them. "There are many indigenous people in Guatemala," Josefina re-minds us—but what Quiché word has become Duncan's phrase, "indige-nous people"?—"many people have lost their lives."

A young woman in the audience suddenly and unexpectedly stands to introduce herself as a Mayan refugee who has come all the way from Florida because she heard the Mayans were here. What is Duncan's role here? she asks of him, in a voice touched with sorrow and reproach. In measured, conciliatory tones, caressing the long fringes of his poncho with his fingers, Duncan observes that white Anglos like himself are capable of feeling the influence of native cultures. His own relationship to the

Quiché, he recalls, began in childhood, in the long summer excursions by car that he used to take with his parents deep into Central America. He remembers the bedroom curtains his mother had made for him out of a Guatemalan weaving—not unlike the poncho he is wearing now. When his mother died, these holidays ended—but, of course, his love of the Quiché has endured.

The Bauls are a sect from Bengal whose name means "madness." They are descended from Buddhists, and their faith is in personal salvation through yoga. Their ways—the long, flowing hair, for instance—are contrary to established norms and practices. "Oh mother," sings one in a long melismatic chant, accompanying himself on a tiny drum, "will I ever see you again? I was born out of your body, and yet I never come to understand you." Another recites an ancient poem: "I've never known another human being who hasn't given me pain. . . . The lotus flower in the forest understands more than any man. . . . What is caste? I've never seen it with these eyes of mine."

The day is ended; everyone is exhausted. The shuttle bus carries us past the Vietnam Memorial, and one young woman, a member of the grounds crew, is speaking in confidential tones about Maya Lin, the architect. But Tony Latiolais, the Cajun boatbuilder, is a Vietnam veteran. "You couldn't do nothing over there," he says as the memorial drifts by. "You had to get permission to piss."

"I wake up every night in a cold sweat," he says, "afraid they're going to send me back there."

All of Western culture is inescapably violent, says Komal, holding forth at dinner to a group of rapt Festival assistants. Capitalism is to blame— capitalism is inherently violent and destructive. In India, all the daily rituals concentrate on centering the body. Centering, he says, making a circular motion with his palm over his navel, brings peace. The folk culture represented in the Melā is dying out; no—it is already dead. But at least we can try to draw spiritual energy from it.

Later Carolynn, who has been very impressed by the handsome, well-spoken, cosmopolitan young man, tells me that though he himself is of very high caste, Komal has a reputation for devotion to the folk per-formers, people driven into a Delhi ghetto by discriminatory laws that regard them not as artists but as beggars. Did I see the beautiful thirteen-year-old acrobat who walks the tightrope? The story is that in Delhi she has been forced into prostitution.

Tens of thousands: that is Duncan's estimate of the number of people, men, women, and children, who have been killed in Guatemala in the last four or five years, since the army began to remove the Mayan people—more than one million of them—from their ancestral lands. Many, of course, tried to get away; a hundred thousand or so fled into Mexico, into refugee camps established along the border. Some made it into the United States—maybe seventy thousand. Most of them are down in Indiantown, Florida, where Factor and Josefina, as well as Pedro Francisco, Jeronimo Composeco, and Juan Gaspar, the marimba players, all live now. For the rest, the government has built a system of resettlement camps. The countryside has been thoroughly militarized; every able-bodied man must serve one day a week in a paramilitary patrol unit whose work is to identify and root out "subversives."

Duncan has been explaining as best he can, because someone has asked him, the complicated political situation in Guatemala, about which there has been so much talk. Isn't the photograph of the soldiers examining the traditional weaving a political statement? "It is a factual statement," Duncan replies. He wears his white hat even in the dining room, where several curious people have joined him for supper: two of the sound men, a stage manager, the young actor whose photograph has just appeared in *People* magazine, and a folklorist from the National Endowment for the Arts. The brim of his hat bobs gently up and down as Duncan furrows and unfurrows his brow in the vigor and intensity of his speech; his small hands, red and rawboned, rise impulsively from the surface of the table in intermittent bursts of agitation.

He seems to know everything about the country that it is possible to know, to have read every government document, every foundation report, every scholarly article. He has been, moreover, among the Mayans themselves and has partaken of their way of life, framed his vision of things by their lights—and he has become their advocate, and that advocacy his profession. And yet: Though his account is thorough, practiced, and passionate, it is nevertheless difficult to understand, to piece it all together, to see into the causes, to reconstruct precisely the sequence that has led to something appalling, a catastrophe. Our ignorance is too vast, too intractable, the sense of our unwitting complicity too frightful. Why, we wonder together, have we not heard of this? Has there been nothing in the newspapers, the magazines? And our own government—is it merely a matter of acquiescence, or of something more sinister? We have read and heard, even if we have not entirely understood, of outrages in Honduras, in El Salvador, in Nicaragua, but they cannot compare to this.

"Somoza"—that's a name we know. The Mayans call him the Snake. He puts people into vats and boils them when they are too weak and emaciated to work any longer. Or so they say. The oral tradition, Duncan says, has preserved many hideous tales of murder and the torture of families by government soldiers. "Eisenhower"—that's another familiar name. He engineered the military coup in 1954 that overthrew the socialist democracy that ten years earlier had displaced Ubico, the benevolent dictator with the white hat.

Across the cafeteria, a plume of sound rises up from one of the Baul singers, the ones with shoulder-length hair and saffron robes. One drums with his fingers on the table as he calls out his long opalescent syllable with its many ululations, building a delicate architecture of rhythms across the space of the room, where tiny birds might perch and fly about as if among the ruins of a temple made of yellow bones. The other, scarcely more than a boy, with the scandalous darting eyes of a beautiful woman, sips on a throaty bamboo pipe that seems to breathe as it releases, like incense, successive clouds of tone.

The socialists, Duncan goes on, sought land reform—which is to say, they wished the peasants to cultivate with their hoes the idle lands controlled by the giant landowners. Socialists: their vague gray image hovers phantasmally among ballot boxes and bookish men at public meetings, orating and gesticulating . . . and what of the peasants? Out of an old geography text, or perhaps from a film screened one February afternoon in the sixth-grade classroom, there materializes a band of swarthy, sunburned men, bending over their gardens or bowed under sacks of sugar cane or coffee. Among the landowners—these must be the men in white suits again, holding tumblers of gin on some shady verandah and gazing proprietarily out into the dense forests, where keen shafts of sunlight pierce the shadows in meteorlike trajectories, touching the hanging masses of green fruit with a green flame—among these landowners, the most gigantic was the United Fruit Company, whose chairman was married to Eisenhower's personal secretary. Over the wharves, platforms of loaded sacks swing into the riveted holds of ships; uniformed men with rifles arrive at the appointed hour before the presidential palace, springing out of limousines and over the sides of jeeps, and in a matter of minutes the operation is complete.

Duncan's narrative strides into the next decade, when the United States, using advisers who had been trained for or who had actually served in Vietnam, trained a counterinsurgency force to quash resistance to the government's development plan, which proposes to displace the hill-country farmers, the Mayans, with cold-season agriculture in vegetables aimed at the American market. *Vietnam*—by an uneasy surmise we seem to know that there is some connection, some obscure force at large in the world that is one force and yet has erupted into history with violence and disruption at many diverse sites: a connection between our tendentious war and the one billion Whoppers and Big Macs, made with Guatemalan beef, for which we still do not have to pay so much; between the war in Vietnam, or the ideas that became the war, and the asparagus or broccoli we may someday buy, or are already buying, cheap, from the Blue Goose or the Big Bear or the Piggly-Wiggly.

The handful of people seated around Duncan Earle does not disperse until well after the dining room doors have closed and the foodwarmers have been carried back to the kitchen. The group emerges from the building to find that the evening has become cool as the sun sets, paling the skies over the Georgetown clock tower. A few folks linger on the sidewalk that climbs the slope toward the dormitories, while a sporadic traffic of late arrivals empties out of the vans wheeling into the driveway.

Behind one of the blinds at a low second-story window, one can hear an Irish hornpipe; it's coming from Mick Maloney's room, where young Joanie Madden with her flute and her mentor Jack Coen, both from the Bronx, and fiddler Brendan Mulvihill, son of Martin of County Clare, have unpacked their instruments. Others pass by: a distinguished-looking woman with professionally groomed silver hair, wearing a maroon sari and a white shawl, limps forward on a deformed foot. A younger woman with a silk scarf over her head accompanies her, and both wear the *tiki*, the blood-red spot in the middle of their foreheads that signifies a blessing— even the little girls are wearing them. A pair of studious young men, exceptionally dark, follow in their white pajamas, accompanied by an old man with a white beard and a turban.

The old man is Buddha Chacha, the potter, and the younger fellows are the icon makers; the silver-haired woman, who lives in California, is the henna hand-painter, who has already decorated the palms of several of the young women on the staff. Behind them is the bluesman from Baton

Rouge, Silas Hogan, wearing the silver-painted hardhat he won as the pioneer black worker in the oil refineries there. Arthur "Guitar" Kelly, who has played with Silas for years, strolls alongside him, inscrutable behind his red-rimmed sunglasses.

John Cephas and Phil Wiggins, Washington blues singers, are discussing their work with folklorist Barry Lee Pearson. Cephas, who plays in the North Carolina Piedmont style, a form of fingerpicking, represents his own development as a musician with a strong emphasis on community and family occasions—what the folklorists like to stress as the medium of transmission—as if he had never listened to a radio or heard a record, when it is apparent both from his repertoire and his style that he has heard a good many of the classic blues recordings as well as a good deal of contemporary music. He plays a verse of Blind Boy Fuller's old "Untrue Blues":

> Hey hey, hey hey, hey . . . aw shucks!
> Used to be your reg'lar, now I got to be your dog.

Oh god, he's fabulous.

When a young man returns from a period of practicing his guitar alone—called "woodshedding," Barry explains—very dramatically improved, it is sometimes said that he has "made a pact with the devil," particularly because his music, in the view of the church, belongs to a range of behavior condemned as, among other things, a form of idleness connected to drinking, sexual promiscuity, and so on.

Wiggins, a young Washingtonian, locates the origin of his interest in the blues—again, quite ignoring the influence of radio and records—to a Washington street singer, Flora Moulton, and, interestingly, to the 1976 Festival of American Folklife, where he sat in by invitation with Mother Scott's traditional blues band; this is a vivid instance of the Festival's plausible role, Pearson observes, in the actual transmission of folk music.

Not surprisingly, a member of the audience at this discussion workshop, after hearing these narratives, so impregnated with the conventions of such narratives, is helplessly in the grip of a bit of folklore that he wishes to thrust upon Cephas and Wiggins: "Have you had a relationship with the devil, like Robert Johnson?" he asks eagerly, with a kind of guttural, maniacal laughter.

At an afternoon staff meeting we are cautioned about three characters in paramilitary outfits, carrying briefcases and strolling around the site looking threatening and sometimes being abusive. And pickpockets are working the Melā.

Under the hot sun of a July afternoon, we learn that one of the Festival staff has been thrown from a pargo, which staff and workers are using to get around the Mall. She lies on the gravel path, stiff and trembling with pain, and screams when one of the ambulance attendants, whose vehicle with its revolving lamp leans on the grass with its rear door opened toward her, attempts to shift her onto a stretcher. Several of the staff women have rushed across the grass to her aid and seem to be wringing their hands over her.

Moments later, after she has been driven away, a police ambulance rolls silently to a spot on the grass not ten steps from the pargo accident, where a young, shirtless man with long lanky hair lies hugging himself, fetally, on the grass. A uniformed man assists him to his feet and trundles him into the truck: a drug overdose, apparently, or a heatstroke.

Later I wander into the Louisiana crafts tent, where, at this hour of the day, the craftspeople are mostly weary of talking, though most still have visitors, children mainly, clustered around them. But Azzie Roland, the split-oak basketmaker, is alone, so I sit down beside him. Like many folk artisans, he took up basketmaking, of which he knew the rudiments from his youth, after retirement. A month ago, though, he lost his wife of forty-one years, and though he is course happy to be at the Festival, just now he doesn't see the point in weaving baskets. After the Festival, he says, he's going to give it up.

Two-thirty in the afternoon on the Fourth of July, and it must be ninety-eight in the shade. Over the fence, slowly and ponderously, a drumbeat rises from the Melā. We're all very, very tired.

Across Fourteenth Street, near the Washington Monument, the American Indian Heritage Foundation is sponsoring a pantribal powwow, and they are crowning a picture-pretty Indian queen in white buckskin and a feather headdress. Near them the Hare Krishnas are sponsoring a "Festival of India." In the heavy, delirious atmosphere, their festival seems to parody our own.

Masses of people are gathering for the Beach Boys concert. The stage, with its twin mountains of speakers, has been set up just below the Monument at Seventeenth Street. It looks like a launching pad for the Atlas booster. By 3:00 the Mall has become a thoroughfare for what the police later estimate is a crowd of more than three hundred thousand people, pouring up onto the grass from the mouth of the Metro stop and across Hamilton and Jefferson streets from downtown and from the waterfront, carrying blankets, beer coolers, frisbees, softballs and bats, footballs, radios, and umbrellas.

The Festival, today, is sparsely attended, its own dusty corrals and paddocks now largely empty of the thousands of footfalls that have left their imprints in the dirt and trod the grass into extinction.

Silently and facelessly, like strange mollusks from the ocean bottom, their wide maws open, the Luiseño culture bank—three impact-resistant, aerodynamic aluminum suitcases in a glass case in the Cultural Conservation section—records the illusory reducibility of culture to its productions: treasures laid up on earth, which rust will corrupt and moth will steal. In them are old photographs of Luiseño people, an anthropologist's monograph, Kodacolor records of Southern California's wild plants and flowers, and other documents, locked away—as if culture could be transported like the combs and brushes of a traveling salesman or a magician's paraphernalia. It suggests a culture in flight, eternally en route, seeking the place and time at which the suitcases might be opened and a new world blossom out of them.

People begin to gather around nine in the main lounge of the dormitory, a long room with a parquet floor and paneled walls lined with couches. A grand piano stands in one corner; in the other, volunteers have begun to ply the bar, where a keg of beer squats in its tub of ice. Among them is warm-voiced Mary Cliff, Washington's folk music radio hostess.

A few of the Cajuns have gathered near the piano, though no one is playing it: Dewey Balfa, fiddler in the Balfa Brothers band until two of the three were killed in an auto accident; Canray Fontenot, wide-smiling black zydeco fiddler from Welsh Louisiana; and D. L. Menard in his cowboy hat, the Hank Williams of Erath, Louisiana.

Others sit or stand on the periphery, including the young guitarist for the Hayride String Band, Mike Kirkpatrick of Shreveport, and Peter Schwarz, a teenager apprenticed to Dewey Balfa under a grant from the NEA. Peter is the son of fiddler and banjoist Tracy Schwarz, who made a reputation in the 1960s with the New Lost City Ramblers, the revivalist string band that brought old-time music to life by reperforming, with zealous scholarship, accuracy, and passion, the mountain songs and tunes recorded on discs sixty years earlier. Peter cuts a colorful figure in his red Hawaiian shorts, talking T-shirt, and razor haircut, which seems to have piled all of his blond curls onto the top of his head, as if they had fallen there like wool from a shorn ram.

D. L. sings a lonesome mountain song, one from Hank Williams's repertoire, in which lofty black pines and a howling wind offer their grim companionship to a betrayed lover and insinuate into his mind their secret doctrines. D. L. shuts his eyes forcefully and seems to bend his whole face toward the song, as if it were a child, and he were talking to it, while his heavy right hand drops industriously over the guitar strings, forging stout utilitarian chords that roll under the song like steel-belted tires. Menard's hands, it is clear, were formed by hard work, perhaps as a mechanic or farmer; unlike the hands of a classical violinist or cellist, whose grace and strength are precisely proportionate to the requirements of the instrument as, over the years, they have grown to it, Menard's hands and arms so far exceed in strength what his guitar requires that his stout strokes fill every chord with the turmoil of laboring metal and wood, even as their harmonies disclose the exquisite delicacy and tenderness of strength subdued. He sings without restraint, his voiced touched at different points in the song with all those situations in life that harrow it—with the trepidation and strain that might show in a lovers' quarrel, in some brave speech, in a cry of anguish, all gathered onto the stream of the melody and shaped into the buckled words of D. L.'s English, which seems half-buried in his Cajun French.

Somehow it is wrong to say that D. L. sings and plays a song, as if the song were something separate from him; it seems to come from him immediately, originally, even spontaneously, not a song that he performs, but one that possesses and becomes him—a song that sings him.

The room is filling up, and Henry Grey, the blues pianist who played with Muddy Waters, sits down at the piano, joined by Boogie Bill Webb with his guitar and Hezakiah Early; in short order, the entire room is rocking as people move toward the center of the floor and begin to dance. Hezakiah's blues shouts rise above the din, while Henry's hands, striding toward and away from one another across the keyboard, give the piano a strange life of its own, as if it were enchanted, though the pianist himself seems to be paying little attention—instead he is gazing expectantly with his smoky eyes to the people gathered around the piano, one and then another, reading them, as if his music were telling their fortunes.

Rhythms, emerging out of the musical instruments and from the clapping of hands and the pounding of feet, draw all of us into their synthesis and seem to make of the very room the interior of some great living body. They resound like the names of gods, the audible sounds of human forces working through us and upon us, from the most reptilian impulse to the most sublime idea, infinitely ramified from cell to cell along the pathways of the nervous system in the myriad shapes that we call culture when they find expression in all the forms of human invention.

Has there been a time in history when the rhythms of India, in cymbal, drum, and gong, have been woven into the driving beat of a barrelhouse blues? The Delhi drummers, Jamil Khan and Shyam Lal, have entered the room with Jiten Badhayakar, the Bengali, carrying their elbow drums, cymbals, and castanets; even Ramdu Aiyar, the resplendent provincial ghatam or bass drum player, joins them, and the four set up shop a few paces from the piano. A transformation occurs as the massive bolts of energy from the blues backbeat flow into the microcircuitry of the Indian rhythms, filling the atmosphere with new and urgent computations as the two groups of musicians, glancing back and forth across the gap between them, try to understand one another.

Strangers are dancing with strangers: the Indian men in their loose, pajamalike costumes and the women in their saris; Festival workers in blue jeans and T-shirts; visitors from the Washington folklore establishment in light dresses, sport shirts, or summer suits. Near the center of the floor, a young American woman in a sari is revolving in self-made pirouettes, her head thrown back luxuriously; another couple, still in office garb, show off their expertly synchronized jitterbug. Tall, red-faced Glenn Ohrlin, in his cowboy hat and faded jeans, pushes delicately around the floor, as if she were a potted plant, my young Festival volunteer, distinguished by the pastel outfit and fresh yellow tresses that seem to thrust them both far from Georgetown—perhaps to Montana, thirty years ago or more, to a high-school gymnasium where kids are dancing to phonograph records under the red or blue crepe-paper bunting hanging from the ceiling above them.

Meanwhile, near the entrance to the room, through its wide arched door, the great marimba, like some sacred effigy, the relic of some sainted bishop of the Middle Ages, is entering, attended by the Guatemalans and assisted by Duncan Earle, still in his white panama with the black band. Once set up in a corner opposite what has become a Bengali-Punjabi-Cajun-Chicago-Mississippi Delta blues band, the Guatemalans begin to play, bending studiously over the bars to find the undiscovered notes that will bring them into the strange global synthesis of sound that has filled the cavernous room and joined the entire mass, it seems, of Festival partici-pants into the busy human colony in the middle of the floor, where, like the friezes on some ancient temple come to life, the whole repertoire of human postures—the warrior meeting his foe on the battlefield, the beg-gar squatting in the street, the stevedore handling heavy ropes, the lover shortly to gain possession of her beloved—passes from person to person, invisible gods seeking momentary habitation.

And they *do* find the notes, luminescent, mothlike things that fly up and around the music, as if they had been there all along and were now escaping from its heat and turbulence; so bright are they, and so fleeting, that the musicians begin to follow their various tracks, as a child might chase fireflies in the dusk, and soon a new music, unheard before in the world, takes shape in the room, in which the rushlike notes of the ma-rimba, arranged in their girlish scales, are borne in upon us in great tides of rhythm alive with many eddies, currents, and crosscurrents.

Everybody is dancing!

But look: It is the bahrupiyas, Gurmukh and Krishan, the monkey-men, who out of their monkey costumes seem—though they are outcastes and are even forbidden to speak—little more than street-urchins, as nobly formed as young gentlemen. Were it not for their dark complexions and pajamas, they might be boys from some fine old school, the one as studious-looking as one who has read Latin and Greek, the other as lithe, long-boned, and flexible as some champion of the playing field, both with all the beauty and self-assurance that privilege brings with it; thrust to the bottom of society, where their vocation is to burst pretension, to ruffle the smooth demeanor, to amuse children while embarrassing their elders, they are as alert, as free, as invulnerable as young lords—for to have nothing, and to live with the expectation of nothing, is the same as to have everything and to expect everything.

They cannot speak to the women with whom they dance; but of the language of their intense eyes and supernatural movements, which can as likely have come from London discos as from the tops of the banyan trees where the monkeys carry on their interminable chatter, there can be no misunderstanding.

8
Falling in Love

Folk-Lore, which the word's coiner, the British antiquarian William John Thoms, defined as the "manners, customs, observances, superstitions, ballads, proverbs, &c, of the olden time," was a neologism with a strong precedent, as the *Oxford English Dictionary* tells us, in German compounds that linked together areas of human culture bifurcated by social differentiation. "Folk," as everybody knows, means "people"—or, more precisely, "*a* people" or "*the* people"; but the term's etymology as well as its usage seem to insist on the primacy of one of the ideas embodied in its Old Norse meaning, which is "a detachment" or "a division of an army." This notion of a small group set apart, but not isolated, in relation to a hegemony or authority set over or around it persists in all of its derivative meanings: as a race or tribe; as a group of people under a God, king, or priest; as the followers or retainers of such a figure; or as people of a particular party or class, the "common" people. The still-current use of "folks" to mean one's parents or one's clan or race, or to address a social assembly, also reiterates the primary sense of a social form arising out of the relation of one group to another that surrounds, encompasses, and prevails over it.

The lexical momentum of the word *folk* is, consequently, socially downwards or outwards, from the inclusive to the included, the central to the marginal group, from authority to the absence of authority; folk*lore*, moreover, which makes implicit reference to a body of knowledge and to the shaping influences of one mind upon another—what I call *ethnomimesis*—is set in contradistinction to the unbounded field of formally constituted disciplinary knowledge, embedded in literacy or some other intellectual technology, whose authority arises from its connection to social power.

Often, in their elite cultural contexts, the actual historical, social, and practical connections of folk texts and folk performances are unknown to us; hence they have often been attributed to an isolated, "untutored" individual genius or a pristine ethnomimetic community unconnected to the surrounding official or popular or commercial culture. But folklore, in fact, always issues from these relationships. It occurs in the spatial and temporal interstices of otherwise complex and highly differentiated civilizations, noetic vacuums that are themselves a consequence of that complexity and differentiation. It occurs, to paraphrase Raymond Williams, where concentrations of cultural power, owing to practical insulation or disadvantage, or to some form of social discrimination, or to active quotidian resistance, or to all of these, have broken up, worn thin, or come loose: when enclaved groups, such as immigrants or workers, and individual lives and their associations develop beyond the reach of, but often in the framework of, the roles, obligations, duties, and functions through which we participate in and are shaped by the civilization that surrounds us.

The power and authority of folklore consist precisely in the fact that, because it arises where power has lapsed, retreated, or failed, it lies outside all authority and power. Far from a kind of anomaly or residuum, folklore is one of the cultural resources of modern bourgeois civilization, which tirelessly produces it, consumes it, and produces it again. In the postmodern society of the spectacle, however, as we shall suggest, the reproduction of folklore *as* spectacle, far from legitimizing or empowering it, may like the spectacle everywhere uproot and dispel it.

Like stereotype itself, the concept of "folklore" is a compound one, forging meaningful signs out of various conjunctions of folk-cultural productions with certain elite or popular frames of reference. The construction of folklore consequently demands—as a folktale anthology, a folk festival, a folk art gallery, a folk museum, a folk concert, or even a scholarly monograph amply illustrate—the radical decontextualization of the folk-cultural text and its concomitant incorporation with the discourses of its new academic or festival context: the discourse of cultural conservation, say, or, as we saw in the Smithsonian films, a kind of remedialism or counterculturalism. We will find the folk community, in any case, where our social ideologies dictate that we find it. In the romantic period, which coincides with industrialism and hence brings us up almost to our own time, folklore was enlisted in the project of rooting the new imperial Western nationalisms in more ancient and utterly obsolete forms of social organization. It was used in the same way in our own nativist movements of the 1920s and in the regional folk festivals those movements inspired. With the advent of the socialist analysis of Western society, folklore drifted to the left and allied itself both with preindustrial production and with the labor movement; the Festival of American Folklife, extending this tradition, posits cultural communities formed around specific kinds of production and showcases the producer. In the ideology of progress, then, folklore is something backward and primitive. In the ideology of social revolution, it is the culture of the marginal, the oppressed, and the powerless. In the ideology of cultural pluralism, it belongs to the unassimilated ethnic group, and in the fascist state, to a particular race or to speakers of a particular language. The place to look for folklore in the postmodern period—in which, as Fredric Jameson writes, we seem to have lost every possibility of "positioning the cultural act outside the massive Being of capital"—is perhaps at the very heart of social power, where bands of men in high office swear oaths to one another behind the scenes of the corporate and political spectacle, paradoxically all-powerful and yet beyond the reach of all legitimate authority and power.[1]

"Folklife," as constructed by the Festival of American Folklife, is a structure of cultural analysis descended indirectly from the proto-Marxist tradition of class analysis represented by Henry Mayhew and from the socialist response to the aggravated class differences brought about in the nineteenth century by industrialism. In this context, then, it ought to be instructive to consider its genesis in the early years of the Festival.

Festival founder Ralph Rinzler's early experiments with recontextualized presentation on the Mall reflected, like his first crafts exhibits at the Newport Folk Festival, the idealization of cottage crafts and of the pastoral life of Great Britain generally that belonged to the romantic-socialist tradition and the genteel German-Jewish social class in which Rinzler had been reared. At the time of his attachment to the Smithsonian he had won a reputation both as a folk music impresario and as a crafts entrepreneur, the latter as a result of his collaboration with potter Nancy Sweezy in a Cambridge, Massachusetts, outlet for traditional crafts objects he had collected on field trips to Tennessee, Georgia, and North Carolina for the Newport Folk Foundation.[2] Hence these early presentations were characterized by crafts demonstrations and performances that, by virtue of their stereotyped associations with mountain culture, most readily crossed the economic boundary between folk and consumer culture: cornhusk dolls, apple-butter making, blues, and mountain music were all part of the souvenir folk culture that had been bought and sold in this country for several generations and widely depicted in popular culture.

At the 1968 Festival of American Folklife, the carding, spinning, and weaving of wool were featured along with Appalachian quilts, appleface dolls, dulcimers, chairs, whittlers' toys, a blacksmith, a potter, and a rug-hooker; if these pastoral crafts had been stereotyped by several poetic and pictorial traditions, the Appalachian crafts had been stereotyped by a long-standing trade in folk crafts both on roadsides and in urban museums and shops; popular imagery, too, the province of magazine covers and post-cards, had fixed the figures of the sinewy-armed smith and sagacious whittler talking politics "under the spreading chestnut tree" or on the egalitarian crackerbarrel in front of the General Store, emblem of participatory democracy.

But the future direction of the Festival was suggested in 1968 by a strong contingent of Native American exhibits in basketweaving, patch- and ribbonwork, pottery, dollmaking, rug weaving, silversmithing, and sandpainting. Many of these crafts, like their Appalachian counterparts, had the signature of tourism upon them, from Tucson or Santa Fe if not Asheville or Gatlinburg. But they accomplished a decisive break both with Anglo-pastoralism and with the folk revival, in which Native American culture had never played a significant part, and placed the entire event upon a new theoretical foundation.

Rinzler in the meantime had solicited the advice of, among other folk-lore scholars, a young Pennsylvania folklorist, Henry Glassie, who in 1968 published his influential *Pattern in the Material Folk Culture of the Eastern United States*, which placed folk crafts in the context of the social, tech-nological, and aesthetic processes of particular folk communities. In the next two years an emerging configuration built around cotton, corn, and wool brought into the foreground the artifacts and skills connected to these resources, an emphasis that had the effect of elaborating the exhibits and of effacing regional and racial classes, which were superseded by the new economic categories. Thus both Appalachian and Native American exhibitors demonstrated corn milling and grinding along with their displays of other corn products such as pipes and brooms, and the wool-centered exhibits expanded to include sheepshearing, wool dyeing, and even a sheepdog demonstration on the lawn.

This kind of Festival organization, based on economic arrangements flowing from a particular resource, did not survive in precisely the form it followed in the first three years of the Festival; craft presentation came to fall under the aegis of the "featured state"—a program begun with Pennsylvania in 1969, largely as a funding strategy—and of the Native American program. But the perspective it implied, that cultural life is built upon economic necessities arising directly from the encounter of society with the natural environment, was the germ of the Festival's embrace in 1971 of organized labor, a move that, through the initiatives of labor historian and folklorist Archie Green, brought all manner of working people to the Mall, including not only traditional crafts and trades such as meat cutting and carpentry but, in succeeding years, truckers, railroaders, airline pilots, taxi drivers, street vendors, skipjack fishermen, loggers, bartenders, cowboys, and even, in 1986, Washington trial lawyers.

The exhibition of industrial arts, like the Native American ethnographical displays, could be said to have descended historically from the Smithsonian's early participation in the Centennial Exhibition in Philadelphia, to which it contributed an ethnological exhibit of tools, pottery, weapons, and other Native American artifacts and from which it ultimately inherited, in 1879, an international collection of machines and manufactures.[3] But the Native American cultural exhibitions and the industrial arts were, at a deeper anthropological level, joined by the classical perspective pioneered in the nineteenth century by American anthropologist Lewis Morgan, who had articulated a theory of the "primitive communistic society"—a theory elaborated by Karl Marx, who saw the "village community" as the primitive form of society "everywhere from India to Ireland," and who emphasized the historical connection between modern industrial labor and its primitive beginnings. "The modern labor movement," wrote a union member in the 1972 Festival program book, "traces its ancestry back thousands of years to the very first workers who ploughed the fields and, before that, made primitive garments and 'invented' tools for hunting, sewing, and the sustaining of human life."[4]

That Morgan happened to have based his conclusions upon a study of Native Americans, then, is of more than passing interest for the Festival of American Folklife—and not only because the Smithsonian, too, was an early pioneer in the study of American Indian ethnology.[5] Integrated with Marx's dialectical theory of history, Native American culture and the social arrangements it embodied synthesized a number of closely related ideas. In nineteenth-century anthropological theory, it dramatized human economic origins; as such it sanctioned, socially and historically, a program of resistance to market capitalism and hence enabled the Marxian hypothesis for proletarian revolution, which would restore the original and natural, or economically communal, human society. It also embodied the traditional folkloric model of human social organization. Even more recent folklore theory has suggested that under certain social conditions such as those represented by the occupational group, the village community—a small group reliant principally upon "face-to-face" communications—might be reproduced, if not in a strict economic sense then in the secondary social and psychological senses, as the internal impulse of social groups for whom a noetic space has opened in the interstices of civilized life.[6] These groups are "primitive" not evolutionarily but teleologically, exhibiting the form to which human communities return when extrinsic influences upon their development are removed or when barriers against those influences are erected around them.

Thus it appears that, philosophically at least, two of the Festival's most interesting and most characteristic components, its industrial trades and its Native American exhibits, are closely interconnected. Both situate the folk character in economic life, whether in its tribal form or in the form of the occupational community; both further suggest that the folk community, with its communal codes and close interpersonal interactions, is the product of some underlying common purpose and is thus inherently resistant to a society marked by economic competition among self-interested individuals with isolate and distinctive subjectivities or "worldviews." This conception unifies in the Festival two traditions, one social and one political, that independently had idealized folklife as a specially insulated relational condition illustrative of the human social and economic nature and as the embodiment of an economic and social eschatology embodied in Marxist revolution.

To folk revivalists, the proximity of folk crafts to industrial trades may have seemed a rude juxtaposition, particularly against the backdrop of Vietnam-era politics and its vociferous working-class reactionism. But at the heart of both crafts revivals and the labor movement, economically speaking, was the dream of economic independence—called "seizure of the means of production" by Engels, "self-reliance" by Emerson, and "do-it-yourself"-ism by hobbyists of the 1950s, to whom Pete Seeger once compared the folk revivalists—the moral project of Henry David Thoreau; it is, individually or collectively, a dream of liberation from a society that, in order to carry out its economic aims, required that the individual be cramped into a tiny "nutshell of civility" that both Thoreau and Marx despised. Thoreau, perhaps, took the idea of the individual too seriously, and Marx not seriously enough; but it should be apparent that the idealization of the primitive and the politics of the labor movement are, in this context, mutually grounded in the principle of economic self-determination—an idea whose curious circuit in our culture begins, perhaps, with Robinson Crusoe, to whose acquisitive impulse the entire productive output of England had been opened in the hull of a wrecked ship, and who as a man of property naturally acquired a black servant.

Having been subsumed under the twin programs of the featured state and the Native American exhibits, crafts proliferated promisingly at the Festival in 1970, leaving the more facile stereotypes well behind. Biscuit, blintz, wine, butter, and cheese making emerged to initiate the Festival's foodways component, while the Cheyenne and Kickapoo brought tepee building and hide tanning, and from Arkansas came fishing lure crafters, silhouette cutters, a cooper, a fiddle maker, and a log cabin builder. But by far the greatest diversity, and hence the greatest challenge to intellectual organization, lay in the areas of music and dance.

Some of the Festival's musical performers during its first six years had already established themselves in a commercial domain such as country music, black gospel, or blues and continued to flourish in them. These included guitar picker Merle Travis, Grand Ole Opry character Grandpa Jones, Chicago bluesman Muddy Waters, gospel singers called the Swan Silvertones, and two bluegrass bands, Ralph Stanley and the Clinch Mountain Boys and Bill Monroe and the Bluegrass Boys. Others, such as Jimmy Driftwood, Norman Kennedy, and Jean Ritchie, were self-conscious professional and semiprofessional folksingers who had developed largely in the context of the folksong revival or, like Bessie Jones and the Georgia Sea Island Singers, had been brought to public attention by professional folklorists.

Among the black performers in the first six years of the Festival, many had enjoyed a modest commercial success within the black urban subculture at some prior epoch, from which the Festival summoned them: among these were jazz musicians Billie and DeDe Pierce of Preservation Hall; bluesmen "Yank" Rachel, Booker White, Mance Lipscomb, Sleepy John Estes, Skip James, and Sunnyland Slim; and the Martin, Bogan, and Armstrong string band. Several Appalachian performers who had distinguished themselves in the twenties and thirties as old-time recording artists were similarly called back in tribute to their former celebrity, including Maybelle Carter, Wade Mainer, Wade Ward, Wily and Zeke Morris, banjoist Buell Kazee, and Grand Ole Opry stars Sam and Kirk McGee. Among those called from an earlier professional life in 1970 was "Big Boy" Arthur Crudup, the Chicago jump singer who, through his influence on Elvis Presley, figured importantly in the rock-and-roll revolution; his appearance promised that the original Sun Records House musicians— rockabilly guitarists, singers, and a pianist—would find a place in the Festival sixteen years later.

Virtually all of these performers had already been lionized by the folk revival. Many had been brought into the limelight by Festival director Ralph Rinzler himself, or by friends and associates, particularly Mike Seeger, in the years predating the Festival of American Folklife: most conspicuous were North Carolina guitarist Doc Watson and his family; Ozark balladeer Almeda Riddle; Elizabeth Cotten, the Seeger family housekeeper who had composed the popular song "Freight Train"; and coal miner, banjoist, and singer Doc Boggs. Among these were musicians whose participation in the Festival would help spread their celebrity and influence to the revival of the seventies: the black Virginia songster John Jackson; cowboy singer Glenn Ohrlin; fiddler Tommy Jarrell; clawhammer banjoist Kyle Creed; and, most enduringly in the Festival of American Folklife, Cajun fiddlers Canray Fontenot and Dewey Balfa.

Popular anthologies of folksong have typically categorized folk music according to a bewildering mix of thematic, historical, regional, ethnic, ethnomusicological, occupational, and sociopolitical classes. Alan Lomax's *The Folk Songs of North America*, to cite an important example, drew upon Lomax's developing "cantometric" hypothesis, which interprets folksong style as an "indicator of cultural pattern."[7] This collection divides American folk music into four great geoethnic bodies: "The North," which includes such categories as "Yankee Soldiers and Sailors," "Workers and Farmers," and "The Maritime Provinces"; "The Southern Mountains and Back-woods," which includes, among other groupings, "The Old Ballads," "White Spirituals," and "Hard Times and the Hillbilly"; "The West," which includes "Cowboys," "Railroaders and Hoboes," and "Prairie Farmers"; and finally "The Negro South," which includes, predictably, "Spirituals," "Work Songs," and "Blues"—twenty-eight classes in all. As Lomax observes at the opening of his anthology, "the map sings."

A strictly musicological analysis of these types, however, given the errant character of aural traditions and the complex ecology of their movement, would result in a musical map opaqued by its own complications. But that is precisely why such hybrid classes of traditional music—more than crafts, which are largely tied to particular natural resources and social settings—have proved so useful as a paradigm of Festival organization: they record, in the medium of an expressive form that both observes and transgresses cultural boundaries, the drifts, the disruptions, and the conformations in the techtonics of culture. They *are* a map, at a particular historical moment, of ethnomimesis.

The fivefold typology of the 1973 and 1974 Festivals of American Folklife, which initiated the realization of a Bicentennial plan, was a matrix of signification formed on the boundaries between social classes and in the zones between social groups, where one's social identity can be construed as a point on an ethnemic map of society as a whole. The 1973 Festival figured folk culture occupationally in "Working Americans," racially in "Native Americans" (and, in the following year, in the "African Diaspora"), ethnically in "Old Ways in the New World," and regionally in "Regional Americans." Later festivals, as we've seen, took age and family as cultural determinants. Particular intersections of these determinants, such as the culture of the midwestern family farm, have been attempted; specific folkloric genres such as the music of political struggle, the culture of the deaf community, and the medicine show and folk medicine, or folkloric themes such as "American talkers" and the idea of "community" itself, have also been presented on the Mall. The fact remains, however, that the construction of folklife, as all these cases indicate, demanded a kind of dismemberment in which parts or pieces of social identity are deployed as cultural signs, eclipsing the souls of the real people in whom these many forces—race, ethnicity, nativity, occupation, gender, and class—all struggle for integration.

The 1973–74 typology is conservative and to a degree revivalistic, striving against what Festival rhetoric characterizes as the homogenization of the American character by commercial culture, and at the same time redrawing the lines that culture has begun to efface. Hence, in the Festival setting, these classes constitute a form of cultural reinvention, bringing into bold relief, by a kind of social ultraviolet light, those cultural features shaped by the meeting of stereotype and personality and in effect prompting the reconstruction of identity along social rather than personal lines.

At the same time, however, the racial classifications—Native Americans and the African Diaspora—are, paradoxically, politically innovative, urging a reconception of cultural groups whose identities have not only been fixed in stereotypes but have been deeply and tragically shaped by them. *Native* American, of course, draws attention to the historical priority of ancient Asian peoples and silences the stereotyped associations attached to "Indian." "African Diaspora," while implicitly analogizing the Middle Passage to the Jewish Diaspora, at the same time draws the various New World black communities together into a newly configured cultural family with roots in Africa and branches in the outposts of the slave trade, the American South joining the Caribbean as the two nodes of African American cultural transfiguration.

The white representation of black music has of course long been tied to political movements, beginning with abolitionist Lucy McKim Garrison's *Slave Songs of the United States* in 1867, as well as to various bohemian and countercultural traditions, as in the case of jazz and blues. At the Festival of American Folklife, the representation of black culture was linked to the civil rights movement through the influence of outspoken black activist and singer Bernice Johnson Reagon, who later became a Smithsonian anthropologist and leader of the progressive black women's singing group, Sweet Honey in the Rock; it was influenced, too, by Rinzler's friend and associate, folklorist Roger Abrahams, whose work in African American culture has consistently pointed to the cultural kinships between the two venues of his fieldwork: the island of Antigua and urban black Philadelphia.

Although regional, ethnic, and working-class folk artists emerge in the Festival with most of the signs of their participation in contemporary culture occluded—cowboys eat at McDonald's, carry drivers' licenses, and pay income tax, too—Native and African Americans appear as representatives of larger cultural traditions that transcend the histories of these groups within specific polities and identify them instead with global movements belonging to the history, not of nations, but of races and peoples. The Navajo sandpainter who normally photographs his work with a Polaroid camera before the wind blows it away may for that reason be discouraged from doing so at the Festival, just as the blues singer may, for the same reason, be reluctant to discuss his record collection or his enthusiasm for Monday night football. In effect, the political and social marginality of these groups has been turned inside out, granting them a kind of nationhood by redefining those margins as the frontiers of a heterogeneous but unified cultural polity.

In the five new Festival classes, then, five distinct ideological traditions are allied under new names: the socialist political, arts, and labor movements; the popular and populist theater, journalism, literature, and pictorial representation that since the early nineteenth century had traced the emergence of American cultural regions and types; anthropology, with its interest in races and peoples; the black liberation movement in this country; and finally turn-of-the-century social reform, with its internationalist outlook, whose history begins in the settlement house movement and which has emerged from time to time since then as an issue in municipal improvement, educational and recreational innovation, folk revivalism, and, in wartime, as part of the propaganda of national solidarity.

What unifies these perspectives is that each one locates a particular human group outside the domain of ordinary bourgeois or modern cultural life, technological development, and material advantage and at the same time identifies those groups, as Marx identified the working class, as the agents of fundamental historical processes. It defines the group economically and socially, as the engine in the consummation of history through class struggle; it defines it anthropologically, as the site of a search for human essences and origins; or journalistically or poetically, with reference to stereotyped landscapes, characters, and ways of life belonging to the epic, comic, or elegiac frontier or Western story; or ethnopolitically, with reference to black and Third World liberation movements and a program of cultural democracy.[8] Whether rooted in a social philosophy, in commercial entertainment, in popular literature, in late-nineteenth-century social science, in the labor, civil rights, or antiwar movements, or in the expansion of the social role of women, each of these perspectives arises from a drive in the "weightless" modern subject, who has "hardly seen music, or anything else, made by a pair of human hands," to identify with groups through whom—by means of political, social-scientific, or aesthetic interest, participation, and advocacy—it may win a moral imperative and a historical role in a society that cannot offer these things on its own terms.

It is interesting, then, that having established for the 1973 Festival these four new categories (five in 1974), the Festival planners should have chosen to represent each category with its most familiar and stereotypical example, as if to place the Festival squarely in the midst of the popular representations of folk culture, so that the making of sign into signifier to form the new cultural sign, "folklife," might be most forcefully achieved. This was most apparent at the Regional America offering for 1973, featuring the state of Kentucky. That Kentucky had already acquired a purely stereotypical status hardly requires discussion; from the Edenic accounts of seventeenth-century Jesuit missionaries, to the frontier tales of Daniel Boone and the myth of Lincoln, to the idols of the minstrel show and all the popular music inspired by it, even to *Uncle Tom's Cabin*, Kentucky had become almost a pure idea, an archetype of the frontier paradise in which the American character had been bred. Regionalist writers such as Jesse Stuart continued the theme, while various heroes and rogues of folklore—the Kentucky rifleman, the Kentucky Roarer, the Kentucky moonshiner—entered the popular imagination alongside such icons as Kentucky bourbon, the Kentucky thoroughbred, and even the blue moon of Kentucky.

As Rogers Morton, Secretary of the Interior, pointed out in the Festival program book for 1973, the Festival itself, spread out around the Reflecting Pool at the foot of the Lincoln Memorial, was thereby linked symbolically to the state; but it was linked historically, too, by the central role Kentucky had played in the genesis of American folklore, the folk revival, and the folk festival.[9] As Festival director Ralph Rinzler observes in the same program book, folk revivalism flourished early in Kentucky as handmaiden to essentially philanthropic educational experiments and economic self-help programs. Fireside Industries was established at Berea College in 1893 by President William Frost as a retail outlet for such crafts as broom making, woodworking, and weaving, through which the Berea students might pay their college tuition; at the Hindman Settlement School, founded in 1902 after the Berea model, training in native folk music and crafts—and some not so native—was combined with basic vocational training.

Though ostensibly social in their aims, all of these educational programs set out with a cultural agenda deeply informed by the nativist myth that the mountains were a preserve of the old Anglo-Saxon root stock whose hegemony was threatened by massive European immigration; it was this myth that sent Cecil Sharp, and all the ballad collectors whom he inspired, into the Appalachians, or that justified the introduction into settlement-school curricula of the Morris dance, May festivals, and the dulcimer—for which no analogues existed in mountain culture—in addition to the native

crafts these schools aimed to revitalize.[10] One of the earliest concert balladeers, the lachrymose John Jacob Niles, holding in his embrace an
elaborate, outsized dulcimer, his sage white hair streaming behind his ears,
was the product of that movement, as was warbling Jean Ritchie, dressed
in calico, the dulcimer asleep in her lap scarcely out of its diapers. Kentucky, in short, was the unwitting recipient of a late-nineteenth-century
parlor morality that found, in the domestic folklife of the state, modes of
recreation and amusement compatible with current ideals of propriety,
decency, and respectability, ideals principally represented by middle-class
white women and Protestant ministers with a strong stake in identifying
these values with folk tradition—in which, of course, violence and revelry,
associated not with dulcimer players and chairmakers but with fiddlers and
banjo pickers, also had a part. Sarah Gertrude Knott, who founded the
National Folk Festival, Annabel Morris Buchanan, one of the originators
of the White Top Folk Festival, and Jean Thomas, the traveling court
reporter who established the "Traipsin' Woman" festival and promoted the
fictional fiddler Jilson Setters—though ideologically quite distinct, all
three participated in this internal missionary movement.[11]

Can something similar be said of the other presentations at the 1973
Festival of American Folklife? Certainly. "No other Indians," writes John
Ewers, the Smithsonian's senior ethnologist, of the Northern Plains culture presented in 1973, "are more widely known. . . . They and their deeds
as big game hunters, warriors, and horsemen have been most frequently
portrayed in the paintings of George Catlin, Frederic Remington, and
Charles M. Russell; in Wild West shows from the days of Buffalo Bill to
current TV dramas, and in countless books and articles of fact and fiction.
Consequently, millions of non-Indians in this country and abroad tend to
think of Indians in terms of the hard-riding, feather-bonneted warriors of
the Northern Plains."[12]

The 1973 Festival's working people and European Americans had not,
perhaps, been as richly elaborated in popular romance as had the Ken-
tuckian and the Indian; but their trades conformed nevertheless to familiar
occupational stereotypes. These are, first, the building trades: carpenters,
plumbers, and electricians; stonemasons, bricklayers, lathers, and plas-
terers; millwrights, pipe and steam fitters, sheet metal workers, and opera-
tives—the laborers whose work surrounds us and upon which we most
directly and palpably depend. They are the working-class and the union
people, just as Serbs and Croatians, settled for two generations in seaports

or near steel mills and coal mines, are representatives of the Slavic peoples who supplied immigrant labor to the burgeoning factories of our delayed industrial revolution: the Popoviches, Karovidovics, and Jovanoves who—in classrooms, labor unions, and city governments—disturbed the composure of a society that habitually conceived of itself as a covenant of Smiths and Joneses.

On the National Mall, then, forms of folklife have become articulations not only of the social institutions whose authority we acknowledged by coming to Washington in the first place, but of the traditions of representation that surround them. Hence it is inevitable that the Festival visitor will see in the presentation a compatibility with some prejudice that will shape his response—"the Ink Spots"—with its particular articulation of social power. But too perfect a compatibility will throw an air of fraudulence over the presentation, a quality of farce or of melodrama. We know we are being hoodwinked when our conceptions, which we use to recognize but not to know, prove too perfect; it is a form of flattery, slippery and self-interested. The Festival visitor, as we've seen, may seek to discover in the Festival presentations evidence of earlier encounters with folklore, or with the presentations themselves in their own settings, and may judge the accuracy of the scholarship, or the authenticity of the presentation, accordingly. In any case, the Festival experience will displace, not supplant, her thought, but beyond that, it will inspire thought of its own, about which it is impossible to generalize except to say that the successful presentation is one that strikes home by virtue of its sheer excellence, power, and beauty, all the more so because it has been highlighted by means of standards belonging to the visitor's own culture. And if the presentation is successful, the Festival visitor will never again identify the object, the performance, or its maker, whether it be bricklaying or bluegrass music, as unalloyed stereotype, even while stereotype persists as the infrastructure of the Festival experience.

The 1973 Festival, then, presented certain traditional cultures whose stereotypes, developed in popular language and art out of myriad social encounters, have become complex national symbols of defining moments upon which the historical spotlight has, at different periods, shone: the transmontane settlement, the westward expansion, the great immigrations, and the industrial triumph. But stereotypes, like all romantic conceptions, are deeply ambivalent—glorious in memory, degraded and comical in actuality, the brunt of habitual contempt and ceaseless caricature. In the language of stereotypes, the brave and independent frontiersman of legend had by 1973 become a welfare casualty; the noble savage of the Plains a drunk; the aspiring peasant of Europe, sailing past the Statue of Liberty, a prole; and the muscled laborer, who built the Grand Coulee, the Empire State Building, and the Golden Gate, a bloated reactionary.

The Festival of American Folklife attempts to harness these forces, the forces of stereotype, which at the most fundamental level have already wedded participant and visitor together in passionate antipathy or love, and to power the Festival's system of human relations by means of them. The Festival's ductile system of framing devices, ranging from theaterlike performance stages to the smaller and more intimate workshop and discussion stages and crafts booths, both reiterates and evacuates persistent and daunting hierarchical class attitudes, reducing them to a set of ephemeral physical structures that, in their physicality, provide the sense of social immunity essential to representation but, in their slightness and ephemerality, ephemeralize social distance itself and open the visitor to the unmediated impact of a living performance. The structure of stereotype, with its mediating sign that absorbs performance and performer into the cultural discourse of the subject and at the same time opens out, over the social boundary, into a broad cultural generalization, is preserved; but the immediacy of presence empties that structure and fills it with a new cultural content that reshapes not only the visitor's perception of the participant's cultural identity but also, it is hoped, given the interactive character of the encounter, the participant's perception of herself.

That is why it was important, in 1973, to bring together under the banner of the institution, in a daylit social setting and in a structure of formal presentation, realms of folklife to which, in one way or another, most of us had already been exposed. For these preconditions replicate originally and concretely, almost as if in a laboratory, the inherited social and psychological preconditions of cultural participation: the attachment of legitimacy, worthiness, and beauty to what culture has marked as legitimate, worthy, and beautiful; a sense of social consensus to which we naturally strive to conform; an authority around which that consensus may form; formal insulation against other concerns that may disrupt or inhibit our willing appreciation, such as prejudice or fear; and, finally, a class or kind in relation to which we place the experience among our other experiences of a similar kind.

It is an effective formula, but one that cannot account, by itself, for the tremendous power, the sense of exhilaration and transport, that emanates from the Festival's best performances. For that we must look into the cultural memory and the power of festivity to unlock it.

The cultural sign is meaningful only in a total order of meaning, which is itself dynamic, going into retreat with historical change or dimmed by the forgetfulness that comes with the evolution of the individual life and of the generation, reemerging from obscurity into a new social present, so utterly uncoupled from its original world as to constitute something entirely novel and strange, meaningful only in a new order of signs equally strange and new. Where orders of meaning have vanished entirely, and the sign erupts in its incandescence onto the cultural surface, we begin history anew and call our epoch by new names; the more deeply hidden the old order of meaning, the more powerful and persistent is our passion to interpret the isolate material sign—a turbulent, urgent desire to remember what we know we know.

At a certain early period of our lives—beginning perhaps with the acquisition of language and our primal naming, extending into youth, and then expiring, though never entirely departing from us but rather leaving its traces throughout our lives in moments of recognition and luminosity, sometimes renewing itself in periods of intense stress or trauma—all our impressions of the world come to us, as Wordsworth knew, in relation only to themselves, originally and in their utter novelty; they become, as our original impressions of the expanding world, the initial, the definitive, and the final expression of that world, as solid, as impenetrable, and as timeless as we suppose the world to be, the entire field of perception being sweepingly and uniformly present. But gradually, as our experience unfolds, memory leaves behind us a wake in which the debris of experience appears and disappears, and vaguely we become aware that the world is transient, that time changes and swallows it; as we wake into adulthood, an impression of spurious novelty, and with it an irritating sense of fraudulence or decadence, lays itself over everything, while behind us stands in its fullness and sufficiency that permanent world, permanently lost, that opened to us with the opening of consciousness.

This vanished world—and the relics of it that survive into our ongoing present—is of course the world of our security, our childhood, not only in some sentimental pastoral sense but psychosocially, as an original pattern and ontological touchstone of learned experiences, expectations, and representations; in the same way that the lover permits the collapse of his will before the unconscious promise of unlimited nurture he attributes to his beloved, unconsciously recognizing in her the signs he associates with that power, so does the imagery of our childhood unconsciously acquire the quality of unabridged reality that comes of our inability to see it in relation to anything but itself, originating nowhere and destined to nothing—as nothing, indeed, but a benchmark or gold standard in the economy of our own minds.

Some icon from our childhood, then, when we recover it later in life, may be enchanted, but more enchanted still are the people and the scenes we first encountered not only in childhood but in representations of the world outside of the confines of childhood, the world yet to be discovered: the world that as children, and as members of a particular class and its culture, we learn either to aspire to or to flee from and, learning this, learn to accept or reject the lesson, depending upon the manner in which it was taught. For the landscape of childhood includes not only its palpable surface, but the windows that open through that surface into imagined worlds, the worlds of stories and tales, of pictures, and of music, crossing physical and social frontiers, all the more powerful and impressive because as children, having not yet learned to apply the standards of evaluation belonging to our social class, we confront these representations baldly and nakedly for what they are: signifiers seeking to become signs.

The consequence of all this is that, as adults, we may irrationally yearn for or aspire toward, or unconsciously be driven by, or conversely, irrationally repudiate the cultural promise that the actual circumstances of class and culture have either bestowed impersonally upon us or will prevent us from ever realizing. We may be quite irrationally enthralled by images first inculcated, say, by popular culture, scenes and images in the world whose distant analogues are a magazine cover, a popular song, a movie, or a storybook, the actual occasion and context of which will never be known to us. And in seeking to establish these scenes and images in our own lives, we may find it necessary—our taste and judgment having passed beyond the innocent receptivity of childhood and shaped themselves fully to the contours of class—to displace them by the cunning belonging to unconscious aims, that is, to transfigure them in ways that makes them acceptable to the standards of our own station and to our sense of the historical and personal moment. By such a process is fashion elaborated, tradition continued, and culture communicated and established, through our own representations, in the imagination of the next generation, which will find its own means of transfiguring it.

It is impossible, after more than thirty years, to look at the original historical context of the Festival of American Folklife, the folk revival of the 1960s—reflecting now upon its surface of images, symbols, and signs—without detecting below its surface the agitation of the popular culture that touched the childhoods of revivalists, a culture whose roots were in the nineteenth century and whose social, economic, and other preconditions had by the late 1950s largely disappeared from the American scene. A man or woman born between, roughly, 1941 and 1948 or 1950—born, that is, into the new postwar middle class—grew up in a reality perplexingly divided by the intermingling of an emerging information society and a decaying industrial culture, a society in which the automobile, the television, the research laboratory, and the transcontinental market would begin to displace the railroad, the radio, the factory, and the regional market—changes that, in less than a generation, would reshape patterns of settlement, the structure of the family, networks of communication, and the material environment itself. Obscurely taking shape around this postwar generation, then, of a definite order and texture, was an environment of new neighborhoods, new schools, new businesses, new forms of recreation and entertainment, and new technologies that in the course of the 1950s would virtually remake the world in which their parents had grown up, a world whose representations nevertheless still surrounded them.

First of those representations to come to mind is the romantic interest in wild and picturesque natural scenes and rustic life, which of course began in the gallery art of the nineteenth century but which, in the age of cheap reproduction of images, ultimately became as commonplace as salt. By the 1950s, long-familiar genre scenes of the rural South, of New England winters, of the Western plains with their wild horsemen and lone Indian braves, had become the stock-in-trade of Christmas cards, picture postcards, magazine covers, art reproductions, and decorative designs of a million varieties on such objects as schoolbook covers and notebooks, calendars, and cereal boxes. In the period preceding the saturation of culture by electronic imagery, these scenes at once informed and guaranteed, mapping the public imagination and opening a window on a national culture in the construction of which commerce, education, and government, brought into unprecedented alliance by depression and war, all shared.

Much of the romance of the American landscape was centered on the railroad, itself a powerful folk symbol, which typically entered the lives of middle-class children of the fifties under the Christmas tree; the railroads had capitalized on and promoted the national interest in the West by adorning their advertisements, depots, restaurants, and hotels with Western and Indian icons and pictures. Other corporations associated with travel, such as the oil and automobile industries, placed commercial images of their products in such settings as the open highway or the small town street, suggesting that the vanishing life of agrarian America was still accessible by automobile.

The railroad and the automobile, then, aside from their purely practical functions, came to be regarded as a means of access to America's romantic realms and vacation paradises, which were themselves scenic, historic, or rustic, usually an association of all three. The architecture of state and national park lodges and restaurants built by the WPA in the early thirties showed the influence of the arts and crafts movement, and historical restorations such as Old Sturbridge Village, Colonial Williamsburg, and Lincoln's New Salem became at once tourist attractions, subjects for travel and commercial photography, and models for domestic design.

Of all of America's romantic images of itself, the most ubiquitous, of course, was the cowboy, who, having made his appearance in the dime novels of the late nineteenth century, established a continuous presence as a singer, dramatic character, and idol on radio, in the movies, and finally on television; his romance provided the motif for hundreds of commercial products, most of which were aimed at children. The influence of his costume, as Hollywood interpreted it, would ultimately be visible in the folk revivalists' passion for leather vests and belts, boots, jeans, and hats and in their constant companion, the guitar.

The career of one of the best-known revivalists, Bob Dylan, illustrates the movement of the displaced cowboy figure up the social ladder. As a high school student in the 1950s, Dylan, still Robert Zimmerman at that point, had been a motorcyclist and a rock-and-roll pianist-singer. Contact with folk revivalists at the University of Minnesota, however, alerted him to the possibility of carrying his project into a new realm, that of the folk hobo epitomized, of course, by Woody Guthrie, a hillbilly singer-songwriter who had won the endorsement of the educated, or the educable, class and who was himself, as a public presence, largely the construction of Alan Lomax and the left-wing folksong revival community in New York.[13] This shift in tone and color—reflected quite literally in the change from black leathers to the natural hide of Dylan's well-known chamois rancher's jacket—although apparently a movement socially downward and culturally westward, in fact signified Dylan's social elevation, as did his adoptive name, which, if nothing else, indicated matriculation in a freshman English course—a gesture in the ritual of disaffection made all the more authentic because, after a few weeks, he dropped the course.[14] Not surprisingly, then, the transformed folk-hero surfaced again, not with second-generation Okies in Bakersfield, but among folkies and beatniks in Greenwich Village.

It is intriguing, I think, that the folklorists of the 1980s, many of whom were revivalists in their adolescence, retrieved the cowboy from concealment in his various displaced manifestations and made him, as an occupational figure, one of the darlings of public folklore: the American Folklife Center, the National Council for the Traditional Arts, and the Smithsonian all mounted exhibits and presentations about him in the 1980s; the Country Music Foundation issued a superb collection of cowboy songs, *Back In the Saddle Again*; and three revivalist musicians formed a trio called Riders in the Sky, devoted to the revival of cowboy songs.

All this makes sense psychologically, for as Freud taught, the growth of consciousness consists in recovering the influences by which behavior is unconsciously prompted in order to install them in the field of conscious awareness. The folk revival perpetuated itself by penetrating into popular culture and depositing seeds of influence that would work upon the succeeding generation. Indeed, it seems that it is just this cycle of recovery and regeneration that now defines generational shift, a movement in the strata of culture more closely linked to the marketplace than to biological regeneration. Many of the young people who carried banjos and guitars to Washington Square in the late fifties and early sixties had, as children, had folksongs sung to them by Popular Front and other politically motivated folksingers at the northeastern summer camps and in the grammar schools where folk revivalists, suppressed in popular entertainment by McCarthyism, had made conscientious inroads.

In the late forties, folksong and dance had come to be associated both with education and with recreation: songbook covers ornamented with the stylized images of various folk heroes and heroines or with ethnic stereotypes could be seen on the pianos of music teachers and choral directors; and among the children's offerings in record shops, in the period immediately preceding the rock-and-roll revolution, might be found the children's songs not only of Woody Guthrie, Huddie Ledbetter, and Pete Seeger, but also those of commercially more successful singers such as Burl Ives, for whom folksinging—in the days of Broadway's *Sing Out, Sweet*

Land, *Oklahoma!*, *Finian's Rainbow*, and *Show Boat*—was ancillary to a career on the stage. Thus one phase of the folk revival planted the psycho-cultural seeds of the next; the rising generation, who as young children had not felt the chill of anticommunism, grew into adolescence with folk images deeply impressed, largely purified of their originally political associations and at the same time connected with the aims of education, music, and theater, which, as children of the urban middle class, they were bound to embrace.

In a sense, then, the folk revival ended before it began; or, to put it another way, the postwar folk revival began at approximately the moment at which all the psychological influences that had prompted it began very swiftly and bewilderingly to disappear on the social landscape. Let historians document the transformation—but the triumph of suburbanization in America is at least indicated, if it was not actually caused, by innovations in existing technologies that finally thrust the residua of prewar popular culture into history: jet travel, commuter expressways and interstate highways, and above all television, which brought a sweeping shift from earlier theatrical and cinematic forms to videoistic sitcoms, news broadcasts, and commercialized children's programming—all of which occurred simultaneously with the consolidation of national networks and the ultimate eclipse of print, cinema, and radio as the principal means by which we mediate the imaginary world.

Railroads and the landscape and mythology summoned into existence by them largely disappeared; representations of the American visage and the American landscape in magazines and other popular media dissolved before the new economic power to travel independently by car, recording the scene with one's camera. A new landscape, characterized by economic and technological power on a vast scale, replaced the old romantic landscape of wilderness, plain, desert, farm, plantation, cattle ranch, village, town, and neighborhood, while wish-fulfillment fantasy and commercialized "news" replaced romance as the prevailing genres of popular entertainment—reflecting, perhaps, a fission in the commercial market, and more fundamentally in the family itself, toward adolescent and pre-adolescent children on one side and toward the nationwide consolidation of a prime-time consumer audience on the other.

As the mode of America's representation of itself to itself changed—more fundamentally and more comprehensively, of course, than the American cultural landscape, which retained many of its cultural residues—we grew up with a new sense of what lay around us in realms not immediately and concretely present and, with a changed sense of the accessibility of those realms, learned to regard them with new attitudes. Indeed, the only instrument through which the old romantic world, which is always the world at a distance, might still be reached was perhaps the phonograph, where folk and regional America still lived precisely *because* they lived, invisibly but audibly, at a distance.

The folk revival, then, was a response to a sense of betrayal or loss; but not three years behind the revivalists came yet a new "generation"—the generation, indeed, whose emergence seemed to call for a metaphorical shift in the meaning of the word—their imaginations furnished not with images of distant places or times but with the commodity culture of the late fifties and sixties, which it seemed only social and political revolution could displace but which time has shown to be far more adaptable to cultural resistance than anyone could have dreamed, because it has absorbed and appropriated that resistance as its modus operandi.

As much of this discussion has emphasized, folk revivalism is deeply bound up with social class and with the prestige accorded to those cultural forms endorsed or valorized by culturally influential people and institutions. It may seem immediately paradoxical to say that folklife, normally identified with lowly, marginal, and disadvantaged peoples, should occupy a position of social prestige, that it is a phenomenon of a rarefied intellectual culture, extending itself into society along pathways formed by power and working its magic by joining that power irresistibly to idealized images of human life. Folksongs have been sung and folk dances danced as much in the name of racial purity as of proletarian revolution—but almost always under the ideological tutelage of elites. Early settlement-house "folk festivals" exhibited traditional culture under the banner of extending the blessings of middle-class culture and affluence to ignorant and poverty-stricken immigrants; early gallery exhibitions of folk art offered to the new rich an education in the iconography of cultural authenticity. Much of the folk revival of the early 1960s was simply and straightforwardly commercial; contemporary folk festivals, by a kind of inverse logic, purify the cultural performance of its commercial affiliations by identifying it with race, class, ethnicity, gender, or some other category of an elitist politics bred in the universities. This is not to say that an intimate acquaintance with actual folklife, beyond the concert hall or the folk festival, cannot be legitimately radicalizing—as folk groups are usually poor, marginal, dispossessed, or dislocated—but that is a consequence of contact with poverty, not with folklife.

The folk revival in every phase consisted of the representation of folklife by influential people and institutions: by photographers, writers, and collectors; by social reformers and educators; by rich aficionados such as the Rockefellers; by museum curators; by Franklin Roosevelt, his government, and its culture workers; by the commercial record, radio, and broadcast establishment; and, in our own period, by the Festival of American Folklife and the many public folklore programs in the various states and communities that have grown out of it—and out of the funding of the National Endowment for the Arts, several important academic programs, and the American Folklife Center of the Library of Congress.

In this context, "folklife" is an elegant, exquisite, or mandarin cultural construction whose venue is the esoteric or connoisseur's record label, the gallery-quality photograph, the avant-garde publication and broadside, the bohemian coffee shop with graffiti from Nietzsche and Wittgenstein on its walls, the university concert hall or common room, the summer watering spot like Newport with its weekend folk festivals, and, of course, the Smithsonian and the Library of Congress; at a deeper layer in its history lie the country dance society, the outing club, the private preparatory school, and the left-wing summer camp.

Into this almost ethereally elevated and rarefied social atmosphere comes the young student singing folksongs, with ever deeper seriousness styling himself or herself as a marginal or alienated social type; as the movement evolves, revivalists "discover" the Mississippi sharecropper with a guitar, the bluegrass band fresh from the coalfield circuit, the mountaineer who has not played a banjo or fiddle for twenty-five years; and, increasingly, recordings of these people, as well as reissues of them and of others like them made thirty years earlier, proliferate until the social atmosphere is saturated with a reality of images and sounds elaborated out of these highly sophisticated representations of extraordinarily unsophisticated, underprivileged, and often primitive culture-bearers, annexing that underprivilege as a covert sign of discontent, alienation, and opposition and laying upon it a powerful charge of beauty, ideality, and desire. The social framework of these representations recedes, withdraws, or disappears, and the revivalist thus emerges, engrossed, into a strange divided world, on one side invisibly supported by high culture's most cosmopolitan and advance-guard tendencies, and on the other ambiguously beckoning from those quarters of American society least touched by its many institutional influences and material advantages.

How did this happen? I suggest that, in one dimension at least, the folk revival was the return on a cultural investment that the postwar parent generation had already made in its children in the form of richly and broadly distributed cultural images in various legitimating official venues such as education, entertainment, and recreation; that, in effect, the imagery of the folk revival was a subtly, even cunningly displaced reappearance of the repressed official and popular cultural imagery that had constituted the imaginary world of at least one sector of the postwar middle-class household—that is, the household whose cultural memory extended into the prewar period. "Repressed," first and foremost, because, in a new social and political atmosphere, the corporate and political establishment had repressed it. But repressed, too, because it no longer enjoyed the sanctions of fashion, taste, distinction, or other forces of class consolidation and aspiration; "displaced" and, through unprecedented means of cultural representation, sublimated, because the 1950s had promised to the generation that would inherit it an America that, like Tom O'Bedlam, wasn't really there.

This reality—that the promised America had vanished—the folk revival never really accepted. It aimed to bring America back from oblivion, or even to make it anew in its own social, political, and personal program. The powerful claim of the revival upon the imagination and the short-lived but exhilarating solidarity of the social formation it produced arose, I think, out of the extraordinary social and psychic utility of its paradoxical and self-contradictory cultural synthesis. The familiar generalization that the revival and the various countercultural movements that surrounded and followed it were reactions against postwar regimentation, conformity, and pseudo-aristocratic pretension in middle-class culture is true as far as it goes; but within this reaction were many kinds of positive cultural syntheses nuanced by variations in the social standing and the individual experiences of the revivalists.

Let us reflect—if I may construct a typical or representative figure—upon the folk revivalist at the instant the defining motive rises upon his or her psychic horizon. From many different commercial and political influences converging in the entertainment industry and its urban centers, a kind of legitimate, collegiate, commercial "folk music" has already appeared in pop culture to displace, but at the same time subtly to resemble, the rock-and-roll music so vigorously discredited by the old commercial music establishment it has nearly destroyed. In pursuit of the new fad, our young man or woman makes a pilgrimage to one of the emergent meccas of folksinging: to Harvard Square, to Newport, to North Beach, to Washington Square Park, to Club 47, the Hungry i, or Gerde's Folk City. Or, equally likely, these places have come to him or her in the form of esoteric record albums, folksong magazines, songbooks, and concerts.

And, in these spots, what does the college freshman from the Midwest or the new postwar suburbia discover? Something unanticipated and probably unrecognized—the children of privilege, enjoying as always the prerogatives of their class: the enlarged confidence, the precocious and liberal attitudes, the style, dash, and daring, and the sheer beauty of money that from Dreiser and Fitzgerald to Salinger and Cheever have so infatuated the American middle class whose economic, social, and cultural condition has amounted, for them, to a rigid and elaborate law of exclusion that cannot be transcended because, among other reasons, it cannot be read or even detected. But at this moment the children of privilege are enacting their power in a strange and bewildering new mode: not with debutante picnics, expensive sports cars, or summer excursions on the family yacht, but with exquisitely shabby blue jeans, untended, unshorn hair, a battered but fine old guitar or banjo (indeed, a very antique), a repertoire of esoteric mountain songs or blues ballads, a complicated instrumental technique, and a dog-eared paperback copy of *Reality Sandwiches* or *On the Road*.

To the young person who, until this moment, has never experienced respectable suburban impecuniosity, ethnic or minority identification, or the gilded provincialism of small-town and suburban life as anything but the field of a dutiful idealism and cautious respectability, such a figure is not only disarming, but enthralling. Without any real awareness of what force has, at bottom, worked its irresistible influence, he or she suddenly becomes conscious of his or her own—unwarranted and impossible—social exclusion, and at the same moment of the possibility of rectifying it through personal transformation. For what, as an object of social aspiration, can be more accessible, or as a symbol of achieved status more thoroughly egalitarian, than a pair of dusty old boots, a pair of worn jeans, a mass of tousled, home-shorn hair, and a few guitar chords? What can be more ductile, moreover, as a vocabulary of status within a particular social formation, than the many inflections of this style, revolving around certain heroes and heroines—not only Woody Guthrie and Pete Seeger, but also Joan Baez and Bob Dylan, who on any college campus in 1963 could be seen in ten thousand different incarnations—as well as certain consumer fetishes such as Gibson banjos, Martin guitars, and Levi's denim jackets?

The folk revival then, through the familiar cultural mechanisms of commodity appropriation and class aspiration, was a site at which an entire generation of young people representing a broad social spectrum might converge, not only the middle class, of course, but again the children of privilege in whose circles the folk revival had begun among affluent social-ists, jazz and blues impresarios, captains of entertainment, and leftist intellectuals, in preparatory schools, colleges, and summer watering-spots. Ultimately, in the fullness of the revival, ethnic and working-class young people would seek to reclaim a marginal or minority cultural tradition newly legitimized by the revival. Now, thirty years later, the folk revival has acquired much larger political significance, history having shown it to have been bound up with still deeper tremors in the strata of society such as the civil rights movement and, more broadly, the threat of nuclear annihilation.

In the folk revival, as in other representations of culture, we can under-stand social class not simply as an arrangement of economic, social, and political power, or even as an ideal system of signs, but as the dehistori-cized ethnemic surface of culture as it has deposited itself over time in the social and economic realms, transforming genuine cultural life and its genuine transformations into a standard by which we measure those deposits in relation to one another—which we do, of course, hierarchi-cally. In this realm, social class is a public fiction—the ethnemic face of history, a masquerade, the form that cultural life has when we see it in one dimension only, without its pasts; this is the way that Marx was able to use social class as a basis for a mythology of evolutionary social struggle.

Yet with many cultures having established themselves on the American landscape, their particular histories eclipsed and only the face of culture exposed, each finding, or struggling to find, a place in the social and economic hierarchy, a system of prestige, standards of taste, manners and modes of conduct, and all else that goes with a class system have indeed developed, in a way perhaps unique in America, around the particular cultural deposits that form the semiology of class. In America class has become, in the context of the myth of social mobility, a semiotic field that not only tends toward the reproduction of the social hierarchy but pro-vides for the symbolic manipulation of it—where social life itself is imbued with the spirit of festivity. Though grounded in the concept of the intimate interdependence of culture and the social process, folk revivalism also asserts the radical independence of culture from the material social process in which it is embedded, not only as an appearance but as a practice; further, it asserts the priority of culture, through the efficacy of the sign, in the genesis of social practice: in short, we are free not only to do but to be what we will. Thus, if at some point we find the upward rungs of the social ladder blocked to us, we simply adopt the expedient of turning the social ladder upside down, converting our own social immobility into an exotic kind of social power and thus salvaging the myth upon which our social lives have been founded.

Barred by class, race, ethnicity, or gender from the regular routes to cultural power, we discover in the folk community and its symbols a social prestige the actual carriers of vernacular culture do not enjoy, and by identifying with the folk we incorporate that prestige at the same time that we enact the sense of our own marginality. This was the strategy of Irish American blackface minstrels in the mid-nineteenth century and of second-generation white ethnic jazz musicians in the 1920s. Though in our own time it enjoys a higher social valuation, folk revivalism is at one with the cacophony of bumper stickers, lapel pins, brand names and logos, school decals, credit cards, club memberships, and the like that mark our almost universal struggle for distinction in an essentially festive society where identity is often, it seems, *only* the identity we present or put on, even at the lowest reaches of the society. The inexhaustible cultural resourcefulness of the black underclass, for example, in a period when hopelessness and desperation are at their apogee, continually shows itself in novel ways of combining and wearing the expensive designer clothing of the shopping mall, annexing its commercial prestige and at the same time wresting out of it a completely original cultural statement. Is it any surprise, then, that the young, white, upper-middle-class suburban fashion plates are wearing their baseball caps backward, their basketball shoes with laces dragging, their stonewashed overalls with one strap unbuttoned?

This is the very important sense in which a folk festival such as the Smithsonian's Festival of American Folklife, though underwritten by powerful commercial and political institutions, performs some of the same work as certain unofficially festive social arenas, for example, those gay and bohemian urban districts in which, by tacit agreement, social dissidents joined together in their collective differences rifle the ethnonoetic plenum for a new identity, putting their "real" identities behind them and exhibiting such imagination and originality that these sites seem to become— often on particular days of the week such as Sunday afternoons or particular occasions and dates such as Halloween, and in particular places such as San Francisco's Castro Street or Washington's Adams-Morgan district— outpourings from the ethnomimetic fountainhead of culture. The folk festival and the alternative social arena differ, of course, in the discourses of identity upon which they draw and in their temporal, spatial, and sociological status; but as instances of festivity they have in common their oblique relation to the commercial and political culture in which both are embedded and from which each conscientiously distinguishes itself socially and politically.

The folk festivals of the sixties gave added legitimacy to the already broadly expressed impulse of middle-class youngsters to migrate symbolically down the social ladder, adopting the costumes and the music of sharecroppers, farmers, peasants, migrant workers, milkmaids, hoboes, cowboys, and the like, and ultimately they opened the door to the wildly festive cultural movement we now associate with San Francisco's Haight-Ashbury. In historical perspective, this moment of cultural transition appears more and more like a cultural revolution, festivity being, in this case, not incidental but fundamental to the process—but a revolution so threatening as to have inspired, once oil-price inflation began to erode its economic foundations, a massive reaction whose consolidation still dominates the social, cultural, and political field.

The folk festival, then, belongs to a wider festive culture into which society itself regularly reaches in order to renew itself, insulated from the ethnemic forms of regular social life by the coherent and bounded character of the symbolic inventories upon which it draws. Festivity, however, can transgress even these boundaries. When social roles are inverted or exchanged symbolically without reference to such a traditional or conventional vocabulary—within the semiology of the social system as it is at a particular historical moment and outside an officially or unofficially festive context or enclave—then we have entered the perfidious but grimly festive world of the infiltrator, the confidence man, the impostor.

Outside the context of the festival, the ethnemic mask can become a sinister, unwholesome power, deeply threatening to the social order: one thinks of the junior chamber of commerce executive who arrives at a first job interview in a three-hundred-dollar suit fit for a partner in a Washington law firm; or of the high school biology teacher who, on weekends, patrols the city streets in combat boots, camouflage dress, and aviator sunglasses. The outright impostor, indeed, posing as a surgeon, an heiress, a pilot, with sometimes fantastic powers of deception and of access, suggests, disquietingly, the extent of fabrication, invention, and representation in the formation even of social identities normally accepted as authentic; it seems that the festive, as an element of ordinary social behavior, continuously undermines the inherent stasis of social structures on behalf of the rearticulation of personality to them—a process that can restore and perpetuate, transfigure or destroy.

What is festivity?

We spin our lives out of care and catch ourselves in its web; life proves itself in care and elaborates itself out of care, burdening and unburdening itself in a perpetual cycle. The codes of care are written into our very substance; among these is the power of human recognition that links us together in the bond of care: the primal recognition of the mother's breast, of the face of the nurturing parent who cares and cares for, in whose frame are the discoverable features that will be the pattern of all subsequent recognitions—and, collaterally, recognition of the signifiers of sexuality and of all the natural languages, with their cultural inflections, of the body.

In caring and in being cared for, our nature continually expresses and experiences itself: infant and parent, self and society, creature and Creator realize themselves and their relation in care. There is little human failure that is not rooted in the failure of care, and much human excess and monstrosity that can be laid to it. Care many times transfigured and sublimated brings great human energy and power, growing with and upon itself; without care, caring, and life itself, shrinks, becomes grotesque, and dies. Human value lies along the axis of care and turns on it. Nothing more obfuscates and confounds our sense of what is primary and what is secondary than the prolonged release from care in continual safety, security, and comfort; nothing more swiftly acquaints us with what is fundamental than care stirring in its own vast helplessness before sickness, suffering, pain, isolation, loneliness, and death.

Festivity is the suspension of care, and the suspension of care always awakens the spirit of festivity. It arises in the pause or repose that follows the consummation, or the promise of consummation, of a career of love or work, and it is, like the wedding or harvest feast, the first enjoyment of the fruits of our labor. Hence festivity visits us at once with all its power in the moment—and it is *only* a moment—that the barns are full, the corn heaped high, the plenum stored to capacity with accumulated human labor, the moment at which we face the promise of indulgence, play, and abandon, the broad freedom from want that in the course of days or weeks gradually erodes; for even in the most festive settings, habits and customs, ranks and classes, duties and responsibilities reassert themselves as the sheer traffic and business of festivity gradually reanimate its initiating surcease. In thus forgetting ourselves we remember, as we cannot in the daily round of ceaseless immediate concerns, our dark dependencies and secret purposes and permit ourselves the pleasures that lie in the gratification of desire, paradoxically bringing into being, or at least arousing the sensation of, a world without desire—that is, a world in which the suspension of care awakens with fresh and original vitality all the imperatives of care.

Suspension, that is, not emancipation from, care: for the trajectory, the shape, of festival, from its exhilarating opening moment, when the cares of the world are put behind us, to its close in rituals of social bonding and solidarity, is a gradual reconsolidation of care and its forms within the space of festivity itself. Festivity is always a microcosm of and an object lesson in the economy of care. As life is formed of care, perfect release from care would be a kind of nonlife; hence festivity is always framed by care, and insofar as festivity is temporal, it is, and must be, temporary. And as, in society, the medium, the agent, and the issue of care is identity, so does festivity untie the moorings of identity and all the laws and structures that constitute it, causing it to lie idle or to drift; festivity takes up identity and steals it away, scattering the keys of recognition so that all its doors may be thrown open, exposing all, revealing all, and, ultimately, reconstituting identity in new forms.

In this sense festivity, the suspension of care, is primordially an infantile state, our condition at the mother's breast, and all festivity partakes of the maternal, awakening that enchantment that comes of infant and parent's mutual absorption in mutual recognition, at once the field of individuation and selfhood and the total absorption of self into other. In the first instant after birth, our independent existence is already shockingly unfamiliar, already demanding its own repeal. That the end—as a purpose, a tendency, and a terminus—of life is our ultimate emancipation from it is the irresistible logic, the permanent lesson, and the unconscious expectation read into us by the processes of the womb, the expulsion from it, the nurturing parent, and our eventual separation from the sources of nurture. As the most unrememberable of our unremembered memories, these processes are the geothermal engine of the erotic field that surrounds us, with its two poles, the cultural and the natural, festivity and sexuality. Thus, in a sense, though born into suffering we are delivered into festivity, for festivity is the very condition of love, in which care cares for itself, released from care in the perpetual renewal of care.

Tourism is a kind of festivity that sends the tourist out of his or her native element at the end of a social and economic lifeline extending from it; but festivity as microcosm can arise, too, in specially bounded environments whose role in culture we can perhaps best understand in relation to festivity. These are, of course, the entire range of gardens, parks, malls, and other environments in which representation inscribes itself upon and compromises the actual, promising plenitude, adventure, pleasure, and diversion set over and against the world outside their boundaries. The shopping mall and the hotel megastructure, which place everything "at our fingertips," arouse festive expectations and shape our behavior accordingly. The holiday and the tour, insofar as they promise concentrated pleasure and diversion and represent a suspension of ordinary care, are essentially festive, with concomitant festive masking, license, and the ultimate transformation of masking and license into some new configuration of care.

A familiar illustrative form of festivity is perhaps the inversion holiday, in which the lowest social groups temporarily occupy the stations of the highest, and the highest those of the low. By detaching the role from its player and its office, the inversion renews the general dedication to the social order by converting it to play and revealing momentarily its deeply dramatic and artificial character, loosening the bonds of habit and custom that dull the perception of one's place in the hierarchy and at the same time restoring, through symbolic displays and enactments, a sense of self-esteem and personal significance, an awareness of the reality as well as the experiences of others, and, finally, a larger conviction of collective destiny that is often of a religious or cosmic character. Having dissolved the social structure, though only symbolically and temporarily, we resume our ranks and stations, our roles and functions, restored in the conviction that society is a kind of natural imperative. It is the paradox of the inversion holiday, however, that a temporary and symbolic destabilization of social power in an atmosphere of indulgence, license, and play works through the inherently transitory nature of this state to restore social power, for it is by the very measure and standard of that power and its symbols that festive symbols and displays achieve their purpose.

That the inversion *is* transitory and symbolic should point us toward those social forces out of which festivity arises, as well as toward the ways in which festivity and the festive spirit inform human occasions not formally designated as festive. Inversion by rank, indeed, is usually far less flatly literal than it was in the medieval up-so-doun day, when mayors and aldermen exchanged places with beggars and fools; far more often, it occurs theatrically by means of masks and costumes, and moreover it sweeps over the whole range of social difference, inverting not only social and political ranks but also class and sex as well as certain socially ordained forms of self-representation that determine the frontier between public and private. Thus cross-dressing and clowning, which, as Bakhtin points out, often involve public displays of sexual and eliminative behavior, are a normal part of festivity. All of these inversions are furthermore accomplished, not by a kind of universal exchange of roles, through masking, but by calling upon a traditional vocabulary of symbols, effigies, signs, and emblems.

The Festival of American Folklife is an inversion holiday in at least two senses. It brings representatives of enclaved communities and economically marginal or archaic activities, whether established in a marginal community or sequestered in the private life, into the view of the public culture and into a relationship with it, in wholesale fashion transforming this or that role, function, or pastime into an ethnemic mask through which most, but not all, of the new social negotiation must occur. In some cases, such a transformation is a regular part of the participant's interaction with the public culture, and it sometimes invites the same sad reliance on stereotyped expectations and responses; in other cases, as with displaced folk cultures like that of the refugee Kmhmu, who have not yet developed a mask with which to mediate their interactions with the public culture, the sheer vulnerability of the exposed social self so sensitizes visitor and participant alike that meaningful encounter may be impossible. On such occasions society, indeed, has been turned both upside down *and* inside out; the close and sequestered areas of life, of individuals and communities, have been opened to exhibition, transformed from private to public, from functions into performances, and the social mask and the personality, as the immediate environment of the self, have been brought into alignment. At the same time, a social hierarchy has been inverted, elevating visions of working-class, peasant, and other unofficial cultures into the precincts of elite culture and powerful institutions and to the center of the touristic gaze, which in turn descends socially to experiment with the identity of the folk—putting it on, in a sense, imaginatively.

Herein lies the social as well as the sacred efficacy of festivity—the deep influence of the mask upon its wearer, and its power to awaken in him or her the passion or the virtue that it signifies. Like lovers we become what our beloved has attributed to us, and we love because we love ourselves as he or she has conceived us. The mask of the folk artist cultivates in her the very quality that prevailing social attitudes, perhaps, have compelled her to devalue; her participation in the festival sends her back to her community a changed person—it even makes her, perhaps, into what the folklorist has believed her to be. Thus, by empowering the folk artist in his practice, the festival in fact enforces the academic or romantic conception that defined the folk artist to begin with; and thus, like other inversion rituals, the folk festival practically enforces or constitutes those social structures that it has symbolically inverted.

Social hierarchy deteriorates, more or less briefly, when the clown exposes the commonplaces of the human body, which level distinctions of rank. The ludic masks of carnival, moreover, replace those distinctions with symbolic and traditional inversions of them. The ethnemic mask, on the other hand, effaces the signs of our participation in the surrounding social and economic order and exposes, sometimes shockingly, the visible human initiatives that in simpler economies and cultures are practically and materially the basis of life, just as eating, digestion and elimination, and sexuality and death—the clown's perennial subjects—are biologically the basis of life. If the clown embarrasses us, shows us how, at *bottom*, we are no different from anyone else, so does the folk artist in a sense embarrass us, showing us that in the end the status we claim for ourselves—the social, economic, and cultural status, even the personal record—is nothing of our own but is, rather, an elaborate effect of the civilization in which we have only an obscure and ineffectual part, a part that is itself very likely an effect of remote, inconceivable, and even sinister causes.

As the ludic mask undermines social pretension, then, the Festival's basic cultural proposition undermines our easy and habitual dependence upon the invisible agents that, in all spheres of human activity, underwrite our material existence, define the realms in which we contribute our own exertions to the common purpose as well as the manner in which we contribute them, and even supply the forms of the imaginative life through which we complete ourselves, whether or not that life has any grounding in the actual lives we lead. Something in us—the framework of our social identity—collapses, but its collapse at the same time exposes, as if that framework were so much stage machinery, the mimetic grounds of identity, at once releasing us from identity and holding out the possibility of its total rejuvenation.

This is a disorienting, a disabling moment. We are in love, and in our awakened sense of unworthiness lies the urgency to reform, to grasp life anew, to redeem ourselves in the approbation of the person who has thus revealed us to ourselves.

In traditional societies, festivals, carnivals, and other symbolic enactments regularly recirculate the cultural message, rearticulating the imaginary to the actual structures of social life and to the familiar forms of authority and power. A world that cannot be thus renegotiated is one that, though perceived, cannot be experienced; this is precisely the condition of the bereaved person, the exile, or the culturally dislocated group, lost in an unreal world, a sheer surface that does not, so to speak, come home to us.

But as the folk revival illustrates, the emergent, in our culture, resembles more a kind of dreamwork in which, by Freud's unforgettable account of it, allusion and shift of accent, condensation, pictorialization, elaboration, and other displacements impart to ordinary social life a festive and imaginary character that indicates a return, in disguise, of the repressed or unremembered cultural memory. This process is rarely a simple and straightforward recovery of childhood, any more than the adult dream is the simple and straightforward fulfillment of a wish. We do not literally reproduce the past or adopt without modification the stereotyped manners and styles of our social class. Nor does the displaced ethnic group adopt without revision what it supposes are the manners and customs of the dominant culture, unless its cultural will has collapsed under the weight of some terrible oppression, producing in its distorted reflection of the oppressor unwitting cultural travesties—class stereotypes eerily embodied in real people and, more cruelly, in abject and exacting conformity to them. Consequently, the folk product is rarely either the original ethnic product or the unmediated hegemonic form—the African counterrhythm or the Irish reel on the one hand, or the European meter or the Resurrection story on the other. The folk product, instead, is a new manifestation—the syncopated reel that becomes the breakdown, the story of a dead child reborn out of a flaming tree—whose form is riven with the mysterious and compelling latency of the retrieved but unremembered cultural dream.

This is the level at which the sympathy of the folk revivalist with the "folk"—both, in a sense, culturally displaced—really lies. As Plato taught and Freud repeated, love carnal and spiritual is aspiring: we love, socially and culturally, above us, sometimes inverting the social hierarchy in order to do so, finding in love the opportunity for realizing an idealized self and at the same time unconsciously displacing the forbidden object of our desire with a symbolic substitute to whom immediate access is denied by social and cultural prohibitions, into which are also written the codes by which access might be opened.

Folk culture defamiliarizes the familiar hegemonic forms with its own technical, stylistic, and formal anomalies, which resonate with a queer and inscrutable familiarity. A fascination with it arises, like sexual desire itself, out of the perception of lack, the desired object having migrated per-fidiously out of consciousness to reside, apparently, with and within the other, through whom, and only through whom, it can be recovered. Falling in love—the sensation that we are falling into the well of person-ality as the will collapses, in spite of our efforts to prevent it—causes exactly this feeling of imbalance or vertigo as, under the impetus of an irresistible sexual prompting, we give away through projection the very grounds of our possibility as personal and social beings. And if the folk revivalist's or folklorist's advocacy of folk culture has sometimes an in-tense, dogmatic, chivalrous, even a passionate character, if it is sometimes bound up with a dedication to the political, social, and economic salvation of that culture, we must remember the lover's advocacy of his beloved, which, however irrational, unconsciously recognizes that it is, ultimately, the championing of some essential and inviolable thing in himself.

The spirit in which, at an unguarded moment, we catch something familiar in unfamiliar eyes is the festive spirit; the moment at which, over the edge of the Festival stage or across one of its enchanted spaces, we catch in the stranger a momentary revelation of something that we have detected, but scarcely acknowledged, in ourselves—that is the festive moment. It is a moment of recognition and of conspiracy, a moment in which the mind seizes and invests the other with an immense possibility that cannot be known in itself, and which, indeed, if encountered in its natural identity, rather than in its apparent difference, could not carry the magic of recognition borne by resemblance.

With the special prerogative of representing ourselves to others as we will and of encountering their representations of themselves to us, the festive atmosphere—replete with the human objects of social aspiration and sexual desire, conscious and unconscious, all framed mimetically but not, as in art, illusory—swells with erotic energy, the energy that through the genesis of cultural forms realizes the forms of human imagination.

Festivity is the social apotheosis of desire; it is essentially utopian. The final social forms of festivity, considered for the moment not as an excep-tional and transitory mode of social behavior but as a manifestation of its essentially semiotic character, and that semiosis as the elaboration and organization of power, are perhaps twofold: the totalitarian state or the theocracy, which projects an entire society into an ideal or sacred realm beyond time, claiming to have transcended ordinary social and moral laws and, in sustaining itself, permitting itself, sometimes horribly, to transgress them; and revolution or war, wherein social inversion, the dissolution of social categories, and the suspension of ordinary cares are all violently literal. Though it is perhaps shocking to detect the spirit of festivity in, say, Hitler's youth rallies, his inversions of power relationships, his mobilization for war, and the monstrous libertinage and cruelty released by his regime, this is the direction in which the logic of festivity, when the boundary between the festive and the quotidian somehow breaks down, inexorably leads.

To be summoned away from hearth and home to some high collective purpose may be exhilarating and irresistible, very like a holiday, but festival follows an inevitable trajectory into care, which here, in revolution and war, finds its extremes of sublimity and horror. It is, I suspect, in the promise of festivity borne by some high purpose that murderous fanaticism takes hold; and it is to festivity that the veterans of wars and revolutions turn, in costume, when the social order has again closed over them and buried their former glory. Think of the holiday parade with its drum majorettes, fireworks, and marching bands; it only recalls, in festive form, the conquering army, rolling in from a distant empire to liberate us from the terrible weight of things as they are. Such events recall, and in recalling they reinvent, the ultimate festive moment, the triumph, when we stand between one society and another, full of joy at our release and hope for our deliverance.

The Empire of Ice Cream

"Call the roller of big cigars," commands Wallace Stevens,

> The muscular one, and bid him whip
> In kitchen cups concupiscent curds.
> Let the wenches dawdle in such dress
> As they are used to wear, and let the boys
> Bring flowers in last month's newspapers.
> Let be be finale of seem.
> The only emperor is the emperor of ice-cream.[1]

When the humidity is 99 percent, and it is 99 degrees in the shade, and the sun rages overhead in its endless silent excoriation, it is concupiscence, that longing of the soul and the body for what will gratify and delight, that guides us as we stroll across the Mall, from India to Louisiana or from Tunisia to Kentucky, toward the vendor under the boxwood tree proffering ice-cream cones. The cone is melting and sweet; there is comfort in it; and from the soft mound of its head to the tiny cream-filled cup in which its form both ends and begins, it is complete.

As Robert Rydell remembers in his excellent book *All the World's a Fair*, the ice-cream cone was invented in

St. Louis, at the great Louisiana Purchase Exposition of 1904, by a resourceful concessionaire who plopped a scoop of the stuff atop a rolled waffle. In the vastness of that exposition, with its twelve hundred acres of plaster palaces, plazas, and parks, its imperial displays of airships and automobiles, its giant floral clock that measured Time in thousandths of seconds, its learned congresses in the natural sciences, philosophy, and mathematics—a fair so vast that doctors warned their neurasthenics away, fearing they might collapse—the ice-cream cone must have been a consoling, childish, even infantile pleasure. With their "visions of empire," dreams of progress, and rituals of Manifest Destiny, the international expositions of the Belle Epoch sounded the utopian themes that a century later, though much elaborated and displaced, are still the shaping myths of public policy even at the Festival of American Folklife; and yet, as the wonderful longevity of the ice-cream cone reveals, the compass of human nature always turns with the rest of nature in a field of vital, not metaphysical, forces.

Where I grew up, in Chicago, site of the great Columbian Exposition of 1893, "Little Egypt," who danced the *danse du ventre* at the Streets of Cairo Theater on the midway, is better preserved in the popular, if not the public, memory than the engineering marvel of the Ferris wheel or the beacon that shone from the tower of the Electricity Building, of which one rarely hears except in museums and in books. The name of Little Egypt, as the very essence of steamy sexuality, would from time to time issue enigmatically from my parents' lips, though both were born in the decade after the fair; and I had an old uncle who had visited the fair at the age of nine and claimed to remember her. I myself first encountered Little Egypt in a Chicago tavern, where, painted in garish oils, she lay luxuriously across the oaken panels above the bar for idlers to gaze upon in the afternoons, and in the evenings presided over the delinquencies of secret men and women.

An old Tin Pan Alley song recalls the hoochee-koochee dance that was all the rage at St. Louis; it had been introduced at Chicago by Fatima, the exotic lovely whom visitors used to wait in line for hours to see. But more popular at St. Louis than the hoochee-koochee, more even than the ice-cream cone, were the Bagobos, Negritos, Igorots, and Moros—"wild tribes" displayed in "ethnological villages" on the forty-seven-acre site of what the chairman of the federal government's Philippine Exposition Board called "an exposition within an exposition," the Philippine "Reservation." As Rydell suggests, the popularity of these exhibits was certainly owing in part to the apparent simplicity and primitiveness of the tribal life, as contrasted with the complex wonders of Industrialism, at least as these were represented in the White City and the Reservation; but far more amusing was the public scandal that erupted when William Howard Taft, then civil governor of the Philippines, sought to put shirts and trousers on the naked or nearly naked Igorot and Negrito men, women, and children, hoping to avoid "any possible impression that the Philippine Government is seeking to make prominent the savageness and barbarism of the wild tribes either for show purposes or to depreciate the popular estimate of the general civilization on these islands."[2]

The "ethnological" interest of nakedness was, however, stoutly defended by the anthropologists connected to the exposition, particularly Professor Frederick Starr, chairman of the Department of Anthropology at the University of Chicago. Artificial costumes on the natives, he wrote, "would change a very interesting ethnological exhibit which shocks no one into a suggestive side-show." Starr brought thirty of his female students, "society" coeds, to study the Igorot in conjunction with his daily lectures on art, sculpture, race, and cannibalism. No doubt they found the spectacle edifying, no doubt instructive; and, as the surviving stereoscopic images and other photographs from the exhibition suggest, no doubt there were many who framed their experiences not only in notebooks and through their opera-glasses but in the viewfinders of yet another technological novelty of the period, their new Kodak "Brownies."[3]

But here we should pause briefly ourselves to contemplate this puzzling reflexive structure, an exposition that frames another exposition, which in turn frames an exhibit itself doubly framed by an intellectual category on the one hand and, on the other, by a camera lens, which in turn frames an image that, once photographed, joins in turn the continuum of photographic images to be framed yet again by the order of photography, as something distinct from the several orders of relation that enclose it: the order of the international exposition and its many discourses of power, the discourse of technology, the discourse of race, and the discourses of the body.

We have seen this structure of reiterated frames posited and repeated throughout our discussion of the representation of culture. We saw how the rite of exorcism was framed for dramatic exhibition by an aristocratic household as a political thrust against an established order, and how its ironic double reframing, first by a priest and then by a playwright, cluttered the speech of a madman framed as a disguise by a young nobleman, who was framed by a conspiracy structurally integral to a plot framed for a stage, which was itself framed by the laws of an increasingly repressive official society. We saw how the ocular framing of newly enclosed property framed by surveyor's devices produced the order of a landscape architecture that anticipated the cultural discourse of our own commercial spaces, where the retail drama frames a spectacle of cultural indicia, emblem, icon, and stereotype. We toured the vast frame of the National Mall, which frames not only its own public space but the interior spaces of the various museums, each in turn framing its exhibits to the various gradients of human desire; and we exited the museum onto the Mall and into the Festival of American Folklife, where through various frames we explored the Festival's process of constructing the idea of folklife, especially in relation to stereotype, in which the social, economic, cultural, and other boundaries of ordinary social life become the structural elements of a concept that, by a kind of metaphor, frames the life of the other as a variant of our own.

In the age of the World's Columbian Exposition, an age of, to us, extreme sexual modesty, I suppose it is not extraordinary that the naked human body should have proved so interesting and so compelling, nor perhaps is it especially puzzling that the weaving of a basket or the picking of a banjo should have proved intriguing in an age of hi-fi, plastics, and punchcards. We no longer flock like our great-grandparents to sculpture gardens or to international expositions in order to gaze upon the undraped human form, being more than amply supplied with images of it by a culture in which the commodity has been almost completely eroticized and the erotic itself, of course, eagerly commodified. Had King Lear attended the fair at St. Louis, in any case, he might have noted in the poor, bare, fork'd animals before him a candid representation of his own condition, and, like Professor Starr, considered them well. Professor Starr understood that beneath his own waistcoat, and under the skirts and bodices of the society coeds, were limbs and breasts as naked as those of the most savage and unashamed Filipino tribe—that the "ethnological" interest of the Igorot lay precisely in the fact that, in the end and at bottom, we secretly know the other to be simply ourselves. Distance them as we might—with cultural arrogance, political intimidation, organized violence—they were and are interesting because in them we see, or imagine we see, something that properly belongs to us, something lost or denied, something to be studied, contemplated, grasped, and in effect possessed, made our own again, even as in gaining possession of the other we lose some or all of ourselves.

This is not to say that there are no erotic interests at work, in our day, at the Festival of American Folklife. No official record exists of the trysts, assignations, flirtations, and affairs that the Festival on the Mall has occasioned—but I imagine it would fill volumes. That many Festival participants seek transient sexual relationships, or may actually fall in love at the Festival, is not some social epiphenomena, a sort of summer opportunism, but the very essence of festivity. Being far removed, some even violently dislocated, from home, many participants, like any strangers in a strange place, form new alliances upon whatever pretext may be available to them. Many testify that the Festival becomes for them a world unto itself; the outside world, its news, its sport, its politics, are all forgotten, while an erotic enthusiasm suffuses all activity, especially the festive activities of the evenings, filling the participants with a preternatural energy and often driving them, as experienced participants and Festival workers know, beyond their physical limits. In a world of people and objects charged with erotic energy, we are like lovers mired in a dream, as unfathomable to those outside it as is our behavior under its influence—as unfathomable, indeed, as culture itself.

Remember, too, that the Festival came into being nearly thirty years ago in what was called, in those days, the country of the young, near the end of the 1960s, when an entire generation, as if by some vast collective natural impulse, was busily jettisoning all the inculcated inhibitions of a regimented, repressive postwar epoch, testing the moral limits of a society that, in its reaction, has not yet exhausted, it seems, its tremendous reserves of intolerance. Only come down to the Mall, even now, in the afternoon, to one of the music stages, and observe what is taking place there, especially on one of those tropically hot and humid days that are typical in Washington during the first week in July.

People—hundreds of them, young people certainly, but parents with babies, too, and retirees, and often it seems every nation and race, from Ukrainian peasant women to Senegalese courtiers—have crowded shoulder to shoulder and back to back to turn, tap, twist, trot, stride, step, shimmy, shake, shuffle, bend, bow, and break to the rhythms of whatever music may be there, and it could be *any* music, save, probably, the European orchestral kind. These people are mostly Washington locals, many of them young workers from the nonprofit sector up at Dupont Circle, or students from the suburbs, or professionals from Georgetown, maybe even a few interns from Capitol Hill or bureaucrats from the agencies and departments, always joined by handfuls of intrepid participants from distant parts with wide smiles on their faces; they have come to dance, to have fun, to let down their hair, to fracture the dull routine of the office and the grim isolation of the apartment with sometimes ostentatious reproofs to propriety and convention. Always there are the one or two exhibitionists and rag dolls, as well as the self-appointed authorities and pensive, hesitating wallflowers. But the sexual thrumping of the music, the exposed arms, legs, and shoulders, the bare chests and unbound breasts—it is too hot to stand on ceremony, and we make ourselves as nearly naked as the Igorot as modesty, or what is left of it, will allow—transform the atmosphere into a medium of erotic possibility in which total strangers, who on the Metro might spend a full twenty minutes pretending not to notice one another, may in an instant be opposing their bodies in symbolic embraces that, over the course of hours or days, may conceivably carry them into that most vexed and indeterminate of Washington institutions, the "relationship," or even, perhaps, into an evasive and theoretical "long-term commitment," which, if it is not exactly life itself, at least holds out the possibility that life is something that may, if we are lucky, happen to us.

How tediously pedantic would be the Festival of American Folklife, how un-festival-like, without the dancers, the hand-clappers, and the foot-stompers! How flat and mechanical would its exterior life become were it not for that hidden, underground erotic life whose force draws the participant, the visitor, and the volunteer, however fleetingly or permanently, into its influence. The Festival of American Folklife, like all true festivals, is—as the dancers understand better, it seems, than the anthropologists and folklorists who produce it—a time for fun and a reservoir of promise: sexual promise, certainly, for in a milieu of relaxed inhibition, blurred or effaced social identity, abandoned roles and functions, and open sexual invitation, anything, sexually, speaking, is possible.

Hence the Festival is erotic in a sense far deeper and broader than the merely sexual, for sexuality is, of course, never merely itself—never simply a matter of secret thoughts, hidden places, and unspoken functions—but a cultural formation that binds to itself and deploys for its own use all the resources of similarity and difference: not only age, gender, family, personality, taste, interest, and experience, but also status and class, ethnicity, tradition, and race and all the attractions and aversions, the dreams and aspirations, the privations and longings that attach to them. Social alignments, economic configurations, class affiliations, and ethnic, cultural, and racial identities, even as they assert themselves in their own continuance, perpetually and blindly carry out, through the synthetic power of human imagination, the inscrutable will of Eros. The dance, as a symbol of his dominion, is an excellent figure for a cultural festival, indicating as it does that Eros is at the same time the engine of festivity and the natural impetus of the cultural process. At the Festival, then, where classes, races, traditions, and cultures, in addition to the sexes, meet, however fractionally or imperfectly its promise is realized or achieved, there is always in it a horizon of limitless and wonderful possibility, as well as a lurking spectre of terror, dislocation, and pain.

The professor with his notebook and the society coed with her camera confront their own nakedness as well as a doubled exposure of the real, the remembered, or the imagined nakedness of the beloved in the Igorot, whose formal insulation invites a contemplative gaze of an intensity that not even communal, domestic, or sexual intimacy would allow. Exhibition itself is a kind of doubled nakedness, an expression of dominance endured, negotiated, or granted and hence always the direct exposure of a real as well as of a putative relation. We cannot put the Philippine Reservation entirely behind us, either in principle, for the nakedness of the Igorot is simply an expression of the principle of exhibition, or in practice, for though it has no place in the Festival's official discourse, in fact the dramatic exposure of the body is an integral part of folklife exhibition— certainly not always with an immediate sexual meaning, though the physical charms of dancers and musicians often reveal themselves in explicitly or symbolically sexual movements—and perhaps may be said to form part of what constitutes the folk performance.

The element that distinguishes the folk festival from the folk museum or the folklore collection or the folksong recording is indisputably the living presence of the folk performer, engaged in an activity that, however ethnographically or historically designated, has this special property: that it engages the physical body in some immediate exhibitory way, either because it requires no mechanical aids whatever, or because such simple instruments or tools as it does require themselves engage the body in significant ways, or because certain kinds of complex technologies such as those involved in the building trades, transportation, or agriculture themselves call upon the resources of the body in dramatic or commanding ways. Some folklife presentations—for example, the medicine show pitchman extolling his elixirs and nostrums, or the herbal remedist adumbrating her teas, pastes, and potions—may consist only of talk, but talk, like song, dance, and musical performance, is also a rich exhibitor of human corporality. Though festival producers tend to regard the display of the body as a limit, one that inhibits or even prohibits certain kinds of presentation except through talk, text, and other kinds of mediation—tale traditions and folk beliefs are especially resistant—we should perhaps regard the body as an informing principle that grounds the festival in its vital medium.

However intelligently presented with exhaustive scholarship and articulate discussion, however richly textualized and contextualized with photographs and text panels, however precisely situated in its structure of stages, platforms, and arenas, the festival exhibit is first and fundamentally an encounter with the corporality of the participant, both in itself and as it is elaborated in his or her performance. The stamina of the Senegalese dancer, pounding his calloused feet in the dust, spittle draining along the corners of his mouth as he grins fixedly through his exhaustion; the fragile bones in the hands of the potter, strung with them like a tiny harp, his long fingers resting in the wet clay like crane's feet in the sand, his mottled teeth clamped on the paper end of a drooping yellow cigarette; the tall, narrow architecture of the Cajun washboard player, as inscrutable behind his sunglasses as a downtown office building; the round hips of the hula dancer, her eyes cast aside to the ground, first one side then the other, her hands floating on the surface of the air; the sinewy forearm of the smith exposed by his rolled-up shirtsleeve, bursting blue veins crawling toward his wrists as if to seize the black hammer out of his huge hand; the gummy eyes of the quilter, the sad eyes of the weaver, the intense eyes of the carver, the gay eyes of the accordionist, the terrified eyes of the Hmong embroiderer—none of this is lost in the encounters on the Mall. Nor are the faces: the creased red cheeks and the jagged teeth of the Ukrainian woman, exactly as you have seen them in some photomagazine; the flashing grimace and shelled eyes of the Haitian vodun dancer, the ebony shine of her skin, the red kerchief around her head, the turquoise skirt with ruffles, a kind of unsettling tempestuousness at once proving on the pulse and violently negating every caricature and airline poster you have ever seen; the round cheeks, the modish hairdo, the blue jeans and running shoes, and the chewing gum of the Irish flautist, who is, after all, just a teenager.

In recognition, which is always reflexive, there is intercourse or congress, and in such intercourse, as between dancers, always a fulcrum of mutuality and an outer limit of its possibility. The intimacy, singularity, and essential insularity of the encounter between and among visitors, participants, volunteers, and tourists on the Mall belongs to the unbounded world of human social experience, one that sometimes runs counter to, or deliberately resists, or remains utterly indifferent to the

Festival's own construction of people and their performances. We have seen how, through the recovery of a series of historical alignments between various ethnic, racial, regional, occupational, and other perceived or postulated groupings and the socially privileged subject, the Festival of American Folklife in its formative years generated an ethnemic system of folklife categories. But on the Mall itself, on the level of personal encounter, a new ethnomimetic process engages the visitor in a struggle against his or her own fragmentation by the opposing forces of absence and presence, abstraction and concretion, generalization and particularization, presentation and representation. Failure in this struggle brings profound disorientation, dejection, and, for some, physical exhaustion; success brings festive joy and enduring love.

As the presentation on the Mall is essentially "framed" in different ways by all who participate in it and hence is essentially a kind of construction or fiction, so the process of recognition is essentially imaginative and, like other acts of imaginative reading, turns on acceptance of its constructed or fictional condition—either a naive and unproblematic belief in folklife, or the willing suspension of one's disbelief—as well as a deliberate analytical procedure of some kind, the "reading" itself. In this case, the power of the festival arises, on the one hand, from the immediate, imperative, and palpable claim of the performer to emancipate the mind, as Coleridge writes, from the "lethargy of custom" and "selfish solicitude"—that is, from the socially received, stereotyped, and habitual devaluation of folk culture and of ordinary people—and to awaken it to "the loveliness and the wonder" of people otherwise alien or invisible, and on the other hand, more mysteriously, to interest the affections "by the dramatic truth of such emotions as would naturally accompany such situations, supposing them real." That folklife, in precisely the relations or purposes presented to us on the Mall, may not exist or that ordinary people are not ordinarily so gifted or so original is immaterial; what is important is that at the Festival, and very likely *only* at the Festival, we are willing, indeed we long, for these things to be so.[4]

The apparently willing exhibit by ordinary people of their extraordinary abilities or picturesque and unusual occupations, while it holds open the social gap that is the structural sine qua non of the event, at the same time temporarily relieves spectators of the burden that is most hateful, because it is the most difficult to throw off—that of their own social privilege, in this setting embodied as an immediate practical advantage. There are some people, of course, who do not wish to shed their privilege, because they know the price of it and remember what it replaces; I believe that such people rarely, if ever, visit the Festival. And there are others who have few privileges to throw off. Such people do occasionally come as visitors, sometimes by invitation, to the Festival, forming what Festival producers call the "inner audience" to the event: people for whom its effects are, it is said, bracing and salutary, tending toward the continued vitality of their own folk culture, and whose enthusiastic participation helps to bring otherwise reluctant visitors into the spirit of things.

But I suspect that for the great majority of Festival visitors by far, the condition of privilege is something familiar and habitual but, unlike the privileges of princes and kings, essentially without a history. In them, the brute fact of social inequality breeds a strange sense of unworthiness, frustration, exclusion, and guilt—a social vertigo that the Festival relieves by officially honoring underprivileged people, authenticating the honor with displays of unimpeachable excellence, and providing the visitor with an opportunity to demonstrate enthusiastically her appreciation and love and perhaps ultimately to pay the compliment of imitation. Above all, the visitor wants the participant to like or approve of him and so will like and approve in his turn. As Stephen Greenblatt says of exorcism, "The treatment is in effect an initiation into the performance of the symptoms, which are then cured precisely because they conform to the stereotype of the healing process."[5]

Stereotype, that is to say, has no more potent antidote than stereotype; and thus it is that the Festival adopts the psychodynamics of stereotype to mount its presentations, preempting its recognitions with categories of its own and, in a necessarily limited way that admits of much semiotic leakage or spillage, controlling the signifiers through which the visitor identifies or fails to identify with the participant. The folklife presentation, like its structural twin, the stereotype, is a social figuration, an invention of thought, and like any figure requires a ductile language in which to work itself out—in this case, the Festival's technical capacity to reconfigure social reality in a way that brings people otherwise estranged into a close but formally controlled proximity; what we called the "ambivalence" of the stereotype, which at once despises and desires the traits of the other, is at the Festival disarmed by a kind of cultural laundering that effaces, or attempts to efface, those social signifiers typically associated with the participant that may embarrass, scandalize, or threaten the visitor.

And yet the theory of stereotype explains what happens on the Mall about as adequately as probability theory explains Las Vegas. Whereas the stereotype forms out of a handful of markers exhibited on the social landscape, naturalized by representations, and immunized by social distance against any real empirical challenge, the Festival presentation captures the visitor in a web of intersecting social and cultural categories that, though it is anchored to a carefully framed set of cultural signifiers and mediated through evolved theatrical and museumic techniques, is itself continually shaken, even rent, by the sheer living presence of the participant and his conscious and unconscious negotiations with the visitor.

In her effort to recognize the participant, the visitor is drawn in at least three directions: toward the Smithsonian's own analysis of the participant, which has the double sanction of both the long history and the prestige of the institution itself; toward the participant's presentation of himself, which has the authority granted by his centrality in the total situation; and toward her own perceptions, inferences, and intimations, which call upon every intellectual and emotional resource she is capable of bringing to the situation. In a context of analysis, the visitor must create a coherent cultural synthesis. Under the influence of ideas and ideologies, she must confirm the message of her perception as it registers the presence, the official and unofficial performances, and the productions of the participant, all of which have been magically wrested out of their own historical, social, material, and other relations—all that goes by the name of "context," which the institution, the participant, and the visitor all struggle, often at odds with one another, to replace, each attempting to affirm a particular reality.

As a recent ethnographic study of the Festival of American Folklife suggests, this process—the reframing of folk culture by an elite cultural institution—can, for the participant at least, be deeply confusing.[6] As observers at the Michigan section of the 1987 Festival discovered, participants in many instances did not understand what a "folk festival" was supposed to be or why they had been invited to one, and in contriving their various performances and demonstrations, they found "a lack of consensus and explicitness" among the Festival staff on the issue. Those who had some understanding of the concept of "folklife" were sometimes insulted to be regarded as members of a folk community, supposing that their professional training or an advanced degree had elevated them out of this status. Some were embarrassed to be viewed in such a way by audiences whom they perceived to belong, for the most part, to the social classes above them. Some repudiated, even in performance, membership in the cultural group with which they had been identified, while others struggled with the definition of their role: were they guests, hirelings, or honorees? Few Festival visitors would have imagined that, as the study reveals, most of the participants came with well-developed and well-articulated political and personal aims: to wield political influence in some important area such as fishing rights; to expand the market for a craft item such as duck decoys; to accomplish a specific project, such as the building of a boat languishing under contract for lack of time; or simply, and perhaps most tellingly, to earn a little money. Some found their personal needs neglected or ignored and occasionally experienced the habits of other participants as grossly discourteous or intrusive, the ideal of cultural tolerance having not, apparently, trickled down to the culture-bearers themselves. Nearly everyone felt strongly the honor conferred by an invitation from the Smithsonian—only to meet, in one or two cases, the resentment of people at home similarly engaged who had not been so honored.

To this interior dimension of the participants' experience, most Festival visitors remain, like tourists, blissfully ignorant, especially because, in time, most participants work out many of these definitional problems to their own satisfaction and devote themselves to constructing and promulgating the image of themselves favored by the institution, in effect playing to the tourists but also, perhaps, to some extent embracing the fabricated identity that after all has been implicitly shaped and endorsed by a prestigious cultural body.

The visitor's recognition of the participant, however, is a more complicated matter. It is a kind of translation, conversion, or movement, one that is somehow never complete. Instead it continually repeats itself; indeed, its pleasure seems to consist in its continual, even compulsive, reversal and repetition of the participant's identity as it is immediately and palpably apparent for the visitor into the system of identification prepared for the visitor by the institution. Or, to put this another way, a kind of alternation or interplay, interesting and pleasurable in itself, arises between the visitor and the institution over the body of the participant, the importance of which lies in the play of recognition itself, not in the stasis that would result should one or the other agent dominate—either the visitor's notions, impressions, intuitions, affections, inferences, expectations, and prejudices, or the institution's discourses, devices, texts, ideologies, and abstractions. In the encounter on the Mall, various independent patterns of identification vie for exclusivity in relation to the participant—precisely what the visitor, as each pattern is meaningful both in relation to the other patterns and in relation to the participant, will not grant.

This process, though it resembles and includes it, goes beyond the simple ethnomimesis from which we make our stereotypes. It is, rather, the capture of the stereotype—that is, of the entire ethnemic message that shapes the visitor's apprehension of the participant—by the institution's presentation and analysis of those signs, which consequently function as signifiers in *its* system, the order of folklife. But with this capture comes an immediate, almost simultaneous rescue, prompted by the performance itself, so that the presentation inspires a peculiar fascination akin to the one that captures us at those odd moments in which a word or name drops from memory just at the point of utterance, with the oscillating, obscure, restless operation of our own minds. Readers may recognize this transit or movement, this capture or theft of the sign from its position in the visitor's system of identification—hardly a "system" at all, but rather a shifting, elusive interplay of many systems—to become a signifier in another system, the order of the Festival, as what Roland Barthes in a famous essay has described as myth: the transformation, by particular ideological interests, of meaning into form.[7] At the Festival of American Folklife, such a transformation is always unstable, volatile, "a constant game of hide and seek"; no sooner are folklife forms *per*formed than they are *trans*formed again into meaning, just as meaning seeks again to embody itself as form.[8]

About Barthes' essay, I shall have more to say shortly. For now, let us look closely at the participant—look, indeed, directly into his face. The visage of the participant, all that is concretely perceptible in or continuous with his corporality, has many significant attributes that may be said to fall into at least four broad kinds. Most immediately impressive, perhaps, is his or her physical body, which exhibits, among other things, its biologicality—its age, race, and sex—and hence often suggests his or her social status as well, and in which the participant's own self-presentation, and what escapes that presentation, is embodied and dramatized. Physical presence is animated by performance, in which the body reveals itself as the seat of multifarious intelligences amplified and extended through the forms and materials in which it works. These, in turn, attach ethnemically to the participant through discrete properties—a costume, instruments, or tools—and attach the participant in turn to the product in which the manipulation of that medium culminates, whether it be song or dance, boat or chair, clay pot or woodcarving.

Let us examine this mythification of the participant's visage, in a sense working backward from the institution's ethnemic transformation of these four classes of attributes, considered as signifiers, to the ethnemic signs into which the visitor has already transformed them by her own imaginative and intellectual operations; we should consider whether there aren't some important structural connections, in this case, between one and the other, and whether in fact the ethnomimetic construction of the participant does not in some suggestive ways trace the historical genesis of the idea of folklife.

The institution's aim, then, is to capture these attributes and transform them ethnemically, in ways we've already partly considered, in relation to its own sociocultural position vis-à-vis the participant. In its identification of the participant with his or her art or craft—which is itself identified with significant palpable properties such as musical instruments ("fiddlers") or equally palpable and material products such as coverlets or pots (weavers, potters, broom makers)—the institution achieves a degree of analytical explicitness and empiricality reminiscent of Henry Mayhew's classification of the London street folk by their economic functions or the commodities in which they traded. There is not much difference, epistemologically speaking, between Mayhew's "Dutch-buy-a-broom girls," "Irish fruit-sellers," and "German brass bands" and the Festival's "Chinese dragon-dancers," "Lummi Indian basketmakers," and "Cape Breton fiddlers."

This identification with and classification through folk-cultural productions themselves is, of course, historically rooted in Western culture's incorporation, from the sixteenth century onward, of the primitive, exotic, or preindustrial product—from the "wonder closets" of the Renaissance to the philological folktale collections and anthropological museums of the nineteenth century to the field recordings, folk art museums, and souvenir shops of our own period; it must be said, though, that from the very beginning, from the public exhibition of Native Americans captured by European sailors to such nineteenth-century venues as the Dahomey Village at the World's Columbian Exposition, the appropriation of the product has also often included the appropriation of the producer.

What is significant, though, about this fundamentally material, even tactile mode of analysis is that the property or product is objective, mobile, portable, and separable from its own cultural context and hence admits of transformation both by science, which may fetishize it, and by trade, which may commodify it. Through it one may come, intellectually or commercially, into ethnomimetic possession of the other, as in a sense the analysis of folklife by properties and products brings the Chinese dragon dancer or the Navajo sandpainter into the possession or under the sovereignty of the Festival. The Pawley's Island basket beside my chair, or the face jug from north Georgia on my hearth, ethnemically incorporates the identity of the basketmaker or the potter with my own and says, in a sense, that I've been there, even if I haven't—a claim that will prove critically important when we consider the *visitor's* apprehension of the folk product.

Closely connected to the folk product analytically is the folk property, the tool or instrument through which the participant produces her product, or the medium in which he works and with which he can be identified as a banjo picker or a stone sculptor or dragon dancer; as suggested earlier, the properties in which the participant works are, for visitor and participant alike, the coefficients through which the body of the participant articulates itself—a condition, I strongly suspect, of its "folk" status. Like the folk product, the folk property—guitar or adze, lyra or embroidery needle—attaches ethnemically to the participant and hence can serve as an element in the Festival's intellectual organization, providing the basis of an exhibit such as the Mississippi fiddlers' convention or the California winery. But as we shall see, the folk property, which extends, amplifies, and exhibits the participant's body, can also become the agent through which the visitor may identify his own body with that of the participant.

If the product is the basis of the Festival's ethnographic analysis of the participant, the property constitutes, with the participant's own body, the medium in which the folk performance (the third of our four kinds of attributes) is carried out; as it does engage the body, the performance provides, in conjunction with the participant's living presence and its biologicality, the basis for the institution's identification of the participant with various kinds of cultural communities, because the participant's performance and, further, her own biological status may in social reality have been the ethnomimetic factor around which her cultural identity, or an aspect of it, has formed. Hence performances that occur within specific technical or economic realms may be ethnemically projected into occupational communities such as loggers, miners, or the family farm, or into particular technical functions such as transportation and communication, whereas performances within specific social realms or milieus may foster such exhibitions as the rehearsals of a drama company or services in a black Baptist church. But as performance really is inseparable from the participant's living presence, classes of performances almost invariably impinge upon the cultural categories that the Festival has extrapolated from the participant's nativity or biologicality: his or her ethnic or racial identity, sex, or place in the human life cycle. Thus: *Tunisian* belly dancer, *Iroquois* lacrosse player, *children's* games, *family* folklore, or the *Grand* Generation.

The many attributes of the participant's visage, then, embodied in her physical presence, her performance, the properties through and in which she works, and the product she produces, form a set of signifiers to which the Festival assigns ethnemically specific significances, transforming them into cultural signs that, taken together, constitute the participant for the Festival's purposes. Out of a spectrum of visible and material attributes ranging from folk texts, crafts, and arts through technical, occupational, racial, ethnic, and biological traits, the Festival has generated its own folk-cultural map, with conspicuous continental shapes such as Old Ways in the New World, the African Diaspora, Native Americans, Regional Americans, and Working Americans, subcontinental formations such as Family and Children's Folklore, innumerable local features such as the Chesapeake Bay Fishery or American Talkers, and finally the concrete arts and crafts of individual participants themselves. Moreover, given on the one hand the materiality and immediacy of the folk product and the analytical explicitness it provides for, and on the other the breadth and capaciousness of ethnic and racial classes conceived as cultural communities, this transformation of signifiers seems to have a definite trajectory, one that proceeds from the decontextualized folk product or text, through the entire order of folk culture as the Festival has mapped it, to the overarching idea of folklife, of which every participant is supposed to be an example. The Festival has joined the visage of the participant—in some, but not all, of its attributes—to a complex *image* of folklife that semiotically creates the cultural sign; but this sign's mythic potency lies in the countersemiosis or cosemiosis in which the visitor, in his meeting with the participant, has been engaged.

Or not engaged. Like the dismissive young man who in an instant converted the Fairfield Four into the "Ink Spots," there are Festival visitors, many of them I fear, for whom the presentation is simply—well, nothing at all. As I have suggested, the mythification of the participant is a kind of capture or theft, and the rescue or recovery of the participant out of the institution's own mythology demands the visitor's own captivation or arrest by the participant's performance. The visitor, we can reasonably suppose, has come to the Festival to have fun, to dance, to be entertained, to find transport in music or absorption in another's work, to engage in conversation with some strange new man or woman, perhaps to meet someone or to feel a part of things. As one visitor put it, "I'm here on the Mall, glad to get away from the office, an anonymous person bumping up against other anonymous people, and I feel that all these people who've come from Tennessee, the marble-maker and the moonshiner and the quilter, must somehow know each other back at home—that they're one big community of folks. And I can talk to them. I can be a part of it." The curious fellow who pauses in front of the text-panel that the learned heads of the Office of Folklife Programs have spent weeks composing, slurping on an ice-cream cone and forgetting half of what he reads as he reads it, is far more typical. He likes Cajun music, and he's interested in the Cajuns, but not as interested as he is in the girl who spoke to him yesterday afternoon at the dance party and whom he spied a moment ago heading off toward the Fourteenth Street stage. For as I've suggested, his encounter here is fundamentally with the human body as, in its own vitality, it betrays the ten thousand forms of desire we can bestow upon it.

But let him be momentarily impressed by the swift, almost imperceptible strokes with which the shingle-river transmogrifies a block of cedar or by the pot that stands up in the potter's hands as if it had come to life; let him be touched in some faraway part of him by a few spruce notes from a banjo or distracted by the grace of a Javanese finger-dance; let him be captured, and then his imagination will be aroused and he will begin—albeit, of course, fitfully and partially—that process of investigation we have attempted to describe, until he is caught between two poles, that of the moment of the awakening of his desire and that of the knowledge through which he hopes to, but never really can, allay it. For though he may not know it, the visitor has been distracted, irritated by some sympathetic vibration deep within the harp of himself, deeper than identity, to an unknown energy in the surrounding human atmosphere, *the influence of ethnomimesis itself.*

If the Festival's own analysis of the participant begins with her products and properties, the visitor's apprehension begins with her person; those signs that the institution takes as indicators of broad cultural affiliation, such as race and ethnicity, mark for the visitor the frontier at which his encounter with the other *as* other begins. Around the Eskimo or African or Cherokee or Mexican or West Virginian plays an obscure, distended music, agitated and uneasy like indigestion, of fugitive associations, ill-formed memories, and ugly, impoverished fears and prejudices, all of them pressing like spectres at the gates of a consciousness ingeniously circumscribed by the frame in which the Festival has placed the participant—well within reach, close enough even to touch, and yet on the other side of some boundary, perhaps merely formal or symbolic, formed by a platform or a table. These are the goblins of gender, class, and racial stereotype, a kind of dreamy twilight sleep traversed by the imagery that clings to the margins of awareness: the youth with the curly hair mopping a restaurant floor at midnight or the fellow at the gas station; the blazing eyes and the kitchen knife at your throat; the reeking drunk plunging his thick hand toward you as you pass; the men with lunch pails and dented hats who used to linger sullenly at the chain-link factory gates on the mornings you walked to school; the beauty operator with the lipstick, smoking; the bearded man at the door . . .

But these phantasms are vaporous, dim, hardly present to the mind at all except in the form of the strange sensations of corrosion or imbalance that their images once seemed to engender in one's own body. In this setting, indeed, they are for some reason almost unreal, a kind of refuse left behind in another world. More real to you, perhaps, is the vast, mostly unremembered, but now, here, startlingly recalled to life, imagery of representations: the educational film about Costa Rica they screened in the cafeteria when you were in the seventh grade; the postcard an old teacher sent to you from her retirement home in Asheville, with its picture of a potter; a folksong anthology with its arty lithographs of pile drivers and cowpokes; a travelogue about Arizona or Mexico; your roommate's poster from the Caribbean; the novel about Kentuckians; a photomagazine spread about Indonesia; a television documentary—this repertoire of associations constitutes a kind of knowledge, the indistinct features of some interiorized social landscape in which, however crudely and imperfectly, the participant may be situated, even if only for an initial moment, merely as a structure with which to frame in one's own imagination the encounter with a man or woman who is neither stereotype nor representation but only him- or herself, a living presence endowed with what, against this background of hallucination and fantasy, is the chastening and at times shocking fullness of his or her humanity.

To the visitor, the visage of the participant is a kind of summons—like those films shot from the lead car of a plummeting roller coaster—to a reserve of learned responses so habitual as to have the character of instinct, which even as they are actuated are simultaneously discredited by the invented and represented character of the encounter itself. It is at this moment in the visitor's construction of the participant that a kind of dialogue or struggle ensues between the various kinds of information offered to the visitor by the Festival in the form of text panels, photographs, presenters' discourses, and of course by the participant herself on the one hand, and by the actual message of the senses on the other. Whatever else may be said about the nature of this encounter, it has been to some degree shaped by the very structure of the Festival production: its authorizing situation on the National Mall, under the auspices of the well-known and august Smithsonian Institution; the relatively intimate performance venues, which enrich and intensify the visitor's interaction with the participant and in many cases permit actual dialogue between them; and the "inner audience," whose presence may unconsciously prompt the visitor's response in culturally appropriate ways through which, by enacting them, the visitor unwittingly receives instruction in a certain course of conduct.

On the personal level, then, there is much of the participant's visage that is controlled by the presentation itself, and much that is not. Costume, for example: It is disarming when a man or woman presented as an exemplar of a particular art or craft appears in ordinary working-class garb, just as if he or she were simply the farmer who once pulled your car out of a snowbank with a tractor, the plumber who fixed your toilet, or your favorite waitress at the Dew Drop Inn—or, for that matter, your own uncle or your grandmother or yourself. The familiarity is both reassuring and mollifying, as it may place the visitor—or may only appear to place him—socially above the participant at the same time that it permits the participant to dignify her own station with the exhibition of her officially acknowledged achievements, which in yet another sense places her culturally, though only temporarily and ceremonially, *above* the visitor.

Yet a visitor's perceptions can be sharp. On occasion—when, for example, a well-known blues singer, who has appeared in nightclubs and been photographed on record albums in a tuxedo, appears on the Mall in a brand-new pair of overalls—the working-class costume can be seen to be just that: a costume motivated by a particular outlook. An officially "ethnic" costume of sequins and rayon, which a troupe of Hungarian folk dancers might wear in defiance of the institution's stated policy, deceives no one and is not meant to deceive. It merely indicates the dancers' own understanding of the cultural status that has been ascribed to them, and it represents a gesture of respect, according to their own social and political standards, toward the institution that has invited them (who would wear actual *peasant* clothes to perform for the public in Washington?); it is, in any case, clearly and conspicuously a *costume*, intended to imitate but not to replicate the peasant costume belonging to the European class in which the folk dances originated and out of which the Hungarian participants have happily risen. Is it "authentic"? If you want real peasants, no; if you want people who know what it is to have been peasants, yes.

The "ethnemization" (if the reader will temporarily accept this barbaric term) of the participant is on both sides a complex and dynamic process that may defy analysis, but it seems clear at least that, as in stereotype itself, the links between the participant and the participant's attributes are essentially metonymic. If the participant's race, nativity, and ethnicity can be captured by the institution's signifying machinery, however, his or her personality cannot be. To a suburban Anglo-American visitor, a Hmong or Pakistani participant may be simply inscrutable, for these people share with the visitor almost none of the codes through which culture provides for the articulation of personality, and any interaction in which they may engage is potentially fraught with misunderstanding, often turning out to be nothing more than a ritual of smiles and nods. A visitor may find himself unaccountably angered to discover that a person from whom he might normally expect deference or even servility is unwilling to discuss his method of carving for the two-hundredth time that day; or, conversely, she may be elated to find herself in an honest, easygoing exchange with a fishnet weaver from Mandeville, Louisiana, or a blues guitar player from Ferriday—in short, to find herself accepted for no other reason than that she is a member of the human race. This is certainly one of the happiest experiences the Festival has to offer.

But, as noted above, in the institution's presentation as well as in the participant's presentation of her- or himself, there is a good deal of semiotic spillage or leakage. The almost maniacal intensity with which the Japanese potter's eyes fix upon his work is impressive, very impressive; but in the end, perhaps, it is more of a conscious effort on behalf of his audience than anything really required by the work. The singer of labor songs presents a persona that is perhaps a bit too stagy and a little narcissistic; the Hawaiian guitarist thanks his audience and the institution with a lachrymose speech, which, although affording a certain self-congratulatory latitude to the visitor, also arouses a painful consciousness of a status the visitor does not in fact enjoy and the impression of which she is powerless to dispel. Is there perhaps a touch of sarcasm in the singer's words? One participant may seem to be making a pitch, another to be grinding an axe, one is a bit self-important, another inexplicably melancholy; they have perhaps mistaken the nature of the occasion or have been mistaken themselves by some coarse, unthinking spectator. And, sadly, a visitor must from time to time observe or overhear or experience what perhaps it is better that he or she did not: a virulently racist remark made by a participant to his colleague about another visitor; what appears to be a participant's somewhat abusive treatment of the child accompanying her; or, in fact, an aggressive physical threat, accompanied by foul language, from a very large, strong, and intoxicated participant to a frightened female tourist, which in a stroke brings the real world of social inequality and cultural conflict home to the Mall.

But, for the visitor, the complex message of the participant's person and personality flows into and is inseparable from the participant's performance, in which her or his beauty or strength, grace, dexterity or precision—aspects of the human endowment that transcend cultural difference—touch the visitor in some way, perhaps all the more powerfully because such revelations and intimations, properly speaking, cannot have been captured by institutional discourse, because even in the visitor there may be some conscious or unconscious resistance to acknowledging one's own spontaneous notice of the participant's physical body and its attributes, however inevitably our attention is drawn to such things, particularly, as in dance, where the exhibit is quite deliberate and often exquisitely formal.

And finally, of course, there is the product itself, ethnemically the most concrete, immediate, and palpable element of the participant's visage, placed both by the institutional framework and its devices of presentation in the foreground and at the center of the visitor's attention. There are few visitors who arrive on the Mall without some resources of recognition, especially in the form of remembered representations of folklife; and there are, I suspect, few visitors who are not struck by the strange tuberculosis that attacks that representational image, to which it utterly succumbs as the actual folk product gradually, by increments, and yet swiftly, in a moment's time, replaces it in the visitor's experience. It is not just that we can catch in the performance itself the richness and sophistication of the human resources that the participant has invested in her embroidery or in his song, of which we may not understand a single symbol or word; often, indeed, we have only the finished product—for example, a quilt, whose hallucinatory colors and labyrinthine pattern utterly abolish the hackneyed and sentimental idea of the "quilt"—from which to infer the extent of the intelligence, originality, patience, skill, and, indeed, the sheer human travail of which it is the quilter's patterned expression, belonging to the unprepossessing gray-haired woman in the housedress and pink glasses who sits before us plying her needle.

The visitor's encounter with the participant through her work, then, is a kind of deterioration, as a ghostly and irresolute idea gives way to an affect lodged in a perception, which, even while ideas and associations may play around it, stubbornly defies by its immediacy, density, intensity, vitality, and minute particularity its dissolution into an association or dismissal by an idea; and this affect, moreover, by that same hardness, solidity, and silence, or by that wild, illimitable, and unnameable boldness or that sinister power, arrests the unbinding of thought with a snarl or knot whose mystery, it sometimes seems, must be unraveled before life itself can go on. This is the moment of forgetfulness, of loss, and hence of desire; it is that semiotic emergency, recalling again the dynamic of stereotype, in which the cultural sign threatens to fly apart, flinging the substance of being in opposing directions, toward a real world and an imaginary one, toward an empty abstraction and an obdurate, unintelligible fact.

Here is that realm in which the synthesizing imagination—which knows only similitude and affinity, the absorption of forms into one another, and which turns the dissolution or deterioration of its own categories into the condition of its power—makes shift to fashion a world in which an unfamiliar, even an unknown beauty has an intelligible place. The visitor, again, is pulled in several directions, from the visage before him toward, perhaps, simple denial—"Hey look, the Ink Spots"; or toward the world elaborated ethnographically or folkloristically by the institution in its array of text panels, photographs, and other mediators; toward the participant herself, often with an ardent, almost passionate eagerness; or, perhaps, into his own internal world of remembrance, desire, and dream.

On the Mall, there are many opportunities for understanding culture for what it is not: an essentially frivolous pastiche of color and variety; something essentially inaccessible; a personal catharsis of music and dance; a history, say, of the settlement of Louisiana or the migration of the Acadians; a typology of industrial society, in which a blacksmith can be taken as the type of a foundry and the rain forest can be conceived as a supermarket; an ideology, perhaps feminism or environmentalism, which lends itself to women's folk culture or to Native American culture respectively; or a demonology or a projection of the psychological shadow—traffic with the devil. But readers who have attended the Festival of American Folklife, and who can find in this account some echo of their own experiences, will agree, I think, that in fact we are scattered in all these directions at once. The visage has become a site at which the institution, the participant, and the visitor all compete for dominance in the genesis of an image and, through it, of a meaningful cultural sign signifying the "folk."

And it is in this emergency that the very materiality, discreteness, and empiricality of the folk product, which for the institution has served as a principle of discrimination, becomes for the visitor, for these same reasons, an agency or avenue through which the imagination can recognize and perhaps ultimately identify the participant and, beyond that, identify *with* the participant. In the historical and institutional context, the folk text or artifact belongs to the realm of science, high culture, or trade, being in its materiality a thing separable from its own cultural and historical milieu and, for this reason, a useful way for the institution both to discriminate the participant and through him to generate the idea of folklife. This very separability makes a similar promise to the visitor, one that can be redeemed either in a flatly mechanical and literal way or through exertions and adventures that may prove sublime and life-transforming.

The impulse, of course, is to somehow come into possession of the participant, indeed to *become* the participant. This may demand only a symbolic action—that we *buy* the product, or its equivalent, at a craft tent as a souvenir—but it is precisely to forestall this action that the Festival of American Folklife prohibits the sale of craft items by participants and why, in most years, it has resisted pubic pressure for a crafts or record outlet on the Mall. Thus blocked the visitor may then come into possession of the participant through conversation with her—an interaction sufficient to feel that some bond of mutual acceptance has been formed, but not enough to summon from the world beyond the Festival any of those economic, social, cultural, or other factors that may alienate rather than unite them. Or, as if in a museum, the visitor may be content to possess the participant through information alone; after thoroughly reading the text panels or attentively listening to a workshop, she may feel confident in her ability to carry away from the Mall some understanding of what she has seen and to explain it to others in new social situations, hence in a sense becoming part of her own social construction of herself.

It is important at this point to emphasize that the entire ethnomimesis described here can reverse direction, that the ethneme in the Festival's system of signs, the order of folklife, can become a signifier in the visitor's or the participant's system of signs, which may be the order of art, social class, politics, or romance. The visitor who has no particular knowledge, through representations or otherwise, of folk culture may find herself suddenly moved by the visage of the quilter or the dancer, perhaps from intimately personal or unconscious causes, and ultimately transformed for her lifetime into a champion of folk arts or of the folk themselves, suddenly devoted to the political salvation of the Maya or the Azerbaijanis or to the survival of sweetgrass basket making on the Georgia Sea Islands. In fact, as I have insisted, the cultural sign moves in *both* directions in a kind of perpetual oscillation, the ethneme in the visitor's imaginative life captured by the institution's system of signifiers, the institution's system of signs rescued to become signifiers in the visitor's own ethnemic system, which in turn may be informed, however deeply or superficially, by the Festival's order of ideas.

But fundamentally, because the imagination longs for its own incarnation, the visitor and the participant converge, again, at the folk performance itself and, still more radically, at the folk product, whose folk status, as noted, turns on its capacity to organize the body around itself in a way that recapitulates, at least potentially, the organization of the visitor's own body. I am by no means saying that every visitor to the Festival of American Folklife is going to take up fiddle playing or quilting or chair making, though many do; in any case, I think my point is clear. Whether symbolically, vicariously, virtually, or actually, the end of the folk festival is the cultural union of the body of the visitor with the body of the participant; it is the arousal, elaboration, amplification, and consummation of a cultural love grounded in the desire underwritten by cultural difference, but particularly in inequities of privilege, in which impulses of pity, sympathy, solace, and help, as well as admiration and wonder and especially the power to bestow them, constitute themselves, under pressure of necessity, as love.

Thus, for some at the Festival, the social dominance structurally designed into the exhibition, a precipitate of exhibition itself, is transmuted by a kind of titration into the power to bestow love, which in this or any other context I take to be the will to nurture, to care and to care for, and otherwise to promote the well-being and the realization of life in the beloved. It is for this reason that, on the institutional level, the Office of Folklife Programs has over the years built up around the Festival an ideology and rhetoric, called "cultural conservation" after a federal document of that title, that justifies the Festival in terms of its benefits for the participants: as a morale-builder; as an antidote to cultural dislocation and change; as a corrective to cultural invisibility, a hedge against domination by mass society; as a model for cultural exhibition; and as an instrument of broadened cultural recognition and ultimately of cultural survival.

Whether the Festival actually accomplishes any or all of these purposes, it is not in my power to say; "cultural conservation" is a justification, not an explanation.

To summarize, the Festival is a double process in which the visage of the participant becomes a complex, polysemous ethneme in the folkloric system of the institution on the one hand and in the visitor's own patterns of recognition on the other, each attempting to capture the sign framed by the other as a signifier in its own order of meaning. This double mythification around the body of the participant strives to consummate the relationship between institution and participant, and between visitor and participant, in the restoration of social and cultural equilibrium between them, either through the visitor's total cultural transfiguration, a kind of conversion, or through utopian projects in social, economic, and cultural reform. Like a lover inspired by the image of his beloved toward he knows not what high purpose, who sees in her virtues that others are at a loss to see, so do we somehow need to believe that the visage of the artist before us is just what we imagine it to be, or that we can manipulate the world until it is.

We bring with us to the Festival of American Folklife, then, a great many vague notions, a great many half-formed ideas and untempered memories. Indeed, it is these very ideas and notions that first bring us to the Festival: the image of the lanky mountain boy in overalls, perhaps, with a wayward forelock and a fiddle in his hand, who stood beside Benét's poem "The Mountain Whippoorwill" in a high school literature anthology, evoking fragments of its drawling lines: "So I went to 'gratulate old man Dan / But he put his fiddle into *my* han'"; or perhaps the image of a betrayed lover in some blues shout from the South Side of Chicago, recorded on your anthology of folk blues by a singer who roars like a lion, while his enigmatic lyric summons up smokestacks, freight cars, and a railroad track; or perhaps some sentimental portrait of village life from a magazine article you cannot even remember having read, where quilting bees seem to go on forever in a whitewashed, tree-shaded parish house, while nearby men with pipes seem perpetually to be sitting around a potbellied stove talking politics and whittling.

The Festival educates us out of these illusions. We learn about the Scots-Irish migration and the Anglo-Irish tune tradition, the place of the fiddle and the fiddle contest in mountain life, the Saturday-night dance, regional stylistic variations, the minstrel show and black influences, the nativist revivals of the 1920s; and we learn, too, about the evolution of the blues, its migration to urban areas from the Mississippi Delta, its place in the emergent stratifications of Chicago's African American community; we learn the place of the quilt in the household, in the church, and in the sisterhood of women, about variations on traditional designs, about utility, self-expression, and psychic integration.

It is true, all true. And yet, with white-haired Tommy Jarrell actually before us, scraping out his always rusty "Rockingham Cindy" as elegantly as if he were pruning an azalea; when the giant Howling Wolf, affixed motionless to a folding chair, emits from his chest a sound that could be the entire Corwith freight yards at Forty-seventh Street as they were on the day he arrived in Chicago in 1952; when Ethel Wright Mohammed momentarily raises her eyes from her needlework to point out that the huge tapestry mounted behind her depicts the 1974 Festival of American Folklife, and suddenly we *recognize* the lacrosse players, the sheepshearers, the cotton patch, the telephone lineman—somehow the "film of familiarity falls from our eyes," as Coleridge promised, to reveal "the loveliness and wonders of the world before us," and the old illusions, even as illusions, come back powerfully invested with what we know to be emotions "as would naturally accompany such situations, supposing them real."

Framed by the National Mall and differentiated into several realms, each distinguished by a specific culture or cultural theme, the Festival of American Folklife models, on the scale of a garden or park, the socioeconomic, geographic, cultural, and other boundaries that tourists—and with them folklorists and anthropologists, whose work only rationalizes through analogy to natural science the content of the specular frame in which tourism places the perceptible surfaces of cultural behavior and production—routinely cross for instruction and for delight. A tour of the Festival of American Folklife is not, perhaps, as richly mediated as the encounters with cultures represented by travel accounts, diaries, guidebooks, photo albums, postcards, souvenirs, and other elements of touristic discourse; nevertheless, it is like tourism an encounter surrounded by a complex traffic in representations, mediated by guides, texts, presenters, and other agents and organized around a formal or accidental social interaction.

Like most of what we think of as recreational tourism, the Festival of American Folklife insulates the visitor and the participant from one another in ways that reduce the potential for personal conflict but at the same time may disclose to each the differences that, under other circumstances, might produce such conflict. Over the years, the Festival has elaborated a complex system of framing devices such as platforms, stages, scaffolds, shelters, arenas, tents, and canopies as well as various mock structures and vehicles including an oil derrick, a railroad locomotive, an airliner, a race track, and a tract house, which stand in for and empty barriers of group, class, race, language, culture, and so on, many of them normally insurmountable. Like a tourist attraction, the Festival presentation frames itself in ways that efface the participant's inextricable involvement with the social, economic, technological, and other structures that constitute the participant's whole personality of roles and functions—including, among other things, special kinds of performances and settings designed especially for tourists—and consequently associate some aspects of his identity with the social world the tourist has deliberately left behind and in which both are in some sense involved.

This framework of representation indicates and reestablishes, even as it effectively abolishes, a social or other kind of boundary; but it also conscientiously occludes most of the social, economic, and other factors that account for the boundary to begin with, particularly such potentially alienating differences as those of class, education, and religion. To understand this process, it is only necessary to consider for a moment what the Festival would be like were the cultural group in question to be fully represented in its own home circumstances, complete with such signifiers of disadvantage as a diurnal diet of fast food and daytime television, or with such epicultural forms as develop among disadvantaged or displaced groups in urban ghettos or isolated rural hamlets. Or, concomitantly, if the participant's external connections were to be fully disclosed: if we were to learn that the Native American drummer is a university student or the fiddle player a schoolbus driver, that the honky-tonk singer in sequins runs an auto repair shop, the chairmaker sells insurance, the fisherman heads a political coalition, and that the Native American carver has organized an arts cooperative. Instead, participant and visitor meet on the single footing of the folk cultural performance, which metonymically represents an entire way of life, an essence made to stand in for an existence.

In this way, the Festival provides what much of recreational or commercial tourism can only promise: an intimate, authentic encounter with the other; and though it does not offer a commercial product, the souvenir, by means of which the tourist can symbolically carry the participant home with her, it holds out possession of another kind, which is intimate access to and often some form of participation in the arts, crafts, or skills that define the participant. Through identification with the participant, the Festival visitor in effect "puts on" the participant's identity, just as the participant, with the prompting and guidance of the Smithsonian, has put on a folk identity on the visitor's behalf. This is a form of festive masking that can be compared structurally to the contemplation of engineered landscapes framed in picture windows and of the lives of imagined or represented hermit poets installed therein—a contemplation underwritten by the underlying difference in material condition, projected into the formal or theatrical insulation of the spectator from the spectacle.

The Festival, then, may be said on one level to have more thoroughly realized, through bureaucratic organization and planning, swift and wide-ranging fieldwork, a background of anthropological and folkloristic scholarship, large financial resources, and such technical advantages as high-speed auto and air travel, long-distance telephone communications, information processing, and so on, the principle of tourism; in effect, it collapses the cultural universe, formerly diffused on the margins of the social center, into a culturological garden whose margin is the touristic or the social-scientific gaze.

In this respect, the Festival is perhaps a mimesis of what Dean MacCannell calls "a reversal and transformation of the structure of tourism." After centuries in which explorers, soldiers, missionaries, and anthropologists extended the Western world across the globe, MacCannell observes, the dominant cultural movement in our own day is that of

> refugees, "boat people," agricultural laborers, displaced peasants, and others from the periphery to the centers of power and affluence. . . . Entire villages of Hmong peasants and hunters, recently from the highlands of Laos, have been relocated and now live in apartment complexes in Madison, Wisconsin. Refugees from El Salvador work in Manhattan, repackaging cosmetics, removing perfume from Christmas gift boxes, rewrapping it in Valentine gift boxes. Legal and illegal "aliens" weed the agricultural fields of California.[9]

Such a structural shift, however, which nevertheless preserves the central encounter of people essentially strange to one another or conversely makes strange the encounter of people otherwise familiar, suggests that tourism and the Festival arise together from a distinctive condition of consciousness what MacCannell calls a "modern mentality that sets modern society in opposition both to its own past and to those societies of the present that are premodern," a consciousness which tour and festival in their various forms enact and, through enactment, strive more perfectly to realize or to bring to completion the conditions of existence implied in it; the social-structural shift further suggests that as the conditions of technology, leisure, and power evolve, so will the structures of tourism and festivity evolve with them.[10]

MacCannell's thoughtful and thought-provoking book, *The Tourist: A New Theory of the Leisure Class*, deserves some discussion and some interpolation in this connection. Tourism, MacCannell writes, provides an "unplanned typology" of social structure roughly equivalent, ethnographically, to a cycle of myths that constitutes the "grounds of modernity's unifying consciousness." In the modern world, he continues—though from our perspective, with the concept of postmodernism now exhaustively articulated, we should perhaps more accurately say the "postmodern," "postindustrial," or "consumer" society—leisure has displaced work as the center of social arrangements and has bred a new species of leisure-time commodities such as package tours, work-study programs, vacation planners, and do-it-yourself kits, in effect bringing the tourist home and transforming even the workplace, as indicated by factory tours and the like, into a touristic curiosity. "The best indication of the final victory of modernity over other sociocultural arrangements," he writes, "is not the disappearance of the nonmodern world, but its artificial preservation and reconstruction in modern society."

> The separation of nonmodern culture traits from their original contexts and their distribution as modern playthings are evident in the various social movements toward naturalism, so much a feature of modern societies: cults of folk music and medicine, adornment and behavior, peasant dress, Early American decor, efforts, in short, to museumize the premodern. . . . These displaced forms, embedded in modern society, are the spoils of the victory of the modern over the nonmodern world. They establish in consciousness the definition and boundary of modernity by rendering concrete and immediate that which modernity is not.[11]

This is an arresting insight, and one that must give pause to anyone who has reflected upon the Festival of American Folklife or any other such cultural exhibition. To it, I can only add that in the postmodern or consumer period, the evolution that MacCannell describes seems to have arrived at an even more thorough stage of development, as in a consumer culture, immediate practical experience, in which even touristic experience may be said to be grounded, is gradually displaced by a vast leisure-time trade in virtual, represented, or purely imaginary experiences in the video, radio, audio, and tactile spheres, so extensive as to constitute for many people the represented reality or "culture" in which they live. Even the tourist, who, as MacCannell observes, desires above all to transcend "mere" tourism and to experience the world in some authentic way, must be distinguished from his or her postmodern successor, who is blitzed out in front of a video or computer screen on which it seems the entire known world, as well as unprecedented fantasy and hallucination, can be arrestingly promulgated, almost entirely in a commercial context.

But as MacCannell himself concedes, his analysis and others like it may suggest that the fragmentation of consciousness that we now typically associate with such conspicuous postmodern modes as television advertising, or with MTV, which has become the postmodern symbol par excellence, is not, perhaps, as novel as the concept of "postmodernism" might indicate; it has perhaps been a developing feature of the social landscape throughout the modern period: "Modern battleships are berthed near *Old Ironsides*; highrise apartments stand next to restored eighteenth-century townhouses; 'Old Faithful' geyser is surrounded by bleacher seats; all major cities contain wildlife and exotic plant collections; Egyptian Obelisks stand at busy intersections in London and Paris and in Central Park in New York City."[12]

In fact, such fragmentation may conceivably have begun at the dawn of modernity four centuries ago, with the appearance of the museum of wonders, reenactments of New World conquests of native peoples, Jacobean folk festivals, and the like. One might suppose, then, that the postmodern project, whatever it is, has something of the same aim as tourism, which, MacCannell says,

> is a rite performed to the differentiations of society . . . a kind of collective striving for a transcendence of the modern totality, a way of overcoming the discontinuity of modernity, of incorporating its fragments into unified experience. . . . Modernization simultaneously separates these things from the people and places that made them, breaks up the solidarity of the groups in which they originally figured as cultural elements, and brings the people liberated from traditional attachments into the modern world where, as tourists, they may attempt to discover or reconstruct a cultural heritage or social identity.[13]

Such "social structural differentiation," MacCannell says, the "totality of differences between social classes, life-styles, racial and ethnic groups, age grades (the youth, the aged), political and professional groups and the mythic representation of the past to the present," is the "origin of alternatives and the feeling of freedom in modern society" and "the primary ground of the contradiction, conflict, violence, fragmentation, discontinuity and alienation that are such evident features of modern life." Although common sense might suggest that the tourist is in flight from what social differentiation has produced, in fact, says MacCannell, "the differentiations *are* the attractions." Further, he adds, modern international tourism—and here we might easily substitute "postmodernism" or "the society of the spectacle"—"produces juxtapositions of elements from historically separated cultures and thereby speeds up the differentiation and modernization of middle-class consciousness."[14]

To grasp this paradoxical but powerful structural analysis, and to understand how MacCannell's book anticipates such landmark analyses of postmodernism as Fredric Jameson's "Postmodernism: The Cultural Logic of Late Capitalism," we must briefly consider MacCannell's concept of culture and particularly the primacy of representation in it. The data of cultural experience, he writes, lie in representations of life—"fictionalized, idealized, or exaggerated models of social life" that circulate in the public consciousness, "in film, fiction, political rhetoric, small talk, comic strips, expositions, etiquette and spectacles." These representations, he says, shape life according to their own contours, intensifying the conviction of reality when experiences conform to them and driving cultural life toward the reproduction of them. "A bathing suit model is a model," he remarks— quite in the spirit of our discussion—whereas "the desire for a real-life girl friend that looks 'just like a model' is its influence."[15]

These processes, socially coordinated and invested with social power, constitute what MacCannell calls a "cultural production," which can be something as ephemeral, he writes, as a magazine advertisement in which a woman meets her husband at the door of their suburban home proffering a cocktail, or as monumental as "the summer-long and year-long festivals that tie up the entire life of a community."[16] Marx, of course, would say that the most powerful models are those that proceed from the most powerful groups; though we might add that the most powerful groups may turn out to be those that can produce the most powerful models. If a foreign policy adventure such as the Vietnam War, for example, was a "cultural production," then the television networks' control of its presentation can perhaps be held accountable for much of the cultural and political upheaval of the Vietnam period; we consequently should not be

surprised at the efforts of the Executive Branch and the Pentagon a generation later, in the Persian Gulf, to exert complete control over war as a
cultural production, including control of video representations of it, and
thereby overcome "the Vietnam syndrome."

The Festival of American Folklife is, according to this analysis, a cultural
production; so, too, would be the Peckham exorcizings discussed in Chapter 1. As such, the Festival joins "big games, moon shots, mass protests,
Christmas, historical monuments, opening nights, elections and rock music
festivals," and other productions through which the captains of social, political, and economic power in our society attempt to inculcate beliefs and
values and to rally around them the social groupings—markets, constituen-
cies, movements, formations, classes—that will sustain that power.[17]

But MacCannell's discussion of tourism is nowhere more pertinent to
our own, and to the entire issue of ethnomimesis, than in its analysis of the
semiotic relation between "sights" and "markers," which, he suggests,
model the cultural process generally. Tourists, of course, visit "sights"—
that is, touristically constructed sites of scenic, historical, political, or other
public importance that together constitute the social structure of tourism.
The creation of a tourist sight or site can be a lengthy and elaborate or a
low and meretricious process. The tourization of the West, for example,
required a complex historical and cultural evolution involving, among
other influences, the nineteenth-century cult of the picturesque, "muscular
Christianity," the romance of the wilderness, and the expansion of the
western railroads into passenger markets. But a cardboard carton full of
torpid rattlesnakes, on the lot of a gas station on a remote Nevada highway, can be a tourist attraction, too. What is important is that circulating
in the social system—in some instances virtually saturating it—is a body of
representations about significant sights, called "markers" by MacCannell,
in travel books, museum guides, lectures, and so on, without which the
tourist seemingly cannot take pleasure in her discovery of the sight. So
important, apparently, is the marker to the process of sightseeing that a
tourist may content herself *only* with the marker, as did a young couple
whom MacCannell overheard at a zoo in midwinter, as they moved from
empty cage to empty cage in the aviary reading the illustrative markers to
each other.[18]

At this point, we must modify MacCannell's approach somewhat to
bring it into better conformity with our own discussion. In his analysis, the
marker is the signifier and the sight a signified, in a semiotic transformation that, when the marker is replaced by the sight, produces the tourist's

recognition of the sight. From the Eiffel Tower, he notes by way of example, citing an early guidebook, Paris can be viewed as if it were a picture, map, or panorama of itself and hence can represent a pattern of markers that provides for the recognition of the many sights that constitute it. "Apparently," MacCannell writes,

> the instant just before the sightseer completes his recognition of a famed sight is regarded highly enough by some that they will employ mechanical aids to prolong and savor it. . . . When the Louvre first comes into view, then, it may not be recognized at all. Partially recognized, it has the momentary status of information about a famous building which the viewer "should know." It appears as an incomplete plan, model, or image of itself. Its label or name is not attached to the sight; it is said to be, rather, on the "tip of the sightseer's tongue." The uncertain tourist . . . may check the image provided by the actual Louvre against its other markers—a picture in his guide, for example—before he completes first contact recognition.[19]

In completing that recognition and incorporating the Louvre into the body of his experiences, the tourist adds another line to the social résumé that may in the end win him membership in the class that, as tradition dictates, has visited the Louvre and has the capacity, moreover, to report that experience—that is, the cosmopolitan European upper class for whom Paris has always been the capital of high culture and fashion. That tourism has its own social stratifications and that commerce is ever poised to exploit them are well known: while one tourist longs to see the Louvre, and another Yellowstone, still another dreams of Disney World; while one will summer in Northeast Harbor, another will spend a fortune on a week at Dollywood.

The moment that MacCannell describes, and particularly the metaphor he uses to describe it, returns us to the Mall, to the strange arrest we experience in the presence of the actual quilt or pot or fiddle tune, the "semiotic emergency" that arises from the incompatibility between the representation of the object and its urgent, vital, forceful materiality, particularity, and actuality, when recognition of the sight thrusts into obsolescence the representation that provided for it, seeming simultaneously to expose the object to our attention and to remove the grounds of its recognition. But since we are for the moment in Paris, we ought, I think, to reverse MacCannell's formulation and note that what has occurred is exactly what Barthes describes as the formulation of myth, when a sign from one system moves to become a signifier in another—that is, the Louvre, a sign meaningful in French court and bourgeois culture and in European art, is made to be a signifier in the system of tourism, where the host of representations fashioned in its service, its signifieds, rise up like so many deep-feeding creatures to capture it. The Louvre, a sign, has become "the Louvre," a signifier, in a tourist culture in which imaginative life has been elaborately decked out in representations whose purpose on earth is to find their semiotic mates, reproduce, and die.

The semiotic ambition of the signified, or marker, in tourism is perhaps best illustrated by markers that bear certain historical information in blocks of text, realized in brass plaques affixed to boulders, cast iron panels, or similar manifestations; in these, the representation becomes a sight or signifier in itself and is identified as such by its own material durability and monumentality. That the marker or representation is the signified, not the signifier, in the system of tourism does not mean, of course, that in other orders of meaning it cannot be both a signifier and a sign, a signifier in orders of photography, travel literature, advertising, and the like, and a sign in the configurations of culture that inform these arts: the pictorialization of nature, the construction of national and cultural heroes and myths, the idealization of the primitive, the evocation of the earthly paradise, the gratification of class aspiration, and so on. Recognizing the sight, the tourist finds these nimbi of unarticulated meaning imperfectly mingling in and around the borders of his perception, now dissolved in the sight, now evaporated out of it, and, no matter how violently manipulated to shape itself to the sight, always returning like some marvelous new polymer to its own form.

A myth, says Barthes in a famous and much-quoted essay, is a transformation from history into nature, meaning into form; a system of beliefs, an ideology, is formulated as a system of facts. "Myth has an imperative, buttonholing character," he says. "It turns towards me, I am subjected to its intentional force, it summons me to receive its expansive ambiguity."

> If, for instance, I take a walk in Spain, in the Basque country, I may well notice in the houses an architectural unity, a common style, which leads me to acknowledge the Basque house as a definite ethnic product. However, I do not feel personally concerned, nor, so to speak, attacked by this unitary style: I see only too well that it was here before me, without me. It is a complex product which has its determinations at the level of a very wide history: it does not call out to me, it does not

provoke me into naming it, except if I think of inserting it into a vast picture of rural habitat. But if I am in the Paris region and I catch a glimpse, at the end of the rue Gambetta or the rue Jean-Jaures, of a natty white chalet with red tiles, dark brown half-timbering, an asymmetrical roof and a wattle-and-daub front, I feel as if I were personally receiving an imperious injunction to name this object a Basque chalet: or even better, to see it as the very essence of *basquity*. This is because the concept appears to me in all its appropriative nature: it comes and seeks me out in order to oblige me to acknowledge the body of intentions which have motivated it and arranged it there as the signal of an individual history, as a confidence and a complicity: it is a real call, which the owners of the chalet send out to me. And this call, in order to be more imperious, has agreed to all manner of impoverishments: all that justified the Basque house on the plane of technology—the barn, the outside stairs, the dove-cote, etc.—has been dropped; there remains only a brief order, not to be disputed. And the adhomination is so frank that I feel this chalet has just been created on the spot, *for me*, like a magical object springing up in my present life without any trace of the history which caused it.[20]

This is precisely the magic that transfixes the visitor to the Festival of American Folklife, where various intersecting patterns of representation—products of thought, and as mobile as thought—work or seem to have worked like a draftsman's mechanical arm to reproduce themselves in the visage of the participant, obliging the visitor "to acknowledge the body of intentions which have motivated it." The Peckham exorcizings, too, in like fashion transmitted certain marvels from the religious into the political sphere. It is this same magic, finally, that enchants the tourist and arrests her attention, shuttling it hypnotically between sight and marker, marker and sight, for all that is before her is coupled to the orders of intelligibility she has brought with her, not as "a complex product that has its determinations at the level of a very wide history" of its own.

So long as the tourist remains psychologically and economically anchored at home—the very thing that distinguishes the tourist, with his credit cards and travelers' checks, from the wanderer or adventurer—the entire moral order in which he is grounded undergoes not a disappearance, but a transfiguration, as the material order in which he has placed himself becomes the vehicle of a vast ethnemic metaphor for it. For though the tourist may *even in the Basque country* encounter a Basque house or, for that matter, see a colonial house in Connecticut rather than its imitation in a Los Angeles suburb, its ethnic or historical reality remains largely invisible to him, even while he reads of it in his guide, for its real significance for him lies in the language of status and class—of social, political, and cultural desire—into which he has already incorporated it, and which by means of tourism he enunciates to himself and to others. He will have enunciated it at home as well when he builds for himself a colonial or a French Provincial or a Tudor house on the suburban street in which each of these architectural styles belongs to a particular signifying system that has silently articulated such factors as ethnicity and history to hierarchies of social and economic status, definition, and power, dehistoricizing them to fit them for their new social function. The tourist, in other words, has never left home; rather, home has left him and has been sweepingly and comprehensively replaced—one might almost say redecorated—by another.

The time has arrived, however, to reinterpret, as I think Barthes' own language seems to suggest we must, this semiotics into a poetics, in which the processes of multiple framing, the lateral shifting of signifiers, the transformation of signs, and so on may be seen in relation to imitation, representation, impersonation, and figuring forth—in relation, that is, to the processes that are "the data of cultural experience," what I have called ethnomimesis. The idealist distinction between nature and art is, of course, deeply problematic when we consider that most of what we call nature is the cultural construction of traditions of pictorial art, education, literature, and natural science, whereas much of what we call culture can itself be situated in complex social processes proceeding from a natural human endowment that realizes itself in society. But that we are still entangled with enabling distinctions of this kind is, I think, apparent in the very concept of the frame, which fashions, constitutes, and bounds a discrete thing in relation to what lies outside the frame—that is, somehow sets a thing over against that which remains unfashioned, unconstituted, and unbounded by virtue of its exclusion from the frame. The culturally significant gesture, then, is the framing itself.

The Basque house in the Basque region of Spain, although a "definite ethnic product," may appear natural to the tourist, cultural to the anthropologist, or simply practical to the Basque, defined in each case by its situation in a semiotic field, which is itself determined by a particular frame of reference and the assumptions belonging to it. The Basque house on the rue de Gambetta, however, belongs to an order of art—that is, in this instance, to an order of social, political, economic, and other meaning constituted simply by the lateral movement in which we can detect what Barthes calls an intention (though its meaning does not necessarily reside in its intentionality), whose effect is to frame the Basque house in its "basquity," with the necessary attendant "impoverishments" to its historicity and ethnicity and so on that its framing entails. In fact, the Basque house, understood ethnographically, is itself the product of complex intentions in relation to nature and society that are entirely deserving of the name of culture or art, whereas the Basque house in Paris reflects impulses that are entirely natural to human beings in society and that, indeed, can be observed in some form in every society—that is, impulses toward definition, status, and place and the display of them.

The point is that, in cultural operations, the acts of fashioning, of constituting and bounding, and of drawing the distinction between what is fashioned and what is not, what is bounded and what is not, though theoretically arbitrary, are practically absolute and essential; and from within a culture such distinctions will always seem—because of the culture's sociopolitical naturalizing or mythologizing of its own structures and concomitant projection of the practices that occur within them—at some level a distinction between nature and art, a distinction that will itself shift as cultural discourses such as science or education change, narrowing perhaps the social domain of nature while expanding it in the psyche and the environment, extending the reach of art into what have been regarded as natural processes such as genetic selection or the gestation of the fetus, or reconstructing as cultural formerly "natural" categories such as gender.

"The form which an artist imposes on his materials," writes Aristotle's translator and interpreter Kenneth Telford, "is not the essential form of the natural object which actualizes the potentiality of its parts, but the perceptible form which is accidental to that essence. A painting of a tree, for example, makes use of the visual form of the tree, not the intellectual form which the botanist understands." This perceptible form, moreover, "is controlled by a principle which is peculiar to the work of art and is not derived either from the natural object which supplies the perceptible form or from the artist who produces the work."[21] Because botany is culturally constructed as a description of nature, the tree as the botanist understands it is the "natural" product; as the painter or the landscape gardener understands it, it is a cultural product. The Basque house on the rue de Gambetta makes no effort to reproduce the structure that the ethnographer understands but rather appropriates a perceptible form enabled by a category— the category of the private, freestanding bourgeois urban dwelling—"peculiar to the work of art," that is, to the order of meaning into which the perceptible form has been incorporated. There is, in a sense, *no* "Basque house" *as such* in Basque country; the "Basque house" is strictly an artifact of a culture in which such stylistic distinctions, and the framing of them by particular examples, is meaningful, in which such distinctions, moreover, are a function of that culture's own economic and social arrangements. The Basque house, in short, is a mimesis, a representation, a fiction, an invention, in the same sense that the "Dutch buy-a-broom girl" or the "Chinese dragon dancer" is an invention.

So, indeed, is "folklife"—and in the same sense.

What, then, is the status of the house, or the girl, or the dancer? Are they actual in their own spheres and mimetic in ours? Are they, as Barbara Kirshenblatt-Gimblett suggests, "living signs of themselves?"[22] Or are they "demonstrations," as Richard Bauman calls the conceptual frame favored by the participants at the Festival of American Folklife? The "colonial house" in Yorba Linda, with its fiberglass shingles, prefabricated truss roof, vinyl siding, and polyurethane-finished floors, seems both to represent a house and to function as one, not unlike colonial houses themselves, which were built out of wood to resemble Georgian and neoclassical manor houses made of stone. Or is it, as Plato taught, that only their forms are real, and that the living world is merely a series of wretched imitations of imitations? Strolling among the vinyl and fiberglass houses that line our suburban streets, we might imagine ourselves in Plato's world of ideal Forms, because they are far more perfect, as representations, than their models; and if we can't afford to live on such streets, or to sustain their fragile masquerade, we can buy the exhilaration that comes of it in careful reproductions, such as Disney's Main Street, that actually intensify the illusion with strategic reductions in scale and exaggerations of perspective. Or perhaps it is time, rather than formal perfection, that bestows the seal of authenticity, pulling out the nails by their heads, curling the shingles, sagging the floors, cracking the siding, exhibiting the house in its materiality and blurring its mimetic form. If that is the case, then the vinyl and fiberglass house will with time expose its own fraudulence to the eye at the same time that it reveals itself authentically *as* itself.

In distinguishing between signifiers and signifieds, sights and markers, actuality and representation, I think we are often confused by a distinction that effaces the sheer phenomenality of both; both nature and art are grounded at once in consciousness and with consciousness in the noumenality of creation. The ideality, the purity, the ingenuity, the glamour, and the harmony, proportion, and form of the representation in its own phenomenality, all materially realized, have—even in the process of signification or mimesis—already transfigured what is signified or represented; to the extent that we can scarcely conceive of the object world apart from our representations of it, so is that world continually swept up in the ideality and glamour of representation, which its recognition must of course continually both affirm and deny. But at the same time that the representation detemporalizes and dematerializes what is represented, it is itself material and hence inevitably captured by time and change. And most bewilderingly, as in the landscape garden, the representation even *as* representation can materialize in a strange epiphany of form that, even as we can recline in its shade or grow apples in it, seems as unreal as a dream.

It is a fascination, even an obsession, with this enigma that seems to actuate the tourist and to cause her to dwell, as MacCannell observes, upon the moment of recognition itself, as if the object of her desire were neither the sight nor the marker nor the conjunction of the two, which can never be practically achieved, but rather the possibility of their conjunction, the possibility that what is thought and what is experienced might, at some frontier beyond either thought or experience, become one. The actual practice of tourism, as opposed to its total structure, strongly suggests an interplay between representation and actuality whose motive is the sensation of recognition itself. Working within the body of touristic representations, the tourist projects an itinerary of successive sights that will compress or distill the ordinary density of experience with an intensity of recognition, which the tourist is at pains to sustain: no rest for the weary on vacation. Yet the intensity of that experience is consistently compromised by the necessity of representing it in diaries, photographs, postcard mailings, souvenir buying, and other means by which the tourist can construct the tour socially for others, incorporating it as an aspect of her own social identity, as well as for herself, reshaping the tour according to her own lights in a photograph album or a letter, on a souvenir shelf, in memorates and anecdotes, even in the clothes she wears and the language she uses. I have known tourists whose *only* purpose, it seems, is to be able say they've been to a particular place, however perfunctory the visit itself, however awkwardly distanced with cameras and souvenir-buying the actual experience may have been. But the interplay between representation and actuality is never more mesmerizing than at the sight itself, which is always both absolutely identical to or "out of" its representations—as England is always "out of" Dickens and Hardy—and irretrievably different from them, fully invested with their meaning and yet entirely empty of meaning, at once the consummation and the exhaustion of desire.

I suspect that always between representation and actuality, sight and marker, signifier and signified, earth and world, concealed in the sign itself and brooding in the interior of the actual, is a seductive promise at the frontier of consciousness, and perhaps bound up with its erosion or obliteration, into which the human imagination projects itself and pursues as the truth of its experience, which is perhaps always, in the end, the experience of itself. Our tourist, in any case, is heir to King Lear and to the sad Earl of Leicester who had eaten up his neighbors, gazing upon the raving Tom O'Bedlam or upon the hermit in his hermitage with his hourglass and Bible—upon beings in the mask of unaccommodation, through whom the king or the earl may contemplate what the age was determining to be his own essence. For the tourist, however, the thoroughgoing emancipation of self from society is no longer a horror projected by a distracted king, nor a specialized intellectual method associated since Descartes with scientific inquiry, nor an effigy for an Earl to contemplate with the strange piquancy of his sentimental resources; rather, it is a way to restore an otherwise lost conviction of reality, a form of existential consolation. And incidentally, it is a fine way to spend a holiday, if you can afford it.

The gentleman at his garden window—let us think particularly of Henry Hoare, the banker—is one of the earliest visible figures in the high culture of the modern world who, by virtue of his integration into and his social construction out of, say, a mercantile or industrial system that even in the eighteenth century was nearly global in extent, has no psychic investment in the matter of immediate perception other than that he perceives them. He is more or less insulated from the local sensate world, from its conditions and its effects, quite as if the physical world had been framed as a work of art or as a scientific experiment. Hence it is, at worst, of no particular interest, especially if it does not conform to the prevailing standards of beauty, at whatever level, or has not been framed as art; familiarity only makes the scene more contemptible, whereas whatever lies beyond his practical horizon is proportionately more beckoning because it, too, is essentially an imaginative substance, formed from its representations in art or literature as the extraordinary promise that what can be aroused by art can be confirmed in life. The window frame may perhaps only reiterate the picture frame; in fact, however, both have become, as they were not in the Middle Ages, projections of a psychological frame that forms at the boundary between the empirical world and the vast but imperceptible technoeconomic system in which the gentleman's existence is actually grounded.

The ascendant figure of the eighteenth-century social landscape, the mercantile or manufacturer-gentleman, is now the common currency of our cultural life, repeated in every man or woman socially tied to and extended in the global technoeconomic network and hence utterly uncoupled from the actual scenes of existence in every sense except that she exists in them. She is a tourist in her own life, and she may have begun to construct even her immediate object-world—her clothes, the house and its interior, the street, the park—in conformity with the same standards and values that drive the tourist, a masquerade of represented realities seized in a materiality through which nearly all the functions and purposes of life are to be carried out. The end of tourism—the abolition of the condition of consciousness in which it originates—can be achieved only by framing all of life as a tour, replacing it with a skein of representations that perpetually pacify the longing of the imagination for ever new, ever more perfect representation.

It is difficult, for comparison's sake, to evoke out of our shared postmodern consciousness a counterworld in which otherwise familiar human traits dispose themselves so differently that they constitute, in effect, another consciousness. Where power is concentrated at the sources of life and controls those sources, as the old kings and princes controlled with their might the natural reservoirs upon which life depended and organized around themselves societies based on the extension, maintenance, distribution, and descent of that power, power is the radiant ore, the uranium of human cohesion. In such a political economy, obeisance, fealty, service, loyalty, allegiance, gratitude, affection, fear, and love, and their ritual enactments such as we see in Cordelia and Kent, are not mere forms, not mechanical rites; they are, along with the practices that arise from them, the natural response of the heart to that which and upon whom existence depends, naturally appropriate to sustaining the connection between power and its dependencies.

In this psychic economy, self and world are evaluated in relation to power; both social organization and artistic representation reflect that evaluation in their glorification of power, in the hierarchical structures, both social and symbolic, that descend from it, and in the rituals and ceremonies that continually reiterate and reinforce those structures. Identity, in this scheme, is the orientation of oneself in relation to the antipodes of power and to its social and cultural latitudes and longitudes. Such a psychic economy is not unknown to us. Broadly speaking, it is the project of the political right to promulgate such a system; it is also often characteristic, psychosocially, of certain institutional, bureaucratic, occupational, ethnic, and other ethnomimetic groups in which personal welfare is closely bound up with hierarchies of local power and in which, in a sense, personal responsibility and accountability are distributed throughout the social nexus. In such a system, strictly speaking, there is no tourism, for outside the structure of authority there is no personhood, only the derangement of a Tom O'Bedlam, full of a formless, unbodied culture beset by ghosts.

With the evolution of modern society, an alien, disciplinary configuration of power such as Foucault describes grew out of the rationalization of the world-picture and its projection into the organization of the economy, the polity, the society, and the psyche, whose "subjectivity" came to be constituted, not like the old royal subject, in fealty, but by a new form of subjection that, though engineered and managed by people, seemed to have been designed into the structure of society itself and sustained itself in the technical solidarity of that structure. Today a "society of the spectacle" (in Guy Debord's well-known phrase) "colonizes everyday life," writes Michael Rogin, again turning "domestic citizens into imperial subjects."

> Spectacle goes private by organizing mass consumption and leisure; it attaches ordinary, intimate existence to public displays of the private lives of political and other entertainers. Spectacles, in the postmodern view, define the historical rupture between industrial and postindustrial society—the one based on durable goods production, the other on information and service exchange. With the dissolution of individual subjects and differentiated, autonomous spheres, not only does the connection between an object and its use become arbitrary, in this view, but skilled attention to display also deflects notice from the object to its hyperreal, reproducible representation.[23]

What is alarming about this formulation is not only the much-lamented and somewhat obscure "death of the subject," which seems to lie in a kind of spillage of subjectivity across the surfaces of the collective commercial and political spectacle, but, as Rogin goes on to repeat, the power of the information managers in commerce, communications, and government to promulgate unitary and meaningful political, social, and cultural "simulacra" or mythoi that deliver so absolutely into their hands a power that could not have been dreamed of by the most ambitious and tyrannical king.

The folk revival of our epoch, it might perhaps be argued, occurred at the historical juncture when industrial production, as a gradient of social differentiation, began to give way to the new society of consumption—when, with the slow collapse of the social differentiations grounded in production, the will to identity shifted its orientation to the product in its new differentiating power, not as a thing produced but as a thing consumed. This is, perhaps, precisely the frontier at which the folk festival visitor and the participant, the tourist and the tourized, encounter one another: the boundary over which the cultural sign passes back and forth in restless oscillation, at which the folk product itself stands determinedly fixed in its resistance to appropriation by all the signifying forces working upon it.

It seems that the folk festival reaffirms the artisanal myth of independence just as the web of production migrates to the farthest corners of the globe; that it dramatizes bourgeois individualism just as our individuality evaporates in the consumer marketplace and precipitates as a kind of inundating acid rain of cultural dioxides; that it glorifies a working class that has disappeared, either into its own affluence or into impoverished and exploited foreign or domestic exile; that it celebrates community at a time when discontinuity has shattered every traditional human connection and technology has encroached even upon our biological ties; that it cherishes the homemade and the handcrafted in the midst of a culture that seems little more sometimes than a traffic in fantasy, with which it saturates every public and private space.

What then will become of the folklife festival in the fullness of postmodernism, which by then will no doubt have learned its own name, with production driven into exile and the cultural field transformed into a spectacle of commodities: when, as Fredric Jameson puts it, cultural production "has been fully integrated with commodity production generally"; when the ethnemic cornucopia of tools and products has been transformed into its own image; and when, to quote Debord again, "the image has become the final form of commodity reification"? Is there, in a field of awareness dominated by transmissions, recordings, displays, incandescences, luminescences, amplifications, and other emanations of electronic representation, any manifestation of cultural genesis in a recognizable sense, in which ethnomimesis has any role?[24]

In the society of the spectacle, social life as ethnography might describe it is actually a kind of quarantine or confinement, as if the entire society had been kept indoors by a contagion whose first symptoms we experienced in the days immediately following the Kennedy assassination, when we collectively withdrew to our television screens. That momentary crisis has now, it seems, become the archetype of a society entirely swept up in the exchange of information, a society that effectively incarcerates people in their own enclosures, where they endlessly twist the video dial among seventy-five or a hundred channels (now called "grazing," with the appropriate suggestion of the bovine), or withdraw into the catatonic trance of the stereowalkman, or, trapped in the car, hold a demented pantomime of conversation with a cellular phone, or snare themselves in the bizarre drudgery of rebounding answering machines and calls waiting that conspire to keep us on the telephone indefinitely and concomitantly increase the telephone bill exponentially—a society not only quarantined, that is, but wholly atomized, as it was not at the time of the Kennedy assassination, and totally in thrall.

I myself am deeply perplexed to detect, in my own account of the "semiotic emergency" of the Festival of American Folklife, signs of what Jameson, following Lacan, calls a "breakdown in the signifying chain": that condition in which the genesis of meaning out of the extensive interplay among signifiers in a total order of meaning is paralyzed by a breach—the characteristic moment of postmodern culture—in the relations upon which such interplay depends. Such a breach, Jameson argues, is, in the clinical context at least, pathological, the mark of the experience of the schizophrenic who lives in a world of "undescribable vividness, a materiality of perception properly overwhelming, which effectively dramatizes the power of the material—or better still, the literal—Signifier in isolation." "The present of the world or material signifier," he writes, "comes before the subject with heightened intensity, bearing a mysterious charge of affect, here described in the negative terms of anxiety and loss of reality, but which one could just as well imagine in the positive terms of euphoria, the high, the intoxicatory or hallucinogenic intensity."[25]

This remarkable formulation describes, I believe, that moment—and it is only a moment—in the Festival visitor's experience in which the material reality of the folk product or of the musical or other performance is stunningly arrested in its own being, in the vibration of its refusal to reduce itself to its own representations, to become a figure in a mythology that is always, in turn, the reflex of power. It describes the moment at the conclusion of the "From Field to Factory" exhibit when we peer with a vague troubled surmise through a translucent screen into the beginning of the exhibit; it also describes, I think, the excitement of the tourist as he stumbles down the path toward the rocks where the surf breaks just as it did on the postcard, or her enchantment as she wanders among the pines that filter the light just as they did on the poster—but where the surf and the light, though glorified by representation, are, unlike their representations, intractably other, inscrutable, terrible. The achievement of the sight, as it allies us to a social formation, at the same time reveals in an almost theological sense the irreducibility, the unattainability, the unrepresentability of experience. In this lies the thrill of discovery, and as MacCannell rightly points out, we strive to repeat or prolong it. For it is better that the world should return to us, even for a moment, in its original wonder than that it should disappear at once into the engaging lies of peddlers and the hoary tales of old fathers without granting us a moment's acquaintance with its own nature.

With characteristic ingenuity, Jameson associates the schizophrenic "intensities" or "hallucinatory splendour" of postmodern cultural experience with what he calls the "hysterical sublime," a notion that joins what he calls the "derealizing" effect of postmodern art, which can befuddle the complacent binarism of signifier and signified, with the Burkeian Sublime, which, as he reminds us, was "an experience bordering on terror, the fitful glimpse, in astonishment, stupor and awe, of what was so enormous as to crush life altogether."[26]

The concept of the sublime in the eighteenth century was a response to the crisis in the representation of nature, formerly governed by neoclassical standards of harmony and decorum, and particularly of the colossal or monumental in nature, which tested the limits of perception and further exposed "the incapacity of the human mind to give representation to such enormous forces." The "hysterical sublime"—the *derealization* of the whole surrounding world of everyday reality"—poses, however, an epistemological crisis somewhat different in character than that posed in the eighteenth century. The question is no longer, it seems, whether the human mind is capable of representing reality to itself, but rather whether there is a reality at all that is not constituted by its representations, or whether, indeed, "representations" are somehow not "more real" than what can be represented or simulated—whether, that is, the tangible waking world is not now itself simply a reproduction, in the Marxian sense, of socially legitimated cultural models that, through the process of culture, have prepared and shaped our perceptions of it.

If this formerly scholastic question—we are certainly not the first to question the message of the senses—has a new pertinence, it is perhaps because technology has acquired the power to represent the world in ways whose immediate claim upon the senses far exceeds the intensity of ordinary perception; such technological innovations as digital-audio recording, computer-generated "virtual reality," and high-definition television promise a "hallucinatory intensity," which, unlike the monumental natural scenes that in the eighteenth century seemed to presage the deterioration of the sensory apparatus, now seems capable, like hallucinatory drugs, of capturing the human organism with purely sensory ecstasies and is not, finally, hallucinatory at all. Like some Orwellian nightmare, the spectacle threatens to seduce us—and, even more frighteningly, our children—away from any willed participation in the ordinary social world in order to win us to its own commercial and political aggrandizement.

The postmodern universe, says Jameson, has in an analogous way finally exceeded the capacity of our minds "to map the great global multinational and decentered communicational network in which we find ourselves caught as individual subjects," with the resulting loss

> of a certain minimal aesthetic distance, of the possibility of the positioning of the cultural act outside the massive Being of Capital, which serves as an Archimedean point from which to assault this last . . . that distance in general (including "critical distance" in particular) has very precisely been abolished in the new space of postmodernism. We are submerged in its henceforth filled and suffused volumes to the point where our now postmodern bodies are bereft of spatial coordinates and practically (let alone theoretically) incapable of distantiation; meanwhile . . . the prodigious new expansion of multinational capital ends up penetrating and colonizing those very pre-capitalist enclaves (Nature and the Unconscious) which offered extraterritorial and Archimedean footholds for critical effectivity. . . . We all, in one way or another, dimly feel that not only punctual and local countercultural forms of cultural resistance and guerrilla warfare, but also even overtly political interventions . . . are all somehow secretly disarmed and reabsorbed by a system of which they themselves might well be considered a part, since they can achieve no distance from it.[27]

No one, perhaps, can be more sympathetic to this account of the tectonic shifts in contemporary culture than what I imagine to be the principal readership of this book: that phalanx of now middle-aged folk revivalists who in their youth took up the wholesome and idealistic bohemianism of folksong and folk music, finding resources in it for cultural and political resistance and for pastoral and utopian visions, constructing their social identities around it, and, in many cases, building artistic, academic, or public service careers around it. Theirs was the advance guard of postwar youth culture, shaped by a succession of commercial initiatives, largely in the realm of popular music, that produced first the rock-and-roll revolution and, hard upon its heels, the folksong boom and the great folk music festivals at Newport, Philadelphia, Chicago, and Berkeley; it was the backwash of this movement, moreover, at the moment in which what we now call the postmodern began its explosive expansion, that the Festival of American Folklife emerged to preserve in an institutional setting the cultural outlook that had been superseded in the marketplace. The folk revival, in fact, was precisely the first stage of that expansion, the type and the pattern of it—a tidal wave of consumer culturalism.

Yet "to argue that culture is today no longer endowed with the relative autonomy it once enjoyed," writes Jameson, "is not necessarily to imply its disappearance or extinction. On the contrary: we must go on to affirm that the dissolution of an autonomous sphere of culture is rather to be imagined in terms of an explosion: a prodigious expansion of culture throughout the social realm, to the point at which everything in our social life—from economic value and state power to practices and the very structure of the psyche itself—can be said to have become 'cultural' in some original and as yet untheorized sense."[28] It is not only, then, that "aesthetic production has become integrated into commodity production," but that commodity production has perforce become, with the ubiquitous and seemingly universal and continuous movement of signs through orders of signification, pervasively mythological. There is scarcely a cultural surface, including the surface of our own social lives, that has not become, like the Basque house, "a magical object springing up in my present life without any trace of the history which caused it." We search for authenticity in vain, for authenticity has itself been swept up in the transcendent mimesis of postmodernity as simply one form among many others in the articulation of social power.

What we have called the ethnonoetic plenum—still, in the late medieval period, largely absorbed in sacred political and religious institutions, and in the modern period submerged in the newly posited unconscious and sought there in traces, symbols, and symptoms—is now distributed abroad in a universe of spectacle where, thoroughly projected and uttered, it becomes perforce the object of an incoherent and helpless longing. Tom O'Bedlam was mad; now his madness, in the society of the spectacle, is our own cultural condition; what Jameson calls "late capitalism" has learned to reproduce the cultural process no longer through representation but wholly within it.

And yet, even in the society of the spectacle, there is the stirring of an ethnomimetic process within the body of the spectacle itself. A familiar kind of culturality has emerged from within commodity production as the circulation of the commodity, moving from center to margin and back again, or from present to past, retrieves cultural signs that it introduces into the marketplace as signifiers in emergent communities, which are themselves often grounded either in obsolescence or in marginality. A catalog recently arrived in my mailbox argues that "People want things that are hard to find. Things that have romance, but a factual romance, about them." From J. Peterman you can buy, among other things, reproductions of the beret "worn by Che Guevara, Tyrone Power, Groucho Marx"; an English hunting shirt that "you've seen the upper classes wearing for the last 400 years"; a ladies' blouse "straight out of Gainsborough's portraits of 18th-century women"; Charles Lindbergh's goatskin overcoat; James Dean's windbreaker; or one of Jay Gatsby's shirts.[29] There is scarcely a cultural moment, from the heyday of the Edwardian upper class to the soda-fountain culture of the 1950s to present-day Black Sea fishing villages, whose signs cannot be appropriated as signifiers in the commodity system; but they lose their original associations in transit, becoming, like Hoare's peasant cottage or Temple of Flora, signs of a particular socioeconomic status or role.

But as signifiers they can, of course, become the carriers of social statements. Both gay culture and black street culture, to suggest counterexamples, mark points at which the convergence of social marginality on the one hand and peculiar concentrations of licit and illicit buying power on the other have produced fountainheads of cultural signification that, though inevitably swept up in the circle of commodity appropriation, remain closely identified with the communities that produced them and hence function, often with broad irony, as signs of resistance or dissent, in the same way that Peterman's catalog appeals to the vanishing Anglo-American hegemony.

Indeed, it seems—if I may be permitted some speculation even purer than what I have indulged in to this point—that the implacable resistance on the right and the left to the cultural status quo and the consequent polarization, with its attendant decay of political dialogue, has arisen in precisely those cultural fields where the conversion to spectacle—which at this stage includes and is itself the commodity—remains incomplete or impossible. It should surprise no one that the radical left has built its mansion not only within the walls of the academy, but in that stronghold of elite bourgeois romantic individualism, literary criticism; in so doing, it has succeeded both in commodifying Marxist, deconstructionist, feminist, and other counterhegemonic positions—if university press titles are any indication—and in allying the obsolescent literary vocation, grounded in such faculties as taste, discrimination, and introspection, with the post-modern spectacle by colonizing it with its self-immolating analyses. Nor should it surprise us that the reactionary right, having lost the hundred-years' war over sexual morality, has carried its decency campaigns into regions of sexuality that admit of virtually no empirical investigation, representation, or commodification, where Nature still rules as Other: the womb, child abuse, and incest, sacred realms either coaxed out of obscurity and ambiguity like signs of Satanic possession or manufactured whole out of sheer emotional fantasy—a kind of invention of the repressed.

It is only a matter of time, I think, before we discover how decisively the spectacle can be turned back upon itself, for good or ill. In Israel, second-generation Middle Eastern Jews resist the commercial hegemony of Euro-centric popular music with a lively underground traffic in audiocassettes of their own transethnic music.[30] One cannot but wonder what role the global communications network, bouncing words and images off of satel-lites, must have played in the defeat of the August 1991 coup in the Soviet Union, unthinkable in the epoch of government-controlled newspapers and broadcasting stations. The videotape of Rodney King's beating and the civil disturbances that followed the acquittal of his police assailants in criminal court, on the other hand, may suggest a kind of decentralization and redistribution, through technology, of the power of surveillance, throwing a ghastly illumination onto the "darkest region of the political field." Yet the "symmetrical, inverted body" of Rodney King, as it ap-peared before the public gaze in the image of white truck driver Reginald Denny (their very names embody the inversion), diverts real political forces into the purely symbolic realm of the video screen, opening the way for more severe official reprisals and deeper repression. What briefly arouses the national conscience ultimately becomes, it seems, just another television show.

The postmodern analysis, like Marxism itself, is fascinated by capital and its appendages, for it is capital that supports, intellectually and materially, its remarkably capacious and aloof analytical position. In declaring the ascent of the postmodern, the analysis in a sense allies itself to the expansion of capital, achieving precisely the Archimedean position it claims to have lost, announcing the "death of the subject" even while its own subjectivity continues passionately to drive, along the vectors of race, class, ethnicity, and gender, its enactments of political struggle in the personal sphere. This is a vexing and hopeless project, a symptom of political impotence born not, as it seems, from the "prodigious new expansion of multinational capital," but from the withdrawal from the political field into which that expansion has seduced us.

For our quarrel, finally, is not with one another but with the system of practices, regulations, rulings, laws, as well as the avoidance or violation of them, and the wielding of illegitimate political influence wherein the emergence of the postmodern, which is simply more business as usual, really lies. This development is not natural and inevitable, the consequence of these "late eclipses of the sun and moon." It is the effect—at the sites where corporate and political elites commingle—of particular decisions made at particular times and places by particular people, the self-interested conspiratorial Edmunds of our own time. "The labor of plundering a subject people," writes Lewis Lapham, "isn't a freak of nature, or the work of trolls, or the fault of the Japanese. Specific individuals with specific purposes in mind break open the doors and steal the silver."[31]

There is no more powerful indication of the triumph of corporate capitalism over every other institutional, social, cultural, or moral interest than our continuing infatuation with its productions. Folklife is, in one sense, the awakening from that infatuation, a recognition that life, to be lived at all, must be lived not vicariously or for show, but in and for itself. If the meaning of *folklife* seems to have at once violently expanded and contracted, so that it now includes virtually any form of real social interaction at any level of society, as well as the most intimate and inaccessible of those interactions within the family and the person, it is because the structure of social relations within which folklife has its meaning has shifted. A society that was once a great factory, and after that a great department store, is now a vast video screen surrounded by the concomitantly darkened regions of the political field where real human purposes remain in thrall.

As Alan Jabbour of the American Folklife Center has consistently argued, "folklore" in our day describes a vital and original aspect of the highly differentiated postmodern personality, a mode of self-creation capable of embracing its own inventedness even as it deploys itself ethnemically in the social world, where a community—one among the many communities into which such a personality can integrate itself—forms around it. Both as an idea and as a social fact, folklore first appeared perhaps four centuries ago, born from the early modern differentiation of society and of the psyche embedded in it. Now it opens to us, it seems, not only a glimpse of the limits to such differentiation and integration, which those of us exhausted by technological fragmentation may feel we have already reached or exceeded, but a sense of the shape of humanness and its possibilities within those limits. Our cultural project is to determine our new horizon and, in determining it, to forge a discourse of positive values, beyond mere oppositionalism, from which an effective postmodern politics might follow.

For what is new in this moment, in the context of postmodernity, is that not only identity but the whole grounds of identity, in real human association, in personal and social continuities, and in shared human imperatives, must be again recovered. The urgency of this project may have made the folk festival, perhaps only temporarily, seem oddly residual, fading into the background radiation of a consumer society even as we form new cultural and political rationales for its continuing existence. That is because postmodern culture, with its hollow glamour and shallow, spurious historicity, its supersaturation of imagery and information, its hallucinatory intensity, its dispersal if not the actual "death of the subject," has brought us to what appears to be an internally contradictory state of prolonged or permanent festivity—more precisely, has at every level of society promulgated the awful lie that a kind of total emancipation from care is the normal and permanent condition of social life.

This is the effect of what has become, in the century or so of its development, a kind of corporate totalitarianism, which like other totalitarianisms is transforming our institutions and enterprises into a new kind of ideological apparatus and propaganda machine whose sheer ubiquity, penetration, and amplitude dominate the noetic environment, silence the ordinary voice, and extend commercial metaphors, motives, and practices into areas of life in which they do not belong. Such a situation is unprecedented; but we can look to the ancestors of the Festival of American Folklife—the great industrial expositions of the Gilded Age, the White Cities at Chicago and St. Louis and the Dahomey Villages and Philippine Reservations that lay in their shadows—to find the beginnings of the divided civilization in which we now live.

There is no doubt that, in a still largely agrarian society, the original promise of consumer capitalism, with its great power and abundance, was scarcely resistible. But the illusory perpetuation of that promise, which sustains the corporate totality, is making life inside consumer society as shallow and unreal as it makes life outside of it brutal and brutalizing. If, in the midst of the industrial revolution, men and women assimilated themselves to machinery and domestic furniture, it seems that in the age of the commercial spectacle ethnomimesis is turning us all into apparitions—no longer "reified" with the commodity, but on the contrary spectralized and insubstantial, not selves so much as advertisements for selves, mere ghosts, wandering about in an insubstantial world, longing for life.

In the great consuming feast of the twentieth century, it is hardly surprising that we should feel our spirits squandered and our identities fragmented or false: that is in the nature of festivity. But the relentless exploitation of the world's human and natural resources and the despoliation of the earth upon which it all depends cannot go on forever. Ultimately, what we most long for will be thrust upon us: the burden of care in which human purpose and meaning originally and perennially resides— care for one another, for the planet that sustains us, for the cultures that we have arrogantly divided and allowed to be laid waste so that we might "unburthen'd crawl towards death." Now at last we descry in ourselves what we have demanded others to embody, enact, perform, and exhibit to us, our own nakedness and vulnerability—and in it the truth of human suffering that levels all distinctions. That is what we may hope for, when the festival is over: the resurrection of our human community, our cultures, in remembrance of their originating acts of love.

Sign Language

Conclusion

Consider the signers: the men and women who from time to time can be seen stage right or stage left at a musical performance or a workshop, interpreting the words and music to hearing-impaired members of the audience. One of them, a tall, lean, dapper fellow with an air of self-importance and an expression of vague distress, strides over the Festival grounds with a towel draped across his neck like a prizefighter; onstage, he sways and bounces with the music, his long arms spread wide or brought together in a priestlike gesture, almost as entertaining as the performers themselves. Another, younger, new to the work, stands stock-still and poker-faced, vigorously working her hands, almost literally knitting her message together like a pair of socks. Still another, a studious, dignified woman in early middle age, ascends to the stage with an expression somewhat preoccupied, abstracted; she is thinking. She betrays the rhythms of the music only by rocking on her heels; but she moves her hands and fingers with the swiftness and sureness of a weaver and with the gorgeous convolutions of a Javanese finger-dance. It is an urgent charade: so much to say, so little time to say it, each sign captured on the wing while with her mouth she shapes the words as if she means to throw them, in an intimate communication, across a crowded and noisy room.

They speak in signs: familiar gestures, such as putting one's finger to one's lips to signify quiet or raising the back of the palm melodramatically to the forehead; swift and ingenious hand movements that seem to accomplish some invisible small domestic work; exaggerated facial expressions, like a mime's; alphabetic shapes made with the fingers; and visible but silent speech, mouth and lip movements that demonstrate the making of, but do not make, a sound.

Various kinds of signs, in this system, can be combined to make new meanings. The sign for music, for example, is a strumming gesture; combined with an alphabetic "S," it means "song," with a "P," poetry. Some evoke shared sensory experiences, such as the flowing of water or the brilliance of the sun; or shared somatic feelings, such as heartache (under the sternum) or thought (under the brow); or shared ideas, such as that God is above us, in the heavens, and may be referred to by pointing upward.

For those of us blessed with the perception of sound, this pantomime, in which we can catch the occasional sign amusing or delightful in its fitness or enjoy the signer's dramatizations of feeling in her face, her shoulders, her very posture, only approximates what we actually can see and hear. Toward the community of the hearing-impaired, sequestered in their silence, we are much as we are toward all the cultures here on the Mall— hearing impaired, in a sense, ourselves. And as they are to the audible world, so are we to what lies beyond the power of our signs, or more precisely of our signers, to communicate. The cultural message is all we know; it *is* the world, and of the din beyond it, we can know no more than the fifteenth-century peasant knew of the silent planetary motions in schoolmen's tales.

Yet signs are everywhere: the Monument, the Capitol Dome, the Smithsonian towers. A man dressed as a combat soldier, carrying a briefcase and engaged in conversation with a cowboy, finds himself excluded from a reserved area by a staff member, who happens to be black and is wearing a Mickey Mouse T-shirt and an Orioles cap. Actually, we are all wearing signs—my name tag, almost the first thing I put on in the morning, is white, the participants' are orange, the volunteers' yellow. The first two are hand-lettered like wedding invitations; the last are typed out on the Festival site. Because certain small privileges go with these badges—such as access to certain restricted areas—a certain prestige attaches to them, too; taken together, they are actually a kind of honor roll, each name under the heading "Festival of American Folklife," which after the Festival has ended can be displayed in a new context. My own is on a bulletin board, as a sign of my relation to an august body whose name, in the more homely landscape of the midwestern village where I live, has the power almost of an incantation. Indeed, my skewered badge is a sign of my hope that this connection will become known to my friends, associates, and strangers, for it is part of me.

On my bulletin board, too, is a pendant of plastic beads with a crown, symbol of the French monarchy, in gold-colored plastic hanging from it. In itself it is nothing, a bauble; as a sign it is resonant. It is a set of Mardi Gras beads. I caught them as they were flung, by a representative of the Louisiana tourist board, from the Mardi Gras float as it lumbered along the gravel path of the Mall, the Blessed Virgin rocking a bit tipsily back and forth on its bow. In fact, I caught several strings of them. All the staff members had them; some had two or three or more around their necks during the Festival, as if more beads could bring more festivity, and more festivity, more joy.

But through the mysterious generativity of signs, the Mardi Gras beads take me to Mardi Gras in New Orleans. To have them is to say, somehow, like the sailor's earring that shows he's been around Cape Horn, that you've been there. It is not a lie, exactly—no, these are real Mardi Gras beads, and though I've never been to Mardi Gras, they recall that interval of wide-open possibility and relaxed liberality, that mood, that attitude, those affections, that little erosion of one's inhibitions that comes of displaying one or two sets of what amounts to costume jewelry around one's neck in full daylight, among grown-ups. On the Metro, though, I take them off.

Other talismans, from other cultures, mark the Festival visitors and affirm their presence: henna hand-paintings, which children wear on their palms and which they will display to their playmates until, in two weeks or so, the herb has worn off; or cornrows, which Caucasian girls have tied in their hair by the Nigerian cornrower.

Yet even this triangulation—signifier, signified, significatee—does not make a sign. The sign must have its signer, its significator, as well. Consider the signers again. For one, signing is a painstaking and sometimes awkward task, a labor; for another, it is simply part of a confident and conscientious narcissism. Signer and sign, in them, have not really come together. But the third is wholly taken over by it, her one aim being to tell the story being told, sing the song being sung, to those who cannot hear it. And in giving herself so wholly to what is not herself, she becomes herself, paradoxically, wonderfully, wholly, and completely herself.

It is the final evening. The great hall is filled with the music of the St. Landry Playboys; around and around in circles we go to the zydeco!

Everybody's here: Barry, Alicia, Tom, Nick, Margie, Cal, Peter, Diana, Susan, Rayna, Glenn, Louise, Mick, Dan, John, Laurie, Frank, and Richard; Daphne is here, and Barbara, and Arlene; Lee and Pete and John, the sound men, are here, and so are Mike and Al, the stage managers; Dorothy, who drove around on the pargo—she's here; Janet, Diana, and Jean, the signers, are here, and my friends Yvonne and Carolynn. Duncan, jacket off, in his black shirt, silver bolo, and his everlasting hat, is dancing with Tinika. Ralph is here, picking along on his mandolin, suit jacket hung over a chair. I see Hop Kilby, the shingle-river from Columbia, Louisiana. I see Azzie Roland, who seems happier this evening, with the young folks around him; Hezakiah is over there chatting with D. L., and Canray is playing along with the band on his fiddle, smiling that gorgeous smile. I don't see Buddha, the potter—perhaps he's gone to bed; but Subhash and Tarapado, who made the Durga—they're here, and so are Gurmukh and Krishan, the monkey-men. And dancing together with the beautiful Subrata—myself ruefully still undeclared—I see my secret beloved: his admiring eyes, the gay tilt of her head, turning and turning over the gleaming floor.

All of us hundreds, the Festival, are here, and out of the dark well of my grief springs a tide of joy. The meters and pulses of the zydeco seem to flow slowly away from the accordion and the washboard and the bass and into us, resolving themselves into a single oceanic rhythm, a quaking, a contraction, like the beat of a great heart, or like birth pangs, with which all the dancers and all the onlookers and the sitters and standers and talkers, and the vast room itself, are in passionate synchrony.

But it is late, very late. Up come Barry and Alicia, arm in arm—time to form a line. Duncan comes up, and Rayna, and Cal; across the floor a chorus line stretches from corner to corner and turns, all of us weary, mirthful, breathless, and drunk, a giddy phalanx kicking the ragged air with wild imprecision. I hardly know where I am; and through my arm slips another, a delicate limb, cool and white, and a small hand that, just for a moment, grasps my own.

It is she.

In the enclosing dark of the summer night, its womb now full of the morning, we hold one another and, with tender speeches, begin for one another to make ourselves anew. The old life expires in the breath of words. At the top of the hill, above us on the walk, Duncan stands beside his suitcase under the light. He has seen us. But before he goes—the taxi that will take him to the airport is just now pulling into the drive—and as we look up, he waves his hat.

The icon makers have flown home, leaving behind them the bountiful Durga in her sequined costume, her long clay limbs making elegant shapes under the sheer white and yellow veils in which her makers have adorned her. Day after day I have paused to watch her, watched her transformation from straw and earth to naked flesh, her flesh clothed and her face painted, wondering that she cannot descend from her throne to dance, or return my glance, inwardly mortified that a lifeless thing should be capable of making her woman's promise.

It falls upon us, then, to commit her, now that the festivities have ended, to the Potomac. Such is the tradition, and we have made a promise: the figure made of river clay must return to clay. In the car, she lies stiffly on the seat, the flashing, merry eyes that laughed at our mortality staring into the sun, her red lips gleaming as her veils fall around her and expose her clay-red thighs.

Traffic is fierce. For a moment, at the railing, we hold her over the water and then let her go. Her gaze fixes upon us, her children, as she plummets into the current, rolls over as if to sleep, and, as the river carries her into the shadow of the bridge, heaves once and disappears, pulling her veils down after her.

Notes

INTRODUCTION

1. Mullaney, "Strange Things, Gross Terms, Curious Customs," pp. 65–92.
2. Ibid., p. 75.

CHAPTER ONE

1. My use of *folklife* here is roughly synonymous with *common life* as Raymond Williams uses the term, in various contexts, in *Culture and Society*, particularly in the conclusion. "The idea of culture," he writes, "is a general reaction to a general and major change in the conditions of our common life. Its basic element is its effort at total, qualitative assessment. The change in the whole form of our common life produced, as a necessary reaction, an emphasis on attention to this whole form" (p. 295). The context in which I use *folklife* indicates that I wish to include it as a part of the "common life" but to address both from within, avoiding the socially downward or outward semantic momentum of "folklife" as we ordinarily use it. The technical and academic use of *folklife* extends it, though imprecisely, to the entire realm of informal face-to-face communications within social groups, a sense roughly coterminous with *common life* and one that extends the domain of folklife into certain dimensions of the life of institutional or "official" culture; but, whereas *folklife* normally implies a certain *kind* of social experience, with perhaps certain determining conditions and even particular kinds of people, as distinct from other kinds, *common life* points to the shared experiences, and to the quality of that sharing, that extends culture over differences of class, station, role, and so on. Used with reference to the Jacobean period, *common life* refers most narrowly to the ranks below those of the nobility, with concomitant suggestions of the commonplace, commonality, and commonwealth as well as of community. *Common life*, then, in this context, embraces the less technical and more traditional sense of *folklife*, with its suggestions of oral transmission, cultural survival, enclaved or sequestered community, and resistance. See also Williams's *Keywords*, pp. 70–72.
2. Mack, *King Lear in Our Time*, chap. 1.
3. Greenblatt, *Shakespearean Negotiations*, p. 95. Although I have benefited considerably from Greenblatt's perspective, my own was formed, and my discussion drafted, two years before his book appeared.
4. Ibid., pp. 101–2.
5. Murphy, *Darkness and Devils*.
6. Harsnett, *Declaration of Egregious Popish Impostures*, pp. 2–3.
7. Theobald, *Works of William Shakespeare*, 5:163–64.
8. Harsnett, *Declaration of Egregious Popish Impostures*, p. 180.

9. Descartes, *Discourse on Method*, p. 11.

10. Walter Ong, in *Ramus, Method, and the Decay of Dialogue*, initiates the discussion of these changes in pedagogy and culture. Also see Yates, *Art of Memory*, chap. 10, "Ramism as an Art of Memory," and chap. 17, "The Art of Memory and the Growth of the Scientific Method."

11. I adopt this concept of the "disciplinary" from Foucault, *Discipline and Punish*. The "disciplinary" is the extensive distribution and application of social power through institutions such as schools, prisons, military organizations, and factories whose disciplinary or punitive techniques act directly upon behavior, which in turn lends its disciplinary color to the broader culture.

12. Kantorowitz, *King's Two Bodies*.

13. McLuhan, *Gutenberg Galaxy*, p. 11.

14. Foucault, *Discipline and Punish*, pp. 28–29. See also White, "Noble Savage Theme as Fetish."

15. McLuhan, *Gutenberg Galaxy*, pp. 11–17.

16. E. H. Gombrich, *Art and Illusion* (1960), cited in ibid., p. 16.

17. Greenblatt, *Shakespearean Negotiations*, p. 111.

CHAPTER TWO

1. Bacon, "Of the True Greatness of Kingdoms and Estates," p. 148.

2. John Hales, "A Discourse of the Commonweal of This Realm of England" (1549), quoted in Mantoux, *Industrial Revolution*, p. 155.

3. Hill, *Reformation to Industrial Revolution*, 1:115–17. With the abolition in 1646 of feudal tenures or traditional rents owed to the king, landowners gained absolute ownership of their estates, which they could further consolidate by means of new laws of primogeniture; gentlemen became, in effect, the rulers of tiny kingdoms, sending their younger sons into business, the civil service, the military, or to the colonies. Tenants had become landlords and landlords tenants, as a pamphlet declared in 1654, many ancient families, lesser gentry, and embattled yeomen having yielded to the giant estates formed after the Civil War, when, through confiscation and punitive taxation, thousands of acres of ancestral lands fell to new owners.

4. Henry Addington, "An Inquiry into the Reasons for and against Inclosing Open-Fields" , quoted in Mantoux, *Industrial Revolution*, p. 175.

5. Foucault, *Order of Things*, p. 62.

6. Addison, quoted in Hunt, *Figure in the Landscape*, p. 40.

7. Foucault, *Order of Things*, p. 62.

8. John Trusler, "Elements of Modern Gardening" (1784), quoted in Hunt, *English Landscape Garden*.

9. Humphrey Repton, "Red Book" for Blaise Castle (1795–96), quoted in Hunt and Willis, *Genius of the Place*, p. 363.

10. Dutton, *English Garden*, p. 76.

11. Woodbridge, *Landscape and Antiquity*, pp. 11–18.

12. Mantoux, *Industrial Revolution*, p. 171.

13. Woodbridge, *Landscape and Antiquity*, pp. 51–60.

14. Dutton, *English Garden*, p. 118.

15. Morris, "An Essay upon Harmony," p. 74.

16. Hunt, *Figure in the Landscape*, pp. 25, 43–55.

17. Morris, "An Essay upon Harmony," pp. 74–79.

18. Ibid., p. 79.

18. Hunt, *Figure in the Landscape*, pp. 18, 8.

20. Ibid., p. 8.

21. Williams, *Culture and Society*, p. xvii.

22. Trevor-Roper, "Invention of Tradition."

23. Mumford, *Technics and Civilization*, p. 100.

24. Karl Marx, *Das Capital*, quoted in Mantoux, *Industrial Revolution*, p. 180.

CHAPTER THREE

1. Dubivsky, "Some Fresh Air," and Park, "Secretary S. Dillon Ripley Retires."

2. Trollope, *Domestic Manners of the Americans*, p. 181.

3. Ibid., pp. 181–83.

4. Ibid., p. 181.

5. Frye, *Secular Scripture*, pp. 121–26.

6. Quoted in Rydell, *All the World's a Fair*, p. 76.

7. Smithsonian, *Smithsonian Experience*, p. 26.

8. LaCovey, "Secretary Ripley Discusses," p. 4.

9. "From Field to Factory: Afro-American Migration, 1915–1940." Exhibit at the National Museum of American History, Washington, D.C., 1989–. Spenser Crew, curator; James Sims, designer; William Withuhn, project manager.

10. Poulet, "Criticism and the Experience of Interiority," p. 45.

11. Hawes, "Folk Arts and the Elderly," p. 29.

CHAPTER FOUR

1. Hawes, "Official Observer's Report."

2. Dresser and Hardman, "Evaluation of the 1974 Festival of American Folklife."

3. Reagon, "In the Streets," p. 25.

4. Da Matta, "Carnival In Multiple Planes," p. 209.

5. Reagon, "In the Streets," p. 27.

6. Parris, "Carnival and Community," pp. 10–11.

7. Ibid., p. 10.

8. Da Matta, "Carnival in Multiple Planes," pp. 231–32.

9. Ibid., pp. 229–31.

10. Williams, "Costuming," pp. 9–11.

11. Da Matta, "Carnival in Multiple Planes," p. 228.

12. Ibid.

13. Ibid., p. 224.

14. Bryce-Laporte, "New Immigration," pp. 6–8.

15. Hawes, "Official Observer's Report."

16. Scherer, "History of American Indian Research," pp. 19–20

17. "Indians Seek Burial of Museum Skeletons," p. 26.

18. Green, "American Indian Stereotypes," pp. 19–20.

19. Ibid., pp. 19–20.

20. Kavanaugh, "Seeking Out Indian Participation," p. 14.

21. Mitchell, "Mississippi."

22. Toll, *Blacking Up*, pp. 205–6.

23. Hawes, "Folk Arts and the Elderly," pp. 28–30.

24. Ibid.

25. Ibid., p. 30.

26. See Sutton-Smith, "Importance of Children's Folklore," and Hawes, "Law and Order on the Playground."

27. Susanne Roschwalb, ed., *Festival of American Folklife Program Book* (Washington, D.C.: Office of Folklife Programs, 1974), p. 16.

28. Hawes, "Law and Order on the Playground," p. 33.

CHAPTER FIVE

1. "Festival of American Folklife." Film and video. Public service announcement, Smithsonian Institution, 1982.

2. Ibid., 1968.

CHAPTER SIX

1. Charles Camp interview.

2. Glenn Ohrlin interview.

3. See Hunt and Seitel, "Cultural Conservation," and Kurin, "Cultural Conservation through Representation."

4. Geertz, "Thick Description," p. 6.

5. Levine, *Black Culture and Black Consciousness*, p. 337.

6. Mayhew, *London Labour*, p. 13.

7. Ibid., p. 452. Traditionally, Mayhew observes, workmen are classified variously after the articles they make, such as saddlers, glovers, and wheelwrights; or after the kind of work they perform, as joiners, thatchers, and printers; or after the materials they work upon, as goldsmiths and pewterers. A few are named after the tools they use, such as plowmen and sawyers (pp. 452–53). Mayhew then goes on to survey various other systems of classification, including those of the French industrial exhibitions of the early nineteenth century, the Great Exhibition of 1851, and the British census. The French, it seems, attempted arrangements by locality, or by property, such as mechanical or chemical, and finally and most successfully by alignment with the various human "tendencies"—the alimentary, sanitary, vestiary, domiciliar, locomotive, sensitive, intellectual, preparative, or social.

However inadequate, these classifications are to be preferred to the arbitrary system of the Great Exhibition, whose four divisions—raw materials, machinery, manufactures, and plastic arts—are, he says, vague and incomplete, confusing raw materials with items of manufacture and processes with products, and to the several systems of the British and Irish census, which, though comprehensive, are "unphilosophical." The British system, perhaps not surprisingly, reflects the class system with its distinctions among commerce, trade and manufacture, agriculture, nonagricultural labor, the military, the professions, the government, domestic servants, persons of independent means, and the indigent such as almspeople and lunatics; the Irish system is aligned to human wants and needs such as food, clothing, lodging and furniture, health, charity, justice, education, and religion.

Citing John Stuart Mill's analysis of labor with reference to "utilities," as, for example, the rendering of material things into useful objects, or the conferring upon human beings of qualities that render them useful to others, and finally of service rendered or pleasure given (p. 460), Mayhew arrives at his own four classes of workers: *enrichers*, who produce utilities "fixed and embodied in material things"; *auxiliaries*, who aid in "the production of exchangable commodities"; *benefactors*, who produce "utilities fixed and embodied in human beings . . . conferring upon them some permanent good"; and *servitors*, who confer "some temporary good upon another." "I apply the title Worker," writes Mayhew, "to all those who do *anything* for their living, who perform any act whatsoever that is considered worthy of being paid for by others" (p. 462).

8. Ibid., pp. 9–10.

9. Ashmore and Del Boca, "Conceptual Approaches to Stereotypes and Stereotyping."

10. Abrahams, "Phantoms of Romantic Nationalism," p. 28.

11. Toll, *Blacking Up*.

12. Fussell, *Class*, p. 5.

13. Shelley, Percy Bysshe, "A Defense of Poetry," in *The Norton Anthology of English Literature*, edited by M. H. Abrams (New York: Norton, 1988), 2:493.

CHAPTER EIGHT

1. Jameson, "Postmodernism," p. 87.

2. Ralph Rinzler interview.

3. Rydell, *All the World's a Fair*, pp. 22–36.

4. Herling, "Why Are Unions in the Folklife Festival?," p. 43.

5. Scherer, "History of American Indian Research."

6. Paredes and Bauman, *Toward New Perspectives in Folklore*.

7. Lomax, *Folk Song Style and Culture*, pp. 3–33.

8. Lomax, "An Appeal for Cultural Equity." This article was excerpted in the *Festival of American Folklife Program Book* in 1976 and 1985.

9. Morton, "And Living History," p. 5.

10. Whisnant, *All That Is Native and Fine*.

11. Cantwell, "Feasts of Unnaming," pp. 271–74, 284–87.

12. Ewers, "Historic Basis of Northern Plains Culture," p. 9.

13. Klein, *Woody Guthrie*.

14. Scaduto, *Bob Dylan*, p. 6.

CHAPTER NINE

1. Wallace Stevens, "The Emperor of Ice-Cream," in *The Norton Anthology of Poetry*, edited by Alexander W. Allison, Herbert Barrows, Caesar R. Blake, Arthur J. Carr, Arthur M. Eastman, and Hubert M. English, Jr. (New York: Norton, 1975), p. 968.

2. Rydell, *All the World's a Fair*, pp. 167, 172.

3. Ibid., pp. 174, 166.

4. Coleridge, *Biographia Literaria*, pp. 168–69.

5. Greenblatt, *Shakespearean Negotiations*, p. 111.

6. Bauman, "1987 Smithsonian Festival."

7. Other folklorists have made this comparison, notably Charles Camp and Timothy Lloyd in "Six Reasons Not to Produce Folklife Festivals."

8. Barthes, *Mythologies*, p. 118.

9. MacCannell, *The Tourist*, p. xvi.

10. Ibid., pp. 7–8.

11. Ibid., pp. 2, 7–8.

12. Ibid., p. 13.

13. Ibid.

14. Ibid., pp. 11, 26–27.

15. Ibid., p. 24.

16. Ibid., pp. 24–25.

17. Ibid., p. 25.

18. Ibid., p. 115.

19. Ibid., pp. 122–23.

20. Barthes, *Mythologies*, pp. 131, 124, 125.

21. Telford, *Aristotle's Poetics*, p. 65.

22. Kirshenblatt-Gimblett, "Objects of Ethnography," p. 388.

23. Rogin, "Make My Day!," p. 106. See also Debord, *Society of the Spectacle*.

24. Jameson, "Postmodernism," p. 56.

25. Ibid., p. 73.

26. Ibid., pp. 76–77.

27. Ibid., pp. 84, 87.

28. Ibid., p. 87.

29. The Peterman Company, *Owner's Manual No. 12* (Lexington, Ky., Fall 1991), p. 1.

30. Horowitz, "Musica Mizrahit."

31. Lapham, "Storm of Words," p. 8.

References

Abrahams, Roger. "Phantoms of Romantic Nationalism in Folkloristics." *Journal of American Folklore* 106 (Winter 1993): 3–37.

Ashmore, Richard, and Frances Del Boca. "Conceptual Approaches to Stereotypes and Stereotyping." In *Cognitive Processes in Stereotyping and Intergroup Behavior*, edited by David Hamilton. Hillsdale, N.J.: L. Erlbaum Associates, 1981.

Bacon, Francis. "Of the True Greatness of Kingdoms and Estates." In *The Essays*, edited by John Pitcher. New York: Viking Penguin, 1986.

Barthes, Roland. *Mythologies*. Translated by Annette Lavers. New York: Hill and Wang, 1972.

Bauman, Richard, et al. "The 1987 Smithsonian Festival of American Folklife: An Ethnography of Participant Experience." Unpublished manuscript, Folklore Institute, Indiana University, 1988.

Bryce-Laporte, Roy S. "The New Immigration and New Urban Cultures in the Making." In *Festival of American Folklife Program Book*, edited by Jack Santino. Washington, D.C.: Office of Folklife Programs, Smithsonian Institution, 1980.

Camp, Charles. Interview with author, Washington, D.C., June 26, 1985.

Camp, Charles, and Timothy Lloyd. "Six Reasons Not to Produce Folklife Festivals." *Kentucky Folklife Record* 26 (1980): 67–74.

Cantwell, Robert. "Conjuring Culture: Ideology and Magic in the Festival of American Folklife." *Journal of American Folklore* 104 (Spring 1991): 148–63.

———. "Feasts of Unnaming: Folk Festivals and the Representation of Folklife." In *Public Folklore*, edited by Nicholas Spitzer and Robert Baron. Washington, D.C.: Smithsonian Institution Press, 1992.

———. "He Shall Overcome: Pete Seeger." *New England Review* 13 (Fall 1990): 61–75.

———. "Smith's Memory Theater: The Folkways Anthology." *New England Review* 13 (Spring–Summer 1991): 364–97.

———. "When We Were Good: Class and Culture in the Folk Revival." In *Transforming Tradition: Folk Music Revivals Examined*, edited by Neil Rosenberg. Urbana: University of Illinois Press, 1993.

Coleridge, Samuel Taylor. *Biographia Literaria: Or, Biographical Sketches of My Literary Life and Opinions*. Edited by George Watson. London: J. M. Dent and Sons, 1962.

Da Matta, Roberto. "Carnival in Multiple Planes." In *Rite, Drama, Festival, Spectacle: Rehearsals toward a Theory of Cultural Performance*, edited by John MacAloon. Philadelphia, Pa.: Institute for the Study of Human Issues, 1984.

Debord, Guy. *The Society of the Spectacle*. Translated by Malcolm Imrie. London: Verso, 1967.

Descartes, René. *Discourse on Method and Meditations*. Translated by Laurence J. Lafleur. New York: Bobbs-Merrill, 1960.

Dresser, Norine, and Kay Hardman. "Evaluation of the 1974 Festival of American Folklife." Memo, Office of Folklife Programs, undated [probably August 1974].

Dubivsky, Barbara. "Some Fresh Air for the Nation's Attic." *New York Times*, April 9, 1967.

Dutton, Ralph. *The English Garden*. London: N.p., 1937.

Ewers, John C. "Historic Basis of the Northern Plains Culture." In *Festival of American Folklife Program Book*, edited by Gerald Davis and Ralph Rinzler. Washington, D.C.: Office of Folklife Programs, Smithsonian Institution, 1973.

Foucault, Michel. *Discipline and Punish: The Birth of the Prison*. Translated by Alan Sheridan. New York: Vintage Books, 1979.

———. *The Order of Things: An Archaeology of the Human Sciences*. New York: Vintage Books, 1970.

Frye, Northrop. *The Secular Scripture*. Cambridge, Mass.: Harvard University Press, 1976.

Fussell, Paul. *Class: A Painfully Accurate Guide through the American Status System*. New York: Ballantine Books, 1983.

Geertz, Clifford. "Thick Description: Towards an Interpretative Theory of Culture." In *The Interpretation of Cultures*. New York: Basic Books, 1973.

Green, Rayna. "American Indian Stereotypes." In *Festival of American Folklife Program Book*, edited by Peter Seitel. Washington, D.C.: Office of Folklife Programs, Smithsonian Institution, 1979.

Greenblatt, Stephen. *Shakespearean Negotiations: The Circulation of Social Energy in Renaissance England*. Berkeley: University of California Press, 1988.

Haraway, Donna. "Teddy Bear Patriarchy: Taxidermy in the Garden of Eden, New York City, 1908–1936." *Social Text* 11 (Winter 1984–85): 20–64.

Harsnett, Samuel. *A Declaration of Egregious Popish Impostures. To Withdraw the Hearts of Her Maiesties Subjects from Their Allegiance, and from the Truth of the Christian Religion Professed in England, under the Pretence of Casting out Deuils*. London: N.p., 1603.

Hawes, Bess Lomax. "Folk Arts and the Elderly." In *Festival of American Folklife Program Book*, edited by Tom Vennum. Washington, D.C.: Office of Folklife Programs, Smithsonian Institution, 1984.

———. "Law and Order on the Playground." In *Festival of American Folklife Program Book*, edited by Bess Hawes and Susanne Roschwalb. Washington, D.C.: Office of Folklife Programs, Smithsonian Institution, 1976.

———. "Official Observer's Report." Memo, Office of Folklife Programs, August 30, 1974.

Herling, Albert K. "Why Are Unions in the Folklife Festival?" In *Festival of American Folklife Program Book*, edited by Gerald Davis and Ralph Rinzler.

Washington, D.C.: Office of Folklife Programs, Smithsonian Institution, 1972.

Hill, Christopher. *Reformation to Industrial Revolution: The Making of Modern English Society.* Vol. 1, *1530–1780.* New York: Pantheon, 1967.

Horowitz, Amy. "Musica Mizrahit: Cultural Boundaries and Disputed Territory." Paper delivered at the annual meeting of the American Folklife Society, Oakland, Calif., October 19, 1990.

Hunt, John Dixon. *The Figure in the Landscape: Poetry, Painting, and Gardening during the Eighteenth Century.* Baltimore, Md.: Johns Hopkins University Press, 1976.

———, ed. *The English Landscape Garden: Examples of the Important Literature of the English Landscape Garden Movement.* New York: Garland Publishers, 1982.

Hunt, John Dixon, and Peter Willis. *The Genius of the Place: The English Landscape Garden, 1620–1820.* New York: Elek, 1975.

Hunt, Marjorie, and Peter Seitel. "Cultural Conservation." In *Festival of American Folklife Program Book*, edited by Thomas Vennum, Jr. Washington, D.C.: Office of Folklife Programs, Smithsonian Institution, 1985.

"Indians Seek Burial of Museum Skeletons." *New York Times*, December 8, 1987.

Jameson, Fredric. "Postmodernism, or the Cultural Logic of Late Capitalism." *New Left Review* 146 (July–August 1984): 53–93.

Johnson, Samuel. "Notes to *King Lear*." In *Samuel Johnson: Rasselas, Poems, and Selected Prose*, edited by Bertrand H. Bronson. New York: Holt, Rinehart and Winston, 1958.

Kantorowitz, Ernst. *The King's Two Bodies: A Study in Medieval Political Theology.* Princeton, N.J.: Princeton University Press, 1957.

Kavanaugh, Tom. "Seeking Out Indian Participation." In *Festival of American Folklife Program Book*, edited by Gerald Davis and Ralph Rinzler. Washington, D.C.: Office of Folklife Programs, Smithsonian Institution, 1972.

Kirshenblatt-Gimblett, Barbara. "Objects of Ethnography." In *Exhibiting Cultures: The Poetics and Politics of Museum Display*, edited by Ivan Karp and Steven D. Lavine. Washington, D.C.: Smithsonian Institution Press, 1991.

Klein, Joe. *Woody Guthrie: A Life.* New York: Ballantine Books, 1980.

Kurin, Richard. "Cultural Conservation through Representation: Festival of India Folklife Exhibitions at the Smithsonian Institution." In *Exhibiting Cultures: The Poetics and Politics of Museum Display*, edited by Ivan Karp and Steven D. Lavine. Washington, D.C.: Smithsonian Institution Press, 1991.

LaCovey, Joseph. "Secretary Ripley Discusses a Variety of SI Topics." Interview in *Smithsonian Torch*, December 1967, p. 4.

Lapham, Lewis H. "Storm of Words." *Harper's*, June 1992.

Levine, Lawrence. *Black Culture and Black Consciousness: Afro-American Folk Thought from Slavery to Freedom.* New York: Oxford University Press, 1977.

Lomax, Alan. "An Appeal for Cultural Equity." In *The World of Music: Quarterly Journal of the International Music Council* 14, no. 2 (1972): 3–17.

————. *Folk Song Style and Culture*. Washington, D.C.: American Association for the Advancement of Science, 1968.

————. *Folk Songs of North America*. Garden City, N.Y.: Doubleday, 1960.

MacCannell, Dean. *The Tourist: A New Theory of the Leisure Class*. New York: Schocken Books, 1989.

Mack, Maynard. *King Lear in Our Time*. Berkeley: University of California Press, 1965.

Mantoux, Paul. *The Industrial Revolution in the Eighteenth Century: An Outline of the Beginnings of the Modern Factory System in England*. Translated by Marjorie Vernon. 1928. Reprint. Chicago: University of Chicago Press, 1983.

Mayhew, Henry. *London Labour and the London Poor*. Edited by Victor Neuburg. New York: Viking Penguin, 1984.

McLuhan, Marshall. *The Gutenberg Galaxy*. Toronto, Ont.: University of Toronto Press, 1962.

Morris, Robert. "An Essay upon Harmony, as It Relates Chiefly to Situation and Building." In *The English Landscape Garden: Examples of the Important Literature of the English Landscape Garden Movement together with Some Earlier Garden Books*, edited by John Dixon Hunt. New York: Garland Publishers, 1982.

Morton, Rogers C. B. "And Living History." In *Festival of American Folklife Program Book*, edited by Gerald Davis and Ralph Rinzler. Washington, D.C.: Office of Folklife Programs, Smithsonian Institution, 1973.

Mitchell, Henry. "Mississippi: A Kinship of Lore and the Land." *Washington Post*, July 3, 1974.

Mullaney, Steven. "Strange Things, Gross Terms, Curious Customs: The Rehearsal of Cultures in the Late Renaissance." In *Representing the English Renaissance*, edited by Stephen Greenblatt. Berkeley: University of California Press, 1988.

Murphy, John L. *Darkness and Devils: Exorcism in King Lear*. Athens: Ohio University Press, 1984.

Mumford, Lewis. *Technics and Civilization*. New York: Harcourt, Brace, and World, 1963.

Ohrlin, Glenn. Interview with author, Washington, D.C., July 3, 1985.

Ong, Walter. *Ramus, Method, and the Decay of Dialogue*. Cambridge, Mass.: Harvard University Press, 1958.

Paredes, Americo, and Richard Bauman, eds. *Toward New Perspectives in Folklore*. Austin: University of Texas Press, 1972.

Park, Edwards. "Secretary S. Dillon Ripley Retires after Twenty Years of Innovation." *Smithsonian* 15, no. 6 (September 1984): 77–85.

Parris, D. Elliot. "Carnival and Community: Conflict and Fusion." In *Festival of American Folklife Program Book*, edited by Peter Seitel. Washington, D.C.: Office of Folklife Programs, Smithsonian Institution, 1979.

Poulet, Georges. "Criticism and the Experience of Interiority." In *Reader-Response Criticism: From Formalism to Post-Structuralism*, edited by Jane P. Tompkins. Baltimore, Md.: Johns Hopkins University Press, 1980.

Reagon, Bernice. "In the Streets." In *Festival of American Folklife Program Book*, edited by Ralph Rinzler, Robert Byington, Constance Minkin, Nancy Wyeth, and Susanne Roschwalb. Washington, D.C.: Office of Folklife Programs, Smithsonian Institution, 1977.

Rinzler, Ralph. Interview with author, Washington, D.C., January 19–20, 1986.

———. "Kentucky." In *Festival of American Folklife Program Book*, edited by Gerald Davis and Ralph Rinzler. Washington, D.C.: Office of Folklife Programs, Smithsonian Institution, 1973.

Rogin, Michael. "Make My Day!: Spectacle as Amnesia in Imperial Politics." *Representations* 29 (Winter 1990): 99–123.

Rydell, Robert. *All the World's a Fair: Visions of Empire at American International Exhibitions, 1876–1916*. Chicago: University of Chicago Press, 1984.

Scaduto, Anthony. *Bob Dylan: An Intimate Biography*. New York: Grosset and Dunlap, 1971.

Scherer, Joanna Cohan. "The History of American Indian Research at the Smithsonian." In *Festival of American Folklife Program Book*, edited by William O. Craig. Washington, D.C.: Division of Performing Arts, Smithsonian Institution, 1970.

Smithsonian Institution. *The Smithsonian Experience: Science—History—the Arts . . . the Treasures of the Nation*. Washington, D.C.: Smithsonian Institution Press, 1977.

Sutton-Smith, Brian. "The Importance of Children's Folklore." In *Festival of American Folklife Program Book*, edited by Peter Seitel. Washington, D.C.: Office of Folklife Programs, Smithsonian Institution, 1979.

Telford, Kenneth. *Aristotle's Poetics*. Chicago: Henry Regnery Co., 1961.

Theobald, Lewis. *The Works of William Shakespeare, in Seven Volumes*. London: A. Battersworth and C. Hitch, 1734.

Toll, Robert. *Blacking Up: The Minstrel Show in Nineteenth-Century America*. New York: Oxford University Press, 1974.

Trevor-Roper, Hugh. "The Invention of Tradition: The Highland Tradition of Scotland." In *The Invention of Tradition*, edited by Eric Hobsbawm and Terence Ranger. Cambridge: Cambridge University Press, 1983.

Trollope, Fanny. *Domestic Manners of the Americans*. 1832. Reprint. Oxford: Oxford University Press, 1984.

Trusler, John. "Elements of Modern Gardening: Or, the Art of Laying Out of Pleasure Grounds, Ornamenting Farms, and Embellishing the Views Round About our Houses." 1784. Reprinted in *The English Landscape Garden: Examples of the Important Literature of the English Landscape Garden Movement together with Some Earlier Garden Books*, edited by John Dixon Hunt. New York: Garland Publishers, 1982.

Whisnant, David E. *All That Is Native and Fine: The Politics of Culture in an American Region*. Chapel Hill: University of North Carolina Press, 1983.

White, Hayden. "The Noble Savage Theme as Fetish." In *Tropics of Discourse: Essays in Cultural Criticism*. Baltimore, Md.: Johns Hopkins University Press, 1986.

Williams, Katherine. "Costuming: Latin-American and Caribbean Urban Carnivals." In *Festival of American Folklife Program Book*, edited by Jack Santino. Washington, D.C.: Office of Folklife Programs, Smithsonian Institution, 1980.

Williams, Raymond. *Culture and Society, 1780–1950*. New York: Columbia University Press, 1958.

———. *Keywords: A Vocabulary of Culture and Society*. New York: Oxford University Press, 1983.

———. *Marxism and Literature*. New York: Oxford University Press, 1977.

Woodbridge, Kenneth. *Landscape and Antiquity: Aspects of English Culture at Stourhead, 1718 to 1838*. Oxford: Oxford University Press, 1970.

Yates, Frances. *The Art of Memory*. Chicago: University of Chicago Press, 1966.

Index

Early, Hezakiah, 197. *See also* Hezakiah and the Houserockers
Enclosure, 48; and property, 33; and industrialization, 34; as organization of space, 35–36; and landscape gardens, 36; and philosophy, 41
Enclosure Acts, 3, 33–36; and pastoralism, 33; and land tenancy, 34
Ethneme, 179, 184; defined, 171–72
Ethnomimesis, 6–7; defined, 5–7, 81–84
Exorcism, 13, 29; in Peckham household, 13–15, 28–29, 78; as folklore, 17; and established church, 18; and stereotype, 30

Family Folklore (FAF exhibit), 117–21
Fairfield Four (gospel group), 153, 177, 187–88
Ferris, William, 111
Festival of American Folklife (FAF), 48; introduced, 1, 4; and U.S. Bicentennial, 4; ethnomimesis in, 7; audience, 86–87; and stereotype, 87, 223–27, 258; as tourism, 90, 100–103, 274–76; iconography of, 101; and social class, 102; as spectacle, 113–14, 191–92; and identity, 116; promotional films, 126–29; staff meeting, 129–32, 207–8; grounds crew, 137–39; social problems at, 142; opening ceremony, 146–49; as semiotic field, 151; goodwill at, 151–53; and sound, 188–89; physical structures, 190–92; romance at, 193–94; "down day," 195–96; narrative at, 196–97; accidents, 208; on 4th of July, 208–9; social gatherings, 209–12, 304–5; and the erotic, 211–12, 253–55; pastoralism in, 215–16; organized labor in, 217; economic theory in, 217–19; musicians, 219–20; typology of, 221–23; ideologies embodied in, 223; as inversion holiday, 244–46; corporality in, 255–56; ethnomimesis in, 256–74; and social privilege, 257–58; ethnography of, 259–60; recognition in, 259–74; visitor, 260, 264–74; as myth, 261; participant, analysis of, 261–64; identity in, 271–72; as cultural production, 279–80; signification in, 302–4

Festivity, 26; state-sponsored, 1–2; and social class, 238–41; defined, 241–42; inversion holiday, 243–44; in traditional society, 246; and totalitarianism, 247–48
Folk culture: and ethnomimesis, 5–6
Folk festivals, 7
Folklife: as cultural construction, 16–17; and capitalism, 291, 298; 291, 298; and common life, 307 (n. 1)
Folklore: as sentiment, 3; as cultural construction, 7; as performance, 8; and Peckham exorcisms, 15; and exorcism, 17; in *King Lear*, 9–12, 15–16, 18–19; and power, 25, 28; Tunesian, 85–91; African American, 91–99; family, 117, 118–21; children's, 117–18; occupational, 121–23, 225–26; defined, 214–15; and ideology, 215; theory of, 218; as defamiliarization, 247; as projection, 247
Folk-Lore, coinage of term, 213–14
Folk music: African American, 93–94, 112; Anglo-American, 112; *Folk Songs of North America*, 220–21
Folk revival, 52; and popular culture, 230–33; and suburbanization, 233–34; as resistance, 234; and social prestige, 234–39; as sublimation, 236–38; and festivity, 238–41

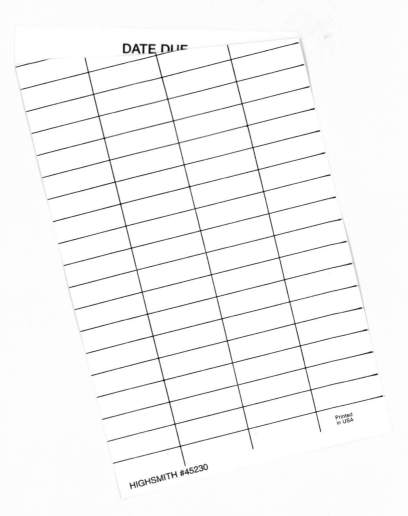

DATE DUE

Printed
in USA

HIGHSMITH #45230

180

160

140

120

100

"...Shit, man.
Don't get so
worked up
over a dumb
game."

Member of Group
Accelerator

"We're busy.
Can we do
this later?"

Leader of Item
Shizuri Mugino

"Damn, I'll have you know, I was the leader of the group that ruled over Skill-Out..."

Former leader of the Level Zero group Skill-Out **Shiage Hamazura**

"An ultra-problematic C-movie presented by the Hong Kong Red Dragon film company... Looks like a real palm sweater in a few different ways, but that's what makes it interesting."

Member of Item **Saiai Kinuhata**

"...Signal coming from south-southwest..."

Member of Item **Rikou Takitsubo**

"Huh? This salmon bento tastes different from yesterday's salmon bento. Hmm?"

Leader of Item **Shizuri Mugino**

"It just means canned mackerel is in vogue right now. Curry is the best—curry!"

Member of Item **Frenda**

A Certain Magical Index

VOLUME 15

KAZUMA KAMACHI
ILLUSTRATION BY: KIYOTAKA HAIMURA

NEW YORK

A CERTAIN MAGICAL INDEX, Volume 15

KAZUMA KAMACHI

Translation by Andrew Prowse

Cover art by Kiyotaka Haimura

TOARU MAJYUTSU NO INDEX Vol.15

©KAZUMA KAMACHI 2008

Edited by ASCII MEDIA WORKS

First published in Japan in 2008 by KADOKAWA CORPORATION, Tokyo.

English translation rights arranged with KADOKAWA CORPORATION, Tokyo, through Tuttle-Mori Agency, Inc., Tokyo.

English translation © 2018 by Yen Press, LLC

Yen On

1290 Avenue of the Americas

New York, NY 10104

Visit us at yenpress.com

facebook.com/yenpress

twitter.com/yenpress

yenpress.tumblr.com

instagram.com/yenpress

First Yen On Edition: May 2018

Yen On is an imprint of Yen Press, LLC.
The Yen On name and logo are trademarks of Yen Press, LLC.

Library of Congress Cataloging-in-Publication Data

Names: Kamachi, Kazuma, author. | Haimura, Kiyotaka, 1973– illustrator. | Prowse, Andrew (Andrew R.), translator. | Hinton, Yoshito, translator.
Title: A certain magical index / Kazuma Kamachi ; illustration by Kiyotaka Haimura.
Other titles: To aru majyutsu no index. (Light novel). English
Description: First Yen On edition. | New York : Yen On, 2014–
Identifiers: LCCN 2014031047 (print) | ISBN 9780316339124 (v. 1 : pbk.) |
  ISBN 9780316259422 (v. 2 : pbk.) | ISBN 9780316340540 (v. 3 : pbk.) |
  ISBN 9780316340564 (v. 4 : pbk.) | ISBN 9780316340595 (v. 5 : pbk.) |
  ISBN 9780316340601 (v. 6 : pbk.) | ISBN 9780316272230 (v. 7 : pbk.) |
  ISBN 9780316359924 (v. 8 : pbk.) | ISBN 9780316359962 (v. 9 : pbk.) |
  ISBN 9780316359986 (v. 10 : pbk.) | ISBN 9780316360005 (v. 11 : pbk.) |
  ISBN 9780316360029 (v. 12 : pbk.) | ISBN 9780316442671 (v. 13 : pbk.) |
  ISBN 9780316442701 (v. 14 : pbk.) | ISBN 9780316442725 (v. 15 : pbk.)
Subjects: | CYAC: Magic—Fiction. | Ability—Fiction. | Nuns—Fiction. | Japan—Fiction. | Science fiction. | BISAC: FICTION / Fantasy / General. | FICTION / Science Fiction / Adventure.
Classification: LCC PZ7.1.K215 Ce 2014 | DDC [Fic]—dc23
LC record available at https://lccn.loc.gov/2014031047

ISBNs: 978-0-316-44272-5 (paperback)
978-0-316-44273-2 (ebook)

1 3 5 7 9 10 8 6 4 2

LSC-C

Printed in the United States of America

PROLOGUE

The Finest Lead Bullet for You, My Beloved
Management.

There are things we call blind spots.

The cleaning room of this major department store, for instance.

The store's employees thought a contract crew used the room, while the contractors believed the employees utilized it. Visitors to the store wouldn't enter a place like that, so there weren't any surveillance cameras inside. Nobody paid any attention to it. As a result, you were left with a room everyone knew about but nobody had ever entered, let alone known where to find its key.

Normally, its iron door was kept locked at all times.

Except for at this moment.

Using a key he'd received in advance, Motoharu Tsuchimikado opened the door in the back of the store. The room was stylishly decorated, resembling a bar: Before him was a sofa large enough to seat at least ten people, with an incongruously small table beside it. At the back of the room, there was a counter. This was clearly a different world than the one outside the door.

A man noticed Tsuchimikado enter and cheerfully said, "Come on in."

This college-aged guy, who was shorter than Tsuchimikado, stood behind the bar. He appeared somewhat comical, wearing a brand-name suit but no necktie, and he had a few shirt buttons undone to show off his chest.

The man, with four or five cell phones hanging from his neck, had a nickname: Management.

As he put an elbow on the counter, he said, "Ah, my bad. I do things casually because this is the service industry. Makes it easier for people to talk to me, y'know? I can stop if you like."

"No, you're fine," said Tsuchimikado, causing the man to grin.

Tsuchimikado threw his key to Management, and he caught it with one hand. Despite what he'd said, once this job was over, the man would take all the furniture and move somewhere else.

"Now then, what might you be after today? I've got a great deal on lock pickers, 'sensor breakers'—cream of the crop, I might add. If you're here for something a little more risqué, I have a few money launderers. We're running low, though, after the new regulations from that 09/30 incident. Other than that, it's what you'd expect."

Some robberies and larcenies took more than one person. When they did, they'd assign roles such as driver, lock picker, burglar, and money launderer, but some ran into a problem where they didn't have enough people. Management would supply the people and profit off the finder's fee.

"I have to say," remarked the man, "I mostly get emails and texts these days. Don't have many coming here personally like you."

"Should I not have come?"

"Oh, no, you're fine. It's not much risk. Oh, right—do you want something to drink?"

Tsuchimikado glanced at the shelves behind the counter, saw the thick cans lined up on them, and frowned slightly. "Not a fan of drinking paint thinner."

"You misunderstand. Those are cleaners for getting rid of oil-based ink. Gotta have 'em in a business like this. The alcohol's over there, in the fridge. Some good stuff in there, have to say."

"Either way, I'll pass."

Despite the refusal, Management's face remained mostly the same. "Too tense to get drunk? Suppose that's how it is before a job. Let's get down to business, then. What are you looking for?"

"Sorry, that actually isn't why I'm here."

"Hmm?"

Management looked at him dubiously. Without skipping a beat, Tsuchimikado said:

"I'm not a customer. I'm the guy who's bringing you in."

For just a moment, Management gave him a blank stare.

But when he saw Tsuchimikado pull a handgun from his belt, he quickly dove behind the counter.

Tsuchimikado pulled the trigger anyway.

Bang, boom, bam!! A series of gunshots followed. A hole appeared in one of the cans of thinner, immediately filling Management's nose with a terrible stench.

Bastard...! The man, still hidden, reached for a bulletproof jacket and a submachine gun underneath the counter.

He popped a magazine into the gun, then cocked it to load the first bullet, when suddenly the enemy gunshots stopped. Management slowly looked around the edge of the counter to check.

Out of ammo? he thought, now covered in thinner—but a moment later, he got a different answer.

The scrape of an oil lighter.

"?!" Management's throat dried up.

Before he could say anything, Tsuchimikado threw the lit lighter behind the counter.

He had no time to think. Management flung the jacket and gun aside, then jumped out from behind the counter to get away from the chemicals.

The lighter dropped into the puddle of paint thinner, and with a *boom*, hurled up explosive flames.

Management had barely escaped its range, but now, unarmed, he noticed the gun pointed at him.

He raised his hands and cried, "Wait, wait, wait! Okay, okay, I won't resist—"

Tsuchimikado pulled the trigger anyway.

Bang!! After he heard the sound of the gun discharging, Management looked at his side in surprise to find a dark-red hole.

"Wh-why, you...I said I wouldn't..."

Before he could finish whatever he was saying, he collapsed to the floor.

Tsuchimikado, expression mostly unchanged, made sure Management was at least breathing, then took out his cell phone.

He dialed a number in his contacts, and when someone picked up, he said simply, *"Collection."*

The voice on the other end of the phone said something.

Tsuchimikado continued, "Look for where this guy lives. We've got a lot to investigate. Notify our ancillary. Actually, wait. We don't need an ambulance, just a patrol wagon. I'll snoop around using his registered address, but I want Accelerator to— He's not around?"

He clicked his tongue in frustration. "Right. He's over there at the moment. No choice, then. Unabara, you go out. Have Musujime switch to backup. Call you later."

He hung up.

Motoharu Tsuchimikado, Accelerator, Mitsuki Unabara, and Awaki Musujime.

The four together were simply called Group.

A small team, working in society's shadows to protect its light.

CHAPTER 1
The Signal Shot Nobody Heard
Compass.

1

October 9.

Today was the anniversary of Academy City's independence, and a holiday within its walls.

The hospital in District 7 was no exception. Since morning, its air had felt relaxed. A frog-faced doctor left through the front entrance and felt the soft morning sunlight on his skin.

Beside him stood a small girl of about ten.

She was called Last Order.

On September 30, the Hound Dogs, led by Amata Kihara, had kidnapped her and used a device called Testament to input specific data into her brain. The hospital had been working to remove that data, but the job was now done and she was being discharged.

"Finally leaving the hospital and nobody's here to greet you," said the doctor, sighing.

Last Order didn't seem too worried. "'Misaka can ride the taxi by herself,' says Misaka says Misaka, sticking out her chest."

"Well, we've eliminated the virus in your brain, so I suppose there's no more cause for worry. I'll put the taxi fare on Ms. Yomikawa's tab, so go straight to her apartment, all right?"

Just then, a taxi arrived at the roundabout in front of the hospital.

The frog-faced doctor waved it down, then put Last Order, who was holding her belongings, into the back seat.

As he watched, the driver asked, "Where to today, miss?"

"'The amusement park in District 6!' says Misaka says Mis—"

"To the Family Side II apartment in District 7. Don't forget, all right?"

The frog-faced doctor had stopped the nonsense about to come out of Last Order's mouth—in the end, he was the one looking after her.

The driver gave a pained grin. "I understand."

"Do you need me to give you directions?"

"No, there aren't many apartments in this city—it's all student dorms. And I can just put it in the car's navigation system."

When the frog-faced doctor pulled his head out of the car, the back door closed automatically. With Last Order on board, her hands on the window and her eyes staring outside, the taxi began to gently roll away from the hospital.

After it vanished from sight, the doctor went back to his hospital. He walked through an uncluttered hallway and into a space for conversation with only a simple sofa and table, then went to the vending machine along the wall and bought a coffee.

This vending machine was the kind that used paper cups. There was no liquid coffee inside the rectangular metal box; instead, it made it automatically, starting with grinding pre-roasted beans. It took a bit longer this way, but it tasted good, and was a nice way for him to switch gears.

The doctor exhaled. *Next I've got to finish the Sisters' adjustments and release them from here as soon as—*

Suddenly, his thoughts were interrupted.

Ker-click.

Someone had pressed a gun to his back.

The doctor froze.

He listened to the shallow breathing directly behind him, thought for a moment, then spoke.

"Already back from Avignon, are we?"

"Shit. Where the hell did you get that information?"

The voice was familiar—Accelerator.

In his right hand, he held a walking cane designed with a modern aesthetic, but since they were in a hospital, it didn't make him stand out very much. And he'd used his body to hide the gun in his left hand from others.

The doctor didn't bother to put his hands up. Instead of acting conspicuously, he spoke quietly, all for the sake of the patient behind him. "…You always have quite the greeting prepared, don't you?"

"I want info. The blueprints for this electrode."

Accelerator was talking about the choker on his neck. It looked like an accessory, but it actually had an electrode fitted in the back that converted his brainwaves into other electric signals. Those signals gave him restricted access to a special electronic communication network called the Misaka network.

The doctor was the very man who'd made the electrode. He kept his face steady and replied, "Why do you need them? If your choker is on the fritz, I can fix it for you."

"Just give me the blueprints."

"Last Order wanted to see you. If only you'd gotten here a little bit earlier…"

"Can it. That has nothing to do with you."

"That isn't true. She was my patient, and she wanted to see you. It's my job to make it work out."

Accelerator quietly cursed. "…I know that. That's why I waited until now, dumbass," he spat, sounding truly bitter.

The frog-faced doctor reached into his white coat pocket and took out what looked like a mechanical pencil's central casing. It was, in fact, a USB drive. He moved his hand behind him.

"You were prepared."

"As I said, it's my job to prepare whatever my patients need," said the doctor, looking at the vending machine, which was still churning. "But it'll be hard to put what's in there to use. I make everything I need myself, you know? If you wanted a second electrode, you'd have to start by manufacturing the machine tools."

" "
...

Accelerator took it, then quietly stepped away from the doctor's back.

The doctor turned around.

There was no one there; not even a trace. He'd probably used his vector-changing ability to jump into the nearby stairwell.

" "
...

The doctor stared silently at the empty space.

An electronic beep went off at his side. The doctor removed his coffee from the vending machine and took a sip of the bitter liquid.

2

Mitsuki Unabara was in a room inside a certain District 7 building.

It was the second of a multi-dwelling apartment complex called Family Side.

The room was designed for a family to use; it was fairly spacious 4DLK, meaning four bedrooms and an open area that served as a living room, dining room, and kitchen. Judging by the furniture, though, only one person probably lived here. All it took was a quick look around the other empty rooms to figure that much out. Maybe it was the same for the rest of the apartments.

He poked around as he talked with Tsuchimikado over his cell. "...Anyway, I've arrived at Management's apartment. I'll start searching now. As for things that he could have stored information in...There's a computer, an HD recorder, and a few game consoles that probably have storage media in them."

"If there's even the slightest possibility, grab it. We could potentially find bits of information stored inside rice cookers or washing machines if we took them apart to get their AI configuration memory cards out."

"It sounds like this will be a pain," muttered Unabara. "I do still wonder what sort of jobs Management was helping with."

"I'm looking into that now," answered Tsuchimikado wearily. *"A new criminal organization just formed a day or two ago, thanks to*

him. He filled their gaps, provided the personnel they needed. And they paid good money for fighting strength to use right away. They're sure to pull something very soon. It's our job to figure out what—and to stop it before it happens."

"Will it be bad enough that Group needs to make an official outing?"

"Look, just get to work. I want to complain about all this just as much as you, but these are the only jobs Group ever gets: piles of shit and nothing else."

"All right," answered Unabara.

He walked through the big apartment, sticking little tags on the computer, the HD recorder, and the rest. He didn't plan on dragging everything, refrigerator and washing machine included, out by himself. For now, he was marking them so that their ancillary organization could carry them out later.

Well, that about does it. Just as Unabara had finished his run-through, he noticed something odd:

Bills.

"..." There were several paper bills on a waist-high shelf.

Nothing about that was unnatural, but they felt strangely isolated from any wallets. Unabara prodded about the room, finding a credit card and a passbook.

The placement of objects in a room said a lot about a person's daily routine. But by Unabara's analysis, the way these bills were sitting on this shelf seemed abnormal. Putting them this far away from a wallet made it seem like the resident was making sure they wouldn't get mixed up with any others.

He looked at them again, then flipped them over and started speaking into the phone. "Tsuchimikado, do we have any equipment that can read IC chip information?"

"What?"

"I found five paper bills here. If I remember correctly, Japanese yen minted and circulated in Academy City come with microchips in them. We should probably investigate these as well."

"Right. I'll get something ready...I didn't find any notable info here.

I'm gonna give up on the department store's cleaning room and head over your wa—"

Unabara didn't get to hear Tsuchimikado's voice until the end.

Boom!!

A rocket suddenly broke through the window, flew inside, and exploded right in the middle of the room.

A clamoring of heavy footfalls rushed the front door.

Men dressed in gray armor moved into the room swiftly yet cautiously. There were five, all with full face masks and identical equipment. Not a single one stood out from the rest.

Without a word, one of the men signaled with a finger to check the charred apartment—the formerly five-room one, given that, as they stepped over an air conditioner that had fallen to the floor, one of its thin interior walls had collapsed.

Not only did no automatic fire-extinguishing system turn on, the regular fire alarms weren't even working. They'd disabled security ahead of time.

They didn't exchange words among themselves, and so the soft clacking of metal stood out—they had their firearms, which were hitting against their hard armor, ready and loaded.

*Seriously...*Mitsuki Unabara sighed as he watched. He was spying on them from a small gap in a door that had been knocked diagonal by the explosive impact, his back against the wall of the kitchen space. He'd jumped into the room the moment the rocket had crashed through the window.

Now he produced an obsidian knife from an interior pocket. *They tried to destroy the information by blowing up the entire room. Must be people who'd be in trouble if we got our hands on Management's info.*

This was the third floor.

Moving slowly so he wouldn't make any noise, he went up to the smashed window. From this view alone he spotted about fifteen more men, all dressed in black. There were probably a lot more waiting out of sight. He was completely surrounded.

"…"

Unabara's dismantling sorcery, the Spear of Tlahuizcalpantecuhtli, was incredibly powerful, able to completely disintegrate objects by concentrating and reflecting the light from Venus onto them.

But on the other hand, he needed to designate his targets one at a time. In exchange for the ability to one-hit kill even the strongest enemies, he could only go one by one for even the weakest.

They're using mainly 9mm submachine guns, plus military handguns of the same caliber. If they started firing in this cramped space, skill wouldn't make a bit of difference—I'd be full of holes in no time.

And furthermore…this is bad. A lot of grunts showing up at a time like this is really bad.

Even if the enemy went all out and had everyone charge inside at once, it would be pointless, since the apartment had limited space, thanks to the doors and hallways. They'd end up packing inside and getting into a jam.

Instead, by keeping their invading team as small as they could and having most of their men surround the apartment complex, they eliminated the possibility that their target could escape. Even if he did wipe out their smaller team, they would either send in a new one or decide that if a rocket launcher couldn't take the enemy out, they'd simply have to blow up the entire building.

…They're experienced. Even if I slip out, I might not be able to get through their encirclement. I'm stuck here…

He adjusted his grip on the obsidian knife.

Sweat had broken out on his palms without him realizing it.

Now, what to do?

3

"Fires in District 7. Five instances confirmed. Relevant buildings' security systems, including automatic fire extinguishers, are inactive. Begin firefighting at once."

In an emergency correspondence center for connecting civilian reports to groups such as Anti-Skill and Judgment, a female opera-tor continued to convey the information coming up on her monitor to the appropriate authorities.

"Requesting criminal identifier dispatch from Anti-Skill to be a witness to the fire brigade's inspections. In addition—"

The operator took up a fire manual, which was propped up against the wall of her communication booth, thus taking her eyes off the monitor for just a few seconds.

During that time, a rep from the team waiting on-site for specific instructions said "*Understood,*" and the call abruptly ended.

"…What?" wondered the female operator.

On her monitor, it said she'd already given them everything they needed.

4

It was fifteen minutes after the rocket had fired into the complex.

Motoharu Tsuchimikado and Awaki Musujime were in one of the apartments of Family Side's second building.

There were no fire brigade or Anti-Skill officers. They spotted a few curious onlookers near the building, but nobody came inside; there had been an explosion, after all. They wouldn't do that, consid-ering the danger of being caught in a fire or building collapse.

The apartments had been built for families, but most of its resi-dents apparently lived alone. Plus, far more teachers and faculty used apartments than students. After Academy City had sent out Anti-Skill to prepare for "war," the strain of making papers and other teaching materials had fallen to the rest of the faculty, so even on a holiday like this they'd be out at work.

"This the place?"

It probably used to be a high-class apartment with four bedrooms plus an open area serving as a kitchen, living room, and dining room, but it was like an explosion had gone off right in the middle of it. Furniture and wallboard had come apart and was scattered everywhere, reducing the unit to only a couple of rooms. They could see the bathroom right after stepping through the front door.

"They cleaned up all the evidence. Even a mind-reading esper might not be able to get anything out of this," muttered Musujime as she gazed at the charred floor.

Accelerator arrived a moment later on his cane. "Damn. Thought you called me for something important. Just some fun little leftovers again?"

"Did you *finish your errand*?" Tsuchimikado asked without looking at him.

"Shut up," said Accelerator flatly, looking around. "This it? The place where that moron Unabara vanished?"

"Yeah," said Tsuchimikado. "For now, we've captured Management, and we got the guys from our ancillary transporting him in an escort car. But whatever info comes from his mouth won't be trustworthy. And if he starts going on about all the information being stored up in his head, we won't get anywhere with him. We wanted hard data to back up what he's saying, which is why I sent Unabara here."

His tone grew weary. "While he was here, he came under attack by a third party. We don't know whether they were after Unabara in particular or just anyone who wanted information on Management, but it's looking like the latter. From his initial report, we knew there was a computer, an HD recorder, and a few other things, but they're all totally gone. Any appliances with AI in them are gone, too—the whole lot of 'em."

"It does seem like there are a few appliances left, though…," said Musujime, using her foot to point at a scorched microwave oven. "They're probably all products without onboard AI. They left behind the stuff you can't put info into."

After more searching, they found a few other things, like a TV with a broken screen and an iron. However, everything important indeed seemed to have been stolen.

Accelerator took a seat on a bed with cotton sticking out and sighed in annoyance. "Damn it, what a pain. Don't know anything about that shithead Management. Don't know what happened to Unabara. Seriously, can't you people do your jobs?" He jabbed his foot at the broken microwave on the floor.

Just then, its plastic door opened up and something came out.

"...Eh?"

Paper bills.

About five, marked with soot, had been in the microwave for some reason.

"Unabara reported these—he was interested in them." With a thin smile, Musujime crouched and picked them up. "There should be microchips in these bills to prevent counterfeiting. Maybe something's written on them. Putting them in the microwave would shut out electromagnetic waves and stuff. This might have been enough to fool the attackers even if they had a way to detect the chips."

"...So our shithead was the one who hid them here?" asked Accelerator.

Then Tsuchimikado, a short distance away, announced, "Hmm?"

They looked over to see that he'd opened a closet, and inside it was a man's corpse. A closer inspection revealed that all the skin around his right calf had been torn off.

Tsuchimikado said, "This is Unabara's doing."

"What's with the foot? Hobby of his?" replied Musujime, put off. Her foot had once been injured in an accident during class. The trauma from the incident hadn't completely left her. It was so bad she had to use a low-frequency oscillation treatment instrument to alleviate the stress whenever she used her ability.

Tsuchimikado shook his head. "He uses human skin to make a certain kind of tag. I'll cut out the explanation, since you two don't know anything about sorcery, but...Basically, *he's got a skill where he can switch places with someone*," he said, looking at the scar on the corpse's foot. "He probably looks just like this guy at the moment. I bet he's waiting among the people who attacked this place, biding his time."

"In other words," he said, pausing, "that chameleon is still alive and smiling. Don't know where, though."

5

What is she doing? wondered Kazari Uiharu, cocking her head to the side.

She saw a girl of about ten, who was inside a stopped taxi—presumably at a light—arguing with the driver...Well, actually, it looked like the girl was one-sidedly biting his head off.

Uiharu didn't have to get any closer to hear their loud voices.

"'I keep saying let me off, let me off, so why won't you let Misaka go?!' argues Misaka argues Misaka, putting her hands on her hips and puffing out her cheek!!"

"Look, miss, I've been paid to drive you to your destination, so I can't let you—"

"'While he's making excuses, Misaka will look for an escape!!' says Misaka says Misaka, quickly getting out of the car and running into a back alley!!"

After shouting that, the little girl disappeared into an alley so narrow you probably couldn't even fit a bicycle through.

The driver scratched his head, at a loss. Uiharu walked up to him.

"Hmm? Oh, are you with Judgment?" asked the driver, looking at Uiharu's armband.

Judgment was a student organization created to help keep the peace in Academy City. Their jurisdiction was mainly limited to school, but apparently, most people weren't aware of the difference.

Uiharu gave him a blank look. "Um, was there some kind of trouble, sir? Did that girl leave without paying?"

"No, just the opposite," said the driver, at his wit's end. "Her, er, *guardian* gave me the money beforehand, and I was supposed to take her to an apartment complex. But now she's left, and I haven't given her back the money."

"Oh. Well, that's up to the passenger, sir. Couldn't you just accept it as a tip?"

"The taxi fare was twelve hundred yen. I got five thousand to begin with. I'd feel bad if I treated it as a tip."

What a nice person, she thought.

The driver glanced at the alley, which he clearly couldn't bring his car into. "...Still, I can't get out of the car and chase her."

"Should I look for her?"

"Yes...yes, if you could, I would greatly appreciate it. Hold on one moment."

The driver had a machine in the car print out a receipt, then handed it, along with the change on top, to Uiharu. Since she was wearing the Judgment armband, he didn't seem particularly cautious when it came to handing the money over to her. "Please, give this back to her."

"I will, sir." Uiharu put them in her skirt pocket. After exchanging contact information with the driver just in case, she set off into the narrow alleyway.

In that dark space where the sun's light couldn't enter, she called out, "Um, what was her name? Hmm...Miss Odd Haaair?!"

"'Hey! Misaka's identifier is Last Order!!' says Misaka says Misa... huh?!"

For the time being, she'd gotten an answer, so Uiharu walked that way in search of the girl.

6

Black smoke billowed.

A boxy escort car had stopped on the road, apparently after crashing into a guardrail. Only the front half, though—something had torn apart the car's frame, and its back half was in the middle of the road.

The car was the same model Anti-Skill used, but it wasn't one of theirs. Instead, Group's ancillary was using it. At Tsuchimikado's command, it was secretly transporting an important witness.

"Ow, damn it..."

A college-aged man came out from the part that was cut away—Management. Handcuffed, he stepped down onto the asphalt, then looked at his side and scowled. The gunshot wound had reopened, and fresh red liquid was starting to spread out on top of the dark-red stain that had already dried.

Nevertheless, after spotting a boy nearby, he gave him a mild smile. "Sorry. I flubbed the job."

"Don't be."

The boy was wearing a pair of metal goggles on his head. No, not goggles—his eyes weren't covered. It was a ring, wrapped around his head like Jupiter. Countless cables plugged into it from all directions, and they connected to a device at his waist.

Management offered his hands to the strangely dressed boy. "Sorry, but could you cut these, too? I can't do first aid like this, but it'll be a pain to find the key, too. I'm pretty sure it would be best to leave here immediately."

"All right," the boy said, moving his fingers as though swiping a card.

A moment later, Management's wrists were shattered.

"Ah, *aaaaaaaaaaaaaaaaaaahhhhhhhhhhhhhhhhhhhhhhhhhhhhhhhhhhhhhhhhhh*?!"

Management writhed in agony, eyes filled with pain and surprise as he looked up at the boy. The boy, taking aim once again—this time at his vitals—spoke simply, without much change in his voice.

"That's too bad."

7

Group was a cruel organization.

The remaining three members took a wait-and-see stance with Unabara, whose whereabouts were still completely unknown. However, they still might not have gone to help him even if they had a hint about his location. Their fundamental policy was that if any of them mismanaged something, they had to fix it themselves.

Therefore:

"Got a call from our ancillary. The escort car with Management on board has been attacked."

"Everyone dead?" Accelerator asked.

"No. They were nice and left everyone but Management unconscious. Either way, there goes our option of getting the man himself to talk."

"Do you think they left a clue as to who did it?" Musujime added.

"Again, it's probably in these bills."

For now, they had the five paper bills.

After leaving the Family Side II apartment complex, Group had decided to return to their hideout and investigate the electronic information contained on the bills' IC chips.

"Man, didn't think our secret hideout would be some empty store in an underground mall. What if some hopeful corporate dropout wanders in for a peek?"

"Then we'll leave," said Tsuchimikado distractedly. "There's hide-outs all over the place, and this one was meant for them originally anyway." He put a device for reading the bills on the floor. It was connected to a laptop via cables.

"...What is that?" asked Musujime, surprised.

Tsuchimikado gave a small smile. It was a cell phone wallet sensor, the kind next to cash registers in convenience stores. "Ugh...It was gonna be a pain in the ass, so I asked someone in the industry and just brought the whole reader here."

"Doesn't matter what we use," said Accelerator, sitting in a pipe chair and cleaning off his handgun. "Just get started already."

"Right," answered Tsuchimikado simply, picking one bill from the stack of five and holding it up to the device.

No discernible language came up on the display. Only a jumble of numbers. Tsuchimikado fiddled with the screen, eventually starting to change them into sentences that made sense.

"That didn't take long. We got a hit." He followed the lines of char-acters on the screen with his eyes. "...It looks like Management's product listing. There was a deal on a professional sniper. He was handling the sniper's weapons, too, apparently."

He ran the second bill over the sensor.

"The sniper's name is Chimitsu Sunazara...though we can't confirm its validity. It has his history and abilities here, too, but we can't trust that, either. But the introduction fee was seven hundred thousand yen, which makes him one of the best 'products' on Management's lineup."

He ran a third bill over the sensor.

"This one has his weapons on it. He's got...an MSR-001, a magnetic sniper rifle," he finished with a foreboding hum.

"Magnetic?" repeated Musujime.

"Just what it sounds like. It uses an electromagnet to launch a steel bullet. Made by Academy City, of course. It's simpler than a railgun on the inside. The bullet's initial speed is two hundred ninety meters per second—not quite supersonic."

"...Does that mean something?" she asked. "It sounds to me like a normal sniper rifle would be better."

But Tsuchimikado grinned and said, "In terms of pure force, sure. But this one doesn't use gunpowder, so it has no recoil. It doesn't have the 'sway' sniper rifles tend to have, so you can attach a delicate, super-precise sighting device to it—if you used gunpowder, you'd need the whole thing to be sturdy enough to handle the recoil from firing. And..."

"And what?"

"If it doesn't use gunpowder, it doesn't make noise. Perfect for doing things in secret."

Tsuchimikado continued, holding a fourth bill up to the sensor.

But this one only put up an error on the screen.

They couldn't read the all-important data.

"Damn. The chip must have gotten hit by the heat or the impact... Just based on the fragments of the header, this one has concrete details on the other end of the deal, the guys who employed him."

Tsuchimikado passed it over the sensor a few more times, but he never got the data inside to show up. He gave up on that one for the time being and held the fifth and final bill to the sensor.

A rough map of somewhere came up on the screen.

It was a simplified map that cut out everything except what was important. A red dot was displayed in the center, with numbers written next to the buildings nearby. But as to what story, or how many meters in length—all of that was unreadable from a top-down map.

Tsuchimikado laughed. "It's a sniper plan. Management was even dealing in these things?"

"Hah," snorted Accelerator. "What, did he run a general store or something?"

"It's showing the plaza in front of District 7's concert hall...," said Musujime, looking up at the ceiling. "Right above us."

"The plaza's been rented out by someone on the General Board for a speech. They must be after the VIP. Name is Monaka Oyafune. Don't know why they're trying to put a hole in her head, but they must have a grand plan in mind if they're trying to assassinate Oyafune. If we stop him, our job's done...As for Unabara, well, you know. He got the lowest score on this job, so we'll rescue him and make him play a penalty game."

"Hah! We going to run over and play tag with a sniper now?" grumbled Accelerator in annoyance. "Sounds like a pain. I'm sure the speech will be boring anyway— Can't we just stop the event?"

Tsuchimikado shook his head. "Probably not."

"Why?"

"Simple—the speech has already started."

8

Accelerator and Motoharu Tsuchimikado had left the underground mall and neared the plaza in front of the concert hall, which was directly below them.

They hadn't taken a sane means of travel, like the stairs or elevator; instead, they'd used Musujime's ability, Move Point. The ability was certainly convenient, but it had a flaw: It was hard for her to warp herself. So she'd remained at the hideout alone, continuing their microchip analysis.

Many students were in the plaza, probably because it was a holiday. They wouldn't have thought an outdoor speech would be interesting, but just at a glance, there were two or three hundred people there.

Around a hundred meters separated Accelerator and the VIP, Monaka Oyafune.

A simple stage was set up in the middle of the plaza, the kind that might be used for a cultural festival, and a middle-aged woman was standing on it. Four escorts dressed in black were waiting around her, but…

"No motivation," said Accelerator, cutting it down to two words. "It's like they're screaming for someone to come put a bullet through whatever organ of hers they want. It's completely obvious that VIP bigshot isn't wearing anything bulletproof when you look at how thin her clothes are, either."

"Stop it. That's why we're doing this."

"That Shiokishi guy is on the General Board, too, and he wears a powered suit around the clock. Apparently, he's not scared of being attacked—it just makes him feel uncomfortable when he's not in it."

"He's an extreme case," muttered Tsuchimikado, standing next to him.

Accelerator glared at him. He jabbed his chin at Monaka Oyafune onstage. "You seriously wanna protect that woman?"

"What do you mean?"

"I mean, I don't. The General Board is a bunch of shitheads. You think they deserve us risking our lives to protect them?"

Accelerator was referring to a man named Thomas Platinaburg. Like Oyafune, he was one of the General Board members. He'd never even talked to him before, but just looking at his furniture had told him right away that the man naturally looked down on everyone else and didn't think anything of it.

"There are two kinds of people at the top of Academy City," said Tsuchimikado quietly, slipping into the crowd in the plaza. "The assholes who deserve to die this instant, and the good people seen as assholes—the diligent ones. In most cases, those types don't fit into the world well and always draw the short stick."

Accelerator stared at Tsuchimikado and let out a quiet hum. Applause and cheering filled the area.

"I hear Monaka Oyafune is trying to give the children in Academy

City the right to vote. Most of the city's residents are minors who don't have that. They can't complain about policies adults decide for them. She says she wants to give them that right." He laughed, his tone light. "If she's not a thorn in their side, I don't know what is. If the kids got voting rights, they could even stop this war."

"Are you dumb? There's no way it'll be that easy. It's a peaceful idea, but not a practical one. It's like they don't understand the meaning of the word *violence*."

"The divides between races and the sexes were the same, too, at first. Special influential people weren't the only ones fixing everything. Sure, they had a lot to do with it, since they were leading the masses. But the big reason was the people who had been thinking they were powerless—they changed their minds. Then they all got together, and history changed."

Accelerator looked back at the plaza—the one with so many students in it, even though it was a holiday.

Tsuchimikado chuckled and said, "I don't know how you feel about it, but I think Monaka Oyafune is at least worth protecting. I would risk my life for her. I won't tell you to do the same, but don't think you can stop me."

Accelerator clicked his tongue in frustration, then used his cane to take a step forward.

"What a pain in the ass. Let's just crush that dumbass sniper already."

9

Accelerator and Tsuchimikado were standing about a hundred meters from the stage Monaka Oyafune was on. They should have been closer—it certainly wasn't what you'd call a good plan—but considering the crowd, this was what they had at the moment: checking the location with their cell phone GPS maps.

"Looks like there's about thirty-two possible sniping positions," said Tsuchimikado. "But with the stainless-steel board behind the stage, any point one hundred and eighty degrees behind it is actually a dead angle. Which means..."

"...It's one of the fifteen spots one hundred and eighty degrees in front. We could probably get the sniper if we went to every single spot..."

"...But there's nothing saying Chimitsu Sunazara is gonna wait around for us once he's in firing position," said Tsuchimikado, surveying the area.

He wasn't looking at Oyafune, as she smiled softly on stage, or the youth, listening to her and applauding. He saw a vehicle—a specially permitted commercial one—parked a short distance from the plaza. Its body resembled a crane truck, but a giant fan-like machine was attached to the top.

"Looks like they do have a Wind Defense set up against sniping, at least."

"Eh?"

"You know how much the wind affects sniping," explained Tsuchimikado. "That machine purposely creates blasts of wind around a VIP to throw off their aim. They're probably using four of them, making a whirlwind all around the plaza. They're third generation, so they should be using a random number generator to make the air currents more chaotic."

But something else seemed to have caught Accelerator's eye, because, as he peered through the edge of the throng, he suddenly darted into the crowd to hide.

Tsuchimikado looked that way and saw, a few meters away, a middle school girl with a lot of flowers decorating her hair holding hands and walking with a girl who seemed around ten or so.

"'I told you, Misaka is looking for a lost child,' says Misaka says Misaka, announcing her intentions."

"Yes, well, um, a lost child?"

"'I don't really know, but I think he's somewhere around here,' says Misaka says Misaka, offering a prediction. 'My head feels like it's getting nervous about something,' says Misaka says Misaka, adding extra sense-based information."

"Right...I knew that silly piece of hair was incredible!"

"It's not silly!!" came the shout, and Accelerator's hand went to his forehead.

"...Why would that brat show up here?! Is God fucking around with me or what?!" he hissed.

"...Ha-ha. That's just how life is," muttered Tsuchimikado off-handedly, but after noticing a girl in maid clothes in the crowd, he buried his own face in his hands.

For once, their opinions matched—they had to ensure no "stray bullets" flew in their direction.

"Anyway, things get complicated with the Wind Defense throwing off the hitman's aim..."

"That truck. Says on the side it's an air-cleaning truck."

"Well, it's not *wrong*. It uses the same principle as the air purifiers that smokers use in schools' faculty rooms. Just on a totally different scale," said Tsuchimikado with pride.

Accelerator's eyes were cold, though. "That's great and all, but it's not on."

"What?!"

Tsuchimikado, startled, checked it himself. Accelerator was right—the giant fan on the big cart truck wasn't doing anything.

"I swear it was just on..." It was protecting a VIP. Could it have possibly had a malfunction?

Then Tsuchimikado heard an odd *bkk* sound ringing through the noisy crowd around him.

It sounded like a metal pot crumpling.

"..."

Accelerator and Tsuchimikado looked in the direction of the ringing at the same time.

There was another Wind Defense–equipped special vehicle parked elsewhere. Its giant fan wasn't on, either. And there was a thumb-sized hole in the cylindrical outer wall around the fan.

"It was him—Chimitsu Sunazara."

"Bastard...," hissed Accelerator. "He's trying to take out the Wind Defenses to give himself a clear shot at Oyafune!!"

"Shit!!" cursed Tsuchimikado, trying to plunge into the crowd to get closer to Oyafune. But there were too many people, and he couldn't get as far as he wanted. Meanwhile, two more metal-pounding *bkk* sounds repeated in succession. Accelerator couldn't see them from where he was, but the sniper was probably taking out the other Wind Defense machines, too, one at a time.

Damn it, thought Accelerator. *Magnetic sniper rifles don't use gunpowder, so nobody would even notice if their equipment was getting shot at!*

The man-made gale barrier was gone now.

Tsuchimikado seemed to be trying to warn Monaka Oyafune of the danger, but it didn't look like he'd make it.

"Great."

Monaka Oyafune's speech from atop the platform continued. The bodyguards in the vicinity were standing still, unaware of the threat.

If this went on much longer, it would be checkmate.

"What a goddamn pain!!"

10

The sniper, Chimitsu Sunazara, brought his magnetic sniper rifle up.

He was in a hotel room. He'd gone up to it without checking in, got its electronic lock open, and went inside. As for the window, in addition to disabling the security, he'd cut a square piece of it away to create a hole, out of which his rifle barrel extended.

A magnetic sniper rifle—although its form differed greatly from other existing guns, it was a metal cylinder as thick as an ankle with a steel box stuck onto it, almost haphazardly. Propped up on a tripod, the barrel was a strong solenoid coil.

A pair of suitcases sat next to him. One was for storing the magnetic sniper rifle after disassembling, while the other was for the rifle's giant battery.

"…"

The range was about seven hundred meters.

He'd destroyed all the Wind Defense machines that were blocking him.

Monaka Oyafune, on the distant stage, seemed close enough to hug through the scope.

He would hit.

He thought so naturally, then relaxed and pulled the trigger.

That's when it happened.

Ga-bam!!

All of a sudden, part of the plaza in front of the concert hall exploded, flinging flames and black smoke into the air.

His target, exposed to the blast, flinched, crouching down. Because she had moved, Sunazara's bullet missed her.

"What was that…?"

Sunazara frowned. The timing was too good. Meanwhile, the big men stationed as guards around Oyafune came down to the platform to surround her.

He had a job to do.

He pulled the trigger again, but the steel bullet struck one of the bodyguards pressed against Oyafune. It flung his body down in spectacular fashion, but there was no blood, so he was probably wearing a bulletproof vest as a shield.

The guards changed positions. Oyafune ended up completely hidden behind the stocky men.

"Looks like that's it for now."

Long-range sniping was delicate. Even if you used a bullet that traveled at the speed of sound, sniping a target from seven hundred meters away would mean the bullet had to travel for almost two seconds before hitting the target. It was one thing if the person was standing still, unguarded, but with her running away—present tense—with multiple bodyguards, it would be very difficult to shoot her in a vital spot.

After thinking for a moment, Chimitsu Sunazara decided not to be stubborn and to withdraw.

"Still, what exploded?"

He looked through his scope, then saw the black smoke rising from one of the special Wind Defense vehicles. He'd shot them in order to stop them, but he was sure he hadn't hit anywhere that would have made them explode.

" "
...

A moment later, Sunazara's breath caught in his throat.

Right next to the special vehicle in flames. A person with white hair, at the scene and yet blending in casually with the background, was looking straight at him—with a cane in one hand and flames and smoke at his back.

"I see."

Sunazara looked away from the scope and immediately began taking apart the magnetic sniper rifle. As he put each part into the suitcase, he said to himself:

"I'll remember that face."

11

When Motoharu Tsuchimikado set foot in the hotel room, it had already been vacated.

But there was a square section of glass unnaturally missing from the window.

"Shit." Tsuchimikado took out his cell phone and called Accelerator. "Retrieval is a failure. But if Sunazara fled, he probably won't be doing any more sniping today. Get Oyafune to stop her speech for now, get security to regroup, and get them out of there."

"I've got a message from Musujime," said Accelerator on the other end. "She managed to read the chip on the fourth bill we couldn't get anything from. Like we thought, it's got the name of the guys who hired Chimitsu Sunazara on it."

"Who was it?" asked Tsuchimikado.

Accelerator answered with an annoyed voice. "...School."

"What?"

"Same as our 'Group'...An organization hiding in the shadows of Academy City."

INTERLUDE ONE

A man was standing around in an open-air café at lunchtime.

Tables crammed with customers were covered with all sorts of food, but his table alone stood empty. Only a big hodgepodge of printer paper was stacked there, not a single coffee mug in sight.

The man was staring at the papers spread out on the table, his hands stuck in the pockets of his white coat. Printed on the dozens of sheets in this bundle was involuntary-diffusion field data on espers from the data banks.

A girl in a red sailor-style school uniform, sitting across from the man's seat, looked at him dubiously. "What do you think you're going to find by looking at them?"

"All sorts of things," he answered without looking up. "You may not know this, given that *you're a sorcerer*, but this has all kinds of information in it. It's not just a weak power that vents from espers—it's them unconsciously interfering with reality...By examining the infinite variety of types and strengths of powers, one can explore the minds of espers, too."

"Unconscious interference...?" repeated the girl, not understanding.

"If we advance our understanding of involuntary diffusion fields, or IDFs, we can highlight the outline of espers' personal realities and use them for data by investigating their personalities and behavioral patterns. Though, I think the resulting parameters would be much more utilitarian and easy to understand than psychological profiles."

A silvery beast was next to the chair the man sat in.

It was a quadrupedal animal made of titanium alloy and synthetic resin. It had the basic form of a carnivore in the Felidae family, but its nose was unnaturally long, like an elephant's. The metallic creature had a seeing-eye dog walking program installed, so it blended into human society with a surprising litheness.

The beast opened its mouth. *"Professor."* The voice didn't sound synthesized—it was the voice of a young man with rich enunciation. *"It appears there has been activity within Group and School."*

The man called Professor looked over at the mechanical creature. Its speech functions weren't produced with a robotic AI; someone in another place was simply speaking through it via a wireless network. One could think of it as a slightly more complicated telephone.

"Did they make contact?"

"No. Group appears to have failed to capture. In this situation, they may not be able to catch School's tail."

"Hmm." The professor sighed just once. "Either way, *the others* will probably act, too."

They were on a team directly under the jurisdiction of Aleister, the Academy City General Board chairperson.

They acted as "that person's" limbs, uncaring of good and evil. That was all that was expected from the small outfit.

"From the outset, *groups like ours* have complicated reasons for acting, but various powers higher up the chain have pressured us and controlled us," the professor said, his tone relaxed. "But after the violence that occurred during the 09/30 incident, most of the powered suits have been sent out to clean up in Avignon. That force makes for effective hands for the man on the telephone. They can't use the suits freely now, which gives us a huge opportunity."

"Then perhaps the time is ripe."

Suddenly, a voice appeared from directly behind the girl in the red uniform.

Nobody had been there a moment ago, but now someone was there. It was a boy covered in a big, baggy down jacket.

It was like he'd appeared out of thin air.

"Yes," the professor said languidly, placing a hand on his nearby creature's head and stroking it lightly. He didn't seem surprised at the boy's appearance. The girl sitting across from him watched their exchange with a lack of interest.

Her expression suspicious, she asked, "How do we know exactly how *they're* moving? The intel from higher up could be wrong."

"They have tech that makes it possible to know with accuracy."

The professor's hand stopped petting the synthetic animal.

He was staring at the sidewalk across the street from the café. A girl, in what might colloquially be called maid clothing, was passing by. But the professor wasn't looking at her. That girl was sitting atop an oil drum–shaped cleaning robot. He watched its very smooth procession down the sidewalk.

He nodded to himself.

He was honestly impressed.

"I never thought of an idea like that."

"Professor, please keep your mind off strange ideas."

Group	 MOTOHARU TSUCHIMIKADO  MITSUKI UNABARA  AWAKI MUSUJIME  ACCELERATOR
School	UNKNOWN UNKNOWN  CHIMITSU SUNAZARA  UNKNOWN

CHAPTER 2

Those Gradually Beginning to Act
Altair_II.

1

Inside an RV that one of their drivers had brought around for them sat Accelerator, Motoharu Tsuchimikado, and Awaki Musujime.

It was noon.

Fast-food meals lined a small table bolted to the floor.

Each was eating the food they'd bought—Accelerator his spicy fried chicken and Tsuchimikado his giant hamburger. They weren't kindred spirits even in what they ate for lunch.

Meanwhile, Awaki Musujime, eating a fancy salad from a direct-delivery brand in the Mediterranean, watched them. "...That stuff will shave years off your life."

"Eating meowthing but green and yellow veggies seems too healthy to meow. You need both meat and vegetables to maintain a healthy body, y'know. You've gotta have a balance."

"Hah. Wouldn't you be happier eating meat and dying? You'd be able to die after doing what you wanted to do until the end," said Accelerator to Musujime, licking grease off his thumb. "Anyway, find out anything about those School guys?"

"I accessed the data banks, but aside from the name, no. It looks like they're as secret as we are. It just says Group and School in there.

"But," she added with a pause, "When I looked around, I found a few more organization names like that."

"There weren't only two?" Tsuchimikado bit into his hamburger and hastily tried to keep the meat from coming out the other side.

"Group, School, Item, Member, Block...," she answered, counting on her fingers. "Five, just from what I can tell. Details are unknown, but they're probably like us—*unofficial teams made up of a small number of people.* School were the ones plotting to snipe Monaka Oyafune. Would that make them the ones who blew up Management's mansion and attacked his escort car? Maybe Mitsuki Unabara infiltrated them, too."

"Who knows? But if he's doing spy work in School, I wish he'd at least give us a sign. We might think he's a baddie and accidentally kill him," said Tsuchimikado, listening to Musujime as Accelerator put a coffee can to his lips.

...But why would School be trying to assassinate Monaka Oyafune?

2

They're doing whatever they want, thought Shiage Hamazura.

Right now, he was in a family restaurant in School District 7. But the woman named Shizuri Mugino, who had installed herself at one of their table's seats, was blatantly eating a convenience store meal she'd bought elsewhere. *That poor, poor little waitress waiting at the edge of the table...*

"Huh? This salmon bento tastes different from yesterday's salmon bento. Hmm?"

The woman, by the window and wearing a short-sleeved coat in bright fall colors even though she was inside, re-crossed her stocking-covered legs and tilted her head in confusion as she mumbled.

It's the same as always, thought Hamazura.

Weirdos, every single person at the table.

"It just means canned mackerel is in vogue right now. Curry is the best—curry!" said a blond, green-eyed high school girl named

Frenda sitting beside Mugino as she wrestled with the can. Maybe she was bad at using can openers, because she wrapped some kind of plastic tape around it, then attached a fuse to the tape and blew the thing open. Hamazura was pretty sure you were supposed to use that for breaking open doors.

Meanwhile, sitting across from Frenda was a mature-looking girl of about twelve named Saiai Kinuhata, who wore a fluffy knit dress. She wasn't paying the least bit of attention to what the weirdos were doing (not that she had common sense or tolerance but because she was *that* kind of weirdo). Instead, she was browsing through a movie pamphlet. "An ultra-problematic C-movie presented by the Hong Kong Red Dragon film company...Looks like a real palm sweater in a few different ways, but that's what makes it interesting. Yes, worth a check. Takitsubo, what do you think?"

She was asking an all-around lethargic girl named Rikou Takitsubo, sitting next to her. She hadn't touched her food; she was just sprawled out on the booth seat, eyes wandering here and there, never focusing. "...Signal coming from south-southwest...," she muttered.

...These girls were a team called Item.

They were an unofficial Academy City organization whose main business was to hold the city's upper echelons, including the General Board, in check. This small group of four had real influence in this city, and by extension, the science faction as a whole. They were treated with the same level of secrecy as Group and School.

Shiage Hamazura wasn't an official member of Item. He belonged to their ancillary organization, doing odd jobs and being their driver.

Before, he'd been the temporary leader of Skill-Out, an armed organization comprising back-alley Level Zeroes. But after their plans fell through and they sustained catastrophic damage, his life of standing above others had come to an end. Now he was doing grunt work in Academy City's underworld.

...*Still, though*, thought Hamazura. Ever since they'd assigned him here, something had been constantly worrying him.

Being the only man in a group of women is really uncomfortable.

This booth seated six, and Hamazura was closest to the aisle. They'd assigned him the job of refilling their drinks.

"So!" said Shizuri Mugino after finishing most of her salmon bento. "About that incident where one of the General Board members, Monaka Oyafune, was almost killed this morning. With that, I think we should start moving, too."

"Actually, I never got any information about that," said Frenda simply.

Mugino paused with a grunt. Then the short-sleeved-coat-wearing woman glanced at Hamazura. "Hamazura, would you forward this incident's details to everyone's phones?"

"Yeah, yeah," answered Hamazura. He wouldn't complain when they gave him orders. This was his job now. He took out his own cell phone, then sent them the saved data.

"Hmm..."

Everyone looked at the information on their phones.

And what came up was an adult video downloaded from the Internet.

A moment later, all four members of Item slapped their cell phones closed. With stares of contempt, they shut the doors to their minds, then barred those mental doors shut, then took their mental underground elevators down to evacuate to their mental nuclear shelters.

"I, wait!! Do-over! There must be some mistake!!"

The delinquent leader who once led over one hundred people in Skill-Out bellowed a plea.

As for the four members of Item...

"Hamazura..."

"Man, you really are a creep."

"Bunny girls are a big hit for you, Hamazura?"

"It's okay, Hamazura. I still support you even though you're like that."

Hamazura, trembling at the warm words, this time sent the correct information about the attempted sniping of Monaka Oyafune.

Kinuhata sighed. "Right, the one School totally planned. I thought we'd, like, totally dealt with their assassin sniper three days ago."

"They must've hired a new one," said Hamazura. "It just means they ignored our warning."

"Man, didn't we argue about why they were after Monaka Oyafune then, too?" said Frenda, stabbing the contents of her can of mackerel with a fork. "Oyafune is on the General Board, but man, she's useless. She has almost no influence. She's not even worth killing. But they still wanted her…"

"School still hired a new sniper after the one they lost, then still tried to assassinate Oyafune even despite our warning," said Takitsubo lazily, continuing for Frenda.

Mugino nodded shortly. "There is no value in killing Monaka Oyafune. Despite the risk of getting found out, they decided to force their plans and shoot her. Why is that? …Hamazura!"

Hamazura's shoulders jerked in surprise. *What?! Why does it seem like she's trying to get me to say something funny now?! D-don't look at me at times like this!!*

"U-um, well!! Wait a sec, it's coming up my throat now, I'll know in a moment!!"

In the end, he had enthusiasm, but couldn't actually say anything.

"Uhh, Hamazura…"

"Man, the way you get flustered is creepy."

"There's totally different kinds of creepy, but Hamazura is the worst kind."

"It's okay, Hamazura. I still support you even though everyone keeps calling you creepy."

The girls gave disappointed sighs. The Level-Zero Hamazura hunkered down on the floor and stopped moving.

Mugino ignored him. "Well, like I said, there's no value in assassinating Monaka Oyafune. She's too straightforward. But School still chose her for their target. So, like, maybe they chose her *because she doesn't have any value.*"

"Because she doesn't? I totally don't get it."

"I mean, like, maybe School just needed *someone*. They only wanted to cause a big fuss, so they chose a VIP whose death wouldn't affect much…In other words, they went after the VIP with the least security." Mugino sounded amused. "As for other VIPs…Well, even in just the General Board, nobody else would have been giving a speech outdoors in the past couple days. That Shiokishi guy wears his powered suit around the clock, right? There's no way they can snipe someone like that, so I think they chose whoever would be easiest. And honestly, Monaka Oyafune didn't have much in the way of protection."

"…Man, poor Oyafune."

"Assuming that's correct, what was School after? I propose this: a system of guaranteed VIP security." Mugino stuck out her chest proudly—a chest visible even outside her short-sleeved coat. "Academy City designates several people and organizations as VIPs, starting with the twelve General Board members. Their protection comes from a different security group. If anyone ends up in a life-threatening situation, they'd call in people from all over. They'd do things like close off roads for ambulances to pass through and get all the biggest names in medicine to do surgery.

"What I'm saying is this," concluded Mugino after a pause. "What do you think would happen if a VIP was almost assassinated?"

"They'd call in other people to defend the medical facility, then get all those special scientists and machines and stuff together," replied Kinuhata. "Heh, you're saying School would use the chaos to do something else? How boring."

It would certainly create an opening, but the method wasn't very decisive. It wouldn't affect District 23's strict security or the Windowless Building much at all. At most, it would raise the possibility of attacks on facilities that were already targets to begin with.

"It could be insurance," said Mugino. "If School got serious, they could break into most facilities by force. However," she added, "they were so intent on obtaining insurance that they hastily replaced the sniper we took care of and plotted to assassinate Monaka Oyafune. It seems like they're pretty high-strung about it."

"Man, that means Oyafune was just a means of insurance, and School plans on attacking somewhere or someone else now."

"Yep," said Mugino, nodding.

Hamazura broke in anxiously. "...Wait, doesn't that mean they *wanted* to fail?"

"I don't think it matters, really. Even if she did die, they'd devote a lot of people to her for heart and lung resuscitation and crime scene inspection and autopsy and stuff. She might not be all that, but she's still one of only twelve members of the General Board—one of the highest VIPs in the city. They would mobilize all sorts of unknown technology for it."

"Urk," said Hamazura, scrunching up his face.

Mugino continued anyway, not so much as batting an eye. "I'll check the facilities with less security because of the attempted assassination of Monaka Oyafune...Actually, maybe that's not enough. I'll check the points that would have changed if it had worked out, too. School must have controlled the situation so they could get to their goal whether or not their sniper succeeded. There must be a facility with less security that matches both conditions. That's probably where School will show up next."

Shizuri Mugino vigorously rose from her seat.

Without sparing a glance at Hamazura, she told him, "Hamazura, go look for a car, please. We'll probably be leaving right away."

Her snobbish tone pricked at Hamazura's nerves, but he couldn't argue with her. He was just a grunt right now. "Damn. I'll have you know, I'm the leader of over a hundred people in Skill-Out...," he muttered anyway, despite himself.

"Yes, and?"

...Damn it, he cursed to himself before leaving the family restaurant ahead of them to find a car.

3

Mitsuki Unabara was in a mixed-residence building in School District 10.

The building was missing a lot of tenants, and now he found himself in another vacant apartment. The sole juvenile reformatory in Academy City being right out the window might have had something to do with it.

There were a dozen or so armed men in the small room—and about four people who clearly looked like bosses—all standing around. On a business desk left haphazardly in the room were the firearms and laptop they'd brought there, as well as a tossing of smaller tools for disguise and hand cream and such.

...My, my. This is a quandary.

Right now, he was not Mitsuki Unabara.

He'd taken out one of the attackers, and now he was "borrowing" the man's face.

Who would have thought someone so weak was central to this organization...

His plan was to disguise himself as one of the grunts at random, wait for an opportunity to go out on an errand or something, sneak away from the group, and flee...But apparently, Unabara had taken out one of the group's bosses.

It would be hard to sneak away from them like this. It wasn't like they were watching his every action, but whenever he moved, the ring of people seemed to move with him and around him.

He lost his chance and ended up coming to District 10 from District 7...

"What is it, Yamate?"

Suddenly, a voice spoke to him from the side.

A tall woman was standing there. Though she was slender, her whole body was covered in hard muscle. She looked built—almost like a statue, actually. He could tell at a glance she did behind-the-scenes jobs, but according to what he heard, she was also an Anti-Skill officer on the surface and had infiltrated their headquarters.

As he thought about all that, he recalled what the muscular woman had said.

Yamate. That seemed to be his name.

"*It's nothin'*," he said.

"Keep it together. Your strength, is vital, to our plan's success."

She spoke politely, stating each word clearly. It sounded like she was being kind while also looking down on him.

"School's started to move," said a bearlike man. "We're the ones who sent them Management's information, but…Damn. If only they'd taken action a little later."

"In the end, attacking the mansion and destroying the information was all pointless," said the muscular woman standing next to Unabara. "Thanks to School's actions, the security level, of the entire Academy City, should have gone up. I just hope, it doesn't impact, what we need to do."

"Looks like this won't be easy. We can't get out of Academy City now, either. Though, it's not like we can stop now anyway."

"…" As Unabara listened to the woman's voice, he pieced together the information in his head.

…This organization was apparently called Block.

…Block was presumably afforded equal secrecy and authority as Group.

…Block seemed to be planning something, but because another organization called School took action on the same day, they were apparently caught up in it.

…In order to correct that impact as much as possible, Block had set off an explosion to clean up after School's mess. That was why Unabara had gotten caught up in this, too.

…Block had apparently given up on doing anything about the negative effects from School's mess and decided to go through with their plans anyway.

School and Block. This is starting to get complicated…

Then the brawny woman spoke to the bearlike man. "What about *him*? Is he all right?"

"…Oh, our telephone man. No problem there. After all, the powered suits he uses to do his bidding are all occupied in the Avignon cleanup. There isn't much the telephone man can do now. He's got it rough, too, eh? Normally he just tosses down orders from above, but if we ever went out of control—well, we're his responsibility, so he'd be executed for it, wouldn't he? And the Hound Dogs were all wiped out, including their leader, Amata Kihara, after the 09/30 incident. They won't get in the way, either."

It seems like the same person is giving this organization its orders as Group, thought Unabara. But was this "telephone man" the same person, or was there more than one? Was more than one person giving orders to one organization, or was there one per team? Maybe he pretended there were several, but he was using a voice changer. That was an unknown factor.

Well, whether it's one or a bunch, they're probably not a very big team. And despite their size, they seem strangely flexible.

The "telephone voice" could come later. Right now, Unabara focused on Block's conversation, converting his thoughts into those of their group's composition and such.

At the very least, it doesn't look like they're acting out the intent of some higher Academy City power. The powered suits aren't around right now, so what are they trying to do?

Unabara glanced to the side. The men from Block's ancillary were there. They were clearly assisting in this rebellious act, but…

No, how many people realize that?

Even if someone in a position of power handed them a command, saying *"It's an emergency. Meet up at location A,"* things like that were commonly lies in the underworld. Nobody took orders at face value with how convoluted everyone's ulterior motives always got. When push came to shove, at the very end, all anyone could do was base their actions on what they'd personally seen.

Their intel could be a lie. Block would immediately shoot him if he turned his back right now. If he was to believe one of them, it had to be the latter. That was how he would live through this.

That's divine punishment for you, I suppose. Every day they deceive those beneath them. Now their information is less trustworthy because of it.

"All right," said the big, bearlike man, appearing to have made up his mind. "No more delays. We're getting started, too. Who cares about Block? I don't plan on living my whole life under *their* thumb."

So he said, but he didn't move right away, instead looking around the room.

Unabara asked, "What's wrong?"

"Nothing, just wanted to do the usual safety check before that."

The bearlike man clapped his large hands twice. At his signal, a gloomy-looking girl moved slowly in front of them.

"Tetsumou…We're borrowing your Skill, Polygraph. Make sure we don't have any traitors, just in case."

"All right. My only value is in reading people's minds, after all."

…?! Mitsuki Unabara almost thought the surprise would show on his face.

He glanced around the room, then pretended to casually take a bottle of hand cream from the business desk. The four members of Block (including him) and the dozen or so in the ancillary group—if he was found out here, he'd be in trouble.

"Oh, one more thing. Anyone who refuses being read will be labeled a traitor on the spot. I like transparency, after all."

After the big man finished talking, the girl he called Tetsumou shook hands with each of her associates in turn. Only a mechanical, inorganic voice came from her lips.

"Tatsuhiko Saku. Age twenty-eight, Block's leader. Main job is to monitor coordination with outside agencies cooperating with Academy City."

The brawny woman spoke after the big, bearlike man.

"Megumi Teshio. Age twenty-five. Official member of Block. Anti-Skill roles include— …?!"

Tetsumou's face twisted in surprise. For a moment, bloodlust filled the air, but Teshio spoke calmly. "…You don't need, to be so enthusiastic, to read me. The reason *she* has no parents, and the cause of her inability to speak, do not make her past, very fun to see."

Tetsumou shook her head lightly, then looked toward Unabara next.

That was when Unabara let the bottle of hand cream slip out of his hand. "…Oh, sorry."

The bottle rolled to one of the men in the ancillary. As he reached out for it, the young man came up and handed it to him.

"Thanks. After you," prompted Unabara. The young man had just stepped in front of Tetsumou, basically interrupting the order, so Tetsumou held out her hand to him instead. She seemed to want to get this check over with promptly.

They shook hands, and then it happened.

"......*Gaaaaaaahhhhhhhhhhhhhhhhhhhhhh?!*"

All of a sudden, a red flame erupted on the man's and Tetsumou's hands. With an explosive *boom*, blood sprayed. Several fingers flew. Tetsumou held her right hand, but she couldn't endure the pain and blood loss. She fell to the floor and stopped moving.

The young man, in a haste, reached for a first-aid kit, but the bearlike man blocked him. "What did you just do?"

"I don't know. How should I know?!"

"I asked you what you did!!"

"I'm a victim here, too!!"

Saku said nothing more. He pulled his handgun from his holster, pressed the muzzle against the young man's forehead, and pulled the trigger.

"Wait, I didn't—?!"

The young man from their ancillary was arrested with surprise... but the gun discharged.

With a thunderous series of bangs, the man, now covered in blood, fell to the floor.

The bearlike Saku threw a glare down at the crimson corpse. "...Well, it's a good thing we found that before we started. Wonder what on earth he did."

"Now what? Do we continue?" asked Unabara.

Saku shook his head. Tetsumou was hurt, and it didn't look like she was getting back up. "No time to replace her. I'll get a new checker later."

Seemingly uninterested in Tetsumou, he instructed those in their ancillary group to dispose of the body.

"..." Unabara glanced at the young man unmoving on the floor.

Just before he'd shaken hands with Tetsumou, he'd handed the bottle of hand cream to Unabara. At the time, *there was cream from Unabara's palm stuck to his hand.* And mixed into that cream was a trace amount of liquid explosive.

Unabara continued to blend the hand cream in his palm. This time, he mixed in a chemical to remove the explosive. *They may be enemies, but...No, there's no time to think about it,* he thought, without letting it show on his face.

Saku, collecting himself, said, "Now, then...Let's get started for real this time."

He sat down in front of a laptop.

4

Beep!! went the electronic warning in the RV.

The Group members had finished their lunches and had been discussing what to investigate next, but their conversation was immediately cut off.

The hurried voice of the driver, also their operator, came over the onboard speakers. *"E-emergency! I'll send you the data now!!"*

Accelerator and the others looked toward the speakers. A screen was set upon the wall to separate the driver's seat from the rear living space, and a map of Academy City came up on it.

"The Virus Storage Center in District 5?"

"They analyze Academy City–made computer viruses and develop anti-virus software there...Looks like they're being hacked," said Tsuchimikado, his eyes following the scrolling lines of characters.

Despite finding out about a crime, the thought of notifying Anti-Skill or asking them for help never crossed their minds. Group never got jobs normal people could do themselves. If normal people could solve everything, Group wouldn't exist.

Accelerator, in an annoyed tone, said, "Do we really have to go out there? You said there's a bunch of others like Group, right? Just leave it to them."

"They probably have different jobs. We don't have a guarantee they'll do anything, and besides, it's pretty likely one of them is betraying Academy City. We have to be the ones to go."

Tsuchimikado continued, "About that Virus Storage Center… Aside from unanalyzed viruses, they have a multitude of experimental ones they made for research agencies in the city. If they end up outside…well, we'd have a panic on our hands."

"How far 'outside' are we talking, here?" asked Musujime, a meaningful smile on her lips.

The scientific technology of inside and outside Academy City differed by two or three decades, and that went for the viruses as well. Even if a virus was an old version for city machines, it could be a completely unknown threat for outside machines. And if a brand-new type of virus that Academy City didn't even have a fix for were to leak outside…

"Let's see if I'm remembering this right. Academy City's security prefers guarding things going out over things coming in, right? There should be some place to do that."

"…The external connection terminals."

Academy City was cut off from the normal Internet—it had formed its own interior network. Every external line hooked up to the Internet had to go through one of the facilities called "external connection terminals" before connecting.

"There're four, right? One at each compass direction," said Musujime.

Then they heard static start to come over the in-vehicle speaker. The hard-pressed voice of their driver and operator came over it:

"*Beginning emergency quarantine of the external connection terminals. District 3 northern terminal, quarantined. District 12 eastern terminal, quarantined. District 2, southern terminal, quarantined…?! No response from District 13, western terminal! Cannot confirm quarantine!!*"

"Ha-ha!" burst out Accelerator at the report. "Predictable once again!!"

Tsuchimikado grinned tenaciously as well. "Odds are ten to one they're luring us there. I don't know who they are, but they must really want us to turn 'em into scrap."

The RV started off toward the district in question, District 13.

Their driver's uneasy voice continued over the speaker. *"Wh-what shall we do about the attempted assassination of Monaka Oyafune?"*

"Put it on the back burner."

"Actually, School might be doing that, too," pointed out Musujime. *"Also...What about Mr. Unabara?"*

"Never cared about that guy anyway."

5

In a back alley, Shiage Hamazura flinched away from the electronic beeping.

The source of the noise was the portable device in Shizuri Mugino's pocket.

"Hey, are we just ignoring that?"

"I'm telling you, it's fine. Someone else will deal with it, so we don't have to."

Nevertheless, the device continued beeping incessantly. Mugino shivered at its awful persistence, then finally snatched the thing and shouted into it.

"Quit your noise, you little shit!! Can't you tell I'm not gonna answer you?!"

"You little...! We're not calling you up because we wanted to!!"

She wasn't on speakerphone, but it was loud enough for it to ring clearly in the nearby Hamazura's ears. The voice belonged to a lady—the mystery woman always giving instructions to Item.

"There's an emergency at the Virus Storage Center in District 5. I want you all to move out and fix the problem!"

"Aw, why?"

"Don't 'Aw, why' me, you little...! Seriously, those powered suits sure are busy cleaning up after Avignon and looking for some Terra of the Left guy's corpse. You should be working, too!"

"We're busy. Can we do this later?"

Mugino sounded incredibly fed up, but the person on the phone again cried out, *"You little...!"* Then, *"Just so you know, it's Item's job to get rid of troublemakers in Academy City. Do your damn jobs!"*

"You say that, but..."

"And you! You said you'd killed School's official sniper already! You said they wouldn't be sniping Monaka Oyafune! You little...! Then why the hell did things come to this?! I thought it was all over, so I reported that the danger had subsided...I'm the one seriously pissed off here, so shape up!!"

The voice sounded like someone telling off a waitress who got her order wrong.

"You've sure done it now, damn it...," the voice continued. *"I'll ask another post to deal with the Virus Storage Center. In the meantime, I want a report on the attempted sniping. Double time that, at least!"*

"Sorry. Can't do that."

"What the hell? What do you mean?!"

"Because we're about to slaughter all the shitheads in School right now."

The yapping female voice stopped abruptly for a moment. *"Um, could I put in a request? Could you put, like, ten bullets in at least one of them?"*

"...Um, on an unrelated note, this is when our supervisor—i.e., you—is supposed to be stopping us."

"Don't give me your sass, you peon. I've hated those School bastards for a long time. And anything that I have to worry about should just get wiped off the face of the planet!!"

With a giant, warlord-like *Gah-ha-ha-ha-ha-ha*, the call ended.

Mugino put her portable terminal back in her pocket and made a face that questioned whether someone like that was really the right person to lead an organization. She glanced around. "By the way, Hamazura, can we really get an assistant?"

"Everything just goes right through you…Anyway, I'll manage on that end," he replied. "More importantly…"

Hamazura walked up to a passenger car parked on the road. He attached a fiberscope device to his cell phone's lower port, ran the light cable, more slender than a *soumen* noodle, into the keyhole, then began looking for where the pin was. Using the data about the keyhole's interior that was coming up on his cell phone screen in conjunction with several wires, he unlocked the door easily.

After climbing into the driver's seat, he studied the engine keyhole under the steering wheel.

"Huh. What a handy skill," said Mugino with genuine admiration as she got into the passenger seat.

Kinuhata, Frenda, and Takitsubo piled themselves into the rear seat. The car was a family four-door, like most taxis, but with five people inside, it felt cramped.

"Where to?"

"Kirigaoka Girls' Academy, in District 18. The Particle Physics Institute is nearby. It was the only place during the Oyafune commotion to be thrown into chaos, with the people there getting called up for emergency security and to transport equipment. Because of that, their guard is pretty much down. A perfectly simple criminal scheme."

"Only that one place? Seems really easy."

"Excuse me, I forgot to say. There was only one place beneficial to them out of several."

"Ah," replied Hamazura effortlessly. "The Particle Physics Institute? Even if that was School's real target, what are they after?"

"Who knows? It would have to be something more important than Monaka Oyafune's life, right? Anyway, time for our little whoop-ass tour."

"Right," mumbled Hamazura as he easily started the engine.

Takitsubo spoke up from the back seat. "Hamazura, I didn't know you had a license."

"The card isn't what you need. It's the skill," answered Hamazura casually, smoothly driving off in the automatic car.

6

The RV Accelerator and the others were riding in charged into District 7.

Attentive to the clock, Tsuchimikado said, "…About ten minutes until we get to District 13."

The deal was that they couldn't quarantine the western terminal, but if they went to the site and directly disconnected the large-capacity cable, they could prevent access for now. The important people, stubborn about their budgets, didn't like this kind of solution, but the situation called for drastic measures.

But then, yet another alarm beep rang.

Tsuchimikado responded harshly, "What now?!"

"*Hacking confirmed in District 23 as well! The Aerospace Engineering Institute's satellite control center is under electronic attack!!*"

"Satellite?" repeated Accelerator, frowning. The ones Academy City had launched were spy satellites pretending to be weather satellites. If you used them, you could have a complete view of all the city and its surrounding areas. "Hey, things are getting interesting after all. The one satellite, *Altair II*—that thing had a large-bore ground-attack laser on board, didn't it?"

"This is bad," said Musujime. "The Virus Storage Center is still being hacked, too, right?"

"The countermeasure team is probably running around like a chicken with its head cut off," mused Tsuchimikado. "Means this is a decoy so they can't bring their full force to bear, but that doesn't mean we can leave the Virus Storage Center alone, either. Even if it is a decoy, it doesn't change how much damage it could do."

"Do you think this is School, too?"

"No idea. It could be different group."

"Wh-what will we do? Which one should we head for?!"

"Ha-ha. That's a stupid question," grunted Accelerator, kicking the RV's side door with the bottom of his foot. He had already turned on his electrode, and the bundle of force, its vector altered, sent the metal door flying and bouncing wildly off the road.

Tsuchimikado, in spite of himself, shouted, "Accelerator!!"

"Dealing with those shitheads' decoy wouldn't be my thing. I'm going to District 23. If I wreck the big ground antenna they use to communicate with the satellites, the hacking will stop, too. Meanwhile, you two can do the grunt work."

After saying his piece, Accelerator jumped out of the RV without hesitation.

Flying in an unnatural trajectory, he passed over the median and came to a *thud* in the passenger seat of a convertible in the opposite lane. A normal person would have been crushed by the relative speed, but with all the vectors on his side, he had no problem.

In fact, the one who flinched was the convertible's driver.

"Whoa, what?! Wh-what?"

"I'll pay for gas and labor."

He heard a small clicking sound.

The driver felt something press against his cheek, but he didn't move his neck. However, in the rearview mirror, he saw the dark shine of what looked like a small gun.

"District 23. No detours."

7

I'm bored, thought Shiage Hamazura idly in the driver's seat of the parked car he'd stolen.

They were near Kirigaoka Girls' Academy in School District 18. The squarish building of the Particle Physics Institute was about a hundred meters ahead, inside which two organizations would be in the midst of a fierce battle—School, assaulting the institute, and Item, intercepting them.

As he gazed that way, Hamazura was muttering to himself. "Wow, crazy…They wrecked half the building. And was that a beam cannon I saw flying out? That was Shizuri Mugino, right? Full steam ahead as usual, that Level Five."

The reinforced concrete building was leaning over, sending columns of gray dust billowing out. Earthquake-like tremors reached all the way to Hamazura's stolen car.

A Level Five, eh...?

Had Ritoku Komaba, former leader of the armed Level Zero organization Skill-Out, really believed he could fight against *that* and win?

And did Skill-Out, now without that leader, still think they could fight?

"...Shit," cursed Hamazura, smacking the steering wheel in annoyance. Either way, now that he had fled Skill-Out and surrendered at the espers' gates, he didn't have the right to talk about it.

Frustrated, he opened the driver's side door and stepped out.

Considering how he had to prepare for Item so they could leave at any time, and how they'd started cracking down on no-parking zones, getting out of the car wasn't a very good plan. But Hamazura wanted a mood change at any cost.

Today was a holiday, so not many people were near Kirigaoka Girls' Academy. And there were three sports cars parallel parked on the road.

Hamazura's eyes lit up. *Whoa?! They're '89 Boosters!! They call it the emperor of four-doors!! W-wait, trying to steal such a remarkable car would just add to the risks...Aw, screw it, we're going home in a Booster today!!*

Imagining the low exhaust of the famous car, one that would make a celebrity's spirit waver, with strangely excited breaths coming from his nose, Hamazura took out his lock-opening tool. The sports cars were that much better than the rest—mature, high-grade vehicles, and he was just going up to one when...

"Hamazura!!"

"Y-yes?!"

Suddenly, a woman's shout came from right behind him, prompting him to hastily pocket the tool and turn around.

It was a female teacher wearing a green tracksuit.

Hamazura could tell how pretty she was despite the tracksuit…
Actually, she was so beautiful he wanted to shout, *Why a tracksuit,
it makes no sense, let's have sex!* but that wasn't the important thing.

She was an Anti-Skill officer—a fated enemy of Skill-Out.

Her name was Aiho Yomikawa, he recalled.

"Huh? What's the matter? I heard you were in custody after the
Dangai University database center incident. Wasn't you after all,
hmm? Well, that's good."

She was speaking casually for some reason, but not because they
were friends. Her kindness was one-sided—besides, he'd never have
a positive response for the woman who'd caught him fourteen times
in the city at night and thrown him into a police cell.

"What the hell are you doing here, you stupid hag?"

"Well, can't you see by looking?" said Yomikawa, pointing with
her thumb at the Particle Physics Institute in question.

Hamazura's hand went to his forehead. Item's ancillary organization was probably suppressing all sorts of things, but even they
couldn't perfectly hide an institute currently half-destroyed.

Yomikawa put her hands on her hips and smiled at him. "You
know, all I ever want is for you to be rehabilitated."

"What? What the hell are you talking ab—"

"Bent over, staring at a car's keyhole—for what? I *know* you don't
want to make me put you in cuffs out here in the open."

Hamazura's shoulders jolted. He couldn't afford to get locked up
here, so he shook his head back and forth. "Y-you've got it all wrong!
A baby!! They left a baby in the car!!"

"What?!" Yomikawa hurriedly approached, then stuck her hands
to the car's window and tried to look in.

The security system kicked in a moment later. The shrill wailing
of the alarm flustered the woman. Meanwhile, Hamazura whistled,
feigning ignorance, as a station wagon barreled toward him from
the Particle Physics Institute that was about to be destroyed.

The station wagon passed by, and then Shizuri Mugino came running from the institute, this time in pursuit. In one hand, she had another Item member, the airhead Rikou Takitsubo, by the neck.

They dove into the original four-door's rear seat, Mugino saying, "Hamazura!! You suck at hitting on women, so come on! Hurry and follow that station wagon!!"

"I wasn't hitting on her, you little twerp!!" Hamazura shouted back, returning to the car. He wished he could have had the '89 Booster, but he obviously couldn't steal it right in front of Yomikawa.

After he got into the driver's seat and the engine roared to life, Yomikawa finally shouted at him. "Hold on, Hamazura!! What's with that car?!"

"Can't you tell?! I got my license!!" he cried, the biggest lie of all, before flooring it so they could get away from the woman as quickly as possible. The engine and tires squealed at the sudden departure, and the family car began to roar down the street, leaving the tracksuit-clad teacher in the dust.

After leaving, Hamazura noticed something. "H-hey, what happened to Kinuhata and Frenda?!"

"It'll take more than that to kill them. That station wagon comes first!!" answered Mugino in irritation.

Hamazura saw through the rearview mirror that the hem of her short-sleeved coat was burned, and her cheek was swollen as though someone had punched her. He tried to imagine what had happened in the institute. "How'd that happen? Thought you were number four."

"They had a Level Five, too. Teitoku Kakine, that number-two pile of shit," she answered, petulant. "But we had something to say about that. We took out one of School's members. Didn't look like he was very strong inside the building."

As a war trophy, she shook a sturdy-looking mechanical piece of headgear at him. It went all around one's head like the rings of Saturn, with what looked like lots of plugs. Cords hung from them, but they'd been severed like mowed grass. He didn't know what the thing was used for, but he was horrifed at the blood stuck to it.

"Anyway, what are we chasing that station wagon for?"

"We've gotta crush the guy in it and grab their cargo."

"Cargo?"

"The Tweezers. Super-precise granule-sized object interference absorption manipulators."

"...You don't even want to explain, do you?"

"Anyway, it's what School was after!! You can chase that station wagon without knowing!! And can this car even catch up to it?!"

"It's all right." This wasn't Hamazura, but Takitsubo. She was sprawled out lazily in the back seat. "My Ability Stalker will perfectly track any involuntary diffusion fields I record. I can always search and find them, even if they escape outside the solar system."

"Exactly," muttered Hamazura. "They're not getting away as long as we have such a good navigation system. More importantly, what are we doing after we stop—"

He broke off. A huge truck had suddenly broken onto the road from the side.

"?!"

He didn't even have time to swing the wheel.

The gargantuan crane truck slammed headlong into the side of their four-door. The deafening *crash* rattled his brain. The sensors reacted, causing the steering wheel airbag to deploy, but given that it was a side impact, that didn't seem to matter.

Hamazura's car, which had been traveling straight, skidded to the side, pushed by the truck. It continued, breaking through the guardrail, running onto the sidewalk, and impacting the side of a building.

Caught between the yellow crane truck and the concrete wall, their car was completely unable to move.

They hadn't considered the show it would make or the collateral damage.

They wanted to kill them, plain and simple, no matter what it took.

"...Ow..."

"Damn...that was School!" snapped Mugino. "They must really want that station wagon to get away. They're stalling for time!!"

The crane truck backed up about ten meters. A girl who looked about fourteen was in the driver's seat behind the protective glass. Despite her petite, slender figure, she wore a short, open-backed dress like a barmaid.

Is she gonna ram us again? thought Hamazura, still reeling from the pain, but that didn't happen:

The girl pulled a lever, and the crane arm extended. Attached to its end wasn't a metal hook designed for lifting up objects.

It was a giant wrecking ball, meters across, for destroying buildings.

"Damn it!!" shouted Mugino, trying to open the rear door. It wouldn't open, though, because the chassis was twisted.

Hamazura used his own lever to put the passenger seat down. "Out through the windshield!! Hurry!!"

He broke open the slightly fractured front windshield and jumped out onto the hood. Mugino and Takitsubo scrabbled over the passenger seat to get to the front.

And then the iron ball started to swing like a pendulum.

With a low, loud rumble, the giant thing headed straight for them. After Mugino climbed onto the hood, Hamazura panicked while grabbing Takitsubo's hand to pull her out. But then the iron ball smashed into the car's side.

A tremendous crash rocked the air.

The impact blew the three off the hood and onto the ground. As Hamazura tried to raise his head, Mugino grabbed the back of it. The next moment, he went fully prone on the ground when the passenger car exploded, shooting flames everywhere. It was a near miracle they were all still alive.

The crane truck's engine gave an eerie rumble.

It was a reaction that paid no attention to the onlookers who had started to gather after hearing the explosion.

Shizuri Mugino tsked in frustration. "We're splitting into three."

"You're not gonna fight, Level Five?!"

"My goal is that station wagon and the Tweezers it's carrying. I'm not about to let some grunt buy any more time—and the girl inside has a really annoying power."

No sooner had she finished than she'd crossed the road and gone into a narrow alley.

Takitsubo, left behind, ran off in another direction.

Hamazura followed suit, thrusting himself into an alley between buildings and running for his life. But behind him, he heard wet footsteps.

Ah, shit, they caught up!!

His throat dried as he ran. The crane truck's operator was a girl with a small frame, but she was also a member of School, who had fought Item on even terms. He had no clue what kind of savage ability she had. Even Mugino, a Level Five, called it "annoying."

He continued to flee, running up a metal emergency staircase on the side of a building and going into a building on a random floor.

It looked like a student dorm.

He ran down the straight hallway, then heard the click of a door opening behind him.

They've got me...?! thought Hamazura, reflexively looking back.

It was indeed the small girl in the gaudy dress who had come out of the door. She held a handgun with an awfully small grip—it was made for women.

I'm dead!! Hamazura slammed his palm into a wall.

There was a button under it, and a steel shutter to protect against berserk espers dropped down like a guillotine. The girl's eyes widened a little before she swiftly brought her gun up and fired at Hamazura.

Bang, bang!! Two high-pitched shots.

Hamazura instinctively shut his eyes, but when he opened them again, there was no hole in the steel shutter. He looked at the monitor next to the button on the wall and saw the girl click her tongue in annoyance. She checked her gun.

It looked like she didn't have enough firepower to get past this shutter.

...Which means no matter what she tries to do, that woman can't get past this wall.

Relief washed over him.

Then he made the world's greatest look of sheer amusement at someone else's stupidity, raised his hands, shook his butt, and shouted, "Eee-hee-hee-hee-hee-hee-hee!!"

"…"

The girl in the dress, also looking at the monitor on the other side, put her gun away in a thigh holster and then reached behind her.

Her hand came away from her hip with a handgun whose barrel was as thick as a coffee can.

Actually, it was a small .40 grenade launcher.

"Oh. Oh shit…Now I'm gonna die for sure!"

Panicked, Hamazura tried to run farther down the hall, but the girl mercilessly pulled the grenade's trigger.

The shutter exploded and burst toward him, the fragments sending Hamazura five meters through the air.

"G-gahhh?!"

He somehow got himself up off the floor. Wobbling, holding the wall with one hand, he ran farther down.

Beyond that was a terrace—a dead end.

It didn't look like the hallway had stairs or an elevator on this end.

Past the railing was a drop about three stories high.

But the unknown girl from School was behind him.

He didn't need to think twice about his choice.

The three-story dive, absolutely!! Using my guts and willpower to jump is a hundred times better than standing up to someone obviously so strong! The small-fry have their own ways of surviving in this world!!

"Ha-ha!! I'm fine being a loooooooooooseeeeeeeeeeeer!!" He laughed as he ran, before jumping up onto the railing and leaping off the third story.

He hadn't looked down before he jumped.

Considering who was chasing him, he hadn't had time to check. And besides, if he had, he knew he'd be too scared to go through with it.

But three stories was no small height.

Damn, anything down there to cushion my fall?!

He looked down for the first time, in midair, to see a young mother happily pushing a stroller.

As Shiage Hamazura fell through the blue sky, his brain shouted *No!* with all its might.

"Gwoooooooooooooooohhhhhhh?!"

He started flapping his arms and legs, trying to airwalk himself out of the way. Fortunately, the move planted his large body five inches from the stroller.

Keee-raaack!! A sharp pain shot through his heels and ankles.

The young mother gracefully put a hand to her mouth in surprise. The baby in the stroller had forgotten to cry—he just stared, eyes wide.

"U-um...Who might you be?"

"The type of hero who falls out of the sky. It's dangerous—please get out of here, miss!" said Hamazura casually with a cool smile, bursting into another alley nearby.

8

"Tsk!!"

The fourteen-year-old in the gaudy dress put away her grenade launcher and handgun, placed her hands on the terrace railing, and glanced down at the road from the third story.

Her target with the stupid expression, the one she'd been chasing, was nowhere to be found.

Only a mother pushing a pram.

The girl took out her cell phone and called one of her allies at School.

"I lost sight of the target. The only thing here is a woman with a stroller...Do you think the target could have disguised himself as a young wife or a stroller?"

"Piss off, idiot" came the answer, so the girl ended the call and returned the phone to her pocket.

I let my guard down because I thought he was a nobody. I should have used my ability to begin with...

After one last hateful glance at the road, she gave up and turned around to look for the dorm's elevator.

9

Accelerator and the convertible headed for District 23.

Watching the panicky young man in the driver's seat next to him out of the corner of his eye, he took his phone out of his pocket.

After thinking for a moment, he punched in the three-digit number for reporting crimes to Anti-Skill.

When he held the phone up to his ear, though, he didn't get the operator at Anti-Skill's call center. Somebody else, the "telephone man" giving orders to Group, broke in.

"What do you think you're doing?"

"Just figured you'd have to intercept if I called 'em. If you don't like other people manipulating you, maybe change your own actions," he said with a shrug. "Anyway, shit's hitting the fan now. School, or whatever they are—they've been busy, too, eh? Looks like you can't completely control people just by talking to them on the phone, after all. If you couldn't find the time to butt into our business until now, you must be in a lot of trouble."

"Do you really think so?"

"Trying to smooth over your mistakes? Pathetic."

For a brief moment, both Accelerator and the man on the phone were silent.

Eventually, Accelerator got to the point: "The satellites being hijacked—I want their data. Especially *Altair II*. How powerful is the military laser on that thing?"

"Oh, was that all you wanted? I would think you'd want to ask more pressing questions."

"I don't trust you enough to put my life in your hands."

"A scathing critique," answered the composed male voice. *"Strictly speaking, the 'laser' on board the* Altair II *is an optical bombing weapon using white light waves. And it's not currently at a military stage, but an experimental one. It uses four-thousand-degree heat to*

burn a target, but the white light waves are strong enough to destroy cell nuclei just like ultraviolet rays. It causes a rapid onset of cancer."

A fool's weapon, thought Accelerator, but he didn't say it. "…Irradiation scope?"

"*It has a five-meter radius at minimum, and three kilometers at maximum. Its rapid-fire capabilities don't amount to much—you* could *maybe be able to fire it once per hour*," explained the man airily. "*Also, since the atmosphere refracts the white light in a random fashion, there is something of a variation regarding precision as well. It's still in the experimental phase, after all.*"

Accelerator said no more and hung up.

He stared at the phone and used the gun in his other hand to prod the driver again, thinking in the convertible's passenger seat, *It can burn a radius of three kilometers? What the hell are they gonna use that for…?*

Then his phone's ringtone went off.

He thought it was the telephone man again, but it wasn't.

"*Accelerator…that's you, right? It's Unabara.*"

He was keeping his voice down—actually, it was like he had his hand over the microphone, making it hard to hear.

"*I'm in disguise, so just talking in* this voice *is dangerous. I'd like to keep it short.*"

"What, slipping out of School's sight to whisper some secrets? Sorry, but I ain't helping you. I have to go stop the satellites from getting hacked. If you're gonna stop 'em, though, I'll gladly hear you out."

"*It's not School.*"

"Eh?"

"*Right now, I'm with Block, not School. They're the ones hacking the satellites.*"

"…"

According to Unabara, another organization besides School, one called Block, was using this day to plot criminal activity. "What a pain. What the hell happened to School trying to snipe Monaka Oyafune, then?"

"Please don't ask me…Wait, sniping?" repeated Unabara dubiously before getting the conversation back on track. *"They attacked the Virus Storage Center and the external connection terminals beforehand, so Academy City's network teams are in total confusion. At this rate…they'll finish the hacking in twenty minutes or so, and* Altair II *will fall into Block's hands."*

"Pieces of shit," spat Accelerator. "…Why doesn't District 23 shut down satellite control temporarily?"

"They probably have a few reasons. I would imagine they need at least an hour to freeze control if they went by the normal manual process."

The money that went into space-related business was on a completely different level. He understood they'd incur heavy damages if they cut off their link to their satellites, even temporarily. *But they should've cut the lines as soon as they saw the hacking attempt,* he thought with irritation.

"What the hell is Block trying to do with *Altair II?*"

"You've probably imagined, but…They want the optical weapon on board."

"A deal?"

"No, it's likely to be a direct attack."

Accelerator swore. "What's their target?"

"…District 13."

"District 13?" Accelerator frowned. Tsuchimikado and Musujime were headed to the external connection terminal there now. *Could they be trying to take out Group…?*

He thought about it for a moment, but decided that wasn't it. They went through all the trouble of hijacking a satellite—it was too big, and too unsure to do the job. Group wouldn't necessarily have jumped in to solve an incident if it happened.

"They're aiming there? The only important place there is the terminal. It's just a clump of kindergartens and elementary schools, isn't it?"

"Yes, but that is their target." Unabara sounded angry in his explanation, and his voice was low and bitter. *"District 13 has the most*

kindergartens and elementary schools in the city. Attacking it will let them massacre most of the city's youngest residents. What happens then? ...Frankly, if I were a parent, I wouldn't want my kids to go there."

" ..."

"Academy City is a city of students. No matter how many people live here, they'll all graduate one day. If they don't have any new students coming in, the population will decrease, and in the end, the city will cease to function."

"...So they want to slowly kill this city over decades?"

In reality, due to all the scientific technology Academy City commanded, from a financial point of view, it wouldn't go down that easily. An Academy City without any children, however, would still be equivalent to taking away its reason for existence.

Accelerator thought for a moment. "Can you stop it from there?"

"If I could, I wouldn't be asking you."

"Can we get everyone in District 13 to evacuate?"

"If we caused a panic, the kids could start falling all over one another throughout the district. And, lest you forget, today is a holiday. The teachers might be able to round up their own kids in the dormitories, but probably not all the ones outside playing."

"Useless. Looks like I'm just gonna have to wreck the ground antenna they use to talk to the satellite."

"I'll leave it in your hands. Meanwhile, I'll continue gathering information and get as much of it to you as I can," said Unabara, hanging up.

Accelerator put the cell back in his pocket and looked ahead at where the convertible was going. *Twenty more minutes, and they'll hijack Altair II.*

The car would get to District 23 in about ten minutes.

It didn't look like he had any time to relax.

"Hurry up. We've got a tight schedule," he said, poking the man with his gun again so he'd understand. The convertible faithfully sped up.

10

Kazari Uiharu and Last Order were on a District 7 station platform. This was apparently Last Order's first time on a train and she wanted to run all over, so Uiharu was holding her hand.

Seriously...Why did this happen to me?

At first, she'd given her the change from the taxi and handed her over to Anti-Skill, but somehow, with some sort of power, Last Order had broken out of the police station before Uiharu knew it and was prowling around the crowds of the city again. Uiharu figured she'd get the same result no matter how many times she left the girl with Anti-Skill, which was why she was helping her look for "the lost child" now.

I wonder what Last Order's ability is.

She'd only asked one question, and that resulted in finding out she had a nickname Uiharu couldn't begin to guess the origin of. Ability names came in two flavors: the simple ones that the school gave you, like *telekinesis* or *electromastery*, and the ones the students gave themselves, like *Railgun*. *She probably decided her own ability name, too*, thought Uiharu offhandedly.

"'Why won't the train come?' asks Misaka asks Misaka, tilting her head in confusion."

"It looks like a freight train is coming through. By the way, where do you think the lost child is right now?"

"'Hmm, well, I feel like he's coming this way,' answers Misaka answers Misaka, making little frowny lines on her forehead."

It seemed as though Last Order was using some kind of ability to search for the missing person, but it didn't appear very precise.

"'I hope we can find him like this,' says Misaka says Misaka, down in the dumps."

"It'll be okay."

"'Thank you for the super-lazy encouragement,' says Misaka says Misaka, thanking her anyway."

"So that your silly hair strand perks back up again, I have a present for you."

"'What?! You can detach your head flowers at will?!' says Misaka says Misaka, obviously shocked and stuff!!"

"Here you are. In the language of flowers, the hibiscus means *just give it a try.*"

"'And now you're boldly mistaking floral language,' says Misaka says Misaka, disturbed!!"

Last Order was going on and on, so Uiharu just smiled and nodded.

But then she heard the *vrooooom* of an engine. The young woman looked, but she couldn't tell what it was. The roar of exhaust told her it was probably a speeding sports car.

"I wonder where they could be going. Hopefully Anti-Skill pulls them over," she said with a sigh. Meanwhile, Last Order was frowning about something, groaning in thought.

11

Shiage Hamazura burst out of an alley and onto a large road.

Heaving, he stopped and looked around.

Boys enjoying their holiday were giving him dubious stares, but for now, he didn't see any attackers. He wiped the sweat on his brow, then went to a nearby vending machine and bought a cold can of oolong tea. Once he drank some, he finally let himself feel relief.

I-I'm alive. For now anyway...I wonder if the higher-up Item girls are okay? Gah. Damn it. I just want to run away from everything and go on vacation.

But then, in an act of coldhearted cruelty, his cell phone rang. He looked at the screen, then moaned.

It was Item's very own Shizuri Mugino.

"*Yo,*" she said. "*Since you picked up, I guess you're alive for the moment...Hopefully this isn't a mistake, and you aren't handcuffed with the phone pressed to your ear right now.*"

"Yeah, I'm alive...I drew the winning number, so I'm sure you're safe."

"*Thanks for that. It made things easy for me. Anyway, sorry, but could you come back right away? We have a lackey kind of job for you.*"

"A job?" said Hamazura, making a sour face.

Mugino continued—without skipping a beat:
"Got a dead person. I wanted you to deal with it."

12

The convertible with Accelerator in it parked near the District 23 terminal station.

He flung several paper bills at the young, dazed driver and exited the vehicle.

This was District 23's only station.

Many lines connected here, but its freight platform was at the very end. Despite this being a terminus, the lines went farther and farther down. They connected to a switchyard for servicing trains, and if one was carrying a lot of shipping containers, it could unload them there as well.

Accelerator, ever more conscious of his cane impediment, moved along the outside of the station building looking for the ground antenna. He was walking through a container depository, whose entrance was restricted to anyone not related to it.

A little under ten minutes. The schedule of a big-time artist.

He turned his attention to the electrode on his neck.

The satellite antenna is a few clicks from here, but I won't be able to take a regular train there.

His battery had about thirty minutes left in it. Though he would have liked to keep consumption to a minimum, he was going to have to use it now. Looking for a car at this point would be a hassle—it seemed faster to use his vector-transforming ability.

Accelerator's hand went for the switch on his neck.

"Oh my. We can't have this, now, can we?"

Suddenly, he heard a soft-spoken male voice behind him.

He didn't think anyone had been nearby.

"!!" Accelerator whipped out the gun tucked into his belt and turned around, but nobody was there.

His body wavered slightly on his modern-design cane.

He tried to use the tip of the gun in his left hand to push the electrode switch at his neck.

"I see that's your weakness."

But they grabbed his hand from behind.

"You may have an awfully strong ability, but you can't turn it on unless you flip the switch."

Before Accelerator could shake the hand off, *wham!!*—a heavy impact shot through the side of his head. It didn't feel like a punch from a fist. It was duller, like a metal pipe or a hammer.

He felt goopy liquid dripping down the side of his face.

"Arg! You…You're with Block?!"

"No, no. Not Block—I'm with Member."

The voice from behind him:

Member.

One of the five organizations, same as Group and School.

Shit, one thing after another…!!

"Although our interests don't align with theirs, I will be stopping you from destroying the satellite's ground antenna now."

As his head swam, Accelerator looked behind him, but once again there was nobody there.

But he didn't hesitate.

Still looking in that direction, he swung out his leg behind him and stomped down on his attacker's foot. The impact freed up his left hand, and without turning around, he pointed his gun behind him and fired three shots in sequence.

"…?! Damn!!"

After getting the sensation that he'd hit, Accelerator swiftly flipped his neck electrode's switch from *normal* to *ability usage* mode.

Then he whirled around.

But once again, nobody was there.

After a quick glance at his surroundings, he saw someone standing behind a startled railroad employee who had heard the gunshots and come over.

The man had light wounds, grazes to his side and thigh, both bleeding. His down jacket was torn, and the down inside was stained red. He looked like he was in high school, and he was pressing a big saw against the railroad worker's neck.

Accelerator snorted. "A teleport esper *who can only go behind other people*? That's a shitty power. Bet it's not even Level Four. Even though, if you can teleport your own body weight, you're normally that high."

The man growled.

"What a loser. You can't calculate eleven-dimensional values by yourself. You need to base it on other people's locations, or else it won't even activate. That power's too good for you."

"…This coming from the one relying on an electrode. In any case, this discussion is over. The professor wants me to do this, so I will stop you here."

"With a hostage? That's a shitty shield. Besides, I'm not after you anyway. I'm after the antenna."

"You wouldn't abandon a hostage," snorted his attacker, who Accelerator decided to call Kill Point. "If you would, you wouldn't be here trying to stop *Altair II* in the first place. If I use another person's life, you'll stop, won't you? And, well, if this isn't enough, I can make a much bigger sea of blood for you."

He pressed the saw against the young worker's neck, causing him to cry out.

"…You lack aesthetic," said Accelerator, slowly raising his gun. "You have none of the values of a villain."

"If you want to shoot me, you may want to stop. I do believe your gun has quite a margin for left-right error."

Now that you mention it, this thing does feel different. When Accelerator had shot at Kill Point when he was right behind him, the youth's hand had probably messed up the aiming mechanism. He could readjust it if he wanted, but the tense situation didn't give him any time for casual maintenance.

With Accelerator's skills, he could easily hit the target even if the sight was somewhat off.

But things changed if he was using a hostage as a shield.

You could act on intuition for some problems, but certainly not for others.

"I see. You're right—this situation sucks."

"What will you do, then?"

"This," he said, pointing the handgun at his own temple.

Before Kill Point had time to think, Accelerator, without hesitation, pulled the trigger.

Bang!!

"Guh...*ahhhhhhhhhhhhhhhhhhhhh*?!"

Kill Point keeled over backward.

There was a dark-red hole in his shoulder. He managed to dig down and endure it, but he still fell to the ground.

Accelerator had changed the vector of the bullet he'd shot at his head and directed it at Kill Point.

He waggled the gun in front of him, signaling for the railroad worker to move. The worker complied, rolling aside in a fluster, and then Accelerator pointed the gun forward again.

"Yeah, looks like the gun's aim is off."

His finger rested on the trigger.

"I can fix it by using my body to control its vector. My power is way more precise than this gun's stupid sight."

"Urgh..." Kill Point, face still pointed at Accelerator, used his eyes to observe his surroundings.

Accelerator saw that and sneered. "Go right ahead. I don't care who you warp behind. I'll still shoot you. Wherever you run, my next move will destroy you. So run, you pig. Hope you're impressed enough to be terrified now."

"...!" Kill Point's throat dried.

Accelerator ignored his expression. "Now let me teach you something about aesthetics."

He smiled, then quietly said:

"This is what a first-rate villain looks like, shithead."

Bang bang!! came the gunshots.

Kill Point resisted somewhat, but soon, he was no longer able to move.

13

Shiage Hamazura was in a big, open space.

The job waiting for him after shaking off his School pursuer was a suspicious one involving incineration.

Nobody was using this place at the moment. The building had been abandoned. For some reason, a giant, thick metal device was placed in the middle of its incomplete floor. About as large as a shipping container, it was an electric furnace used to dispose of experimental animals. Using immense heat, almost 3,500 degrees Celsius, it sterilized and burned their corpses and all sorts of microbes at once.

"…Wonder how it's powered. Seems too large for a wall plug," muttered Hamazura, looking at the big, out-of-place device.

His job was simple.

Open the oversized, steel, safe-like lid by its handle, toss the black sleeping bag inside, close the lid, and turn on the furnace. It had been tuned up beforehand, so all he had to do was press the conspicuously red ignition button.

He was better off not thinking about what was inside the bag. Item's Shizuri Mugino had warned him as much—not that Hamazura wanted to.

Item, School—as a lackey, Hamazura didn't think too much about what these top-secret teams were after. He was only here because he wouldn't survive in this city otherwise.

"…"

But every time he felt the black sleeping bag's oddly vivid weight, every time the spongy sensation came through the thick synthetic fabric and into his palms, he imagined the face of someone he'd never seen before. He forced himself to shrug it off, threw the bag into the furnace, secured the thick metal lid, and locked it.

Now he just had to push the red button.

The electrically created 3,500-degree heat would incinerate the body in minutes, even destroying DNA information, changing a person into nothing but ashes.

Hamazura considered, for a moment, the person in that sleeping bag, but still put his thumb on the button.

The passing thought gave him fear, and the tip of his thumb trembled—before his thumb pressed the button anyway.

Vrrrgg. The "disposal" began with a low rumble.

Hamazura gazed at it for a short while in silence, but he eventually took one step back, then another, then sat down on the dusty floor.

"…"

Who could have been in that sleeping bag?

It could have been a lackey Level Zero like Hamazura, and it could have been a much stronger esper. It wasn't necessarily a child, but he couldn't say for certain it was an adult. Was it an enemy? Mugino might even kill an ally if they blundered. He didn't know the story behind them, and they could have even been entirely unrelated, simply swept up in the chaos.

All of it burned to nothing.

Inside that thick metal machine, the person changed into something else entirely.

The ashes, no longer legally a "person," would disappear off somewhere. It might end up thrown into some garbage-disposing automation, blended into a mush, and shipped out as fertilizer. Even if someone found the ashes in the garbage, they wouldn't treat it as a person. The flesh had lost its DNA information, so it couldn't be used as physical proof.

"Hamazura."

Even when someone addressed him from behind, Shiage Hamazura couldn't move.

The electric furnace gave a few shrill beeps, letters coming up on its monitor to indicate the incineration was complete.

"Hamazura, what's wrong?"

It was probably Rikou Takitsubo, from Item, talking to him.

Her other name was Ability Stalker.

Unlike Hamazura, she was a very powerful Level Four esper. That power was what had led him astray, but he still envied it more than anything else.

"...What does human life mean?" said Hamazura, letting the energy drain from his body while simply staring at the furnace.

It wasn't like this was his first time seeing a corpse, and yet he felt considerable pressure in his heart.

"Damn it. When did Level Zero lives get this cheap...?"

He heard a voice say his name.

He stood, ignoring it, then opened the furnace lid and collected the ashes within.

Shiage Hamazura's job wasn't over yet.

14

Mitsuki Unabara was in a multi-tenant building in District 10.

The place operated as one of Block's hideouts.

Right now, there were three official Block members present, along with a dozen or so combat personnel belonging to their ancillary organization. Of course, Mitsuki Unabara had secretly switched places with one of their official members.

"...Not much longer now," said Tatsuhiko Saku, his big, bearlike body shifting.

A laptop was in front of him. It looked compact, but a cord came out of it and connected to what looked like an overstuffed sandwich. Apparently, it was almost fifteen store-bought CPUs stacked on top of one another, with liquid cooling tubes running through the gaps between them.

The brawny woman, Teshio, her eyes on the screen, spoke to Saku. "Has it worked?"

"Mostly, yeah. Thanks to the dummy we used on the Virus Storage Center, District 23 thinned out, too." Saku spoke without looking at his companion. "Now we can say good-bye to this shitpile of a world with Aleister's stink permeating every last corner. This is our first step in that direction."

He wasn't giving a speech; not many people were particularly listening. He was practically talking to himself.

Even so, Unabara could feel strength in his words.

"But this is just the first step. There's a long way to go before reaching our goal, but still, it's the first step."

"..." Unabara casually glanced over at the clock on the wall. It would only be a few more minutes before the satellite was hijacked.

He'd gotten no message from Accelerator. He didn't know if he'd managed to destroy the ground antenna. Unabara turned his attention to his inside pocket, thinking on the Spear of Tlahuizcalpantecuhtli within.

...I could just destroy that computer, but if I do, it would be at the cost of my life.

His palms began to clam up with perspiration.

He didn't have much time to make a decision.

But then, Megumi Teshio said, "It would appear, there has been some action, in District 23. A number of on-site Anti-Skill officers, have gone down. But as far as I can tell, from intercepting communications, there is no danger to their lives, the likes of which, would cause rescue teams any confusion."

Everyone there looked at the woman.

"We can understand, by connecting the points, at which the Anti-Skill officers went down, that they're lined up, straight from the terminal station, to the ground antenna. Such incredible speed. It certainly doesn't seem, like he walked."

"Who, and from where?" asked Saku.

"Nobody honest, I'm sure. Is it one of Aleister's dogs, part of Member?"

"No," said Teshio simply. "Group, most likely. I remember, that white-haired kid. If I recall correctly, he's the Level Five esper, who came here recently."

...She remembers seeing him? wondered Unabara, but the question was soon answered.

Teshio had a small business instrument in her hand, a device with somewhat more functionality than a cell phone. And on its screen was a rough video, probably taken by a telescope.

According to the number in the corner, it was magnified four thousand times. One of Block's subordinates was probably outside District 23 recording it right now.

On the monitor, it showed Accelerator heading for the ground antenna.

With his ability, destroying the twenty-five-meter-across parabola would be as easy as swatting a fly.

And he didn't think Block was about to wait quietly for it to happen.

Not good—or wait, maybe it's fine…? Even if he was captured, they couldn't accurately snipe him from that range.

"What now?" asked Megumi Teshio curtly, awaiting instructions.

Everyone's gaze turned to Saku's bear-like frame.

"That much is obvious," came the reply, not particularly hurried, sending tension through Unabara.

They had a plan to deal with him.

Could there be a wireless bomb or something set up near the ground antenna? he thought, before the bear of a man gave a different answer.

"We just have to pray that he succeeds."

For a moment, Mitsuki Unabara couldn't understand it.

But soon his thoughts recovered.

No…That was their aim?!

"Breaking through District 23 would have been too difficult for our abilities. Still, we can't get anywhere while that ground antenna is still up. We needed a more capable idiot to help us."

"Actually, we might have been, thinking too much. The Level Five is, already at the antenna."

"Someone watching from 'above' probably cleared the way for him. The district is loaded with air force-related weapons. Normally, unmanned weapons, namely HsAFH-11 attack helicopters, would have gone to intercept him. 'Course, that Level Five could probably wipe them out, too."

We were so preoccupied with the optical weapon on board that we forgot Altair II's main usage—to monitor Academy City and the surrounding areas...Taking away that ground antenna doesn't only disable its ability to attack—it paralyzes all its surveillance functions, too!!

Unabara's thoughts went to the cell phone in his pocket, but no matter how he looked at it, he couldn't get away to contact anyone.

Teshio's eyes went to Saku. "They're actually useful, right? The ones standing by, outside the wall, of District 11?"

"This is one project those kinds of guys are the right choice for. What? You're not worried about getting unrelated people wrapped up in this, are you?"

The big man stopped the hacking program on his laptop, which they no longer needed, then turned the machine off and tossed it to one of the underlings.

"Let's go. Five thousand mercenaries are waiting on the other side of that wall."

October 9, 1:29 PM.

With the destruction of the ground antenna that communicated with the satellites, they all lost function.

Academy City, without its surveillance system in the skies, had lost a significant chunk of its defenses.

INTERLUDE TWO

School's Level Five esper, Teitoku Kakine, was in District 4.

The district was home to many eateries, even in Academy City, with a host of other facilities related to food as well. He had hidden their station wagon in one of them, a meat freezer warehouse.

"No sign of Item. I guess they got away for now."

Kakine opened the station wagon's rear door and checked inside.

There was no frozen meat. Instead, there was a giant metal box the size of a small closet.

"...So these are the Tweezers...," groaned the driver, one of School's subordinates.

A grin came to Kakine's face. "Superfine object interference absorption manipulators. In short, mechanical fingers that can grab tiny particles smaller than atoms. That's why they're called Tweezers."

All matter in the world was composed of several elementary particles combined with one another. The Particle Physics Institute had apparently been running experiments where they purposely removed elementary particles from objects to create unstable matter.

Normal robotic arms had a hard time grabbing anything smaller than atoms. But with the Tweezers, they created a way to "suck them out" using magnet force, light waves, and electricity.

"But one wrong step and they could have caused an atomic collapse."

"What?"

"Nothing," said Kakine. "Getting a new sniper to replace the one Item killed, shooting Oyafune—a lot of work went into this, but it seems like we got a lot out of it. That's a relief."

The driver stared at the big device for a few moments. "But what on earth are you going to do now that you've stolen it?"

"What do you mean, what? Exactly what it's meant for. I want to grab something really small. *It'll give me a way to break through to Aleister.*"

"???" The driver looked confused, but Kakine didn't bother to explain more. He opened a toolbox in the station wagon's trunk, took out a screwdriver, and started loosening the Tweezers' screws.

"A-are you going to break it?"

"I'm making it better," said Kakine, annoyed. "You want to know why this thing's so big? It's to prevent theft. If you just had the bare minimum parts, you could make it smaller."

The clacking sounds continued for a while.

Soon, the Tweezers were remade, changed into its original, optimized form.

Kakine now held what looked like a metal glove. Long, glass-like nails came out of the index finger and middle finger, and inside the nails were even smaller parts that appeared to be metal stakes. There was a small monitor the size of a cell phone screen on the back of the hand.

From what it looked like, it extracted elementary particles from the glass nails, then performed measurements with the metal stakes.

"Y-you can make it that small?"

"Well, it's brand-spanking-new Academy City tech. If they go too far, that's their problem, eh?" answered Kakine, putting the glove on his right hand and checking it. "Great, feels good...Contact the others. We're moving to the next phase."

"Right away," nodded the driver, and that was when it happened:

Ba-geen!! A sharp, metallic sound rang out through the warehouse.

Kakine and the driver looked over to see a square hole cut into the thick warehouse wall like a door. Bright midday sunlight shone in through it, as the dismembered section of wall fell inward.

Nobody was outside.

But the attacker was definitely aiming for them.

"Gyah...*Gwahhhhhhhhhhh?!*" the driver screamed suddenly.

Kakine looked over just as the skin on the driver's face disappeared. Then his fat and muscle disappeared, too, in that order, and in the end even his brain vanished as well, leaving only clothing and bones to fall to the ground.

The clattering sound was light, like plastic.

Kakine frowned slightly.

"Teitoku Kakine? It would be a waste to lose a Level Five right now."

A voice from an unclear direction came to Kakine's ears.

Staying alert in all directions, he activated the Tweezers he'd just finished rebuilding. *Didn't think I'd have to use it so soon.* "...Group, is it? Or maybe Item?"

"Unfortunately, I'm with Member. By the way, young man, have you ever smoked a cigarette before?" The middle-aged male voice, source unknown, was calm. "You know how when you take one out of the box, you tap the box with your finger? When I was a child, I didn't understand the point. Still, it made a fine show. That's why I started tapping on my boxes of cookies."

"Yeah?"

"That's exactly what you're doing right now."

"Talking down to me? Looks like you really want me to make your corpse a good one."

A mechanical blip came from the Tweezers equipped to his right hand.

He looked at the monitor, and among the air particles it had gathered were, it seemed, little droplets of machines. Something clearly artificial had mixed into the electron-microscopic world.

"Nanodevices? You plucked out every single cell he had."

"No, *mine* aren't that excessive. They don't have circuits, or power. They're simple granules of reflective alloy; they only show a specific reaction in response to specific frequencies. I call them the Bowing Images, though."

The middle-aged male voice, which he still couldn't locate, continued,

tone vaguely annoyed. "But if you use several frequencies, you can control it, kind of like using a television remote to control a radio-controlled car. Normally, I attach them to bacteria in the air, and let the bacteria disperse naturally."

Whooshing noises surrounded Teitoku Kakine.

His eyes darted all around, but before he could find an escape route, the Bowing Images attacked.

Member's "Professor," having taken the mechanical beast along with him, stood relaxed outside the freezer warehouse. In his hand, on a small device, it showed the operation status of the program controlling the Bowing Images.

Right then, he was in a bazaar built along the sidewalk. In that area, you could only park your car on the road if it was for business use; food trucks, such as crepe stands, lined the street.

The mechanical beast next to him spoke. "Our superiors' information was right. He was in the District 4 freezer warehouse."

"That goes to show how strong they are. Academy City is their territory. It's spilling over with strange technology. There's nowhere to run, no matter how much we struggle."

He took a bite into a tropical fruit, red enough to seem poisonous, and continued quietly, "It was my twelfth winter when I lost all hope in the arts."

The mechanical beast listened quietly to the professor's words.

"I admired European architecture. I was in love with the scale, of using so much time and manpower to construct a work of art, to complete just one piece of beauty. But at the same time, I found it hard to understand. It's easy to gaze at the outside of a building and say how beautiful it is. But when you try to understand the design in-depth, down to its fundamental layers, you need a ton of time because of the building's scale. Quite frankly, it's tiring—there are too many points of interest."

"Is that why you discovered a connection with mathematics?"

"Indeed," the professor said, nodding. "Ah, numerical formulae. They have no excess, they're like machines, they hold a rainbow of aesthetic in the smallest space possible. The very formulae have an artistic beauty, but also the poetic beauty of a haiku. And all these aesthetics can be enjoyed just by unraveling a single line, leaving nothing left over...I want to find the beauty hidden in the world's crevices, to take that wonderful beauty and cherish and adore it. I would throw myself at the feet of my worst enemies to do so—even if it meant others calling me Aleister's dog."

The professor looked at his wristwatch.

His Bowing Images would be almost finished eliminating the hostile.

Aleister probably wouldn't look kindly upon him bringing down the second-place Level Five, but if he made a new Level Five in his place, it would solve the problem.

"Let's get going. We need to retrieve the Tweezers and crush the other official members from the rebellious School, and then our job is done."

"What about our own Saraku going down near the District 23 terminal station?"

"If I recall, Accelerator was calling him Kill Point. Well, if he's not dead, we can leave him be. If you have time, you should retrieve him," said the professor.

But the mechanical beast didn't answer.

Because, with an explosive *boom*...

...the freezer warehouse burst apart from within, into tiny pieces.

The extreme force shattered all the windows in the surrounding buildings. People screamed, ran around in a frenzy trying to escape, causing minor chaos among the food trucks at the bazaar.

The dust billowed up.

Teitoku Kakine pierced through the cloud, slowly walking over to them.

There wasn't a scratch on his body.

Not one.

"Yo. You said you lost hope when you were twelve, right?"

The professor frantically gave orders to his Bowing Images, but he got no response. The explosion had cleared away the particles in the air, and his nearby airborne Images had been blown far away.

Kakine looked at the professor's desperate expression and chuckled. As he chuckled, he said this:

"Time to lose hope again, asshole."

Item

Leader

SHIZURI MUGINO

SAIAI KINUHATA

FRENDA

RIKOU TAKITSUBO

Member

Leader

PROFESSOR

UNKNOWN

UNKNOWN

SARAKU

Group	 MOTOHARU TSUCHIMIKADO	MITSUKI UNABARA	 AWAKI MUSUJIIME	 ACCELERATOR

School	Leader  TEITOKU KAKINE	 UNKNOWN	 CHIMITSU SUNAZARA	 UNKNOWN

Block	Leader  TATSUHIKO SAKU	 MEGUMI TESHIO	 YAMATE (UNABARA)	 TETSUMOU

Transmission data from "UNDER_LINE"

CHAPTER 3

In a Land Where Abilities Are Forbidden
Reformatory.

1

A cold sweat broke out all over Yoshio Baba.

He was in Member, just like the professor. He'd been remotely controlling a quadrupedal walking robot to support said professor, but…

"That bastard…Damn you! How could you die so quickly?!" he swore.

But a dead man wasn't going to help him. He tsked, then began preparing to withdraw. He was in School District 23—in an underground town under development hundreds of meters belowground, a nuclear shelter for VIPs called Summer Resort. Originally, it was the private property of one of the General Board members, but they almost never used it, so Baba had taken it upon himself to disable the security systems and make himself at home. The "resort" had grand, villa-like furnishings, and even a special line for Net conferencing. It was a wonderful environment for Baba, a hacker. He'd had his eyes on it for a while, but getting to actually experience it that day was really something else.

But this wasn't a perfectly safe place, either.

The enemy's ability was unknown, but if it was a form of teleportation, the walls' thickness wouldn't do him much good. The person to easily kill the professor had been one of only seven Level Five espers in Academy City. Someone like that could tear open the shelter door with brute force. Plus, it was possible they'd bring some brand-new equipment, like an anti-bulkhead shotgun.

They'll notice this place soon. All I can do is get out before that happens!!

He stuffed several devices, most importantly a laptop computer, into his bag. Then, after grabbing a sheaf of papers preserved inside the Summer Resort on the way, he headed for the exit elevator.

But when he pushed the button, there was no response.

"...?"

He headed for the door to the staircase instead, but that was locked, too, and wouldn't open.

Then the lighting in the shelter changed to bright red. Dumbfounded, Baba looked at the control monitor for shelter safety. On it was displayed "For safety reasons, all locks have been set."

When Baba's eyes nearly popped out of his head, he began to hear something strange:

*Shhhhhhhhhhhhhh...*It sounded almost like a waterfall.

It was considerably loud. After all, it was coming through the shelter's thick walls.

"Water...?!"

Terrible images raced through Yoshio Baba's mind.

If someone had used a fire hose or something and was pouring tons of water into the elevator shaft or underground stairs...

With such an immense water pressure against every door in the shelter, neither human hands nor the monitor's automatic controls could make them move again. And even if they did open, an overwhelming devastation from terrible quantities of water would be waiting for him.

There had been a teleport-type esper in Member, Saraku—whom Accelerator called Kill Point—but he'd been taken down in District 23 already, too. He wouldn't save him from this situation.

"Damn!!"

Baba frantically took the laptop out of his bag and booted it up, before connecting to the Net conference line and contacting another person in Member. Now that the professor and Kill Point were gone, he only had one ally left—a girl the professor had dubbed a sorcerer.

But the answer from his ally, who had learned of things through text messages, was very simple.

"The data you were collecting on the other organizations was saved on another server, right? I just need that, not you. I'm chasing down my own enemies—I don't have time to wipe your ass for you."

"You piece of shit!!" exclaimed Baba out of reflex. He considered abandoning all shame and reputation and calling their ancillary organization or the "voice on the telephone" for help, but then his laptop screen suddenly froze. A bad premonition began to set in as he tried to get it working again, but the cable for the line must have been physically cut. That was why the information stopped updating.

He pulled the cord out of the laptop and wailed. He tried to force himself to think optimistically, but no matter how he tried, he always returned to the same answer.

He was trapped.

As Baba admitted that fact to himself, the thick walls, which had seemed reliable before, came at him from all directions with a dark pressure. How many rations were down here? Was there enough oxygen? When would help arrive? Would help ever arrive?

With his panic accelerating just from the whirling images in his mind, he eventually slammed his bag on the floor, tore at his hair with his hands, and screamed like an animal.

In the safest place in the world, which actually had enough oxygen and food to last him another year without trouble, Yoshio Baba's mind began to disintegrate, eaten alive by the beast called imagination.

2

School District 11.

Since Academy City wasn't on the sea, goods could only come to it two ways: by land or air. And District 11, which was on the outer wall, served as a front door to the largest of those land routes.

That was where the members of Block, including Mitsuki Unabara, were.

Squared-off buildings were lined up around him. Unlike normal buildings, these had no walls, which made them look like parking garages. Academy City–made self-driving electric cars waited inside for shipments.

District 11 exchanged over seven thousand metric tons of goods per day, and its "town of warehouses" was immense.

Control near the gates directly managing entry and exit was very strict, but they couldn't keep an eye on every nook and cranny of the warehouse town. This district probably closely resembled a pier at a normal port. Just like the fondly remembered mafia movies of old, it was quite often used as a spot for shady deals, night after night.

And...

So that's the outer wall...

Unabara directed his gaze at it.

Despite being easily over five hundred meters away, the wall was giant, palpably displaying its grandeur. Like the Great Wall of China, there was a path on top of the wall, and if you checked with binoculars, you'd see oil drum–shaped security robots going back and forth.

Certain sorcerers had climbed over the outer wall. However, that was because the wall's security was protected by *scientific* sensors, and tended to be weak to *magical* ploys (...or, at least, Unabara wanted to believe that. He didn't want to think Aleister's calculations went that far, and that he was toying with them).

Presently, though, because their satellite-based surveillance was gone, the security had grown incredibly weak. Now, even regular people who didn't use magical means would have a chance.

Five thousand mercenaries, summoned by Saku, would be waiting on the other side.

They'd probably been waiting for Academy City's satellite security to cut out, hiding in nearby buildings or scattered cars.

Yet despite knowing that, Unabara was never blessed with the chance to relay that information.

Those in Group didn't know of this place. Even the city's higher echelons might not have figured it out. They'd personally resolved the immediate threat of attack from the satellite, so it was likely they felt relieved.

Block's objective is to let those mercenaries in and do…what? Where on earth do they plan to attack…?

"Yamate. Are you, worried about something?" asked Megumi Teshio suddenly from nearby.

Yamate was the name of the man Unabara was disguised as. "No…," he answered shortly.

Normally, he did at least a week-long investigation of the person he would impersonate. He couldn't make any careless remarks before he knew more about his model's personality.

Teshio didn't seem to think much of Unabara's attitude, either.

She'd probably decided he was nervous, since they were in the middle of a huge operation.

"Sure, we got rid of the satellites, but those security robots are still up and rolling around," said Tatsuhiko Saku.

Teshio turned to face the bearlike man. "Is there, a problem?"

"Nah. Those bots don't have any firearms, so they won't be an obstacle. We just have to get the timing right, and they can cross the wall."

"Why *aren't* they armed?" asked Unabara, deciding to get into the conversation.

Saku glanced at him. "Bunch of reasons. The robots up there are always protecting the periphery. They can't risk malfunctions causing them to shoot people walking around outside the wall. Then there's the ammunition issue. That type of robot isn't designed to swap out magazines, so once it runs out, that's it."

"Then even if they are spotted, they would only, trigger an alarm?" said Megumi Teshio, sounding deflated. "In that case, instead of going through the work, couldn't we have just, staged a brute-force breakthrough?"

"Nope. Those outer wall security bots have a special comm line. Once the warning comes in, they'll send a message directly to

District 23 control and call in their unmanned attack helicopters. Right now, the main one being the Hexawing, a brand-new model that showed up at the interception weaponry show. If they get spotted, we'll have problems."

Saku glanced at the watch around his thick arm. "In ten minutes, the security robots on the wall will rotate out."

"…"

"They run on electricity, after all. They can't operate twenty-four hours a day, so they've gotta recharge somewhere. Which means the ones currently operating will naturally split away from the ones recharging."

Because of this guard rotation, once per day, a twenty- to thirty-minute gap would open up in the robot-based wall security.

Typically, that wouldn't be a problem.

Because normally, Academy City's satellites kept a never-ending watch over the city and its periphery.

But not right then.

Those twenty minutes would turn into a full-blown blackout.

"Get as many cars as possible. And don't forget to swap their license plates," instructed Tatsuhiko Saku to Block's underlings. "The electric self-driving cars for planned shipment parked in the garages—we need to transport five thousand people in them, after all."

3

The twenty minutes of blackout began.

In the District 11 warehouse town, surrounded by squarish parking garage buildings, Mitsuki Unabara directed his attention to the obsidian knife in his inside pocket.

He wouldn't get the chance to contact Accelerator and Group.

Even if he did so right now, there was no guarantee they'd come running here right away.

From what he'd gleaned by eavesdropping on Tatsuhiko Saku's radio chatter, the mercenaries were throwing ropes up the wall to secure a path. And Unabara could already see several scaling the wall by peering through binoculars an "ally" had handed him.

...*I have to do it*, he thought.

The Spear of Tlahuizcalpantecuhtli reflected Venus's light, then dismantled whatever that light touched. It was a projectile spell. As long as the light directly hit, it would break apart any kind of matter, but he couldn't aim for multiple targets at the same time.

The problem is finding where to aim that one attack.

There were five thousand mercenaries in total.

Aiming the Spear at them wouldn't mean much. It would just reduce the number of perpetrators to 4,999.

He could aim at Block's official members.

...Taking down Saku, the commander, would have some effect, but now that their plan had already progressed this far, losing their leader probably wouldn't completely stop them.

I need a more effective point..., thought Unabara, taking his eyes from the binoculars. *A target that would bring this all to a halt in one strike...*

He then averted his gaze from the climbing mercenaries and set it in a completely different direction.

An intense tremble ran through him, but he didn't have the time to hesitate.

...*It's there!!*

He slipped his obsidian knife out.

The light of Venus reflected toward...

...the parking garage right next to them.

Although Tatsuhiko Saku and Megumi Teshio saw him bring out the obsidian knife, they just stared blankly. They had no knowledge of sorcery, so they didn't understand what he was doing.

But when Unabara suddenly broke out into a run toward the building, and then the parking garage began to collapse without warning, they put two and two together.

A sharp *ba-keen* rang out.

The reinforced concrete parking garage in Unabara's path began to break into pieces, as though the pillars supporting it were being pulled out one by one. Every time one of the building fragments collided with the ground, it smashed the asphalt and whipped up clouds of dust.

"What…? *Yaaaaaaaaaaaaaaaamate!!*"

Unabara heard Saku's scream from behind.

The sound of several guns being leveled at him followed.

Unabara ignored them and ran.

With clatters and rumbles, the giant concrete fell at him like a cave-in. The pieces actually shielded Unabara's back from the rain of gunfire. A self-driving electric car, crushed in midair, stabbed into the ground with its sharp cross section. The only good thing was the lack of an explosion, since it didn't use gasoline.

Unabara pointed the obsidian knife down.

Venus's light destroyed the ground. He jumped down into a sewer to try to protect himself from the concrete falling above.

However, there were so many fragments that they began to crush the sewer itself, quickly approaching Unabara.

"*Ohhhhhhhhhhhhhh!!*"

He ran, tumbling, then actually tripped and fell, but still got up and crawled forward.

Eventually, the rumble of the parking garage's collapse ended.

The impact had damaged every part of this sewer; the area behind him was blocked, of course, but even in front of him was collapsed, too.

The ceiling had crumbled, and bright light shone in from above.

Unabara looked up at the dusty-blue sky as he grabbed a ruined wall with his hands and climbed up.

There, he saw…

4

District 23's air control center received an emergency signal from District 11 near the outer wall.

But the unmanned helicopters wouldn't immediately launch from there. It was possible the signal was incorrect. Final judgment was left to an operator, who would personally connect the line's plug and input the command. Only then would the helicopters take defensive action.

Normally, there was a complicated manual, dozens of pages long, waiting.

But the control center, having temporarily lost hold of the satellites, had taken up a special security status. The operator didn't do a single check against the manual before promptly pushing the plug in and issuing the dispatch order.

Three unmanned attack helicopters were standing by on the vast asphalt ground.

They were HsAFH-11s, code-named Hexawings.

When they got the order, they increased the rotational frequency of their blades and slowly lifted off.

5

The unmanned Hexawings flew through the air above District 11.

They were similar to AH-64 Apaches, with "wings" along either side of the fuselage for loading machine guns and missiles.

The definition of a helicopter is an aircraft that generates lift using rotors attached on its vertical axis and uses the angle of those "wings" to move.

By that definition, you could certainly call the Hexawing a helicopter.

However, whether or not you could really call the Hexawing a helicopter—when it contained two rocket engines as auxiliary power sources and could, at max speed, reach Mach 2.5—was up for debate.

The unmanned attack helicopters' arithmetic processors first confirmed the collapse of the parking garage, and then the group of suspicious persons scaling the outer wall of Academy City just a few hundred meters away.

There were about five thousand.

Acknowledging them as hostiles, their processors quickly and automatically began to attack.

"Damn that Yamate bastard…!!" shouted Tatsuhiko Saku bitterly as the Hexawings moved.

With a metallic *ga-shoo*, the wings on either side of the machines split into three. They were indeed six-winged, and the slender wings even had joints in them. They pointed their weapons in six different directions with movements like human arms.

"Here they come!!" shouted Megumi Teshio.

The Hexawings' machine guns began to wail.

It was less a rake of gunfire and more a series of blasts.

Megumi Teshio dove behind the station wagon they'd been using, but then the shield took the machine gun fire, becoming dented and misshapen. An orange glow engulfed the vehicle, and a moment later, the whole thing blew. Teshio was sent flying meters back, but after hitting the ground, she ran off to look for another shield.

"Frictional bullet tips?!"

Super-heat-resistant metallic bullets, with special grooves in them so they could use air resistance to heat up to 2,500 degrees Celsius. When one hit armor, it would quickly burn up circuitry and fuel from within.

Hundreds of meters in front of her, the helicopters had begun their attack on the mercenaries scaling the outer wall as well.

Whole groups blasted apart like popped balloons. It was so terrible that she could see the crimson splashes even from her distance. Other mercenaries who were safe were pushed by the force of the blasts and starting falling off. They were strafing the ones who could counterattack first.

At this rate, they'd kill everyone.

Megumi Teshio shouted over to Tatsuhiko Saku, who was some distance away. "The mercenaries, should give up!! They may be moving, as a large group, but from above, they're nothing but a giant target!!"

"There's five thousand of them! How hard do you think we worked for this single moment?! Are you telling us to let it go to waste?!"

"They mistakenly think, they've been betrayed, anyway. The ones, on the other side of the wall, won't be coming now. We're getting, the ones who fell inside, and leaving!!"

"Yamate, you bastard...I'll kill you, I swear it!!" bellowed Saku from his thick throat.

"Ha-ha...I should have expected as much from lethal weapons that cost two hundred fifty billion yen each...," muttered Unabara to himself, having crawled out of the sewers and behind some rubble. He was the one who'd done it, but the scene was still spine-chilling.

He looked into the distance and saw several groups hoisting anti-air missiles on their shoulders and firing them.

But the Hexawings fired things that looked like softballs at the missiles. Iron sand exploded from them, and a high-tension current went through. An entire area, twenty meters square, turned into an electrical current zone, the missiles flying into it exploded of their own accord.

In response to the attack, the Hexawings fired a barrage of anti-surface missiles, transforming the entire plane into a sea of crimson flames.

For now, it looks like I prevented the mercenaries' entrance as much as I could, but...

Unabara pressed his back to a giant concrete chunk and covered his face with his hands.

He ripped away the protective skin talisman he'd used to create the false countenance of Yamate and pulled his Mitsuki Unabara face back on. A moment later, his entire physique and voice, not just his face, had switched to a different person.

He didn't need the Block's face anymore.

The problem is how to survive this. Those Hexawings' arithmetic processors probably won't object to labeling me an enemy, too.

For now, the Hexawings' objective was the elimination of the soldiers scaling the outer wall.

If he stayed hidden until they left, the helicopters would leave on their own, but...

A *brat-rat-rat-rat-rat* sound splitting the air squeezed Unabara's heart.

He looked out from behind the rubble and saw a Hexawing taking aim at him.

"I suppose it won't be…that easy!!" he shouted, no sooner than jumping out and swinging his obsidian knife.

It reflected Venus's light, triggered the Spear of Tlahuizcalpantecuhtli, and broke apart the Hexawing in a surprise attack.

Another Hexawing, notified of what happened, pointed one of its wing-mounted machine guns at him. It was positioned so that its flank was facing him, but that didn't pose an issue. Its six-jointed guns aimed at Unabara.

The Spear of Tlahuizcalpantecuhtli could break any object apart.

However, it couldn't aim for multiple targets at once.

"Argh!!"

He quickly tried to dive behind cover, but the helicopter was far, far faster.

The Hexawings he'd called here were trying to blow him to bits.

So this is the end…!!

Unabara brought up his obsidian knife, knowing it was futile, but before he could do anything—

Bang!!

A white-haired Level Five dropped down hard on top of the unmanned helicopter. He grabbed the fast-spinning rotors and stopped them. The Hexawing couldn't deal with such an insane action, and it fell to the ground and exploded everywhere.

"He" came walking slowly out of the flames.

The tension finally left Mitsuki Unabara's body. "Accelerator…"

"Heard something was goin' on near the outer wall, so I came. Man, what a shit show," said Accelerator, sounding bored, returning his electrode switch to normal and leaning on his cane. "Looks like Tsuchimikado and Musujime cleaned things up at the external connection terminal, and I thought busting their satellite antenna would put an end to things. And now control is crying there's some invaders making a mess of things on the outskirts."

"Ha-ha. I suppose you realized they were using you, too."

"You didn't call the Hexawings for no reason, yeah? Where's Block?"

"They got away," said Unabara, wiping his sweat. "I think they brought about a hundred of the mercenaries from outside."

"From outside...Damn it, that's what the satellite thing was for? Block, Member, mercenaries...Too many shitheads running around," grumbled Accelerator, realizing he'd been played. "Still, didn't think we'd let people break in. What a bunch of useless idiots."

"To be fair, they said they had about five thousand at first."

"Here's a neat little expression. A miss is as good as a mile."

A Hexawing sliced through the sky, interrupting him.

This time, though, it wasn't aiming at them.

After a general scan of the area, the last remaining helicopter began to fly back toward District 23.

"Looks like they're done cleaning up."

"They probably don't want their allies breaking another one," said Unabara, shrugging. "They apparently cost two hundred fifty billion each."

6

Motoharu Tsuchimikado, Accelerator, Awaki Musujime, and Mitsuki Unabara all met up in the District 11 warehouse town. Mitsuki Unabara, who had been out of the loop until now, asked Tsuchimikado, "What's an 'external connection terminal'?"

"Just some building. The paperwork would have been a pain, and they wouldn't answer us, so Musujime and I blew up their core. Anyway, there's three more terminals, so there shouldn't be any issues with the access situation."

Musujime, who had been with Tsuchimikado, asked Unabara, "Should I take this to mean Block were the masterminds behind these incidents? I think I remember School being the ones behind the attempted Monaka Oyafune assassination."

"It doesn't seem like Block and School were directly cooperating," he replied. "The two organizations were acting on their own, causing those incidents independently. Although, they probably had some contact due to Management's introductions and such."

"Shit. Member's been crawling around, too. This is getting out of hand."

As Tsuchimikado listened to Unabara and Accelerator, he moved his gaze elsewhere.

Blood and flesh were sprayed around the outer wall, but survivors still remained. Mercenaries unable to die, unable to run—and not recovered by Block, either.

"All right, question time," said Tsuchimikado bluntly. "What were you five thousand mercenaries going to attack?"

"Wh-what do you mean?"

"Five thousand may sound like a lot, but it's not enough to take down Academy City. Tell us your *business* here, mercenary. What was this plan of yours that needed so many people?"

"..." The mercenary looked at the four members of Group in turn. He seemed to be mentally at a loss. He hesitated, looking at this disaster, wondering if his Block allies had failed or if they'd been planning on betraying them all along. Eventually, he opened his mouth and spoke.

"...School District 10."

"District 10?"

With the cheapest land prices in the city, it was home to all sorts of unsavory facilities, like abandoned animal testing sites and nuclear power-related laboratories.

The mercenary continued, "We planned to attack the juvenile reformatory there."

"!!" Awaki Musujime grabbed the mercenary's collar. "Why attack a place like that...? Trying to save some VIP criminals, were you?!"

Accelerator, staring at Musujime being driven by impatience, took the time to think.

Academy City's juvenile reformatory was a facility for holding criminals who had used abilities during their crime. Nobody knew the details, but he'd heard stories that they had anti-esper measures there. That meant a regular military combat force would have a much higher success rate for an assault.

The mercenary Musujime was holding by the collar eventually said, "Our target…was Move Point."

Her eyebrow twitched.

The mercenary didn't seem to have any idea who the girl in front of him was.

"We heard…that Move Point's allies are being held there. We wanted to capture them…and use them to negotiate with Move Point."

Why did they bring up that name in particular? thought Musujime to herself. She soon realized the answer. "The guide…to the Windowless Building where Aleister is…"

"Yeah. The guide's identity is top secret. They're directly linked to Aleister, after all. But Block found out that Move Point was the guide. So we decided to investigate her, then get resources we could use to bargain."

"What did you want to bargain with the guide for?" asked Tsuchimikado.

"For info on how goods get inside—the Windowless Building, that is," the mercenary answered. "Even nukes can't destroy it from the outside, but what about from the inside? They say it has no entrance or exit, but they have to be bringing goods in and out somehow. We were going to use that and blow the Windowless Building apart from within."

"Blow it apart?"

"Block said they had procured multi-synchronous bombs. You're all tactical weapons made by Academy City, right?"

Multi-synchronous bombs were large-scale bombs where you systematically set up multiple high explosives. While normal tactical weapons tried to make ever more massive blasts that would spread out farther, multi-synchronous bombs aimed to focus the high-energy blasts on a single, extremely small target and destroy it thoroughly. They were devised to blow up enemy fortresses in urban areas without causing civilian casualties.

"We had to stop the worldwide chaos. I'm a mercenary by trade, so I understand: The world is on the brink. Strife is going to start all over soon. Wars have to be stopped before they happen."

The mercenary looked at each of the faces in Group in turn.

"It would have been too much to ask for Move Point herself to join us. Anyone you can't trust—well, you can never trust them in the future, either. We wouldn't pursue that very far. If the info is right about Move Point's ability, things would have gone much easier with her cooperation, but it's one thing we couldn't do anything about. We assumed we wouldn't get her cooperation to begin with—"

"You're right about that," interrupted Musujime. "By the way, do you know who's standing in front of you right now?"

"What?" said the mercenary, frowning—before his face went beet-red a moment later. "N-no, that can't be, that's not...!!"

Before he could finish speaking, there were almost ten iron nail-like objects pierced through his body.

He lost consciousness because of the shock from the pain, but he still seemed to be alive. Musujime let go of the ragged mercenary and stood there, head down, clenching her teeth.

That which she wanted to protect most—that which she had to protect no matter the cost—was being stolen away at this very moment. In the face of that, the other three were silent. Each carried something similar, so they said nothing.

Aleister was probably using some unknown tech to watch all this from on high. And though he watched, he wouldn't want to intervene. He was, without a doubt, watching and laughing at the little people floundering in the miniature garden he'd created.

"Let's go."

Eventually, Tsuchimikado prompted the group onward.

Everything to come wouldn't be a Group problem but an Awaki Musujime problem. But nobody was willing to point that out. The situation had changed from each Group individual having to overcome the hardships that came with their own assignments by themselves, like it had been for Unabara when he was within Block's ranks.

"To District 10. Block's still got almost a hundred mercs with 'em.

We don't know what they're armed with, but one thing's certain: We can't be optimistic about this."

7

Accelerator and the rest of Group used a transport ambulance to get out of District 11. Their destination: a certain juvenile reformatory in District 10.

"This is the only juvenile reformatory in Academy City. Looks like it's split half and half, with a boys' block and a girls' block," said Tsuchimikado, pressing a few buttons on his laptop. "Academy City doesn't consider treason a crime right now. That means Musujime's allies can't be legally sentenced. They wouldn't put people like that into one of the normal houses."

"Which means…there must be a hidden room?" Unabara looked at Musujime, but she didn't seem to know.

"What a pain," muttered Accelerator. "Don't we have a map of the place? If we can't hack their data, including hidden passages from their facility, can't we just steal it from the construction company's computer?"

"It's not a normal building. I don't think that sort of data would still be at the company."

Tsuchimikado looked at the screen.

It showed several data points on the reformatory, but the map itself was designated secret. They wouldn't be able to touch it from here.

Accelerator, who was also peering at the screen, noticed something. "This place doesn't have a fire office." He looked over the data again. "There wouldn't be many fires in the facility, so they left it out to cut costs. But that means if there *was* a fire, the fire station would act. They would have gotten a rough map beforehand to be able to move cleanly through that maze."

Tsuchimikado directed his hacking attempt elsewhere.

He got results quickly.

"Here we go. Part of the secret area is blotted out, but if we assume there's a hidden staircase, then construction-wise, it has to be here. Beyond that is the underground block for traitors."

Judging from how there was only one predictable location for the hidden stairs, the traitors' block must not have been separated between male and female. They were all individual cells, with no common spaces at all.

"Technically, it is hidden," said Musujime. "From Block, too, who are attacking the place."

"Hah. Group and Block have equal authority. Anything we can get our hands on is free game for them, too, right? You're the one who said our secrecy levels in the data banks were the same, idiot."

Musujime glared at Accelerator, but he didn't budge.

"Tsuchimikado," he said instead, "what about security?"

"The guards are using MPS-79s—an old powered-suit model. Anti-esper equipment, but we can't expect much from them. They're only using self-defense tools to stop out-of-control espers, but Block has real lethal weapons. The mercenaries left in District 11 had the whole nine yards of outside equipment—knives, guns, rifles, blast-ing powder, you name it—but they probably have Block's brand-new stuff now. From what Unabara said, they've still got almost a hundred mercs with them. We don't know how many people Block has, or their abilities. What's important is whether or not they have lethal abilities. Powered suits are really just big, rugged targets, after all."

"Not that," interrupted Accelerator casually. "That reformatory holds brutal espers, right? What about their anti-abilities setup?"

"Mostly IDF jammers—around twenty-five."

"So, what? We can't use our abilities inside?"

"No, it just ruins your focus or purposely leaves thoughts easy for psychometer espers to track. Your abilities will be somewhat weaker, but it won't completely erase them. Those prison guards are appar-ently in one of the three professions most hated by insurance com-panies. It means they can't fully neutralize everything, even though the facility is so large in scale.

"But," warned Tsuchimikado, "using your abilities carelessly could make them go out of control. Especially ones that need complex calculations. It's too dangerous for you and Musujime. Be careful. That would be a stupid way to kill yourself."

8

When the ambulance stopped in front of the juvenile reformatory in School District 10, Accelerator, Motoharu Tsuchimikado, Mitsuki Unabara, and Awaki Musujime burst out of its back door.

From there, they couldn't spy the actual reformatory. Walls almost fifteen meters high were in the way. But even from where they stood, the sickening scent of smoke reached their noses.

"...!!"

Musujime grated her teeth and immediately tried to dash in through the already destroyed gate, but Accelerator, leaning on his modern-design cane, frowned.

"Does this seem odd to anyone else?"

"You noticed, too?" said Tsuchimikado slowly, pulling a military pistol from his inside pocket. "No noise. If Block is in combat with the reformatory guards, we should be able to hear gunfire, at least."

The four passed through the gate, which also served as a checkpoint. Beyond it was a roundabout for police wagons. As they stepped toward the edge of the asphalt surface, twenty meters long per side, Accelerator felt a slight pain around his temples.

"...The IDF jammers, eh?"

He looked up and saw a net of thin wires drawn over the entire grounds, from one fifteen-meter-high wall to another. Were they emitting special EM waves or something?

They were probably causing espers to interfere with their own abilities by throwing their involuntary diffusion fields into chaos. He'd never heard of Anti-Skill using them, so they likely needed immense electricity or processing instruments, making them usable only in limited spaces like this one.

Doesn't look like I'm having a problem walking, at least...But I should probably stay away from ability usage mode, since it uses proxy calculations.

Still, Accelerator wasn't under the impression he couldn't use his ability here. They seemed to be stimulating abilities to run out of control instead, so he couldn't use it carelessly. His arms and legs could fly off if he got caught in his own ability.

They're using a bunch of other machines, too. Purposely getting them to interfere with one another.

If he could figure out what sort of devices they were manipulating, he might have been able to find a countermeasure, but there, Accelerator stopped thinking. He'd found the reason the whole reformatory seemed odd.

Corpses.

Probably the mercenaries Block had called in from outside. Close to fifty big men were lying in pools of their own blood. Some were shot through the temple, others were missing parts of their heads from close-range shotgun blasts, and yet others had their necks cut with knives... There were many causes for death, but all had one thing in common.

"They...All of them were ended by their own weapons...," muttered Tsuchimikado.

"Suicide...? No, wait, this is—"

Unabara didn't get to finish.

"I've found you."

They heard a voice behind them.

Accelerator turned around to see a girl standing in the destroyed gate. A small girl, wearing a red sailor-style suit that looked like a school uniform. But there was a glint in her eyes. She wasn't just any killer.

"If you're here, does that make you one of Block's shitheads?"

"No, I'm with Member. I was only using them, though, so I don't care who I belong to," she answered coolly. She was probably the one who'd attacked the mercenaries lying around. That would mean she took down fifty without a single wound, but she didn't brag about it. She really didn't seem to have any interest in either the mercenaries or Block.

Another from Member...

Accelerator had run into someone from Member a short while ago in District 23, too. They didn't seem to be on friendly terms with Block. He didn't quite know what their goals were, or which organizations they were hostile toward. Whatever the case, though, if they were hostile, their response wouldn't change.

But one person overreacted to seeing her face.

"...Wait, could you be..."

Mitsuki Unabara—an agent, whose name and face were known to none.

"You would ask me my identity at this point, Etzali?"

The girl looked at Mitsuki Unabara and called him a completely different name.

Or perhaps that was his true name.

As Unabara stood frozen in surprise, the girl wiped her face with a hand. Her face was no longer there. Her Asian features disappeared, leaving a girl with a dark complexion and sculpted features.

"I'll have to thank Block. Esper powers are reduced here. I don't have to worry as much about your allies or whatever getting in my way."

After seeing her face and hearing her voice, Unabara's face twisted.

"Xóchitl? What are you doing out here? You don't have a spell like this, and even in the organization, nobody would ever give you the dirty jobs!!"

"I have only one reason," stated the brown-skinned girl named Xóchitl, face steady. "You turned coats to Academy City, you traitor. I abandoned everything to come here and destroy you."

"So that's it," muttered Tsuchimikado, looking over at Unabara.

"...I'll hold her here. You all go on ahead," Unabara stated quietly, his voice strained. "She's Xóchitl. An Aztecan sorcerer who belonged to the same organization as I did before I came here."

The girl called Xóchitl didn't change her expression even after hearing Unabara's words. "I only have business with Etzali. I don't care if the rest of you leave, but will *they* let you go?"

A gunshot rang out.

Accelerator and Tsuchimikado ducked behind a patrol wagon parked in the roundabout. Meanwhile, they heard several feet running out of the reformatory building.

"The Block mercs who were waiting...Don't you have to deal with them?" said Tsuchimikado to Xóchitl. She ignored him. She really had only eliminated the ones in her way; she wasn't interested in Block or their mercenaries.

But as the mercenaries stopped them there, Block was getting deeper and deeper into the reformatory—to use Awaki Musujime's allies as hostages.

Accelerator tsked in frustration. "Bullshit. Get going already."

"But...," began Musujime.

"I can't walk without a cane. If we can't use abilities, then I can't expect anything from your Move Point, either. The slowest guy gets to hold them off," said Accelerator quickly. "Tsuchimikado, you're Musujime's backup. We don't know how many guys Block has. Go into it ready to fight a lot of them."

As for Unabara, he didn't need to give him any directions at this point.

Accelerator would intercept the mercenaries coming out of the building, Unabara would settle the score with Member's Xóchitl, and Tsuchimikado and Musujime would rescue the kids in the special block.

With each of their own goals in mind, the four members of Group glanced at one another and nodded.

"Let's go!!"

They all got started.

9

Tsuchimikado and Musujime went down the hidden staircase the map's contradictions had shown them and headed to the special insurgent block which, on paper, didn't exist.

They came across a few men on the way who appeared to be mercenaries, but Tsuchimikado used his gun to silence them. Xóchitl must have gotten a lot of them. Thanks to Accelerator taking on her job, they seemed to have mostly run out.

Then Musujime felt a cold, slight pain in her head.

"...IDF jammers. They're getting stronger."

"They've got machines outside, in the building, and in the rooms. Their effects are probably overlapping. This is the only juvenile reformatory in Academy City, and the only anti-esper holding facility in the world. You can't have normal security in a place like this."

Tsuchimikado was probably feeling a similar pain.

She felt less like it was holding back her ability, restraining it, and more like it was throwing her aim off. If she used her ability without thinking, she could catch herself in it.

"Musujime. Your ability is extremely strong, but one misfire and you'll die. You shouldn't use it here."

"You make it sound like my ability is the only thing I'm good for."

"Shh!" Tsuchimikado held up his index finger to quiet her.

The passage stuck out the side of the stairwell, and from around the corner he heard a heavy clattering, like someone forcing open a bolted metal wall by driving a nail into the gaps between plates. Tsuchimikado silently brought his pistol back up. The completely ability-reliant Musujime must not have had her normal throwing weapons with her, because she removed the flashlight-slash-nightstick from her waist.

They burst out into the passage.

It was narrow. Metal doors for solitary confinement cells lined the walls on either side, and a big, bearlike man had stuck some kind of clay on one. Next to him, a sinewy woman watched.

When they saw Tsuchimikado and Musujime, the bearlike man said, "Good timing...You must be Group."

Musujime didn't immediately move, probably due to the IDF jammers. Tsuchimikado, on the other hand, aimed his barrel right between the big man's eyes. But before he could fire, the man stuck a long, needlelike object into the clay on the door.

"A plastic bomb, and this is the fuse."

The muscly woman's eyes sharpened. "Saku!!"

"We have to, Teshio. We have to use hostages here."

The large man called Saku slowly removed his hand from the bomb with the fuse stuck in it. His hand held a wireless device—the switch to set off the bomb.

"...If you use that now, it'll blow you two to smithereens first."

"I've already set the amount of gunpowder and direction. The blast will only go into the door." Saku pointed to the bomb on the door with his index finger. "But the shockwave will rip through the cell. Along with the blown-apart fragments of this metal door. Breaking the door is easy, but caring about those inside isn't. We have to be hasty, thanks to the lot of you getting in the way."

"...!!" Suddenly, there was a boom of wind.

Musujime had bared her fangs, and her ability had accidentally discharged. Several fluorescent lights on the ceiling went out, sticking to the walls and floor in a muddle.

Even then, Saku and Teshio didn't look disturbed.

"...Awaki Musujime. The famous Move Point," said Saku with a grin, reaffirming his grip on the device to blow the bomb. "That's good. Less work for us. We have the hostages and the other party all right here. Let's get straight to negotiations, shall we? You be the guide to the Windowless Building."

"And if I refuse?"

"You can't refuse. Would you rather your ability go berserk?"

That made Musujime clam up. If not for the anti-esper setup, she'd have skewered Saku a long time ago.

"Still...Group, eh? What did you learn after experiencing the 09/30 incident?"

"What?"

"We learned something. We thought Aleister governed every last corner of this insane world, but he doesn't. There are ways to escape his sway, places to flee his control. Isn't that a fun little fact? Academy City restricting us almost seems absurd now. And with the disturbance in Avignon after the 09/30 incident, we have the chance of a lifetime. You can't tell us to stay put."

"A new world built on the backs of others? That isn't something you can speak of so haughtily. All it makes me think of are the massacres during the Age of Discovery."

"Really? It's human nature to desire a heaven or a paradise that isn't here for them right now."

As he listened to their exchange, Tsuchimikado watched the device Saku held.

He was good enough to shoot it down. But he couldn't deny the possibility that he'd fail, nor that falling to the floor would coincidentally hit the button and blow the door to bits. If that happened, it didn't matter where in that small cell Musujime's ally hid—the hail of metal shards would get to them.

Musujime's jaw was clenched so tightly she could have broken all her teeth.

The burly woman, Teshio, saw that and spoke to Saku next to her. "...Using hostages won't make this better."

"What are you saying, Teshio? This is where it gets real. This hostage's worth has gone through the roof."

"That was only something we needed, before negotiating with Move Point, before we knew where she was. Musujime is in, our hands now. The hostage, has served his purpose. If you use that bomb, she'll be even more stubborn." Teshio glared at the bomb on the door. "Come to think of it, I was against this from the start. I only agreed to the hostage plan, because it was absolutely necessary, to achieve our goals. Now that we know, that's not true, we don't have to keep them."

"No, Teshio. We have thirty-eight hostages right in front of us! Don't you get it?! They're our assets. We have so much capital that we can treat a few recklessly and it won't even itch!! ...Did you spend too long on the Anti-Skill job? Did you start having feelings for these brats?!"

"...Saku."

"Don't get in my way!! I'm gonna fucking kill Aleister!! This is the first step. I can't let it end here!! Like hell I'll let you take up my precious time. If you hold me back, Teshio, I'll kill you first!! If you don't want that, then—"

Saku couldn't finish his sentence.

*   *   *

Ga-thud!!
Teshio crashed her fist into Saku's body with all her might.

They could discern the incredible force behind the punch just from hearing it. The man from Block probably had no idea what had just happened to his body. Suddenly, he'd slammed into the wall and slid down to the floor in a heap. That was the first time Awaki Musujime saw the spittle actually come out of someone's mouth. That's how merciless the strike had been.

"…Don't waste time, on nonsense."

The woman known as Teshio reached for the metal door. She pulled the fuse out of the plastic bomb stuck to it, removed the bomb itself, and casually tossed them to the floor.

"Is this, better?" she said slowly.

Her face grim, Musujime asked quietly, "…What's your game?"

"I apologize, for our rudeness. Feel free, to beat me, until you're satisfied." Teshio's eyes held steady, even after Tsuchimikado pointed his gun at her. "But I will not yield to you, until you win. I, too, have a reason, I need to kill Aleister. I won't, use hostages. I *will*, however, inflict pain on you, and get the information I need."

10

Mitsuki Unabara and Xóchitl stood in the reformatory gymnasium.

The brown-skinned girl took a feather out of her pocket and held it to the side of her ear, saying, "Is looking at me with a false face your version of courtesy, Etzali?"

"…Unfortunately, I happen to rather like this face. You, on the other hand, have no right to use that face after leaving the organization."

"You're wrong," cut in Xóchitl quietly. "You don't even have the right to *live* anymore."

"!!" Feeling a peculiar bloodlust, Unabara immediately drew the obsidian knife from his inside pocket. He hadn't been planning on using the Spear of Tlahuizcalpantecuhtli on his former ally.

"What have you been looking at this whole time?" asked Xóchitl, exasperated.

A moment later, everything from Unabara's right wrist to his elbow stopped moving. Before he could grunt in surprise, the obsidian knife he gripped *began to move toward his face without his command.*

"Wh...what?!"

He wasted no time in grabbing his wrist with his other hand.

Little by little, the knife's tip inched closer to his eyeball. It was his dominant hand, which might have been why he couldn't keep it farther away.

Xóchitl's face remained steady.

Not even joy for her advantageous position marked her expression. It felt like she was watching a boring play.

Argh...! At...this rate...!!

"*Raaaaaaahhhhhhhhhhhh!!*" shouted Unabara.

He forced his left hand to move and dislocate his right wrist joint. The pain of scraping bones tore through him before all feeling left his hand. Without any gripping force, the knife finally slid out and fell to the ground.

Holding his wrist, he took a big jump back.

Xóchitl pointed at the ground and said impassively, "You dropped something. Gonna pick it up?"

Her spell probably interfered with the weapons others held. It captured the weapon, then borrowed its force to cause the enemy to kill himself without her needing to get her hands dirty. To avoid that attack, he'd have to abandon all weapons and Soul Arms and fight either barehanded or with spells he could cast with only his body. Meanwhile, Xóchitl could use whatever weapon she wanted for her strikes.

It rejected human civilization itself, this overwhelming handicap.

However, thought Unabara.

The Xóchitl he remembered didn't use spells like this. Though her nickname was ghastly—the Corpse Artisan—her actual job was to extract information leftover in corpses, determining whether their last words were true or consolidating burial methods. She was just an aftercare provider for the dead.

She'd studied all the world's necromancy, but purely for a peaceful purpose. The brown-skinned girl named Xóchitl shouldn't have been accustomed to hurting others.

"...What happened? Or, rather, what on Earth is happening in the organization right now?!" demanded Unabara in spite of himself.

Xóchitl didn't even answer. She swung her hand and produced a giant sword that, no matter how he looked at it, couldn't fit in her hand. Unlike Unabara's blade, this was a traditional sword made of white chalcedony. It was technically a double-sided blade, but sharp grooves had been carved into the left and right like the back of a survival knife.

A macuahuitl...?!

It was a sword used by Aztecan warriors. In Aztecan civilization, which didn't use metal in weapons, several small stone razors would be lined up on the sides of wooden blades, so instead of cutting by striking like katanas, it would cut by pulling across something, like a saw.

"I'll hear what you have to say later. If you're lucky, and the brain damage is minor."

Xóchitl raised her *macuahuitl* and sprang into motion, dashing toward him.

Given that he had to fight barehanded, Unabara was at a severe disadvantage.

"Damn it!!"

But he couldn't lose here.

He stepped back to create distance. When Xóchitl, her timing thrown off, tried to step in more deeply, Unabara dug his shoe into the dirt and flung it in front of him. Blinded, Xóchitl stopped moving. He tried to aim a second kick at her gut.

But with a *vwoosh*, Xóchitl's *macuahuitl* swept to the side.

Unabara hastily pulled his foot back, but it left a mark on his leather shoe like a razor had cut it.

"That's a traitor for you. Makeshift ploys suit you well."

Xóchitl's voice was calm. Even that struck Unabara as strange. Before, she would have hesitated to even pick up a weapon made for killing. Her job was to read the residual information from corpses, so she knew the terror of weapons like that far more than normal people did.

And yet...

"But no matter how much you struggle, you need to fight barehanded. I'll give you the right to defend yourself, at least, but each time you do, it'll tear up your body a little bit more."

"...Weapons like that don't suit you."

"Then is this the real you? You, who abandoned the organization, went into hiding, and grew fat on the tranquility of Academy City?"

"Xóchitl..."

"If the answer is yes, then you are indeed a traitor. If not, then you're lying to yourself—and a liar has no place to criticize me. Either option means you have to die here!!"

Gripping her Aztecan sword, the *macuahuitl*, Xóchitl charged straight into range. He could sense no mercy—not in her eyes, her face, her hands, or her movements.

She was serious about killing him.

Maybe he could avoid one or two attacks. But he couldn't keep that up forever. And if she successfully landed even one clean hit, the grievous blood loss would end his life. He couldn't retreat for now, either. He needed more leeway for that. He could only choose that option once he decided she wouldn't kill him if he turned his back.

Still, so long as her weapon-breaking spell was in effect, he also couldn't use any tools to defend himself. If he tried, he'd end up attacking himself with it.

He was against the wall.

"Damn it!!" he swore, trying to back up.

A swing from the *macuahuitl* tore through his jacket, sending several cuttings of hair flying.

"It's over."

Thump!! Xóchitl stomped on the ground. Then, this time in range for a sure kill, she brought her *macuahuitl* up—a strike with timing Unabara would never be able to dodge.

She had no emotional connection from Unabara being a former ally, someone from the same organization, or anything.

Roar!! She cleaved down the sword.

...?! Unabara thrust his right arm, its wrist dislocated, over his head. She saw it and laughed. She must not have thought it would provide any defense. The *macuahuitl*, with its sawlike blades, descended with all her body weight behind it at a terrible speed.

Shrripp!! It tore apart his jacket, and then the jagged blade dug into the flesh of his arm. The grating, sawing noise reached his bones. His face distorted in pain.

But...

...that was all.

Mitsuki Unabara's arm was still attached.

In fact, with the *macuahuitl* buried in his arm, he rallied all his strength and tried to push it away.

"What...?!" exclaimed Xóchitl in surprise before he slammed her in the side with a kick. Her petite frame gave way to momentum and crashed to the ground.

"...The Aztecs had no way of processing metal into weapons, so their swords aren't that sharp. Instead of having a single chunk of iron for a blade, it uses many small, jagged stones along the sides of a wooden club. Even an expert couldn't cleave bone; it's made so you have to sweep the whole thing across arteries. In short, I can stop your sword with my bones."

With the Aztecan sword still lodged in his right arm, he coughed, then continued, "Why did you think I gave up on dodging and got my arm ready? If I thought it would get through my arm and cut me in half, I wouldn't have tried to defend like that. I decided that if I kept on evading, I'd lose due to blood loss."

His tactic was possible because of Xóchitl's relatively small stature and lack of skill with the weapon. A true warrior would still have broken his arm even if she couldn't cut the bone.

"That's why I said that weapon doesn't suit you."

Unabara looked down at the immobilized, laboriously breathing Xóchitl.

He still couldn't use weapons. But she had let go of her *macua-huitl*, too. In this state, he could win by strangling her, or hitting her hard enough. Given the differences in their physiques, it would be easy to straddle her to stop her from moving before she got her hands on another weapon.

Xóchitl...

But he couldn't do that.

No matter how much he wanted to.

"I will not take your life. Disappear, and don't come back," he said bitterly, popping his wrist joint back into place and swinging his right hand to send the sword to the ground.

When Xóchitl heard that, a subtle smile came to her lips.

And a moment later, the brown-skinned girl's body began to crumble.

11

The underground passage was straight and narrow.

And inside the facility, the myriad of anti-esper measures employed—IDF jammers first and foremost—made Musujime's ability unreliable. If anything went wrong, things could get really bad, even to the point of killing everyone instantly.

That was why Tsuchimikado didn't rely on her, nor did he attempt to approach Teshio when he didn't know what sort of attacks she would use. Instead, he just brought up his gun, intending to fire bullets in a spread pattern that would leave her no room for escape.

In response, Teshio kicked something at her feet into the air.

It was a cloth bag with ammunition that Saku, now lying on the ground, had been holding. If he accidentally hit that, it would send a spray of bullets out into the narrow passage, ricocheting off the walls and quite possibly him. By the time he was startled into stopping his trigger finger, Teshio had begun running up the passage, her fist clenched tight.

"!!"

Tsuchimikado squeezed the trigger, just barely before her fist was in range.

But Teshio assumed a boxer-like stance, low enough to kiss his knees, in order to let the bullet go past.

Before Tsuchimikado could fix his aim, Teshio sprang out of her low stance and tackled him right in the stomach. The blow was strong enough to destroy doors, and even thin walls, and it sent his body flying several meters back.

A terrible sound rang out, and he almost stopped breathing. "Those movements...Anti-Skill arrest techniques...?"

"This is, my spin on it. If I used, something like this, on a child, it would kill them."

Tsuchimikado fired his gun even as they spoke, but Teshio easily avoided it by swinging her upper body out of the way. The moment he was out of bullets, she sent out a kick that tore the gun from his hand.

Then she came in for another tackle.

With a dull *thud*, Teshio trapped Tsuchimikado between her shoulder and the wall. When she quietly stepped away, he slumped to the floor, limp.

"!!" That was when Awaki Musujime swung her flashlight down behind Teshio.

By simply raising her hand, Teshio caught the blunt weapon. "A professional needs, no eccentric abilities, nor any one-shot skills."

Returning the favor, she used her other hand to backhand Musujime across the face.

Thwop!! The blow sent her careening to the side, and she collided with one of the solitary confinement cell doors along the wall.

"We only need, an array of basic tactics, to defeat our enemies, in a logical manner."

Teshio delivered a kick.

With a terrible *ga-bam,* Musujime tumbled into the cell along with the door, which should have been sturdily made. The extreme impact made her think her internal organs had been wrecked. Despite feeling a strange urge to vomit, nothing came out—it was like her throat was plugged shut.

One of her allies must have been in this cell as well, because she heard them immediately call out her name. That alone gave her completely worn body a little bit of energy.

Ka-click. Teshio set her foot down in the broken cell entrance, blocking her path.

Musujime put a hand on the wall and wobbled to her feet, bringing her flashlight up. After telling her nearby ally to back up, she said, "...You were talking about forcing me to spit out the route they use to send goods into the nuke-proof Windowless Building, then trying to destroy it from within with multi-synchronous bombs, right?"

"Feel like, talking now?"

"You can't possibly believe you can take down Aleister like that. If that was all it took, anyone with a teleportation ability could kill him in his sleep. You really don't think Aleister has a plan for that?"

"You're right—perhaps I cannot, kill Aleister. He is, in the truest sense, a monster.

"However," she said, "the life support machines, keeping him alive, are different."

"..."

"Those are just, machines. The reason, a monster like Aleister, would be holed up, in a fortress sturdier than a nuclear shelter, is plain to see. I've heard, those machines, have no replacement. If they're blown up, he would be in trouble."

"No, he wouldn't," retorted Musujime, trying to catch what breath she could. "It's not a *windowless building* in the first place. If you don't even understand that, then you don't have any useful information. Plan all you want, but nothing will work."

"What?"

"Didn't you realize it? A building without any doors or windows would never normally exist. But there are a bunch of hints connect-

· ing to the right answer. For example, being able to produce every-thing he needs to live, including oxygen, inside. The fact that it can withstand a nuclear attack also means it blocks radiation. All sorts of cosmic rays from the stars."

"Cosmic rays? …Could that mean—?"

"No," interrupted Musujime.

"It's not like that."

Feeling her own powerlessness, she smiled thinly. Her answer sure seemed to have caught Teshio off-guard. "With these many hints, there's a few possibilities. I have a couple theories of my own. But answers about Aleister himself aren't part of them. My theories at this point in time are nothing more than guesses based on the infor-mation I've been shown up to the here and now. And I'm pretty sure Aleister hasn't shown me all the information."

"…"

"The only thing I can say is that his plan is far beyond what we can imagine. For Aleister, this entire planet is probably just a disposable tool. And you think your banal methods could possibly defeat him?"

Musujime had only been trying to buy a little time. She just wanted to let out some of the damage she'd accumulated.

But Teshio said, "That's a great story, but my intentions, will not change."

"…Why are you so intent on taking Aleister's head?"

"I, too, have seen, my fair share of tragedy, in this city. And I wanted to ask Aleister, whether he was involved, or if he knew noth-ing at all. That's it."

Teshio's tone was curt. It wasn't a desire for revenge burning in her heart. Because of that, though, Musujime felt the truth behind her words. No unnecessary emotions were driving her actions.

"That's a corny request."

"Maybe so."

"I was possessed by this 'need for truth' thing once, too. But going after something like that won't get your peace of mind back."

Musujime's voice was quiet. "If Aleister admitted he caused those tragedies, would you accept that? If he said he wasn't involved, would you accept that? Whichever answer you get, you'll probably think he's lying. That there was something more to it. The question wouldn't mean anything, and so there's no point in asking it."

"...I see."

Teshio said no more. She'd probably decided on her answer by now—so she didn't waver one bit.

"Then what are you, going to do?"

Musujime couldn't answer that.

Even inside this reformatory that held criminal espers, they were in a top-secret area. The anti-esper measures, including the IDF jammers, were probably firmly optimized for those specific people. Still, she couldn't attack with her special ability, Move Point.

And without that, Awaki Musujime was just a girl. She didn't have firing skills like Accelerator, and she wasn't proficient in close-quarter combat like Tsuchimikado.

After thinking it through, she smiled a little and said:

"...If I keep thinking like that, I'll never be able to protect anyone."

As her lips moved, her hand went around to her back. She grabbed the bundle of cords there and yanked.

A low-frequency oscillation treatment device. They were electrodes, aids that measured the disorder in her brain waves and gave her mild shocks to induce stress-relieving effects, and she tore them all off at once. She tossed the flashlight to the side, too.

Musujime, having lost everything, still didn't stop smiling.

When Block's Teshio saw that, she looked at her with interest. "You're going to use it."

"Yes," answered Musujime clearly, without a moment's pause.

"Sorry, but I'm going all out."

Suddenly, a metal nail appeared in Musujime's empty hand. It was probably from the sturdy bolt on the solitary confinement cell door.

But her Move Point wasn't precise enough. She felt it tearing up the skin of her clenched palm.

The trauma haunting the depths of her heart came on all at once.

She forced it down, then triggered Move Point again.

This time, her very body disappeared.

Using logical eleven-dimensional vectors, she overcame her three-dimensional limitations and snuck right up to the brawny woman. A crushing pressure assailed her stomach as she teleported, but she ignored it and tried to jam the nail into Teshio's gut.

In response, Teshio backed up.

Musujime's instincts told her that if she got away now, she wouldn't be able to win. But when she tried to step forward, she realized her right leg wasn't moving. It felt like it was stuck to the ground with superglue, but her memory had very clearly felt this sensation before.

The root of this terrible feeling was that, as a result of mistaking her teleport positioning, everything from halfway down her calf and below was buried inside the floor.

Suffering.

Terror.

Shock.

All those emotions she's experienced before came surging up from her stomach at once, but...

I'll overcome this...

With a *creak*, she squeezed the iron nail tight and bit her lips to hold everything in. Behind her was an ally she needed to protect. There was a life she needed to protect right now, and for that, Awaki Musujime crushed the past creeping out of her.

I'll overcome this infuriating scar, damn it!!

She gritted her teeth, then moved her leg in one motion as if to yank it out of mud.

In that moment, she heard a ripping noise.

Awaki Musujime didn't look away from any of it.

And she went forward.

Right up to the Block killer threatening her ally's life she went, ignoring her mutilated foot, simply gripping that iron nail, shooting forward like a bullet.

Thud!
An explosively dull noise rattled the cell.

The power drained from Teshio's body. As she tottered forward as if to lean on Musujime, she brought her lips to Musujime's ear and muttered into it.

"...Awfully confident, of you."

The iron nail was in Musujime's hand. But right before impact, she'd spun it around in her hand and struck Teshio not with the sharp end, but with the middle of its flat back end.

"Unfortunately," she answered indifferently, "this is the leadership they need from me."

12

Mitsuki Unabara couldn't believe what he was seeing.

He'd beaten Xóchitl in the reformatory gym. Now, her right arm had suddenly crumbled. It wasn't biological decomposition.

It was like an invisible person taking off bandages.

The texture of the outside of her skin was incredibly human, but after the bandages came off, there was only a void. The change, which started from her fingertips, ate its way up to her elbows in the blink of an eye.

"Xóchitl...? What on Earth...?!"

"My body's hit its limit, that's all," said the brown-haired girl with a thin smile as she slowly came undone from the tips of her hands and feet. "Hope you learned something. When you try to compensate for a lack of ability with a grimoire, this is the result you get."

"Wait...*You read a grimoire?*"

"Even more than that, actually. As an Aztecan sorcerer yourself, you'd know. In our rituals, we reach heaven by eating the flesh of man. Basically, a magical conduit connects me to any flesh cut from my body."

Hearing those few words, Unabara was shocked. Now he knew the *real* meaning behind the spell, which used someone else's weapon to make them kill themselves. She dried her own skin, made it into a powder, and scattered it around. Magically speaking, that powder was a part of Xóchitl's body, so she could control them like limbs just by thinking at them. The same applied to things they stuck to tightly.

She made other people's weapons part of her own body. That was the true identity of Xóchitl's spell.

But...

"Any spell that gets rid of your own body like that is quick to fail! This is already past the point where Soul Arms could assist you! You must have at least known that much, Xóchitl!!"

"It doesn't matter. The organization demanded disposal of the traitor, and I answered. If I can kill you before my expiration date, the organization's goal will be achieved."

"Damn!! The organization I knew was already terrible, but it wasn't this bad! What the hell happened there while I was away?!" exclaimed Unabara.

Xóchitl only smiled mysteriously.

The brown-skinned girl was swiftly crumbling. By Unabara's estimation, there was only a third of her physical body left. Naturally, that wasn't enough to preserve her life. It was leaving her flesh and organs out in the open air.

...I don't think any ordinary spell or Soul Arm could have caused this bad of a situation.

Unabara watched the destruction, far past her limbs now and at her gut, and thought desperately:

If there's anything more esoteric than those...all I can think of is an original copy!!

Via a fusion with an original grimoire, which was indestructible by anyone and could act entirely on its own—or rather, by becoming one of its parts—Xóchitl had attained power. Things made sense when he thought of it that way. Causing people who were holding weapons to kill themselves with those weapons was very much in the vein of the defenses original copies had. And the Aztecs had books called *codices*, which wrote characters in animal skin.

Animal skin…Wait!!

Unabara stared dumbly at the girl's brown skin, which was literally coming apart at the seams.

And inside was written——

"Guh, *urgh, ahhhhhhhhhhhhhhhhhhhhhhhhhhhhhhhhhhhhhhh*!!"

When he carelessly peered inside, he screamed.

Just a few characters. He hadn't even seen them—they'd only gotten into his peripheral vision, and it almost broke his mind. It wasn't a written, less-pure copy, a reinterpretation for the average person. It was a bona fide original.

He grasped at his pounding temples and staggered, but he continued to think.

Ugh…A derivation of the calendar stone?

The calendar stone was an Aztecan calendar arranged in a circle. However, the Aztec empire used two different calendars at the same time. They also believed in the sun's death and rebirth, among other things, so the calendars became incredibly complex. On the underside of Xóchitl's skin, there was only an extraction of the time portions relating to life and death, themselves developed into a religious discourse.

Unabara couldn't handle something like this. The very idea of fighting against it was a mistake. Even the index of forbidden books was said to be incapable of destroying these evil writings—a mere sorcerer was helpless against one.

However,

even so,

I won't…let you die…

Xóchitl was a noncombat personnel. How did she sneak all the way in? What was happening with the organization? He had a pile of questions to ask. He couldn't let her die there.

Original grimoire copies were indestructible.

Even if they could be destroyed, Xóchitl's life depended on this one, so she wouldn't last.

With Mitsuki Unabara's power alone, it was impossible to solve this problem.

Which meant...

If human power can't realize it, then I just need to borrow this grimoire's!!

Original copies defended all attacks, and nobody could damage them. But there was one exception: showing the knowledge contained within one to someone who wanted it. If they truly prevented any interference whatsoever, nobody would be able to flip through their pages, and the very reason for a grimoire's existence would be lost. He didn't know how, but original copies could differentiate between readers and everyone else, and tended to cooperate with those broadening their knowledge.

Which was why Unabara thought this: *I'll inherit this grimoire.*

If he could obtain ownership of the grimoire, its automatic interception spells would cease to function. And by inheriting it, he could naturally tear the grimoire from Xóchitl's body, too. It wasn't cooperating with Xóchitl because it liked her personality or anything. It was just seeking those who would disseminate the knowledge within it.

On top of that...

I'll fool the grimoire's judgment. I can make it think that I can't inherit it if Xóchitl dies! Then it should save her life on its own!!

Mitsuki Unabara wasn't able to save Xóchitl. Because of that, he just had to make a stronger force act on her instead. There was no precedent, of course. If he couldn't completely deceive a phenomenal original copy, his reward would rebound in the form of death.

But Mitsuki Unabara didn't hesitate.

To save this brown-skinned girl, he would accept everything.

13

Dragging her bloodied foot, Awaki Musujime slowly exited the cell.

The other cells were locked. Her allies wouldn't be coming out. Even if they took more forceful measures, the higher powers in Academy City might still set to work erasing them.

She may have gotten Block out of the way, but she hadn't resolved the fundamental problem. She hadn't overturned the situation—how their lives were in someone else's hands.

But Musujime heard somebody say "I always believed in you."

She heard her allies' voices through a small window installed in the cells' iron doors where food was passed through, like a mail slot. They said they believed in her. They said they knew they were right to believe in her. She could sense the relief in their voices. Relief that she'd saved their lives, of course—but also that Musujime had come running here for them.

For a short while, Awaki Musujime couldn't move a muscle.

Finally, she slowly opened her mouth. But no words would come out. Her lips were trembling harder than she thought. Even so, she began, little by little, to speak.

Over a long period of time, just two or three words eventually made it out.

But that was all they needed.

"Good now?" said Tsuchimikado.

Musujime pushed him out of the way with a hand and headed for the exit.

Accelerator and Mitsuki Unabara, too, were outside. They'd each been fighting their own battles—nobody was unharmed. But the four members of Group had still come together again.

Musujime didn't say anything.

Tsuchimikado looked at her and sighed.

"Then back to the dark we go."

INTERLUDE THREE

She walked slowly down the street.

Considering the position she was in, being there was unthinkable. Anyone had free passage through the streets—and she, without any bodyguards, simply blended in with the crowd. In her hand were five balloons filled with helium, which drew yearning stares from passing children.

She held a cell phone in her other hand.

"Hey, like, Item's the one I'm in charge of, you know. Seriously... I'm not getting any overtime pay for this call."

"What are you saying? I'll admit they got the better of me with Block. But I can recover anything I need to with my strength. Take down the quarantine on Block's position and info! If I can find them again, I can prevent damage to Academy City—"

"The damage thing is fine. It looks like the Group kids just disabled Block at the juvenile reformatory. They won't be causing you trouble anymore."

"O-oh." The person on the phone sounded relieved. *"In that case, I'll..."*

"Yes," she continued, also relieved.

*   *   *

"The Block threat is gone, so we don't need you controlling them anymore."

She heard the person on the other end gasp.

He panicked and began to argue vehemently about something, but she wasn't listening anymore. This was something they'd all decided on. She hung up, then walked back into the crowds.

She let go of one of the balloons in her hand. It flew high into the sky.

"Anyway," she said, not watching it go, fingering the strings of the others. "I wonder what the person controlling School is named."

Item

SHIZURI MUGINO — Leader

SAIAI KINUHATA

FRENDA

RIKOU TAKITSUBO

Member

PROFESSOR — Leader

YOSHIO BABA

XÓCHITL

SARAKU

Group MOTOHARU TSUCHIMIKADO	MITSUKI UNABARA	AWAKI MUSUJIME	ACCELERATOR

Leader **School** TEITOKU KAKINE	UNKNOWN	CHIMITSU SUNAZARA	UNKNOWN

Leader **Block** TATSUHIKO SAKU	MEGUMI TESHIO	YAMATE	TETSUMOU

Transmission data from "UNDER_LINE"

CHAPTER 4

The Paper-Thin Line Between Self-Loathing and Pride

Enemy_Level5.

1

In the end, he washed the ashes down a river.

Shiage Hamazura just couldn't bring himself to throw them into an automatic raw garbage disposer. He knew it had only satisfied himself—and contaminated the environment—but he still resisted discarding into the garbage what had once been human.

...*This sucks*, he thought idly. He'd split up with Takitsubo, and he was now walking along the river alone. *It's not like I sympathized with whoever was in the bag. I was just scared to think it could be me next. I wouldn't like it if someone threw me out like trash when I die.*

"Damn it..." Resisting the urge to mutter *and now I have to go back to them*, Hamazura started back on his way to where Item was waiting.

Then he heard a voice call out to him, saying, "Hey!"

He tried to ignore it and keep going, but someone grabbed his shoulder from behind.

The impact hit him before he turned.

Thud!! A blow to his head, and Hamazura fell to the dirt below.

He heard laughing. When he looked that way, he saw a few young men he'd never met. One was holding a golf club. That was probably what he'd hit Hamazura with.

...?! Are they burglars?

Eighty percent of Academy City's population was students. Depending on the time of day, there would be almost nobody in the student dorms. Some delinquents had formed armed groups, which would plunder the rooms while their owners were away.

"See, I told you. I've seen this guy before. Skill-Out, from District 7, yeah?"

"Didn't they go down?"

"Doesn't matter. We just have to beat him here."

They all laughed. Before Hamazura could speak, they began kicking him from all directions. And all they did was laugh.

"Get this, Skill-Out. We've had it real rough until just recently."

"That leader of yours—Komaba or something? That guy was fucking annoying. We couldn't do our jobs with him around."

"Anyway, we're gonna beat your face in so hard you'll look like an extra on a movie set. You hearin' us?"

Hamazura tried to say that wasn't his fault, but another kick dug into his side before he could. Now that he was having trouble breathing, he couldn't talk to begin with.

Damn...it...

The unknown person resting in the sleeping bag flashed across his mind. Burned by the electric furnace, turned into ash, and washed down the river—he couldn't get the sights out of his mind. Now he'd be erased like that soon. How cheap Level Zero lives went for. It was all making him angry.

And next to him on the dirt-covered road was a metal pipe for propane gas about the width of his thumb.

He didn't hesitate.

"!!" He grabbed the L-shaped pipe and fiercely swung.

It struck the golf club–wielding shit in the ankle, and he could feel the cracking of bones breaking in his hand. As the screaming idiot fell, the bloody Hamazura rose, bringing down the pipe again and landing another blow.

The other two delinquents shouted something, but he ignored them.

Once again, he brought the pipe down on the guy, and was rewarded with a comforting scream.

When one of the other kids heard that, he took a hammer out of his bag.

That might kill me, thought Hamazura. An iron pipe was plenty destructive, but he couldn't knock someone out in one hit with it. If this came down to a straight brawl, they could easily both end up dead, too.

But at that point, he didn't feel like stopping. The sensation of the sleeping bag's synthetic fabric weighed on his palms with amazing vividness.

And then...

"Over here, Hamazura!!"

Right as he heard the shout, the hammer-gripping boy's neck bounced to the side with a *grrk!* Before Hamazura realized it, someone had thrown a brick-like object at him, and someone else grabbed his arm.

"Come on, idiot! We're getting out of here!!"

In a strange display of lethargy, Hamazura let the person pull him into a run.

After a few moments like that, he finally put a name to the voice. "You're...Hanzou, right?"

Hanzou used to be another member of Skill-Out, one he'd been on a few jobs with. If he was hanging around a place like this, maybe he was considering robbing an ATM again, thought Hamazura, remembering part of his old habits.

Exasperated, Hanzou answered, "Did you forget the back-alley rules or what, stupid? If you're too obsessed with winning, you'll end up dead. If you want to concentrate on life or death, then give up on winning!"

He glanced behind him to make sure nobody was following, and then they stopped.

Hamazura gave Hanzou a mystified look. "Why did you help me? I'm the one who ruined Skill-Out and ran from punishment."

"That's not something you gotta say," replied Hanzou in irritation.

"I mean, don't you get it by now? We don't hate you, and we don't think it's your fault. With what happened, it didn't matter who ended up as Skill-Out's leader. We were ruined anyway."

"..."

"Clinging to the past might look good on TV, but we're not walking down that road. Although, I'll admit those were some fun times...me making plans, you getting assistants, Komaba leading the attacks."

"Yeah," said Hamazura impassively. "I'll admit it. It was a shitty life, but it was still fun."

"...What are you gonna do now?"

"Hell if I know. It doesn't matter where I roll into. It wouldn't be the same if I went back to Skill-Out, though. I don't think there's much value in that," he spat, about to turn his back to Hanzou.

But just then, Hanzou reached for something in his pocket and tossed it at him. "Take this. Doesn't look like you have a good weapon."

It was a small handgun, its grip only half the size of his palm.

"...This is a ladies' gun."

"Who cares? The harder a weapon is to use, the better. Get too used to one and you'll spill more blood than you need to."

Hamazura spun it lightly in his hand, then stowed it in his sleeve.

This time, without looking at Hanzou, he left the alley alone.

Item probably had his next job waiting.

2

Shiage Hamazura returned to one of Item's hideouts.

"Hey, Hamazura, you're late," Shizuri Mugino lobbed at him lazily.

They were in part of a high-rise building in School District 3. The facility consisted of sports gyms and pools; all the indoor leisure activities it could fit—and those who used them—were of fairly high grade. You needed to show your member card just to enter the building, and whenever you wanted to use one of its facilities, they'd look at your member rank. Apparently, a membership here was one of the first things people of the so-called upper crust would acquire for their status.

Hamazura and the others were in a VIP lounge, made to look like a European-style "salon"—a fancy suite of private rooms rented out on a yearly contract. You couldn't even use it temporarily without at least a two-star membership rank—truly a top-notch room. Even though it was considered private, it was easily bigger than a four-room apartment, and Mugino had made herself at home on a sofa.

Hamazura looked at the people gathered there, then asked dubiously, "What happened to Frenda?"

"Vanished," answered Mugino curtly. "Either she died or got caught. We don't have time to replace her, so in any case, Item will have to settle for three for now. 'Course, School's missing one of theirs, too, so our numbers match. It won't be hard to recover. Item's got Takitsubo, after all."

Mugino had said *three*: Hamazura frowned at not being counted, but pointing it out wouldn't get him anywhere.

"Hamazura. You're hurt," said Takitsubo, looking at his face.

"It's nothing," he replied, blowing it off. "What do we do now? School stole the Tweezers, right?"

"Yup," admitted Mugino easily. "So now it's our turn to counterattack. Takitsubo's Ability Stalker can search for a specific esper's location with any involuntary diffusion field she remembers. And we fought them at the Particle Physics Institute already. That means we can chase them down. Item's purpose is to protect against the higher-ups and top-secret organizations running amok. Let's do our duty, shall we?"

Hamazura looked at Takitsubo. As always, she had her arms and legs sprawled out lazily. Maybe she was always acting unstable because of the never-ending IDF effects.

"Should I search for Dark Matter?"

"Who's that?" he asked.

"The number-two Level Five," said Mugino. "And the asshole leading School."

Meanwhile, Takitsubo brought out a small case from her pocket with white powder in it.

Kinuhata looked at the see-through case, mystified. "You've, like, got it super-rough. You can't use your ability without Crystals, can you?"

"It's no big deal. This was always normal for me," said Takitsubo, licking just a little bit of the powder.

The glow returned to her eyes. She straightened up and paused, as though this was her regular state.

"Beginning involuntary diffusion field-based search. Stopping pickup of approximate and resemblant IDFs. Limiting search results to a single matching IDF. Time to completion: five seconds."

Her voice came out like a machine.

And then came the right answer.

"Result: Dark Matter is in this building."

Before everyone could give a start and shout "What?!" it happened:

The door to the private lounge was decisively kicked in.

A man came walking in from behind it.

Shizuri Mugino saw him and growled. "Dark Matter...!!"

"I'd rather you call me by name. It's Teitoku Kakine, in case you didn't know."

The man's hands had peculiar "nails" made of machines. "The Tweezers...," said Mugino.

"Sweet, right? Came to declare victory."

"Hah. What's some secondary candidate Aleister didn't choose getting all excited for? You ran away before. Now it looks like you had an attitude change."

"Nah, look. That was some good shit at the Particle Physics Institute. Thanks to you, we lost one of our only four official School members."

"Aren't you forgetting someone? We killed your sniper a few days ago. You get a new one?"

The conversation between Level Fives was suddenly interrupted.

The cause was Saiai Kinuhata. Without rising from the sofa, she had lifted up a nearby table with one hand. The table was covered excessively in decorations and looked like it weighed at least two dozen pounds—and now this girl, who looked no older than twelve, hurled it at Teitoku Kakine.

Ga-slam!!

The table shattered, but Teitoku kept a straight face.

"That hurt," he said, so naturally nobody could tell if he meant it. "And it made me mad. I'll smash you to pieces first."

Kinuhata still didn't respond. She ran to the side of the room, and with her tiny fist, mercilessly broke through the lounge wall. Then she grabbed Hamazura's and Takitsubo's hands, shot a quick glance at Mugino, and dove into the broken wall.

A luxurious lounge of similar construction was on the other side. People were inside, but Kinuhata punched them unconscious. When they got into the hallway, there was a man there who was probably one of School's subordinates, but she knocked him out, too.

Saiai Kinuhata wasn't monstrously strong; she was an esper who could freely control the nitrogen in the air. The skill was incredibly powerful, and by manipulating chunks of compressed nitrogen, she could lift cars and even stop bullets—but its scope was very small and only reached a few centimeters out from her palms. That was why it had looked like she'd been lifting up the table.

"Hamazura, find us a car, like, super-quick, please," said Kinuhata. "Takitsubo is probably one of School's targets. Now that they found this hideout, it'd be extra safe to assume they found other info, too. They probably discovered Takitsubo's troublesome ability and came to crush us all to throw off pursuit."

"You mean her search ability?" asked Hamazura. In terms of visible power, Mugino and Kinuhata seemed a lot flashier, but...

"They don't have to kill everyone in Item—they can severely limit our operations just by taking out Takitsubo. Her being here or not decides who's being chased and who's doing the chasing. If it was me, I'd go for her first."

"..."

"But as long as Takitsubo is safe, we can recover the situation. So please get her in a car and get really far away. If you avoid Item's hideouts, you should be able to buy a lot of time." Kinuhata took a stun gun out of her pocket and made Takitsubo hold it. "You always seem super-unsteady, so this weapon is good for you. Even if it misfires, you won't die."

Bang!! An explosion ripped through a nearby room.

It was from the lounge where Mugino and Kakine were.

"Get going, like, crazy fast, please!" said Kinuhata, turning her back to them.

Before he could say anything, the small girl had already run off toward the battlefield.

3

The explosion's impact made the entire building shake helplessly.

As the chief guests ran about, trying to escape the indoor leisure facilities, Saiai Kinuhata walked through the lobby.

Men from School's ancillary organization were lying on the floor. Kinuhata had thrashed them. She walked next to them, kicking away nearby guns and rifles.

Then suddenly, her face jolted to the side.

By the time she realized she'd been shot, a second and third impact flashed through her, and her small body was sent flying to the floor. She let herself land, then slid across and hid herself behind a nearby pillar.

...A sniper. Where?

The impacts had struck her in the head, chest, and lower gut—all vital spots. If not for the shield from her ability, she'd have died for certain. She placed her palm on a crushed bullet on the floor.

Steel rounds...The magnetic sniper rifle from before? If its initial speed is subsonic, then judging by the way this thing is crushed, they're five to seven hundred away.

As she thought, she reached into an inside pocket. Her fingers came out with pieces of metal between them, about the size of juice cans, with thirty-centimeter metal rods on the ends. They looked kind of like maracas, or maybe old-fashioned grenades, but it was neither.

*   *   *

They were portable anti-tank missile tips.

The fleeing patrons looked at her in shock, but she ignored them.

She would aim the tips between her fingers in that direction, then pull the short strings attached to their back with her other hand. It would look like setting off crackers at a party or drawing back the string of a bow. After a breath, she jumped out from behind the pillar and looked straight out the broken window. A bullet hit between her eyes that very moment, but she ignored it and took aim.

Then, without hesitating, she pulled the strings.

With a dull *shhhp* noise, the power of compressed air sent the missile tips flying from their grips. After traveling about ten meters forward, they ignited—and, scattering flames behind them, closed the five-hundred-meter distance in the blink of an eye.

When all the missiles crashed into the side of the building, the building blew up like crushed mille-feuille. Perhaps as a gift of its excellent aseismic construction, it managed to at least avoid coming down entirely.

"Whoa, that's crazy. I bet Sunazara and his magnetic sniper rifle are a goopy mess now, eh? Maybe that's all someone we got in a hurry could manage."

A bright voice came to her.

When Kinuhata turned around, Teitoku "Dark Matter" Kakine was just coming out of the hallway.

"Heh, wreckage from Project Dark May? You must have it tough. That was the one where they took Accelerator's calculation patterns and used them to optimize a bunch of espers' personal realities, right?"

"..."

"And you ended up with a self-defense ability. Though originally, it was an air control–type ability. Automatically deploying a defensive field made from your ability around you, same as Accelerator, is all you can do, eh? Haven't you ever felt sorry for yourself?"

"Not really," answered Kinuhata shortly. "I'm super–well off compared to the PRODUCE test subjects. They got their brains sliced up like birthday cakes so people could figure out where personal realities come from."

"Right," said Kakine, sounding uninterested.

Still on her guard against the man before her, she asked, "What happened to Mugino?"

"Right, well. Nothing much."

His words were blunt. Just from that, Kinuhata knew: As a Level Four, she couldn't stand up to someone who treated the fourth-most-powerful Level Five in Academy City like that. She'd gotten a vague impression to that end when they'd fought in the Particle Physics Institute, and now she knew she was right.

"So where's the Ability Stalker? That's all I want to know. Tell me where she is and I'll let you go."

"Who would be stupid enough to make a deal like that?"

"Oh, I don't know. Frenda, for example."

"..."

"I'm just saying you've got the choice. And to make things clear, your Level Four Nitrogen Armor can't beat my Dark Matter. No fancy tricks are gonna close that gap, either."

Kinuhata said nothing.

As she glared silently at him, Kakine said, "Where is the Ability Stalker?"

"It doesn't seem like I have the right to refuse...," said Kinuhata, smiling a little.

As she spoke, she grabbed a nearby bench and hurled it.

But...

With a roar, a strange explosion burst out from Kakine.

It shattered the bench flying at him and even batted Kinuhata's body to the side.

Her small frame flew ten meters through the air, then crashed through a thin wall and into another room.

Kakine watched and smiled thinly. "Weighed your pride against death, eh? Emotional, but certainly not practical."

Then he turned to a nearby subordinate and said, "Retrieve her."

"Retrieve...You mean she's still alive after that?"

"That's the sort of esper she is."

4

Shiage Hamazura and Rikou Takitsubo made it to the elevator lobby.

He hit the button on the wall, and the display—paused on floor 48—quickly began to descend to the twenty-fifth floor, where they were. Meanwhile, Hamazura took out a lock-picking tool...*Parking garage must be underground. Everyone here's probably got a fancy car, but no time to be picky. We'll go for the one closest to the elevators—*

The elevator stopped on floor 25.

With a gentle electronic ding, the metal doors automatically parted.

"Oh, there you are."

And then Hamazura heard the voice of despair.

One of School's members came walking out into the hallway: The number-two Level Five who could even fight Shizuri Mugino. With strange nails attached to his right hand, the man approached slowly.

"I was looking all over for you, y'know! You're the search esper, right?" he said, tossing *something* he'd been dragging with his left hand to them. "It" flew a few meters and landed at Hamazura's feet.

"It" was Saiai Kinuhata, with whom they'd just parted.

"...!!"

"She made a good decision. Item's core isn't the Level Five—it's you, right? Man, if you'd gotten out of here, that would've been rough. On the other hand..." Teitoku's voice lowered. "You can't run away at this point."

Each of his steps counted down the lives of Hamazura and Takitsubo.

Hamazura turned his attention to the gun up his sleeve. Then, looking at the open elevator out of the corner of his eye, he spoke to Takitsubo in as quiet a voice as he could. "(...You get on the elevator and go down.)"

"(...But Hamazura—,)" she whispered back.

"(...Either way, if I abandoned you and ran away from School, it would mean the end of Item! Damn it, I'm caught between a rock and a hard place!!)"

Teitoku Kakine stopped walking.

He wasn't hesitating, nor was he trying to let them go. He was already in effective range as a Level Five. "So what're you gonna do? How long do good-byes usually take?"

"...!! Go!!"

Hamazura tried to push Takitsubo into the elevator.

But instead, she reached for his hand.

Their positions whirled around like they were ballroom dancing, and then she pushed him toward the elevator. Hamazura, confused at the sudden act, fell onto his rear.

Only Takitsubo's hand went into the elevator.

She pressed the B1 button—for the underground parking garage.

"What the hell are you—?"

"Sorry, Hamazura." From the other side of the automatically closing doors, Takitsubo gazed at him. "I asked everyone about the furnace. I don't want you to turn into ashes like that."

Her eyes were smiling softly.

"It's okay. I'm a Level Four, and you're a Level Zero. I promise I'll protect you."

"...!!"

Before he could say anything, the door finished closing and the elevator began dropping like a rock. Something absurd had just happened, but on the other hand, he was out of immediate danger, and he felt an odd sense of relief wash over him.

Still sitting on the floor, he put his back to the wall and looked up at the ceiling.

Weren't espers supposed to think our lives weren't worth anything? he thought as the floaty sensation unique to fast-moving elevators came over him. He put a hand over his face, still looking up. *There are heaps of us. We're like disposable umbrellas. Even if we die, we're supposed to get burned to a crisp in an incinerator and our ashes thrown out with the rest of the trash.*

"Damn it," he mumbled.

Hamazura probably hadn't been the only one experiencing shock when he cooked the black sleeping bag in that furnace. The girl watching from behind him had been shocked just the same. Had Rikou Takitsubo always wanted to protect people like him, or had the furnace incident given her a change of heart? He didn't know.

But he did know one thing.

Rikou Takitsubo had stood up to the number-two man in Academy City to save him, a Level Zero.

"…This is a load of crap," he mumbled, putting a hand on the wall and slowly getting up. "This is a load of bullshit!!"

He slammed the wall with his open hand, pounding a button on it and causing the elevator to stop.

Clenching his teeth, he took a few deep breaths. To be honest, he had virtually no chance of winning. That Kakine guy was a Level Five, and he wasn't the only bad guy. He at least had those black-clothed guys, probably from their ancillary organization.

But…

"Is there even a place for Level Zeroes? Of course there is. Can you get by without victimizing other people? Of course you can, damn it!!"

Once, he'd met a Level Zero completely different from him in the Dangai University database center, and now his words naturally came to mind.

"You had enough strength to form Skill-Out— If you'd used that to help people in weaker positions, you'd all be in a different place right now!! You had the strength to fight back against strong espers— If you'd used that to reach out to people in need, everyone in Academy City would have accepted you!!"

"…Yeah."

Shiage Hamazura pushed the button for the twenty-fifth floor again, where he'd parted with Takitsubo, and closed the elevator doors.

"*That's right, asshole,*" he declared, cutting off his own retreat and returning to the battlefield where the Level Five waited.

5

The elevator stopped on the twenty-fifth floor.

The automatic doors opened, and Hamazura passed through them to find the scene he'd predicted.

"What? Came back, eh?" stated School's Level Five, Teitoku Kakine.

Near him, in the same position as she had been when he'd thrown her, was Saia Kinuhata.

And at the unscathed man's feet was Rikou Takitsubo, head down, face unreadable, limp on the floor. He couldn't even tell whether she was alive or dead.

Kakine cracked his neck joints. "I gotta tell you, she's got no direct combat skills, but she came at me pretty hard. Must have been an application of her search ability—she interfered with my involuntary diffusion field and then reversed it, trying to hijack my own ability. Sheesh, if she'd developed normally, she could have been the eighth one."

Each word of praise just sounded like he was making a fool of her.

Hamazura didn't say a word. Silently, he whipped out the gun hidden up his sleeve and pointed it at him.

"Oh, you weren't finished yet?"

Suddenly, another voice.

A girl wearing a fancy dress came around the corner behind Kakine.

The…the crane girl from before?!

Hamazura hesitated for a moment about where to aim.

"You'd better not."

That moment, Shiage Hamazura lost the ability to move even a finger.

"I would've needed to kill you before, but now that I have the Tweezers, I don't have to—you're only part of their ancillary organization."

His body wasn't paralyzed for any reason. Physically, he was totally fine. But there was an idea blossoming in his mind—one that he couldn't shoot even if he wanted to.

He felt like he was trying to stomp on a kitten taking a nap.

He felt like he was trying to kill a sick kid to steal his valuables.

He felt like he was accidentally pointing his gun at Rikou Takitsubo.

"You've got a mean face, but you're a nice person on the inside. I knew I should have used my power from the start," said the girl in the dress, smiling. "My Heart Measure can freely control the distance between people's hearts. What do you think would happen if I set us to the same distance as all of your friends?"

"Ugh…!!" *What is this? Some kind of telepathy?!*

"Why not call it quits?" she continued. "Right now, I'm at a distance of twenty units…In other words, the same distance as between Shiage Hamazura and Rikou Takitsubo. You can't shoot Takitsubo, so you can't shoot me. I know you came all the way back up here for her sake. You'd never be able to hurt her, would you?"

The gun clattered, shaking in his trembling hand.

He couldn't do it. He knew Takitsubo and the girl in the dress were different people, but he just couldn't do it.

Kakine made a look like his fun was spoiled. "This is dumb. Now it seems like we're the bad guys."

"Hey, a boy and a girl protecting each other is romantic. It's so rare I almost don't want to break it."

"Yeah. It's too bad. Wonder if she'll do us a favor and die without us doing anything."

Hamazura's shoulders jolted at that. "What the hell…? What do you mean?"

Kakine kicked the clear case near Takitsubo over in his direction. "The Crystals. Did you know she was using them?"

"…Yeah, for her ability…"

"Strictly speaking, they induce a physical rejection and make her ability go out of control. More specifically, they used 'em in the Explosion Experiment for Analyzing Runaway Ability Laws. Most of the time, it's nothing but a disadvantage—but in really rare cases, someone'll be able to get better results when berserked. This girl was probably one of them."

Kakine sounded like having to explain every little thing was boring him.

"She won't last long in this state. She might be fine if she never uses her ability again, but one or two more times and she'll break down."

Break down. The unsettling phrase made Hamazura grimace.

Kakine ignored him and went on. "We don't even need to finish her off like this. Without her search ability, her death doesn't mean much."

"Just so we're clear, she collapsed of her own volition," the girl said flatly. "It's because she kept forcing herself to use those Crystals to fight against School in this building—if we were really going in for the kill, there'd be nothing left."

Hamazura glared at her, unable to move in any meaningful way, even as the two School members ignored him and pushed the elevator button.

"Anyway, now what?" said Kakine simply as they waited. "Kill him, or let him live?"

"Leaving him be won't be a problem, will it? Item's on the brink of destruction anyway. They can't stop us."

Hamazura gnashed his teeth at the words "brink of destruction," but he just couldn't pull the trigger. Her Heart Measure ability had him completely under her control.

"Killing him would be easier."

"Look, didn't your personal reality get messed up through your IDF because of the search ability? Shouldn't you check yourself? You going out of control is a lot more dangerous than a near-dead Item. I'd rather not die because an ally went on a berserk rampage."

Teitoku Kakine cracked his neck again, annoyed. He wasn't holding a gun. He must have had just that much faith in his ability. But if worse came to worst and his ability *did* go haywire, Kakine himself would be the first one caught up in it.

"Guess I don't have a choice. Let's go back. The check is simple, but we don't have the machine here."

As though timed, the elevator arrived on this floor.

Shit!! Hamazura pushed the gun's hammer up with his thumb.

But the dress girl's face remained steady. "Our current distance is twenty. The same as between Shiage Hamazura and Rikou Takitsubo. But I can make the distance even shorter, you know."

"!!"

"There's nothing sadder than plastering false emotions over real ones. You should share your happiness of surviving this with that near-dead girl over there."

The two got into the elevator, Hamazura unable to stop them, and the automatic doors closed.

He looked down at the Crystal case at his feet, then at the unresponsive Rikou Takitsubo, and slowly sat down.

If she uses her ability a couple more times, she'll break down...

Hamazura, being a stupid delinquent, didn't know what "break down" entailed, exactly. But he could guess it was nothing good.

What should I do?

He peered at her face. Her body wasn't even twitching. No sign of her waking up, either. She must have put a lot of excess strain on herself, too, since she was covered in a layer of thick sweat.

Rikou Takitsubo had fought Kakine until she'd gotten like this.

Probably to save Shiage Hamazura.

While borrowing the power of these Crystals he didn't understand.

"..." He quietly clenched his teeth.

It didn't amount to enough to be called resolve, and it wasn't refined enough to be called determination. But he still had something now—something to drive him, to move his own arms and legs with.

"Damn it..."

He couldn't return Rikou Takitsubo to Item. Their system would gladly replace official members if they disappeared. Even if he brought her there in her critical state, they'd cruelly force her to use her ability.

As his hands trembled, he took the ladies' gun out of his sleeve. He pulled the magazine out and checked his ammunition. It couldn't hold much, given how narrow the grip was built to be. Besides, even with thousands of bullets on him, could he really overcome the crisis he was about to face? Academy City's underworld would chase Takitsubo down, and even Item had enemies. Could he fight them all?

"God damn it!!"

He had to.

If they made Takitsubo use her ability any more than this, it would really be over.

Then Kinuhata, lying on the floor with her, looked over at him without moving anything else. She seemed to guess the situation from his irritation. "...Well, that's probably the right thing. Take Takitsubo somewhere else and disappear, please."

"Thanks."

"I didn't say anything you needed to thank me for. I'm just insulting you. I'm saying that the only thing super-useless people like you and her are good for in Item is holding us back anyway."

Despite that, a little smile was on her lips.

She wasn't unharmed, either. Blood was trickling from her lips. But she saw him act for Takitsubo's sake and smiled anyway.

"Is there anything I can do before I leave?"

"...Well, you could use code five-two to contact our ancillary organization and get an information concealing unit and an ambulance here, please. As you can see, I can't move."

"All right," said Hamazura. It pained him to leave her here, but for now, he had to take Takitsubo and escape.

In any case, we're fine as long as she doesn't use her ability. She'll have to retire from Item, but that's a lot better than "breaking down" or whatever, he thought.

But just then, his cell phone rang.

On the other end was Shizuri Mugino.

"Haamaazuraaaa. Would Rikou Takitsubo happen to be with you?"

"...Are you all right?! You were fighting Kakine, and, and...!!"

"Quit making such a fuss. It's time we started our counterattack on School. We're using Takitsubo's power and chasing them. If she's there, bring her here, now. *We're getting results even if it kills her.*"

6

Hamazura, with the corpse-like, unmoving Takitsubo on his back, left the building. He wasn't obeying Shizuri Mugino's orders and making her use her ability. Quite the opposite. He would run as far away as he could, so that she would have no part in Item in the future.

He was on a short bridge now. It wasn't water flowing underneath, but a railroad track. It was one of the parts of the subway line that went aboveground. A sports car was parked on the other side of the bridge.

"So I don't know what's going on, but you want me to take her, yeah?"

It was an Anti-Skill officer named Aiho Yomikawa who had gotten out of said car and was now putting a hand on her hip in exasperation.

The escape routes and hiding places they used were also used by all of Item, which meant Mugino would easily find out. He decided the better plan would be to give her to someone with a completely different escape route.

"Hamazura, you know what my job is, right? I'm an Anti-Skill officer, 'kay? You think I'd let you escape alone after coming to me in this extremely suspicious situation with an unconscious girl on your back?"

"…Shut up," said Hamazura, gritting his teeth. Yomikawa frowned a little—his irritation seemed different. He went on, "If you want an explanation, I'll tell you whatever you want later. I'll attend whatever I need to! Take her and bring her somewhere safe, and fast!! She's seriously messed up right now. She was using some Crystal things and now she could break down any second!!"

"Crystals…? Wait, Hamazura, did you just say Crystals?!"

Yomikawa's expression changed completely just from that one word, but Hamazura didn't explain.

He didn't have the time.

"…Haaamazuraaa."

Suddenly, he heard a voice from behind.

He turned around and saw Shizuri Mugino, covered in blood, on the other side of the short bridge. Some blood was hers, some wasn't. She was dragging some rags in her right hand—and he knew what they were.

"Frenda…"

To be more accurate, only her upper half.

Her lower half was nowhere in sight, and dark red dripped and dropped from her terminus.

"Oh, yes. It looks like School scared her, so she betrayed Item and tried to go into hiding. I cleaned her up real nice…And what's this, now? I don't have to clean *you* up, too, do I?"

Mugino let go, and what was left of Frenda dropped to the ground with a *blotch*.

She wasn't paying attention to her trophy anymore.

That showed the depth of their friendship.

Hamazura grimaced at the sight—clearly a corpse, unlike Takitsubo. But he still wouldn't waver. He pushed the girl on his back onto Yomikawa and said quietly, "…Please, go."

"Hamazura, like I said, I'm an Anti-Skill officer. I could never use a child as a shield in this situation—"

"Go, damn it!!" he shouted, interrupting her. "I know you can't leave a murder case alone. But she's in a different dimension! I can't tell you the details, but Frenda was really strong herself. And that woman killed her, no problem! Just take Takitsubo and get out of here!!"

After that, his expression about to break down, he looked at the unconscious Takitsubo.

"Please…I don't want to let her die. For a while, I haven't had any idea what to do, but now I finally found something. So please, go. I can't protect her alone. Without your help, I'll lose everything!!"

"Hamazura…"

"Anyway, what chance would you have alone?! She's a Level Five. The fourth-most-terrifying monster in Academy City! I'll buy you time, so you get Takitsubo out of here!!"

The words seemed to tear his throat apart. Yomikawa sucked in her breath at his fierce look. She hesitated—but nevertheless, spurred by the glint in his eyes, nodded at last.

"Once I've brought her somewhere safe, I'll get fully equipped officers here right away. Don't die before then."

"...Right," he answered.

Yomikawa decisively got into the car and stepped on the accelerator. The sports car, with Rikou Takitsubo on board, quickly sped away.

He heard someone whistling.

Hamazura looked over just as the Level Five Shizuri Mugino was crossing the bridge and approaching him.

"A fight with your life on the line? How exhilarating, Hamazura."

"I—"

It was just when he tried to say something.

Mugino, now close to him, waved her hand horizontally. He took the hit, and his body went flying to the side. With a dull crack, the bridge's metal handrail dug into his gut. The shock brought bile up into his throat. The power almost left his limbs as he hung across the railing like a futon set out to dry. Right under the bridge, he saw a subway train going by on the tracks.

"Quiet. I didn't ask for your opinion."

Ignoring Hamazura's moans, Mugino crossed the rest of the bridge.

She hadn't used her power as a Level Five. It was just brute force. She'd purposely made him yield to physical strength so he couldn't use their relative levels as an excuse.

She hadn't given up yet. She wanted to know where School was even if Takitsubo "broke down" because of it.

"Ha-ha," he laughed anyway, still limp on the handrail. "You sure you don't want to just finish me off?"

"Eh?" Mugino turned an indignant glare on him.

Then her eyes went wide.

The case of Crystals that Rikou Takitsubo had been using was in Shiage Hamazura's hand.

"She absolutely needs these to use Ability Stalker, doesn't she?"

"You bastard...!!"

Before clear rage could make it into her eyes, Hamazura went over the metal handrail and jumped off the bridge.

A subway car was passing by just at that moment.

He crashed into the car's roof. People usually perceived them as flat, but subway cars actually had outer air conditioners and such on their roofs, making them fairly uneven. When he landed, he rolled several times, his skin tearing as though he'd been dragged over a grater, and the momentum almost carried him straight off the car. But he managed to dig in and stop.

Sprawled out on the subway car's roof, he grinned. *Looks like I managed to shake her off. Without these Crystals, she can't make Takitsubo use her ability. I don't have to fight her. As long as these don't make it into Mugino's hands—*

Suddenly, with a massive jolt, the train car stopped.

He slid across the roof. As he stopped himself and looked up, startled, he saw Mugino standing far behind them on the rails. Like Hamazura, she'd jumped off the bridge. Her hand was deep inside the ground—the ground within which the electric cables for Academy City's subways ran. Mugino had used her ability to sever those cables, forcing the train car to come to a stop.

A few hundred meters away, Shizuri Mugino said something.

He couldn't hear her, but he could read her lips.

Now. You're. Dead. For. Sure.

7

Hamazura, on the train car roof, got the message from Mugino.

The Level Five had stopped the car by force, and now she had a sharp, enraged grin on her face.

"...!!" Hamazura's hair stood on end. He quickly jumped from the car roof and ran across the gravel. He was blocked off on either side by concrete walls, like this was a man-made river, but spotted a metal staircase interrupting one. He ran up those stairs and burst out into the streets aboveground.

He cast a glance over his shoulder.

Mugino was ascending the stairs, not far behind. In spite of the twenty or thirty meters between them, she was staring straight at

him through the crowds. She'd already locked onto Shiage Hamazura as her prey.

Shit!! I can't even shake her in a crowd!!

He kept on running, slipping between the people enjoying their days off. But he soon reached his limit. He looked around, then headed for a nearby building. Without checking if the door was locked, he basically gave it a shoulder tackle to force open the entrance and rolled inside.

"...Damn. Where am I...?"

This wasn't a normal company building. Trees a little taller than Hamazura were planted all over the floor. A wire netting hung overhead, and the trees' branches tangled around it. Grapes. He looked down and saw a line of hydroponic containers. The bluish-purple illumination must have been ultraviolet light to stimulate photosynthesis.

An automatic manufacturing plant for vegetable ethanol fuel?

Research on gasoline substitutes had come a long way. Sugar cane and corn were the usual culprits, but judging by the purposeful choice of grapes, which had a low alcohol production rate, it probably meant the grapes were of the finest quality, with a serious consideration on branding. Apparently District 3's celebrities wanted even the fuel they put in their cars to be different from the norm. Were they trying to make their engines drink wine, or what?

"What a nice place."

The voice came from directly behind him. He tensed.

"That's some good sense to choose an unmanned facility, Hamazura. It's best if you're the only one to die."

Before he could turn around in a panic, he felt the impact.

Gwa-thud!! With a nasty noise, Hamazura's body flew several meters away before hitting the ground. In grand style, he overturned the hydroponic containers, cracked through several grape vines, and kept on rolling along.

The one hit, liable to kill him outright, caused intense pain all over.

It was very strange that none of his bones were broken.

"Damn it...!!"

Hamazura dragged his bruised body out of the room. There was a staircase, so he went up it. Upstairs, he found rows of silver machines twice his height and straight metal piping connected to them. It looked like a beer production plant, the kind he saw in commercials once in a while. They were fermenting grapes and using the alcohol content from them, after all, so it was probably mostly the same on the inside. There would have also been machines to concentrate the alcohol and convert it into automobile fuel.

Compared to before, there were more blind spots.

She might be a Level Five, but that doesn't mean she's invincible.

Hamazura wriggled through the intricate pipes, then pushed his back up against the wall of a machine the size of a small room, desperately searching for an advantage.

Back when I got attacked by that crane truck outside the Particle Physics Institute, she didn't use her power to destroy the wrecking ball. And with the subway before, too—she didn't try to stop the speeding car itself. She aimed for the power line in the ground.

He clenched his teeth against the pain going through him and looked for a way out.

She's incredibly strong, but I bet she needs a certain amount of time to take aim. In other words, she's weak to surprise attacks. She shouldn't be able to deal with a sudden attack from the shadows.

That wasn't because her power was commonplace, but rather a weakness born of it being too strong. Unless she was meticulous and defined her ability's area of effect, she could get herself caught in it.

Whatever the reason, he didn't care, as long as she had a disadvantage.

With all the obstacles there, Shiage Hamazura should have had some chance at victory.

But...

"Haaamazuraaa."

One word. Just hearing the voice made Hamazura's body scream of danger.

Abandoning all logic, he went down to the floor—and a moment later, it came.

*   *   *

Zzzhhhaaa!! A rain of light rays.

Pure-white, unhealthy-looking rays of light lashed out in all directions from around the woman named Shizuri Mugino. They were special electron beams, each fired with as much energy as a lightning strike. Electrons, like light, exhibited properties of both particles and waves, depending on the situation, but Mugino could control electrons in a vague state between those.

When these electrons, stuck in an ambiguous state, collided with an object, they wouldn't be able to determine which response to exhibit—a wave or a particle—and would end up "stopping" in place. The mass of an electron was supposed to be infinitely close to zero, but because of this stopping effect, they would turn into a pseudo-wall, which would smash into the target with terrible force, given the speed the electrons were fired at.

That was Meltdown.

Its formal classification: a high-speed particle-wave cannon.

Unlike the number-three Railgun, this Level Five could control electrons without using either waves or particles.

Each of the light beams destroyed metal like it was paper, melted down thick walls, and painted everything in an orange hue. As though heat had made it to the already-produced alcohol, small explosions were triggered in a few places. Hamazura managed to avoid a direct hit, but a metal fragment the size of a guitar pick stabbed into his left shoulder. And it didn't stop at one—three or four more followed.

"Guh, *ahhhhhhhh!!*" he screamed, holding his bloody shoulder.

If his cover was in her way, she would make short work of it. With everything reduced to rubble and the room now flattened, Hamazura and Mugino hopelessly faced each other.

"The machines around here—they're just like those things you use to scoop goldfish. Uhh, I forget the name. Anyway, none of this can block my Meltdown."

Academy City's number four.

She'd reduced all the machines covering the room to rubble in a single attack. She'd wrecked all possible cover, even doing major damage to the outer walls—and with the building itself now in danger of falling, Mugino stood in the center of the destruction and slowly, slowly widened her smile.

"According to those shithead scholars, my biological instincts put a safety on my ability, so this is all the power I can use. But I hear that originally, it could instantly kill Railgun. I guess that's just me complaining, though—if I actually did it, the recoil would apparently blow my own body to pieces, too."

Fear washed over Shiage Hamazura like a wave.

The Level Five monster merely approached him without a word.

8

Shizuri Mugino's Meltdown fired with overwhelming force.

With the rubble behind him, Hamazura ran for his life, trying to get as far away from her as he could.

As he fled from the vegetable ethanol plant to another part of the building, Mugino called out.

"Hamazuraaa. Couldn't you please stop making this difficult and hand over the Crystals and Takitsubo already? I won't be satisfied until I've killed every single person in School."

As he ran, Hamazura rejected her words. "I refuse. I'm not letting Takitsubo use the Crystals anymore. She's at her limit!"

"So what? If Takitsubo dies, we can just get another esper to replace her. She's probably the only one who can search for people by their involuntary diffusion fields, but I don't mind having an esper who does it differently. As long as we know where the School bastards are, we don't have any problem."

Hamazura made it to the area where the remnants of grapes were temporarily gathered once the alcohol had been wrung out. But Mugino's Meltdown reduced that place to a mountain of debris in mere seconds.

As he hid behind a heap of hot metal, Hamazura said, "...Sorry, but I can't go with you."

"Eh?"

"You can't beat that Kakine guy. You've already *run away twice*—once at the Particle Physics Institute, and again during the last battle."

He thought he heard her grating her teeth.

But he continued anyway. "Now that I faced him personally, I know. It's not about you being fourth place and him being second. You'd lose to him in a different way. What good is it going to do for you now, finding out where he is?"

The people in School were perverted in their own way, but they at least let people farther down the scale escape. Even when their enemy, Takitsubo, exhausted her strength, they didn't move in for the kill.

Meanwhile, Shizuri Mugino was baring her fangs at even her allies, just because she didn't like it. She didn't seem stronger than them. However overwhelming her power, that impression didn't change.

"Being able to win or not isn't the problem. Even if you risked your life and won, all anyone would get out of it is self-satisfaction. I can't let Takitsubo go along with something that petty. You'd squander her life away on that?"

"Hah. Ha-ha!!"

Even when she heard Shiage Hamazura's answer, Mugino just laughed it off. She slowly followed him as he changed cover, from rubble to rubble, to get away from her.

"How did she train you, Hamazura? Did her cute face make you do it? Or was it because she was nice to you even though you're a Level Zero?"

When Hamazura stayed silent, Mugino's smile deepened.

"There's a word for you: an idiot. Is everyone who says nice things to you a good person, and everything who says harsh things to you a bad guy?! You talk like you're the center of the world!!"

"…I know that."

Hamazura didn't deny it.

If Rikou Takitsubo hadn't said those nice things to him, he wouldn't have changed his mind.

"But she said she didn't want me to die to some calculating bastard like you. She's capable of saying things like that, you know! A girl like her deserves to be happy. Neither of us is fit to stand above others. If a nice idiot doesn't get to the top and lead us all to a new kind of society, this shithole of a world will never be saved!!"

He didn't get an answer.

Instead, with a *roar*, light rays so white it was like a nuclear explosion blew away both Hamazura and the pile of metal he was hiding behind. The blast sent him careening back, but suddenly, he felt the presence of someone right along his back.

Before he turned around, he noticed something felt off in his right ear.

Shizuri Mugino had stuck a screwdriver into it.

"Hey, wait. It looks like you have a screw loose in your head."

Slshh... The screwdriver's tip slowly went into his ear.

"Want me to screw it back in for you?"

He couldn't move. If he moved his head at all, it would damage the inside of his ear and he'd start bleeding everywhere. As Mugino maintained their positions, she brought her empty left hand in front of him and held out her palm.

She was telling him to give her the Crystals.

Hamazura reached into his pocket.

The clear case with the Crystals was inside.

Damn it...

He clenched his teeth, shut his eyes, and made up his mind.

Whirl!!

He disregarded the screwdriver and whipped around.

9

Shiage Hamazura ignored the screwdriver in his ear and twisted his body.

"Wha—?"

Even Mugino seemed a little surprised.

The screwdriver chewed up the inside of his ear. Unimaginably intense pain exploded in his head, and sounds on his right became muted like he had put in an earplug. On top of that, for some reason, half his vision seemed faintly red.

He ignored it all and took the Crystal case out of his pocket.

It was a small, rectangular, clear case, like the tubing inside a mechanical pencil.

He squeezed it, and using its corner, shoved it lengthways into the clinging Mugino's face.

It crushed her right eye in an instant, like a pirate captain.

"Guh, *ooohhhhhhhhhhhhhhhhhhhhhhhhhhhhhhhhhhh*!!"

Mugino wobbled backward, grasping at her red, dripping face with her hands.

Hamazura watched quietly and smiled. "A Level Five's eye for a Level Zero's ear…Bargain shopping, am I right?"

When Mugino heard that, her face distorted in anger. "Hamazu-raaaaa!!"

Bam!! A flash of light burst from her.

Her left arm, from hand to elbow, blew away as though it had melted. The pure-white light it created aimed at Hamazura's face. She was trying to fire her weapon without taking precise aim first.

"…!!"

Hamazura swung his head out of the way a moment before.

It was total coincidence that he dodged an overwhelming attack like that.

Mugino reached out with her blood-covered right hand, shoved Hamazura to the ground—he had lost his balance, and was unsteady—and climbed on top of him. As she did, the case of Crystals left his hand and clattered across the floor. Mugino wasn't paying attention to that anymore.

Glaring at Hamazura through her remaining left eye, she screamed, overtaken with fury. "It doesn't matter!! *It doesn't fucking matter!!* An ear? An eye?! You can break off my limbs and crush my heart and it wouldn't change the fact that I'm stronger than you! This is what a Level Five is. I am the fourth-ranked Meltdown!! Don't get full of yourself, bastard. I could kill a hundred of you fucking Level Zeroes without even moving a finger!!"

As spittle flew from her mouth, Mugino grabbed Hamazura's neck with her right hand. If she activated her ability like this, she'd definitely annihilate his head.

Hamazura smiled as she held his neck like a can of juice.

The strength left his body as though he had given up on something.

"...Hey, I'm no idiot. I figured this would happen," he said, listening to Mugino's ragged breathing. "You're the kind of person who can't be satisfied unless she can beat a video game without dying. The slightest mistake, and you fly into a rage—and even if you see the ending, you're not happy."

"Eh?"

"When people like that make a tiny mistake, they'll find another goal so they can write it off. If you can't win without dying, you'll get a new high score and be satisfied...You never needed to obsess over some boring Level Zero. You should have just used your Level Five shit and sniped me from far away."

He grinned.

"What I'm saying is that wasting time to come here and declare victory was a fatal opening!"

Shka!!

It was the sound of Shiage Hamazura stretching his arm, and the ladies' gun up his sleeve sliding out.

"Wha—?"

Before Mugino could say anything, Hamazura pulled the trigger.

Bang, bang, bam!! With a series of dry sounds, several holes opened up in her upper body. Hamazura kept on firing until he ran out of bullets, and even after that, his index finger continued to move for a while.

"..."

Mugino looked at the blood all over her, surprised.

Eventually, she rolled limply to the side, fell to the floor, and stopped moving.

"Easy win, Level Five," said Hamazura casually, dragging his own beat-up body to its feet. He picked up the case of Crystals and put it back in his pocket.

He probably couldn't have beaten her if he'd taken his gun out right away. She would have easily used her ability to protect herself. He needed to be stingy about it until the very last moment. Even when she put the screwdriver in his ear, he hadn't taken it out—to lull her into a false sense of security, that he had no actual weapons.

Ritoku Komaba, Skill-Out's leader, had once locked out Academy City's strongest Level Five's ability and gotten within inches of taking his life. Hamazura had done the same kind of thing.

He pushed his pinkie into his wounded right ear.

The eardrum didn't seem damaged. His finger came out with a clump of blood, and some of his hearing returned.

"…Sheesh. Bargain shopping indeed," he grumbled, about to leave.

"…ma…zura…"

Then a voice, as though from the depths of hell, gave Hamazura a terrible chill up his spine.

He slowly turned around.

"Hamazuraaaaaaaaaaaaaaaaaaaaaaaaaaaaaaaaaaaaaaaaaaaaaaaaaaa!!"

Despite the dark-red holes in her body, a left arm missing from the elbow down, and a right eye crushed into mush, she was just shooting to her feet. An all-too-unhealthy white light surrounded her right hand. She was probably looping her high-speed wave-particle cannon, which used an immense number of electron beams. One hit from that would wipe Hamazura clear off the map.

The handgun in his right hand had no ammo left.

He wouldn't be relying on it.

"Ohh…*Oooooooooohhhhhhhhhhhhhhhhhhhhhhhhhhhhhhhhhhhh!!*"

He flung the gun aside and charged straight into Mugino's zone.

Their arms intersected.

The slightest hesitation would have created an opening.

The slightest opening would have ensured his death.

But Shiage Hamazura had made up his mind. He simply stepped forcefully in, gripped his fist tight as a boulder, stared straight into the face of the enemy he had to defeat, and let loose the strongest, fastest attack he could.

A loud *slam* thundered through the room.

The energy left Shizuri Mugino's body; she crumpled to her knees, then to the floor. The terrible white light in her hand melted into the air and vanished. There was no danger there.

Hamazura picked up the gun he'd thrown away, then looked down at the unmoving Mugino and took his cell phone out of his pocket. He called up Yomikawa, who had given him her number when she'd put him in custody, saying something about being there if he wanted to talk.

"It's Hamazura. Don't need Anti-Skill support anymore," he said, walking through the demolished building, heading for the exit.

"Yeah. I ended it all."

10

Shiage Hamazura left the District 3 vegetable ethanol plant. Several people from Item's ancillary were standing by to erase all the evidence, but nobody stopped him. From the looks of things, he'd just crushed the fourth-ranked Level Five in Academy City. Nobody would want to foolishly lay a hand on him.

"Yo."

A figure standing a short distance away from the building saw him and spoke up.

"Hanzou?"

Delinquent members with their bases in District 7 had nothing to do with the celebrity-filled District 3. It couldn't have been a coincidence he was there. Had he tapped into their radio or something?

"Heard all about it, Hamazura."

"What, and how much?"

"You beat a Level Five on your own, right?"

Some information source he's got, thought Hamazura with a sigh, then he remembered something. "It came in handy, by the way."

"It?"

"The girl gun. If you hadn't given it to me, I'd be dead."

"Hah. If you took down a Level Five with that tiny little gun, that makes you a real beast." Hanzou took out a cigarette, then handed a second one to Hamazura. "Well, isn't that a nice little present? With all this under your belt, nobody would turn you down. Not that many people actually hate you anyway."

"..."

"Your old position's available, Hamazura. A bunch of others are waiting for you, too."

"Sorry," said Hamazura, lighting the cigarette and grinning. "I found something else to do."

"*Pfft.* Now I'm jealous."

Nevertheless, Hanzou didn't persist. The fact that Hamazura, of all people, had stood up to the monster that was Shizuri Mugino all on his own—he could sense something different about his state of mind.

"Whatever. I'll round up Skill-Out for the time being."

"Thanks."

"But don't forget about us. We'll save you a seat. Come on back when you're done."

They talked, they laughed, and they bumped fists, before each headed for his own destination.

INTERLUDE
FOUR

After holing up in a hotel room for about an hour, the girl in the dress went back to School's hideout. Teitoku Kakine, Level Five, was in there.

"Huh? Where'd you go, exactly?"

"Just making a little pocket change. Academics are the worst, you know. They calculate a base rate and don't bother tipping."

"Hmm. One hour—sounds like a rousing time."

"I wasn't doing anything shameful. We got a hotel room, sure, but we just flipped through magazines and talked a bit."

"…Not having sex?"

"No! And I didn't need to. It depends on the person, but my 'customers' don't generally come looking for something like that. Do you know why rich people go to stores and give money to women? It's not because they have some sexual desires they want to fulfill. They just want to form a personal relationship by themselves outside of work."

"Strange world," said Kakine.

The girl in the dress seemed half-exasperated. "You know workaholics, right? Their jobs are so much fun for them that they wreck their families because of it. For them, relationships they can build with money are like salvation. Money is the result of their work. They use it to buy friendship and love, and then get the satisfaction that they made personal relationships on their own, or really are fit for this society. I'm just relieving some of the complex they feel by having money."

"Right," said Kakine, his voice perfectly uninterested.

The girl in the dress lost the will to explain. "Oh, right," she said. "Looks like Item, the ones we were after, are out of business. Infighting. Shizuri Mugino, number four, went down, and now they can't keep their group together."

"Huh? Infighting— So Mugino escaped my attack…But wait, who took her out? Frenda ran away after making a deal with us, and we crushed Saiai Kinuhata. Rikou Takitsubo doesn't have any direct fighting power, so…"

He stopped. "No…"

"Yes. If it wasn't an official member, it's most likely someone from their ancillary group."

They both thought of the Level Zero who had come back up into the elevator lobby to protect Rikou Takitsubo. Kakine whistled in praise.

The girl stared at him. "Anyway, how's the analysis on the Tweezers going?"

Teitoku Kakine wore a mechanical glove on his right hand, and two clear nails were equipped to its index and middle fingers. Plus, though you couldn't see it with the naked eye; the nails were filled with silicon chunks absorbed from the air. Although they were chunks, they were only seventy nanometers across—you'd have to use an electron microscope to observe them.

"I always had doubts," said Kakine, clicking the nails together. "That jackass Aleister *always knows too much about what we're doing.* He's not just watching through the surveillance cameras, security robots, or satellites. I was always confused about how he got his information."

"…"

"Turns out, it's nothing much. He just has about fifty million invisible machines floating around the city he pulls intel from. It's no wonder he knows the place inside and out."

It was called the Underline.

It took the form of a spherical body, with three wiry cilia extending from each side. It didn't walk along the ground to move—it was closer to drifting through the air.

These ultra-small machines rode on convection currents in the air to generate their own power, pseudo-perpetually gathering information and using a straight electron beam to send internally produced quantum signals to and from the Underline, creating a sort of network. The Underline was the only place information entered the Windowless Building, and naturally, the little things would contain several pieces of information powerful enough to shake the world.

"But even knowing the Underline exists, it's really hard to find machines you'd need an electron microscope for. And even if I did catch them, I'd have no way to get information out of them. After all, you'd have to pry open a nano-sized device and hook up to its circuitry. On top of that, I hear the quantum signals inside them would get changed if an outside source carelessly observed it."

That was where the Tweezers came in.

However small the nanodevices were, the Tweezers would have no problems, since they were developed to grab elementary particles themselves. They would make it possible to extract information from the Underline.

The girl in the dress looked at Kakine and asked, "What did the analysis show?"

"What we thought it would," answered Kakine. "It won't work. There's a lot of data stored in the Underline, but I don't think this by itself will put us on an equal playing field with Aleister. We'll need one last push, in addition to this data."

"Then we're going to do it?"

"...Yeah. We'll kill Academy City's number one. That's the only way. If we want to have an advantage negotiating with Aleister, a spare won't cut it. Instead, I'll have to become a main."

"I see," replied the girl, not particularly emotive. "Doesn't matter to me. I'm still not getting involved in the Accelerator fight."

"What?"

"My Heart Measure ability changes the distance between people's hearts. So if I held the same distance to Accelerator as whomever he's closest to, I might be able to force him to hesitate to attack."

"And?"

"But that doesn't guarantee he'll stop when confronting the person closest to him. Some people go crazy and attack even more fiercely. *Why'd you betray me, bastard*—that kind of thing...Could you trust Accelerator on that front? I'm sorry, but I feel like no matter how I adjusted the distance between us, he'd attack me. He's a mess, and I can't predict what he's going to do."

"Huh," answered Kakine boredly. He didn't sound disappointed— he must not have been expecting much from the girl in terms of fighting force.

She looked at the nails on his right arm. "Once you've got a result, tell me. Once we have direct bargaining rights with Aleister."

"Right," said Kakine, before the girl in the dress left School's hideout.

Teitoku Kakine stared at the Tweezers and grinned lethargically.

"...Accelerator, eh?"

Item

Leader

SHIZURI MUGINO SAIAI KINUHATA FRENDA RIKOU TAKITSUBO

Member

Leader

PROFESSOR YOSHIO BABA XOCHITL SARAKU

Group MOTOHARU TSUCHIMIKADO	MITSUKI UNABARA	AWAKI MUSUJIME	ACCELERATOR
 Leader			
School TEITOKU KAKINE	UNKNOWN	CHIMITSU SUNAZARA	UNKNOWN

Leader			
Block TATSUHIKO SAKU	MEGUMI TESHIO	YAMATE	TETSUMOU

CHAPTER 5

One to Overcome the Strongest Black Wings
Dark_Matter.

1

With Block's eradication, the incidents had ended for the moment.

Tsuchimikado was cleaning up the mess it caused, Musujime was tending to her wounds, and who knew where Unabara was or what he was doing, though he was probably fine. Accelerator, without anything in particular to do (nor the motivation to do it), took the train back to District 7, went into the first convenience store he saw, and got a can of coffee.

Then his phone rang.

On the screen was Tsuchimikado's number, registered as "Contact 3," but when he picked up, someone else was on the other end.

"Excellent work, Accelerator. Block's attempt on the General Board chairperson's life has terminated. This is all thanks to you and Group."

"You again?" answered Accelerator, clearly annoyed.

"I'm happy to have such capable subordinates."

"…It sounds a lot like you want me to kill you."

"No, not at all. I really am grateful this time. So in addition to the stipulated payment for your normal business operations, as personal thanks, I have a useful piece of information for you."

"Useful info?"

"Yes. Information regarding a fatal threat to Serial Number 20001—Last Order."

2

Kazari Uiharu and Last Order were at an open-air café.

Last Order was really worked up about searching for this lost child, but since they'd been walking so long, her feet hurt, and now she was slumped over the table. Uiharu, for her part, was taking on the shop's specialty: a huge, sweetly flavored parfait.

"So what happened to the child? Did your silly hair stop reacting to him?"

"'...Misaka doesn't have silly hair,' answers Misaka answers Misaka, wilting."

Despite what she said, that one piece of hair on the top of the ten-or-so-year-old girl's head was drifting left and right in the autumn wind. The oddly sticking-out piece of hair was certainly very silly—you probably couldn't find a sillier one if you searched the whole world, thought Uiharu.

Misaka groaned. "'I definitely sensed him wandering around here before, but it looks like he went somewhere in the meantime,' says Misaka says Misaka, fed up with all the fruitless walking."

Abruptly, the flabby Last Order's face shot up.

Did she find him? thought Uiharu, but it looked like she was wrong:

Last Order was staring at a group of girls walking by, each with a key holder that came with meal sets at a different café chain.

"'M-Misaka wants that, too,' says Misaka says Misaka even though she doesn't have a wallet so she starts making her eyes sparkle at the nice lady Uiharu!!"

"Oh, come on. Weren't you looking for someone who got lost?"

"Mgh! Misaka senses that he's in that café over there—!!"

"You mustn't be so quick to tell lies like that. Besides, I've only just gotten past the fresh-cream-zone prologue of this big parfait, so I couldn't possibly leave now."

"'How can you be so relaxed?!' says Misaka says Misaka, banging on the table, throwing a tantrum!!"

"Come to think of it, didn't you get a lot of change from the taxi?"

"'Ah!! Now that you mention it,' says Misaka says Misaka, reaching into her pocket and grabbing a bunch of coins and dashing out of the café!!"

Before she even finished talking, she had run off. Uiharu waved a handkerchief after her, figuring she'd give her a cursory warning, saying "Be sure to come back here!"

With that, Uiharu set to work, diving into her large, sweet parfait's ice cream zone...

"Excuse me, miss."

...when suddenly, a voice addressed her from the side.

She put her awfully small spoon down and looked over to see a somewhat ill-bred-looking boy standing there. He had suspicious nails made of machines on his right hand.

He smiled gently, which didn't suit his appearance.

"Yes...? Who might you be?"

"Teitoku Kakine. I'm looking for someone," he said, handing her a photograph. "Would you happen to know where this girl went? She's called Last Order."

"..." For a few seconds, Uiharu stared intently at the girl in the picture.

She looked back and forth between it and Kakine several times before shaking her head. "No. *I'm sorry, but I haven't seen her.*"

"Oh."

"If you really can't find her, you should probably put in a report at an Anti-Skill office."

"Okay. I'll try looking for her a little bit longer before that. Thanks," said Kakine with a smile, walking away.

Uiharu stuck her slender spoon into her parfait and was about to dive back in.

"Oh, right, miss? I forgot something I wanted to say."

"?" Before Uiharu could look up, the next words came.

*   *   *

"I know you were with Last Order, you fucking imbecile."

Wham!! An impact shot through her temple.

Before she realized she'd been punched, she'd already fallen out of her chair. Her legs swung out wildly, knocking over the chair and her table. Her parfait, almost entirely uneaten, splattered all over the road like a crushed fruit.

Several nearby pedestrians screamed.

Still unable to figure out what had happened, Kakine stomped on her with his sole, holding her to the ground. "That's why I asked that question. Not *Have you seen this girl?* but *Do you know where she went?*"

He leaned into his foot.

With a dull crack, the intense pain of bones scraping together tore through her. Her joint had popped out. It hurt so much that she wanted to writhe around, but Kakine's iron foot wouldn't move.

She let out not so much a cry as a scream, but Kakine's face didn't change in the slightest. "I'm certain you didn't let her escape because you knew I was coming. I may be a wicked asshole, but I try my best not to get normal people wrapped up in my business. Just work with me, here, and I won't have to resort to violence."

The open-air café was next to a major road, and it was a holiday afternoon. There was a lot of pedestrian traffic nearby, but they'd all distanced themselves from the scene—not a one ran to Uiharu.

Which made sense.

She had a Judgment band on her arm. Judgment was really for dealing with disputes in school, and even had its fair share of elites and dropouts. But any normal student who didn't know much of its inner workings would simply think "anyone with an armband is part of a peacekeeping organization." They were like the police or the self-defense force. Seeing the consummate ease with which one had been overpowered made it unthinkable for anyone to jump to her aid.

With Uiharu left high and dry, Kakine's sole dug farther into her dislocated shoulder. "...But I don't have mercy on my enemies. It's one thing if you were with her by coincidence and don't know anything, but if you're voluntarily protecting her, that's different. Please, miss. Don't make me kill you."

Crick-crack-creak!! Another wave of vicious pain hit her as her dislocated bone was manipulated even more.

By the time she decided she'd endure it, there were already tears falling from her eyes. She felt unfairness at not knowing why this was happening, fear at the overwhelming violence rendering her helpless, and frustration at her inability to break free. All the negative emotions mixed and muddled together, turning into a great pressure beginning to blossom within her very personality.

And now, purposely presented to her: a single escape route.

"Where is Last Order?"

As her consciousness flashed in pain, only Teitoku Kakine's voice came to it.

"That's all you need to tell me, and I'll let you go."

She looked back and forth, but there was no sign of an exit from this labyrinth—just a goal set up at a single point. Thrown into the darkness of violence as she was, she couldn't help but consider giving up. Her pride as a member of Judgment and her personality as Kazari Uiharu both began to waste away under the temptation to be released from pain.

Her lips slowly moved.

As her tears fell in big drops, her mouth moved.

She couldn't just remain silent.

Mortified at her own ungainliness, she said her last words.

"...What...?"

Teitoku Kakine's eyebrows knotted, as though he didn't understand.

Kazari Uiharu worked her trembling lips again.

"Did you...not hear me...?" she said with all the power she could muster. "I said she's in a place you'll never, ever find her. I don't remember…telling you any lies," she said, even sticking her tongue out at him, trying to make as much of a fool of him as she could.

Teitoku Kakine was silent for a moment.

"…All right, fine," he said, taking his foot off Uiharu's shoulder.

But he didn't set it back on the ground—instead, he moved it above Uiharu's head and stopped. "I don't lay a hand on civilians, but like I said, I don't have any mercy on my enemies. You knew that, and you still decided to refuse to help me. You leave me no choice."

Teitoku Kakine's raised foot tensed.

Then it moved, with the same casual fluidity as someone stomping on an empty can.

"This is where we say good-bye."

A burst of wind hit her, and Uiharu shut her teary eyes. That was about the only thing she could do.

But his foot didn't crush her head.

A new roar thundered through the city streets.

Grrushh!!

A gale kicked up. A massive one—practically a shock wave. When Uiharu opened her eyes, she saw an ATM machine shatter to pieces, its walls and glass exploding, its fragments forming a whirlwind and zipping at Teitoku Kakine, colliding with him. The attack threw him off-balance. His foot, which he'd planned to crush her head with, had stopped on the ground mere centimeters away.

Paper bills fluttered out of the utterly demolished ATM like feathers.

And then she heard it.

"…Shit, man. Don't get so worked up over a dumb game."

The white-hot, clouded, insane, demonic voice of Academy City's strongest Level Five.

"Let's do something a little more fun. I'll give you a nice lesson in how villains are supposed to act."

3

"That hurt."

Teitoku Kakine shifted his gaze from Uiharu to Accelerator and spoke quietly.

"And it made me mad. I figured the number one would be crazy good at making me mad. Looks like I'll just have to kill you first after all."

"Hah. You're intimidating me, you chicken? *You're the one who was too scared to fight me and went looking for a handicap.* The moment you decided to go after that brat, we all knew the difference between us."

"What are you, stupid? She was insurance. Who'd ever challenge you to a fifty-fifty fight, asshole? You're such a pain. You think you're worth that much?"

Academy City's number one and number two.

Accelerator and Teitoku Kakine didn't bother to keep everything secret.

Cleanup was a job for someone else, not them.

"You swine. Your prep work done now, or what?"

"I gotta say, Underline is something. You showed up way earlier than I thought."

"Eh?"

"Don't make me laugh, you lapdog. You think fighting for the weak like this is gonna make you a good person?"

"Hah. You don't get it, do you?" said Accelerator quietly, tossing his cane to the side. "This is great. I'll show you how villains come in many colors."

Bwoom!! An explosion rang out.

Accelerator and Teitoku Kakine clashed head-on. The aftermath shock wave blazed through their surroundings equally, mowing people down, shattering glass to smithereens. In every direction, clamors broke out—but neither paid attention.

Their clash had shown clear results.

Accelerator's attack had sent Teitoku Kakine flying back. He shot into a café on the road, and a series of cracking and breaking noises followed as he tore through furniture. Accelerator's expression, however, was nothing if not displeased. The feeling of his punch having purposely gone awry remained in his palm.

"You control the vectors here and now," said the voice from inside the shop, which looked like it had been bombed by terrorists. "I thought I could manage by using so much mass you didn't have enough vectors to move it, but I guess that won't work. I can't do anything if you're controlling my own vectors, too."

Unharmed.

When Kakine came out of the store, he was wrapped in a white cocoon. No, not a cocoon—they were wings, spread on their own. Six angelic wings flapped slowly behind him.

Accelerator frowned a bit. "Those look terrible on you. What are you, from a fucking fairy tale?"

"Don't worry, I know."

With those words, they moved again.

Accelerator charged straight at him while manipulating the vector of his legs' power, while Kakine made a leap to the side, wings batting the air. He shot dozens of meters over and landed on the road's central divider; meanwhile, Accelerator swung his arm, cutting through the air and literally grabbing hold of the air flow's vector.

Roar!! A blast of wind burst forth from behind him. The air hit 120 meters per second, turning into a cannonball to knock Kakine off the divider.

"!!" Deftly moving his wings, Kakine avoided it.

And then he heard a *clack*. When he looked, he saw that Accelerator had just put a foot on the side of the road next to the divider Kakine was standing on. How had he gotten so close—when had he done that? Before he got answers, Accelerator charged into range and thrust out his right hand.

Kakine said, "Fun fact. Everything in the universe is made up of elementary particles."

As he spoke, he protected himself with a wing. When Accelerator's hand pierced it, he changed his own wing into countless feathers, preventing the impact from reaching his body.

"I'm talking about particles even smaller than molecules and atoms. Gauge particles, leptons, quarks...Even hadrons, made from antiparticles and quarks combined, but, eh—you can group them into a few things. Anyway, these are the particles that make up this world."

"However," he said in a low voice:

"My Dark Matter doesn't play by those rules."

With a loud roar of wind, six new wings grew out of Teitoku Kakine's back.

"The Dark Matter I create is something that doesn't exist anywhere in the universe. Not because we haven't found it, or because theoretically it should exist, or anything dumb like that. *It doesn't actually exist.*"

A new type of matter created by a Level Five that didn't fit into any academic categories.

His white wings ignored the laws of physics, as though he'd dragged them straight out of an alternate universe. But Accelerator wasn't shaken at all.

Whatever they were made of, he would crush all of it with his vector control ability.

"'Kay. I'll bury you with the rest of the trash."

Accelerator stepped in closer, trying to grasp at Teitoku Kakine's heart.

But...

"You don't get it, do you?"

As soon as Kakine said that, his white wings suddenly let out an intense, bright light.

"?!"

Accelerator felt a pain like he was being slowly roasted, and reflexively got away from Kakine. Then he realized the strangeness of what had just happened.

Accelerator, who reflected every vector, *had just been affected by an outside force.*

"That was diffraction. When light waves and electrons pass through a slit, the waves scatter in different directions. It's in high school textbooks. If you make more than one slit, you can make the waves interfere with one another."

Basically, his white wings had tiny gaps too small to see, and those gaps changed the nature of the sunlight coming through them and attacked him…or so Accelerator figured. His wings hadn't made light—they'd altered the light passing through them.

"Yeah, like everything, it all depends on how you use it. How's it feel to die from a sunburn?"

But…

"…Looks like you flunked physics, moron. Use diffraction all you want—you can't change sunlight into a death beam."

"Maybe not, if I was obeying this universe's physics."

Kakine began to boost his wings with power as though drawing back a bowstring.

"But my Dark Matter is a new kind of matter that doesn't exist in this universe. Our existing laws of physics don't apply to it. Any sunlight that touches the Dark Matter and reflects off it starts working on independent laws. It's called a foreign substance for a reason. A tiny bit of it and the world changes completely."

Zhaa!! The six wings flapped. They stirred up a gale, and as Accelerator buffeted it with his reflection, he realized what Kakine was after. He looked right at him to see him smiling thinly.

"…I'm done reverse-engineering it."

"!!"

Accelerator tried to get out of the way, but Kakine had already unleashed his six wings: as simple blunt killing instruments.

Crack, thud, crush!! Dull sounds ripped through Accelerator's innards.

His body, reflecting every vector, was blown away. He crashed into a tree over ten meters away, breaking its thick trunk in one go.

"Guh, pah...?!"

The sunlight, the gale...their meaning...!!

"Accelerator, you say you reflect everything, but that's not quite accurate."

Kakine's wings silently extended.

They looked like giant swords now, over twenty meters long. Accelerator jumped over a building top, but the wings, positioned vertically, struck him like a crumbling tower.

"If you reflect sound, you can't hear anything. If you reflect matter, you can't hold anything. You unconsciously filter out the harmful from the beneficial, and you only reflect what you don't need."

As Accelerator coughed up blood, he jumped to the side, breaking through the remains of a water storage tank.

The white wings swung down, ripping through the building from its roof to midway through, spreading dust everywhere.

"My Dark Matter affected that sunlight and wind just now. I injected them with twenty-five thousand vectors each. After that, your reflection used its good-bad filter—I just had to attack from the direction of a vector you're unconsciously letting through."

Even if Accelerator changed his reflection's composition, Kakine would redo his search in an instant. It would trap him in a vicious cycle. He'd just accumulate damage while switching between attack and defense.

"This is Dark Matter," grinned Teitoku Kakine, holding his six wings at the ready. "A space filled with a foreign substance. A space you don't know shit about."

Meanwhile, Accelerator manipulated the air to cause four tornadoes around him.

And then he charged.

His tornadoes wrenched Kakine's white wings away, and Kakine's white wings, along with their gales, erased Accelerator's tornadoes. By the time the reinforced concrete structure began to creak and sway unreliably from the aftermath, the two were no longer there. They were moving parallel to each other, crashing their abilities

together, sometimes jumping onto wind turbine propellers and sometimes leaping off traffic lights, dashing at an intense speed through the city streets.

"I invented a bunch of schemes—stealing the Tweezers, taking a look into the Underline—but none worked," shouted Kakine as he swung his dozen-meter-long wings around. "Looks like killing your number-one ass is the fastest route after all!!"

"What's that, small fry? Didn't know you still had such a complex about being number two!!"

"It's not about that. I just wanted direct bargaining rights with Aleister!!"

Accelerator ignored him and purposely crashed down onto the asphalt below. The impact caused pebbles to pop into the air; he flung out a hard, two-stage kick at them.

A tremendous roaring noise split the air.

The pebbles, their vectors altered, flew out faster than a Railgun shot, but disintegrated just four or five centimeters later. But the shock wave remained; the speed had already broken the sound barrier. However, Kakine, putting all his strength into his white wings, used them to disperse it. Their respective waves clashed between them, and the resulting surge of air ripped signboards and traffic lights from their fixtures.

"That shithead Aleister has a bunch of plans going at once. Seems like they're his highest priority. But even if you stop his crazy plans, he'll switch to some alternative scheme, then go back to the original plan. Terrible guy. It's like a game of Amidakuji—he goes to a different line for a bit, but he ends up right back on the track where he started."

Accelerator and Teitoku Kakine, who'd been running parallel, now made sharp turns, running at each other to clash at point-blank range. They were at a giant scrambled intersection, with four lanes on each side. Their clash completely cut off the flow of traffic, but nobody was complaining. Nobody *could* complain. Everyone instinctively knew that secrecy wasn't the issue here—if they said something, they'd die.

The two bodies crossed.

Air exploded, and after a few seconds, a *zbaaahhh* rattled through it.

"Which makes things simple. Just smash all his backup plans, and he won't be able to compromise by going to a different line. And if I set myself up as the real core of it, rather than just a spare plan, Aleister can't ignore me. It's not like I want to destroy Academy City. I can use it. That's why I'll worm my way into the middle and get it all in the palm of my hand!!"

Blood flew from both Accelerator and Teitoku Kakine.

"Right. If you kill the current 'core' now, you'll take over his plans."

They stopped, then slowly turned around to face each other.

Teitoku Kakine was probably confident, beyond his big talk, that he could get accurate information on just how many plans Aleister had running at the same time.

And Teitoku Kakine had a reason, something making him go that far. Accelerator didn't think too much about that point. Wander into Academy City's underbelly and you'd realize tragedies were as numerous as hills and stars. Teitoku Kakine had probably experienced one and broken. Just like how Accelerator had killed over ten thousand people for the experiment. And how he had thrown away his life for the sake of one person.

"Worthless," he said, having predicted that. "Maybe you're trying to give me sound arguments like you're some perfect person, but it's still all shit coming out of a filthy mouth."

"Hah. You don't have the right to tell me off when you don't even know how valuable your own position is. You're the closest to having direct bargaining rights with Aleister."

"That's all you had to say to prove what a cheap villain you are," said Accelerator in disappointment from the wrecked intersection. "You can use a tragedy a bunch of ways. You can carry it with you, you can tell others about it, and you can use it to decide what direction to take your life in. But just because it happens doesn't make it right for you to go after totally unrelated little brats, got it? The moment you start to think your grand cause makes it okay for you to kill civilians, you've cheapened yourself as a villain."

"Right, sure. That means a lot, coming from you," replied Teitoku Kakine, sounding uninterested. He went on, "I'm not going after civilians because I like it or something. If I'm in a good mood, I'll even let lower villains go free. But not if it's a threat to my life. How many random onlookers and pedestrians have you crushed in this battle so far? You just sent pieces of asphalt flying faster than the speed of sound. The shock wave leveled everything. It was our battle."

"..."

"That's why I went after Last Order—and that brat who looked like her guardian. Don't lecture me from on high, murderer. You've got no right to tell me shit when you've let those onlookers die just to kill me. You think you're an exception or something?"

"Hah. Let onlookers die just to kill you, eh?" But Accelerator, denounced, laughed. "You really are third-rate. You don't have the *aesthetic*, and that's why you can only spout bullshit like that."

"Eh?"

"Do you even know why I'm number one and you're number two?"

Laughing, Accelerator slowly spread his hands.

"It's because there's a wall between us you can never get past."

Teitoku Kakine felt his head nearly explode with anger, but then he noticed something.

What it was like around them.

True, Accelerator and Dark Matter's clash had messed up the city streets. High-rise building windows had been shattered, broken traffic lights were strewn about the roads, and roadside trees had been whipped around so hard they were now stuck in concrete walls.

But something was missing.

The tragedy.

Despite the glass fragments pouring down like rain, nobody was injured. The raging winds had diverted their course and the signboards had shielded people late to escape, miraculously protecting the crowds. The rest was the same. Not a single person hurt.

He couldn't check every single one, but he knew if he went back along the course of their battle, there would be many who had been defended by invisible hands.

*Are...are you...*Kakine's throat dried up.

"Are you telling me you protected them...?"

He thought back to the first shots. Accelerator had fired a gale at Teitoku Kakine, but he could have done a more powerful surprise attack as well. But if he had, the aftermath would have blown away Last Order's acquaintance, but...

In short, that was his way of life.

Even embroiled in a Level Five death match, number one in the city vs. number two, even though the slightest diversion of his attention would have created a fatal opening, Accelerator had continued to protect innocent people.

"You've...gotta be shitting me. How much can you fucking control?"

Accelerator looked bored. He just grinned scornfully, as if this much was only natural—why couldn't Teitoku Kakine do it?

"*You angry now, small-timer?*" said Accelerator, as though this were all absurd, to Teitoku Kakine, awash with shock. "*This is a true villain.*"

Even after all that, he was still a villain. How amazing did *good* people have to be in his mind?

"!! Don't get full of yourself, Acceleratoooooorrrrrrr!!"

With a shout, Teitoku Kakine's six wings immediately swelled with power. He changed their length, then their properties—until the white wings spread out as lethal weapons. They were tense as a fully drawn bowstring, and their sights were set perfectly on six of Accelerator's vital points.

Accelerator just laughed. "Come on."

"Don't get complacent. I've already analyzed your reflection's filter. That fraud of a defensive power won't work on these."

"Yeah, maybe this Dark Matter you control doesn't exist in this universe," said Accelerator, beckoning with his index finger. "Textbook laws don't apply, and light waves and EM waves that touch those elementary particles go off in vectors they're not supposed to. So yeah, I guess trying to use this universe's vector calculations for it ends up putting holes in my armor."

The bloodlust between them expanded.

The center of the busy intersection was covered up with death.

"I'll just have to redo my calculations to include it. I'll redefine the universe so that it's constructed of particles including your Dark Matter, and then, once I officially unveil your 'new world' to the public, it'll be checkmate."

"You think…you can use your vector control on my Dark Matter…?"

"You think I can't?"

"Hah. You think you've got me all figured out, do you?"

"Wouldn't be much of an issue."

"…!!"

"And sorry, but I don't need to know everything about you anyway."

There was an explosive *ga-bam!!*

They crossed for an instant.

And thus, the match between number one and number two was settled.

4

Accelerator looked toward the ground. His crutch was there. It was probably one of the things that came flying from the direction of the onlookers as a side effect of the battle. He picked it up and returned his choker electrode's switch to normal mode. A moment later, it sounded like the noise from around the busy intersection had gotten closer. About a hundred, a hundred fifty witnesses. But he wasn't about to try to hide any of this. That was for the underlings to do. It was too trivial for him to worry about.

"…" He turned around.

Teitoku Kakine was lying on his face in the middle of the intricate intersection—the vectors of the white wings he'd created had been predicted, their control wrested from him, and then his body skewered. Red blood spread out in the middle of the intersection like some strange magic circle.

But Dark Matter still wasn't dead.

And Accelerator wasn't a good guy—he was a villain.

That detestable "good guy" probably wouldn't finish him off right now. He'd just pick up and leave. He might even meddle in the villain's affairs and leave him away to get back on his feet. But Accelerator instead pulled the gun from his belt. The option of letting Teitoku Kakine go, when he'd chosen to use Last Order and civilians as his weakness to defeat Accelerator, didn't cross his mind. *Guess that's the difference between a good guy and a villain*, he thought distractedly.

"See you, third-rate," he muttered to the unconscious Kakine, flicking up the hammer on his gun with his thumb. "Less pathetic than a good guy taking you down anyway."

He rested his index finger on the trigger. This was the end. He wouldn't rely on man's goodwill or God's miracles—his was the path of evil, a future created simply as a result of his actions. Intending to live his own way, he lined up the barrel with his enemy's head and began to put one last bit of energy into his right hand.

About to accomplish everything, with a peace built upon death just moments away...

"Wait up, there, Accelerator!!"

A loud, out-of-sight voice interrupted him. He looked over as a familiar face jumped out from the wall of curious onlookers. One wearing an unbelievably unstylish green jersey and no makeup. She was both a school teacher and a member of the peacekeeping organization Anti-Skill.

Aiho Yomikawa.

She ran straight over to him.

"I don't know where you've been this whole time. I couldn't tell you what any of this means. But I can say one thing—give me that gun. You don't need something like that!!"

Yomikawa wasn't carrying one. She wasn't even carrying the bare minimum for self-defense, like those distinct batons or stun guns. The onlookers nearby must have thought she was an idiot. That it was an act of suicide to go up to an out-of-control esper, one who had just committed so much havoc unarmed.

Yomikawa probably understood the dangers just fine.

In fact, as a front-line Anti-Skill officer, she knew it a lot better than those onlookers.

"I'm a villain."

"Then I'll stop you."

"Are you serious?"

"Stopping you is the only choice I know."

She said *stop*, not *defeat* or *kill*. That was how she did things. Just as Accelerator had chosen the life of a villain, Aiho Yomikawa would never agree to point a weapon at a child she should be protecting. Accelerator stared right into her eyes. The strength of her will was in them. From his point of view, the compass she used to decide her actions was nonsensical. She'd probably found enough value in this to be worth giving up her life for.

"Accelerator, it doesn't matter if you're a good guy or a bad guy. It doesn't matter what kind of world you're immersed in, either. What matters is me bringing you back, 'kay? However dark your world, however deep it runs, I will never give up on you. I promise you that I will pull you out of there."

At that moment, the two were on a level playing field. He was Academy City's strongest Level Five, and she was an adult with no power whatsoever—but all that belonged in a different dimension now as Aiho Yomikawa stood in his way.

"That's why I'll stand in your way. I do it for the children I need to protect, and for this peace we love. In that, I see you and Last Order there, and everyone living happily. You won't need that gun in that future."

"..." Accelerator, for a little while, stayed silent and listened to her words.

And then he came to a conclusion.

He turned his gun, aimed at Kakine, and pointed it at Yomikawa.

That's why...

Aiho Yomikawa was an enemy. Even if she was a "good guy," even if the reason for her actions was so Accelerator could be happy, she was obstructing the path of evil he needed to dominate. So he would get rid of her. Not kill her. He was good enough with a gun to go easy on her.

...right here...

Accelerator had people he needed to protect. Last Order, the Sisters, Kikyou Yoshikawa, and Aiho Yomikawa. That was why he would stick to his cruel nature. Even if the whole world, *even if the people he needed to protect turned into enemies*, he was determined to save those people from the darkness.

...I'll shoot her!!

"You can't."

The next thing he knew, Aiho Yomikawa was close to him, gently holding Accelerator's gun-wielding hand in hers.

"I know you're a better villain than that."

The match was decided. Yomikawa began to take each of Accelerator's fingers off the gun. She took the magazine out from under the grip, pulled the slide, and removed the bullets already loaded, too. Accelerator watched in a daze as she finished the job.

And then...

Crash!!

Teitoku Kakine's Dark Matter attacked, putting an end to Accelerator's train of thought.

He hadn't been the target.

Aiho Yomikawa's eyes opened wide with shock. Then she slowly looked down at herself. The tip of one of those unknown white wings was sticking through her gut like a sword. Her green jersey was stained red with blood. Already red, and it didn't take much time for it to start spreading terribly fast.

Yomikawa tried to say something. But her body wavered, and she fell to the asphalt without resistance. Accelerator watched. Beyond where Aiho Yomikawa fell was a single figure. It was Teitoku Kakine, who should have been unconscious.

On his back were six wings.

What had happened didn't bear any explanation.

Slllp. The sharp feather thrust through the woman quickly removed itself.

"…However dark your world, however deep it runs, I promise you that I'll pull you out of there, eh…"

Teitoku Kakine, face covered in blood, was saying something.

He hadn't gone after Yomikawa because she was in the way; Kakine had only ever been watching Accelerator. It was that slight moment of hesitation when, before Yomikawa, he'd been about to stop the *evil*. The act that would have withdrawn his very reason for killing Teitoku Kakine. *That* was what was in the way.

Now he barely knew why he'd even lost.

And that was why Teitoku Kakine flew into a rage.

"You could never do that. It would never be that easy! This is our world. This is where the darkness and the despair lead!! You were condescending to me before, and at the very end, you still cling to it…Is this the fucking *aesthetic* you were talking about?!"

Incoherent words. His anger and malice came first, and what resulted were words that had lost logic and consistency. They were just shock waves slamming into Accelerator's body.

"In the end, you're the same as I am. You can't protect anyone. And a lot more people will die after this, too. Killed by people like me. Isn't that right, Accelerator?! You only got this far after making a lot of fucking people die!!"

Teitoku Kakine unsteadily dragged his blood-covered body to its feet.

Not to bare his fangs at Accelerator. Accelerator could tell—he knew malice personally. Kakine's was directed somewhere else.

Namely, to Aiho Yomikawa, crumpled on the ground.

"St...op."

"I can't hear you!"

He identified a grinding noise. He didn't know what had happened. Kakine hadn't touched Yomikawa, but something invisible trampled over her. Her body twitched. The dark red on her, under pressure, started to expand a lot more quickly.

"Stop!!"

"I said I can't fucking hear you!!"

Kakine's roar drowned out Accelerator's words.

"Don't let that bitch decide things, idiot! Why the fuck are you trying to resolve things through talking, villain?! That's not what we are. That's not how we do things and you know it!!"

Kakine's ability further increased in pressure.

Now, not only her side but her mouth began to drip with viscous red fluid.

"If you want someone to stop moving, just kill them. If you don't like something, just break it. That's what it means to be evil! Don't start wanting to be saved!! Don't start trying to laugh it off like an idiot!! There's no way a dumbass like you would ever be given that!! Come on, show me. Show me that evil you were lecturing me about before like some kind of fucking god!!"

——*Idiot*, he spat.

He said he wouldn't get civilians and pedestrians involved in the battle, and look what had happened. He'd abandoned the path of light, he'd decided to rule from the pinnacle of darkness, and he almost took the hand extended to him, fooled by warm words. He almost looked away from the dark world he was in, just for a moment, and almost touched the world of light. As a result, he lost sight of his top priority—removing the threat of Teitoku Kakine as soon as he could—and it gave way to a tragedy he could have prevented.

Therefore...

*　　*　　*

This time, Accelerator would become altogether evil.

He swore then and there to rend Teitoku Kakine to pieces, no matter what he lost.

He felt like his right and left brain had split. And he definitely felt like something sharp, something with an edge, had come up out of it and stabbed the inside of his skull. It wedged itself into his brain, that something, and immediately swallowed up Accelerator. He heard a squish, like a fruit being crushed. Something like tears flowed from his eyes. But they weren't tears. This fluid was darker, redder, dirtier, more uncomfortable, and smelled like iron. Anything spilling from his lachrymal glands was now only hatred.

And with it brought...

a loss of control.

"Oo..."

He heard a pillar supporting his identity break. A thick, syrupy emotion washed over everything, from his center to his extremities. He clenched his teeth, his eyes turned red, and Accelerator let loose a howl that could be heard to the ends of the earth.

"Ooooooooooohhhhhhhhhhhhhhhhhhhhhhhhhhhhhhhhhhhhhhh!!"

His back burst open. From it burst murky black wings. Black wings like jet sprays. The anger had removed his very consciousness, crushed his very sense of self, and the pair of wings had exploded out of it. In moments, they stretched dozens of meters, parted the asphalt, and scraped against building walls.

"Ha..."

When Teitoku Kakine saw that, he knew.

His Dark Matter, his elementary particles that supposedly didn't exist in this universe. What on earth was it? Where was he pulling it out of? What did it mean?

"Crazy...That's some crazy evil. See, you can do it after all, villain. I see why Dark Matter's just a spare plan now. But that doesn't necessarily mean victory is assured!!"

As though answering his cry, Teitoku Kakine's six wings exploded

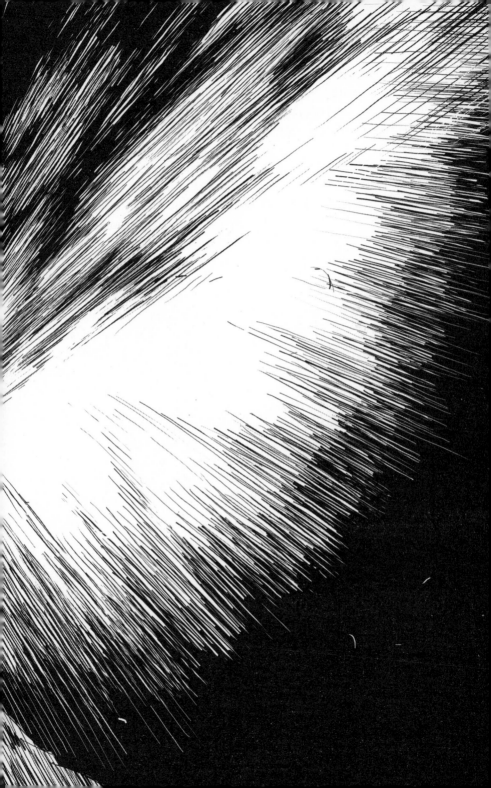

out. They reached dozens of meters in length, filled with both a mystical light and an inorganic, machinelike quality. Just like a giant weapon that God or angels would use.

Bawoo!! cried the air touched by the six wings.

What Accelerator and Dark Matter possessed, respectively, were organicity and inorganicity. And those terms applied to a different world than this one. One wielded a part of a power equal to God, and one wielded part of the heavenly plane in which God lived. With these conditions, the match was even. And Teitoku Kakine, unlike Accelerator, hadn't lost himself.

Power the likes of which he'd never felt before raged within him.

And he felt like he had perfect control over every last bit of it.

Kakine thought to himself that their number one and number two positions had just reversed. It wasn't an empty act of courage, nor was it him being a sore loser. It had none of the dramatization the emotion did. It was a simple impression. Right now, even against all the armies in the world, even against all the espers in Academy City at once, he could beat them without a scratch. Those were his honest thoughts.

"Ha-ha-ha-ha-ha!! *Ha-ha-ha-ha-ha-ha-ha-ha-ha-ha-ha!!*"

Laughing and laughing some more, Kakine took his six truly awakened wings and slammed them into Accelerator.

He didn't even care about Accelerator anymore. He just wanted to test this on something nearby. That was all Kakine was thinking.

But then, a *crack*.

A moment later, his body, hit with a massive force, was buried in the asphalt.

"Guh…?!"

He didn't know what had happened.

Accelerator's black wings hadn't moved. He'd simply looked his way and waved a hand. With just that, Kakine, who thought he was in an absolutely dominant position, lost, crushed deep down into the ground.

He heard cricking and cracking.

It was his right hand, with the Tweezers equipped, being instantly cut off at the elbow.

Gah...ah...!! Wh-what the...hell...?!

Accelerator had picked up some kind of vector, changed its direction, concentrated it at one point, and attacked him with it. He knew that, but even with all the world's vectors, he couldn't have caused something like this. Right now, Teitoku Kakine was sure he couldn't lose in this world.

It didn't make sense.

He couldn't comprehend it.

The supremely overwhelming Accelerator simply walked toward him, slowly, one step at a time, toward where he was smashed. Kakine realized that every footfall was his life ticking away. When the distance came to zero, his life would end. And Accelerator had already taken the final step.

"Ha-ha..."

"...yjrpevilqw"

"Damn it...So that's it!! That's what you were for?!"

No response—just a lethal fist coming down on him.

The overwhelming butchery had begun.

5

Only the sounds of pounding meat echoed through Academy City. With each hit, the asphalt cracked, the earth rumbled like an aftershock, and the buildings shook ominously. None of the onlookers could say a word. Even looking away took courage. Most people did nothing but gaze at the overpowering scene.

"Ugh..."

Amidst all that, Aiho Yomikawa woke up.

In the haze in her mind, she heard a roar. A roar more fearsome than a beast's and more horrible than a demon's. But to Yomikawa, it sounded like a child crying.

I have to stop him, she thought in spite of herself.

"Yomikawa!!"

But before the collapsed Yomikawa could move, someone grabbed her arm. They picked her up, got under her shoulder, and swiftly moved away from the site of the incident. The deftness belonged to another Anti-Skill officer. But unlike Yomikawa's jersey, this one was fully armed with a gun and body armor.

"...Urgh...Saigou? Let me go...I still have to...!!"

"You can't, Yomikawa!!"

She tried to fling him away, but she didn't have her normal strength. Meanwhile, she heard a series of bangs and booms, the air being struck. She looked up and saw a black combat helicopter soaring through the blue sky. It was one of the brand-new Hexawings.

"The satellites just came online again temporarily, and they detected an abnormality. A distortion the law of relativity can't explain has expanded over one hundred meters around us. The analysis team says it's probably bizarre interference from involuntary diffusion fields."

"And you're attacking the source, even though it might kill you? Give me a break!!"

She coughed up blood when she shouted, but this time, she wrested herself free from Saigou's arm. She took another look around. Many other fully armed officers were here, and they even had units of powered suits and armored cars. It was like a scene out of a nightmare. For Yomikawa, who had investigated Accelerator's earlier years to some degree, it gave her a sense of déjà vu. He'd been surrounded like this once when he was younger, and he'd surrendered, having lost any hope at life—and then they threw him into a dark research facility.

She couldn't let that happen again.

Not paying any mind to the wound in her side, the blood-soaked Yomikawa stood in the officers' way.

"Lower your guns!! We don't need them to persuade Accelerator!!"

"But Yomikawa!!"

"Don't you know who that is? That's a child we're supposed to protect! I won't accept it. I'll never allow anyone to point a weapon at him!!"

That was when Accelerator looked up to the skies.

His black wings began spurting out with even more force.

"Ooooooooooooooohhhhhhhhhhhhhhhhhhhhhhhhhhhhhhhhhhh!!"

Ba-boom!! An impact shot through everyone present.

It wasn't a physical one; it was a simple threat to their lives. Their animalistic instincts had gripped and squeezed their hearts. The pressure she felt was so strong it felt like she'd crumple to the ground if she relaxed. Accelerator's anger wasn't directed at the onlookers or the officers; they were below his attention. Nevertheless, with just the scrap of that emotion, he dominated the world, forced it to yield to him, and nearly destroyed it.

Accelerator was supposed to be after Teitoku Kakine.

But who would believe, looking at him now, that he'd stop there? Once his target was gone, and his anger had nowhere left to go, would he point it somewhere else? Nobody there let that possibility—no, that danger—go unconsidered. Yomikawa knew Accelerator well— and she knew his actions were too hard to predict.

Damn. Can't I...do anything...?

When Yomikawa tried to get closer to him, she coughed up blood. Saigou frantically pinioned her, stopping her from moving. Even restrained, however, she watched Accelerator through blurred eyes, thinking, *Isn't there some way to stop him? Is...is this stupid nonsense really going to end his future?!*

He let out another roar, painting over the world with black. The black wings on his back granted despair beyond the realm of man. She saw some Anti-Skill officers get their guns ready out of reflex, without being ordered. But if they pulled the trigger, it would all be over. The act would be tantamount to rejection from society, and it would break him again. And she wasn't sure anyone would be able to bring him back a second time.

Faced with such overwhelming power, everyone had lost hope.

All they could do was cringe out of the way of that power's rampage and tremble.

And then, before their eyes...

*   *   *

...their last hope came down to them.

It looked like a ten-year-old girl. Shoulder-length brown hair and energetic features. Clothed in a sky-blue camisole with a baggy men's button-down over it, their "hope" pushed terror-stricken onlookers out of the way as best she could and came to the busy intersection.

She said she was looking for someone lost.

Now that she'd found him, she didn't hesitate. Even with the overpowering scene spread out before her, she went straight up to Accelerator. Everyone who saw her thought it was over—but none could reach out to stop her, either. She'd already gotten too close to the destruction's center point.

"'I found you,' says Misaka says Misaka, relaxed."

She approached Accelerator's back as he continued to howl.

Accelerator slowly turned around.

Vwooh!! A burst of roaring wind.

Academy City's strongest Level Five had just done something very simple: His jetlike black wings had sliced through the air. His backward-facing wings were packed with incredible power, and he'd inadvertantly let loose a massive yet casual attack.

Everyone there visualized the tragedy.

They imagined her young body torn apart, crushed, and scattered across the road.

But...

With a tremendous *gkkkeeee*, the black wings stopped right in front of Last Order.

An invisible wall had blocked Accelerator's attack. It was just a few centimeters from her face, and though his wings trembled and shook, they didn't get any closer. The girl shouldn't have had any abilities that could ward off his black wings. Even if someone searched the whole world, they might not find anyone like that.

If she couldn't do it, and if nobody in the world could do it, then who had stopped them, and how?

As Yomikawa stared in stupefaction, she eventually came to an answer.

"*Accelerator...*"

Academy City's strongest Level Five. The One-Way Road. If anyone could stop this overwhelming power that nobody could reach, it would have to be the man creating that power himself. At the very end of the end of the critical moment, Accelerator had stopped his wings.

The black wings trembled, squealing and cracking.

They trembled like the sobbing of a beast.

And then the *bang* of gunpowder rang out.

Yomikawa, startled, looked over to see that one of the Anti-Skill officers had just discharged his gun.

Shit, she thought.

He'd fired at Accelerator with Last Order nearby. His black wings had torn apart and transformed into several sharp feathers. They were aimed at the Anti-Skill officers nearby. He had taken it as an attack against the girl.

Accelerator unleashed a booming attack right away, with himself at the center, but...

"'Stop,' advises Misaka advises Misaka."

One word from Last Order.

As soon as it came out, the feather tips at the Anti-Skill officers' throats stopped dead in their tracks.

"'It'll be all right,' says Misaka says Misaka, extending her hand."

It wasn't that the little girl didn't understand the situation. She knew how dangerous Accelerator was, but she still reached out to him with a delicate hand.

"'You don't have to do this anymore,' says Misaka says Misaka, telling you what the right thing is."

As if to swat away her words, Accelerator crashed his black wings into her again.

But once again, they stopped centimeters before her face. A sharp *ggkkkeeee* was the only sound that came out. It was Accelerator's internal conflict. His heart was telling him to get rid of her. If it meant feeling like this, if it meant tragedies repeating, he should abandon everything. But he just couldn't do it. He could kill her at the twitch of a finger. It would be so easy to send that tiny body flying. But no matter what he did, he couldn't let go of that hope.

"*Aaahhhhhhhhhhhhh!! Gaaaaahhhhhhhhhhhhhhhhhh!!*"

He burst into a roar.

For a few moments, the only sound was the angry flapping of his black wings.

But the overwhelming sense of pressure they'd been exerting was gone. Now he seemed like a young child throwing a tantrum. The girl watched. When those next attacks came, she didn't even shut her eyes. She trusted him—so she wasn't surprised.

He swung his wings much wider, then brought them down at her in one final, determined attack.

When they stopped dead in front of her face, Accelerator stopped as well.

His head was down—nobody could see his face.

Without a sound, the pair of wings on his back melted into the air and vanished. At the same time, all the strength left his body. She spread her arms to accept him. He wavered, then slowly fell toward her.

Accelerator's weight seemed like it would crush her, but she held onto him anyway.

She brought her mouth to his ear and whispered into it.

"'That's good,' says Misaka says Misaka."

EPILOGUE

To the Survivors Go the Spoils

Nano_Size_Data.

When he came to, Accelerator was riding in an ambulance.

But the machines inside it weren't the same as an actual ambulance. This one probably wasn't heading for a hospital. He was being brought somewhere else.

Someone must have been driving it, but he couldn't see them. Nobody else was riding with him, either. His cell phone was on the floor beside him. When Accelerator noticed it, his ringtone went off, as though somebody was keeping a close eye on him.

Accelerator picked it up and heard a voice that was familiar, in a way.

"It looks like you overdid it this time."

"…You again? None of you could do shit. You all just watched from on high. You don't have the right to lecture me. The only one who can act high and mighty is the one who *actually* risked her life to stop me."

"You understand."

"Shit," spat Accelerator bitterly at the voice on the telephone that wasn't listening. *"Yeah, I get it."*

"Anyway, I was the one who gave you the information regarding Teitoku Kakine, so I can't be too hard on you. I would like you to be more efficient in utilizing my information, that's all."

"What's the penalty?"

"What should it be, indeed. I could increase your debt, but for you,

that wouldn't be much of a punishment. And you're too important to get rid of. Yes, what shall I do?"

Those words were filled with implication. It got on Accelerator's nerves, but the telephone voice abruptly said, *"By the way, do you really plan on going back?"*

"Eh?"

"I ask out of simple interest. After falling so far, declaring that you'd stand at the top of the darkness— Will you still not give up on that warmth?"

"Do you even have to ask?" he spat back.

"I see."

"Not gonna stop me?"

"I'll at least give you the right to struggle. Not necessarily the right to succeed, though."

"Perfect," said Accelerator, hanging up.

He stared at the screen for a few moments, but eventually put it in his pocket, opened the window hidden behind the curtains, and looked out at the scenery.

...Oh.

He still felt that little girl's warmth in his arms.

He clenched his fist and tried to will the sensation away, quietly thinking, *I'll outwit them for sure. Academy City, those shitheads at the top—everyone.*

In his inside pocket was a USB drive with his choker electrode's blueprints.

He'd checked it between operations, but it was no simple device. Just to make one part needed two or three ingredients or devices, and to make them he'd need four or five pieces of equipment—and those were all made by the frog-faced doctor himself. He felt like he was looking at Princess Kaguya's impossible tasks. It looked like it would take considerable time to break down the electrode, remove the useless parts, and make a copy of it.

But Accelerator still swore he'd do it as he hid that little hint he'd finally gotten in his pocket.

* * *

Mitsuki Unabara left through the hospital's front entrance.

Xóchitl had come here as an assassin from the organization. She'd probably hate this ending. Unable to accomplish her goal or to even meet her end through death, he had let her live, only to steal her strongest weapon, the original copy of her grimoire. All she could feel right then was suffering.

But she was still alive.

Even with less than a third of her original body left, and though what remained was not much more than a simulacrum wrapped in skin, she still had life. Unabara was happy for it. It may have been pure self-satisfaction, but for Mitsuki Unabara, it was a kind of salvation.

"Urgh…"

His consciousness swayed.

Taking in the grimoire meant immense knowledge was now stored in his mind. But it wasn't used to a human body. It felt like iron fragments scraping through the wrinkles on his brain, strong enough to shoot through him from head to toe if he let it.

I must have lost too much blood…

Mitsuki Unabara reached into his inside pocket.

His hand came out with the original copy, which he'd separated from Xóchitl. An extremely long grimoire in the form of a scroll, made out of animal skin. He unrolled the meters' worth of knowledge and cast his eye over the contents.

Gradually, the pain decreased.

Once it was completely gone, he would understand this "original copy."

Ha-ha. If the English Puritan Church found me, they'd get rid of me, no questions asked.

But this grimoire had power.

And at the moment, he desperately needed power.

…I was so intent on staying hidden in Academy City's underworld.

He rolled the scroll back up neatly, then put it back into his inside pocket.

What's happening with the organization right now? Why did a nice girl like Xóchitl transform into an assassin? ...I'm going to have to confront the organization again.

With a new power in hand, he looked forward.

Unable to look too deep into the dark—but the Aztecan sorcerer didn't hesitate.

From afar, Awaki Musujime stared at the juvenile reformatory as dark smoke rose from it.

A bandage-like thing was wrapped around her bloody foot. It was an organic artificial skin that used corn fibers. It still felt strange to her, but eventually it would fuse with her—thanks to the regenerative capabilities of flesh—and create such natural "human skin" that it wouldn't leave any marks.

"..."

Without looking at her painful wounds, she kept her gaze fixed on the reformatory.

She thought becoming a playing piece for Academy City's underworld had guaranteed her allies' safety. But when push came to shove and the reformatory fell under attack, the city hadn't even sent in Anti-Skill reinforcements—even though they had those brand-new HsAFH-11 attack helicopters out and ready by the time the mercenaries scaled Academy City's wall.

I figured there would be a limit to how much I could trust those people.

Nevertheless, she couldn't immediately start waving a flag of rebellion. "Those people" were the ones with all the real power in Academy City. Even if she liberated her allies from that juvenile reformatory's special block, they'd have nowhere to run. Not too long ago, she'd put down another back-alley group, Skill-Out. If she let her allies escape haphazardly, a similar end would be waiting for them. "Those people" could have even assigned her that mission to let her know that.

Still…

I swear I'll get them back for this.

Musujime promised herself. She decided to hold tight to the truth of that day, and the emotion that had begun to sprout from it. The phase of her relying on other people or other things she'd never seen or met before to protect her allies was over. Going forward, she would only believe what she saw with her own eyes and felt with her own hands, and use that to build up a protective wall.

She cast one last gaze in the reformatory's direction, then turned her back to it.

She left without a sound, thinking to herself.

I'll rescue them from that place, for sure.

And so, at an unspecified time, in an unspecified place, Accelerator, Motoharu Tsuchimikado, Mitsuki Unabara, and Awaki Musujime gathered back together.

Tsuchimikado had a machine glove on his hand. His index finger and middle finger each had a long, glass nail attached to it. The bloodstained tool was the exact one Kakine had been in possession of.

It was called the Tweezers.

Accelerator looked at it and sighed. "Slipped in during the chaos and snatched it, huh? Surprised you were hiding with the rubberneckers."

"Apparently, nanodevices called the Underline are inside this. It looks like the reason for School's actions was to collect them from the air and analyze them."

Accelerator wondered how he knew all that, but decided he'd probably been scurrying around without him knowing.

Then Unabara, who didn't look very good, asked a question, his speech slower than usual. "What data do they contain?"

"The Underline is the core of Aleister's direct information network in Academy City. The stuff inside the nanomachines is on a different level than the city data banks."

Now that he mentioned it, when Accelerator had attacked a

General Board member named Thomas Platinaburg in his mansion some time ago, he'd tried to steal data from him. He could only get so much at the time—maybe he was splitting up information based on its secrecy between the regular network and the special one that used the Underline.

Musujime, with a bored look, said, "Sounds like work. What kind of info is in those nanomachines anyway?"

"One second. We're about to find out."

The small monitor on the back of the Tweezers' gloves made a blip. A jumble of random-looking characters scrolled by quickly—results of the analysis—and after that, began to change into actual words and sentences.

"Looks like a bunch of secret codes for the Academy City underworld."

"You think it'll give us a hint on how to get out of this?"

"The names here are…Group, School, Item, Member, Block…This one is Tweezers…Here's the *Altair II*'s data and a rough map of the juvenile reformatory…"

"What do you mean secret codes?" said Musujime. "Sounds better than it actually is. Doesn't this just mean the higher-ups were keeping an eye on Group and gathering information? Why show us this data now?"

"There's one more," said Tsuchimikado.

All of Group looked at the Tweezers' screen. Tsuchimikado had set it apart from the others, and they took that to mean it was some different information.

Newly acquired intel.

Motoharu Tsuchimikado read aloud the characters displayed there.

"The last one here…is 'Dragon.'"

At the end of the battles, they'd gotten an all-too-tiny opening.

But it was still a key, and now that they had it, the four members of Group got to work once again.

Item

Leader

SHIZURI MUGINO · SAIAI KINUHATA · FRENDA · RIKOU TAKITSUBO

Member

Leader

PROFESSOR · YOSHIO BABA · XÓCHITL · SARAKU

Dragon

Group				
	MOTOHARU TSUCHIMIKADO	MITSUKI UNABARA	AWAKI MUSUJIME	ACCELERATOR

School	Leader 			
	TEITOKU KAKINE	UNKNOWN	CHIMITSU SUNAZARA	UNKNOWN

Block	Leader 			
	TATSUHIKO SAKU	MEGUMI TESHIO	YAMATE	TETSUMOU

AFTERWORD

To those of you purchasing these books one at a time, it's good to see you again.

To those of you who bought all of them at once, pleased to meet you. I'm Kazuma Kamachi.

I went all out on the science for Volume 15. The seven Level Fives, agricultural buildings, nanodevices, unmanned attack helicopters, satellites, computer viruses, Skill-Out...I brought out all the little science key words that have popped up in the past and delivered them in bulk.

The themes of this volume were the Academy City underworld and forlorn stories. Accelerator's viciousness as he sprints down the path of evil was another major point. Though it was evil, it wasn't the kind that left a bad aftertaste—I was aiming for an ending where the reader would feel refreshed after getting through the whole thing. Did I succeed?

I think this was the most new characters appearing in a single book in the series (leaving aside groups like the Sisters). But his circle will never grow—perhaps one of the differences between Touma Kamijou and Accelerator.

Thank you to my illustrator, Mr. Haimura, and my editor, Mr. Miki. It ended up being a chaotic story, so I really appreciate you two sticking with me all the way through.

And thank you to all my readers. It felt like we were dashing down a side road again, but seriously, thank you for making it through all these pages.

Now then, as I close the pages on this book,
and as I pray you'll make it through even more pages in the future, today, at this hour, I lay down my pen.

...That white one—people might start calling him Robin Hood soon.

Kazuma Kamachi